MINUTES OF THE

VIENNA PSYCHOANALYTIC SOCIETY

VOLUME II:

1908 — 1910

MINUTES OF THE VIENNA PSYCHOANALYTIC SOCIETY

Volume II: 1908–1910

EDITED BY

HERMAN NUNBERG

ERNST FEDERN

Translated by M. Nunberg

New York

INTERNATIONAL UNIVERSITIES PRESS, INC.

Library of Congress Catalog Card Number: 62-15591

Manufactured in the United States of America

CONTENTS

Prof. Freud betont die Schwierigkeit des Themas, die es notwendig mache, sich in der Sache zu beschränken. Er erklärt Sadgers Beobachtung für bedeutungsvoll, da sie den Nachweis der infantilen Wurzeln erbringt. In der Auffassung des Falles selbst würde er in einigen wesentlichen Punkten vom Vortragenden abweichen. Besonders störend sei der Sprung, den es bei Sadger immer gebe zwischen der eingehenden Detailbeobachtung und der unvermittelt als Fassade daran geklebten Theorie.

Beim Asthma nervosum liegt es nahe sich nach den ähnlichen Zuständen umzusehen; da ist zunächst die Migräne, dann gewisse Formen von neuropathischen Oedemen und gewisse Formen von Urtica. Am auffälligsten sei die Ähnlichkeit mit den Oedemen, welche die Neurotiker oft unter Umständen bekommen, unter denen andere sie nicht bekommen. Über den psychischen Faktor bei diesen Anfällen kann kein Zweifel sein, ebensowenig wie bei der Migräne, bei der der Charakter der Verschiebbarkeit und psychischen Auslösbarkeit wiederkehrt. Sie ist kein hysterisches Symptom sondern ein sozusagen organisches Leiden; sie hält sonst ihre eigenen Perioden ein, kann aber vom Individuum auf bestimmte Zeiten verlegt werden. Das sind lauter Syndrome an denen neben organischen Bedingungen auch das Psychische einen grossen Anteil hat; die Frage ist wie sich diese beiden Faktoren in die Verursachung teilen, eine Frage, die mit grosser Vorsicht angefasst werden muss.

Sadgers Mitteilung zeigt in 2 Punkten eine Unvollständigkeit. Die 1.) hat Stekel richtig herausgegriffen. Wenn Pat. Knaben zwischen 11 und 13 Jahren, also sich selbst in diesem Alter, zu Liebesobjekten wählt, so hat uns die Analyse zu zeigen warum er sich in diesem Alter gerade hervorhebt; was ihm damals passiert ist und welche Befriedigungen in dieses Alter fallen.

2.) erhebt sich die Frage ob auch dieser Pat. nach dem von Sadger aufgezeigten Mechanismus (frühzeitige Bindung an das Weib, baldige Verdrängung dieser Neigung, Identifizierung mit dem Weib und

REFERENCES

Key to Abbreviations

C.P. Sigmund Freud: *Collected Papers*, 5 Volumes. London: Hogarth Press, 1924-1950.

G.S. Sigmund Freud: *Gesammelte Schriften*, 13 Volumes. Vienna: Internationaler psychoanalytischer Verlag, 1924-1934.

G.W. Sigmund Freud: *Gesammelte Werke*, 17 Volumes. London: Imago Publishing Company, 1940-1952.

J. *International Journal of Psycho-Analysis*

Jb. *Jahrbuch für Psychoanalyse*

S.E. *The Standard Edition of the Complete Psychological Works of Sigmund Freud*, 24 Volumes. London: Hogarth Press, 1953-

Yb. *The Yearbook of Psychoanalysis*, 10 Volumes. New York: International Universities Press, 1945-1954.

Z. *Internationale Zeitschrift für Psychoanalyse*

Zb. *Zentralblatt für Psychoanalyse*

ACKNOWLEDGMENTS

The editors regret that it was not possible to present this second volume of the Minutes of the Vienna Psychoanalytic Society to the public before a span of several years had elapsed since the publication of the first volume.

We wish to express our deep gratitude to Miss Ursula Sommer and especially to Mr. Harold Collins for their excellent work in carefully editing the translation from the German.

54A

SCIENTIFIC MEETING *on October 7, 1908*[1]

Present: Prof. Freud, Adler, Bass, [A.] Deutsch, Federn, Häutler, Hitschmann, Hollerung, Joachim, Rank, Reitler, Rie, Sadger, Steiner, Stekel, Wittels.

COMMUNICATIONS

Dr. Rie[2] and Ferenczi[3] are nominated as new members by Prof. Freud; unanimously accepted by all present.

Papers announced:

1. Stekel: "*A Dream is Life* and Its Connection with Grillparzer's Neurosis"
2. Sadger: "Analysis of a Hysteric Pseudoepilepsy"
3. Häutler: "*Ecce Homo*"

Planned for later in the year: Prof. Freud on dementia praecox; Adler, Hitschmann on diseases of the endocrine glands; Graf (Odyssee); Rank; Stekel: "Professional Choice and Neurosis"; Heller: "History of the Devil."

Reporter: Prof. W. Hellpach;[4] Bass, Hitschmann.

[1] The Minutes for this evening have not been preserved. The scientific meeting on October 14, 1908, is recorded as the first lecture meeting of the new working year. The attendance lists do not tally with the protocols in this, as in several other cases.

[2] Oskar Rie was a distinguished pediatrician in Vienna, and a close friend of Freud. He was Wilhelm Fliess' brother-in-law.

[3] Sandor Ferenczi is so well known that it seems superfluous to indicate who he was. A warm human being, full of ideas and interested in many fields, he was Freud's favorite pupil.

[4] The work of the renowned German psychologist and political figure, W. Hellpach, has been mentioned in earlier Minutes (see Vol. I, Minutes 28, 43, 46, 53). Jones, in his biography of Freud, does not mention Hellpach.

54B

SCIENTIFIC MEETING *on October 14, 1908*

Present: Prof. Freud, Adler, [A.] Deutsch, Federn, Hitschmann, Joachim, Rank, Rie, Reitler, Sadger, Schwerdtner, Steiner, Stekel, Wittels.

Dr. Rie and Ferenczi definitely accepted.

PRESENTATION

A Dream Is Life[1] and Its Connection with Grillparzer's Neurosis

SPEAKER: DR. STEKEL

STEKEL introduces his presentation by stating that all the valuable knowledge about the dream that Freud has imparted to us has been expressed by the poets. They too could not help but become aware

[1] *Der Traum, ein Leben* [*A Dream Is Life: A Dramatic Fantasy in Four Acts*] tr. H. H. Stevens. (Yarmouth Port, Mass.: Register Press, 1946) is a play in verse by the great Austrian dramatist and poet, Franz Grillparzer (1791-1872). Grillparzer had been interested in this theme as early as 1813; the play, however, was not staged at the Vienna Burgtheater until 1834. For a better understanding of these minutes, we append a very brief summary of the play's content.

The protagonist is Rustan, a young Persian who lives in the home of his uncle

of the connection between the dream and the poet's creation (Jean - Paul and Hebbel, in particular). Grillparzer was also greatly preoccupied with the problem of the dream, and with his own dreams. Since the chief problems of the dream have been pretty nearly solved, we are now interested in the finer details—for instance, the dream within a dream. Using two examples from his practice, Stekel tries to prove that the dream within a dream serves to expunge unwelcome facts, that it is, as it were, an expression of the saying: "Anyway, all this is nothing but a dream." This is also the case with Grillparzer's play. It, too, is a dream within a dream, since the entire play is to be viewed as the poet's dream.

The speaker now proceeds, not from Grillparzer's work, but from Grillparzer the man, and especially from his neurosis. Grillparzer, Stekel asserts, suffered from a compulsive neurosis; *A Dream is Life* is the dream of an obsessional neurotic. According to Freud, the

---

Massud, a landowner. Instead of working on the farm, the restless youth spends his days hunting from early morning till late at night, which greatly disturbs and distresses his cousin, Mirtza, who is in love with him. He dreams of great deeds and successes as a warrior. These ambitions are nurtured by his uncle's Negro slave, Tsanga. With his support, Rustan decides to leave for Samarkand to offer the beleaguered king his services, and eventually to win the king's daughter and with her the throne. He is spurred on to this decision by an insult he has suffered at the hands of a young nobleman, Osmin. During the night preceding his intended departure, Rustan has a dream: he encounters the King of Samarkand, who is fleeing from a gigantic serpent. Rustan tries unsuccessfully to kill the serpent; it succumbs to the spear of a man clad in a brown cloak, who throws his weapon from a high cliff down onto the monster. Egged on by Tsanga, Rustan claims the deed as his own, and is rewarded by the king with the leadership of the army and the promise of the hand of his daughter, Gylnara. When Rustan and Tsanga are alone, the man in the brown cloak reappears and warns Rustan that he will claim the reward for himself. Since the man does not yield to Rustan's entreaties and threats, Rustan, at the instigation of Tsanga, stabs him and throws him over the bridge into the water. Although he is successful as a warrior, Rustan stumbles from one lie to another, from one ruthless deed to another, until finally, after several murders, he himself is about to perish on the same bridge on which he had killed the man in the brown cloak. Tsanga has turned into the Devil, who ultimately drives him to death. At this point, Rustan awakens from his dream; at first unable to distinguish between reality and dream, then overcome by emotion, he begs his uncle's forgiveness, asks for Mirtza's hand, and prevails upon his uncle to set Tsanga free, under the condition that the latter leave immediately.

Stekel published this paper as the last chapter of his book *Dichtung und Neurose. Bausteine zur Psychologie des Künstlers und des Kunstwerkes.* Wiesbaden: Bergmann, 1909 ["Poetry and Neurosis. Contributions to the Psychology of the Artist and of Artistic Creative Ability." *Psychoanal. Rev.* 10:73-96, 190-208, 316-328, 457-466, 1923; 11:48-60, 1924].

obsessional neurotic is characterized by doubt—that is, doubt about love.[2] [Hans] Rau (*Grillparzer und sein Liebesleben* ["Grillparzer and his Love Life"] [1904]) maintains that Grillparzer's works contain nothing personal, that they give us no clue to the man Grillparzer. But this is not true; on the contrary, Grillparzer has woven all his sufferings into his works.

His doubts about everything are expressed in the poem *Incubus,* written when he was thirty years old. He was subject to a number of obsessional ideas and compulsive acts. His behavior toward the actress, Kati Frölich, was very peculiar indeed. The speaker now reads a passage from Grillparzer's diary, in which he ponders the cause of his aversion. . . .[3] Grillparzer is engaged in a constant struggle between sexual love and aversion. He is tugged hither and yon by two powerful currents: homosexuality and heterosexuality.

The speaker then relates a few facts about Grillparzer's sex life. First, about his parents. A burning hatred for his strict, sober, pedantic father was hidden under the cloak of love. When Grillparzer approached his father's deathbed, the latter said: "Now it is too late." Such utterances are disastrous in the life of a neurotic. This hatred of the father has repeatedly been carried over into Grillparzer's writings, e.g., in the poem *The Tragic Muse,* and in the drama *The Ancestress,* which deals with parricide. In this drama, a sister has been substituted for the mother, by way of displacement. Franz was hostile

2 This reference is not altogether accurate; Freud never characterized the obsessional neurotic merely in terms of this *single* symptom.

3 The sentence is left incomplete in the original protocol. The passage referred to is very likely the following in the Diaries (May, 1826; *Gesammelte Werke*, Vol. 8, edited by Rollet & Sauer, 1924):

"In the end it was mainly my resolution *not* to enjoy the girl, a resolution peculiarly adhered to, which brought me into this lamentable state. Peculiarly adhered to, I say, because it was not a truly virtuous decision; rather it was engendered by a pleasure, perhaps merely aesthetic, artistic, in the girl's purity, which restrained me from doing what I was almost irresistibly driven to do by all my feelings and thoughts. Thus I spent myself in the struggle against the almost continuous excitement; and the heated atmosphere which, emanating from me, passed over to the innocent creature, and without her knowing it also set her in motion, finally provoked in her all the effects of ungratified sexual love. She became suspicious, violent, even contentious. Thus, this relationship was also disturbed in its spiritual components, which had made it so unbelievably beautiful.

"My fantasy, by the way, has not yet recovered from this defeat. It is as if it has become impossible for me to portray any tender feelings, after I have seen my own emotion, beautiful beyond description, change into coldness and baseness."

to his brother Karl, and he did not have any special liking for Kamillo, his mother's favorite. Not much is known about Grillparzer's relationship with his mother. Referring to the fact that he was taking care of the household expenses, he once said that he was her son and husband.[4] His first love was a cousin, Marie Rizj;[5] Mirtza is a contraction of this name. His homosexual component expresses itself in his relationship to Altmütter, whom he called "dear Karl." The fact that Altmütter had the same first name as Grillparzer's brother probably had some bearing on Grillparzer's love for Altmütter, since in general the symbolism of the identical name plays an important role. In his diaries, Grillparzer speaks very candidly about his own characteristics: jealousy, hate, love, and envy play important roles, as they do in all obsessional neurotics. Also, the sudden misfiring of the mental apparatus is characteristic. That is to say, the forgotten theme for *Medea* suddenly came back to him as he was listening to a symphony by Haydn which his mother liked very much.[6]

Stekel then discusses Grillparzer's dream analysis of the Martine dream[7] and remarks that poisoning plays an important role in obsessional neurosis, as it does in the play under discussion.

[4] "Since I was the only one who took care of the household needs after her own resources had been exhausted, she combined in me, for herself, son and husband" (Autobiography).

[5] This and the following statements made by Stekel are not correct. Grillparzer's love was his cousin's wife, Charlotte von Paumgarten. The first name of Altmütter, a close friend of Grillparzer's, was Georg. "Dear Karl" was a friend of Altmütter's, not of Grillparzer. In fact, Grillparzer became very jealous of Karl when he saw a letter addressed to Karl on Altmütter's desk.

[6] Stekel's rendition of "the forgotten theme" differs from what Grillparzer tells us in his autobiography. However, Stekel profited from the criticisms offered in the discussion of his paper and corrected the inaccuracies when he published his book.

[7] "How strange, indeed almost mechanical, is the meddling of recollection in the dreams, I experienced again today. Toward morning I dreamed that I was reading some verses that my brother Karl had composed for a 'Lady Martine.' I woke up from this dream seeing nothing peculiar in it but the name Martine, which I could not recall having ever heard at any other time, nor could I convince myself that it was likely that it was used anywhere in the world. Still reflecting on the working of fantasy in the creation of this name, I sat down to breakfast and began to read Tacitus. In order to reread a passage that I had forgotten, I turned back a good many pages until I came upon the death of Germanicus, about which I had read several days before, and lo and behold! the woman whom Piso allegedly used for the poisoning of Augustus' grandson was called—Martine [*Annales*, III, 7; II, 74]. With my bad memory, I had forgotten this so completely that even the repetition of the name in the dream did not bring back to me a vague recollection that I had heard it once before and—the dream knew what I myself did not. . . ." (*Diaries*, 1830).

In addition to the doubting, the inability to make decisions is of great significance. Rustan, too, acts only under the pressure of external circumstances.

The speaker now turns to the dramatic tale itself. Grillparzer took the subject matter from a story by Voltaire, *Le blanc et le noir* ("The Black and the White"), which contains some ideas about the dream. In Voltaire's work, the princes of that region are called Mirza.[8] In an earlier version, [the figure of] Rustan was called Ismael, a name that contains the same three vowels that appear in the poet's own name (*i, a, e*). The various recastings best show what was initially intended.

Mirza has the same relationship to Rustan as Grillparzer's first love, his cousin, had to him. His father appears in many forms in succession, one of which—in his positive aspects—is no doubt Massud. Tsanga is the personified unconscious, the suppressed, and also bears many traits of his brother Karl. Osmin, Rustan's rival, was originally named Sapor and represents, according to his description (Act I), Grillparzer's womanish brother K*a*mill*o* (vowels *a* and *o*). In the first version, he played an important role; later, he was relegated to a minor part; as a rival, he deprived Rustan of the princess' favor, just as Kamillo had robbed Grillparzer of his mother's love. It has been said that it was Napoleon's fate that induced Grillparzer to finish the play. But Napoleon was, like Grillparzer, a lawyer's son; thus it seems likely that some fantasies of grandeur were operative in Grillparzer, since they are also indicated in the play (Tsanga obliterates the traces of Rustan's origin). Grillparzer, by the way, hated his own name, as do all people who hate their fathers.

The speaker then discusses the play scene by scene, reading some particularly significant passages, and interpreting them. In the first act, Mirza places herself at the table between Massud and Rustan, in order to protect Rustan from the old man's wrath. This scene was surely modeled after a domestic scene in which the mother intervened between father and son.

In the dream itself (Act II), the scenery clearly is an expression of sexual symbolism; the symbolism of right and left is carried through, just as it is in analyses.

[8] Mirza is a general honorary title in Persia.

Mention must also be made of the symbolism of the snake. The Cliff-man is one of the representations of the father. Grillparzer intended to write a play *The Purple Mantle* (royal mantle, father's mantle); the man in the play has a brown mantle. Gylnara, the princess, who corresponds to the mother, is represented as being beyond all human love only in the last version. The Cliff-man (father) reminds him of Osmin (the brother); he wanted to murder his father and brother. Rustan says of him: "His touch is unmanning"—which may go back to an infantile experience with the father (castration-threat complex). The wish fulfillment of the first act of the dream is this: he renders a great service to the king (father and mother), and kills father and brother. The old mute Caleb, who accuses him of murder, is again the murdered father. The old witch personifies his mother, who thus also appears in two figures. In this a fantasy of rape is also indicated. In Osmin's report, which the king reads, Mirtza is directly identified with Gylnara. It shows Rustan's homosexual tendencies when he orders Tsanga to stab him in the back with his dagger. Rustan then dies on the same bridge on which his father died. Tsanga is transformed into the Devil, the tempter. Finally, a feeling of release takes hold of Rustan when he feels that it is all nothing but a dream, that he hates no one, and that, with regard to murder, he can have a free conscience. At the end Grillparzer expresses a thought that is not very far from Freud's dream theory: he says that the dream does not create wishes, it awakens those already present.

DISCUSSION

FEDERN sees in this paper the whole Stekel, with all his faults and his merits. With his customary lack of critical judgment, Stekel jumbles up everything, and is utterly arbitrary about details. Federn does not want to go into this, but he does wish to stress emphatically that the material presented in no way justifies the assumption that Grillparzer was a compulsive neurotic.

REITLER, by contrast with Federn, states that Stekel's paper is sound and shows evidence of hard work. He raises this objection: that inversions and transformations of father and mother, such as Stekel makes much of, do not take place. It is incompatible with the dream mechanism of condensation for Stekel to find the father represented in so many different shapes.[9] He, too, would rule out the diagnosis of obsessional neurosis; he sees in all this the hysteria of an impotent man. That the words "too late" played an important role in Grillparzer's life is evident from Zipper's biography,[10] according to which Grillparzer later used this phrase repeatedly. Grillparzer's wild devotion to Austria might be regarded as a neurotic symptom; this love for the fatherland could be a reaction formation to the hatred of his father.

WITTELS remarks that a drama, according to the well-known definition, ought to evoke terror and pity; this is not the case in Stekel's presentation; it is his interpretation that is more likely to evoke these emotions.[11] He deals with the drama as if it were a picture puzzle, in which one has to try to find the father everywhere. If one persists in this type of interpretive technique, it will not be long before one sees a penis in every convex object and a vagina in every concave one. It is true, one cannot deny Stekel a certain skill in the character and application of his method. Nevertheless, it is inadmissible to seek out the hidden symbolism behind a writer's every word, because after all the writer has no means other than language, and language, moreover, may not have the same significance for the writer that it has for the neurotic.

STEINER merely wants to refer most strenuously to the viewpoint of impotence.

RIE would divide the paper into two parts, of totally unequal value. In one, Stekel illuminates the creative process by using biographical material—as Brandes did with Shakespeare's plays; from this part of the paper Rie has learned something new. The details that Stekel has presented, on the other hand, seem to him inferior; Stekel's need to particularize seems to be too strong. Moreover, the dream within a dream is not the same in the neurotic and the poet.

[9] This statement of Reitler's is incorrect. Among the dream mechanisms is not only condensation, but also fragmentation. See Freud's *The Interpretation of Dreams* (1900), *S.E.*, 4 & 5.

[10] Albert Zipper: *Franz Grillparzer*. Vienna: Reclams Universal Bibliothek.

[11] The German original has "*erwecken*" ["arouse" or "evoke"]. If this is not a slip, if it should not be "*ersticken*" ["smother"], then this remark can only be understood as a sarcastic critique of Stekel's interpretation.

SADGER this time agrees with Federn's judgment. What Stekel adduces in support of Grillparzer's obsessional neurosis also occurs in other people; the important issue is only the way in which these drives are dealt with and worked up. Grillparzer was definitely not an obsessional neurotic. To conclude from Grillparzer's chastity vis-à-vis Kati Frölich—to whom he had obviously transferred the love for his mother—that he was impotent would be very risky. Contemporaries of Grillparzer describe him as a "wolf."

Furthermore, there are many incorrect details. For instance, Grillparzer's relationship with Karl was not bad at all. The assertion that the incestuous thoughts in *The Ancestress* refer to the mother has not been substantiated, nor have many other assertions [made by Stekel]. In general, there are limits to the interpretation of a poet's creations, because we do not know the most important factor—that is, the type and degree of distortion.

RANK points out that, in his paper on the incest theme,[12] he has already furnished the major portion of what Dr. Rie called the first part of Stekel's paper. However, at that time he had for good reasons refrained from embarking on an interpretation of the drama discussed by Stekel today, because the supporting evidence is missing, although in some instances Stekel's interpretation may be correct.

PROF. FREUD first expresses the fear that the criticism directed against Stekel today will make no impression on him, although if he did take the objections into account and eliminated certain exaggerations, the work would have some merit.

To begin with, there is not the slightest evidence that Grillparzer was an obsessional neurotic; on the contrary, many things in his character traits actually speak against such an assumption. With regard to doubt about love, Stekel has misunderstood matters, for what is involved here is always doubt only in one's own love, and not in that of others. Furthermore, Stekel's analytic method is too radical; everything he finds in Grillparzer can be found in every neurotic, as well as in all normal persons. It is not enough to demonstrate [the existence of] these complexes, which, as we know, must be present; the problem is rather to demonstrate their psychic localization. The main

12 Compare Volume I, Minutes 3.

reproach to be leveled against Stekel is: this is not the way to make an analysis, nor is it the way to present one. Sadger is quite right in contending that certain things cannot be dealt with. It is not permissible to interpret a drama sentence by sentence. Some passages can be traced to recent impressions, others to inhibitions; in this way, one gradually comes upon the impressions of childhood, and then one can, in some instances, demonstrate the intimate connections. In short, a presentation must take into account the fact that psychic processes occur on different levels. No doubt, the drama contains elements that essentially confirm Stekel's presentation. He has a flair for psychogenic complexes (for instance, "unmanning"); the trouble is that he relies exclusively on his inspirations, instead of submitting them to the control of conscious thinking. His paper contains many more valuable thoughts than appear at first glance.

The title of the play is not correct; for what it portrays is not a dream but a fantasy (the dream never works that way)—which might better be compared to a myth. Myth and fantasy, in comparison to the dream, are both paranoid;[13] they decompose instead of condensing, and for this reason they frequently contain duplications; the same person, even the same motif, appears in several duplications. In these fantasies, we find one element that is well known to us—namely, the rescue of the emperor or king, which plays an important role in many fantasies (that is, the rescue of the kind father). In contrast to this—and hence in a certain sense identical with it—is the father's murder.

The interpretation [of the dream landscape] as a sexual landscape may or may not be correct. The only proof in such cases is to be found in whether the interpretation yields a new connection. The scene in which the father (the Cliff-man) is thrown from a bridge into the water is reminiscent of something that belongs in the "family romance"—namely, infants being cast into the water (the representation of birth). Here, however, both the rescue fantasy and the exposure fantasy have been transferred onto the father.[14] As to the idea of impotence, it is significant that Rustan does not become Gylnara's husband; this circumstance does seem to point to the mother.

[13] This is a very important differentiation between dream and fantasy.

[14] These ideas of Freud's are contained in Rank's *The Myth of the Birth of the Hero*, which appeared later (1909).

JOACHIM doubts that a poet's work can really be interpreted consistently. There can never be any certainty in this. Moreover, in the psychoanalytic sense, little can be gained thereby and rather [much] lost. An artist's creation resembles only in part that of the neurotic. To attribute to homosexual tendencies Grillparzer's rapidly cooling inclination does not seem to be satisfactory enough; in all neurotics love cools rather quickly, and this circumstance could perhaps be more appropriately explained in terms of the incongruence of his fantasy image with reality.

[A.] DEUTSCH is certain that Stekel was conscious of the boldness of his interpretations; in writing this paper, he has elucidated much.

HITSCHMANN hopes that the speaker will have better patients than Grillparzer, who could only have been harmed by psychoanalysis. Grillparzer was an impotent, physically ill man, whose sexuality was severely suppressed. He is frightened when he recognizes himself in Rousseau's *Confessions*. Stekel reasons that Grillparzer could not possess Kati because he had not possessed his mother. In view of the fact that very many men do not possess their mothers, and yet do not become sexually impotent, this argument becomes quite dubious.

Nothing was said about the extent to which wish fulfillment can be recognized: perhaps the wish can be characterized briefly as the desire to obtain a woman after a battle. In his opinion, Stekel should not have placed so much weight on the parents; in this respect, one must in general be on guard against exaggerations (see Goethe's parents).

ADLER regrets that he must increase the number of critics. One cannot make an interpretation of a poet's work by lining up single elements one behind the other, and then making a scribble out of all this. Above all, one must give due regard to the fact that these various details stem from different phases of the poet's life.

In this case, it would have been important to point out the connection with recent material. It has to do with Osmin and the events occurring at the hunt on the day preceding the dream. The dissatisfaction that results from the failure of Rustan's revenge leads to the dream. Rustan's tendency to aggressive acts fits in with this. He attempts to attain in the dream what he was unable to attain when he faced Osmin. From here, one could gain access to the experiences of childhood:

these are the revenges that he was denied, which he could not carry out against father and brother.

STEKEL, in his concluding remarks, stresses that his paper fulfilled its purpose if it accomplished no more than to serve as the occasion for the Professor's reply. He is aware of the boldnesses; he always goes somewhat further than he himself believes. Nevertheless, it is his conviction that he has accomplished somewhat more than some people believe he has.

55

SCIENTIFIC MEETING *on October 21, 1908*

Present: Freud, Adler, Bass, Hitschmann, Hollerung, Joachim, Rank, Reitler, Rie, Sadger, Steiner, Stekel, Wittels.

PRESENTATION

Analysis of a Case of Hysterical Pseudoepilepsy[1]

SPEAKER: DR. STEKEL

The case has to do with a young man, eighteen years old, who was sent to Sadger with a diagnosis of hysterical pseudoepilepsy and obsessional neurosis. He complained of states of confusion of short duration, fainting spells, loss of consciousness, biting his tongue, and impotence. He also stated that he had previously suffered from convulsions; this, however, proved to be incorrect.

On the second day of his analysis, the patient went into a state of confusion: he stopped in the middle of a sentence, his mind wholly

[1] The paper was published in *Wiener klinische Rundschau,* 14-17, 1909, under the title "*Ein Fall von Pseudoepilepsia hysterica psychoanalytisch erklärt*" ["A Case of Hysterical Pseudoepilepsy Psychoanalytically Explained"].

elsewhere, and he spoke no more. Upon being questioned, he said, "Just now I was with the girl with whom I am in love" (he had numerous love affairs); "that's the reason for the confusion." He said that, in such a state, "I have an empty page in my brain." For a while, during the time he was in treatment with a professor to whom he was homosexually attached, these states of confusion ceased to appear. He felt for this professor, as he said, simultaneously fear and love—that is, obviously, a transference from the father. He had been in love with his father, but also had seen in him a rival for the mother [and] the Devil (his fear of the Devil!).

The speaker then passes on to the major attacks. These occurred at short intervals, especially when the patient was ten and eleven years old. In describing one of these attacks, the patient relates that one morning, before school, he had gone to a rather primitive toilet, had fallen asleep there, and awoke only when his father, worried by his long absence, searched for him and found him there; this attack is said to have lasted two hours. His second attack occurred at home, in the presence of his tutor, who seems to have been a sadist and with whom he was homosexually in love; he was looking into the light, as in hypnosis, and fainted (a kind of autohypnosis). He had a third attack in school during a lecture. He stared continuously at the teacher in a vacant manner, had a feeling as if he had an empty page in his brain (just as during the minor states of confusion), and then fell asleep. Even before this incident he had tried to suppress the urge to urinate, but had not been successful, with the result that he was made fun of and felt deeply ashamed. This time too he had suppressed the urge to urinate and had been afraid that he might not succeed. He suppressed the urge because he was used to doing so at night, when he chose to suppress his needs for fear of meeting ghosts outside his room.

Later the attacks were replaced by congestions that lasted from twenty-four to thirty hours, and by fear of death and nausea. At the age of 20, the patient, stimulated by seduction, also began to indulge in masturbation.

Among the events in his life history, one should stress the fact that from his fifteenth year on his love for a girl, Dora, played an important role; but behind her one could detect his sister, who had died at the age of seven. In addition, two other amorous relationships were significant. When he was about five or six years old, he was in a room with a girl three years his senior. He urinated, but wet the floor beside the chamberpot. The girl beat him. He had the same sensation in his penis then as he has now during intercourse. This feeling provokes his congestion. At twelve, he made his first declaration of love to a girl of the same age; however, she reacted very coolly.

At twelve, also, he began to practice his own special method of masturbation: with a finger in the anus and in front on the penis. He said: "While I am doing this, I feel like a woman." Obviously, he is representing simultaneously a woman who is being masturbated and a man who is masturbating.

He knew his sister Emilie, who plays the most important role in his illness, for only one year.[2] She seemed to him more like a cousin, as he says, and she loved him dearly. He indulged in various forms of sexual play with her, looking at her anus (not her vagina!), etc. He enjoyed most putting various objects in his anus and beating [himself] on the buttocks.[3] After his sister's death, he blamed himself for having possibly caused it by his sexual play. He believes that one dies with each coition; therefore, it is not only prostitutes that he fears. Were his sister still alive, he says, she would—out of love—permit him to have intercourse with her.

He uses his masturbation, which gives him a twofold autoerotic pleasure and complete independence, as a means of self-punishment; for he feels pain when he introduces his finger into the anus; moreover, he beats himself on the buttocks.

He spoke also of one attack which, as he himself admitted, was simulated. Between the ages of twelve and fourteen, he wished to have epileptic attacks, because [he says] they gain love. He also simulated a fit of fury, which was preceded by great sexual excitement. Later he believed that masturbation caused illnesses of the brain and the spinal cord. At that time, he frequently had suicidal ideas; he wanted to stab himself in the chest with a penknife (symbol of the penis), or to cut

[2] Up to her seventh year, Emilie had been living at her grandmother's. She died one year after coming to stay at her parental home.

[3] The original does not make altogether clear at this point whose buttocks he beats. But see later in the presentation.

his arteries. Even as a small child, he often spoke of death. If he fell, for instance, he would ask whether he had not died. Often he would threaten [his parents] with his death.

He also tells of the attacks of the last three years up to his masturbation. From his fourteenth to his seventeenth year, he had had no attack.

Now he writes—poems and plays, also musicals; nothing but love stories. In his poems, he calls all the loved ones "sister." Yet he has forgotten what his sister looked like. Later, he saw her in a photograph that impressed him deeply; she wore white (the white, empty page of his attacks). When he was studying hard, he masturbated more, and thought of his sister, whom he wanted to call back to life. After masturbating, he would think of intercourse with his sister. He accepts the surmise that while masturbating he was, in his way, having intercourse with the sister. Thus he uses the compulsive masturbation as a way of performing by himself, without outside help, the coition with the sister that is impossible in actuality, since she is dead. The confusion of his mind is merely the searching for his sister: the white page seems to be the airy specter he imagines his sister to be. The "white" leads to nightgown and to the shroud of Jewish ritual [for the dead]. The patient is now given the explanation that his "epilepsy," too, is caused by his desire to have his sister always at hand for intercourse.

The patient supplements his report by mentioning still another attack, which he had at the health resort where his sister's last friend died; from then on, his epileptic attacks became more severe. On the twenty-third day of his analysis, he had a minor epileptic attack. During the preceding night he had dreamed that his father had died (he had just learned of the murder of the king of Portugal: king = father). Later the same night, he had the same dream once again. He also dreamed that his mother was beating him on his naked buttocks. Upon awakening, he thinks of the operetta which he is now occupied in writing and is very happy about it. Then he feels nauseous. The joy about his creation is a displacement of the joy about his father's death; in the operetta he plays the part of the lover vis-à-vis mother, sister and Dora; at the same time, he dreams of the greatest feeling of pleasure he knows—that of being beaten.

On the thirteenth day, he has a major "epileptic" attack. In the morning, he is awakened by a knocking on the door, and thinks that ghosts are there, that his dead sister wants to open the door and to come to him. He falls asleep again and dreams about his usual act of masturbation. Upon awakening, he feels a pain in his chest and on his tongue; he sees a wound on his tongue. The preceding evening, the conversation had been about the theater (Krastel[4] had died); he wanted to act the lover's parts with a girl who had the same first name as his sister. While relating this, he constantly moves his legs. To bite india-rubber comes to his mind; rubber, a symbol for labia and navel. As a child of five or six years, he bit his mother; later, he bit his own arm and hand. An aunt of his comes to mind; she had the habit of biting little children on their bellies.

The pain in his chest is the substitute for his desire to bite Emilie's breast, as he had bitten his mother's. The latter used to take him into her bed up to his ninth year, and he would pinch her breasts. He imagines fingernails as a symbol of the tongue. He still sucks his fingers. A colleague told him about *minette;*[5] he felt the desire to do that with Dora. Probably he wanted to do it with his mother and sister too.

At fourteen and fifteen, he frequently went to his mother's bed at night, allegedly because of fear of ghosts and burglars. However, he may have done so in order to disturb the parents' intercourse. Occasionally his mother would change beds with him, which gave him great pleasure. Once he said to his father: "Give me a woman or I will shoot you."

He now begins to understand his feelings of anxiety during the attacks: they arise from incestuous sources. He was afraid that, owing to his thoughts about his mother, his father, who is a notary—that is, the guardian and representative of the law—would call him to account and sentence him to death.

Ever since he stopped sleeping with his mother, he has been able to sleep only with the light on. At four or five years, he suffered from attacks of migraine; at that time, his mother would turn the light on, in order to give him wet dressings. When he hypnotizes himself, he also stares at shining objects (*light!*).

He had one epileptic attack in which his sister came to him, and

[4] A famous actor of the Vienna *Burgtheater*, at the beginning of this century.
[5] Cunnilingus.

another in which it was his mother: each time, one of the two beloved persons. He admits the possibility that behind Dora and his mother may be hidden the sister.

It is interesting that his fantasies about hypnosis are wish fulfillments; he imagines that he is given an order to perform rapes, for which he is then not responsible.

His fainting spells are instances of autohypnosis, from which he wakes himself. During his epileptic attacks, he is not completely unconscious but thinking of sexual matters.

The homosexual roots of every hysterical symptom are laid bare in a homosexually motivated attack, during which he fantasied that he pressed his brother to his body and kissed him. At the same time, he felt congestions in his head—that is to say, an erection displaced from below upwards. Before falling asleep, he had thought of *The Ancestress*,[6] and of Jaromir in particular, who loves his sister and gives her poison in order for her to kill herself and her father. Thus, the patient wants to poison his brother and father. At present, he very much loves this brother, whom once, as a child, he had wanted to kill.

It is clear to the speaker that he has not elucidated everything—for instance, the first attack on the toilet, which, with its relation to feces, surely goes back to earliest childhood. The migraine has likewise remained unsolved. On the other hand, the analysis has clearly demonstrated that this case, which had been diagnosed as typical epilepsy, was actually not that at all. The analysis of the individual attacks makes this quite apparent. In such cases, for which the diagnosis is still so uncertain, one must be very cautious. Perhaps with the help of the psychoanalytic method one can succeed in unmasking some of these unfortunate people for what they usually are—namely, hysterics—and lead them to recovery.

DISCUSSION

JOACHIM is of the opinion that, from the patient's accounts, it is not possible to distinguish what kind of attack it was. The post-epileptic states of confusion, which do not appear after hysterical attacks, might perhaps be regarded as a distinguishing sign.

[6] See Minutes 54B, this volume.

HOLLERUNG remarks that he, too, has treated such cases of "epilepsy," which later proved to be hysterical.

PROF. FREUD considers the paper to be praiseworthy in various respects. A few minor critical objections should not detract from this essential appreciation. One must reproach the speaker a little for the fact that he introduces surprising pronouncements with "as everybody knows"—a journalistic mannerism (for instance, "the piece of apple stuck in the esophagus is the penis, as everybody knows"; this is, however, by no means always obvious).

In general, Prof. Freud asks the speaker to give up one part of his technique—namely, writing down verbatim whatever the patient says. This leads—to use a simile—to the speaker's presenting the pitchblende instead of the radium that is to be gained from it. Many of the associations are wrong connections—that is, they are secondary elaborations—and to treat them in the same way as the valuable ones would easily give the impression of a lack of judgment [on the speaker's part].

Other objections are answered by the speaker's remark that he has presented a fragment only.

As far as the subject matter is concerned, it is to be noted that, apart from the distorted memories and fantasies that make their appearance at the beginning of every analysis, a good deal was well understood and interpreted. Especially with regard to the question of the differential diagnosis of hysteria and epilepsy, there was much that was eminently correct; it is quite true that we do not know of a distinguishing sign that would help us to sort out the attacks anamnestically. Even urinary incontinence and biting of the tongue are found in the most unquestionable hysterias. Incontinence of feces is rarer in hysterias. The old dispute can probably be solved in line with Sadger's thinking: there are hysterias and there are epilepsies; occasionally, the two may combine, but all those illnesses that are called hysteroepilepsy are simply hysterias.[7]

Of theoretical interest in this case is the question of how this patient, whom Sadger himself called a "pig," came to develop a hysteria. Actu-

[7] Freud wrote in "Dostoevsky and Parricide" (1928): "It is therefore quite right to distinguish between an organic and an 'affective' epilepsy. The practical significance of this is that a person who suffers from the first kind has a disease of the brain, while a person who suffers from the second kind is a neurotic" (*S.E.*, 21:181).

ally, he should be consistent and remain a pig. In what way does he acquire repressions? Adler will certainly be able to answer this question in a way which, from his point of view, is very simple and justified.[8]

The experiences that are characteristic of hysteria occur at a very early age, probably in the second or third year; by the time it is at an end, the fourth year may perhaps be already too late.[9] An indication of this can also be found in this case, and the repression must be connected with this enigma: at an early age there are manifestations of strong instincts of cruelty, which do not persist with the same intensity in later years. He has remained a pig in sexual matters, but he is no savage in cultural ones. Perhaps the instincts of cruelty have fallen victim to the suppression that is inherent in civilization, and this may be the root of his hysteria.

It is strange, moreover, that this child, as early as at the age of two and three, spoke so much of death. The death complex must have been within his range of ideas as early as that. And as chance would have it, moreover, his sex object died soon thereafter. Then he probably began to suffer from the infantile complex, which is the cause of every neurosis. Indeed, we are more and more inclined to believe that it is only one complex that causes man to become ill, and that this complex is always in the sphere: father-mother. Each and every neurosis can be traced back to this complex.[10] In this way, matters that initially appear to be very complex gradually become much simpler, here as everywhere.

Yet the question of the choice of neurosis has thereby become even more difficult to answer. If all neuroses go back to similar complexes, what then is the source of the different forms of neurosis, whose determinants must be specific? No doubt, a certain violence of the motor

8 This is the first indication in these protocols that Freud makes a distinction between his own opinions and those of Adler.

9 This remark is very important. The form of the neurosis is probably dependent upon the age at which the determining event took place. Perhaps this is the time element to which Freud ascribes importance in the choice of neurosis.

10 This statement is still valid today. All attempts to minimize the importance of the oedipus complex for the causation of the neuroses must fail, for the so-called "preoedipal" causations are reflected in the oedipus complex, which then takes the lead by itself in the formation of the neurosis.

apparatus plays an important role in this respect. The motor components that otherwise spend their aggressive force in coition fuel the attack, which is the purest equivalent of coition. Thus an ancient saying by Galen is confirmed: intercourse is a minor epileptic attack; only we would say it the other way around.[11]

Freud fully agrees with Sadger's interpretation of the fear of ghosts (the same is true with regard to the fear of burglars): they are indeed the white-gowned nocturnal visitors of the child. The burglar is invariably the father; this is also evident in the dreams of adults, in which this figure is sometimes clearly recognizable.

To Dr. Joachim one must reply that the postepileptic states are not an unfailing criterion, either.

HITSCHMANN makes the point that, according to common clinical knowledge, no greater mistake could be made than to question an epileptic, even a merely potential one, about himself. In this case, Hitschmann misses the information [that one can gain] from those around the patient, especially from his closest relatives. On the basis of what he has heard, Hitschmann could not be prevailed upon to swear that this man is not an epileptic, especially since no reason has yet been given for the patient's recovery. It seemed remarkable to him that this patient could talk consciously about so many matters. To regard the penknife with which the patient wanted to cut his arteries as a penis appears to be a very forced interpretation. Furthermore, the photograph of the sister, which the patient saw only later, was used to

[11] In "Some General Remarks on Hysterical Attacks" (1909), Freud wrote: "Already in ancient times coition was described as a 'minor epilepsy'. We might alter this and say that a convulsive hysterical attack is an equivalent of coition. The analogy with the epileptic fit helps us little, since its genesis is even less understood than that of hysterical attacks" (*S.E.*, 9:234). In 1923, in *The Ego and the Id*, Freud elaborated on the idea set forth here, that heightened motor excitability and excessive rage are involved in epilepsy. He wrote: "We perceive that for purposes of discharge the instinct of destruction is habitually brought into the service of Eros; we suspect that the epileptic fit is a product and an indication of an instinctual defusion" (*S.E.*, 19:41). See also *Beyond the Pleasure Principle* (1920) (*S.E.*, 18).

The following may be of some interest in this context: Freud sent an epileptic to me for treatment, a patient who was under heavy bromide sedation. The treatment did not progress satisfactorily, and I therefore asked Freud whether I should not withdraw the drug from the patient. His answer was: "Of course you can do that, if you want to risk a *status epilepticus*" (that is, a state of constant convulsions, which may well lead to death).

interpret earlier events. Aside from these minor matters, the paper was quite nicely done.

RIE would like to ask only one question, which the speaker himself has already raised—namely, the question concerning the relation of the migraine to the total picture. The patient himself saw an analogy between the migraine and the attacks; hence it does not seem impossible that both were hysterical.

In reference to the differential diagnosis of hysteria and epilepsy, Rie mentions the case of a woman whose illness had all the appearances of a hysteria, yet was finally proven to be an epilepsy, from which she died.

PROF. FREUD mentions, in this context, that death also occurs in hysteria. The decrease in intelligence also proves nothing, for in hysterics it is caused by the power of the unconscious complexes. The "petit mal" is completely analogous to the brief loss of consciousness at the acme of sexual gratification [our "to the point of unconsciousness" (*bis zur Bewusstlosigkeit*)].[12]

STEKEL considers what has been said as indisputable and, with regard to the problem of hysteria fully agrees with Sadger and Prof. Freud. The question of why this patient fell ill has probably not been fully answered by Freud's remark. This man may perhaps have struggled through a severe conflict; perhaps he believed that in the eyes of the world he was carrying a crime around with him. The pleasure in flagellation, masochism, often has a peculiar root. Originally, it is the punishment for the incestuous wish.

With respect to the method of taking shorthand notes of the analysis, Eulenburg's[13] criticism of Sadger's analysis of a homosexual (in Hirschfeld's *Jahrbuch*)[14] is justified; it is true that it is tiring.

REITLER has nothing to add to the general expressions of appreciation. He has encountered the fantasy of watering the sister's grave

[12] See footnote 11. In fact, according to the theory current at that time, migraine was a minor epileptic attack.

[13] Albert Eulenburg, German professor of pharmacology and neurology (1840-1917).

[14] *Fragment der Psychoanalyse eines Homosexuellen* ["Fragment of the Psychoanalysis of a Homosexual"], *Jb. für sex. Zwischenst.*, 9, 1908.

in order to awaken her, in the case of a sadist, in which it had the meaning of intercourse ("wetting"), coupled with desecration of the dead (sadist: defenselessness of the object).

ADLER wants to make only some brief and general remarks. The distinction between hysteria and epilepsy is indeed quite difficult to make. In his practice, he has rarely seen a genuine epilepsy; almost invariably, the cases turn out to be hysterias. It is correct that none of the commonly accepted signs of distinction are valid. However, from the description of the patient's character, one can make a diagnosis with a fair degree of certainty, often without even having seen him. Hysteria on the whole resembles the picture that Prof. Freud sketched of the anal character. The latter is frequent and plays a prominent role.

In these fits, rage plays an important part, which Adler has related to the aggressive drive. It is of the utmost importance to establish the connection with the recent events that triggered these attacks. Only from an understanding of the attack can an understanding of the nature of the illness be gained.

In these cases, migraine almost regularly plays an important role; in his Salzburg paper, Adler characterized migraine as an attack of rage.

The congestions, which can be traced back to a choking sensation, also admit of an interpretation. He can suggest a way of explaining the mutual relationships among these phenomena. There are many cases that are distinguished by the patient's having suffered a spasm of the glottis in the second year. But, as Adler knows from personal experience, these spasms of the glottis always appear only after temper tantrums. These are specific spasms of the glottis: they begin with wheezing and are followed by dyspnoea and, almost regularly, by loss of consciousness. It can be clearly demonstrated that such cases are the typical representatives of the anal character, with its usual component of aggression.

PROF. FREUD remarks that this (Adler's) view coincides in its essentials with his own—namely, that, in the hysterical attack, two components are regularly present: aggression and affection, which Adler has not directly mentioned.

MINUTES 55

SADGER, in his concluding remarks, states that on the whole he feels satisfied with the success of this evening. He then makes a few supplementary remarks: the patient's mother is looked upon as a paragon of cleanliness in their small community; she is her husband's cousin.

56

SCIENTIFIC MEETING *on October 28, 1908*

Present: Freud, Adler, [A.] Deutsch, Federn, Häutler, Hollerung, Joachim, Rank, Rie, Sadger, Stekel.

Dr. Friedman and Mr. Frey as guests.

PRESENTATION

Nietzsche's *Ecce Homo*[1]

SPEAKER: HÄUTLER

Ecce Homo was the last work that Nietzsche finished in publishable form. Before the book could be made public, the catastrophe had happened. For this reason the book was not published at that time, and his sister continued to postpone publication. Nevertheless she made ample use of the manuscript in her biography of Nietzsche, especially in the second volume. Had *Ecce Homo* been available earlier, it could have contributed to a better understanding and ap-

[1] This is the second evening devoted to a discussion of Nietzsche. The topic for the first evening was "On the Ascetic Ideal" (Vol. I, Minutes 45).

Nietzsche wrote *Ecce Homo*, his autobiography, between October 15, his forty-fourth birthday, and November 4, 1888. His mental breakdown occurred in January, 1889.

preciation of Nietzsche. Even if the picture he paints of himself does not entirely correspond to the truth, it still represents a wish fulfillment: this was how Nietzsche wanted to be seen. In any case, he characterizes himself by this presentation.

In this work, there is a restyling of his life, for a very definite purpose: he represents himself as the opposite of Christ; it is the Antichrist whom he depicts in portraying himself as Dionysus.[2] As one who has been prepared by everything to assume this position of confronting Christ, he accords himself the right, as it were, to create, in words, an Antichrist. It is characteristic of Nietzsche that he is able to recognize himself only in someone else; when he talks about Dionysus, he is simply speaking of himself in that guise.

The book is divided into chapters, which have very curious titles, such as: "Why I am so clever," "Why I am so wise," "Why I write such excellent books." The titles, which are not really related to the contents of the chapters, seem to have been chosen to contrast with some sayings of the Gospel—for instance: "Blessed are the meek."

To Nietzsche, the nature of his wisdom appears to be founded on the contrast between his father and mother. From his father (who died when he was 36), he has his morbid disposition. To this he then adds: "Now I continue to live as my mother."[3] By virtue of his paternal heritage, he is destined to be at home in all forms of decadence. What enables him to overcome this is what he has inherited from his mother. He defines the essence of illness as the will not to recover. Nevertheless, he feels indebted to his illness, because illness is necessary for spiritual development.

His second major investigation concerns resentment.

As another trait that is characteristic of himself, Nietzsche refers

[2] The work ends with the following words: "Have you understood me? *Dionysus versus Christ. . . .*" See *Ecce Homo*, tr. C. P. Fadiman. New York: Modern Library, p. 145. (All subsequent quotations are taken from this Fadiman translation.)

[3] Häutler's report of this passage is not quite correct. The first chapter begins with these words: "The happiness of my existence, its unique character perhaps, lies in its fatefulness: expressing it in the form of a riddle, as my own father I am already dead, as my own mother I still live and grow old." And a few lines further: "My father died in his thirty-sixth year: he was delicate, lovable and morbid, like one fated for but a short life—a gracious reminder of life rather than life itself. In the same year that his life declined mine also declined: in my thirty-sixth year my vitality reached its lowest point . . ." (pp. 3-4).

to his attitude toward war which, as Heraclitus did, he represents as the father of all good things.

The essence of his wisdom is that he has wasted his strength.[4] His hatred of the Germans and of all things German is, to a great extent, a reaction against their conspiracy of silence against him.

Heine embodies for Nietzsche the very essence of the lyricist. Shakespeare's crowning achievement lies, according to Nietzsche, in his having conceived the character of Caesar.

Nietzsche speaks with regret about his book *Contra Wagner*.[5]

He then turns to answer the essential question: how one becomes what one is. His guess is that a person has no idea of what he is; that even mistakes are valuable, an overriding wisdom expresses itself in them; in this context, he takes the side of the selfless drives, which here work in the service of selfishness.[6]

Nietzsche then justifies his relating trivial matters, which have hitherto been too much neglected.

He discusses his way of writing, the art of style, and finally, in the spirit of his last prefaces, he reviews his books one by one.

The question posed in the last chapter, "Why I am a fatality," is answered in *Thus Spake Zarathustra.*

Nietzsche views Christianity as the essence of a complete rescaling of all natural and all moral values. In the chapter on the Ascetic Ideal (in *The Genealogy of Morals*), discussed here previously, Nietzsche analyzes one specific case and then, in the figure of the Antichrist, gives it a general meaning; the author's conception of the Antichrist is set forth in *Ecce Homo.*

Only now, by calling himself Dionysus, does he indicate what stands out as most essential in this book, as well as in his other writings. Two

[4] In the recording of this sentence, the word "never" was apparently omitted. What Nietzsche says is: "I have *never* wasted my strength" (p. 23).

[5] *Der Fall Wagner. Nietzsche contra Wagner* ["The Wagner Case. Nietzsche versus Wagner"). Leipzig: Naumann, 1895.

[6] Again the rendering of Nietzsche's passage is not quite correct. Moreover, the contents have here been so condensed that they cannot be understood. Nietzsche says:

"The fact that one becomes what one is presupposes that one has not the remotest suspicion of what one is. From this standpoint a unique meaning and value is given to even the blunders of one's life, the temporary deviations and aberrations, the hesitations, the timidities, the earnestness wasted upon tasks remote from the central one. In these matters there is opportunity for great wisdom, perhaps even the highest wisdom" (p. 44).

notes written in his last lucid period have become known; one of them, addressed to [Georg] Brandes, is signed: "The Crucified"; the other, to [Erwin] Rohde, "Dionysus greets his disciple."

It is doubtful whether Nietzsche's conception of Dionysus was based on factual knowledge. He believed the cult of Dionysus to have been an indigenous one, whereas Rohde proves quite the opposite. In dealing with the problem of Dionysus, Nietzsche contributed to the illumination of the romantic period between Homer and Pindar, the period of the lyrical-mythical contemplation of nature in the sixth century. Nietzsche finds himself again in late antiquity. What was still lacking was something that is known to us from classical Greece: that irresistible inner drive to give form and expression to passion, to spend oneself in one's work. This is linked with the high regard for passion itself and for those who are ruled by it. In Nietzsche's character we find essentially the dionysiac—i.e., the orgiastic—trait. When we ask what this means, the information given us by Deussen[7] may perhaps provide a small clue; Deussen asserts, surely without justification: *nullam mulierem attigit* ["He touched no woman"]. Even though it has been attested on good authority that he did not shun all contact with women, it is still certain that he felt much less attracted to women than is normal. There was never more than a flirtation and a single, although erotically highly charged, meeting with Lou.[8]

Nietzsche had a strong need for friendship; and his relationships with his friends were intense, although devoid of any conscious sexual feeling. His abstention from normal sexual gratification was coupled with a powerful repression of moral and cultural values. A peculiar trait is related to this, a trait of which he accused Wagner, but toward which he himself strongly leaned—that is, dramatizing. He is driven to try himself out in ever new forms. This is expressed also in his forever discovering himself in a superior being: in Schopenhauer, Wagner, Zarathustra and, finally, in Dionysus. This last symbol is eminently well chosen, because Dionysus was also the god of masks and of drama in general. In depicting him and his vicissitudes, the Greek Dionysus enthusiast would work himself into such a state of ecstasy that in the

[7] Paul Deussen (1845-1919), German philosopher and Sanskrit scholar.

[8] Lou Andreas-Salomé, German writer and philosopher, became famous as Nietzsche's friend; she was also a close friend of Rilke and of Freud.

end he believed that he himself had become divine. Here, however, that circle closes which, beginning with *The Birth of Tragedy*, now permits Nietzsche to sense even these supreme enchantments.

DISCUSSION

FRIEDMAN and FREY are most interested in the struggle of Nietzsche's nature against his own illness, and in the way by which Nietzsche believed that he had found health again. Without knowing Freud's teachings, Nietzsche has sensed and anticipated a great deal [that appeared in them]: for instance, the significance of forgetting, of the ability to forget; or the fact that he regards illness as an excessive sensitivity to life, and so forth. Certainly, a neurosis consists to a large extent in the distortion of perspective on the importance of individuals or of the external world in general. Something that has hurt the neurotic assumes excessive importance and obscures his ability to see life in its many aspects. This is a state that could perhaps be termed, to use Mach's expression, the "shrinking together" of the ego. In *Ecce Homo* the striving to "stylize" himself, as Häutler put it, is prevalent; that is to say, the striving to kill what is one's own nature. The tender, sensitive, affectionate Nietzsche re-creates himself as Dionysus, as the man who submits completely to his instincts.

FEDERN mentions a report according to which Nietzsche is supposed to have been homosexually active and in this way to have been infected.

Nietzsche displays the symptoms of a severe neurosis. Many neurotics produce theories according to which illness is a grave sin; what made Nietzsche ill is the illness also of mankind.

One could wish that many poets, founders of religions, and other men of stature had submitted to therapy; then they might have accomplished great things.

RANK thinks that there is no basis for making a diagnosis of neurosis in Nietzsche. The characteristics that would seem to indicate [the presence of] one are present in all unusual men, and even in the normal human being. Now, as before, Rank can find the mainspring of Nietzsche's entire creativity only in his originally "sadistic" disposition and its tremendous repression. Seen from this point of view, his negative attitude toward "masochistic" Christianity is self-evident.

RIE remarks that, although he has read *Ecce Homo* attentively, Häutler has enlightened him a great deal. He regrets the omission of a reference to the passage in which Nietzsche himself speaks about sexuality and advocates normal sexual activity in the broadest sense. There has been mention made here only of neurosis, but not of psychosis, although several clues point in that direction. Nietzsche makes a sharp distinction between Christianity and Christ; he is Antichrist only vis-à-vis Christianity.

HOLLERUNG merely wants to raise the question of whether Nietzsche did not regret having written one or another of his books, since he himself said: only he who changes is kin to me.

PROF. FREUD says that today he would have liked to hear from a psychiatrist;[9] then the discussion would have been simple: Nietzsche was a paretic. The euphoria is beautifully developed, and so on, and so on. However, this would also oversimplify the problem. It is very doubtful whether paresis can be held responsible for the contents of *Ecce Homo*. In cases in which paresis struck at men of great genius, extraordinary accomplishments were achieved until a short time before the outbreak of illness (Maupassant). The indication that this work of Nietzsche is fully valid and to be taken seriously is the preservation of the mastery of form.[10] The fact that Nietzsche was at first the victim of a conspiracy of silence, and then later became a fashionable idol, is almost comical. To all of us, he is an enigmatic personality. The lack of understanding of Nietzsche may be due to the fact that there really is something un-Germanic in his nature. We just have not succeeded in understanding Nietzsche's personality. One could look at the matter this way: this is an individual about whom we lack some prerequisite information.[11] Some sexual abnormality is certainly present. Jung claims to have learned that Nietzsche acquired syphilis in a homosexual brothel; however, this is immaterial. From his child-

[9] Häutler was not a physician.

[10] The original has: ". . . *die Erhaltung der Meisterschaft in der Form*," literally: ". . . the preservation of the masterfulness in the form."

[11] This is a free translation; literally it would be ". . . an individual whose prerequisites (*Voraussetzung*) we do not know."

hood, one thing stands out: he lost his father at an early age and grew up in a family of women. Several points are of interest here: for instance, in his autobiography Nietzsche kills his father once again. A few other echoes from childhood can easily be detected. When a person is an Antichrist at the end of his life, we are reminded of the fantasies of being Christ that are frequent among adolescents. In any event, we are far too little aware of the difference that exists between our emotional life and that of a Christian. Most likely, Nietzsche had a Christ fantasy during his puberty.

Then one sees how, in his life, illness becomes his fate. This illness is probably also responsible for all the disturbing elements in the picture [of his personality]. But there is no evidence whatsoever of a neurotic illness. Completely cut off from life by illness, he turns to the only object of investigation that is still accessible to him and which, in any event, is close to him as a homosexual, i.e., the ego.[12] And thus he begins with great perspicacity— in endopsychic perception, as it were—to recognize the strata of his self. He makes a number of brilliant discoveries in himself. But now illness takes hold. Nietzsche is not satisfied with correctly fathoming these connections, but projects the insight gained about himself outward as a general imperative [*Lebensanforderung*].[13]

To his psychological insight is added the teaching, the pastoral element that derives from his Christ ideal. The confusing, although basically correct, results of Nietzsche's views come about in this way. That is the formula which Freud has arrived at for [an understanding of] Nietzsche. In a similar way, as has already been indicated (*The Psychopathology of Everyday Life*), mankind has created for itself through projection a moral view of the world that mirrors endopsychically perceived elements.[14] The degree of introspection achieved

12 Obviously even at that time the concept of narcissism and its connection with homosexuality was already in Freud's mind.

13 The mentally deranged person sees in the external world the reflection of his inner world.

14 The original has: "*In ähnlicher Weise habe sich . . . die ganze Menschheit eine moralische Schattenwelt geschaffen, durch Projektion der endopsychisch wahrgenommenen Substanzen.*" [Literally: "In similar fashion . . . mankind created for itself a moral shadow-world, through projection of endopsychically perceived substances."] We assume that Freud's reference is to the following passage in *The Psychopathology of Everyday Life* (1905): "In point of fact I believe that a large part of the mythological

by Nietzsche had never been achieved by anyone, nor is it likely ever to be reached again. What disturbs us is that Nietzsche transformed "is" into "ought," which is alien to science. In this he has remained, after all, the moralist; he could not free himself of the theologian.

Prof. Freud would like to mention that he has never been able to study Nietzsche, partly because of the resemblance of Nietzsche's intuitive insights to our laborious investigations, and partly because of the wealth of ideas, which has always prevented Freud from getting beyond the first half page whenever he has tried to read him.

The most essential factor must still be added: the role that paresis played in Nietzsche's life. It is the loosening process resulting from paresis that gave him the capacity for the quite extraordinary achievement of seeing through all layers and recognizing the instincts at the very base [of everything]. In that way, he placed his paretic disposition at the service of science.

The entire design of the book suggests that a chapter "On My Sexuality" belongs in it and may even have been written.

SADGER finds in Nietzsche, in a certain sense, a sinking down to [the stage of] the child, a well-known phenomenon in paresis. The fact that neurosis and paresis seldom occur together speaks against Federn's assumption of the presence of a neurosis. The chapter titles are reminiscent of the praise given a small child when he behaves himself. The amoral position—"beyond good and evil"—also refers to the child.

[A.] DEUTSCH mentions a feuilleton which appeared about a year ago in the *Neue Freie Presse*,[15] in which one of Nietzsche's disciples emphasized Nietzsche's homosexual tendencies.

---

view of the world, which extends a long way into the most modern religions, *is nothing but psychology projected into the external world*. The obscure recognition (the endopsychic perception, as it were) of psychical factors and relations in the unconscious is mirrored—it is difficult to express it in other terms, and here the analogy with paranoia must come to our aid—in the construction of a *supernatural reality*, which is destined to be changed back once more by science into the *psychology of the unconscious*" (*S.E.*, Vol. VI, pp. 258-259).

[15] A Viennese newspaper, comparable in its standing in Vienna to *The New York Times*.

ADLER stresses that we should not be surprised to rediscover here all the elements that we find in the analyses of neuroses; yet this does not prove that we can consider Nietzsche a neurotic. Neither his homosexual tendencies nor his relationship to his father has any significance, since we are justified in regarding these matters as perfectly normal. It is only a question of degree. The problem has not yet been solved, but one need not *a priori* disagree with Federn. If we found in a patient some of the things [mentioned], we would not hesitate to diagnose them as neurotic. The question is only what Nietzsche's reaction would have been. Similar doubts arise when one puts the instinct of aggression in the foreground—as Rank has done. We must maintain that this "sadism" too is part of the equipment of the normal individual. All these tendencies can explain only the "how" of neurosis; they do not provide the key to neurosis itself. Once one disregards the differences among the neuroses and considers instead what they have in common, one can see very clearly in Nietzsche those tendencies that point to the deepest root of the neurosis. Unquestionably Nietzsche would at present have to be considered a neurotic.

Throughout this last work of Nietzsche's, paresis played the role that Freud has explained with regard to it. At the earlier meeting devoted to Nietzsche,[16] Adler had already stressed the fact that in paretics one often finds extraordinary accomplishments, and an intensification of those characteristics that we can uncover in analysis. The explanation cannot be looked for in the luetic toxin, since it is not possible to construct a postluetic psyche. Rather, psychic processes that had previously been masked become evident; what had been under the pressure of the censor emerges. The censorship in Nietzsche was certainly different from that in other human beings—namely, it was weaker. His considerable [capacity for] introspection must be due to this condition. Paresis then further weakened this censorship—which explains why in *Ecce Homo* the usual paretic characteristics are present, and yet intelligence is preserved on Nietzsche's level.

HÄUTLER thinks it superfluous to speak in conclusion.[17]

[16] April 1, 1908 (see Vol. I, Minutes 45).

[17] It is interesting that in this discussion some beginnings of ego psychology are simply and lucidly set forth.

57

SCIENTIFIC MEETING *on November 4, 1908*

Present: Freud, Adler, [A.] Deutsch, Graf, Hitschmann, Rank, Reitler, Rie, Sadger, Schwerdtner, Stekel, Wittels.

COMMUNICATIONS

Papers announced:
[A.] Deutsch: Phenomena of Skin Magnetism (January)
Adler: On the Oneness of the Neuroses
Stekel: Analysis of a Case of Female *Interruptas*; The Sexual Root of Kleptomania
Prof. Freud: Discussion of the additions to the second edition of *The Interpretation of Dreams*

Reviews and Case Reports by All Present

[A.] DEUTSCH reports that he has not come across any publications of particular interest, with the exception of two books by Flammarion: *Unknown Forces of Nature* and *Unexplored Psychic Forces,*[1]

[1] Camille Flammarion (1842-1925): *Unbekannte Naturkräfte* [*Unknown Forces of Nature*] (Stuttgart, 1908) and *Rätsel des Seelenlebens* [*Enigmas of Psychic Life*], originally published in French in 1900 (German translations by Gustav Meyrinck). Both books deal with parapsychic phenomena.

which he will discuss when he gives his paper on "Phenomena of Skin Magnetism."

Then he quotes two passages from Langmann's collection of short novels, *The Influence of Woman.*

STEINER reports on a paper on papillomas in the posterior urethra and their relationship to sexual neurasthenia in the *Zeitschrift für Urologie* [*Journal of Urology*], 1908; Frank in Berlin, by removing the papillomas, succeeded in eliminating the neurasthenic state.[2] An interesting but by no means entirely new idea.

Then Steiner supplements a case report that he had presented at the end of the previous season: a case of psychic impotence that at that time he thought had been cured, but which, it now turns out, is linked at its roots to the patient's relationship with his sister.[3]

Steiner then tells about a dream that a patient who was suffering from gonorrhea had interpreted to his mistress rather correctly—except for one point: he could not recognize himself in the corpse that appeared in her dream.

HITSCHMANN remarks that Steiner's treatments seem to be strikingly short and successful. Actually, they are on the borderline between psychoanalysis and history-taking.

PROF. FREUD, in the discussion that follows this remark, comments that the patient gains nothing from the physician's confronting him directly with his complexes [direct analysis]; for even when a patient occasionally becomes aware of the correct solution, he will reject it if there is any chance to do so.[4]

REITLER reviews the *Zeitschrift für Sexualwissenschaft* from June to October [1908]. Abraham's essay on "The Psychological Relations between Sexuality and Alcoholism"[5] leads to an extensive discussion.

[2] E. R. W. Frank: "Über die Beziehungen der papillomatösen Wucherungen des Blasenhalses und der hinteren Harnröhre zum Mechanismus der Harnentleerung und zur sexuellen Neurasthenie" ["On the Relationship of Papillomatous Growths of the Bladder Neck and the Posterior Urethra to the Mechanism of Voiding and to Sexual Neurasthenia"].

[3] See Volume I, Minutes 52.

[4] An important technical hint, repeatedly found in Freud's writings, as was stressed in the Introduction to the Minutes (see Volume I).

[5] Abraham's paper was published in #8 of the *Zeitschrift für Sexualwissenschaft*, 1908. In the *Jahrbuch für Psychoanalyse und psychoanalytische Forschung* (I, 1909) he summarized it as follows: "The old experience that alcohol removes psychic inhibitions must be defined more precisely, in that alcohol nullifies the effects of repres-

RIE supposes that probably not everyone is in agreement with Abraham. The release of instinctual drives follows from the fact that the toxin removes *all* repressions, not only the sexual ones. Nor does Rie agree with what Abraham says about differences between the sexes with regard to alcohol. This can be traced back to the fact that in former times customs were determined by men. Essentially, Abraham is merely describing the harmful effects of alcohol.

WITTELS refers to his remark in [the chapter on] "Interdiction of Forced Abortion,"[6] that one of the most important social effects of alcohol is the increase in childbirth among the lower classes, since under the influence of alcohol people fail to use precautionary measures.

HITSCHMANN thinks that Abraham's paper is one-sided. For instance, the convivial habits of students can just as well serve to protect some of them from harmful sexual experiences. However, alcohol does not always act as a stimulant.

ADLER confirms this observation.

GRAF remarks that women, who are kept from alcoholism by external circumstances, find a certain substitute in the coffee circle and the confectioners.

PROF. FREUD mentions a large group of people who hold the same view as Abraham, Wittels, and others—namely, the anti-alcoholics. This movement, to judge from the entire bearing of its adherents, seems to be [based on] a displacement of sex abstinence. Alcohol lends itself particularly well not only to the generation of primitive

---

sion and sublimation and increases sexual activity. Under the influence of alcohol, the repressed component drives again come to the fore. Inasmuch as alcohol engenders sexual excitement, it flatters the sense of masculinity. Man identifies alcohol with his procreative prowess. This identification can already be found in ancient myths. Woman, whose sexuality, as a consequence of the renewed repression at puberty, is of a more passive nature, loses her special characteristic and therefore her charm under the influence of alcohol.

"Chronic alcoholism continually produces the same results. To the alcoholic, pleasure in drinking becomes a substitute for sexual pleasure. He represses this fact and displaces his feeling of guilt in the form of an accusation (delusion of jealousy) onto his wife. The sexual components affect the drinker in a manner very similar to the way in which they affect the neurotic."

[6] Chapter I in Wittels' *Sexuelle Not*, Vienna: Stern, 1907.

pleasure, but also, when taken excessively, to a disturbance of functioning.

Justified as Rie's doubts may be, they do not get to the core of the question. The removal of sexual inhibitions is indeed of particular interest to us, and in any case is worthy of interest insofar as it is a fact. The difference between the sexes in this respect is likewise undeniable; of course, the constitutional factor must also be held responsible. Here, as everywhere, the presence of external social connections does not exclude deeper relations and associations.

Superficially, the explanation for jealousy in this context seems to be: simple projection of the man's own impotence. The paranoid jealousy can be seen through clearly: it always involves the emergence of the suppressed or sublimated homosexual component.[7] For instance, the wife suspects her husband in the most peculiar way: not with her beautiful friends but with persons whom she likes, often with old women and especially with those who clearly revive an infantile attachment, such as a housemaid, a nurse, a wet nurse, and the like. The wife herself is on quite friendly terms with these very people; *thus she projects her homosexual liking in the form of jealousy onto her husband.* The same is true with regard to a man's delusion of jealousy. The unconsciousness of the whole process, however, is expressed in the reversal of the entire relationship.

Paranoia as a rule has as its starting point the rejection of a newly emerging homosexual inclination. A number of characteristic details support this view. An analogy to this—in a totally different area—would be, for instance, the peculiar sympathy of the deceived husband for his wife's friend. He uses his homosexual affection for her lover not to notice anything. Behind Abraham's "alcoholic" conception of sexual life lies hidden the "toxic" conception of sexual life which common man had discovered and had been aware of long ago.[8] We simply transform the "love potion" of legend into science. Things of such magnitude can only be *re*discovered.

REITLER continues his review with Rohleder's article on *masturbatio interrupta.*[9]

[7] This seems to be the first time that Freud mentions the relationship between pathological jealousy and homosexuality.

[8] Literally: "which folk consciousness [*Volksbewusstsein*] had discovered long ago."

[9] Hermann Rohleder: "Masturbatio Interrupta." *Zeitschrift für Sexualwissenschaft,* 458-478, 1908.

JOACHIM comments that in such cases there occur ejaculations into the bladder, which Steiner has also observed in the case of *coitus reservatus* (habitual in Siebenbürgen, according to Bloch).[10]

STEKEL relates an observation made on himself: after frequent interrupted masturbation in adolescence, he was later unable to achieve ejaculation in intercourse; further, when he had dreams of emission, he would awake before ejaculation with a fear of the loss of semen. He also mentions a similar case concerning a lady who before orgasm suddenly and forcibly interrupted coitus with her husband. *Masturbatio interrupta* is surely one of the causes of anxiety neuroses.

PROF. FREUD observes that *masturbatio interrupta* has the same significance as a severe form of frustrated excitement.

HITSCHMANN, in relation to Stekel's case, refers to a case that had been discussed earlier. This lady also practiced a kind of interrupted masturbation.[11]

STEKEL believes that the psychic mechanism in *masturbatio interrupta* lies in the fact that these persons struggle for a long time with the temptation to masturbate, but then, no sooner has the first step been taken than the inhibiting ideas re-emerge.

ADLER also recounts two cases of *masturbatio interrupta.* However, this is never the only symptom, but is always at bottom interwoven with others. Moreover, it is not the beginning of a neurosis, but occurs in the midst of one. Stekel's explanation is insufficient and incomplete, although the observation can be confirmed. There exists also a form of psychic impotence in which an erection occurs, but no ejaculation. Adler promises to shed light on these processes in a paper on "The Oneness of the Neuroses."[12]

HITSCHMANN first mentions once again the case of the woman with spasms of the glottis. Asked by the Professor whether the patient had previously suffered from vaginism, he replies that he has no information about this. Then he mentions some cases of so-called psychogenic dyspepsia. Actually, one should also consult a neurologist in

[10] Iwan Bloch (1872-1922), a well-known German sexologist, published two great works: *Sexualleben unserer Zeit in seinen Beziehungen zur modernen Kultur* [*The Sexual Life of Our Time in Its Relations to Modern Civilization*], Berlin, 1907; and *Beiträge zur Ätiologie der Psychopathia sexualis* [*Contributions to the Etiology of Psychopathia Sexualis*], Berlin, 1902-1903.

[11] See Volume I, Minutes 37.

[12] See Minutes 82, this volume.

every case of appendicitis, because so frequently these cases are unnecessarily operated on, and later turn out to be hysterias.

He reports that a colleague began to suffer from an anxiety neurosis when he stopped masturbation after he had become engaged.

Hitschmann also tells about a dream whose interpretation permitted one to recognize clearly a direct connection with external events.

As to reviews, he speaks about an article by Forel,[13] "On the Present State of Psychotherapy: A Recommendation" (in the *Journal für Psychologie und Neurologie* [Vol. 11, 1908]). Forel includes, in addition to Freud's method, that of Bernheim, Dubois, and others. This quite intelligent article also contains a mild attack (on Jung).

Hitschmann further points out that Näcke, in a review of Muthmann's book,[14] is gradually coming closer to our views. Finally, he mentions Kronthal's *Nerves and Soul*[15] (a purely anatomical book) and closes by reading two interesting passages from [Gustav] Frenssen's novel Hilligenlei.

STEKEL, in connection with a remark in Abraham's essay on the crude customs among students, refers to such a description in the memoirs of Master Laukhard.[16]

In Zola's novel, *Au bonheur des dames* [*Ladies' Delight*], there is a passage that points to the sexual root of kleptomania.

Stekel then refers to a French essay on priapism, which the author distinguishes from satyriasis. The latter is characterized by pleasure without pain, priapism by the opposite.[17]

[13] August Forel (1848-1931), the distinguished Swiss psychiatrist and neurologist, was Bleuler's predecessor in Burghölzli. He was one of the most important leaders in the movement for sexual reform and mental hygiene in Europe. At the same time he conducted outstanding research work on ants. Forel rejected psychoanalysis because of Freud's "exaggerated" emphasis on infantile sexuality (*Out of My Life and Work*, New York: Norton, 1938).

[14] "Beiträge zu den sexuellen Träumen," *Arch. für Krim.-Anthrop. u. Kriminalist.*, xxix, 363-371, 1908. Muthmann's book is probably *Zur Psychologie und Therapie neurotischer Symptome; eine Studie auf Grund der Neurosenlehre Freuds.* Halle: Marhold, 1907.

[15] Paul Kronthal: *Nerven und Seele*, Jena: Fischer, 1908.

[16] Friedrich Christian Laukhard (1758-1822): *Friedrich Christian Laukhards Leben und Schicksale, von ihm selbst beschrieben, Deutsche und Französische Kultur und Sittenbilder aus dem 18. Jahrhundert* [*Friedrich Christian Laukhard's Life and Fortunes, Described by Himself. Pictures of German and French Civilization and Morals in the Eighteenth Century*]. Edited by Viktor Petersen. Stuttgart: 1908-1909. These memoirs first appeared in 1792-1802.

[17] C. Laurent & Nové-Josserand: "Le Priapisme," *Gazette des hôpitaux civils et militaires*, 1908.

In general, the French are now very much interested in Freud's work, although they do not accept his teachings. For instance, in the current *Gazette* there is a report of a case of astasia-abasia in a little girl; although the author assumes an *idée fixe* to be operative, rather than the plausible wish to be carried in her parents' arms, he finally adopted a therapy which, though correct on the whole, nevertheless used strong methods.[18]

Since neurasthenia has come into ill repute, Janet is striving hard to make a differential diagnosis between psychasthenia and hysteria.

The *Presse Médicale* contains a paper that describes the anxiety-neurotic characteristics of certain stomach ailments in the same way as Stekel did in his book.

In the *Juristisch-psychiatrische Grenzfragen* is a paper "On the Influence of the Sexual Functions on Female Criminality" [*Über den Einfluss der Geschlechtsfunktionen auf die weibliche Kriminalität*], in which [Siegfried] Weinberg demonstrates that 80 to 85 per cent of all female crimes (including kleptomania) are committed during pregnancy, menstruation, etc.

The utter helplessness of modern neurology is demonstrated by a case reported by Boulanger, a neurologist in Brussels, in the *Journal de Neurologie*.[19] The sexual etiology is unusually clear in this case, and yet the physician did not see it. (RIE mentions in this context that he knows of three cases in which religious madness is coupled with murderous impulses toward the child.)

Other items that should be mentioned are: a paper by Hellpach on the unconscious in the *Zeitschrift für Psychologie und Physiologie der Sinnesorgane*;[20] a book by Bernheim: *Neurasthenia and Psychoneuroses*;[21] an essay by Hartenberg on psychotherapy (*Archive de neurologie*); Fleury on psychotherapy (in the *Archive générale de médecine*); Eulenburg on neurasthenia (*in Entwicklung der Medizin*).[22]

18 L. Babonneix: "Un cas d'astasie-abasie chez une enfant de dix ans." *Gazette des hôpitaux civils et militaires*, 1908.

19 Boulanger: "Alcoölisme chronique chez un enfant."

20 Wilhelm Hellpach: "Unbewusstes oder Wechselwirkung: Eine Untersuchung über die Denkmöglichkeit der Psychologischen Deutungsprinzipien" ["Unconscious or Reciprocal Action: An Examination of the Possibilities of the Principles of Psychological Interpretation"].

21 Probably, Bernheim: *Neurasthenies et Psychoneuroses, Rev. Méd. de l'est*, XXXIX, 753-773, 1907.

22 Eulenburg, A. "Ueber Neurasthenie-Behandlung," *Therapie der Gegenwart*, XLIX, 337-353, 1908.

WITTELS refers to the smooth successes quickly achieved by Steiner, in which Wittels misses the patient's affective involvement. In this context he reports a case of psychic impotence that did not yield to the most assiduous and thorough psychoanalytic efforts. He does not know where the mistake lay. The patient, an intelligent man who was already acquainted with Freud's work, came to him and, in the course of the interview, said that he was glad to be ill because now at last he would have a chance to test the validity of these doctrines.

STEKEL, to whom Wittels had sent the patient in consultation, thought that the patient had been overtreated, much as overtreatment in a case of gonorrhea is injurious. In cases of psychic impotence, it can happen that inhibiting ideas suddenly appear. These ideas may then disappear spontaneously, but they can become fixated if they are discussed continually. Stekel told the man that he did not have a neurosis at all, and that he was not in need of treatment. He explained to the patient that he had such inhibiting ideas because he was afraid of impregnating a decent girl and of its consequences; this had happened to the patient once before (there had been a miscarriage). But in spite of this explanation, the patient did not improve, and Wittels dismissed him.

PROF. FREUD terms this case a very important one, on the one hand because of methodological considerations, and on the other hand because of its specific nature. With regard to the first point, he must agree with Wittels and emphatically disagree with Stekel. He does not know of any damage that has resulted from overtreatment. *Nothing is accomplished therapeutically by the discovery of the solution.* Rather one has to induce the patient to accept this solution.[23] About the enigmatic aspect of the case, the following should be said: any man who is impotent and who declares that it is more important to him to find out whether certain theories are correct than it is to be cured must attract our attention. A person who feels so little unhappiness about his ailment is actually glad to be ill. For some reason or other, this man has turned away from women, to begin with, owing to his homosexual component; and Wittels correctly recognized the transference of this component onto himself to be one of the causes

[23] This view is frequently met with in Freud's work; however, it is often misunderstood or ignored. On the other hand, Freud never stated directly how the patient can be induced to "accept interpretations."

of the patient's desire to be perpetually treated by him. This man does not want to be cured; rather he has ulterior motives: he wants to "pull the doctor's leg." The father, whose image is before him in the homosexual transference onto the physician, is the main resistance to the cure. The patient wants to prove (to the father!) that he is impotent—therefore cannot be a "bad" son. For this reason both Stekel, who turned him away, and Wittels, who finally dismissed him, expressing regrets that he could not help him, instinctively employed the proper therapy. Some day this man's urge to have intercourse will become more powerful than all these ideas, and he will be cured.

The affect, which Wittels found missing from the history of the illness, was concealed in the patient's behavior toward the physician.

SCHWERDTNER mentions that the Sicilian tragic actress [Mimi] Aguglia, who can be seen at present on the stage in Vienna, is said to be a hysteric, who invariably has her attack in the second act of *Malia* [*The Possessed*]. Then he speaks about the relations between mechanotherapy[24] and psychotherapy.

PROF. FREUD remarks that Schwerdtner is quite right in attributing the unconscious effect of mechanotherapy to the fact that it offers certain substitutes for sexual gratification.

ADLER reviews an article by Kahane, who communicates a laboratory finding: namely, that treatment with high frequency can induce attacks in hysterics.[25] The validity of the observation can hardly be doubted; the question is only whether this fact is as transparent as Kahane thinks, and whether it can lead via a physical path to an organic, and, as Kahane expresses it, "exact biological basis" for hysteria.

PROF. FREUD thinks that the fact appears to be comprehensible, since hysteria surely has its own metabolism, but these characteristics can never replace the psychological ones.

[24] Mechanotherapy is hygienic gymnastics with the use of apparatus.

[25] M. Kahane: "Hysterie und Hochfrequenzströme, nebst Bemerkungen zur Pathogenese der Hysterie" ["Hysteria and High-frequency Currents; With Some Remarks on the Pathogenesis of Hysteria"]. *Medizinische Klinik*, 1908.

58

SCIENTIFIC MEETING *on November 11, 1908*

Present: Prof. Freud, Baas, Federn, Graf, Hitschmann, Joachim, Rank, Reitler, Rie, Sadger, Steiner, Wittels.

PRESENTATION

Discussion of Moll's Book: *The Sexual Life of the Child*[1]

REVIEWER: DR. RIE

DISCUSSION

SADGER first stresses that Rie's presentation of Moll's attitude toward Freud is probably correct. Moll, who had gotten himself introduced to the literature through Krafft-Ebing, and who was the first after Krafft-Ebing to devote himself to these matters, considers it an intrusion into his personal domain if another person has also achieved

[1] *Das Sexualleben des Kindes.* Leipzig: Vogel, 1908 [*The Sexual Life of the Child.* New York: Macmillan, 1912]. Albert Moll was a German sexologist of whom Freud did not think very highly.

something in this field. Such is his relationship to Hirschfeld as well. A second characteristic of Moll's is his dialectical sharpness.

Detumescence and contrectation, the question of acquired or congenital perversions, etc., are nothing but empty phrases: new labels to cover up for deficient knowledge. Both may be true in a certain sense, as Freud's analyses show. The remark about the frequent incidence of hysteria in girls and boys is quite interesting. The fact that hysteria occurs in men, as well as in children, was first understood by Freud.[2] According to Sadger's experience, hysteria occurs far more frequently in men than was hitherto assumed. It is true, however, that it is a minor hysteria, whereas the so-called "screaming hysteria" is rare in men. In certain races (Russian and Polish Jews), almost every man is hysterical. Moll's undifferentiated state is also a catchword of the kind mentioned above. Indeed, in childhood everybody passes through such a stage, which corresponds to the bisexual constitution.

Sadger can confirm Dr. Rie's statement about the favorable effects of a meatless diet on states of sexual excitement.

HITSCHMANN's impression is that Moll's book is a reaction to the *Three Essays on the Theory of Sexuality*, as well as, in part, to Bloch's book.[3] It is a semi-scientific work, unsystematic, a mere compilation, in which there is nothing original. The "stage of interference" is not a new idea either.

As far as the book is concerned, one can discuss only some details. With regard to the harmfulness or harmlessness of masturbation, Moll does not maintain the view that masturbation must be rigorously fought against. However, Hitschmann thinks that one could go even further and attribute a certain value to masturbation. Masturbation in childhood—that is, the second period of masturbation, from four to seven, not the masturbation of infancy—seems to be necessary; it is important, especially for the man, in so far as he begins to learn at the right time about this drive to mastery, this grasping of the penis. Later, it is trying to take hold of the organ of the sexual partner. Hitschmann knows of two cases of psychic impotence and feeble erections, in both of which masturbation had been absent.

2 Before Freud, hysteria was believed to occur only in women. The term "hysteria," derived from the Greek *hysteron* implies this belief.

3 Cf. Minutes 57, this volume.

Concerning the causes of perversions and of inversion, one cannot blame the author for an unsystematic presentation. We ourselves have not succeeded in solving these problems.

In the *Three Essays*, Freud remarks that the sexual life of the normal individual probably does not differ from that of the patients whom we have examined. But then we do not analyze healthy people!

It is surprising that such valuable concepts as autoerotism or the perseveration of the infantile, the dream, and so on, are not mentioned. However, the "indifferent stage," as seen in this light, is new. One must take exception to the restriction of the concept of sexuality and the omission of all platonic and erotic tendencies.

Prof. Freud answers the question of whether it is true that "wet dreams" usually bring on emission in the preliminary stage of coitus by pointing out that the wet dream repeats masturbatory fantasies.[4]

Instead of saying, as Moll does, that anxiety causes emissions, we would say that anxiety causes masturbation. As far as the effect of a meatless diet is concerned, Hitschmann thinks that symbolism is probably also involved.

Moll may be right in considering the precocious development of sex life to be evidence of hereditary degeneration, particularly in view of the fact that the boundaries of the pathological are by no means precisely drawn. Perhaps it should be pointed out that the number of children with strong sexuality is much smaller in certain circles than we think. It is striking, not only that neuroses, psychoses, suicides, etc., play a more important role among the Jews, but also that they have many more sexual experiences than others and—a fact that must be particularly emphasized—take them much more seriously.[5]

Here again we must raise the question of the guilt feeling connected with sexuality. For instance, where does the child—who has not suffered the trauma of prohibition—get the feeling of guilt that accompanies masturbation? Does a genuine feeling of guilt exist or not?

[4] The original record does not make it clear whether Freud made this statement in the discussion, or Hitschmann is quoting Freud.

[5] Hitschmann is speaking from the point of view of the bourgeois Jew of Vienna in those days, just as Sadger did before him. While the predominantly Catholic population of Austria was by no means totally opposed to sexual freedom, the Jewish middle class of this earlier period clung far more strictly to the moral standards of "middle-class propriety." The aristocracy has always allowed itself full sexual freedom.

According to Moll, nail biting is a tic. But what actually is a tic? Is there not a sexual factor behind a tic, and could it not be treated psychoanalytically?

BASS would merely like to try to explain Moll's attitude to Freud. The reviewer has already pointed out the main factor—namely, a reaction to and an acting out against an intruder. However, the entirely different methodological point of view probably plays a role too. Most likely, Moll is not equal to psychoanalysis and has not grasped its essence—hence his reaction.

Just one word about the question of meat: Bass belongs to the school of thought that believes in giving only minimal quantities of meat under all circumstances. The states of sexual excitement in children can be understood in the following way: children who get a lot of meat are usually members of well-to-do families and are altogether too well fed; consequently, they develop early and for that reason may also be sexually precocious

WITTELS wishes to refrain from saying anything about perversions today, since he plans to discuss them next time. In the introduction to his book (on "the sexual misery,")[6] he has referred to Freud as the discoverer of the child's sexual life. This may quite effectively counterbalance Moll's point of view. Hitschmann's opinion, which seems to be that only Jewish children have a sexual life, has no foundation whatsoever.

As far as sexual enlightenment is concerned, Wittels' opinion differs perhaps from that of most of the group. It is still a question whether risks are not necessary for the development of personality. Someone has already pointed to the positive aspects of masturbation. Sexual enlightenment is something inorganic, as it were, something not provided for by nature.

Certainly, children should eat as little meat as possible; but for the adult the quantity of meat should by no means be restricted, but rather increased, even if the matter of the states of excitement were true.

FEDERN, in connection with the Jewish question, refers immediately to some "Christian" psychoanalyses. Neuroses, he says, are more

[6] *Die sexuelle Not.* Vienna: C. W. Stern, 1907 and 1909. (There is no English translation.)

frequent among Jews because the preconditions for it are present more frequently in that group. The most serious cases of male hysteria have occurred in meat-eating families. He refers to an article in the *Münchener medizinische Wochenschrift,* in which it is reported that severely neurasthenic children were cured when all meat was eliminated from their diet. In general, one must not forget that there are certain people who have a lower tolerance for certain poisons.

Federn does not think that the second period of masturbation, which Hitschmann brought into the discussion, is normal, let alone necessary. In regard to the question of whether strong sexual stirrings in early childhood are normal, one must state that, to be sure, some normal people had nothing resembling them in their childhood, yet in these same families severe neuroses occurred. Moll maintains that the impulses of the child are not sexual, even though later in life sexual impulses may attach themselves to these infantile stirrings. From the Freudian standpoint, however, one must assume that infantile sexuality, because later it decisively influences adult sexuality, is connected with the latter and represents its first stirring. Anal erotism is the best proof. Federn mentions the case of a five-month-old boy whose penis moves upward when he is sucking his thumb.

Moll finds detumescence so rarely in children because he does not seem to know anything about enuresis. [Federn also speaks of] a case of genital discharge in a three-year-old.

Moll's book was written for practical purposes and—like all such works—has no scientific value.

JOACHIM: When an author speaks from ethical viewpoints in connection with problems of the natural sciences, one should generally stop concerning oneself with him any further. It is precisely the ethical point of view that causes Moll to deny things that must be obvious to every naïve observer. Otherwise, it would not be possible to assert that there is nothing sexual about tenderness; it is impossible to imagine tenderness without sexuality.

Personally, Joachim is inclined to believe that a masochistic component is partly responsible for emissions of children in anxiety states. He has a childhood recollection from his very early life (fourth year): he was expecting to be beaten by his father; when his father did approach him, he had a sensation of pleasure and urinated. He did not get a beating after all and subsequently had a feeling as if of a tension that could not reach discharge. This experience was then repeated in fantasies and dreams; later Joachim suffered from emissions during school examinations, and while working on difficult problems that he could not solve. Even now, he often has anxiety dreams of being pursued, the anxiety subsiding with ejaculation.

Concerning the question of meat, he refers to the treatment to which patients with skin diseases submit. As a result of their generally undereating, their skin eruptions subside. Following the withdrawal of meat, there occurs a decrease of all organic and psychic energies. [On this, PROF. FREUD comments that undereating makes a man a meat-eater since he is then forced to nourish himself on his own flesh.]

PROF. FREUD stresses first that he had expected something from this book, but since listening [to the report], he must now term it an inadequate, inferior, and above all dishonest book. There are two evidences of its dishonesty. Dr. Rie has already pointed out one of them. Strange as it may sound, infantile sexuality was really discovered by him—Freud; before that, no hint of it existed in the literature. The best evidence for this state of affairs can be found in the explorations of the *libido sexualis* by Bloch (Moll).[7] In that work, not a single word is said about the great importance of childhood sexuality, which now, in this book by Moll, it has suddenly assumed. Moll gleaned the importance of infantile sexuality from the *Three Essays*, and then proceeded to write his book. For that reason, Moll's whole book is permeated by the desire to deny Freud's influence.

The second evidence has to do with the question of whether Moll read Freud's *Theory of Sexuality*, and in what way he may have read it. He apparently read it selectively, with the result that he failed to draw from it its most important parts. The real significance of the *Three Essays* lies in the fact that it achieves a unification of normal sex life, perversion, and neurosis—that is to say, in the assumption of a polymorphous-perverse undifferentiated *Anlage*, from which the various forms of sexual life develop under the influence of life experi-

[7] The reference is probably to Bloch's *Beiträge zur Ätiologie der Psychopathia sexualis* ["Contribution to the etiology of psychopathia sexualis"], Berlin, 1902-1903. It is not clear what Rank meant to indicate by inserting Moll's name here.

ences. But the intimate relationships between perversions and normal sexual life, along with the question of what is genuine sexuality and what is not, cannot be understood unless those interrelationships are kept in mind.

For if one restricts the consideration of sexuality to genital activity, then its relationship to the other [erotogenic] zones is lost. The justification for thus extending the concept of sexuality, however, derives precisely from the consideration of perversion. Yet in [Moll's chapter on] perversion, Freud's name is not mentioned. Nor does Moll mention the connection of perversion with neurosis and infantile sexual life. This omission can only be intentional—Moll's character is only too well known. Hirschfeld has complained bitterly about him. He is a petty, malicious, narrow-minded individual. He never expresses a firm opinion; this is supposed to impress people as circumspection. In science, the essential thing is not exactitude, but decision. Unwillingness to make a decision is also a decision; Moll always wavers and remains wholly undecided. One thing Moll has turned to his advantage —the inability of the general public to imagine that a number of thoughts can be represented in a few pages.

What he had expected from the book, Freud continues, was the following: the weakness of our conception has been that one cannot define precisely what is to be called sexuality and what is not. In the *Three Essays*, he had spared a lengthy discussion of this question, because the justification for extending the concept of sexuality so far is inherent in the contents. He would have expected a critique to single out this point, in order to separate what is actually called sexuality from the rest. In rebuttal, one would then focus attention on the significant connections that follow from our conception. Actually, Moll regards sexuality as being really "genitality."

Now to some specific points. With regard to frigidity in women, Moll seems to be ignorant of a few things. In many cases one is probably dealing with a local, merely relative, topical anesthesia. Statistical surveys of male and female hysteria are simply not possible—as they are in most sciences—because the basis is missing—i.e., the certainty of the diagnosis of hysteria.

It is a great misfortune when a man who is destitute, as Moll is, of original ideas, nevertheless does have an idea for once. This is the case with Moll's detumescence and contrectation—an utterly impossible and artificial concept, which turns up throughout the book, as though pasted on, and which leads Moll into the following trap: detumescence cannot be applied to the child (Moll introduced this term at a time when the idea of infantile sexuality was still remote from his thinking). He differentiates three stages. The first, the one that he reserves for the child, would be contrectation without an object. But contrectation as such implies relationship with an object, so that the concept collapses right there.

The castration experiment that Moll cites is indeed a warning not to overestimate the role of the genitals. The question of " 'innate' or 'acquired' " is, as Sadger has already noted, no longer germane, because of polymorphous infantile sexuality. Such a question does not fit the facts. Between the innate and the acquired intervene the experiences and developments of infancy.

That in his opposition to psychoanalysis Moll also attacks symbolism merely shows a general ignorance of human ways. After all, we did not invent symbolism; it is a universal age-old activity of the human imagination.

The experiences with the milk diet are probably true, but they should not be overestimated. One must not forget how much is due to the contrast; the change itself is of more importance than what is changed. With great masses of people, however, this does not work. The proletarians in our country certainly eat little meat, yet they show sexual precociousness and full sexual activity. And the English are no more nervous than other peoples, and English children certainly least of all. There are peoples who neither drink alcohol nor eat meat, yet mature at an early age and are sexually very potent (for instance, the Brahmanic Indians).

There is no quick answer to the question concerning the source of the feeling of guilt. No doubt many factors are operative here. It is certain that the feeling of guilt comes about as a consequence of the disappearance of sexual impulses.[8]

Freud does not agree with Wittels in regard to sexual enlightenment. Wittels is opposed to enlightenment on sexual-aesthetic grounds.

[8] This sentence belongs, of course, to the period preceding *Totem and Taboo.*

This, too, is a matter of posing the wrong question. One permits children to grow up in sexual ignorance; whether one then leaves them to their own resources or enlightens them makes no difference, the alternatives are equally harmful. Children should be gradually enlightened from the very beginning. Sexual life must, from the start, be treated without secretiveness in the presence of children. It seems that it is the quality of being forbidden that is the essential factor. Children do precisely the forbidden thing in their leading desire to do "what the grownups do."

GRAF wonders whether sleep in children should not be viewed in part as a sexual activity (the blissful face of a sleeping child).

PROF. FREUD replies that general activities and sexual ones cannot be sharply separated from each other. Sexual life, as he said in the *Theory of Sexuality*, is organized in such a way that it draws upon all the important processes in the organism.

One can make no statements about the connection between anxiety and emissions in any individual case (for instance, Joachim), unless one knows how long masturbation was practiced. Masturbation serves as a consolation; the child escapes to masturbation. Emissions, which occur later, have this same function. This can be seen clearly in hysteria. If a female hysteric is made angry, she suffers an attack. It is a substitute for masturbation—for sexual activity in general. She now gets a hysterical attack in the same set of circumstances that previously caused her to masturbate.

HITSCHMANN remarks that one usually wants to have coitus when one is unhappy; thus it too is a solace. (Intercourse, the supper of the poor!) PROF. FREUD adds that the same is true of drinking, as Abraham has recently demonstrated.

RIE would like to correct a minor omission, which will be of special interest to Adler—namely, that for certain perversions Moll assumes a weakness in the *Anlage*.

Concerning meat diets, Rie must stress again that the withdrawal of meat has favorable effects on masturbation. On this point, he cannot agree with Freud's view.

To Wittels one must reply that nature also wanted the child to see, for example, the mother's menstruation, and the like.

Rosegger,[9] in his *Childhood Recollections*, tells a story that resembles Joachim's story about his father. He describes his beloved father—and how he always waited for the father's angry face.

[9] Peter Rosegger (1843-1919) was a distinguished Austrian poet.

59

SCIENTIFIC MEETING *on November 18, 1908*

Present: Prof. Freud, Federn, Hitschmann, Hollerung, Joachim, Rank, Reitler, Rie, Sadger, Schwerdtner, Steiner, Stekel, Wittels.

Dr. Hitschmann proposes Dr. Victor Blum, urologist, assistant of Prof. Frisch, as a member.

PRESENTATION

Sexual Perversity

SPEAKER: DR. FRITZ WITTELS

The speaker introduces his paper by saying that he has not succeeded in finding the guiding thread that ought to go through the topic from beginning to end, and on which the separate thoughts could be strung. He can therefore offer only some random observations.

First, one should examine the nature of perversity and ask: what is it? Then one should consider the relationship of perversity to the normal sex instinct: that is, whether perversity is an illness, and if so, how it should be kept under control. Then, from the legal point of view, one should ask whether perversity is punishable, whether the lawmakers could come into possession of essential facts for the codification of laws relating to perversion and for its suppression. In this connection, one should look at the official position on the perversions to see whether the state has any interest in suppressing perversions, and if so, which ones, and also whether the state can do so. Then would come, as a follow-up, an investigation into the choice of perversion—that is, why certain persons and national groups have a preference for certain perversions, etc. (the naming of some perversions after such groups).

The speaker now turns to a consideration of specific topics.

First: what is perversity? According to conventional opinion, it is only a method of obtaining sensual pleasure. But why then is this method judged so differently? The most obvious assumption would be: for statistical reasons, because the most widely practiced activity is the normal one. This, however, is very unlikely. In the world today, there is a lot more masturbation—not to speak of the rest of the perversions—than there is intercourse.

Then there are various ethical aspects brought forward. In this respect, matters are easiest for the theologians: they say that normal activity comes from God, the other from the Devil. The physicians maintain that sexual activities other than intercourse are contrary to the purpose of the sex instinct. One could reply that there are even more reliable methods of insuring propagation: injecting sperm directly into the uterus (similar experiments have been made in the field of nutrition: concentrated pills). Finally, there are some natural scientists who maintain that all sexual activity other than intercourse must be rejected because it does not occur elsewhere in nature: perversion is a human aberration. However, one finds perversities as curiosities (the highly developed sexuality of the baboon) in domestic animals—which, it is true, live under "perverse" conditions (in a certain amount of luxury, without having to worry about food). Besides, even property, which indeed is considered to be a human achievement, exists among some animals. The argument that perversities deserve to be condemned because they do not occur elsewhere must also be refuted. Property is also an aberration, a perversity in some people (the analogies and relationships between money and sexuality would deserve closer scrutiny): "Property is theft."[1]

[1] This tenet of the French anarchist and political theoretician, Pierre Joseph Prouchon (1809-1865), referred, of course, to economic conditions.

The ancient straight trunk of sexuality has branched out among men, into a broad crown, within whose wide compass properly fall not only the perversities, but also all that is called sublimation of the sexual instinct. In this sense it could be said that a rich personality would actually have to have been perverse in a certain phase; for as man has achieved sublimations that are generally accepted, he must also have encountered the perversions that underlie them. And in fact, many of the greatest and most versatile personalities (Leonardo, Michelangelo, and others) are said to have been perverted. On the other hand, no physician can deny that there are perversions that are pathological, but it is impossible to decide which. The same perversion with which one man is quite content will cause another severe suffering. The sole reason for saying that a person is ill is that he is suffering.

Perhaps one could most properly say that perversity is a disturbance in psychic metabolism; the mentally normal person does not fall ill of perversity. Another reason for classifying perversity as pathological is that some perversions are so dreadful. This, however, is not a permissible basis for classification; disgust and dreadfulness are not objective symptoms. Only that perversion is morbid that appears dreadful to the person who practices it. Accordingly, a masturbator may be ill and a licker of feces healthy.

Our morality does not tolerate perversity. Whoever practices forbidden perversions is a criminal. But the prohibitions of perversity are not systematic. Some dangerous perversions are allowed (masochism), and vice versa. Masturbation—which, if practiced continuously, may cause severe damage—is not prohibited; the horrible custom of an old man marrying a young girl and begetting children by her is permitted; and so forth.

As to the legal aspect, there is first of all the question of whether it is in the interest of the state to proceed against perversion; and if so, whether it can do so, and then, against which ones? Above all, it is quite certain that nothing that two *lovers* do together can be called perverse. Whatever they may do with their bodies is the right thing, whether they are of the same or the opposite sex; for one is upon this earth to be happy. Whatever lovers do is, from a higher point of view, ethical (Nietzsche: whatever is done out of love is beyond good and evil).

The opposite of a lover would be, for instance, the "rake";[2] he is incapable of love. In between the two, there would be the large group of average people. In the rake, everything is unethical. This antithesis would gain in value, if we could compare it with areas bordering on love.[3] But first we would have to know what love is. If we wished, for instance, to explain it to an inhabitant of Mars, we would have to assume that he has a feeling for music. In that case, there would be a much greater likelihood that one could succeed in giving him a human notion of love than would be possible through words. Dr. Wittels dwells for some time on this musical parallel and compares lovers to those who, being connoisseurs, see in Wagner a great advance over the older musicians and for that reason hold him in such high esteem, whereas the rake, who knows nothing about the nature of love, is comparable to the overenthusiastic Wagner fans who do not have any notion of music. And in between there are those who, without any deeper understanding, assert that Wagner means the end of all music—they like Mozart.

To explain love as an intoxication is of as little use as are all materialistic explanations. All psychic processes are accompanied by intoxication. It is a step further to say that love is a transference; this statement contains the whole solution, in the Freudian sense. Whatever is connected with erotogenic zones and infantile sexuality is then also transferred.

The speaker next discusses the various perversions and, to begin with, divides them into two main groups: those that are practiced by one person alone and those that are practiced by two persons together. The latter are further subdivided into perversions practiced with the same sex and those practiced with the opposite sex. And each of these groups would have to be still further divided into an equal number of subdivisions, enumerating all the forms of perversion.

Whether masturbation is physiologically harmful no one can tell. That it is psychologically harmful has been emphatically stressed by

[2] *Wüstling:* literally, a dissolute person.

[3] What Wittels had in mind when he spoke of *Nachbargebiete der Liebe* [neighboring areas of love] we do not know.

Freud; and that fact does not change, whether a person practices his sexual activity by himself, with animals, or with prostitutes. (There are even men who, in having intercourse, use the woman to masturbate.) The fetishists belong in the same category. It is impossible, however, to establish who is an onanist in this sense (in any case, it is a great number of people; it seems, for instance, that all Jesuits were). They represent a definite type, in their behavior and their faces (the image of Savonarola). One hides himself timidly in a corner, while others are the most arrant troublemakers, persons attuned to indignation. This spirit of ill-will, of envy, which may spread over larger or smaller areas, stems from masturbating. If there is a Napoleon, then one hears about great revolutionary changes; Napoleon, too, despite his numerous love affairs, must be counted among the masturbators, just like Don Juan, who is the counterpart of the onanist and therefore identical with him. Don Juan cannot be faithful to any woman because he cannot develop a psychic attachment to her. One has to be an onanist in this sense in order to be able to reach the ultimate limits of one's nature; but it seems that man is not meant to do so, for such people are usually felt to be destructive, noxious creatures. In any event, the state can do nothing against masturbation.

The speaker now turns his attention to the perversions that involve more than one person. Actually, each perversion should be discussed in detail, but he will focus on masochism. In this, too, the physical act must be separated from the psychic consequences. The most essential feature of masochism is the fact that the relationship of man and woman is reversed; for woman, being masochistically inclined by nature and in the core of her being, and having learned to gain a certain amount of pleasure from this, is forced into the opposite behavior toward the man (there is the expression: "a slave to women"; no analogous term exists for women who permit themselves to be tormented by men). A woman who feels pleasure while performing sadistic acts must be characterized as masculine. And just as there are homosexuals who really are heterosexual, there are, from this point of view, heterosexuals who are basically homosexual.

It is doubtful whether sadism and masochism always occur together; there are masochists who have no sadistic traits at all. If sadism occurs in women, they must be regarded as homosexuals. It is no accident that in Berlin, where homosexuality is so widespread, there are so many whipping prostitutes. Homosexuality is so widespread there because the Prussian woman is very prudish and therefore unattractive; the men are more dashing. If the man, then, wants to get his pleasure from a woman, he has to transform her into a man and let her beat him.

There does not seem to be any reason for the state to fight the practice of homosexuality. There are homosexuals who are extremely happy. Besides, homosexuals, individually as well as in groups (the Knights Templar), have accomplished great things.

The laws prohibiting perversions are neither systematic nor justified. The law does not cover all perversions, nor has it made the proper selection. No doubt, it would be in the state's interest to suppress some perversions, if it could do so—however, not by means of prohibition but by influencing the public mind; and for that, nothing need be done except to leave the public unfettered. Then, surely, many perversions would occur less frequently, particularly if at the same time access to women were made easier. At present this is difficult, not only because of external obstacles (infection and pregnancy), but also because of our customs.

The psychological difference in the conception of perversion is that in perversion a barrier (disgust, anxiety, pride) must be overcome, whereas lovers have already overcome it. Thus the pleasure afforded by perversion does not stem from overcoming this barrier because it is not always present. The different evaluation of perversion therefore depends on whether the person is in love or not.[4]

This, Wittels says, concludes his random remarks.

DISCUSSION

STEINER feels that this presentation contains some pearls, though many a shell will have to be opened and discarded before one can get to them. He does not believe that we have gained any general and new points of view. For the time being we can be content with the answers offered in the *Theory of Sexuality*. However, he had expected at least a definition of terms.

[4] This entire paragraph is unclear.

Among the permitted perversions, one should also mention kissing, but of course only when kissing is the sole aim.

STEKEL comments that, on the whole, nothing new has been said about the subject. Wittels and Kraus[5] advocate a point of view according to which perversion is merely a variation. Wittels has revealed himself to be a reactionary, in a sense, and betrayed a hatred of old age in his condemnation of the marriage of old men to young girls.

It is difficult to define perversion; we might say that perversion is an individual's reaction to his infantile experiences.

Stekel is unable to understand Wittels' assertion that a normal person does not fall ill because of perversion. It is the person with inhibiting ideas who falls ill with perversion. Equally unintelligible are Wittels' ideas about the rake and his extension of the concept of masturbation, the dangers of which, incidentally, Wittels exaggerates considerably. Stekel would not attribute neurasthenia to the harmful effects of masturbation. It is true that neurasthenics masturbate; however, it is not the masturbation that leads to neurosis, but the psychic conflict.

On the other hand, we are indebted to Wittels for having broached the topic, which is in need of a thorough examination and discussion.

Masochism is a complicated topic. However, this much can be stated: out of some kind of religious feeling of guilt, these persons tie punishment and pleasure together (mass epidemics). Such general considerations are justified only when they are rooted in a wealth of personal experience. What Wittels has offered us is an interesting extract from his *Weltanschauung*, but he has not given us any new insight.

JOACHIM thinks that Wittels can be blamed only for having offered too much. To give a definition is not possible, but that was not Wittels' intention.

It is questionable whether there exists anything but perversions. In these circumstances, intercourse, as Wittels thinks, could really be regarded as normal only if the sperm reaches the uterus directly and in the absence of any preliminaries. All love play would then have to be considered a perversion.

[5] Karl Kraus. (See Volume I, Minutes 24, footnote 3; also Minutes 93, this volume.)

For the rest, Joachim is in agreement with the speaker's main points. It would have been interesting to learn what ideas Wittels has about the origin of perversions, aside from infantile memories. Wittels believes that it is not a matter of overcoming barriers. That forepleasure is extended, and the way [to satisfaction] made more difficult by inhibitions, does seem to be the case in many perversions.

PROF. FREUD notes with astonishment that he must be under a misconception: everything that was solved in the *Theory of Sexuality* makes its appearance here as a riddle, and the trouble is that he cannot repeat over and over again what he has already stated. Otherwise, he liked the paper quite well and must defend it against Stekel.

The paper centers around the topic of perversion, and that also needed to be done. In this, two difficulties have not been sufficiently overcome. (1) Wittels used the concept of perversion that is antiquated, purely practical and legal, and with that one cannot do very much. (2) He let himself be seduced into diluting the concept too much.

The way society deals with perversions can be, from one viewpoint, justified. It is like what happens with a state monopoly: in the same way, the enjoyment of love is a monopoly of society; and just as the penalties for infringements of the tax laws are disproportionately high, so are they in the case of the perversions—since one cannot, after all, look into things everywhere. The state regulates matters in such a way that the enjoyment of love is reserved for marriage; to keep things as they are, nature takes care to attach certain dangers to coitus. But if a man tries to obtain pleasure from the convenient form of perversity in the midst of married life, he withdraws a portion of his strength from the state, and this "tax exemption" no one is willing to grant him. This is clear and logical. The woman who finds enjoyment in perversion has considerably reduced her capacity for enjoyment in the genital zone. If anybody maintains a perverse relationship with a woman, he thereby deprives her future husband of much of her value as a sexual object.

In his paper, Wittels actually endeavored to fathom the nature of love. It was a correct hunch of his to attempt this via the study of perversions. In fact, however, the problem was solved long ago. Prof.

Freud continues that he himself is planning a paper on this topic, but for practical reasons will keep it until the time when his own sexuality has been extinguished.

As far as the old controversy with Stekel about masturbation is concerned, Freud's opinion still differs from Stekel's. Masturbation as such may cause purely somatic damage, what we see as common neurasthenia. It is true, however, that the greater harm of masturbation is done in the psychic sphere—namely, in the character change that is brought about through this short-circuiting between desire and satisfaction, by a bypassing of the external world, and particularly through thus setting up a prototypical pattern [*Vorbildlichkeit*] for the entire [future] sexual life.

Somatic masturbation may also ensue in the absence of psychic conflict, just as neurasthenia has occurred in persons who have nocturnal emissions, and for whom the emissions have had decidedly harmful consequences. Of course, the psychic conflict may then, in addition, contribute a further injurious influence.

STEKEL takes exception to this statement; [he maintains] that a person who has nocturnal emissions is an anxiety neurotic because of sexual abstinence.

PROF. FREUD replies that Stekel is here falling into the mistake for which he [Freud] has often reproved him: establishing a general principle from his personal experience.

REITLER was pleased with the remark that the Don Juans are onanists in the real sense of the term; he has observed such cases.

The association of masochism and sadism can always be demonstrated. As a rule, children become sexually excited when they see their siblings being beaten: in this, both currents are already linked together. One reason why many perverts remain stalled at the level of infantile practices may perhaps be that, in their puberty, adults instilled in them such a loathing of sexuality that they have acquired a feeling of disgust for their genitals; homosexuality, on the other hand, remains permissible to them.

FEDERN emphasizes that a good deal can be said in favor of Wittels' attempt to establish a connection between masochism and homosexuality. On the whole, he has not been disappointed in the paper.

A merely subjective meaning of the concept of illness is probably not sufficient. The Freudian viewpoints also do not explain why the state prohibits certain perversions and not others. The fact that the state does not interfere with masochism may have as its reason the fundamentally masochistic character of Christianity.

In Federn's opinion, the distinction between lovers, normal individuals, and rakes is very strained. Everyone who is anesthetic during intercourse has remained a masturbator. But Federn cannot conceive either of Napoleon or of Don Juan as onanists. As literary sources for Don Juan, he mentions [E. T. A.] Hoffmann and [Alfred de] Musset. Musset's Don Juan is a man who never finds his woman, even though he believes that he does. Perhaps the mother is behind it. The pervert, too, must long since have carried through the overcoming of these barriers. There are certain people who become perverts because of a defect in or a surplus of sexuality.

SCHWERDTNER defends Wittels' kind of presentation and settles some misunderstanding and differences of opinion between the speaker and the discussants.

SADGER stresses that Wittels had an advantage because he came to psychoanalysis late [in its development] and therefore could acquire a great deal of ready-made knowledge, thus leaving him free to adopt broader perspectives.

Don Juan seeks his mother in every woman, and can never find her; and this is the basis of all of man's love. In the relationship between mother and child also lies the basis of all perversions.

One can speak of perversion only when a person himself feels he is sick. The sense of guilt has to be artificially implanted in man. The discussion referred only to individual masturbation, and not to the almost equally frequent mutual masturbation (homosexuality),[6] which does not lead to the typical character of masturbators. Thus, the finding of the other object apparently constitutes an important psychic component.

RIE finds a wealth of stimulation in this avowedly unsystematic paper. He wishes to refer only to the comparisons. Ownership: money

[6] For instance, in prisons and in the army.

often stands for the sexual act; Zola depicted the hero of his *L'argent* as a pervert.

The second comparison, that with music, is a good one, but unfortunate for Wittels, for it proves him to be wrong: the rakes are just as far from being sick—unless they are anesthetic—as the unmusical person is from healthy enjoyment.

HITSCHMANN sees little value in continuing the discussion. The paper did not offer much that was new. The prerequisite would have been sharply defined concepts, and these were missing. Wittels should have started with Freud's assumptions, and should not have used the word perversion with so much affect and disapproval. Nor can one understand why he suddenly extended the concept of masturbation to such a degree. One must go back to the *Theory of Sexuality*.

Wittels failed to mention those perversions that appear in later life. Moreover, occasionally perversions play a different role from those that come along with a person from childhood. Whether or not a gratification obtained through perversions is physically harmful is determined by whether it is genuine or has been acquired later. The condemnation of old men's marriages is the expression of a kind of sexual envy, and it is by no means proven that a child born out of such a marriage is inferior. The whole business of preventing perversity can best be achieved by rooting out the examples of it.

WITTELS, in his concluding words, attempts to draw the guideline that was missing in his paper. He does not discuss the individual objections. He wishes only to specify the general difference between Freud's *Theory of Sexuality* and what he himself has said. It is impossible to begin with the *Theory of Sexuality*, because its framework is too solidly put together. He has adopted a different—in a sense a higher—position.[7] The natural scientist is a dogmatist; he lays down a principle and declares: that is the way it is. On this, Wittels had nothing new to say; so he chose the skeptical point of view, which asserts that matters are not so, they merely seem to be so. The natural scientist, if he has stated the truth, need not concern himself with the opinion of others, but a person working in other fields can engage in a discussion with other people and can shake up what they consider

[7] Precisely what Wittels wanted to express is not clear.

to be undisplaceable. Seen from this point of view, the medical man must ask himself what he can cure and what he cannot. The Freudian theory holds a danger for the man who is not philosophically inclined: it rationalizes something that was previously considered to be unrationalizable (the most extreme result was that the penis and the vagina were seen in everything). It will hardly be possible to explain all of love rationally; there will always remain something inexplicable, without which one would not care to live. The skeptical point of view is that of the artist. By pursuing the line of thought presented in his paper, one might produce something theoretical. Perhaps this will happen in the future.

Finally, Wittels corrects a few minor misunderstandings and refutes some objections.

60

SCIENTIFIC MEETING *on November 25, 1908*

Present: Prof. Freud, Adler, [A.] Deutsch, Federn, Hitschmann, Hollerung, Joachim, Rank, Sadger, Stekel.

Blum was not accepted as a member.

PRESENTATION

The Myth of the Birth of the Hero: A Psychological Interpretation of Mythology

SPEAKER: OTTO RANK

The contents of this paper will be published shortly as the fifth issue of *Schriften zur angewandten Seelenkunde.*[1]

[1] In the previously cited review of the literature of the *Jahrbuch für psychoanalytische und psychologische Forschungen,* Vol. I, Abraham gives the following summary: "In myths of heroes of the most diverse nations, the hero's birth and childhood have certain recurrent elements in common. The hero is of noble descent, but after an ominous prediction he is cast out in his early infancy (most often onto water, on which he floats in a small chest); he is rescued, and is raised by humble parents; later he emerges from obscurity and goes on to power and glory. Rank demonstrated the pervading analogy of these myths with childhood fantasies, such as are also preserved in dream and neurosis. Mankind creates the hero and his fate out of its own childhood memories and fantasies. Some of these fantasies are symbolically disguised in the myths. For instance, being cast out in the small chest is a symbolic representation of pregnancy and birth." Rank's book contains a long passage written by Freud, in which Freud introduces and formulates the idea of the "family romance."

DISCUSSION

ADLER remarks that the material is unexpected and overwhelming. He finds many a fine thought in the paper but, with all the recognition that is due these, nevertheless while listening he had the impression that the speaker was not successful in tracing the matter through to its core, although he came close to it. The aspect of the problem that has been represented as most significant could, perhaps, be gone into in greater depth. The author did not bring out with sufficient clarity the compulsion toward the formation of myths.

The sore spot is this: it seems that Rank attributes the formation of myths to the child. That the impulse toward myth-formation comes from the child cannot be surprising to us, in view of the importance of the infantile in the adult. However, this point deserves special clarification and cannot be passed over lightly.

Sexuality takes up comparatively little space [in Rank's presentation]. It is questionable whether by and large this is tenable. Adler believes that he is correct in assuming that it was the Professor's idea to trace the myth back to the act of birth. In his own analyses, this [sort of] material does not present itself frequently; and he suspects that all of it cannot be interpreted without any more ado as representing the act of birth, even if reversal and the other mechanisms are taken into account. The casting out of the child could perhaps also be explained in a different way. Adler is here referring to a thought that is contained in his paper on the aggressive drive.[2]

There are many possible ways of fulfilling one's ambition in fantasies, but their number is limited. As for the exchange of parents, there is only a small number of ways of acquiring other parents. Amidst these means, among primitive peoples, floating on the water, etc., naturally has a dominant role. This point may deserve a certain amount of consideration.

FEDERN stresses the fact that the inherent probability that these things have for the initiated also provides a degree of security to the seemingly most arbitrary productions and interpretations. In view of these basic agreements, one can do no more than argue about details.

[2] See Volume I, Minutes 53.

Federn's first objection is the same as Adler's; in this, however, he sees not a contradiction, but a supplement. A contributing factor in myth-formation is the reaction of adults to the strange phenomenon of the formation of a hero (*Heldenbildung*), which has always been a chamber of horrors for the older generation. For instance, the parents' hatred against a rebellious son may be expressed in their desire to cast out the child, and perhaps also in the idea that this child, who is so unlike them, must be a stranger.

Ominous dreams are later creations: the father who has such a son is afraid of him.

The "inversion" of the Moses legend may perhaps owe its origin to the fact that the legend came out of a suppressed people (whereas other legends came from ruling peoples).

The attitude of parents can be recognized in the fact that the first child, after its death, is replaced by another child.

The simulation of insanity may perhaps have its root in observation of the incredible development of these extraordinary children.

HITSCHMANN emphasizes that this time the plausibility was most impressive. He himself has had no experience that would specifically confirm these birth fantasies.

Even if the myths are really not different, still, when a nation assimilates a myth that pleases it, this is almost equivalent to the creation of one. [The recurrence of] shepherds and animals finds its explanation, perhaps, in the period when people led a nomadic life. And besides, the child is closely related to the animal.

The fact that the human part of the sphinx shows that portion of the body that the suckling infant sees, i.e., the breasts, seems to support Rank's view. The content of the myth is not exactly infantile, but rather corresponds to the psychological situation of the young boy (where there is already jealousy with regard to the mother, etc.). Hitschmann is struck by the fact that the myth has been given a purely masculine interpretation. There are some elements that could be regarded as feminine—such as a virgin giving birth to a child, a woman bearing another child to replace the stillborn, the helping sister participating in the brother's fate, a mother fondling her son, among others.

The motif of simulation may perhaps be altogether in keeping with children's behavior—specifically with the fact that a child always knows more than he admits, that he is actually always pretending to be ignorant. It goes without saying that the content of these myths has to do with something repressed.

PROF. FREUD first stresses that the main purpose of this paper was to demonstrate the share that psychic life has in the formation of myths, because the prevalent theory of myth-formation, operating as it does on a purely linear hypothesis, has taken great pains to ignore the general human content of myths; in other words, [the main task was] to take a step of no small importance, by way of which a second advance into the field of mythology is made (the first one was made by Abraham, as we all know).[3]

Rank cannot be altogether spared a certain amount of criticism. He has not yet attained the art of self-discipline, which would enable him to give up not only the superfluous but occasionally also the pertinent, for the sake of his didactic purposes. It would, therefore, be advisable to limit the discussion to matters that are plausible and easily demonstrated. This should be placed in the foreground, while certain complications and some secondary items should be relegated to the background. In this category belong primarily complications of our myth

[3] Karl Abraham's "Dreams and Myth: A Study in Folk-Psychology" appeared (in German) as the fourth issue of the *Schriften zur angewandten Seelenkunde* in 1909, but was obviously known to Freud and his followers earlier in manuscript form. A brief summary given by the author himself in the *Jahrbuch* follows:

"Just as the dream arises from the individual's fantasy, so is the myth engendered by a people's fantasy. The myth also tends toward wish fulfillment. Many myths even express the same wishes as certain dreams (Freud's 'typical dreams'). Most myths contain a symbolic fulfillment of desires from a people's childhood. This symbolism is discussed in detail; we encounter it in our language, in customs, in dreams, and so on. The legends of the descent of fire (the Prometheus myth), and of the divine potion, are analyzed in connection with Kuhn's investigations. The fire legend, in symbolic form, originally represents procreation; the divine potion is originally the human semen. Both procreation and semen are deified in the two myths. Man's desires, which are connected with his consciousness of manhood (complex of sexual greatness), are represented as fulfilled. It is, of course, true that in the usual tradition of the myth the wish fulfillment occurs in a deeply disguised form. Here too censorship is active and enforces the distortion of the very thoughts on which the myth is based, by means of condensation, displacement, and the like, just as in the dream. The effect of this psychological process is demonstrated in the legends of Moses, Samson, and others.

"The wish theory of the myth deserves to be given preference over the older theories because it affords insight into the motives of myth formation."

with other myths—for instance, that of the hostile brothers as rivals. It would be better to leave aside a number of motifs, such as those of the several children, the animal, stupidity, the physical defects and their relationship to Adler's theory, etc., and to limit oneself to the core of the whole problem.

In the foreground one should keep, above all, the fact that the myth has a paranoid quality. In keeping with this is the fact that in paranoia the story is told plainly, although without affording any insight into its motivations. Intimately linked with the paranoid quality is the characteristic of separating that which is connected in fantasy; hence the multiplications, the splittings, etc. This same characteristic expresses itself in the reversal, in the projection onto the father, and in other details; insight into the paranoid quality [of the myth] makes all this easily understandable.

Prof. Freud then takes up some points that have been mentioned already in the discussion. Before doing so, he calls attention to the fact that the legends of the great flood are likewise myths of the father's wrath, carried over from the individual to the whole of mankind: the floating on the water in a chest; the casting out and the simultaneous deliverance; the rebirth of mankind. This leads to the conclusion that these are secondary legends, that they could have been formed only at a later time, during a period when a monotheistic view must have prevailed.

Adler's doubt about the validity of interpreting these dreams as dreams of birth is totally unjustified. There is a very good reason why the act of birth is represented in different ways in dreams and in myths.

The name *Moses* is Egyptian and is often attached as a suffix to the names of Egyptian kings; for instance, Rameses (*Meses* = Moses), rebirth of Rah; Thotmeses, etc. The name Moses, then, means "birth"; and this meaning of the name is explained by the princess herself when she says: "I have pulled him out of the water."[4]

As far as the animal motif is concerned, one may content himself with seeing it as the motif of the helpful animals. Animals are well

[4] See Freud, *Moses and Monotheism* (1937-1939), New York: Knopf, 1947. The problem of the origin of monotheism was already occupying Freud's mind at an early time.

suited for this role, because they readily lend themselves to the observation of sexual processes; moreover, it is precisely in this area that there arises the child's first rebellion against his father, who conceals the facts about birth from him. In accepting what the parents have told him, the child says, in a somewhat parodistic way: "If an animal was capable of bringing me, it was capable of suckling me, too."

As for the motifs of stupidity, physical defects, etc., Freud does not want to go into the biological bases, but will limit himself to the psychological aspects. The child incorporates into the myths, with a corresponding emphasis, the reproaches that he hears from his father about his physical defects, and he equips the heroes with those same defects that press down upon his own self-esteem.

Myths are not, as had been assumed, formed by the child but by a group [*Volk*] of adults. The impulse for this is obviously provided by amazement about the appearance of the hero, who must therefore have had such a childhood. The amazement about the development of the ingenious child, the rebellious son, provokes the invention, in the myth, of the hero's extraordinary childhood. This they fashion out of their own childhood consciousness.[5] And by endowing the hero with their own childhood history, they are identifying with him and saying, as it were, "I was such a hero, too." Thus the real hero of the romance is the ego, which rediscovers itself in the hero by placing itself back in the time when it was a hero, by virtue of its first heroic deed—the rebellion against the father.[6] The adult thus creates myths by way of a fantasied return to childhood, and the substitution of this childhood for that of the hero. Thus, on the one hand, the myth contains the justification for the ego's objective rebellion; on the other hand, it contains the justification for the individual's rebellion against the father (which comes out especially clearly in epics). This is the real tendency, this is what has been oppressing him: the fact that he did not become a hero later. Now he justifies himself by saying that the father has given him reason for antagonism. The antagonism was

[5] We must not forget that the small child's consciousness differs from that of the adult. It is, rather, preconscious and often very close to the unconscious. Therefore, if Freud speaks here of the child's consciousness, we may understand him to mean the unconscious impressions of childhood.

[6] See also Freud, *Totem and Taboo* (1913), *S.E.*, 13.

primarily caused, however, by the fact that the boy was shut out from knowledge of the sexual processes of birth.

The weak point in the motif of the casting out, which cannot be immediately explained by the content known to us, can be shored up by other material—that is, by two points: (1) The fantasy of the rescue of the emperor, as mentioned in [the discussion of] *A Dream Is Life*, which regularly appears in neurotics.[7] Saving a life is the opposite of casting out; the fantasy of rescue is represented by its opposite: the hero is placed in mortal danger (as a rule, cast out into water). Hence casting out means nothing else than rescue. From the modern pessimistic point of view, the hero even has a certain right to look upon this gift of life as being cast out into the hostile world. (2) The so-called "maternal etiology," in persons who have not succeeded in giving up the prototype of their sexual object, i.e., the mother. These persons represent a special type of love life, a type that includes some unconnected characteristics: (i) they have a long string of love affairs; (ii) they are very faithful in each of these relationships, and free themselves [each time] with great difficulty; (iii) they are attracted only by women who belong to another man, and who (iv) have a bad reputation as far as sex is concerned; (v) these men feel a need to make such women their mistresses, in order to rescue them.[8] The first characteristic (i) signifies that the mother is irreplaceable; in (ii), the faithfulness and the high esteem refer to the personality of the mother; (iv) is an indication that these boys attribute love affairs to the mother in their fantasies; in them, the enmity to the father comes to the fore, and the boy himself has a chance to come closer to the mother. The lovers show traits of the father and of the son himself. (v) The woman must be rescued for reasons similar to those for which the emperor is rescued. This is a characteristic feature of the child's relationship to his parents. The saving of their lives is his revenge for their gift of life, for the fact that he owes his life to them. There is, thus, a danger inherent in the gift of life, and, in fact, this danger lies in the act of birth. For this deliverance from the danger of suffocation, the son feels bound, on his part, to rescue his parents (the act of birth

[7] See Minutes 54B, in this volume.

[8] The thoughts expressed here were later elaborated by Freud in "Contributions to the Psychology of Love" (1910, 1912, 1918), *S.E.*, 11.

as a source of anxiety).[9] If we keep in mind these reinforcements of the rescue motive, we will find the interpretation of the casting out as birth far more convincing.

These myths are a combination of two opposing motifs, both of which are subordinate to the main theme of the individual's vindication through the hero. The two motifs are: (1) gratitude and tender feelings toward the parents, and (2) rebellion against the father. Here, however, the conflict with the father has its origin not in sexual rivalry for the mother, but in the father's concealment of the facts about the sexual processes connected with birth.[10]

[9] These are the earliest precursors of the later theory of anxiety. Cf. especially Lecture XXXII in *New Introductory Lectures on Psychoanalysis* (1932). New York: Norton, 1933.

[10] It is apparent that Rank has considerably abbreviated Freud's contribution to the discussion, and therefore some passages are not entirely clear. Nevertheless, this contribution should be read with the utmost attention, for it contains a wealth of ideas, including some seeds of important later works.

61

SCIENTIFIC MEETING *on December 9, 1908*

Present: Prof. Freud, Federn, Graf, Hitschmann, Joachim, Rank, Sadger, Stekel, Wittels.

Reviews and Case Reports by All Present

WITTELS presents the case of a young man, about thirty years old, who lives in the delusion that he is suffering from anti-Semitic persecution, for which he holds his inconspicuously Semitic nose responsible. He therefore plans to have the shape of his nose changed by plastic surgery. The patient has a terrible and quite childish fear of his strict mother and a special predilection for elderly, corpulent women. Wittels tried to explain to him that his "nasal symptoms" are displacements from the penis; this the patient declared to be a good joke. He had masturbated from the time he was seven, until he was caught at it. From then on, his mother kept after him and punished him quite severely. A short time ago, he brought with him an article by Tolstoy, which contained the statement that anti-Semitism is a sexual business; this impressed him very much. The patient's confidence in Wittels dates from one of the latter's very early writings on baptism.

PROF. FREUD comments that it is not in keeping with our aim to make the patient a present, as it were, of the correct solution, as Wittels did in this case. A somewhat redeeming factor in this procedure, however, is the fact that the case is of a paranoid character, and therefore in any event unsuitable for psychoanalysis.[1] In his experience all cases that, in similar ways, come to focus on physical matters (beauty blemishes, disfigurations) are cases of paranoia.[2] Obviously, the man is unhappy about being a Jew and wants to be baptized. (At this point Wittels remarks that the patient is an ardent Jew.) Nevertheless, he does not undergo baptism. In this fact lies the conflict that has absorbed the meaning of other conflicts. (Wittels now mentions the name of the patient, whose father is known to Professor Freud as an ardent Zionist.) The opposition to the father, on the one hand, and the attachment to him, on the other hand, are contained in this conflict.

HITSCHMANN first offers the genesis and analysis of a joke he made up on some occasion.

Next he mentions an article on the Steinheil case by Attorney General Wülffen, published in the *Berliner Tageblatt*, in which Wülffen makes full use of our terminology.

Further, he presents two dreams from Gottfried Keller's dream book (which is reported in Baechtold's biography[3]); in one of these dreams, the symbolism of the serpent comes out very clearly.

He then mentions two articles by Ferenczi. One of them, entitled "The Analytic Interpretation and Treatment of Psychosexual Impotence in Men," was published in Bresler's *Psychiatrisch-Neurologische*

[1] Later one often heard (and nowadays particularly one hears) about attempts to apply psychoanalytic therapy to schizophrenics. Whether all these patients warrant the diagnosis of "schizophrenia" is another question. Freud predicted that the psychoanalysis of some schizophrenics would probably become possible through a specific variation of technique resembling child analysis, in which contact must be kept up with parents and teachers in order to obtain information about the child's behavior outside of the therapeutic session, especially with reference to his "acting out."

[2] Obviously Freud had in mind the hypochondriacal ideas of schizophrenics; for an example see H. Nunberg, "On the Catatonic Attack" (1920), *Practice and Theory of Psychoanalysis*. New York: International Universities Press, 1961, note 14.

[3] J. Baechtold, *Gottfried Kellers Leben. Seine Briefe und Tagebücher* [*Gottfried Keller's Life. His Letters and Diaries*]. Berlin: W. Hertz, 1894-1897.

Wochenschrift [1908].[4] Hitschmann gives a short report of its contents and conclusions, supplementing the report with a case of his own: a man, married for three years, who has been incapable of *immissio penis*. The man had three brothers but no sister (Steiner!). The basic experience goes back to the time when his tutor, if the child had to urinate, would carry him into another room and ask him to urinate into his mouth, which was very distressing for the child. Later on, he had fantasies during which he masturbated mentally. He saw himself as a favorite of the Empress Catherine of Russia. Later, he occasionally went to prostitutes and had them masturbate him (also fellatio). Twice he attempted in vain to rape servant girls. He entered matrimony fearfully. His analysis disclosed that he had once seen his mother naked. In addition to the analysis, he was given encouragement, advice to avoid frustrating excitement, and the like. After a relatively short treatment, the man was cured.

Another work of Ferenczi is just beginning to appear in the *Wiener klinische Rundschau*.[5] It starts with a restatement of Freud's views.

Hitschmann goes on to mention an article "On Dismenorrhea" by Prof. Veith, who arrives at the conclusion that this subject belongs in the province of the neurologist.

In Brodmann's *Journal* [*für Psychologie und Neurologie*], M. Levy (Berlin) reports that, in order to induce hypnosis, he uses a piece of colored glass with a piece of gray paper in the center; he tells the patient that, as the first sign of his falling asleep, he will see the complementary color (which, of course, appears to everybody).[6]

[4] Abraham gave the following summary of this paper in the *Jahrbuch*, 1:582, 1909: "According to Ferenczi, sexual inhibition is a prohibition by the unconscious, originally directed against the realization of repressed sexual childhood wishes, a prohibition that, however, interferes with all sexual activity in order to secure complete repression. The incestuous fixation on parents and siblings is of the utmost importance. Psychic impotence is in most instances linked with other neurotic symptoms. Mild cases may be cured by even a superficial psychoanalysis; a psychoanalysis correctly carried through may achieve a cure, even in severe cases."

[5] "Actual- and Psycho-Neuroses in the Light of Freud's Investigations and Psycho-Analysis" (1908). *Further Contributions to the Theory and Technique of Psycho-Analysis.* London: Hogarth Press, 1926.

[6] "Über ein leicht anwendbares Hilfsmittel bei der Einleitung der Hypnose" ["On an Easily Applicable Aid in the Induction of Hypnosis"] (Further bibliographical data are unavailable.)

In the *Berliner psychologische Gesellschaft* ["Berlin Psychological Society"[7]], Abraham presented a paper on marriage between blood relations and their consequences (according to Freud, this will be published in the first *Jahrbuch*).[8] A very animated discussion is said to have followed this presentation.

STEKEL presents an example of a slip of the tongue. The case involves an obsessional neurotic who has the idea that he is being poisoned by a bookcase that his mother sent him. The bookcase stands for his cook, and his fear that he might make her pregnant. Wanting to say that the bookcase has now been "eliminated," the patient says that it is "*a*liminated."

PROF. FREUD, incidentally, finds in this nice slip of the tongue evidence of something that could become fundamental to our conception. It permits us to anticipate that one day we may be able to trace typical symptoms back to certain basic complexes. Wherever there is poison, or being poisoned in any form—from fantasy to actual murder by poisoning—this complex at first always means pregnancy. Poisoning is invariably the chief impression a child has when he sees a pregnant woman vomiting. Poisoning is the substitute for the complex of pregnancy. (Federn mentions a short novel by Mann, in which a little boy likewise believes his pregnant mother to have been poisoned.)[9]

[7] The paper was read before the Berlin Society for Psychiatry and Nervous Disease, Nov. 9, 1908.

[8] We append Abraham's summary of his paper, "The Significance of Intermarriage Between Close Relations in the Psychology of the Neuroses," first published in the *Jahrbuch für psychoanalytische und psychopathologische Forschungen*, 1:110-118, 1909. "In neurotic families one frequently finds an abnormal fixation of the infantile sexual transference onto blood relatives, with the result that the ability to transfer libido onto strangers is rarely sufficient. Marriage to a blood relative represents for the man a substitute for the unattainable gratification of his infantile incestuous desires. Members of such families, in many instances, remain in a state of childlike dependence on their parents, because in puberty they did not fully succeed in detaching their libido from the sexual objects of childhood. Such persons frequently remain unmarried or at least show outspoken monogamous inclinations. The fixation of infantile incestuous tendencies is furthermore of great significance for the development of certain neurotic symptoms—as, for instance, psychic impotence in the man and frigidity in the woman. Marriage among blood relations should be regarded primarily as a consequence of a neurotic disposition; thus such a marriage becomes a breeding ground for this kind of neurotic disposition in the descendants."

[9] Heinrich Mann: "The Unknown," contained in the collection *Stürmische Morgen* [Stormy Mornings], Munich, 1906. Federn's report is not quite precise: It is not his

STEKEL adds that, to his patient, poison primarily means "sperm." The fantasy described was the replica of an earlier one in which the mother was the bookcase (this time she sent him one), and the patient intended to poison his brother. From observing many neuroses Stekel has gained the impression that, in the end, after one believes that one has resolved everything, the patient projects the whole thing onto a servant girl.

He mentions two minor, but nevertheless characteristic, traits from Grillparzer's *King Ottocar, His Rise and Fall.* The main impression one gets is that Rudolf von Habsburg represents Grillparzer's father. Grillparzer's father was angry about the first poetic attempts of his son. In the play Rudolf gives his chain to the poet. Then Katharina Frölich appears as a little bourgeois girl and Rudolf says to her: "Don't fall, Katharina; just go back to your mother, Katharina": [this represents Grillparzer's] desire to give her back, unhurt, to her mother.

Lastly, Stekel reads some characteristic passages from Artemidorus' dream book.

PROF. FREUD mentions a paper by Frank[10] of Zürich, who, in curing several cases of hysteria by hypnosis, could not, of course, discover the sexual factor in hysteria.

---

mother whom the little boy thinks to be poisoned, but another woman, with whom he is passionately in love; poisoning by her husband is the only way he can explain the change in her appearance.

It seems pertinent to mention here that the derivation of the paranoid delusion of poisoning is a projection of the passive homosexual desire. (See Freud, "Psycho-Analytic Notes on an Autobiographical Account of a Case of Paranoia [Dementia Paranoides]" 1911. *S.E.*, 12:3-82.)

[10] Ludwig Frank, a neurologist in Zürich, achieved successes with the cathartic method.

While it does not immediately touch upon the subject of these Minutes, we have deemed C. G. Jung's review of Frank's paper of sufficient historical interest to reprint it here. Frank's article, "Zur Psychoanalyse" ["On Psychoanalysis"] appeared in a Festschrift in honor of Forel in the *Journal für Psychologie und Neurologie,* 1908. Jung's abstract was published in the *Jahrbuch für Psychoanalyse,* 2:361-362, 1910.

"After a short historical introduction based on the studies by Breuer and Freud, the author expresses his regret that Freud has abandoned the original method without giving his reasons for so doing. (Attentive reading of Freud's subsequent writings discloses soon enough why he preferred the perfected technique to the originally imperfect one.—*The reviewer.*) The author restricts himself to the use of the original cathartic method in conjunction with hypnosis, and his case reports prove that he is working with a valuable, practically useful method, which shows rewarding results. The inevitable attack on Freud's theory of sexuality is consequently set forth in more temperate tones; the author poses the question: 'Why should just the sexual affects,

Next Freud mentions an essay by A. A. Brill of New York on "Psychological Factors in Dementia Praecox [An Analysis]" (in Morton Prince's *Journal [of Abnormal Psychology]*, 1908).[11] The analysis dates back to the time Brill spent in Zürich. The main points are these: the patient, a native of Zürich, had gone to America and returned home. He was a freethinker and a friend of the Jews. His father was a powerful figure, tyrannical, bigoted, and anti-Semitic. Despite their contrasting personalities, the patient had always remained dependent upon his father. He had had various love affairs. He can, of course, be made use of only for the association experiment. He ridicules the physicians, he is a mystic, and his father in his eyes has become God the Father. He undergoes a change of character and turns again to his father. This relationship to the father was not brought out clearly enough by Brill.

---

among all the many affects with which the psyche is endowed, give rise to disturbances? Or, why should the sexual affect even be at the root of all others?' (The role of sexuality in the neuroses was not invented *a priori*, but was discovered empirically through the use of psychoanalysis; and this is something different from the cathartic method.—*The reviewer*.) The author does not use psychoanalysis because 'a practicing physician should not be obliged, in each case, to carry the psychoanalysis through to its very end for theoretical reasons only.' [This obligation exists nowhere, but for *practical* reasons one has to go farther than one did in 1895; had the method of that time accomplished everything, there would have been no need for going further.] The author gained the impression that Freud mastered hypnosis and suggestion theoretically, but by no means in its practical application. 'I can understand his [Freud's] constant change of method only on the basis of the fact that, *dissatisfied with his insufficiently thorough hypnotic treatments and their results*, he, as a theoretician, was constantly trying to find new methods.' A little earlier in his paper, the author says, 'Freud has relinquished these methods *in spite of his successes*.' In connection with this contradiction, it should be mentioned that Frank *utterly ignores* Freud's later works, as well as the writings of other authors and the Clinic in Zürich; otherwise he could not possibly assert—and in 1908—that the cathartic method and its results remained 'unnoticed' and that only 'now and then was a verification attempted.'

"(The reviewer cannot refrain from pointing out how simple it is to become informed about these seemingly difficult problems. If, for instance, an author is faced with the problem of why Freud may have given up hypnosis, he need only compose a letter to Prof. Freud and inquire about it. On this point the reporter is insistent because it is the basic illness of German psychiatry that one is never eager to *understand*, but only to *misunderstand*. In these matters a *personal discussion* is necessary for the reduction of all superfluous difficulties and misunderstandings. If this principle, which is fully accepted in America, for example, were only acknowledged on our continent, not so many otherwise deserving authors would have to discredit themselves by their criticism, which is frequently couched in a language that renders any reply impossible.)"

[11] See Minutes 54B, in this volume.

Two items in the analysis that shed some light on the case are worth mentioning. In his mystical fantasies, the patient is also under the influence of the two Egyptian deities, Isis and Osiris. In Zürich he was a bank clerk; recently, a multimillionaire banker by the name of Osiris died there. One can easily understand his desire to be heir to this man. This fantasy is related, of course, to his father's death. Isis, who is automatically associated with Osiris, is his mother.

Another bit of interpretation is very daring, but it does seem plausible. The patient constantly reiterates the question: "Am I Parsifal, the pure *Tor?*"[12] He has a mistress who writes him letters from America, and there is a sentence in her first letter: "I am in Pittsburgh, Pennsylvania, staying with the Thaw family." He says he has become possessed by this sentence, and repeats over and over again the words "Pittsburgh, Pennsylvania, Thaw." The American abbreviation for Pennsylvania is "Pa." This "Pa" he turns into Parsifal and Thaw becomes *Thor;* thus one stereotype becomes the substitute for the other. We could go further and ask: What is the meaning of this question, which has become the substitute for another question? Obviously, the question that torments him is: Is she faithful to me? This question has been transformed, as it were, into the homosexual [counterpart]. The word "purest," used with regard to faithfulness, contains a hint of what is animating, so to speak, the entire obsession.

In contrast to this intelligent analysis by Brill, there is a paper by a Dr. Steyerthal of Mecklenburg, which appeared in Hoche's collection.[13] Its title is "What is Hysteria? A Nosological Study." In the form of a historical presentation (Havelock Ellis used this form in "The Evolution of Modesty" in his *Studies in the Psychology of Sex*), Dr. Steyerthal, after describing the development of the concept of hysteria up to the present time, offers an analysis of this concept and comes to the conclusion that there is no such thing as hysteria.

FEDERN reports that, after he read the second edition of *The Interpretation of Dreams*, his doubts concerning the explanation for coun-

[12] It is necessary to give the German word here because the interpretation deals with the sound association. *Tor* means fool; *reine Tor* = pure, or innocent fool.

[13] *Sammlung zwangloser Abhandlungen aus dem Gebiet der Nerven-und Geisteskrankheiten* [*A Collection of Informal Treatises in the Field of Nervous and Mental Diseases*].

terwish dreams were dispelled by several clear and transparent wish dreams which confirmed the validity of the dream theory.

He reports a case from his psychoanalytic practice. This patient's anxiety attack was connected with being locked up. As a child, he had been locked up frequently. From the time he was eight, he believed himself to be rather "limited" [*beschränkt*[14]], while his brother was gifted.

PROF. FREUD comments that this connection is of basic significance. This example demonstrates with particular clarity the difference between nonpsychological and psychological psychiatry. The clinical textbooks describe claustrophobic patients as people with lowered self-esteem. Analysis reveals that an immense number of shattered fantasies of ambition are hidden behind claustrophobia. Thus the old clinical view hit upon something that was correct. Of course, this connection leads to all sorts of plays upon words and symbolic references ("limited," "to confine," "to lock in," "to encounter barriers," "to fail to advance," etc.).[15]

FEDERN mentions a few more reviews: first, a review of Sadger's "Fragment of the Psychoanalysis of a Homosexual" (*Jahrbuch für sexuelle Zwischenstufen*) by Havelock Ellis in *Journal of Mental Science*;[16] second, a review of Muthmann's book by Bernhard Hart;[17] third, two Italian articles on the erotic dreams of healthy people in the *Rivista Psichologica* of January/February, 1908;[18] finally, a psychological essay by Mercier on memory, thinking, and wishing, etc.[19]

GRAF presents a short analysis of the draft of a play (composed during the summer), whose subject is also a conflict between father

14 *Beschränkt* means constricted, narrow, limited, "rather dull."

15 Freud refers to the play upon the words *Schrank*, which means cabinet; *Schranke*—barrier or enclosure; *einschränken*, which means to restrict; *eingeschränkt*, which means confined and, in a figurative sense, limited, narrow-minded. The root of this word is *Schrank*; hence *einschränken* = to enclose in a limited area.

16 In this review Ellis praises Sadger as the most remarkable of Freud's disciples.

17 Hart's review also appeared in the *Journal of Mental Science*, under the title *Psychotherapy*. Muthmann's book, *On the Psychology and Therapy of Neurotic Symptoms: A Study Based on Freud's Theory of Neuroses*, has already been mentioned (Minutes 57, this volume, note 14).

18 Havelock Ellis reviewed Lorenzo Gualino's paper "Il Sogno Erotica nell' Uomo Normale" ["Erotic Dreams in Normal Persons"] in the same *Journal*.

19 C. Mercier: "The Physical Basis of Mind," Presidential Address delivered at the 67th Annual Meeting of the Medico-Psychological Association in London, July, 1908.

and son. Two months before he conceived the plan for this sketch in three acts, his father died; he had always lived in conflict with him. In connection with this sketch, memories of Schiller and Hebbel come back to him: both, in spite of their living in conflict with their fathers, achieved prominence. Thus his play is his own personal justification.

SADGER mentions that Ferenczi, in the paper that is just now appearing in the *Wiener klinische Rundschau*,[20] has omitted stomach symptoms in his discussion of neurasthenia.

Then he briefly reviews the first volume of Reibmayr's book.[21]

[20] See footnote 5 above.

[21] *Die Entwicklungsgeschichte des Talentes und Genies.* Band I. *Die Züchtung des individuellen Talentes und Genies in Familien und Kasten.* [Developmental History of Talent and Genius. Volume I: The Breeding of Individual Talent and Genius in Families and Castes.] Munich, 1908.

62

SCIENTIFIC MEETING *on December 16, 1908*

Present: Prof. Freud, Adler, Bass, [A.] Deutsch, Federn, Hitschmann, Hollerung, Joachim, Rank, Rie, Sadger, Schwerdtner, Steiner, Stekel, Wittels.

Prof. Ehrenfels as a guest.

PRESENTATION

Die Sexuelle Not, by Fritz Wittels[1]

SPEAKER: PROF. EHRENFELS[2]

After first expressing his gratitude and his appreciation to Wittels, the speaker then raises his objections to *Die Sexuelle Not.*

1 Wittels' book was published by C. W. Stern, Vienna and Leipzig, in 1909. (It has not been translated into English.) Its motto is: "Man must give free rein to his sexuality, or else he becomes crippled." The chapter headings are: I. The Injunction against Abortion; II. Venereal Disease; III. The Family; IV. About the Child: The Ego of the Child, Emotional Brutality, Problems and Worries, Explorations, Sexual Enlightenment; V. The Masculine Woman, Female Assassins, Women Physicians; VI. The Child-Woman.

In the second Volume of the *Psychoanalytisches Jahrbuch*, Jung reviewed Wittels' book. Because of its historical interest, we quote the last paragraph of that review:

"I have not read a book on the problem of sexuality that so harshly and mercilessly tears to pieces our present-day morality, and yet in the main is so right; it is for just this reason that Wittels deserves to be read; but so do many others who write about the same topic. For it is not the single book that is of importance, but the problem common to them."

2 Cf. Volume I, Minutes 5.

The first question has to do with Wittels' low opinion of women's intellectual work, which Wittels regards as converted sexuality. This opinion is in contradiction to Freud's view (which very much appeals to the speaker), that there exist only two basic instincts: hunger and love, and that all other drives stem from these. If one accepts this point of view, then the male's quest for knowledge must also be derived from sexuality. If, however, one assumes the existence of a multitude of drives—e.g., a drive for knowledge alongside the sexual drive—it would seem most unlikely for this drive to exist in men only. There is, therefore, no foundation for Wittels' thesis from any point of view. Nevertheless, *de facto*, the speaker's own point of view does not differ very widely from Wittels'. The scientific works of women he has seen have all been of inferior quality. It is true that there are some rare exceptions; on the whole, however, in this respect woman seems to be less developed.

The social views expressed in the book are closer to the speaker's personal feelings. Wittels makes demands that, in his own opinion, can never be realized. It would be too good if they were ever realized, and it will never happen. One cannot but doubt the sincerity of this prediction; perhaps the author just wanted to captivate the reader.

In one of his proposals, he suggests the elimination of all social pressure, moral as well as legal, that prohibits sexual activity. All sane people should be allowed sexual activity according to their wishes; and nobody should have the right to find fault with them—either morally or legally. The manner in which this demand is put forestalls the objection: what is the way to its fulfillment? For Wittels explicitly states that it will never be realized. But that does not rule out the objection that this state would be untenable even if it could be reached, for it would lead ultimately to the destruction of human society. Wittels has anticipated this objection, too, by a reference to his point of view as a physician, in which he says that, if this "libertinage" existed, men would be sexually healthy. From the purely medical point of view, one may not have any right to express such general demands. One would have to put it this way: for the health of the individual, this would be best. But this leads to the question of whether the health of the individual is that valuable. That question the speaker would like to answer in a different way, from a standpoint that follows directly from the Darwinian ethic: there is also the health of the species, and this, in many instances, conflicts with that of the individual. This seeming paradox is dissolved when the existence of future individuals is also taken into consideration. As a result of selection, there developed instincts, even in the animal kingdom, that are fateful for the individual. Thus, for example, the bee's mania for work is detrimental to the individual, and the sting that it uses to defend its work kills the individual.

Wittels gives two reasons why "libertinage" contributes to health: (1) Unrestrained sexual activity [*Ausleben*—what American slang calls "living it up"] would spare man the damages that are brought on by suppression. (2) The elimination of all condemnation, moral and other, is the only basis for a successful battle against venereal disease. This second reason is all the more plausible to the speaker in that he himself has expressed similar ideas. The only reason why we do not fight these illnesses as energetically as we do the plague and cholera is moral prejudice. There remains only the question of whether such moral license would not be detrimental to us in other ways.

Concerning the first point, which is also expressed in the book's motto, I [*sic*—Rank means Ehrenfels] say that man could not satisfy all his sexual desires, even if the state of "libertinage" were realized. As a natural consequence, the next step would of course be the permitting of abortion. But even then people could not fully satisfy their sexuality, for there is something else that belongs to sexuality, something that is connected essentially with it. The thought of procreation is not an essential factor in the sexual act, but the procreative urge is. And where men have been conscious of this procreative urge, the fruits have been of the highest biological order. In this respect, Christianity has brought about a regression. The urge to overcome female resistance by force, the instinct to fight, and so forth, are also essential constituents of sexuality, as are the worries that come with progeny. These instincts would be switched off by "libertinage" together with the instincts of modesty and rivalry. But then other individual illnesses would arise. In the type represented by the Roman Caesars, we find examples: first, normal desires become blunted; then a hunger for new [forms of] stimulation sets in; abandonment of these too follows; finally, there is nothing left but disgust and weariness.

Therefore, I dispute the thesis that this situation would be altogether salutary, even for the individual. Now the question arises: which state would be desirable and attainable, or what can we do to help people give full reign to their sexuality? I would answer: this is simply impossible. People cannot give full reign to their sexuality. The social reformer cannot be expected to do more than to find those norms that would make it possible for worthwhile people to fulfill their sexual needs.

WITTELS, after some personal remarks, willingly admits that his thesis may be going too far; but there is no doubt that conditions could be improved, with a little good will. And if people only come to understand that one has to go just a little way toward the other side, his book will have fulfilled its purpose.

But he also wants to plead his own basic point of view. The speaker has postulated an antithesis between the individual and society, giving as an illustration the example of the worker bee. There is, however, this great difference between the worker bee and the human female: the worker bee has no sexual function.

Before going on, Wittels wants to stress that it was not his intention to express a low opinion of the work of women; if he gave that impression, he has expressed himself inadequately. In judging the activity of men, one must stress the difference between conversion and sublimation. It makes a difference whether a free-floating affect is directed toward scientific work—as with the woman—or whether the drive to know stems from a sublimation, while the sexual instinct is satisfied independently and only the surplus is realized in art and science. Hence, it is not because of any inferior brain capacity that woman's mental work is inferior, but for the reason just mentioned. Perhaps it is precisely full sexual activity that enables the man to sublimate successfully. In our culture, there is usually nothing left for the woman to sublimate; the reason may be that she does have to give birth to children and to take care of them. If placed on the right path, the drive for knowledge may become valuable in women too. Some women satisfy this drive for knowledge out of love for a man, and this may well be the basis for all accomplishments by women. And it need not even be a man of flesh and blood. That does not mean that man's supreme achievements are not also brought about in the same way (Goethe's seal: "All for Love"). All sorts of things are also accomplished out of hate, but that is basically the same as [accomplishing things] out of love. Both man and woman achieve the greatest things when they act out of love. The difference is that it is only in this way that the woman can accomplish something that is psychologically irreproachable while the man, even when he is handicapped by circumstances, can do [things, and] not out of love.

It was not caution that made Wittels cast his demands in the form of a utopia, but the fact that he really was unable to visualize this situation. As far as he himself is concerned, "libertinage" goes against his grain. Even if he had known what this situation would look like, he would not have spoken about it, because the possibilities of what the future may hold are too varied. In regard to this subject, he feels that he should take the standpoint of the natural scientist. He does not know whether it would be better if thought played a part in propelling toward procreation; but he does know that, at present, it acts to inhibit it; so does the concern about progeny. Rivalry would continue to exist, as is shown by the example of pimps, among whom one finds the most jealous and pugnacious fellows.

Wittels goes on to discuss the speaker's most important argument—namely, that it is not possible for all people to satisfy their sexuality fully. In asserting the opposite, he only wanted to say: things cannot go on as they are today. How to bring about a change, he does not know. However, he considers it even more impossible that only the "most worthwhile" people should be given sexual freedom. How is one to discover who are the most worthwhile people? Indeed, their worth starts with their fully satisfying their sexuality—or, under certain conditions, not satisfying it.

The less tangible results of moral hypocrisy are far more dangerous than the tangible ones: venereal diseases. The latter can be combatted with a law on infectious disease. But what is one to do with those people who, as the result of suppressing their sexual drives, have become ill, maladjusted, neurotic—have become medical students or killers of women? It was the purpose of the book to point out the conditions; he is not able to show the road to improvement.

In conclusion, Wittels thanks the speaker for the extraordinary praise that he allowed the book to have at the outset. Certainly, he overestimated it. Not only is the book based exclusively on Freud's findings, it makes use of them, except that it groups them somewhat differently.

PROF. EHRENFELS is pleased that, thanks to these expositions, their viewpoints do not seem as far apart as they did at the beginning. Since Wittels states that he does not demand "libertinage," but instead wishes to see our present conditions modified in that direction, there exists no basic disagreement, but merely some details that need to be discussed. Of course, Prof. Ehrenfels did not want to cite the example of the bee as a close analogy to woman. He has not yet made the distinction between conversion and sublimation, although it seems quite plausible to him and, with regard to this point, he is entirely in the position of one who wishes to be enlightened. He was puzzled by the conception of love and hate as identical. That they should have a common root in sexuality seems to be plausible, but he would like to learn more about what is meant beyond that.

He did not refer to the conscious thought of procreation, which Wittels calls an inhibiting factor, but to the instinct for procreation. Generally it is a mistake, made by psychologists as well, to assume that a strong drive cannot be directed toward abstractions; one needs only to think of the drives for possession, for honor, etc. The same thing holds true for the drive toward procreation.

He must admit the validity of the objection Wittels made when he pointed to the jealousy of pimps. Hence, while the damaging effect of "libertinage" on the individual may be somehow restricted, not so, however, the social effect. Even the concern for his progeny sometimes has a salutary effect on the individual.

Finally, he would like to emphasize that the selection of those who are of greatest worth can be achieved to a certain degree, although not by means of conscious, deliberate sorting out. The selection of persons of greater worth can be achieved in a way similar to the one nature chose in the evolution from animal to man; there will always be a certain margin of error. All we have to do is to re-establish natural selection which, at present, is completely paralyzed by our leveling educational morality. This can be achieved only by social measures aimed at the establishment of a genuine culture.

DISCUSSION

SADGER would like to make only a few minor remarks. The fact that [there are] women physicians [who], once they are married, see their drive for knowledge vanish is evidence of the fact that their sexuality had been converted into a drive for knowledge. Even Sonya Kovalevska,[3] the most brilliant woman known to Sadger, gave up working after she entered into a sexual relationship with that student. Sadger knows no details about Mrs. Curg.

The example of the Roman Caesars does not seem to fit into this context, for, according to general opinion, they were mentally sick, and that is why they displayed such abnormalities in their sexual life.

To be sure, Wittels has exaggerated considerably; but in science, too, one must exaggerate in order to achieve something. Wittels, by the way, merely became the most outspoken standard bearer of a movement that was unjustly accused of sexual libertinage. It is true that complete fulfillment of one's sexual needs is advocated, but not without consideration of the partner, and this always sets certain limits to the fulfillment. Besides, the institution of marriage is in process of undergoing a great transformation; a way is being sought out of this form. Nevertheless, it is still maintained because, in our present social order, this institution is the only solution for women. But something else is in the making: greater freedom in sexual life. The "affair" in every form is more widespread today than marriage. In this may lie the future solution of the whole problem, for it would also lead us closer to selection in the Darwinian sense.

PROF. EHRENFELS comments that this point of view is frequently advocated; it would result in selection for pleasure, not in selection for procreation.

RIE stresses two points that seem to contradict one another. The most worthwhile individuals should be allowed to give free reign to

[3] Sonya Kovalevska (1850-1891), a famous Russian mathematician, married a young scholar when she was eighteen, but separated from him a few years later. Her biography by Anna Leffler, based on an autobiography, was published in 1892.

their desires, while at the same time regard for the following generation should be kept in mind. Yet, when we speak of the most worthwhile persons, we are thinking mainly of their spiritual progeny.

PROF. EHRENFELS comments that this is merely an apparent contradiction; it disappears when the biological viewpoint is adopted. His conception of physical excellence includes not merely a beautiful appearance, figure, etc., but also the capacity for survival in the struggle for existence. Furthermore, all psychic phenomena and processes have a physical basis. Abnormal individuals, in whom intellectual capacities are developed at the expense of their sexuality, cannot survive in the struggle for existence. Abnormal formations must be eliminated. It is not the genius who should propagate, but a generation psychologically just a little above average; out of this generation there will grow a few abnormal [outstanding] individuals. This could be achieved by means of selective breeding.

PROF. FREUD first makes two personal requests of Prof. Ehrenfels: would he be willing to tell us something about his positive proposals for reform next Wednesday, and would he be willing to publish his review of Wittels' book? (Prof. Ehrenfels is glad to comply with both requests.)

Freud personally takes no stand with regard to the efforts at reform. Wittels' book, which presents proposals for reform, stems from two different sources—from, so to say, a paternal and a maternal source. The first one, represented by the *Fackel*,[4] goes part of the way with us in its assertion that suppression of sexuality is the root of all evil. But we go further, and say: we liberate sexuality through our treatment, but not in order that man may from now on be dominated by sexuality, but in order to make a suppression possible—a rejection of the instincts under the guidance of a higher agency. The *Fackel* stands for "living out" one's instinctual desires to the point of satiating them [*ausleben*]; we distinguish, however, between a pathological process of repression and one that is to be regarded as normal. We try to replace the pathological process with rejection. This is also the only way open to society; society too must first revoke its suppressions, in order to be able to repudiate anew [what had been suppressed, this

[4] Cf. Volume I, Minutes 24.

time doing it in full consciousness and judiciously]. That is why Freud strongly dislikes the motto of the book.

In agreement with Prof. Ehrenfels, Freud thinks that the example of the worker bee may be able to show the way to the solution of the problem. The sublimations of the worker bee are determined by her sexual organization. And the distinction between this suppression and that which is acquired later in life is of decisive importance.[5] Once, in a discussion with Prof. Ehrenfels, Freud tried to define the etiology of the neuroses on this basis; it is the conflict between the cultural and the organic demands that explains the neuroses. The preservation of our culture by means of suppressions—this capability has its foundations in our organic constitution. For many persons who are, to begin with, set up and suited for sublimating, this does not present any difficulties.

The terrifying picture that is painted of "libertinage" is an exaggeration: we can be sure that all the instincts would continue to exist alongside of liberty. Social need would take care of that. He is not inclined to regard the Caesars as mentally sick. It was their position that drove them to their excesses; we must not give people that unlimited sense of power.

Actually, the best selection would be achieved by establishing "libertinage" for one generation; for then the inferior individuals would automatically eliminate themselves in sterile indulgences in love. The number of those who are worthwhile and have offspring is too small; hence the state cannot make use of that situation. With regard to hate and love, we have learned from analyses that they not only have a common root, but are identical, and that there is no love without an admixture of hatred. One can easily turn into the other through a reversal of affect, a change of sign.[6]

FEDERN first opposes Wittels' attitude toward the work accomplished by women. There is no justification for preventing a woman

[5] It seems that Freud has in mind here the two kinds of repression: repression proper and primary repression. He considered the latter to be an organic process, as he often indicated.

[6] Later on, Freud changed his opinion: he found that love cannot turn into hate, and vice versa: the two instincts are independent of each other, although they always occur fused in a certain proportion.

who does not succeed in suppressing her sexual drives from fulfilling them in the intellectual sphere.

HITSCHMANN notes that we ourselves in our debates came out against Wittels much more than Prof. Ehrenfels today, even though Wittels' demands are in direct contrast to Ehrenfels' point of view concerning sexual ethics. Although we have not stressed Ehrenfels' point of view, it has certainly always played a role as a half-unconscious limitation on our discussions. Finally, Hitschmann takes exception to Sadger's argumentation.

ADLER emphasizes that Wittels' most outstanding characteristic is his underestimation of women, and in particular of their intellectual work; this is an attitude that he shares with the philistine. We must not forget that woman has only just begun her fight, and that in all such movements the early pioneers have to be sacrificed. One can point to such a large number of women of intellectual merit that a comparison with the average accomplishments of men would not be to the woman's disadvantage. To the question of conversion and sublimation, there is no unequivocal answer, with regard to man either. Perhaps conversion and sublimation occur at the same time.[7]

Last, Adler refers to the process that is evolving in [Tsarist] Russia's intellectual circles, where uninhibited sexual expression has come into its own.[8] It is not enough to express the demand, "You must yield to [the demands of] your sexuality"; first the barriers must be removed. We know from individual psychology that this can be done only by broadening consciousness. That is how one learns to recognize and master one's instincts and no longer to be at their mercy.

WITTELS speaks against Adler's arguments, to begin with, and justifies his "philistine" point of view with regard to women. Not everything, indeed, is progress that looks like progress. Women fight for their sexual freedom, but in different ways. To show this was the purpose of his book. In that sense Wittels feels entitled to consider himself a friend, nay an enthusiastic admirer, of women. The example

[7] It must be emphasized that the analytic concepts of conversion and sublimation have nothing in common. In the same way, the concept of "repression" must be strictly distinguished from the concept of "suppression," as Freud has stressed.

[8] Cf. Volume I, Minutes 19.

of Russia also supports his view: the women who threw themselves into the business of revolution were taken seriously by the men, which means that the men misunderstood them. Now they demonstrate what they really wanted to have and fling themselves into the arms of full sexual freedom.

In reference to a misunderstanding by Prof. Ehrenfels, Wittels remarks that we must not forget that we have no influence over the quality of our progeny, since there are any number of unpredictable variants. Moreover, the greatness of a person probably has its roots in his experiences rather than in the germ [cell]. Hence, we cannot provide for our offspring. In the greatest love affairs (Romeo and Juliet, Tristan and Isolde) there is no mention of progeny. It is Christianity that must be blamed for the fact that this thought has gained such prominence.

PROF. EHRENFELS, in conclusion, replies briefly to these arguments. Our task is to improve the average quality of progeny. Contrary to Wittels, he believes that Christianity has pushed the thought of breeding into the background. As proof for this thesis, Ehrenfels mentions the breeding policies commonly followed in ancient times—for example, by the Spartans—of which traces can be found in Plato's ideal state. The most sublime developments of what we call love may be the flourishing of marvelous cultures, but biologically these are of no value.

63

SCIENTIFIC MEETING *on December 23, 1908*

Present: Prof. Freud, Adler, Bass, Federn, Hitschmann, Joachim, Rank, Rie, Sadger, Stekel, Urbanschitsch, Wittels.
Prof. Ehrenfels as guest.

PRESENTATION

A Program for Breeding Reform

SPEAKER: PROF. EHRENFELS, PRAGUE

The speaker begins by commenting that the title is not altogether adequate. His proposals are intended to raise the level, not only of constitutional life but of cultural life as well. Because of its significance this contrast, which has been emphasized by Freud, needs to be briefly defined. We call constitutional those characteristics of an organism that are inborn and can be transmitted by physiological procreation. Everything else belongs to the cultural realm. This distinction was, in fact, first made by Darwin and was then defined more precisely by Weismann.[1]

[1] August Weismann (1834-1914), German biologist.

The core of the proposal itself is: to fight against monogamy for both constitutional and cultural reasons (an appreciation of the positive achievements of this institution may be found in *Sexual Ethics*).

The first part of the paper will present the negative aspects, the "debit," of monogamy in the constitutional and cultural realms. The second part will offer a proposal for reform on a polygamous basis, and the third part will briefly show the way to attain such an arrangement.

Ad 1. The constitutional damages caused by monogamy become evident if one fully understands what selection means and what it achieves. In civilized man, pure selection is modified by humane and hygienic considerations. As a result of monogamy, sexual selection is far more in the man's province. And this tempering of selection occurs in just those situations in which the change of living conditions (industry, etc.) makes stricter selection a necessity. As a result, a marked constitutional decline is to be expected. This conclusion was arrived at by deductive reasoning. We can confirm it, however, by inductive reasoning, through comparing our cultural development with that of the Chinese, who have an older civilization and are more advanced in their physiological development. The reason for their constitutional superiority lies in their favorable conditions of selection. In the end, if there is no change in current practices, this will lead to the annihilation of the white race by the yellow race.

Connected with their constitutional superiority is their conscious drive for propagation. Another basis is the fact that the Chinese do not use contraceptives, which have enabled us to attain full enjoyment while still preventing conception.

The third reason follows the lines of Wittels' arguments: the fight against venereal disease must remain unsuccessful as long as extramarital sexual activities are morally proscribed. But, for the time being, this moral proscription cannot be abolished, because otherwise far too small a segment of the population would propagate. As a consequence, the race would be swallowed up in courtesanry. Thus the conscious drive for propagation is the prerequisite for a successful fight against venereal disease. This striving for propagation is, however, choked off by monogamy.

Further damaging effects of monogamy are: it not only tones down the process of selection, and permits inferior individuals to propagate, but brings about counterselection. Monogamy is harmful in any event from the point of view of health alone, because of the restriction of sexual life that generally comes about.

Nor are the damaging effects of monogamy on *cultural life* negligible. Above all, woman's economic potentialities remain unused. Secondly, monogamy is the cause of the "double standard." Thirdly, monogamy calls for the establishment of hereditary family privileges. Monogamy imposes the *duty* (not only the desire) upon everyone to see to it that his descendants can continue to enjoy the same privileges. This principle is unjust; for it is not always valuable characteristics (those that make people successful in life) that are transmitted to their descendants.

The question arises: how can we improve the situation so that the most worthwhile individuals come into possession of greater power and wealth? At the moment, the only conceivable opposition to that goal lies in the demand for social leveling. This absurd demand, which does not take into account the fact that men are not equal, is presented to us in an idealizing, glorifying light. Thus we perceive these two contrasts in our social life; but the sound principle that power and wealth should be distributed among those who are most capable, the principle of merit, is crushed between them. What is lacking is close association among intellectual workers—that is, those who are the rightful representatives of merit; they do not yet realize the justice of their demands. The same situation prevails in the realm of the political power struggle. The ones who should really be in our *Herrenhaus*[2] are the intellectuals.

In conclusion, I should like to stress that we must introduce a new sexual order, not only because we are driven by constitutional necessity, but also for the purpose of reaching a higher and more permanent level of culture. So far for the criticism.

Ad 2. The question now is this: What kind of social order would fulfill these demands? First of all, what would be its sexual basis? It is important to realize that the harmful effects of monogamy are essentially connected with the principle of the close family life of husband,

[2] The Upper House of the Austrian Parliament [literally: the House of Lords].

wife, and children. Hence, this principle has to be abandoned. Women would then have to form an association among themselves in order to safeguard their family and household tasks. The men who have intercourse with the mothers of their children would be obliged to support these associations. Even this, however, would not provide a favorable basis for selection because in this arrangement the wealthiest would have the best chance for propagation. Potentiality for achievement would have to become the guiding principle. In order to make such a selection possible at an early age, a combination of teachers' and pupils' vote should make that choice. The point is not to breed geniuses but, by way of this *self-judgment*, to discover those who are somehow superior. This principle should be further developed and retained later in life, through the formation of similarly organized professional associations.

Ad 3. The main question as to how one can achieve this goal is still to be answered. From the biological as well as from the sexual point of view, it can be justified that a man have sexual relations with several women, but not the other way round. The only way to get from our form of marriage to the desirable order is the conclusion of a sexual contract with a unilateral obligation. The man, in return, is bound to support the children materially. Since legal approval for such a relationship cannot be achieved at present, it must first be started as an illegitimate relationship. In this case, however, the woman would be the only one who would have to suffer and to endure the whole social struggle. Thus nothing else can be done but to get married legally and to enter privately into a supplementary agreement, according to which the man would retain the right to beget children with other women, if the auspices were favorable. Besides, the wife would have to stay in her parents' home. However, it can be immediately objected that, in order to enjoy that kind of sexual freedom, one must have money. Thus only a few could take this path. But what are the others supposed to do? The only advice one could give them would be: to act out their sexual drives in asexual fields; they should abstain, but under protest (Freud). Such an abreaction by cultural means would be possible first in school life, etc. All these things could now be worked on: people should enter marriage in the proposed fashion at an early age, the self-judgment should be instituted at school, and the intellectuals should associate as a conscious, more consolidated group.

I do not say that all this is going to happen. Perhaps our humane-Christian point of view has made us too soft. But I see no other way by which to escape certain extinction in the cultural struggle with the Mongolian race.[3]

DISCUSSION

ADLER begins by attempting to characterize the position of these proposals within the framework of the sciences. To him they appear to be the result of an idealist philosophy, the ideas of a man who by speculative means arrives at proposals that he deems will remedy certain abuses.

It must be emphasized that Ehrenfels seems to ignore the meaning of the "leveling" [*nivellistische*] *Weltanschauung*. There is no prevailing tendency toward a general leveling in such a broad sense—only the intention to effect the transforming of conditions that is called for in Marxian doctrine, not on the basis of an idea, but in close connection with and looking toward reality, with the aim of attaining equal rights for all. It was the existence of sexual bondage in our social order that gave rise to our deliberations. This would be reduced to a tolerable measure if that doctrine proved correct and if we succeeded in restraining the capitalistic way of life.

We should emphasize one point that was merely implied by Ehrenfels. It was asserted that there is a relationship between safeguarding the law of inheritance and securing the foundation of the family on the one hand, and the disinclination to let oneself be degraded on the other. This seems to be a necessary concomitant of culture. In a paper on "The Psychology of the Class Struggle,"[4] which Adler is

[3] The slogan of the "Yellow Danger" had come up again and again in German and Austrian politics and was familiar to the audience. Paradoxically, thirty years later Ehrenfels' views were nearly turned into reality by the National-Socialists. (There is even a hint of such principles in the American immigration quota system.) Ehrenfels, professor at the University of Prague from 1896 to 1932, was a philosopher of repute. Even if we take into account that Ehrenfels was a member of the nobility and enjoyed certain privileges, it still seems remarkable that so much intellectual freedom could be enjoyed in the Catholic Austro-Hungarian monarchy.

[4] Cf. Minutes 72, in this volume.

planning to present in the near future, he arrives at the conclusion that the motive behind class struggle is the same fear of being degraded that maintains the right of inheritance.[5] Two conclusions can be drawn from this point of view: (1) The fear of degradation forces man into this leveling tendency, and (2) the same culture that has generated this fear in the privileged classes generates it in woman, too. And only by violence would it be possible to assign a more unfavorable position to woman than the one she holds at present. This fear, which also sets the direction for woman's striving for emancipation, is connected with organic conditions and is sustained by the rapidity of technical development.

BASS raises the objection that, with regard to the principle of [controlled] breeding, one cannot simply make a comparison between civilized man and animal. The term "selection" has meaning only for man in the primordial condition. In holding monogamy responsible for lowering the possibilities of propagation, one should consider whether this is not a case of *hysteron proteron*—that is, whether in this respect it should not have a regulating effect. A similar objection must be raised with regard to privileges. Unilateral obligation seems unjust to him.

SADGER, after making a few critical remarks, voices doubts as to the possibility of bringing about the proposed relationship between husband and wife. It is often precisely the prospect of sharing his life with a woman that induces a man to get married.

He assumes that there is a personal story behind this entire conception, most likely discontent on the speaker's part with the way in which he has solved his own sexual problems. To Sadger, all of this seems like an adolescent sexual fantasy.

FEDERN thinks that the dangers of such arbitrary selection by means of self-judgment, as proposed by Ehrenfels, would be far greater than those of natural selection—which, in spite of all modifications and all limitations, nevertheless has enough vital power and always prevails.

[5] This is difficult to understand unless one bears in mind Adler's "masculine protest."

WITTELS is diametrically opposed to the opinions expressed. To him the most important thing would be to remove the taint of shame from venereal disease. One must object to the proposal that the man, who can father 365 children a year whereas the woman can give birth to only one [in that same time], should have the right to many wives, while the woman, with her unlimited capacity for sexual pleasure, which requires more than one man, should be restricted to a single one. What is to become of these women who are reckoned merely as breeding machines? Indeed, people are in every respect more concerned with gaining pleasure than with the danger of becoming "mongolized." Women too would oppose such a reform for many reasons. If one were to enforce it, men would have more to suffer from this enforcement, because women would take revenge by way of hysteria.

URBANSCHITSCH expresses the conviction that such reform neither will nor can ever come to pass. It would be incompatible with our culture in every respect.

HITSCHMANN, on the other hand, does not consider its realization impossible. But one must doubt that this "gospel" will find a large enough following to sustain this "gospel." Besides, our culture might still be able to produce many achievements that would prevent the extinction of a race. Leaving aside the fact that a victory of the Mongols is very doubtful, he would not regard it as such a great disaster if they should come to dominate the world. This would not necessarily have to be brought about by violence and extermination, but could happen quite gradually, by assimilation.

He dislikes the fact that there is no consideration for woman's will and woman's welfare; this is entirely a man's philosophy. Further: one is supposed to renounce the family; but it has developed organically and has a deep meaning. Moreover, it would be harmful for children to be brought up by women alone. The self-judgment in school would not be reliable, in view of the changes in personality that take place later in life.

RIE would like to bring up some questions for the purpose of clarifying the discussion. Would the Mongols, in taking over our culture, not take over our potentialities for degeneration as well—with the result that, in a hundred years, the danger would no longer be as great? Furthermore, he missed the conclusion: the postulation of thoroughgoing changes in the marriage law.

PROF. FREUD points out a difficulty that only Hitschmann touched upon. Starting from the present situation, the speaker did not take into account sufficiently either the emotional life or the distribution of libido in our society, which is based on sublimated homosexual feelings. We have acquired this libido distribution and it is continually transmitted by way of childhood impressions; it will hardly be possible to succeed in any effort to change that situation.

PROF. EHRENFELS first expresses his gratitude for the criticisms, which he sought, and then states that the almost unanimous objection was: "It cannot be done." In so far as the objections mean no more than this, he has nothing to reply. Then the alternative will take its place. But he wants now to turn to details, and comment on a number of things.

For instance, he thinks that we should alter our entire way of life, not out of fear of the Mongols, but out of the inner need of men to give full rein to their desires. He himself has felt that need, knowing full well that he was in diametrical opposition to our moral code. His proposal grew on him, as he came to realize that it was not that he had to suppress his instincts but that the whole of morality was an aberration. And his hopes [for acceptance of his proposal] are based on these instincts being just as powerful in other men.

PROF. FREUD finally raises the objection that, in his opinion, family life is the basis for the striving for propagation; with the dissolution of family life, the drive for propagation would also become extinguished. It is from the desire to imitate the father that the son's desire arises to become a father. Where there is no father, there is no such wish.

64

SCIENTIFIC MEETING *on January 13, 1909*

Present: Prof. Freud, Federn, Graf, Hitschmann, Hollerung, Joachim, Rank, Sadger, Steiner, Stekel.

PRESENTATION

Poetry and Neurosis

SPEAKER: DR. STEKEL

STEKEL presents parts of his paper "Poetry and Neurosis." It will soon be published in Löwenfeld's collection, *Grenzfragen des Nerven- und Seelenlebens* [*Borderline Problems of Neurological and Psychic Life*].[1]

DISCUSSION

HOLLERUNG mentions the fact that in some cases creative writers are no longer able to work in later life. He cites Peter Altenberg as an example.

[1] See Minutes 54B, in this volume.

STEKEL comments that there are periods in the life of every writer when he is unable to create. He points particularly to the fact that almost all great writers suffer from the fear of losing their creative power.

STEINER remarks that the speaker presented too much material and yet he also made, on the other hand, many assertions that cannot be verified. In this case, less would have been more. He missed a precise statement of Stekel's views. It is hard to contradict his contention that every creative writer is a neurotic. For there are in general few people who are not at one time or another, neurotic. On the other hand, everyone is a poet at a certain period (in puberty); this, however, must be taken as sublimation and not as repression. He cannot see in this a symptom, a stigma of hysteria. Such a view can be neither theoretically supported nor confirmed by actual examples. Therefore, he cannot agree with the view that neurosis is a prerequisite for poetic creation. There is a certain correctness in saying that great poets sometimes also happen to be neurotics. It lies in the nature of artists generally to be endowed with an abundance of fantasy; that is why they are easily susceptible to neuroses. If one includes in the neurosis as much as Stekel does, then of course his theses cannot be contradicted.

GRAF criticizes the loose style of the paper and its lack of continuity in thinking. One cannot argue against it, in part because of the banalities of the statements, in part because Stekel has failed to define his position exactly. First of all, the topic—that is, the relationship between artistic creativity and neurosis—should not be confined to poets. Along with other artists, one should consider the imaginative average man, the "misunderstood genius," and also the adolescent in his creative period. The relationship between poetic power and mental illness can be varied. There are cases in which illness inhibits creativity (for instance, Grabbe, or Zacharias Werner).[2] In another group we find no signs whatever of neurosis; these are the artists who have kept a childlike quality—for instance, Mozart. The main point, however, is that we understand neurosis to be something that inhibits

[2] Christian Dietrich Grabbe, German poet (1801-1836); Zacharias Werner, German poet (1768-1825).

man's capacity for a full life and for work, and not something that promotes these capacities, as we see them in the great poets.

Then again there are morbid epochs, during which all artists have a neurotic coloration; two such epochs are the romantic and baroque periods. We see, however, that the works of these epochs are of no lasting value. We must not forget that all those who are engaged in intellectual work are prone to neurosis; one might say that it is their occupational disease. The fact that, in the artist, failures of repression can readily occur is not difficult to understand. The finest characterization of poetic creation is found in [Richard] Wagner's dictum: "The poet is he who knows the unconscious."

PROF. FREUD does not doubt that the lecture when published will impress the general public; it will please them because of its abundance of "interesting" material. We ourselves, however, cannot but feel that this work does not bear the stamp of necessity. It is too general on the one hand, too superficial on the other. Rank had a deeper conception of the topic. Some of Stekel's theses are not new; others lack justification—as, for example, his assertion that all poets are hysterics. While Stekel views repression as the sole characteristic of hysteria, this indeed is a general property, not only of all neuroses, but also of other psychic processes. Moreover, there are great writers who were paranoiacs or obsessional neurotics—e.g., Zola, whose entire development as a writer runs parallel, on a higher level, to his obsessional neurosis.[3] Besides these, we find even healthy persons among the poets; Schiller is a particularly fine example of a normal man.

In regard to the question of the sexual precociousness of poets, the material is of very uneven value. We simply do not know what sexual precocity is. In the phobia of five-year-old Hans, published in the *Jahrbuch*,[4] the state of being in love was clearly evident, and an American magazine has published interesting statistics about the loves of schoolchildren. It showed that tender affectionate relationships and states of being in love can be observed clearly in three- and four-year-old children. As long as our experiences are not verified, we cannot

[3] Cf. Volume I, Minutes 11.

[4] "Analysis of the Phobia of a Five-Year-Old Boy" (originally in *Jahrbuch für psychoanalytische und psychopathologische Forschung*, 1:1-109, 1909). *S.E.*, 10:5-147.

say whether the poets who fall in love at the age of eight or nine are not in reality retarded [in their sexual development].

SADGER thinks that Stekel's views, despite his arguments to the contrary, come close to his own. What Sadger called hereditary taint Stekel calls neurosis. Stekel really has offered substantiating material in only three cases: Dostoyevsky, Rousseau, and Grillparzer. The most important traits that we find in poets, do not permit themselves to be fitted into the neurotic. Whether they are now called inferiority, or anything else, has nothing to do with it. Their chief characteristic is that they cannot be analyzed psychosexually. We can even state a certain contrast: neurotic symptoms are comparatively minor in the case of a severe hereditary taint (for instance, Lenau);[5] it kills the neurosis, as it were.

JOACHIM, after defending Stekel against some, especially formal, objections, voices his agreement with other criticisms. He strongly objects to the arbitrary way in which one group of neuroses, that of the poets, was singled out. This group is too narrowly conceived, since the other artists also belong in it. The remark that everyone is a poet from birth should rather be defined more accurately, to this effect: that everyone is a neurotic from birth, with a rich fantasy life. On the other hand, an unlimited fantasy life is not favorable even for artistic endeavors; we find it in abundance in the mentally ill and in inferior artistic products (dime novels, and the like). The nature of the relationship between poetic creation and neurosis is extremely variable. The terms "degeneration," "morbidity," are somewhat out of place here. One forgets that the development of new forms will always bring about deviations, but these need not signify a decline.

HITSCHMANN remarks that he does not have much more that is new to add to the discussion. The genesis of Stekel's work is approximately as follows: one day he decided to become interested in Grillparzer; of course, he found many neurotic traits in him. He then searched further in other writers' biographies without trying to reach definite results, and found what he was looking for—because he was looking for it. This is all the easier when people speak about them-

[5] Cf. Volume I, Minutes 8.

selves—which is what the poets do. What is missing is the actual analysis of a poet; that is what should be undertaken. A poet once told Hitschmann that his dreams were not unconscious, but conscious fantasies.

Stekel did not take into account Freud's remarks about creative writers and fantasying.[6] Altogether, one gets the impression that the poet really cannot be seriously neurotic or else he would not be able to create. Besides, it would be more correct to say that those who are mildly neurotic become intellectual workers than that intellectual workers easily acquire a neurosis.

RANK regards Stekel's point of view as too "psychiatric"; he would rather attempt to stress the relations to the normal. But it is just as incorrect to say that the poet is in no way different from the normal person as it is to say that the poet is a neurotic. Indeed, one frequently sees quite clearly how the poet, through his work, liberates himself from neurosis, or rather how he staves off neurosis.

FEDERN emphasizes that in his experience the dreams of poets are in no way different from those of normal persons. A musician developed a neurosis because those around him tried to suppress his musical gifts. Neurosis frequently inhibits production; the great poets produced without neurosis. Creative writing can be understood only as a reaction of especially endowed parts of the brain.

STEKEL stresses the fact that there are always disadvantages in presenting parts of a larger work out of the context, when, as in this instance, he did not find the time necessary to tie these parts into a single whole. Besides, everybody misunderstood him. What he meant to say was that the drive toward creation is in part the product of the neurosis latent in every human being. Of course, he agrees with the statement that a really severe neurosis inhibits poetic creation. He does not venture to define at what degree of severity this occurs. Nor does he have any pretensions to profundity in his presentation; it is rather meant to be a piece of propaganda for laymen, so as to bring them, in an easily intelligible form, new insights.

[6] "Creative Writers and Day-dreaming" (1908). *S.E.*, 9.

65

SCIENTIFIC MEETING *on January 20, 1909*

Present: Freud, Adler, Bass, Federn, Heller, Hitschmann, Rank, Stekel, Wittels.

PRESENTATION

Neurosis and Toxicosis

SPEAKER: DR. HITSCHMANN

The speaker begins by emphasizing the changes that the concept of nervous disease has undergone, from the purely anatomical obscurity of hospital practice up to the current classification of all these phenomena into one of three groups: uric acid, anemia, and nervous diseases. This change in views becomes evident if one looks into one of the older books on this topic. We find many diseases listed in these books which today are no longer classified as neuroses—for example, epilepsy, which is believed today to be caused by an anatomical change in the cortex. The views about certain spastic and paralytic symptoms (e.g., spasm of the glottis, *hyperemesis gravidarum,* asthma, etc.) have also undergone important changes; thus nothing actually is left but the so-called "vagospasms"—and even these one cannot speak of as neuroses—and, still, nervous constipation and dyspepsia. The climacteric must also be regarded as due to the fact that an endocrine gland ["blood gland"] ceases to function. Consequently, the only diseases that are still left as neuroses are: hysteria, neurasthenia, obsessional neurosis, anxiety neurosis, and traumatic neurosis. Originally, everything was considered a neurosis that was temporary, not fatal, not clearly traceable to its causes—in short, everything that had to be explained in general terms. But even at that time there were some references to these "nervous" phenomena as emanating in reflex style from the genitals.

From these [unspecified] nervous complaints are derived several syndromes, such as *morbus Basedowi*. Other diseases, however—for instance, whooping cough—were definitely no longer considered to belong among the neuroses (Note: the speaker mentions a paper reporting that dogs infected with whooping cough bacillus show similar symptoms.). For nervous dyspepsia, too, an anatomical basis was found which expressed itself in a characteristic *habitus*. The discovery of the so-called diseases of the endocrine glands led to a new humoral pathology. Experiments with animals clearly proved the important role that the *nervus sympathicus* plays in these diseases.

The climacteric, mentioned above, furnishes an excellent example for our discussion. It takes a typical course, whether it is brought on by nature or by removal of the female organs. Its symptoms are: hot flushes, constriction of the heart, pains in the small of the back, paresthesias, and pains in the limbs. Freud was the first (?)[1] to call attention to the fact that there is a climacteric in men, too. In women, this illness is caused by the cessation of ovarian as well as uterine activity. Without going into details, we must postulate that the uterus too is capable of internal secretion. We now have to draw attention to the fact that some of the symptoms of this illness, which we regard as toxic, are subject to psychological influence (e.g., hyperemesis, menstruation and, according to Bernheim, constipation). But we must not rush to the conclusion that this fact constitutes evidence against autointoxication.

Only brief mention can be made of the connection that exists between some of the conditions enumerated above and the lower nasal

[1] The question mark indicates, of course, that Rank doubted the validity of Hitschmann's statement that Freud was the discoverer of the climacteric in men.

conchae. Labor pains, asthma, and dysmenorrhea can be successfully treated by means of the conchae.

It must also be stressed that diseases of the endocrine glands clearly show a connection with psychoses: for instance, such autotoxicoses as Basedow's disease, Addison's disease, and tetanus. Since this is true also of pregnancy and menses, we may conclude that the reproductive glands play an important role among the endocrine glands.

We may now turn to the genuine neuroses and pursue their history in the course of these developments. Freud's classical description of the anxiety neurosis and his reference to the sexual etiology of neuroses[2] in a narrower sense have completely changed this picture. For Freud himself the insight was not closed off that anxiety neurosis and neurasthenia will one day have to be conceived of as toxicoses; indeed, he himself points to the great similarity between anxiety neurosis and Basedow's disease; similarly, neurasthenia has some similarity to Addison's disease. Even in antiquity there was clear insight into the fact that the reproductive and genital glands play an important role in the neuroses (see the term "hysteria"). And this is the point at which we should mention the hereditary taint, to which the sexual etiology of neurosis itself points back. First to be abused by nervous progenitors were the reproductive glands. It may be that thereafter an inferior organ (Adler) acts as a carrier in the transmission. In the *Short Writings*[3] Freud mentions that the anxiety in anxiety neurosis allows of no psychic derivation.[4] Some confusion has been brought into the matter by Stekel since, in his cases of anxiety hysteria, the anxiety has a psychic derivation.

All this—and especially the similarity of the symptoms of anxiety neurosis and neurasthenia to those of the above-mentioned diseases of the endocrine glands—encourages us to consider these neuroses as diseases of the endocrine glands, and to trace them back to a diseased

[2] "On the Grounds for Detaching a Particular Syndrome from Neurasthenia under the Description 'Anxiety Neurosis'" (1895), *S.E.*, 3; "Sexuality in the Aetiology of the Neurosis" (1898), *S.E.*, 3.

[3] *Sammlung kleiner Schriften zur Neurosenlehre aus den Jahren (1893-1906)* [*Collection of Short Writings on the Theory of Neuroses (1893-1906)*]. Vienna: Deuticke, 1906.

[4] See "On the Grounds for Detaching a Particular Syndrome from Neurasthenia under the Description 'Anxiety Neurosis'" (1895). *S.E.*, 3:107.

prostate in men, a diseased uterus in women. (These two organs seem to have an evolutionary and histological likeness.) It would then appear as if neurasthenia were the result of a misuse of secretion—that is, the result of abnormal secretion; anxiety neurosis would seem to be the result of a kind of damming-up of secretion. Thus in men a kind of hyperprostatism and dysprostratism respectively would be at the bottom of these two diseases. Of course, both these glands can be diseased without neurosis; on the other hand, such abuse of sexual life can also occur without [these] consequences. At this point, the speaker comments that he himself would not have conceived this theory, had it not been in part suggested by Freud and had he not received some stimulating ideas from Stekel's book.[5] The writings of, and personal discussions with urologists in particular have confirmed him even more strongly in this conception and its validity. Freud gives a detailed description of the causes of anxiety neurosis in his "Short Writings." Among these he stresses in particular voluntary abstinence on the part of the man (similarly, frustrated excitation, *coitus reservatus*, climacteric).

Two points should be clarified in detail: (1) The similarity of anxiety neurosis and neurasthenia to diseases of the endocrine glands, as expressed in their symptoms. (2) An interpretation of the psychic disturbances in neurasthenia and anxiety neurosis that allows us to trace them back, in part to the originally diseased organs, in part to sexual abuses.

A case in point is the striking similarity between the symptoms of anxiety neurosis and those of Basedow's disease, tetanus, and the climacteric. There is a similar relationship between neurasthenia and obsessional neurosis and hysteria.

The speaker now tries to show how the psychic symptoms of neurasthenia can be explained in connection with the toxically diseased organs. There is, for instance, a masturbator type of personality, whose characteristic traits the speaker demonstrates in a specific case: a deep dejection resulting from sexual failures after he has given up masturbation; hypochondria as a result of reading stories about the terrible consequences of masturbation; shyness; timidity; self-reproaches; sub-

[5] *Disturbances of the Impulses and the Emotions: Conditions of Nervous Anxiety and Their Treatment* (1908). New York: Liveright, 1950.

jective olfactory sensations; disgust with work; etc. When one considers the nervous symptoms of the neurasthenic, one is bound to say that they can be explained in terms of his toxins, and in terms of the primary, as well as secondary, diseases of his organs.

The speaker then proceeds to the anxiety neurosis, whose great resemblance to Basedow's disease was mentioned earlier. Even more striking, perhaps, is its resemblance to the climacteric, especially in respect to the vasomotor symptoms (the climacteric is partly the result of atrophy of the uterus). In anxiety neurosis, the typical symptoms of neurosis can again be found: transition to normalcy, a typical psychological picture, variability of symptoms, susceptibility to psychological influence. The psychic mechanism of anxiety neurosis has been elucidated by Freud in the "Short Writings." The major part of its psychic details is interpreted in terms of anxiety. If the anxiety itself were understood, the psyche [psychology] of the anxiety neurosis would also be completely explained.

In Stekel's presentation, one misses any evidence for the hysterical stigmata.[6]

One neurosis must be here interpolated, which, to the detriment of our theory, does not clearly show any connection with sexuality: it is the traumatic neurosis, which is like a combination of anxiety neurosis and hysteria; it is caused by fright, by a strong shock; according to some authors, Basedow's disease can likewise be caused by fright. In any event, Basedow's disease presents the picture of fright in a frozen state, as it were. Income is also said to play a major role in the traumatic neurosis. It seems doubtful whether fright alone is the cause; the illness does not set in immediately after the frightening experience; therefore, prolonged bed rest and the sexual abstinence, that goes with it, among other factors, may also play a certain role. Altogether, however, the traumatic neurosis has remained unexplained.

Thus an apparent transition can be found from the traumatic neurosis to hysteria; it is not a tenet of even our school that hysteria is a purely psychological phenomenon (see Freud, *Short Writings*). If we consider hysteria in the context of this study, we must say the following: hysteria has certain psychic mechanisms; like the diseases of

[6] At that time one spoke of a "hysterical stigma" when referring to certain anesthesias, hyperesthesias, or a lack of certain reflexes.

the endocrine glands, it has an inclination toward psychosis; its symptoms are variable; there is a transition to normalcy, and a connection with hereditary taint, and with sexual life and the sexual organs. In this connection, one should also try to learn more about the childhood sexuality of the hysteric.

If one were to assume an extreme point of view, one could say that all symptoms of hysteria are based on the conversion of incompatible ideas. Here again we encounter the shortcoming mentioned before: the utter neglect of the hysterical stigmata, which, in part, bear great resemblance to the symptoms of the diseases of the endocrine glands.

One must not overlook, either, that Freud states in his writings that the repressions very frequently proceed in a definite direction; he calls this "somatic compliance" ("Fragment of an Analysis of a Case of Hysteria").[7] This apparently implies that the multiple determination of individual symptoms is also a somatic affair. But the stigmata of hysteria, too, are somatically determined. In hysteria—and here we must refer once again to the necessity of distinguishing real hysteria from the other type (with stigmata)—there are symptoms and stigmata that cannot be explained in psychological terms (e.g., unusually prolonged sleep without any food intake, from which one may infer an entirely abnormal metabolism, and other phenomena).

The speaker, after briefly mentioning those symptoms occurring in hysteria that show a resemblance to diseases of the endocrine glands, finally summarizes the results of his investigations:

First, he would caution against a somewhat one-sided conception of neuroses, such as is found in Stekel's book, although this one-sidedness—like any other—has proven to be immensely fruitful. The one-sided point of view presented here may not be completely fruitless either. It must be stressed that, particularly with regard to the toxins, the "detoxicating therapy" cannot be abandoned. Of course, this therapy has to be applied in conjunction with psychoanalytic, local, general, and hygienic therapies. Aside from that, Hitschmann wishes to call attention to the enormous significance in pathology of the genital glands, and to the fact that by means of the toxins a certain connection exists between the diseases of the genital glands and actual neuroses.

[7] (1905), *S.E.*, 7.

In conclusion, the speaker refers to a passage in Freud's *Short Writings* (p. 223)[8] which anticipates the contents of this paper.

DISCUSSION

STEKEL points to the fact that others have already thoroughly proven that the endocrine glands must play a large role. But as to having raised this question in regard to our field, that he must claim for himself. For a long time he has been approaching this problem theoretically as well as therapeutically—whereupon, he refers to passages from his book. All his attempts to heal patients by prescribing glandular material [hormones] failed. Stekel misses in Hitschmann's report an evaluation of the very extensive French literature on this topic. In his opinion, it is a quite one-sided approach to take into account, as Hitschmann does, only the sex glands. Stekel, as he has already mentioned in his book, is firmly convinced, and can prove for all stigmata, that the primary source of the illness is psychological. At the very least, it is from the psychic sphere that the first stimulus comes that later brings about the illness. Hitschmann criticized Stekel for failing to mention the uterus in his book, whereas he himself attempted to trace things back to these two organs. Stekel expresses doubt that the uterus is capable of internal secretion.

ADLER calls attention to an additional complication of this very complex field. Hitschmann, in speaking of an inferiority of the sex organs in connection with changes in secretion there, said that this disturbance could not arise without its bringing about changes in other places. This example demonstrates how the injuries of the ancestors are visited, so to speak, upon the descendants. He himself tried to show that changes in the secretion of the sex organs are compensated for in other organs. It is his view that there is a compensation for inferiority, such that either no conspicuous disturbances appear at all or, at least, only under certain conditions. And yet this compensation does not take place altogether smoothly. Adler emphasized that, in all these cases, we find an inferiority of the sexual apparatus and an inferiority of the brain or—less shocking—variations. If, in addition to

[8] "My Views on the Part Played by Sexuality in the Aetiology of the Neuroses" (1906). *S.E.*, 7:278.

the others, one takes into account this point of view, an immense number of possibilities and difficulties will arise.

One cannot with certainty attribute the origin of anxiety neurosis to the prostate; it could just as well be another organ. Adler confirms the finding that some people with so-called neurasthenic symptoms have a small prostate. The symptoms, however, cannot be explained from *one single* point.

One cannot view psychotherapy, as Hitschmann does, as something that is effective even though the causal conditions still exist.

In conclusion, Adler remarks that he could bring to bear only a principled position on the conclusions, and gladly concedes that they were very stimulating.

SADGER finds the approach too generalized and too far-reaching, in view of the scanty positive knowledge we possess about the endocrine glands and their secretions.

A few minor details ought to be mentioned: it seems to have escaped Hitschmann's attention that [W.] Fliess had already pointed to the relationship between stomachache and the nasal conchae. On the basis of his experiences, Sadger considers a connection between hemorrhoids and sexual life to be very dubious. Sadger, too, considers it a serious gap in our understanding of neuroses that we know nothing about the stigmata.

He is inclined to doubt the effectiveness of a sweat cure for expelling the toxins in the treatment of neuroses. In Gräfenberg, Priessnitz[9] subjected all his patients to sweat cures; however, he strictly excluded neurotics from such treatment.

FEDERN considers it a praiseworthy accomplishment to demonstrate how many illnesses that are undoubtedly toxic bear a striking resemblance all told to neurotic disturbances. While one can hardly contradict Hitschmann's essential mode of reasoning, one cannot, on the other hand, refrain from blaming him for making things too easy for himself by believing that a toxic effect can take the place directly of complicated psychic symptoms.

There is no doubt that the specific secretion of the sex organs exercises a considerable influence on psychic processes. But whether this

[9] Vincenz Priessnitz (1801-1851) was the founder of hydrotherapy.

stimulating effect leads to activity or to anxiety must certainly be independent of the secretion. From still another angle, a new complication arises: the psychic processes of neurosis, being linked with emotions, can on their own incite the glands to abnormal secretion. In general, we must admit that we are not yet fully equal to the whole problem.

STEINER comments that Hitschmann, in his interesting and instructive presentation, was unwise to leave the safe ground of the actual neurosis and permit himself to become involved with psychoneuroses. We cannot yet enter upon a study of the role played by the chemistry of psychic life. Perhaps there is some probability in the assumption that the psychic is the primary, the intoxication the secondary factor. He would not like to follow Hitschmann into this field. Steiner sticks to the actual neuroses, which daily demonstrate to him that treatment of the prostate completely eliminates not only the local complaints but also the neurasthenic symptoms.

PROF. FREUD sees the merit of this interesting paper in two areas: (1) Hitschmann endeavors to emphasize the connection of our work with broad clinical interests; and (2) by this detour, he draws our attention to where we stand and how narrow our field is.

There is much to support the plausible idea that there is a connection between actual neuroses and the diseases of the endocrine glands. Prof. Freud would have liked some clarification of one problem: Are we to assume that the two types of actual neurosis have their origin in different processes, which take place in one single substance or in two different substances? It would be important to reach a decision on this question, so that one could then leave the realm of vague possibilities and proceed to the formulation of a theory. Does Hitschmann believe that there exists a male and a female sexual substance, or that it is a question of one identical substance, for the effects of deficiency or accumulation? Neurasthenia, which is caused by a process of impoverishment, has the greatest clinical resemblance to intoxications; anxiety neurosis, which is caused by insufficient discharge, has the greatest resemblance to symptoms of abstinence. At this point, we are faced with the necessity of assuming the existence of an antisubstance.

It was the realization that this problem cannot be solved by speculating about the material [at hand] that induced Freud to stop at this point. Another reason was the fact that the foreseeable complications of the phenomena cannot be unraveled at the present time. The symptoms may have their source in a, "so to speak," primary insufficiency of the psyche. Is this, then, the original cause, or is it the direct toxic effect of the substances? Or is there perhaps a third possibility—namely, that a number of symptoms are brought about through normal reflex actions of the nervous pathways? Certainly, there are quite extensive interactions between the somatic and the psychic. But here a new problem arises: is there a theory that would permit us to conceive of a toxic stimulus being transformed into a psychic one, and, similarly, of psychic activity detoxifying the toxic stimulus? Whoever could show us that all toxic substances become poisonous if the psyche does not digest them would render us a great service. In view of such a state of affairs, Prof. Freud turned to another field of research and carried out the psychological investigation of the subject, without forgetting that it borders so closely on the organic. But after one has surveyed only very cursorily the psychological realm, it is still premature to direct one's efforts toward the organic. He has been satisfied to set up such psychological postulates as sexual excitation and libido, which to begin with completely disregard the organic. The unity of the concept of neurosis rests on the concept of libido and its vicissitudes; this makes it possible to classify, to understand, and, to a certain degree, to influence neurotic phenomena.

The group of neuroses with which we are concerned can conveniently be distinguished, as sexual neuroses, from disturbances of a similar kind, caused by a similar chemical process. In traumatic neurosis, we have things that are similar to what can be caused in the sexual neuroses, but they are caused by different mechanisms. There seems to be a remote possibility of finding a link between the traumatic neuroses and the sexual neuroses, in view of the fact, stated in "The Theory of Sexuality,"[10] that pleasurable sensations are experienced in connection with games involving movement, the shaking of railroad carriages, and the like. In traumatic neuroses, we are faced with the effect of a mechanical impact.

We do not pay much attention to the stigmata because, therapeu-

[10] See *S.E.*, 7:201-202.

tically, there is no reason to do so; moreover, they play no role in the patient's awareness. We consider them to be secondary physical changes that take place as accessories to serious psychic disturbances. As a rule, they are symptoms of excitation derived from strongly stimulated erotogenic zones.

Perhaps the only objection that can be raised against the paper is its emphasis on detoxification therapy. Leaving aside the therapeutic failures, it is very questionable whether the normal toxins can be connected with the alien toxins.

HITSCHMANN in conclusion expresses regret that he cannot give any answer, particularly to the questions and problems raised by Prof. Freud. One thing he would like to point out: he thought, especially in regard to hysteria, that it is by way of these purely hypothetical toxic substances that the possibility is established for convulsions, attacks, etc., which are anomalous in a healthy individual.[11]

[11] We have to look at these discussions *sub specie aeternitatis*: at that time, the controversy about actual neuroses versus psychoneuroses was very intense; later, it subsided to a great extent. But to the very last, Freud did not abandon his concept of actual-neuroses—a concept which, it seems to me, forms the basis of the present concept of psychosomatic neurosis.

66

SCIENTIFIC MEETING *on January 27, 1909*

Present: Prof. Freud, Adler, Heller, Hitschmann, Hollerung, Rank, Rie, Sadger, Steiner, Stekel, Wittels.

PRESENTATION

On the History of the Devil

SPEAKER: HUGO HELLER

By way of introduction to his paper, the speaker remarks that he can present only a review of Gustav Roskoff's History of the Devil[1] and that he sees the value of his discourse primarily in the fact that it may stimulate a thorough discussion of the topic.

The heading of one chapter in particular spurred his interest in a

[1] *Geschichte des Teufels*, 2 vols. Leipzig: F. A. Brockhaus, 1869. In the first volume, the author reports that very old data on the outward appearance of the devil can be found in Theodoret (Greek theologian of the fifth century A.D.). With the help of the prefect, Bishop Marcellus of Apamea in Syria (fourth century) attempts to burn down a temple of Jupiter. But a *black* devil extinguishes the fire again and again. After Marcellus places a vessel filled with water on the altar, prays and makes the sign of the cross, the water starts burning like oil, and Marcellus succeeds in burning down the pagan temple (*Hist. eccles., Lib.* V.).

further study of the subject: "Abasement of the Gods by the Fathers of the Church."[2] An additional incentive was his interest in examining to what extent the theories that Prof. Freud has evolved from and for the individual psyche are, as a heuristic principle, valid for mass psychology; especially whether unsuccessful repression, which can generate hysteria in the individual case, may not have played its part also in the mass hysterias of the Middle Ages, in the belief in devils, witches, etc. To shed some light on these matters from our point of view would require greater familiarity with them than the speaker has. That is why he will content himself with giving a brief review of the book.

In the first volume, Roskoff, with verbose casuistry, describes the dualism in the religions of civilized peoples. The speaker feels all the more able to pass lightly over this volume, since all this has nothing to do with the history of the Devil, but is rather a prehistory of the Devil.

The actual history of the Devil begins with the founding of Christianity. It is true that Satan is mentioned in the Old Testament (though not yet in the Pentateuch): he appears first in the Book of Job, as an accuser, but not as the principle of evil. Nor does the New Testament tell us anything about his shape.

The shaping and development of the figure of Satan began with the Fathers of the Church, during the first three Christian centuries. In this period, the devil always appears—that is, incognito—as the tempter; and it is typical that he is invariably the stupid, the duped devil, right down to the sixteenth century (cf. August Wünsche: *Der Sagenkreis vom geprellten Teufel* [*The Cycle of Legends on the Duped Devil*]. Leipzig: Akademie Verlag, 1905). With the beginning of the Reformation, however, the Devil's power increases in a quite significant way. From then on, with a curious abruptness, he is [transformed into] the Evil One, who comes to fetch people.

The development of the Devil took place along two lines: on the one hand, by way of Christian mythologizing, on the other by way of the Jewish [variety]. There was a rapid transformation from the accuser to the tempter who implants lust and instinctual drives in men. In the fourth century, for the first time, the Devil is described as

[2] The chapter heading actually is: "The Method of Abasement Employed by the Teachers of the Church."

"black." Simultaneously we find, for the first time, the idea that it is possible, of one's own free will, to enter into a pact with the Devil for the purpose of enjoying sensual pleasure (the Faust legend); indeed, those temptations of the Devil to which saints fall victim are almost exclusively in the realm of sensuality. It is an interesting fact for us that the Devil also endeavors to get the better of his victims in the opposite way: if he does not succeed by way of sensual temptation, he impersonates a pious penitent, who calls upon the saint to lead an even more ascetic life.

From the seventh to the thirteenth centuries, the further development of the belief in the Devil takes place simultaneously with the development of the worship of Mary and the cult of the Saints—actually, that is to say, as their counterpart. The idealized figures of the imagination are confronted by the increasingly powerful figure of the Devil, either as a werewolf or, preferably, as an animal symbolizing sex: the male goat and the tomcat. This development of the figure of the Devil significantly keeps pace with the downgrading of the pagan gods into demons, who likewise personify certain sensual drives. The fear of ghosts and of the devil grows in proportion to the suppression of the cheerful spirits of paganism. What was branded as sinful by the asceticism of Christianity was not the open worship of [pagan] religious images but the way the people had lived earlier, happy in their sensual pleasure and without fear. That is how psychic conflict was carried into the masses.

Thus we can understand that the incarnation of the figure of the Devil shows features that point to suppressed sexual drives—in particular, the long tail, the horns, and the animals. That this development generates pathological phenomena in the psyche of the masses is further borne out by the witch trials, which we cannot discuss here at any great length. It is interesting to note that, contrary to all expectations, the persecutions of witches in Catholic areas became more frequent with the advent of the Reformation; this was connected with the entrenchment of the belief in the Devil. It is also worth noting that the Devil, who gradually developed into the one who brings about all evil, often appears in the shape of a serpent—for instance, in exorcism where, in that form, he is wont to creep out of the mouth of the possessed. In the course of time, he acquires an additional characteristic:

by contrast with the saint, who is enveloped in a sweet scent, the devil on disappearing always leaves behind him an infernal stench. His activity consists almost exclusively of tempting saints and luring people into sin. In the witch trials, he plays his big sexual role as incubus and succubus. By the way, it should be noted that not all of the confessions obtained by torture were merely forced admissions of what the person had been accused of: a great deal of such testimony was based on the delusions of the accused themselves. It should further be noted that the combination of lust and cruelty is a characteristic feature of the belief in the Devil and in witches.

Thus our approach may shed much light on the history of the Devil and, on the other hand, we may gain some insight from that history into what we call diseases of the psyche of the masses.

DISCUSSION

ADLER thinks that the creation of the Devil should be regarded as a parallel formation—a concept to which he also attributes great value in psychology. In all probability, the figure of the Devil was not deliberately created. It developed rather as a compendium of all that was condemned by the growing civilization—which, not being able to destroy completely the vestiges of the past, uses the figure of the Devil as a screen figure.

As we develop our psychology, the next question must be—and it comes up in regard to the figure of the devil, too—what psychic force it is that incessantly compels us to keep beneath the threshold of consciousness those human impulses that are doomed to perish, and to move contrary currents into the foreground in their place. In general, the answer is easily found: an individual's existence in his social milieu would indeed be impossible if those of his impulses that are destined for suppression were to become apparent. In regard to the problem of the Devil, the purpose of his creation was to give the various images that comprise his figure a shape in which they are capable of representation in consciousness and can be acknowledged.

A second salient point briefly touched on in the paper has to do with the distinct traits of cruelty connected with the devil's image; Adler himself has called attention to this at some length ("The Aggressive Drive in Life and in Neurosis"[3]). This connection becomes even clearer in witch trials (cf. "the witches' hammer"), where exact details about stigmata, certain anomalies, defects, and the like (that is, references to specific anomalies of the sexual organs, anesthesia, etc.) play an enormous role. It was not the belief in the Devil that brought these traits of cruelty into the witch trials; other factors were responsible: (1) the Jesuits' craving for power, and their cruelty; (2) the collaboration of public authorities and government with the Jesuits (confiscation of property, etc.); (3) the fact that the persecution of witches was always directed against the weak, a trait inherent in human cruelty. These three factors play the most important role in witch trials. The influence attributed to the Devil derives from man's own impulses, which would not have needed the help of that embodiment.

HOLLERUNG relates that in the year 1885 he himself was present at a rite of exorcism.

SADGER comments that, in psychoanalysis, God and Devil lead back to the parent complex. As a rule, early in life the father is identified with God by both sexes; later on, when detachment begins, the father becomes the Devil, to whom all evil is ascribed. Thus it is easy to explain why the Devil is endowed with sexual attributes. The witches, too, who are forced to have intercourse with the Devil, are easier to understand when one assumes that this idea stems from girls. Some other specific features would seem to speak in favor of this view.

RIE believes that not all representations of the Devil can be viewed from the psychosexual standpoint. In different periods, the Devil has represented what at each particular time has been viewed with the greatest abhorrence (as Hauff demonstrated in *Satan's Memoirs*[4]).

WITTELS stresses that the Devil, as we know him today, is a sexual symbol, which does not even lack the anal character. He is a "penis."

That which produces symptoms of repression in the individual produces myths in the masses. The capacity for creating myths and believing in them seems to safeguard the well-being of a people. It is a good thing that the psyche of the individual finds "symptoms" ready for his

[3] Cf. Volume I, Minutes 53.

[4] Wilhelm Hauff (1802-1827), German poet and writer, author of *Mitteilungen aus den Memoiren des Satans.*

abreaction, without his being compelled to produce new "symptoms" by himself. In no other nation has the myth played as prominent a role as it did with the Greeks; but it would be mistaken to conclude from this that they were hysterical. Myths must form the proper symbols for everything that is to be repressed; later on, of course, the adult must free himself of these symbols. Repression may already set in at the time when the child's training in cleanliness begins, as a reference to animal psychology indicates. Who knows whether the mythos of the dog is not that his god (man) becomes in some way linked to the repression that he has to accomplish? We, however, need to create for ourselves a superior being; it would seem, therefore, that, from this standpoint, there are strong arguments against unconditional enforcement of enlightenment.[5]

The transformation of the Devil by the Reformation is influenced by the simultaneous thrust of repression. This in turn coincided with the first occurrence of Lues (as mentioned by Freud in a lecture). It would be interesting to learn whether that was the time when the Devil became red.

HITSCHMANN misses in the paper any reference to the question of how man came to construct a supernatural principle of evil altogether. One cannot understand the concept of the Devil if one does not completely grasp the concept of God. Too little was said about Hell.

The Devil seems to represent various things: he is, for instance, a clear example of the unconscious, etc. He is the substance of the automatic sexual excitement in the witch trials, and so on; with his clubfoot he is reminiscent of the Faun.

PROF. FREUD, after having expressed his appreciation of the importance of the problem and the suggestion raised by Heller, proceeds to discuss the theme itself: the Devil, in the completed shape in which he stands before us today, represents, one might say, the personification of the unconscious and repressed instincts, of the repressed sexual components of man, down to the last detail (e.g., anal erotism). With this explanation, however, one does not do justice to him.

The development that led to the creation of the highly complex

[5] Again, Wittels' contribution to the discussion is recorded in such a condensed form that it cannot be fully understood.

personality of the Devil—his prehistory—is an interesting subject for research. This history has two sources. The first is the deities of suppressed peoples—which would involve the racial problem. If Bishop Marcellus, the first one to describe the Devil, had lived in Africa, it would be understandable that the Devil acquired the color of the then despised black race. The second source is the deities of the underworld, which have long been endowed with a devil's nature. However, they differ from the Devil in that they were on an equal footing with the gods: they were their adversaries and not their creatures.

Thus all the features of this figure of the Devil, complex as a dream image, must point to their varied origins (one part of it stems from the ancient satyrs and beast-men, and the Devil's connection with the he-goat of classic tragedy; the clubfoot, a result of his fall from Heaven, just like Hephaestos, etc.).

The transformation of the Devil's personality is connected with the upsurge of repression in the Reformation (syphilis), which saved Italian Christendom from disintegrating during the early Renaissance.

We can see in the Devil nothing but a mass fantasy, constructed along the lines of a paranoiac delusion which contains a justification fantasy. The masses, who cannot put up with this contrast between the demands of the Christian doctrine and their personal feelings, thereby make an excuse for the sinfulness of man. At the same time, however, the characteristic of self-punishment is clearly evident in the person of the Devil (he comes to get the sinner, etc.). The child, having no need for the Devil, transfers that role to God and uses Him—as the Middle Ages used the Devil—to exculpate itself: it shoves onto Him the impulses that it does not want to acknowledge, even though it senses them.

Only a few comments on the very interesting witch trials. In them, obviously, perversions play the main role. We find unmistakably infantile elements in those fantasies that were not created under torture but merely squeezed out by it. The entire picture of the proceedings in the witch trials calls to mind children's games on a meadow, which often enough degenerate into sexual orgies.

Freud is not inclined to join Sadger in his somewhat too orthodox view that devil and witch are father and mother, just as he does not agree with the opinion that the Devil is simply a penis, even though

Boccaccio hints at this in one of his tales (to send the Devil to Hell = to have intercourse).

Finally, attention should be drawn to the fact that the Devil is a masculine personality *par excellence*, thus supporting the thesis of the sex theory that wherever the libido may appear, it is masculine (the only popular female devil-creature is the Devil's grandmother).[6]

STEKEL has little to contribute on this subject. In his eyes, the Devil is, like every superstition, a projection of the consciousness of guilt into the external world. It is regrettable that Heller did not include in his considerations the modern figures of the Devil (Mephisto, Tsanga[7]), to illustrate the transition from the Devil of antiquity to the modern Devil.

[6] See Freud: "A Seventeenth-Century Demonological Neurosis" (1923). *S.E.*, 19.
[7] See this Volume, Minutes 54B.

67

SCIENTIFIC MEETING *on February 3, 1909*

Present: Prof. Freud, Adler, Federn, Graf, Hitschmann, Joachim, Rank, Sadger, Wittels.

PRESENTATION

A Case of Compulsive Blushing[1]

SPEAKER: DR. ADLER

The speaker, after emphasizing that he is well aware of the difficulties he faces in undertaking to present the analysis of an erythrophobia, announces his intention of discussing several points on which he lays special stress. Noteworthy among these are: he seeks the cause of the neuroses in an organ inferiority; furthermore, his critique of the view that we have all held, but about which no clarity seems yet to prevail—namely, on the immediate cause of the outbreak of a neu-

[1] Adler never published this paper. However, some of the thoughts he expressed here can be found in his essay "Über neurotische Disposition. Zugleich ein Beitrag zur Ätiologie und zur Frage der Neurosenwahl" ["Concerning Neurotic Disposition. At the Same Time a Contribution to the Etiology and to the Question of the Choice of Neurosis"]. *Jahrbuch,* 1:526-545, 1909.

rosis, and several other points—will be discussed in the course of the analysis. Adler intends to make a few introductory remarks in order to limit the discussion to the most essential points.

He is not inclined to regard erythrophobia or compulsive blushing as an obsessional neurosis because the most significant characteristics of obsessional neurosis are completely absent. Although the blushing seems to occur as though the patient were under a compulsion, it is his fear of blushing that is invariably in the foreground of the clinical picture. To classify this phenomenon in one of the clinical pictures that are familiar to us, is not an easy thing to do. One would be most inclined to consider it a hysteria, although, depending upon the observer's point of view, one could see the predominance of the so-called neurasthenic complex, or one could lay particular stress on the paranoid character, or—and this seems most likely—one could take the hysteric structure as one's starting point.

Other difficulties in the analysis are the following: Adler is not able to offer a complete elaboration of this clinical picture, with which he has been occupied for over three quarters of a year; however, he plans to give a detailed presentation of the subtle connections in this case, in so far as his memory will permit and the material is available. This "connection" [*Zusammenhang*] is the most important aspect of an analysis; why this is so needs some explanation. If one looks into the literature of the Freudian school, one does not often find the connection [between the separate elements] brought forth in an analysis; one has to be content if connections come forth in a fragment. The majority of publications do not bring forth connections. This is not only the speaker's impression; it has been continued even in recent times. The best of the publications do no more than take up once again things that Freud emphasized, and affirm that "it is all there."

In Adler's analysis, too, everything of course occurs again, and he does not believe that there is a single one of the required traits that he could not easily show. Thus there are perversions of all kinds, distinct or merely indicated; incestuous thoughts, particularly in regard to the mother, but also incestuous acts with siblings, with brothers, as well as with sisters; finally, all the other so-called complexes which we do not have any occasion to *miss* in any one of our cases. Adler's position with regard to this question is the same as that of

Freud, who stressed that these relationships are present in every case, even in the normal individual. Besides, Adler could cite a number of infantile traumata, all of which would have been suitable to provoke the neurosis; they did not do so.

For instance, the child repeatedly overheard parental intercourse, etc. And yet, the young man, at present twenty-five years old, fell ill only four years ago, while the experience of overhearing intercourse occurred during the period from his fourth to eighth year. Nor did he fall ill as a result of the homosexual perversions that he practiced with schoolmates in his ninth and tenth year. The patient began to masturbate at an early age and has continued to do so until very recently. His masturbation has the character of a compulsion; if anything in this clinical picture is analogous to an obsessional neurosis, it is the compulsive masturbation.

The speaker now proceeds to describe the clinical picture of the patient at the time when he presented himself for treatment. The patient complains of blushing which, for unknown reasons, set in four years ago; first it appeared comparatively rarely, later more frequently, bothering him to the extent that a number of relationships in social life were made impossible for him. It is not so much blushing itself [that disturbs him] as the fear that he is going to blush; this, after a short time, is followed by blushing, unless he avoids certain precipitating factors—for example, certain words that might be spoken at a social gathering, such as: "syphilis" and "civilization," which have a similar sound; furthermore, "*anstecken*" ["to infect"] or "*Ansteckung*" ["infection"], and "*anstellen*" ["to employ," but also "to line up" or "to put against something"], which have a similar sound.

All this leads back to thoughts of syphilis, which he contracted six years earlier. During its course, he began a mercury treatment, which allegedly did not agree with him. He then went to Lindewiese[2] to be cured. For five years he has had no symptoms; however, he does not believe in his complete recovery, and thinks he needs some additional treatments in Lindewiese. His blushing, however, occurs not only in connection with the words mentioned, but even fragments of such

[2] A health resort.

a constellation are sufficient [to provoke it]—for instance, if he goes to a party, or if someone looks him sharply in the eye, or if he is in a brightly illuminated hall. Even being in a room with several people calls forth this fear. He feels better in the open air and in the cold. That this connection is untenable becomes evident from the following: in the beginning, he stresses that he is better off in the cold; at the end, he feels better in a warm place. The speaker will again take up, later, this apparently unimportant point, which became very important for an understanding [of the illness].

The patient also suffered from anxieties during examinations (he is an engineer)—which, of course, is a great hindrance to his studies. This caused great difficulties with his father, of whom he now begins to speak. From childhood on, the father has been very strict with his son; he is generally a severe man—in our jargon we would call him a sadist—a man who pushes his son to make money soon and who used to keep him on short allowances. As was shown above, the patient was very fond of his mother. For a long time he slept in the parents' bedroom, repeatedly saw their intercourse, and, at four, was completely informed about all sexual relationships. He received his first enlightenment from older schoolmates in a Jewish nursery school; he remembers that even at that time he enjoyed pressing himself against girls or women.

This leads to another point having to do with infantile sexual traumata. A female cousin, and—of especial importance—an aunt who excited him sexually at an early age, lived in the same house. This aunt, however, always preferred a cousin to him; yet she was not the only female person who fascinated him: there were quite a number of girls and women with whom he was involved. Especially marked and more extensive were his relations with a girl cousin, with whom, in his seventh year, he planned to have a sexual relationship—however, nothing came of it because a mutual aunt watched them too closely. He tried to take the girl aside, and she was willing to go with him. Several times he succeeded in touching her genitals and pressing himself against her body, a sexual activity which was, in general, his specialty. The fate of this girl is not uninteresting, either; later on she became a hysteric, and she is still living in an institution. A break between the two had occurred later on; the cause for it was rather strange. When the patient, after finishing his studies at the secondary school, gave his books away, she received nothing; this she took as a reason for breaking with him, at the same time prophesying that misfortune would befall him.

The patient grew up in orthodox [Jewish] circles and is actually himself orthodox even today. Whenever he allows himself to give in to an urge to commit actions which in his opinion are irreligious, he does so with great reluctance. This is paralleled by a strong inclination toward superstition, which manifests itself very clearly. He reproaches himself severely for acting in a way forbidden by Bible or Talmud. Formerly he frequently tried to purify himself by prayer; he has a predilection for prolonged fasting, etc.

Among his other characteristics is his inclination to dress particularly neatly, an inclination which he cannot ever really indulge in because he does not have the money [for it]. His financial situation on the whole is very precarious. His father is niggardly and sends him his small allowance at irregular intervals; the patient frequently gets into financial difficulties and is forced to borrow money from colleagues, who are also very stingy and do not behave very fairly. The life he leads cannot be called a very comfortable one. He lives in one room with a colleague who helps him with his studies; this relationship frequently leads to confusion when the rent is to be paid, or when the problem comes up of keeping the room warm (in this there is a reference to the coldness complex).

Continuing to describe his symptoms, the patient tells of a frequent feeling of dizziness, which befalls him while he is standing, and combines with a weakness in the legs and a feeling of trembling. Masturbation distresses him somewhat, but not excessively. It should be added that, somewhat earlier than is usual, he had his first sexual intercourse with a prostitute, without encountering any difficulties, and that he has been having intercourse rather regularly ever since; until recently no anomalies or difficulties of any kind have arisen (such as impotence, *ejaculatio praecox*, etc.).

His inability to work, although it did not go so far that he was completely unable to work, proved to be a very important symptom; it was severe enough to make him exceed by half the time allotted for an examination. Once he even flunked; this brought him the most violent reproaches from his father; the patient dislikes talking about it and is glad if examination or *Anstellung* [employment] ("*anstellen*") after the examination do not come up for discussion; if this does happen, the fear of blushing arises. On the whole, he feels unsatisfied, has an anxious and expectant look, but talks rather courageously about most things. Initially, one has to overcome little resistance in his analysis.

In his twenty-first year, this man (whose early life will still have to be discussed in many of its aspects) gets syphilis, which deeply distresses him and brings on a tremendous depression. Having read Hermann's writings, he gives up his mercury treatment and even today does not want to have anything to do with it, but believes that he will be cured in Lindewiese. As far as that is concerned, he is deaf to any objections. In his depression, he abandoned his studies and—vacation being close at hand, anyway—went home. There his depression was noticed, and, questioned about it, he confessed everything to his father, declaring that he was going to commit suicide. He did in fact attempt suicide, in a most awkward manner, by winding a handkerchief around his neck and pulling it tight; when he began to choke, he relaxed his grip. Later on he remembered that, at that time, he had had the sensation of blushing, as well as a feeling of dizziness. Other persons around him soon learned about all this; since everyone was intent on comforting him in his depression, even his father held himself back. The patient visited the synagogue, prayed and asked forgiveness, for now he regarded his illness as a retribution for his former sins. And then something new occurred. In the café where he used to have his breakfast, an acquaintance told him that he did not look well. When he heard these words, the patient was overcome by a feeling of dizziness and a sensation of having to fall down. Afterwards he thought that this is the sensation an epileptic must have, when he becomes unconscious.

Subsequently, the interrelationships [determining] his blushing proved to be far more varied. Some of them will be mentioned: fear of blushing also appears when somebody mentions a "thermometer"—that is, in connection with blushing; if a "mirror" is mentioned, or if he sees a mirror, the thought that mercury is involved comes to his mind. But even there, there were other misgivings involved. A matchmaker plays an important role in the patient's family, a woman who has managed all his relatives' marriages and whose name is *Spiegel* [mirror]. He already sees himself as her victim, and his blushing is further determined by her. His father's marriage plans are repugnant to him. He himself would like to get married, but as soon as he tries to reach an understanding with a suitable girl, the relationship is broken off, for the most varied reasons. One girl, after a half year's acquaintance, does not seem beautiful enough, after all; another is not wealthy; a third proves to be coquettish, etc. Moreover, he cannot go to parties, and thus it is understandable that his own efforts to get married—which is indeed identical with providing for oneself—must miscarry.

The patient's first dreams—many of them were interpreted during the course of his analysis—have to do with marriage plans and thoughts of marriage, and it happens consistently in his dreams that either he or his father wants to have nothing to do with it. In this connection, he mentions that they want to marry him off to certain girls from his home town, and that his father has made the most strenuous efforts in that direction. One gets the impression that the patient's condition has the purpose, among other things, of keeping him from getting married; when one draws his attention to this, he expresses a number of different thoughts, which reveal that actually he would not like to get married: (1) because of the syphilis, and (2) because one never knows what might happen to the children, and he would have to reproach himself most severely if anything were to happen to his wife.

In short, these are trains of thought that the speaker had already some time ago brought together under the concept of aggressive thoughts. The dreams and the analysis of occasional attacks make it evident that the patient has had such aggressions, of an active as well as a passive nature. For instance, at the barber's, he was always seized by [an attack of] blushing, and by the fear that the man who would get a shave after him might also be infected with syphilis; connected with this idea is the wish that the whole world would be syphilitic, so that he would not be the only degraded one.

He always wants to "impress" people (as he says); it is an *idée fixe* with him: if he cannot make an impression, the result for him is a depression. Actually, each of his attacks is permeated by the thought that "here he cannot make an impression." If one keeps in mind this connection [in his] thought, one comes to something like the following conclusion: whenever, for instance, syphilis is mentioned, he thinks, "I have had syphilis, I can no longer make an impression" (the same thing occurs when "employment" [*Anstellung*] is mentioned). This connection is exceedingly manifold; if one were to go into details, one could easily show that these were the thoughts that moved him in all situations.

Some more details should be reported about the patient himself. He is a small, stocky individual, whereas, according to the patient's account, his brother is slender and elegantly built. The patient was envious of him, and there was rivalry between them. The brother was called "handsome," "well-built"—which was indeed the goal of the patient's own great longing. He got the greatest pleasure out of playing soldiers, and it was his ideal to wear a uniform. Because of his small build, however, he was not kept in military service. His attempt to make up for the missing uniform by way of a student's cap likewise miscarried. At that time, having already caught his infection, he was not sociable and did not dress elegantly enough. The result was that he was kept out of a fraternity: they had learned—or so he assumed—about his infection. Nor did his fear of blushing fail to appear when somebody drank after him [from the same glass], etc.

Something else should be mentioned briefly here; it will have to be thoroughly discussed later on. He had a squint as a child, and even now a slight squint can be discerned. Other childhood defects are: he remembers having soiled himself with feces and also having wet his bed. One sexual fantasy that he frequently had, had as its substance his observing the performance of sexual intercourse between a girl and an army officer.

The analyst soon noticed that the patient would more often be seized by fear of blushing when he did not have enough money or when he was hungry; this could easily be related to his being unable, in such a condition, to impress anyone. We can see now how complicated this analysis was and how, despite all these findings, it is not yet always evident what his blushing and his fear of blushing stem from.

One additional circumstance of importance must be mentioned. Being poor, the patient was forced to give lessons, a difficult matter, in which one also had little opportunity to make an impression. He had accepted this tutoring job four years previously; he was engaged to tutor some ill-mannered boys, and a girl who had very peculiar traits. Their parents did not pay much attention to him, and if they did, it was to find fault, which he usually accepted silently (inhibition of aggression). These conditions finally brought him to a state that will be described from his own notes. These notes were written down at a late point in the analysis, when the battle was actually already won, in that most of the connections were already clear to the physician, although the patient did not yet see them.

"In the morning," he wrote on the day when the notes were taken, "I thought of the manifold humiliations that I had to suffer, and how they enraged me." Then the patient enumerated eight items—not a few, indeed, if one considers that this was a matter of regular, almost daily recurrence:

"1. Frequently I sit for more than two hours (actually he was supposed to teach for only one hour); sometimes the children's afternoon tea causes an interruption. Wednesday I spent the whole afternoon there, waiting, without being invited to join [them].

"2. Indifferent answers to my greeting, or no greeting at all.

"3. When I came to take my leave before vacation, I went to the store, and nobody offered me a seat.

"4. Never did I receive an invitation to accompany them to the theater, although I was often present when they left [at this point it is important to note that the sensation in his legs and the dizziness are connected with the fact that he had to stand while talking to the lady; this, in turn, is related to his unsatisfied yearning: to be able to make an impression].

"5. When the pupil had a preliminary examination, I tutored him from 4 to 6, once even until 8 o'clock, without being invited for supper.

"6. Frequently the lady addresses him while he is giving a lesson, and when he is about to answer she does not listen to him.[3]

"7. The girl pupil has the habit of wiping her fingers off after I

[3] In the third person in the original [*hört sie mich nicht an*].

have touched them (for instance, when greeting her, but the patient also touches her at other times during the course of his lessons. This was a fourteen-year-old-girl, of whom he was very fond, but he did not talk about her until late [in the treatment], and then he said nothing essential).

"8. The girl pupil did not like it when her aunt from America spoke to me; by the way, on that occasion too, no chair was offered me."

The relationship to this pupil, which became increasingly clear, was of the following nature: the girl, not very beautiful, yet pretty and tall, was very proud in her attitude toward the teacher. After he had once spoken about her, she soon began to play a role in his dreams. Sometimes she changes roles with his mother, sometimes with his sister. These connections become evident; we speak of it as a transference of his love onto this pupil, a love inhibited in a way similar to that for his mother and sister. His behavior toward his sister, however, was not very inhibited. He would lie in bed with his younger sister, with no sexual activity taking place, however.

Before throwing more light on the patient's relationship to his pupil, the key to the explanation of the whole business, we must mention one more event. One evening, the patient visited a prostitute in the vicinity of his pupils' apartment. He got into a quarrel with her over the payment and, during the course of the quarrel, grabbed a watch that was lying on a table and took to his heels. Shortly thereafter, this deed seemed totally incomprehensible to him, and he zealously took pains to make good for the damage [it did]. The following morning he returned the watch by messenger; since he was afraid that the whole matter could have bad consequences, he remembers well having for a long time avoided the section in which the prostitute lived.

During his treatment, too, he was involved in a minor scandal. There was a fourteen-year-old daughter in the family with whom he lived; she too excited him sexually. It becomes generally evident that his love-relationships are directed toward younger girls, a clear [case of] "leaning upon" [*anlehnung*] his relationship to his younger sister. One day, he caught this young girl by her apron and tore her blouse. Her aunt berated him violently and threatened to inform the police, since that sort of thing was a crime. For several days he lived in fear, until he calmed down again. Thus this side of the neurotic, which we encounter frequently, is illustrated in our patient too.

The problem now is: what caused the young man to become ill? How does it happen that he blushes when he hears the words "*anstellen*" ["to employ"], "civilization," etc.? *Anstellen* has yet another determination. It goes back to one of his earliest sexual impressions—one we have already mentioned—that is, pressing [*andrücken*] himself against somebody. This he did on a wide scale, and especially when he lined up for the theater [*anstellen* also means "to line up"]. Indeed, his interest in literature and art goes back to this *Anstellen* ["lining up"], during which he also had ejaculations. But he was always afraid that he might be caught at it. It was only with great reluctance, but compulsively, that he followed this urge. The [idea of] "not being able to make an impression" fits into this picture: for he who is caught in a punishable action certainly has no chance to impress anybody. But there is a deeper determination for this, connected with an event that occurred during his tenth year, and left an indelible impression on him for the rest of his life. During his entrance examination for the *Gymnasium* (here again we see the trend toward something "higher": studying Latin, etc.) he was caught copying an exercise and, without further ado, he was sent out of the room by the teacher. On that embarrassing occasion, he had not impressed anybody, either. But things became even worse: for years a teacher in the *Realschule*[4] teased him about this incident. For this reason, he was not able to cheat [*schwindeln*] in this school; he became very upset when he felt the temptation to do so, or when he was not well prepared. Of all his sufferings in the secondary school, Adler wants to mention only that the fear of cheating [*schwindeln*],[5] which pursued him in the last days [there], also tormented him during his examinations at the technical institute, for he saw himself deprived of that very widely used and popular expedient. He feared that he might be discovered, which again would rob him of the chance to make an impression. Blushing and attacks of dizziness [*Schwindel*]

[4] *Realschule* is a technical secondary school geared toward preparing students for the sciences, whereas the *Gymnasium* provides instruction essentially in the classical languages and the humanities.

[5] The German equivalent for "cheating," "swindle," is *Schwindel, schwindeln;* this, however, also means "dizziness"—which is relevant to the patient's symptoms.

set in regularly, whenever he is afraid of being found out (for instance, while lining up). And even after the blushing had been eliminated, dizziness [*Schwindel*] and fear still persisted, as long as he was still afraid of being caught in the act while cheating [*schwindeln*]. It should be stressed that he would regard as [an instance of] "cheating," something we would not even think of as being so—for instance, standing behind a lady and pressing himself against her, without her apparently noticing it. For him, then, the concept of cheating has undergone an enormous broadening—a phenomenon that exists regularly in the neurotic's thought processes, in the form of the extension of an idea. This extension, while tenable, does not enter into our thinking; it is one part of what still remains incomprehensible in neurosis.

The speaker then mentions cursorily the patient's relationship to himself, the physician, and in this context refers to the remark that traces of a homosexual inclination could be shown [to exist] in the patient. The essential thing in this case was the transference of rage onto the physician, perhaps not without some fault on the part of the physician, who was very uncongenial toward the patient.

The keystone of the explanation fits into the patient's history as follows: he was in love with his pupil, and his cure was effected when he became conscious of this love. If anyone had made the attempt to enlighten him earlier about this, it would have had no effect at all. It is something altogether different whether it is logical insight or feeling that settles the matter. This [feeling], however, he can produce only at the end of the analysis. This becomes clear from the following: when the patient was already feeling well, he voiced his intention to woo the girl. He loves her, he claims; he cannot live without her; and he asks his physician's advice whether he should propose to her right away. The answer is that caution cannot do any harm; he ought to wait a little while. Besides, he is told, it is doubtful whether the parents would agree to give him a fourteen-year-old girl [in marriage]. He replies that he will gladly wait any length of time and meanwhile will try to finish his studies.

Two weeks ago, Adler met the patient, who is quite well now and did not say one word about the girl at all. It was evident that his full realization of his love for the girl was responsible for his becoming a different person. This is also demonstrated by the fact that none of the earlier eight points bothers him any longer. He has begun to rebel and no longer puts up with anything; he will take a chair himself, if none is offered to him, etc.

Another point must finally be mentioned, a point that belongs in this context and which, even though it was not the most important one, contributed much to the understanding [of the case]. It takes us back to the mirror [*Spiegel*] and the woman of that same name. Having completed his studies, the patient had the choice of either becoming an independent engineer or entering the civil service. In view of his hankering for the uniform and the prestige of "the official with the sword," it would not have come as a surprise had the patient preferred the civil service position, even though he was also tempted by the high income of an independent engineer in America. This doubting is characteristic of him; it is connected with his desire to make an impression and his inability to do so. He thought that, when he applied for a position in the civil service, he would have to submit to an examination by a physician, and that the latter, upon discovering that the patient had had syphilis, would reject him for that reason.

When his mind had been set at rest about this, one last point was left: he was afraid that, if he were to marry, he would have the same experience as many of his friends and relatives had had. The family of his fiancée would receive letters informing them of his infection. And if Mrs. Spiegel, of all people, should learn about anything of this kind, what would be easier for her than to set the whole business in motion in order to take revenge on him for getting married without her help? Now he is falling in love with the girl whose family is connected with his home town. There is a series of other related factors that could easily lead to a mishap.

His aversion to mercury has not been fully explained. The speaker, knowing the patient as thoroughly as he does, thinks that he himself may be more inclined toward the following explanation than an outsider would: the aversion is related to another area of the patient's psyche. Like anyone else who wants to make an impression, the patient is from the start against *everything;* he is also against psychoanalysis and wants to be hypnotized. He does not want to learn anything from anyone, because he thinks he knows everything; were it not so, once again he would be unable to make an impression.

Finally, someone will rightly ask the question: why does the man blush? This does not become evident from the material. It is an interesting fact that this blushing did not appear [for the first time] as recently as four years ago, but that the patient had already blushed as a child of four or five. Indeed, he blushes even now—after his recovery—just as he did before; but it does not matter to him any more. Previously he would blush, for instance, when he had to take off his hat to greet his aunt; one might call this a kind of exhibitionism, and there is something to that. But of greater significance is the fact that it was this aunt who taught him that one has to take one's hat off—which to him was an unpleasant lesson. And his small build was responsible for all of this. At this juncture one should also mention a fact—insignificant and natural in itself—which emerges again and again. It plays a minor role for the understanding of such a neurosis, but it is important for normal psychology: the patient would compare his penis with that of others, and found his father's in particular larger and more handsome.

Thus, at the root of his neurotic condition, there is the impossibility of impressing others, an impossibility that has led to a general inhibition of aggression and several ramifications.

DISCUSSION

PROF. FREUD welcomes as particularly interesting this paper on erythrophobia, since he himself has gained intensive experience with this disease, through the analyses of three cases. One of them occupied him, with brief interruptions, for five years; the later fate of this person is also known to him. The second case Freud saw for only two weeks; he took many notes about it; however, the patient suddenly broke off the treatment. The case involved a young man who was a great rogue [*Hauptgauner*]. The third case is still in treatment with him: this is the case of an intelligent, extremely peculiar man, who continues the treatment forever because it enables him to cope with life.

On the basis of these numerous experiences, Freud supports Adler's remarks on erythrophobia. It is, in fact, a unique condition, for which it is very difficult to find a place among the sexual neuroses. One would be most inclined to consider it an anxiety hysteria; but it also has a number of suspiciously paranoid traits, so that one may have to assign it to a position in between these two conditions.

The first case was not cured, but the person was enabled to cope with life. After his treatment, he went on a trip, and sent his physician picture-postcards from two places that had also been the object of the physician's longing. On both occasions, he had an attack at the moment he put the cards in the mailbox. This patient presented the complete picture of an erythrophobia, showing a symptom that even Adler's patient did not display. There are outbreaks of perspiration, in addition to the spells of blushing, in the "major cases." In this case, too, blushing could be traced back to the earlier years; it had already been noticed during the patient's sixth to eighth years. The most important factor is anxiety, as, of course, Adler also saw. This man too continues to have his attacks. But he has become capable of carrying on his profession and has married—in short, he is cured, from a practical point of view; from the theoretical point of view, of course, he is not. He has remained ill for the sole purpose, it would almost seem, of annoying the physician.

It was interesting to learn which traits Adler's case has in common with the cases mentioned; just a few will be cited: for instance, the assertion that the patient feels well only where it is cold; this is a false connection, established via the association of blushing and sweat, from which the patients fling themselves onto coldness. It is noteworthy that one factor stressed by Adler also plays the main role in two of the cases mentioned: it is evident that a substitution took place. Both these patients, having early been ashamed of something, in later life transferred this feeling of shame onto something else. Erythrophobia consists of *being ashamed for unconscious reasons*. This contains within it the inability-to-impress, for being ashamed is the term by which we designate this affect.

The first thing these patients were ashamed of was usually masturbation; more generally, the secret of their early sexual knowledge (case 3 was ashamed at six years, when his parents discussed matters that they thought the boy did not yet understand). This shame about premature sexual knowledge is closely connected with the secret and the surreptitious sexual enjoyment—phenomena that then recur in [connection with] syphilis (the second patient also had it) and which promote the carry-over.

A trait that Adler also stressed was particularly prominent in case 3. There were far fewer sexual repressions than one usually finds in the sexual neuroses. This patient was a "sex scoundrel" [*"Sexual-Lump"*]; in case 1, too, only slight traces of sexual repression could be noticed.

Case 1 is an exceedingly handsome man, slender, of tall build, etc.

Case 2 is inconspicuous, but with a remarkable head, and also tall.

Case 3 is a weak juvenile individual.

Ad 1. Fear that his penis is too small (the other patient had no such idea), and a classical case of an anal character (one of the meanings of his condition was: to sit on the toilet and press until one gets red in the face).

Ad 2. He was concerned that he might get caught.

Ad 3. An ambitious and sensitive man who was bent on making an impression.

All three cases had in common a fear of shaving.

It is an essentially paranoid trait—the fact that these people maintain that they are ashamed for others, too: they get attacks by putting themselves in somebody else's place. A new feature in Adler's case, because it did not appear with such clarity in the other cases, was the desire to infect the whole world.

Subsequently it turned out that the first interpretation—i.e., being ashamed for an unconscious reason—was incomplete: the neuroses cannot be explained in terms of a single emotion, but only by a pair of opposites; these are, in fact, *shame* and *rage*. Only this coexistence of active and passive emotions explains the cases of erythrophobia: it is the coming together of these two emotions that brings on an attack. At this point, one must state—and this is a bit of criticism—that Adler's analysis did not get beyond this formula. The next problem that remains to be solved is the choice of neurosis,[6] and that point Adler's paper did not elucidate, either.

Concerning the inhibition of aggression, which Adler calls the

[6] This is an ever-recurring problem.

immediate cause of the neurosis, Freud noted that Adler actually places his emphasis on the second part of this expression, whereas he himself would stress its first part. Incidentally, Adler's case itself makes it evident that it was not the inhibition of aggression that evoked the neurosis, but the inhibition of sexuality; the patient became ill only after he had fallen in love.

FEDERN, referring to the inability to make an impression, remarks that to wish and not to be able to attain [one's wish] seemed to him to be a prerequisite for neurosis in general. It is not inconceivable that the trend of a neurosis could be derived in part from the interconnections among these failures.

As a counterpart to erythrophobia, with its strong moral inhibitions, one might place "moral insanity."[7] Whereas, in the rest of the neuroses, the inhibitions seem to grow out of an inner evaluation, the erythrophobic seems to regard as important the evaluation of the outside world.[8] In this may lie one clue to the choice of neurosis. Erythrophobes seem to be poorly endowed hysterics who, out of their scant means, produce a neurosis that inhibits them in the same way as the most severe symptoms inhibit a hysteric.

SADGER: The wish to make an impression over a rival goes back—as Adler also indicated—to the relationship to a younger brother. What Sadger missed was any mention of the person in whose eyes the patient wanted to outshine his brother. Probably it was the father. At the bottom of the patient's inability to complete his studies, there is the wish that the father would always take care of him. (This came out clearly in a similar case.) It might be advisable, therefore, to put more stress on the homosexual factor.

Sadger had two patients with obsessional neurosis, both of whom acquired syphilis during treatment—but they took it remarkably lightly. To these patients, the neurosis is so important that, [in comparison with it], everything organic disappears from sight. In general, it is striking how lightly hysterics take organic afflictions and how easily—both subjectively and objectively—these illnesses run their course in hysterics.

[7] English in the original.
[8] This is the paranoid aspect of his attitude.

HITSCHMANN remarks that he too cannot pass over this case without looking for the relationship to the organic. Blushing is clearly a vasomotor symptom, which is described as appearing without concomitant affect in certain illnesses (climacteric; the typical congestions; neurasthenia, etc.). It is also a phenomenon that corresponds to the physiological affect of sexual shame. Persons who blush easily from childhood on may have different types of vessels, and one might perhaps say that it is just for this reason that they are predisposed to the affects of shame and rage. Looking at the case superficially, one would be inclined to call it neurasthenia; although local symptoms are missing, the weakness in the legs, the dizziness, and other symptoms do remind one of neurasthenia. The anxiety connected with his eyes (inability to look into the mirror), his poor appearance, etc.—these are also reminiscent of masturbation symptoms; in addition, the patient is prone to self-reproach. To round out his paper, Adler really should discuss the question: "What is psychogenic?"

Hitschmann sees no justification for emphasizing especially the wish to make an impression. It is a rather common component of self-esteem, and belongs to the psychic instinct of self-preservation. Nor does Hitschmann consider it fully proven that the recovery is simply due to the patient's becoming conscious of his love for the girl, for the suggestion, reassurance, raising of self-esteem, etc., that takes place during such an analysis is beyond measure.

WITTELS has seen several persons afflicted with syphilis who were not neurotic and who, in the most thoughtless manner, exposed other people to the danger of infection. He finds too much of a generalization in Adler's contention that the key to the solution of this neurosis lies in this small and insignificant person's wish to make an impression. Besides, Adler's stressing that the numerous traumata of childhood had not caused a neurosis does not seem correct; the effect of a trauma is, after all, not at once visible. And on the basis of his limited experience, Wittels can by no means agree with the statement that the battle is won when the physician has grasped the connections and constructed a framework.

ADLER begins his concluding words with some general remarks. Some of the deficiencies in this paper were due to his deficient preparation. For instance, he did not even present everything he had written down about organic inferiority, such as the congenital weakness of the vasomotor system; Hitschmann deserves thanks for having mentioned this. The analysis proved that this was an inheritance from the patient's father, an irascible, brutal man, who was given to frequent fits of rage.

In answer to Wittels, the framework is not arbitrary. While the "desire to make an impression" (the patient's own expression) belongs, of course, to his conscious character (Hitschmann), it is unconscious during the attack. The desire to make an impression can manifest itself in hundreds of ways—and the whole concept of the feeling of shame (when there is an inhibition of rage) is part of this. While [the phrase] "the battle was won" was more a manner of speaking, Adler was nevertheless convinced that this framework fits everything. It is true, of course, that many cases are cured without one's knowing anything about the framework. Adler's viewpoint on this question is: it is not sufficient that the physician know what it is all about; nor is it enough that the patient be shown the way by which he can reach this insight; he must, in addition, attain the feeling for it. The patient fell ill because he "looked away" from this love; the reason for this might help to explain much about the choice of neurosis. The liking for coldness or warmth is an incidental symptom, and probably does not appear in all cases. The patient also wanted to make an impression by going out into the cold. This too can be understood only if one broadens the concept of "making an impression."

With regard to the small penis, Adler had an interesting experience with two brothers, both of whom had great difficulties in their analyses: each believed that the other one had a larger penis.

In order to avoid misunderstandings, more needs to be said about the inhibition of aggression. It does not produce the illness, but it is its form. What is left is [to determine] where it stems from. This again leads back to the problem of why the patient "looked away" from his feelings of love. Adler wishes to stress that the outbreak of an illness requires, in all cases of neurosis, a constellation of recent events, and that this constellation is the immediate triggering factor. As far as the sexual [factor] is concerned, Adler is well known to be a little in opposition to this view, because, in his opinion, sexual and other childhood defects intermingle; he believes that those other childhood defects are originally lacking in any sexual tinge, whereas the sexual does have the coloration of childhood defects.

In answer to Federn, Adler remarks that there is only one evaluation, for which both subject and object are invariably necessary; the different forms of this tension result from the individual constellation in each case.

Adler has never encountered a neurosis that did not display the anal character. But one comes to this only after one thinks of the broadening of concepts.

It is certainly correct that the "neurasthenic" symptoms predominate (Hitschmann), but [the classification of] neurasthenia as such must simply be given up. The trembling in the legs, for instance, results from the patient's desire to stretch whenever he had to stand.

Hitschmann's remarks about all the things that enter incidentally into an analysis is, of course, important. What we can comprehend conceptually is merely the nodal points; what lies in between, one has to fill in or drop. It is the same thing as with the Chladni acoustic figures.[9]

[9] Ernst F. Chladni (1756-1827), German physicist, made studies of the transmission of sound, e.g., in metal covered with sand.

68

SCIENTIFIC MEETING *on February 10, 1909*

Present: Prof. Freud, Adler, Federn, Graf, Heller, Hitschmann, Rank, Sadger, Steiner, Stekel, Wittels.
Dr. A. Muthmann as guest.[1]

Reviews and Case Reports by All Members Present

RANK: From the "German Fairy Tales" collected by the Grimm Brothers, Rank selects one: "Cursed [*Verwünscht*] to Stand." It tells of a boy who did not immediately obey an order given by his father, whereupon the enraged man shouted at the boy that he wished that the boy would remain standing forever on the spot. The father's curse was immediately fulfilled, and, after some years of standing, the boy died. We may comment that, in this case of hysterical paralysis, the psychic motivation—that is, the stubborn boy's resistance against his father's order—is very clearly expressed.

STEKEL comments that this seems to be a symbolic representation of priapism.

[1] Dr. Muthmann was one of Freud's first followers in Germany.

PROF. FREUD mentions that, in neuroses, one very frequently finds a counterpart to this story in the phenomenon of "delayed obedience," when persons, many years later, in their neurosis obey commands and prohibitions that had been given to them unsuccessfully in their childhood. Disobedience is followed by excessive obedience, and this is what the story represents, in abbreviated form. Indeed, it is a frequent characteristic of sagas and fairy tales ("the three wishes") that a wish that is not immediately fulfilled later comes true in a troublesome manner.

WITTELS would like to mediate between Prof. Freud's view, which interprets the story as a case history, and Stekel's view, which sees in it a symbolic myth. One may assume that the story could be both; it may further be that the story was fixated in the consciousness of the people because it could be given a meaning that found a resonance in the people's consciousness—for example, in the consciousness of those who were suffering from the contrary of priapism.

FEDERN observes that in delayed obedience it is not only apparent compliance that is given expression but also defiance; one might formulate it in the thought: now look at what happens when I am obedient!

ADLER too thinks that the condition should be understood as a compromise formation. It calls to mind similar states that can be provoked by suggestion (for instance, someone is told he will be unable to reach beyond a drawn line, and this actually happens). The boy punishes the father whom he originally did not want to obey.

PROF. FREUD comments, finally, that this is the prototype of passive resistance.

RANK then mentions a remark by Rosegger (in the monthly *Heimgarten*) in which the poet admits that the love between mother and son is erotic.

Furthermore, in an article on "Hysteria in Animals"[2] it is argued that "an imaginary pregnancy," observed in an old bitch and in a goat, is of a hysterical nature. The reviewer is inclined to doubt this.

[2] By Dr. Paul Vögeler in *Umschau.*

STEKEL makes a preliminary reference to a French paper on Maupassant's illness.[3] It includes analyses of several of his works; he will review it in detail on some later occasion. He also mentions Swoboda's last book, *Man's Critical Days.*[4]

STEINER reviews the literature on the inner secretion of the prostate, and the relation of the endocrine glands to the genitals; he gives a survey of the whole theory of inner secretion.

PROF. FREUD raises the question: what has remained valid of the findings, made twenty years ago, concerning the effects of sperm and testicle secretions?

HITSCHMANN considers the review to be uncritical.

STEINER replies that he cannot be expected to offer criticism in such an enormous field which, moreover, is not altogether at the center of his interest. However, he is convinced that much can be expected from organotherapy.

ADLER remarks that it becomes more and more clear that the most significant problem of organotherapy lies in the correlation—which all the works cited have failed to mention. He is no expert in this field, and yet he believes that he is right in asserting that, until two years ago, there existed no work on correlation. In his [own] work on organ inferiority, he pointed to the connection with the sex glands, which has since played a role in the literature. It is his hypothesis that a correlation exists among all organs and, in addition, a correlation of all organs with the sex organ. He used heredity as the basis for his hypothesis; while heredity must make its way via the sexual organs, it may already find expression in a number of anomalies in the carrier himself.

HITSCHMANN mentions the following literature:

Berlin: klinische Wochenschrift: "On Two Analyses" by Otto Juliusberger,[5] who quotes Freud and Stekel.

[3] Probably Lucien Lagriffe: "Guy de Maupassant, Etude de Psychologie Pathologique," *Annales Médico-Psychologiques*, 9 (9:5) :177, 1909.

[4] Full title: *Die kritischen Tage des Menschen und ihre Berechnung mit dem Periodenschieber* [*Man's Critical Days and How to Figure Them Out with the Help of the Period Slide*]. Wien: Deuticke, 1909.

[5] *Zur Psychotherapie und Psychoanalyse* ["On Psychotherapy and Psychoanalysis"], 1909.

Gaupp'sches *Zentralblatt*, Bleuler: on a work by Birnbaum, *Psychoses with Formation of Delusions in Degenerates.*[6]

In an essay reviewed in the *Archives de Psychologie*, "Les Idéals d'Enfants," it is stated that school children, when asked, wanted (until their seventh year) to become like their fathers and mothers, who were subsequently replaced by heroes.[7]

"Psychology of the Criminal" by Public Prosecutor Dr. Erich Wulffen.[8]

Wiener klinische Wochenschrift: Wagusski suggests a separation of the psychological from the vasomotor symptoms.[9]

According to a forthcoming work from Kraepelin's clinic, epileptic seizures are precipitated by a toxic process in the blood.

Hitschmann then reports the case of a woman whose fear of having "appendicitis" proved entirely unfounded when she was operated on.

DR. MUTHMANN from Bad Nassau, present as a guest, reports that he had the same experience with a male patient.

STEKEL, in the analysis of such a case, uncovered the unmistakable wish to be a woman. Besides, far too little attention is paid to the sexual meaning of such an operation to a woman (she lies naked in front of a man, whose knife—penis—enters her body, etc.). These fantasies explain the frequency of mild mental derangements after such operations; they are usually attributed to excitement, narcosis, and the like.

MUTHMANN knows a great number of such cases; he mentions, for example, the case of a woman who, as a child, was fondled by

6 Karl Birnbaum, *Psychosen mit Wahnbildung und wahnhafte Einbildungen bei Degenerativen* [*Psychoses with Delusion Formation and Delusionlike Imaginations in Degenerates*]. Halle: Marhold, 1908. Bleuler's article is probably "Wahnhafte Einbildungen der Degenerierten." *Zentralbl. f. Nervenh. u. Psychiat.*, 32:77-80, 1909.

7 Julian Varendonck: "Les Idéals d'Enfants" ["The Ideals of Children"], 1908.

Hitschmann refers to the following passage in the above-mentioned work: "The child first idealizes the characters of his immediate environment; later on he chooses his ideals among persons of his own age who, in one way or another, stimulate his imagination. Finally, he turns to persons with whom he has become acquainted, either in school or in books. The question addressed to them had been: 'Among the persons you came to know in your studies or in your conversations, whom would you like to resemble most of all?'"

8 Cf. Volume I, Minutes 46.

9 Neither an author of this name nor an essay of such content could be found in the *Wiener klinische Wochenschrift*.

her father (later by her lover), in the region of the gall bladder; this resulted in that part of her body becoming an erotogenic zone.

PROF. FREUD: Where the penis is, there is the vagina.

HITSCHMANN further reports on two books (*Wiener klinische Rundschau*, 23). Joire: *Handbook of Hypnotism*[10] and Walstein: *The Subconscious.*[11] In the latter there is [as Prof. Freud adds] a pathological explanation of the *déjà vu,*[12] which Prof. Freud rejects by referring to his own explanation of this phenomenon in the *Psychopathology of Everyday Life:* it always involves the recollection of an unconscious fantasy.

PROF. FREUD reports on the first issue of Moll's *Zeitschrift für Psychotherapie und medizinische Psychologie* which has just appeared; it does not seem to accomplish what it had promised.[13]

Prof. Freud further reports on an essay, "Psychoanalytic Pastoral Care and Experimental Moral Pedagogy," by Reverend Dr. Pfister in Zürich; he considers it interesting in several respects (published in *Protestantische Monatshefte*, Vol. 13, No. 1, 1909).

Prof. Freud does not give a detailed review of this work (which is in our archives), but only a survey of the author's method and viewpoint. The author did not fully grasp one point: he does not sufficiently stress that initially these successful results are merely the effect of transference. This may be due to the fact that it is easy for Pfister to manage this transference. Religion is the most convenient form of sublimating, easily achieved by many people. The pastor turns toward God the love that is tendered him; and this path has long since been smoothed out. With the physician, on the other hand, the patient often fails when it comes to resolving the transference, since the physician cannot offer him any substitute for it. In this context it seems plausible [to assume] that the increase in neuroses is connected with the decrease in religiosity. With regard to Pfister's technique, one must

[10] Paul Joire: *Handbuch des Hypnotismus und seine Anwendung in Medizin, Erziehung und Psychologie* [*Handbook of Hypnotism, and Its Application in Medicine, Education and Psychology*].

[11] Louis Walstein: *Des unterbewusste Ich und sein Verhältnis zu Gesundheit und Erziehung* [*The Subconscious Ego and Its Relation to Health and Education*].

[12] By Theodor Meynert.

[13] Freud published his essay, "Some General Remarks on Hysterical Attacks," (1909) in this journal.

mention that he prefers to use Jung's association method. As a rule, however, this indicates an imperfect mastery of the analytic technique. It [Jung's method] might become valuable only with resistant people, and it is, of course, indispensable in [the treatment of] dementia, and the like.[14]

What is noteworthy is the fundamental difference in the criticism of Stekel's book, a difference that is, of course, determined by the different points of view. Pfister's objections to it are not altogether justified; sexual activity is just not a sin. His criticism is correct in so far as two different ways are open: the normal discharge in gratification, on the one hand, and sublimation, on the other hand. We must frequently take the former way; the pastor will, of course, prefer the latter. In addition, the psychoanalytic pastor has the advantage of the fact that he can undertake the work without pay, thus practicing on a purely ethical basis. It has become evident, on the other hand, that the physician does not gain anything therapeutically by conducting the treatment gratis. Besides, we have overestimated the significance of money as a factor impeding treatment. It carries no weight by comparison with the other forces (such as love) that are operative in this situation.

ADLER reports on an actor whom he treated for a short time (anxiety, *taedium vitae,* disgust; general neurasthenic symptoms). One detail of the analysis is especially noteworthy. During a performance, he had a typical attack of his: he turns cold on one side, and at the same time anxiety sets in. Nevertheless, he held on to his skill and carried his role through to the end. The attack was traceable to an actual incident, which occurred immediately before the performance. (We shall omit its interpretation.) Two days later, the patient requested the physician to come and visit him because as the result of a new attack, he was unable to go out of his house. But this time, by way of exception, the attack affected the left side, and was not "cold" but "hot"—that is, it was *reversed.* Investigation disclosed that he was performing every day in a certain play, and that he had

[14] This remark is particularly interesting in view of the modifications of classical analytic technique in the treatment of psychoses (Federn, Schwing, Sèchehaye, and others), which were to take place some thirty years later.

expected his physician to attend the performance the day before in order to see him. With this he associated the thought that no one wanted to come see him; this again refers to the physician. Furthermore, something has to be inverted; it is not he who has to go to the physician, but the physician has to come to see him; and this too he accomplished. But his fiancee too had to come and visit him on that day, since he felt incapable of going out. In addition, there was a rival who wanted to see him in this role. The patient instead went to the other theater in order to observe the rival, and at that time he was angry that the situation was reversed. Probably, the wish to be attacked is behind the whole matter.

PROF. FREUD comments that the inversion of symptoms is invariably the result of homosexual motives; crudely expressed, this means: reversed (inverted love), from behind.

ADLER thereupon remarks that there are some dreams in which the dreamer does things that another person has done. The analysis of such dreams uniformly discloses that they express the wish to be in the other person's place. This exchange of roles is of great significance.

GRAF tells about his self-analysis of so-called "spontaneously emerging melodies," which he regularly found to be associatively linked with the text. (PROF. FREUD comments that one should perhaps make a distinction between associations that are connected with the wording of the text, with the content, or with the situation.)

FEDERN speaks about, among other things, a dream in which part of the content (*wiping* the anus in childhood) is used in an evaluation of the dream ("The dream is blurred beyond recognition" [*verwischt*—"wiped out"]).

PROF. FREUD reports a similar example: a man dreams that he confuses hotel rooms and thus enters a strange room, in which three ladies are just going to bed; he continues his account: "There are gaps here; something is missing." If we consider this judgment about the dream as its content, it makes good sense: the gaps are [in] the ladies' genitals, which he sees; what is missing is the penis, which his infantile imagination attributes to every human being.

SADGER reports on a book, *Maupassant's Illness*, by Vorberg (Löwenfeld's *Sammlung*). The work is an example of how one should not write a pathography. For instance, the author completely disregards the writer's relationship to his severely hysterical mother. It is an interesting fact that a brother of Maupassant's also became a victim of paralysis.[15]

SUPPLEMENT

FERENCZI

Medical Logic, by Bieganski[1]

From our specific point of view, the following comments are to be made: The author raises the question of whether a "medical logic" is necessary, in addition to the generally valid logic; we agree with his affirmative answer, because medicine, like any other applied science, does require special working methods.

The book's first section deals with "medicine and medical science" in general.

What is emphasized here is a correct stress on the practical-heuristic importance of purely theoretical research, devoid of any utilitarianism. He expresses the view, furthermore, that medicine is an art as well as a science.

The chapter on "Observation" begins with the psychologically sound statement that an observation (perception) is determined not so much by the impression received as by the properly directed work of the intellect. We can support this voluntaristic view on the basis of our

15 Sadger's review appeared in the *Wiener klinische Rundschau*, 23, 1909.

1 W. Bieganski, *Medizinische Logik. Kritik der ärztlichen Erkenntnis* [*Medical Logic. A Critique of Medical Knowledge*]. Würzburg: Kabitzsch, 1909.

This review was apparently never printed. The manuscript, in Ferenczi's handwriting, is attached to the Minutes of this meeting. The following book notice by Ferenczi —showing the same incorrect spelling "Biegansky" as is found in the manuscript— appeared in the *Wiener klinische Rundschau*, 23, 1909.

"In a clear and lucid presentation, the renowned Polish methodologist gives us a detailed report about the logical thinking of the physician, about the limits of medical knowledge, about the most frequent errors in the thinking of physicians. A large number of aptly chosen examples elucidate the theoretical discussions. This book can be highly recommended to every scholar and also to every practitioner interested in the unvarnished truth in medicine."—Dr. F.

knowledge about the unconscious; and we can add that "primacy of will" would be more correctly characterized as the primacy of unconscious trains of thought and wishes.

Many incorrect observations are made, the author very rightly explains, because of the emotions of the observer, for instance, while he is making a diagnosis. Unfortunately, the author, who knows nothing of psychoanalysis, is unable to explain why, and on the basis of which mechanisms, physicians are so frequently wrong in their observations of members of their own families.

Without mentioning the unconscious (which would, indeed, be far more intelligible), the author maintains the view that in perception there are no pure impressions, that there is something more to it: "a judgment that states the resemblance of the present sensation to traces, recollections, of earlier ones." While these observations as such are correct, the author could have arrived at a better formulation if he had been familiar with the unconscious processes of association. It would be a task of practical value if one were to undertake a psychoanalysis of wrong diagnoses. The author, however, follows Wundt[2] in believing that the "elements of assimilation" cannot be broken down further.

The psychology of affects (tendency to wish fulfillment) would explain wrong diagnoses better than the psychology of attention, to which the author adheres, although he admits the role of affects (p. 37).

He emphasizes that the belief in authorities is a frequent cause of psychic blindness; in his remark that we do not perceive that which is actually there but that which we wish to happen, he comes very close to a pure pleasure-unpleasure psychology (p. 39).

The author has a very reasonable opinion that a preconceived theory often has a detrimental influence on the perception of facts. On the other hand, he is right in stressing that theory is indispensable to scientific research. Without theory, no scientific progress. Even erroneous theories may lead to the discovery of true facts. The author quotes Claude Bernard's condemnation of the [practice of] clinging to obsolete theories despite new evidence contradicting them.

[2] Wilhelm Max Wundt (1832-1920), German psychologist and philosopher.

The section on "Anamnesis" would have turned out quite differently if the author had taken into consideration as well those recollections that are forgotten, but which can be revived by way of associations (analysis).

An interesting section deals with the definition of the concept of illness; the author avoids any onesidedness, although it is true that he draws somewhat too sharp a line—in any event an artificial one—between pathology and physiology. The distinction between function-disturbing and compensatory symptoms is carried through very well.

From the methodological point of view, the classification of diseases is correct, but it does not sufficiently take into account the specific needs of neurology and psychiatry. The chapter on diagnosis and the causes of diseases is very good; the various concepts designated by the word "cause" are clearly distinguished from one another. A defense of the teleological point of view in medicine concludes this section. The author demonstrates that the rejection of teleology was suitable only for the inorganic sciences; thereafter, it was carried over uncritically into the biological disciplines.

A special section deals with experimentation in medicine and its indissoluble relationship to a preconceived hypothesis, which it is intended to confirm. The scholars in the field of the biological sciences, who are usually so proud of their "exactitude," might feel more modest, if they were to read this chapter. The author uses convincing examples to demonstrate how small a measure of "exactness" can be attained in experiments with living organisms. At this point, the author might have discussed the limits on the possibilities of attaining evidence in psychology, but his examples deal only with physiology or pathology. The foundations of clinical and therapeutic experiments, of course, seem to him to be the most uncertain of all.

The eighth section deals with the role of generalization and hypothesis in medical research. There is an interesting quotation from Claude Bernard on the capacity for creation: "it cannot be analyzed, it is a mystery that remains beneath the threshold of consciousness, and has its source in incomprehensible innate qualities of the psychic organization." We know, since Freud, that the congenital *Anlage* truly defines the latitude of the developmental potentialities; but within this latitude, it is the influence of environments and postnatal development that determine the capabilities. *Faute de mieux,* the author considers conclusions by analogy to be permissible in the medical sciences; he proves that important discoveries were made with the help of this thought process. A chapter each on medical statistics and indications for therapy conclude this well-written book. I would like to recommend the reading of it to my colleagues.

Dr. Ferenczi

69

SCIENTIFIC MEETING *on February 17, 1909*

Present: Prof. Freud, Bass, Federn, Graf, Hitschmann, Joachim, Rank, Sadger, Stekel.

PRESENTATION

From the Recollections of a "Sweet Girl"[1]

SPEAKER: DR. SADGER

The patient was a severely hysterical girl who came from a very degenerate family; at the time of treatment, she was twenty-three years old and suffered from hysterical vomiting and nausea. Her mother was a severe hysteric (sadist, sleepwalker); her oldest brother suffered from paranoia, and one sister from dementia praecox; another sister came close to the borderline of psychosis.

Vomiting had set in for homosexual reasons; as a telephone operator, she worked in a room together with 200 [other] women, and fell in love with one of them.

[1] "*Süsses Mädel*" is an idiomatic Viennese term; it corresponds to the French "grisette."

She had had innumerable love affairs and relationships; during the course of treatment, she wrote down the story of her heterosexual love life. After nine months of treatment, she also wrote down the story of her homosexual love life. From these confessions the speaker reads word for word those sections that are the most important ones for the genesis of the patient's illness, as well as others of more general interest.

It is the patient's mother who plays the most important role in her life; her vomiting goes back to imitation (or, as the case may be, to repression) of her mother. It is noteworthy that, in spite of her numerous "normal" love affairs, the patient was more homosexual than heterosexual. This may perhaps indicate the nature of a born prostitute; she constantly changed relationships because she was never able to gain the homosexual love she had once known with her mother. Indeed, the only relationships that lasted for any length of time were those in which the man resembled her mother in some way, particularly in his cruelty.[2]

DISCUSSION

STEKEL is mistrustful of the case history; it shows too much evidence of later retouching. The whole thing gives the impression of a regressive fantasy, though much real material may have been worked into it. But the quality and style of the patient's childhood life, as they were described, cannot possibly correspond to the facts. Stekel thinks that Sadger's remark about the psychology of the Don Juans and the Messalinas is his most valuable contribution, especially his explanation of Don Juan's way of life as motivated by a homosexuality that was never gratified.

FEDERN, on the contrary, is inclined to regard Don Juan as a man who finds satisfaction with every woman and, precisely for this reason, constantly goes on to another. Again in contrast to Stekel, Federn has the definite impression that the material bears the stamp of reality.

[2] This seems to be a counterpart to a type of homosexual object choice that Freud described later: the homosexual object often retains some traits of the original, heterosexual, object.

It is striking that masturbation is not mentioned anywhere in the childhood history; instead the term *begeilen*[3]—a term from Sadger's vocabulary—is often used, even in passages where it is quite out of place. If this were true, the patient—like all prostitutes—would have failed to find the path from the masculine clitoris masturbation to vaginal excitability. It is also noteworthy that the patient, although she had often played a variety of sexual games with her brother (probably mutual masturbation, and not, as the patient erroneously calls it, "homosexual intercourse"), showed almost no interest in the penis.

JOACHIM, also referring to the remark about Don Juan and prostitutes, comments that not all [such] cases may have a homosexual root. It is, however, true that some of these people look for a form of sexuality, which they have constructed out of fantasy and experience, and which it is hard [for them] to find.

It is interesting to note that the patient experienced feelings of sensual pleasure when relatives expressed grief after her father's death. This might also be true in the case of normal individuals.

RANK says that, according to his experience, sadism is in the foreground and plays the chief role in the Don Juan [type]. Don Juan is far less concerned with sexual intercourse than with conquest. Where he finds no resistance, he desists immediately (aversion to prostitutes). That is the actual picture; behind this, there seems to be a strong homosexual tendency, which has been repressed early in life.

GRAF sees in the figure of Don Juan the polymorphous-perverse type of the erotic state of childhood. There seems to be no repressed homosexuality in the genuine Don Juan type (Mozart's Don Juan), who is often mistaken for the romantic, Faustian type (Byron). There are two types of prostitutes: (1) one who corresponds to Don Juan and can accommodate herself to all men, as it were; (2) one in whom there is much repression and hysteria (as well as lesbianism). Messalina is the direct counterpart to the Don Juan type (a view that Prof. Freud refutes by pointing out that Messalina is forever unsatisfied, and this is not the case with Don Juan).

Graf thinks that Mozart must also be numbered among the genuine

[3] To indulge in lascivious, lewd fantasies.

Don Juan types because he always remained a child; this finds beautiful expression in the letters of the young Mozart.

(PROF. FREUD suggests to Graf that he work up the theme of "Mozart and his Relationship to Don Juan" for the *Sammlungen.*[4])

PROF. FREUD notes that, on first impression, this case history is repelling. The dissolution of this impression is in the direction indicated by Stekel: the representation of childhood by a sexually adult person, who has become licentious. Her childhood recollections are represented [as they appear to the patient] in the mirror of her present life. It would be undiscriminating to accept all parts of the story as equally genuine. Indeed, all childhood recollections are created at a later period,[5] the genuine ones as well as the others. Even though some doubts must be permitted about the reliability of the story, it still remains a valuable human document. If one were to ask which part might be regarded as genuine and which part as false, the answer would have to be that a great part is to be regarded as genuine and true; it strikes us as strange only because we are not familiar with these things. The sadistic impulses, for instance, are quite correctly conceived, although at that time they did not exist in that form, but only in a germinal state.

Federn quite correctly called attention to the fact that masturbation was not mentioned. This seems to be a "case of worms"[6] par excellence: first, the anal component is stimulated, and in this way the individual subsequently arrives at masturbation. There exists, however, a general childhood tendency toward alloying, in later reflection, the common autoerotism of [early] childhood with the object love of later years because at that time one is ashamed of autoerotism, so to speak. In the case presented, we thus have the life of one who became a courtesan projected into the nursery.

[4] Prof. Freud probably refers to *Sammlungen kleiner Schriften zur Neurosenlehre.*

[5] This sentence can be amplified in the following way: an experience leaves certain traces in the preconscious or in the unconscious; when the experience is reproduced at a later time, it is called a memory. This memory or recollection receives its final formulation when it is raised to consciousness; often it is distorted, serving the purposes of repression. Totally unadulterated recollections are rare; however, they can be obtained through hard psychoanalytic work.

[6] Freud obviously refers to those intestinal parasites that frequently irritate the anal region.

In accordance with Graf's correct remark, the "blood complex," as usual, goes back to the mother's menstrual bleeding (not to her coughing blood, etc.); it arouses the area of sadistic impulses. The patient accepted the other explanation, to which she refers as a fact that was told to her, in order to avoid remembering.

Some problems that are inherent in this case: we learn, for instance, what frigidity in women is all about, that innumerable women do not even get to trying out their sexuality. The sexual life of women is far more restricted than we know; in most cases it is confined not only to a single man but also to a single component of the sexual instinct. Nearly all so-called "anesthetic" women are anesthetic only as far as the vagina is concerned; therefore one could probably find in most women that component that would yield full gratification (in which sadism most likely plays the leading role).

There is another problem involved in this case: how could this person, who could justifiably be called polymorphous-perverse, also develop a hysteria at the same time? And this is by no means an exception. One would not even be at a loss for an explanation; one might say that, in such individuals, the repression is labile, and the like. However, one clue to the solution might be homosexuality. Thus, if certain individuals become neurotic, in spite of enormous sexual activities, their neuroses may have their source in the suppression of instinctual homosexual inclinations. It is, however, a serious misconception to assume the existence of a specific homosexual instinct; the objects are after all different, even though they are equivalent for the child. The patient may not be, as Sadger put it, essentially more homosexual than heterosexual; rather, her heterosexuality is just uninhibited and free; in regard to homosexuality, however, this patient is subject to the same restrictions as any ordinary woman is in regard to her heterosexuality. The resistances (in Rank's sense) against the instincts[7] which we can subsume under [the term] heterosexual are too weak; yet these resistances are necessary for heightening the pleasure gain. Because it is offered freely, heterosexuality has lost its value

[7] The original has "*der Triebe*," "*of* the instincts," which must, of course, be a mistake. To do Rank justice, we must admit, however, that we may, in certain rare situations, be entitled to speak of the resistance *of* an instinct.

for them;[8] that is why they try to find the strong resistance—valuable because of its infrequency—which corresponds to what the lover finds in a normal woman.

A few comments on the analysis of Don Juan: to consider Don Juan, as he is characterized in the history of literature, as a homosexual is an error, which Stekel too will soon realize; Rank's formulation, on the other hand, according to which Don Juan is a sexually normal sadist, is much more to the point. Nor can he be called polymorphous-perverse. Rank is right again in saying that suppression of the homosexual component at an early age is a prerequisite for such development; only this explains why he can turn so completely to the woman. When all these conditions coincide, then a Don Juan may develop. Poetically, one could construct these conditions approximately in the following manner: the mother is very affectionate and has a great need for love; initially she was conquered gallantly by the father, but later she was neglected by him; he is a stern, cruel, but just man, living somewhere far from wife and child. From the beginning, the mother is very affectionate toward her small son, but she must soon die. The boy then grows up in deprivation, which increases his desire for love, while he sees and hears nothing of his father. As the second decisive experience, a girl would have to appear during his earliest years of puberty; this girl makes many advances to him, but is suddenly carried off by illness. He grows up and overcomes certain barriers; then comes his first temptation. Again and again he must conquer what he has lost. Don Juan's father, on his deathbed, confesses to him a paranoiac love for the image of a saint. Something like this would be a poetic transcription of what was indicated in Rank's formula.

BASS remarks that the main objections have already been voiced. He, too, has the impression that the details of the story are in accordance with the facts, but that the form in which they are presented is incorrect. The homosexual factor in Don Juan may find its expression in the selection of the heterosexual object (the strong predilection of some men for slender, boyish women may be traceable to such a homosexual influence).

[8] See O. Rank: "*Die Don Juan Gestalt.*" *Imago*, 8:142-196, 1922.

HITSCHMANN thinks it strange that this patient seems to know everything about her youth; also that she seems to have so little interest in the penis. It may be that she did not actually masturbate all the time, but only indulged in lascivious fantasies [“*begeilt*”].

SADGER stresses in his concluding words that he made a point of exerting no influence on the patient’s writing of her story. He would doubt that the patient became a hysteric because she lacked homosexual gratification: from earliest childhood she has held on to the homosexual object, while it is heterosexual gratification that has met with difficulties.

70

SCIENTIFIC MEETING *on February 24, 1909*[1]

Present: Prof. Freud, Adler, Bass, [A.] Deutsch, Federn, Heller, Hitschmann, Hollerung, Joachim, Rank, Sadger, Schwerdtner, Steiner, Stekel.

[1] The Minutes of this meeting have not been preserved. According to the attendance lists, Freud presented a paper "On the Genesis of Fetishism." His article on "Fetishism" did not appear until 1927, in the *Internationale Zeitschrift für Psychoanalyse.* The numbering of the Minutes indicates that the meeting was recorded; unfortunately, this record was lost.

71

SCIENTIFIC MEETING *on March 3, 1909*

Present: Prof. Freud, Adler, Bass, Federn, Hitschmann, Rank, Sadger, Steiner.

Start of the Second Semester

PRESENTATION

Word and Thought

SPEAKER: DR. BASS

The speaker begins with a discussion of the relationship between the conscious and the unconscious, illustrating it by an optical parallel: he compares the conscious with that section of a dark room that is illuminated by a heliostat; the transition to the unconscious proceeds through innumerable, barely noticeable shadings, in unbroken continuity. It is true, however, that the path of our consciousness is anything but straight, its direction being influenced by a multitude of determinants beyond the reach of our will.

Whenever we succeed in lifting thoughts out of the unconscious into the conscious, we have to overcome considerable resistance. The greater the amount of repressed unconscious material that there is clinging to a thought, the greater is the amount of work needed to bring that thought into consciousness; by this formulation we want to re-emphasize the fact that frequently the boundaries between physiological and pathological thought processes are fluctuating and not clearly drawn.

The difficulties of bringing a thought into consciousness may even be surpassed when it becomes a question of verbalizing the conscious thought. One might perhaps conceive of the resulting interrelationships in terms of a formula, by way of the following equation: the word is related to the thought as the conscious is to the unconscious. This formula implies, of course, that it will be all the more difficult for the word to be at our disposal, the more repressed material adheres to the thought that word endeavors to express; and vice versa (compare what is said about these mechanisms in *The Psychopathology of Everyday Life*). But the word also has the function of releasing in the word-receiver an apportionment of the conscious and of the pertinent unconscious, similar in scope and, to the greatest possible extent in character to [that which held true for] the word-sender. This then would be the second criterion of a felicitous or infelicitous choice of word—the "choice," of course, being limited, for the path of the word out of the thought is as precisely determined as is the path of the thought out of the unconscious.

Bass thinks that it must be possible to find a way into the pathological from any point of the physiological. In this connection he is reminded of two borderline cases in which the individual suffers from a tormenting uncertainty with regard to the expression of a thought; this tendency manifests itself in the fact that, close on the heels of every precise word he utters, there follows a qualifying and balancing addition. One would be tempted to consider this a sign of pathological modesty if the following thought did not seem to be close to the truth: this person may, at a crucial moment, have said something without sufficient deliberation, or else, inhibited by deliberation, he may not have uttered the word necessary for bringing about a decision, even though he had the word at the tip of his tongue. The former is typified by the man who has tumbled into an inadequate marriage as a consequence of a rash courtship, the "henpecked husband"; the latter by the shy old bachelor, who missed his imagined or true happiness as a consequence of being too cautious in his pronouncements.

Who knows whether Socrates would have developed that striving for the most exact formulation of his thoughts if, at the critical moment, he had spoken in somewhat more decisive terms to his Xantippe?

DISCUSSION

PROF. FREUD, by way of introduction, comments that the few remarks made by the speaker have an overwhelming suggestive power. They evoke a variety of indefinite notions, but do not permit them to become condensed into definite ideas. The topic raised is worthy of attention from different angles, but first of all one must group together the questions that deal with the relationship between thought and word. Therefore, at the moment one can say only a few things, in no particular order, and without direct reference to the paper. To begin with, one presupposition is implied in the paper: that it is possible to separate the execution of resistance from the choice of a word—in a way, that first a thought struggles with the censor and only thereafter is it put into words. The resistance, of course, continues to be active in the selection of words and exerts an extraordinary influence over it. All we know about the conscious thought is its verbal expression. Hence, the question is: do the processes take place in areas other than the choice of words? or is the field of battle prior to that? or does the struggle go on all the way? The mode of expression then bears the stamp of all the characteristics of this struggle. A number of neurotics can be clearly recognized by their manner of speaking. In this way, a secondary similarity between obsessional neurosis and paranoia becomes evident. It would be impossible for the patients to speak vaguely, for instance, when they are in a bad mood if the resistance did not directly affect the choice of words. In such instances, one often has the impression that the thought was clothed in words that rendered it incapable of communication. The resistance, however, avails itself of still other means. Articulation and vocalization are the last stand on the battlefield (the patients talk so softly, or chew their words in such a way, that it is impossible to understand them). The effects of censorship or resistance reach far beyond the choice of words, and a model that tried to differentiate and localize the different stages would not do justice to the [actual] state of affairs.

Another comment, just as loosely connected with the topic, would be: there is no doubt that our consciousness, which, as we know, behaves like a sense organ, is at first (as one can observe in children and primitive peoples) turned in only one definite direction—that is, toward the *perception of the external world,* not toward psychological processes. In the course of time, this organ loses this one-sided attitude and, as the result of the [specific] qualities of feelings, gains the capacity to turn toward the psychic life. Thus it becomes secondarily the sense organ for our internal processes—to begin with, probably, for our ideas, in that these ideas become bound up with words. Consciousness is, in this respect, merely a sense organ for the residues of our word representations. This, in the last analysis, is the basis for our superiority over the animals. In reference to this, it is also very difficult to determine whether certain emotions are conscious or unconscious in the child. Residues of qualities that are characteristic of those optical and acoustic representations to which our consciousness was originally attuned must be continued in these word representations. The word representations have a very definite role with regard to the conscious and the unconscious, and we are still waiting for the solution to the following problems: what is the nature of this relationship? why is it that the repression of an idea can take place through its becoming unconscious? Nor is the problem solved of why, during the course of repression—which of course pertains to an affect—the corresponding idea also becomes unconscious. For the time being, we can only assume that the key to this problem lies in the word representation.[1]

[1] Later Freud found an answer to this problem in the theory that in repression the energy cathexis is withdrawn from the preconscious verbal idea, and thus the unconscious representation of an object becomes inaccessible to consciousness. (See Freud: *The Interpretation of Dreams* (1900), *S.E.*, 4 & 5; also his metapsychological works, e.g., "The Unconscious" (1915), *S.E.*, 14:166-215; "A Metapsychological Supplement to the Theory of Dreams" (1917), *S.E.*, 14:222-235; "A Note upon the 'Mystic Writing-Pad'" (1925), *S.E.*, 19:227-232; *An Outline of Psychoanalysis* (1939). New York: Norton, 1949; "Instincts and Their Vicissitudes" (1915), *S.E.*, 14:117-140.

We would recommend that the reader examine Freud's comments in this discussion with great attention; they are important not only in a theoretical sense but, if well understood, also in a practical sense. Much can be learned about the meaning of a patient's resistance if one observes his posture, speech, formulation of sentences, etc.

STEINER: In reference to the Professor's discussion, Steiner places in the foreground the practical question of whether it is possible to analyze a neurotic who speaks a foreign language, if the physician does not know or has not fully mastered that language. Steiner believes that it should be possible, since symptomatic actions and facial expressions offer important clues. He thinks, therefore, that the word does not play the exclusive role that we are at first inclined to ascribe to it. In neurotics, the word is anything but the full expression of the thought.

HITSCHMANN would have preferred to hear a more comprehensive presentation on "Speech and Thought"—and, of course, it should have been supported by examples.

The study of dialects would provide important clues to the character of a people; much can also be learned about the character of an individual from the way he expresses even unimportant things (the speed, the tonal quality, etc., of his speech). Even the lonely and taciturn person frequently has much to say; thus his not speaking, his silence at a certain point, is most expressive. And, as Freud has repeatedly pointed out, the chatterbox, in talking about everything under the sun, thereby frequently wants only to conceal a certain thought.

Strictly speaking, words and sentences are always only partially true, since man really communicates but a fraction of his feelings.

It should also be stressed how easily people give themselves away in the first sentence (for instance, when they meet someone); and how from the first utterance one can guess [the existence of] the most consequential complex (he gives some examples).

FEDERN would like to supplement one of the Professor's remarks by adding that the child comes to fantasies before he reflects. Federn thinks that the formation of concepts out of thoughts does not depend on words, but that one always has a dim feeling of the inner process. It may also be that between word and thought an intermediate stage exists.

ADLER emphasizes the fact that, in the course of the discussion, it has been revealed how fruitful and how worthy of attention is the topic the speaker introduced. He then takes off, to begin with, in line with the speaker's method, from the significance of abstract thinking or the importance of theory.

Similarly, in the search for words, it is a matter of setting up symbols for abstract ideas that do not exhaust the entire range of the faculty of intuition. The development of language and of words is merely a special case of human development; it is not so entirely different from processes in the animal kingdom. The animal also has means of communication. However, the fact that in man speech is in the foreground has its special reason; no doubt, it is connected with the development of the mouth as an organ. It seems that speech is nothing but an economical process for the stabilization of one of the means of communication. The relationship of speech to thought, to the intuitive faculty and to the power of discernment, must be regarded historically as a much later development.

The power of discernment is, however, the primary basis of thinking; from there we come to a theory of language that to some extent coincides with Strecker's.[2] But we should go further: thinking is, in all cases, an action that involves motility, an act of aggression (this is shown by the child, to whom a direct instinctual gratification is denied). The detour that leads to instinctual gratification is attained via the organ of the psyche, and fantasies surely make their appearance before word representations. Thus, we must regard the organ of the psyche as an organ of aggression, which directs the organism in such a way that the missing gratification can be attained via a detour, the result of movement. The evolutionary theories take a similar position: it is the change in habitat that plays the paramount role. The development of discernment begins with a change in habitat. From this point of view, one may arrive at the conception of language and thought as acts of aggression.

The psychology of the "old bachelor" plays a large role in analysis (one encounters fear of impotence, or fear that the wife might not be of equal birth, etc.). The "henpecked man" simply shows passive traits: a weak instinct of aggression,[3] pleasure in the passive transformations of instinct, etc.

[2] It has not been possible to find data in reference to Strecker.
[3] This is a theory that Adler carried to the point of absurdity.

RANK: In contrast to Steiner, Rank thinks that the language of psychoanalysis is very difficult to understand, by contrast with the language of love, which is international. The psychoanalyst needs an adequate knowledge of his patient's language, down to its most subtle possibilities for expression, and the nuances of dialect, in order not to throw into question the prospects for a cure.

BASS, in conclusion, stresses that he had merely intended to highlight certain difficulties encountered in the expression of a thought by way of putting it into a precise word; there invariably remain [thought] residues that cannot be expressed satisfactorily. He also refers to the difficulty in which many poets wear themselves out, finding the right expression for a thought. He sees the cause of this difficulty in a censorship that may be inserted between a conscious thought and its expression in words.

PROF. FREUD would like to call attention to a certain kind of dream, and to ask everyone whether this dream is known to him and what is his interpretation of it. Usually, these dreams deal, in numerous variations, with *climbing down a smooth wall or the outside of a house*. The dream usually ends in a feeling of anxiety when the ground is about to be reached.

BASS has such dreams, bound up with the feeling of a tourist's [sort of] gratification.

ADLER tells of two brothers who both have such dreams. One of them is a famous dancer (Bass's tourism!): this man suffered from *pavor nocturnus*, in the course of which he wanted to climb up the wall with his feet and screamed. His dreams were always linked with anxiety. The interpretation led to a scene of persecution (the patients are Russians), and a successful escape from police (father and mother had kept strict guard over the boys). As children, the patients had actually climbed over terrace, porch, and roof. The "smooth" wall is associated with a reminiscence involving a bath.

HITSCHMANN assumes that the smooth wall stands for the mother's body.

SADGER mentions a patient's dream that tends to confirm this assumption. The dreamer tumbles from a steep rock into water at the bottom of the cliff. As a four-year-old, the patient had been taken by his mother into her bath, and had climbed up on her because the water felt too cold. Tumbling down in the dream thus refers to the mother's smooth body, at the bottom of which is the vagina.

FEDERN remarks that the fairy tale of the glass mountain belongs in this context.

STEINER just recently interpreted such a dream to a tall man married to a small woman; the interpretation drew upon the conditions of his marriage.

RANK comments that if the dream deals only with descending, one would have to think of the genitals (*fellatio*, in popular speech, is called "going down," that is, down to the genitals).

PROF. FREUD: Bass' dream is useless, because it is too well rationalized. Adler's interesting considerations do not properly belong to the language of dreams. These dreams deal with climbing up on a smooth male body ("she has something substantial to hold on to" means well-rounded shapes): these are dreams of homosexual pleasure, deriving from the experiences of the child who climbs up on the father's body; at the point where the anxiety appears (just before touching the ground), one would have to insert the repressed pleasure in touching the genitals.

72

SCIENTIFIC MEETING *on March 10, 1909*

Present: Prof. Freud, Adler, Federn, Hitschmann, Joachim, Rank, Steiner, Stekel.

PRESENTATION

On the Psychology of Marxism[1]

SPEAKER: DR. ADLER

Since the speaker's discourse is to be published in due course, we shall limit ourselves here to outlining his main points.[2]

After describing and briefly characterizing Marx's achievements, Adler calls attention to the psychological and intellectual capabilities

[1] At this time, Adler was the only member of the Vienna Society who was a "Marxist," i.e., a member of the Austrian Social Democratic Party. As mentioned before, Freud showed no particular interest in socialist theories, even though he was on friendly terms with some leading socialists.

[2] Adler's bibliography, in *The Individual Psychology of Alfred Adler*, by Heinz and Rowena Ansbacher (New York: Basic Books, 1956), lists no such publication. According to these authors, an article by Adler entitled "Bolschewismus und Seelenkunde" ["Bolshevism and Psychology"] appeared in the *Internationale Rundschau* (Zürich), 4 (15, 16), 1918. That paper, however, is of no interest to us here.

that enabled the great thinker to gain so deep an insight into the process of social development (his analytic and synthetic powers, etc.).

His insight into natural and social processes enabled him, as did his psychological [capacity] for the intensive penetration of his field, to see clearly what is, through [our study of] analytic psychology, beginning to dawn on us with increasing clarity: *the primacy of instinctual life*. On the basis of his studies of political economy, which were guided by practical considerations, he established the foundations of economics, which in his view is to be comprehended as a study of the forms in which the convergence of the instinctual life and tendencies toward gratification finds expression. The gratification is achieved only by a detour of aggression [*Aggressionsumweg*], which encompasses the conditions of production.[3]

On a somewhat higher level of civilization, there appear altruistic ideas (such as sympathy, charity, tenderness, modesty), which are to rule the world from now on. Psychoanalysis, however, has shown us that these so-called "ideas" are neither innate nor derivatives of a moral sense, but are built up out of opposing impulses, which stem directly from the instinctual life. They are *reaction formations, which bring about an affective state that expresses itself as sensitivity* (sensitivity to debasement, degradation, ultimately to soiling). In most instances, the primary instinctual gratification is quite supersaturated, and any further manifestation of that instinct—such as avarice, envy, shamelessness—is answered by a defensive reaction that shows a kinship with the affect of disgust or with idiosyncrasy.

This sensitivity spreads over innumerable relationships in life. Among the proletariat, it exists with regard to every kind of degradation, and is the affect that lies at the root of class consciousness. Because this affective state always seeks to fend off degradation, it is impossible for the class-conscious proletariat to adopt an attitude of fatalistic resignation. This possibility can be believed in only if one does not see the affective state behind the "idea."[4]

[3] Rank's abbreviated recording makes it very difficult to understand Adler's argumentation.

[4] The influence of Trotsky, who was a personal friend of Adler, shows clearly in these reflections. It is perhaps of interest to note that [the practice of] psychoanalysis was forbidden in Russia after the First World War.

Marx's greatest achievement is to be seen in the fact that he brought this sensitivity into consciousness (the first full-scale analysis of masses) and that he then focused it on one point. This bringing of sensitivity into consciousness then carries with it the tendency toward levelling.

In conclusion, the lecturer expresses the hope that his exposition has demonstrated that the theory of class struggle is clearly in harmony with the results of our teachings on instincts.

DISCUSSION

PROF. FREUD opens the discussion with the remark that his attitude toward such lectures, which enlarge our horizon, can only be receptive.

At the beginning of the lecture, a formula came to his mind. The entire development of humanity could also be characterized, from the psychological point of view, by a formula in which two elements stood out: on the one hand, it is a question of an enlargement of the consciousness of mankind (analogous to the coming into consciousness of instincts and forces hitherto operating unconsciously); on the other hand, progress can be described as a repression that progresses over the centuries. Our culture consists in this: that more and more of our instincts become subject to repression, for which there are beautiful illustrations, particularly in poetic productions (see Rank: "The Incest-Motif").

When placed next to each other, these two characteristics seem to be entirely contradictory to each other, for with the progress of repression, more and more should become unconscious, and not the other way round. But then comes the liberating thought that these two processes are the condition for each other: the enlargement of consciousness is what enables mankind to cope with life in the face of the steady progress of repression. Freud believes that Rank expressed this idea in his *The Artist.*[5] That would be the introduction of psychology into historical studies.[6]

[5] *Der Künstler: Ansätze zu einer Sexualpsychologie* [*The Artist: The Beginnings of a Sexual Psychology*]. Vienna: Heller, 1907.

[6] See Freud: *Totem and Taboo* (1913), *S.E.*, 13:1-162; *Civilization and Its Discontents* (1930), *S.E.*, 21:57-145; *Moses and Monotheism* (1937-1939). New York: Vintage Books, 1955.

Turning to the topic of the lecture itself, it must be stated that Adler has failed to offer us any evidence of our line of thought in Marx. Rather, Adler has tried to present the psychological foundation for Marxist positions.

It would be desirable if Adler were to work out this topic and publish it in the *Schriften zur angewandten Seelenkunde.*

Adler's critique of the "ideas" seems to be particularly valuable: he has defined them psychologically in accordance with our views, and acknowledged them to be reaction formations. Freud would now like to make a proposal in regard to terminology. To say that these are not ideas but affective states seems to have departed from the usual mode of expression in psychology. One should say: these are reaction formations; from them are derived the affective states. He himself would not want to introduce sensitivity as a force. Everything that can be subsumed under this rather philosophical term is still an affective state, derived from reaction formations.

It is surprising that Adler should seek his analogies in a field as distant and as little understood as that of idiosyncrasies, while the appropriate and correct ones seem, indeed, to lie in the field of sexuality (shame, disgust, incest barrier). All in all, Freud would see in the emphasis on these analogies an essential impetus to our understanding. The erotic has become accessible through the study of the neuroses. As far as the fortunes of the other instincts (ego instinct, etc.) are concerned, they can probably be explored only through the study of the pathological symptoms of the social body.[7]

FEDERN knows little about this topic. He would only like to stress another point at which Marx and Freud are on common ground. Marx was the first to offer the suppressed classes the chance to free themselves of Christianity—by the new world outlook that he gave them. If sadism was converted into Christianity (masochism), Marx explained to men their masochism, thus making it untenable for them and once again setting free the primary instinct of self-preservation. This illustrates how, by bringing things to consciousness, one can lift

[7] A few years later, Freud turned this sentence around, asserting that it is only by means of the study of the ego instincts that the pathological symptoms of the social body are to be understood. See *Group Psychology and the Analysis of the Ego* (1921). *S.E.*, 18:67-143.

a repression. In this way the instinct of aggression has passed over into class consciousness.

JOACHIM remarks that the subject is too complicated and too remote for a critical evaluation.

The principle presented seems to him to be applicable to all ideas (even religious ones, the idea of God, the idea of the good, etc.); therefore, it is understandable that such theories can never be refuted by logical arguments. It seems to be true, however, that, in the mechanism of obsessional ideas as well as in the field of religion, the affect apparently overpowers these reactive strivings (for instance when, from otherwise religious persons, there suddenly comes forth a blasphemy).

RANK emphasizes one point touched upon by Adler: the entire history of ethics with its continually changing and contrary systems (the latest example: the hard, cruel Nietzsche and the gentle, compassionate Tolstoy) gives the impression of continuous and interdependent manifestations, forms of expression of the sadistic instinct. In Adler's sense, one might offer the following formulation: all ethical ideas are cultural reaction formations to all forms of aggressive impulses.

HITSCHMANN remarks that after the lecture all this appears quite self-evident to the listener, just as it seems natural that Adler had to succeed in the assimilation of social life and instinctual life. Hitschmann had difficulty only with regard to the concept of the enlargement of consciousness.

The individual who takes part in such a movement is aware only of purely personal inclinations as the motive for his participation; in this sense, Hitschmann found it difficult to deal with the concept of class consciousness, which is only a doctrine set forth by the leaders. For it is a question whether we are really faced with a metaphysical (or metapsychological) need, or with a "religious inoculation compulsion" [*Impfzwang*]?

It also would have been interesting to learn in what way Marx's teachings were derived from his personal psychology.

STEINER refers to Federn's comment that socialism is a substitute for religion. It is precisely this characteristic that makes him distrustful of it. To him, too, it looks like a religion, but in a bad sense; that is why he would not like to place it on the same level with analysis. How would it be to conceive of socialism too as a "neurosis"?

PROF. FREUD would like to report what, in the course of a chance conversation with Jung, he found out concerning the mechanism that is probably involved in eating idiosyncrasies. These are negative overcompensations, based on the repression of the coprophilic instinct. In most instances, the idiosyncrasy has to do with food that reminds the child of the excrements (soup, vegetables) (compare, in idiomatic speech: *Alpenspinat-Kuhfladen*, and the like).[8] Instead of refusing the particular food in as inconspicuous a manner as possible, the child raises an enormous fuss at the sight of the food, and declares over and over again that he is certainly not going to eat "that stuff," etc. What does this mean? Apparently the child is conscious of deserving appreciation. He protests loudly—in the form of overcompensation—the successful overcoming of his coprophilic inclinations. However, the child needs to protest in such a conspicuous way because this overcompensation in the repression is linked with a feeling of great insecurity: the child is still aware of a slight temptation.

RANK comments that, among adults, one regularly comes across the saying: "I just love to eat that, but it doesn't agree with me"—which indicates the character of repression.

ADLER, in his concluding remarks, thanks [the discussants] for the reception given to his arguments; he had not felt altogether certain about them. In agreement with Freud, he had characterized the ideas as reaction formations generated by an affective state.

It must be pointed out that the idiosyncrasies cannot be regarded in all instances as coprophilic. The most widely spread idiosyncrasy has to do with milk, [and is thus] obviously connected with the earliest form of nutrition.

Concerning the enlargement of consciousness that is implied in the concept of classes, Rank, in agreement with Freud, stated that what is involved here is an effect of sadism (he [Adler] calls it aggressive instinct), just as ethical ideas are. Furthermore, this makes it

[8] *Alpenspinat* ["spinach of the Alps"] means manure; *Kuhfladen* means cow dung; its literal translation, however, is "cow flat-cake."

clear that, with regard to socialism, it is not a matter of neurosis (Steiner): in the neurotic, we see instinct of aggression inhibited, while class consciousness liberates it; Marx shows how it can be gratified in keeping with the meaning of civilization: by grasping the true causes of oppression and exploitation, and by suitable organization.

Hitschmann's question about the conditions of existence and the vicissitudes of such a genius is quite justified. But we should approach this problem with great tolerance and, first of all, take leave of the ethical idea. The most important external circumstance[9] seems to have been that Marx found it impossible to become recognized as a university lecturer. Besides this, of course, he brought with him something else: his mind.

In conclusion, Adler wishes to stress that Marx's entire work culminates in the demand to make history *consciously*.

[9] The original manuscript has "*Impuls.*"

73

SCIENTIFIC MEETING *on March 24, 1909*

Present: Prof. Freud, Federn, Heller, Hitschmann, Hollerung, Rank, Sadger, Stekel.

Reviews and Case Reports by All Members Present

HITSCHMANN briefly reviews an article by Kotik on "The Emanations of Psychophysical Energy"[1] (review in *Wiener klinische Rundschau,* 23, 1909).

Hitschmann reports further on the case of a young man whose sexual life consists of petting servant girls and letting himself be fondled by them, which leads to an immediate ejaculation. Since his fifteenth year, he has indulged in such activities four to five times a day. One was the maid of his married sister; this explains the neurotic symptoms that appear on such visits. Because of the abnormal expenditure of sexual matter without complete sexual intercourse, the

[1] Original title: "Die Emanationen der psychophysischen Energie. Eine experimentelle Untersuchung über die unmittelbare Gedankenübertragung im Zusammenhang mit der Frage über die Radioaktivität des Gehirnes" ["The Emanations of Psychophysical Energy. An Experimental Study on the Direct Transmission of Thought, in Connection with the Problem of Radioactivity of the Brain"]. In: Löwenfeld's *Grenzfragen des Nerven- und Seelenlebens.*

boy has lapsed into a sort of exhaustion which is now, thanks to an imposed abstinence, slowly abating.

PROF. FREUD comments that this is simply a case of neurasthenia in which psychic factors do not make any contribution.

STEKEL thinks that the improvement is not that definite and, according to his experience, will above all not be a lasting one. Moreover, he does not believe in "neurasthenia"; totally different things lie behind these symptoms (in this case: ideas of incest with the sister).

There exists only one neurosis, with its somatic rudiments (the anxiety neurosis), and its specific variation (the obsessional neurosis). This neurosis consists of a disturbance of affectivity. Intellect and affects clash with each other; the disturbance lies in the subjugation of the intellect by the affects. Hysteria is a disturbance of affectivity brought on by repression. In this sense, the disturbances should be given different names, which correspond with this conception: *parapathy* should be substituted for neurosis, and *paralogia* for psychosis.

SADGER, in contradiction to Stekel, stresses the occurrence of pure emission neurasthenia ["wet dreams"]; these patients certainly have a characteristically sallow, pale complexion.

STEKEL upholds the contrary opinion about emission, maintaining that only fear of the consequences of losing a lot of semen has any damaging effect.

FEDERN refers to the question of the feeling of guilt in connection with emission. He mentions a patient's dream, which clearly shows that this feeling plays a definite role. (In the dream, the patient's mother is watching him, whereupon the dreamer interrupts his activity.)

PROF. FREUD discusses a case reported by Hitschmann. The patient was a girl who suffered from states of excitement and depression. These gradually subsided, during the course of her talks with the physician. Freud comments that, after a hysteria has been removed, a piece of paranoid dementia frequently comes to light. This explains why a number of cases of hysteria cannot be mastered by the [analytic] technique.

STEKEL supplements his recent report on a case of urolagnia [licking of urine] with some further details. The analysis of one of the patient's dreams disclosed that his perversion was just a splinter from a far more horrifying perversion: eating the flesh of the vagina. He performs this act[2] during an attack on the body of a murdered woman. The murdered women are mother and sister. Thus the licking of urine is but a feeble substitute for necrophilia.

PROF. FREUD comments that he has tried to find the proper place for cases of this kind theoretically, and to set up a category for them. Their essential characteristic is that the perversion manifests itself not directly as sexual activity, but as a symptom; it could be called a *compulsive perversion.*[3]

Attention must be called to the fact that the drive that we know as necrophilia very frequently occurs as an unconscious perversion. At present, for instance, Prof. Freud is treating a thirty-seven-year-old impotent man, who is actually an unconscious butcher of women. Until the time of his marriage four years ago, his sexual activity consisted of masturbation; its chief component, however, was the accompanying fantasy—that he would be butchered—which in this way included his desire to butcher, in a masochistically inverted form. The patient was very much in love with his mother and terribly afraid of his father. The passive components of his fantasy are: at bottom, the castration complex, and then the circumcision fantasy; the sacrifice of Isaac and the Esther episode made a deep impression upon him.

FEDERN raises the question of whether these necrophilic appetites are remnants of cannibalism, or are traceable to the child's pleasure in eating.

STEKEL reports about a five-year-old boy whose governess did everything possible with him. He masturbates, and she threatens to cut off [his penis]; the boy then imposes a penance upon himself: he stretches out on his bed, lying on his stomach. Thus he has the highly pleasurable contact of his genitals with what lies underneath

[2] Obviously, "fantasy" should be substituted for "act."

[3] At this time Freud had already recognized that a perversion is not simply the clinging to a component instinct, but has a more complicated structure, similar to that of a neurotic symptom.

him, and at the same time his position protects him from the danger of having his penis cut off.

Then Stekel has something to report on the genesis of a melancholia. The patient is a sixty-one-year-old woman who fell into a severe depression when she learned that a suitor of her daughter had shot himself because of the hopelessness of his love. She reproached herself severely, although actually she had rejected not this man, but another wooer. She loves her daughter so much that she will not grant her to anyone else. Now a homosexual longing has been awakened in her. When she is faced with the *fait accompli* of the daughter's marriage, her condition improves.

PROF. FREUD comments that all neuroses and psychoses have the same etiology and are traceable to analogous disturbances of the same instincts. The diversity of their forms comes about through their resorting to different mechanisms. Thus mania, for example, is nothing but a mechanism of repression, as Otto Gross certainly demonstrated.[4]

STEKEL thinks that every depression is mourning over the renunciation of sexual pleasure.[5]

PROF. FREUD considers this valid only in so far as mourning is nothing but a natural melancholia; this, however, does not explain anything.

HOLLERUNG reviews the contents of Ebstein's *Luther's Illnesses* (review in *Wiener klinische Rundschau*).[6]

PROF. FREUD: Referring to two remarks in French funny papers that were reported to him by a patient, Freud comments that the same symbols that people use and understand over and over again in the

[4] *Das Freudsche Idiogenitätsmoment und seine Bedeutung in manisch-depressivem Irresein Kräpelins* [*The Freudian Theory of the Origin of Concepts and Its Meaning in Kräpelin's Manic-Depressive Psychosis*]. Leipzig: Vogel, 1907.

[5] In "Mourning and Melancholia" (1917; *S.E.*, 14:243-258), Freud says essentially the same thing, when he states that melancholia sets in after the loss of a love object. He does so, of course, from a point of view quite different from Stekel's. In the same paper, Freud draws a parallel between mourning and melancholia, providing deep insight into both processes.

[6] See *Luthers Krankheiten und deren Einfluss auf seinen körperlichen und geistigen Zustand* [*Luther's illnesses and Their Influence on the State of His Body and Mind*]. Stuttgart: Enke, 1908. The review appeared in *Wiener klinische Rundschau*, 23, 1908, but was written by Stekel, not Hollerung.

form of jokes, sayings, couplets, they reject as arbitrary in our interpretations. One joke regards as well-known a piece of fairy-tale interpretation on which we have taken great pains: namely, Tom Thumb as penis (the giant, with the knife, representing the castration complex). The second joke is a striking illustration of what we have only recently said about dreams of climbing down a *smooth* wall; we interpreted these dreams as homosexual; in the joke, a woman's bosom is called a balcony (by contrast to the *smooth* male body, the female body has protuberances).

The difference in the form of suicide chosen by the two sexes demonstrates how symbolism extends even into death. The most primitive sexual symbolism, which has been known to us for the longest time, is revealed in the selection of the means of suicide. A man shoots himself with a revolver—that is, he plays with the penis; or else he hangs himself—that is, he becomes something that as a whole hangs down, a "penis" (*pendere*).

A woman knows three ways of committing suicide: jumping out of a window; throwing herself into the water; poisoning herself. The first means confinement [*Niederkommen* = coming down]; to go into the water means to give birth (since to emerge from the water means being born; see *The Myth of the Birth of the Hero*); and poisoning means pregnancy, first because the mother, suffering from nausea, seems to the child to have been poisoned, and secondly because the child believes that one gets children by eating particular foods (poisoned foods). Thus the woman fulfills her sexual function even in dying. One is reminded of Busch's verses to accompany the chickens' death by hanging: "Each one quickly lays an egg, and then death comes to her." [*Jedes legt noch schnell ein Ei und dann kommt der Tod herbei.*]

HELLER reports the recent publication of the answers sent in to the *Kunstwart* in response to its prize competition on the best solution of the problem of the sexual enlightenment of children.[7]

FEDERN reports on the contents of the last number of the *Journal of Abnormal Psychology*, edited by Morton Prince in Boston. It is his

[7] We have found no reference to such a competition in the *Kunstwart* of 1909. (See, however, Minutes 77 and 79.)

general impression that the apparent adherence [in it] to Freud's teachings is actually nothing but antagonism in disguise. The authors explain everything in a quite jejune fashion, evidently intent on proving that all of Freud's doctrine is superfluous.

Federn reports further on the case of a lady who is anaesthetic, and who suffers from heart palpitations and particularly from a violent itching of the skin. From his previous experience, Federn recognizes such itching of the skin as a consequence of sexual excitement during a period of abstinence. What makes this case interesting is the fact that the patient has no sexual sensations, so that the entire process remains unconscious.

STEKEL remarks that the whole skin is the woman's erotogenic zone.

SADGER: In connection with the case of glove fetishism (paper presented at Salzburg), Sadger adds that the patient was a "smeller": he liked to smell toes. There was also some evidence of foot fetishism. His glove fetishism is connected originally with feces (only smooth and glossy, brown or yellow gloves excite him). Grey gloves are associated in his mind with nasal mucus: he had been threatened with having to wear gloves because he used to pick his nose.

74

SCIENTIFIC MEETING *on March 31, 1909*

Present: Prof. Freud, Federn, Hitschmann, Rank, Sadger, Steiner, Stekel.

PRESENTATION

On the Psychopathology of Hauptmann's *Griselda*

SPEAKER: DR. STEKEL

The speaker opens with the remark that, struck first of all by the emotional tone in the reviews of Hauptmann's new work, he had made up his mind to track down the causes for this violent opposition. After seeing the play, it became clear to him why it was bound to provoke opposition, for the work touches on a sensitive spot in man.

He would like to report on some of his personal impressions of the drama. It is a drama of jealousy, indeed of a quite specific form of jealousy. To him it seems to be the third in an ascending line of dramas: *Othello* [Shakespeare], *Herodes and Mariamne* [Hebbel], *Griselda.* In *Othello* it is the simple jealousy of a man for a woman—a man whose calling is murder and victory, who, in strangling the woman, does the final service of love to her, and at the same time clearly gratifies his sadism. The jealousy of the second drama is more complex: Herodes is so much in love with his wife that he cannot grant her after his death to another man. He therefore gives the order to kill her if he should die. Mariamne, when she hears of this, is so deeply wounded in her feminine pride that she punishes him in the cruelest way—by pretending unfaithfulness—so that he kills her. In this, Herodes, too, is a Tartar, a sadist; thus jealousy is once again linked up with sadism. Hauptmann's drama introduces a new form of jealousy—namely, that toward a son yet unborn. The Griselda theme Hauptmann borrowed from Boccaccio, but there the version is somewhat different. In Boccaccio's tale, Griselda is a simple woman who knows how to adapt herself very skillfully to her actual circumstances as a countess. She is put to the test by her husband in a very hard way: her children are taken away from her, and she herself is driven into solitude. Finally, she is to come to the castle to serve as a maid to the Count's new bride. When she suffers even this in silence, the Count discloses to her that all of these were only tests, which she has endured splendidly. Fully restored to her previous position, she learns that the Count's new bride is her own daughter. Here, then, the daughter appears, so to speak, as her mother's rival.

Using Boccaccio's story as a basis, Halm[1] had already dramatized this legend; there, the end is tragic, in that Griselda finally leaves the tyrant altogether.

Hauptmann created his own version of the legend; he drew the Count as a neurotic; the speaker, in giving a detailed account of the drama's contents, tries to demonstrate this in particulars. The first act presents the couple as both possessed of strong sadistic impulses, while the man shows clear masochistic desires as well. In the second act, we learn about the Count's peculiar mode of living, which is strikingly reminiscent of the penance that neurotics impose upon themselves in order to atone for some wrongdoing. The masochistic component also benefits from this. The Count displays masochistic inclinations in other ways, too, for he is always searching for the powerful woman. He looks for the man in the woman; from this atti-

[1] Friedrich Halm (1806-1871), Austrian poet.

tude, as well as from a remark of his steward ("he is a woman-hater"), we may conclude that homosexual inclinations are not foreign to the Count. Eberhard quite clearly characterizes his nephew as a neurotic when he says that the Count would be a good morsel for the medical faculty and belongs in the Sorbonne. His father, too, is twice referred to as a peculiar man. It is also a neurotic trait that the Count thinks that for him to take a noblewoman as his wife would be a terrible calamity. His aversion to noblewomen, his avoidance of any contact with them, is in striking contrast to his predilection for peasant girls.

In the next scene (the hunting party), the Count overpowers Griselda for a second time, and recognizes that this awakening of her masochistic streak is the surest way to her love. After the wedding, Griselda undergoes a strange change, which has been unjustly criticized as too sudden and altogether impossible. One can accept it quite readily, if one considers how much talent for being a harlot or a noblewoman, for playing "her ladyship" [*Gnädigen*], is hidden in every woman.

After a rather long interval, the poet takes us back to the castle, where soon the birth of a boy will take place. Having lived very happily with Griselda for some time, the Count has become sad and moody upon learning of Griselda's pregnancy. He does not want to obtain medical assistance for her; he is jealous of the physician, too. The latter believes that he has recognized that behind the Count's brutal and tyrannical bearing is concealed a very tender and sensitive heart. The Count now admits to him that he hates the child, because it will take his wife's love away from him, etc. He hates the still unborn child "as if he had had a bloody strife with him in another world." While Griselda is giving birth, he has thoughts of murder; after the delivery, he leaves the castle when Griselda inquires about the baby, who has been sent to relatives. Only after Griselda has returned to her former life—that is, after she has left him—does his love reawaken; he then becomes reconciled with her and [gives up] his hatred for the child.

The speaker considers it unnecessary to go on throwing light on the clearly underlined sado-masochistic character of the two main figures. He is interested only in the jealousy and its sources. Boccaccio had hinted at a jealousy between mother and daughter similar to that between father and son in Hauptmann's work. The Count has a presentiment of the future rival in his son; and we, from our point of view, can only agree with him. Delivery is, indeed, a sexual event, which the mother carries through with the child. But whence could the awareness of this rivalry have come to the Count? Being a neurotic, he has probably experienced it in his own person. We must trace his aversion to noblewomen to the fact that he identifies them with his mother. With them, he is impotent because they conjure up the image of his mother. With whores, he is brutal. He loved his mother and hated his father, and he has become aware of this hatred. In the child he sees the retribution of Fate bursting in upon him for this. This gives him the right to his jealousy. Thus, psychologically speaking, the Count's jealousy is fully justified; the speaker himself has come upon several cases of this kind in his practice.

Therefore, we should protect the poet against the unfounded attacks, which are due to a lack of understanding. The sado-masochistic character of the neurotic is extraordinarily well portrayed. We also see that jealousy is intimately connected with sadism. Jealousy is, one might say, sadism that has been turned against one's own person, and yet [at the same time continues to] seek out opportunities to torment the loved person. Their sadistic streak drives people to seek out objects for their jealousy. Jealousy has yet another root in the projection of one's own unreliability onto the other person.

DISCUSSION

PROF. FREUD, who knows the drama only from this paper, would like to arange the subjects we have before us for evaluation today into three groups: (1) the question of Hauptmann; (2) Stekel; (3) the problem itself.

Ad 1. Today, as often before, Freud asked himself why it is that Hauptmann is such an uncongenial fellow: in spite of all the misgivings about this new drama, one must admit that it deals with an interesting problem. It should have been Hauptmann's task not to show us this problem, but to present it in a poetic form, capable of absorbing and stimulating us. That ability, apparently, Hauptmann does not possess. The naked brutality with which he develops his dramas is as repulsive in *Griselda* as it is in the others. Freud has perceived no poetic beauty in the drama; the hero is a mad dog who belongs in a lunatic asylum. Since Hauptmann created the hero, the poet must be reproached for not knowing how to present psychological problems in a way that might take hold of us. As Bach very rightly pointed out in a *feuilleton* in the *Arbeiterzeitung* just a few days ago, on the occasion of the performance of *Elektra*, the art of the poet does not consist of finding and dealing with problems. That he should leave to the psychologists. Rather, the poet's art consists of obtaining poetic effects out of such problems; experience shows that these problems must be disguised if they are to produce such effects; furthermore, that the effect is by no means diminished if one merely suspects what the problems are and none of the readers or listeners can make out clearly what the effect is. Thus the poet's art consists essentially in covering over. What is unconscious ought not, without more ado, be rendered conscious; of course it must become conscious to a certain degree—that is, to the point at which it still affects us, without our occupying ourselves with it in our conscious thoughts. At the point where this becomes possible, art leaves off. We have the right to analyze a poet's work, but it is not right for the poet to make poetry out of [*poetisieren*] our analyses.[2] Yet, this seems to be a sign of our times. The poets dabble in all possible sorts of sciences, and then proceed to a poetic working up of the knowledge they have acquired. The public is fully justified in rejecting such products. Bribed by the poet's psychological treatment of the problem, we ourselves may become more lenient in our criticism.

Ad 2. Freud can express himself in more pleasant terms. The broaching of this theme is quite praiseworthy. Stekel surely gave an appropriate comment on the work, aided by the fact that the poet himself has underlined almost everything with importunate distinctness. In addition, the speaker imposed upon himself the wise restraint of the interpreter, and his conclusions are irreproachable, if he looks at the work not as a poetic creation but as a "case." Some minor

[2] This is the literal translation of Rank's record. However, the following formulation probably expresses more clearly the meaning of the sentence: "but the poet has no right to use the results of our analyses, in their naked form, for his poetic creations."

details might be interpreted differently. The Count is not impotent with noblewomen; rather, he hates them—that is, he cannot forgive his mother for having preferred his father to him.

Ad 3. As far as the problem itself is concerned, one must reproach Hauptmann for having fused together two problems that have nothing to do with each other: there is no true inner connection between the theme of "jealousy of the son" and the theme of "sadistic marriage."

It is also one of the poet's tasks to facilitate our empathy with his hero, not to draw him as such a repulsive individual that we cannot take any interest in his fate. Such a fusion of problems, for which two reconciliations are then needed, is artistically quite unsuitable. The conclusion in particular is unsuccessful and inconsistent, because the problem of jealousy between father and child is insoluble.

It should also be pointed out that the birth of the boy is a "birth of the hero" (*Myth of the Birth of the Hero*). The entire story rests on the presupposition of the father's hostility toward the son. It is quite apparent here how eminently justified this assumption is and that the father proves the son to be right in this respect.

The Count's Oriental jealousy of the physician is completely out of place and the effect, therefore, is one of madness.

The twofold conception of the hero—on the one hand as the most masculine of men, a sadist, and on the other as a tender-feeling weakling—makes him incomprehensible to us. To present such complicated characters is a matter for a case history. The figure on the stage must bring with him a simple character structure, and the poet must know how to simplify such highly complicated psychic processes.

STEKEL believes that it is unnecessary to defend Hauptmann as a poet. It is self-evident that a judgment of his work cannot be based on a pathological framework. Nor should Hauptmann be reproached for having fused two problems.

Hauptmann chose this material because he himself is the tender, sensitive person whom he was able to portray in the person of the Count. Flight into solitude frequently plays a role in his works. The objection to the lack of disguise in the play is justified.

FEDERN bears out that the play is immensely impressive, even as a work of art—primarily, however, because it deals with deep, generally human problems. The most important of these problems is jealousy. In Hauptmann we see clearly that neurosis is not a prerequisite for, but a disturbance of, poetic creativity. Hauptmann wages a battle against severe unconscious inhibitions; this struggle betrays itself in almost all his works, and particularly in the family dramas (*Michael Kramer*, *Friedensfest* [*The Coming of Peace*], *Einsame Menschen* [*Lonely Lives*]).

As far as Hauptmann's private life is concerned, Federn knows that he left his first wife, who adored and idolized him, and that he insisted on keeping her four sons with him and did not even once allow her to see them. Nothing more cruel could be done to a woman. He was so insanely jealous of his second wife, who is a concert violinist, that he never permitted her to make a public appearance. She must always be near him; indeed, he awakens her even at night to write down an idea that has come to him. His need for solitude can be seen in the fact that he built for himself eight cottages in different localities, where he can work in seclusion and without disturbance.

From the fact that the Count tells the physician that he practices a wicked art, one would conclude that Hauptmann has an idea of Freud's theories.

In the play, it is a question of sheer sexual sadism, and this may very well be related to the problem of jealousy. The Count tries to find the woman on whom he can rely; when he sees Griselda resisting every man, she is exactly the right person. Griselda herself is no "sadist"; like every woman, she defends herself against men, and gives up this defense as soon as she has found her man. In Griselda one cannot find any sadism that could be interpreted as perverse. The person who is only sexually a sadist may be otherwise a very sensitive individual.

Federn thinks that the homosexual tendency that Stekel assumes, could be contested, as well as Stekel's definition of jealousy. Ultimately, jealousy is really nothing but an elementary anxiety about the woman.

HITSCHMANN thinks that the Count's wish not to have a child should be discussed. This wish is met with quite frequently even without regard to financial considerations; the desire not to be disturbed in one's love life certainly plays a great part in this, and one might perhaps explain the Count's psychology in this way. This disturbance of his sexual relations, in conjunction with the ensuing abstinence, may have driven him into an acute psychosis. It is understandable that he should recover, when these difficulties are no longer present. This would mean that his jealousy is in effect nothing but some form of anxiety about the woman.

We must admit that Hauptmann was not successful in all of his plays. One is most deeply impressed by his purely poetic work, such as, e.g., *Hannele*,[3] where he does not deal with subtle [psychological] problems.

Hauptmann's second wife is said to be his first wife's sister or sister-in-law.

RANK, leaving aside altogether Hauptmann's artistic qualities, upholds his right to make a psychological evaluation [of him]. A glance at Hauptmann's works, and especially his latest drama, discloses that he is not, as Stekel thinks, a person of tender feelings but, in terms of his innermost, and probably repressed nature, a cruel, brutal, sadistic character. In daily life, purely on the surface, he may show, as his picture indicates, a delicate, feminine, tender, compassionate nature. The robust, brutal fellows whom he creates over and over again in his dramas (from Moritz Jaeger; via Florian Geyer; to Fuhrmann [Drayman] Henschel, the first ravisher of Rose Bernd—this play, incidentally, like *Griselda*, begins with rape) are men such as he himself would like to be and could be, in accordance with his innermost nature. Juxtaposed to these men of violence are, on the one hand, a group of slavishly submissive young maidens (in *Florian Geyer*, *Der arme Heinrich* [*Henry of Auë*], and others—the problem of Käthchen von Heilbronn;[4] and on the other hand a group of robust women of force (Hanne Schäl, Rose Bernd, etc.); both these types of women are united in Griselda.

In the Griselda problem, Hauptmann was stimulated only by the sado-masochistic theme, as is true for many of his other themes, ([Der] *arme Heinrich*, etc.). He was intent only on explaining psychologically, in which he succeeded; but this cannot be the poet's task,

[3] *Hanneles Himmelfahrt* [*Hannele's Ascension*].

[4] Play by Heinrich von Kleist.

and for this reason he also failed. Having found the theme of the removal of the child alongside that of sadism in the traditional version of the story, he proceeds to explain this trait as well, in a psychologically irreproachable way, in terms of jealousy of the child. It is a striking fact that Hauptmann's interest in the act of birth seems to be exclusively sadistic; this comes out clearly in his first work (*Before Dawn*) as well as in Rose Bernd's animal-like delivery, and elsewhere. This connection between jealousy, especially where it concerns the child, and sadism seems to have deeper roots, for we encounter it also in Hebbel's terrible jealousy of his illegitimate son Max.

As far as the problem of modern poetic art is concerned, Rank can only agree with the Professor's remarks; he himself had earlier indicated, in his *Artist*, that when the unconscious is made conscious art ceases to exist. However, this is by no means a sign of a deficiency of artistic skill in Hauptmann's case; rather, it is an inescapable sign of the development of our times, which documents the deterioration of art as consciousness advances (Hofmannsthal, Wedekind, etc.). The poet can cope with his personal conflicts only if he brings them to consciousness as far as is possible, but then he is not in a position to analyze them in universally valid human terms; they remain all too subjective, and it is understandable that the public must reject them.

SADGER thinks that Hauptmann is lacking in greatness, character, and health. Hebbel and Kleist, for example, were also markedly morbid personalities, yet they kept their greatness as well. Even though they brought all their conflicts into their works, they still rose above their unconscious forces. Hauptmann created no great character, but only weak people. Nevertheless, each of Hauptmann's dramas gives evidence of a genuine poet. He was not able to bring his unconscious down into his writing, and thus to be freed from his neurosis. He is always under the sway of his unconscious, unable to rise above it.

As for a homosexual tendency in the Count, Sadger would also contest the idea. Stekel should have discussed in greater detail the transformation in Griselda, and he should have explained the hero's predilection for strong women.

STEINER is convinced that Hauptmann is evidence of the fact that a neurotic is not suited to be a great poet. Anything else would do for a poet rather than a neurosis. The neurotic is lacking, above all, in unity of character; that is why it is, above all, understandable that he cannot be fully figured out.

PROF. FREUD responds to some attempts at defending Hauptmann by representing him as a neurotic; he asserts that in this defense Hauptmann has actually been given up. Hauptmann invariably depicts only himself and never the problem. The correct evaluation is to be found only through a comparison of Hauptmann with Ibsen. Surely Ibsen is not the more abnormal personality of the two. Ibsen, with his self-containment, unity, and simplification of problems, along with his art of concentration and concealment is a great poet, whereas Hauptman is the neurotic who portrays himself alone.

The one thing Freud is willing to concede is that the two problems—that of jealousy and that of sadism—are interconnected, and not merely superficially. But here the complications make the connection opaque. Jealousy fits quite well into the conception of the Count as a great sadist. But this weakling, who is indicated as a sadist, might well be the poet himself. There is no reason to see in this a sign of the decline of art. Only a few years ago Ibsen showed us the summit of modern art. This is an isolated phenomenon which [historical] development will soon be on its way to bypassing.

75

SCIENTIFIC MEETING *on April 7, 1909*

Present: Prof. Freud, Adler, Federn, Graf, Hitschmann, Hollerung, Joachim, Rank, Sadger, Steiner, Stekel, Wittels.

Dr. M. Karpas from New York as guest [a charter member of the New York Psychoanalytic Society].

PRESENTATION

On the Psychology of Lying

SPEAKER: RANK

Having stated briefly that the comments to follow are based predominantly on the observation of several persons, the speaker then turns to his topic, which he would like to divide into two questions:

1. An examination of the psychology of lying (its characteristics and mechanisms, etc.);

2. An examination of the psychology of the liar (i.e., the character of those given to lying).

Of these two independent questions, only the second one will be the object of today's discussion. Not being at all versed in the pertinent literature, Rank can merely offer a sketch of the first topic.

Ad 1. Because of our strictly deterministic concept of lying, our point of view is bound to differ from all others. From this conception it follows, entirely by deduction, that all lies have the character of a compromise (they contain a bit of truth) as well as a tendency toward wish-fulfillment—characteristics that can easily be ascertained in any lie. The relationship between webs of lies and fantasies is quite varied and instructive, and the speaker, in drawing a parallel between these two psychic phenomena, elaborates on it.

Ad 2. In speaking of the "determination of the lie," we do not, of course, have in mind objective but psychic determination. By this distinction, we really exclude from our examination all sorts of "white lies" ([the outcome of] compelling external motivations) and draw into our examination precisely those lies that appear almost without any external motivation—the so-called "pathological lies." In addition to the absence of external motivation, these lies have several other striking characteristics: they occur, so to speak, for their own sake; they are often so clumsy that they cannot serve any external purpose. It is easy to see that *they are not at all meant to disguise what it is really all about, but spring from the need to conceal some other thought or complex. Concealment* is thus the essential thing (lie = concealment of the truth; otherwise it is a fantasy). Another remarkable characteristic of these pathological lies confirms this conception: their extraordinary *power of resistance,* even in the face of the most striking evidences of their untenability (see the fairy tale of "Our Lady's Child," Grimm #3).[1] If under the persistent pressure of arguments

[1] The substance of the fairy tale is briefly as follows: A young girl in heaven is given the task of keeping the keys while the Virgin Mary is away. The girl is to take care of all the rooms except the thirteenth, whose door she is strictly forbidden to open. However, the girl, unable to resist her curiosity, opens the door and sees the Trinity "in fire and splendor." She touches the light of heaven, and her finger becomes golden. Upon her return, the Virgin Mary asks the girl whether she opened the forbidden door. The girl denies it, although her golden finger betrays her. As punishment, the girl loses her power of speech and is banished to live in a wild forest. A king discovers her and takes her as his wife. She bears him a child; but on the first day after his birth, the Virgin Mary appears to the young queen and demands that she confess to having opened the forbidden door. The young woman denies it again, and Mary takes her child from her. The people accuse the queen of having devoured her child, but the king protects her. However, after the same thing has happened for the third time, the queen, unable to speak and to defend herself, is condemned to burn at the stake. Finally, when the flames are about to consume her, she admits in her thoughts that she opened the door. The Virgin Mary extinguishes the flames and returns her children to her.

[to the contrary], they are conceded, it is by way of an expression of *shame;* this gives us reason to conjecture that we are dealing with the concealing of a *sexual complex.* The compulsion with which this takes place allows us to guess that in this complex there is something unconscious. We can, thus, offer the following formulation: *in pathological lying, it is a question of a compulsion toward the persistent concealment of an unconscious sexual complex.*

In a particularly crass case of pathological lying, it could be ascertained that it was connected with infantile masturbation and its concealment, as well as its subsequent repression. That was as far as observation went. Since it was made without analysis, however, it seems necessary to insert here a piece of theory that will make possible a preliminary explanation of this connection.

Probably all children lie, just as all children masturbate; there must therefore be specific conditions for the development of a pathologically mendacious character. The *first* condition is "pathological" masturbation—that is, masturbation that is very early, excessive, and long continued.[2]

The *second* condition is the fact that masturbation is linked to lying, which in most cases comes into being by way of the concealment of masturbation. On the other hand, through this conjunction, the "normal" mechanism of lying comes to be anchored in sexuality, and its capability emerges for later pathological utilization. By masturbation is always to be understood here the conscious stimulation and gratification of the genital zone, and not the earliest instinctive masturbation that is proper to unconscious eroticism; it is the former that also brings about the conscious concealment of the activity.

The *third* condition for the development of a mendacious character is the success of this concealment, i.e., the fact that the child is not caught masturbating.

All of these, however, are still preliminary conditions. The decisive thing is the fact and the kind of the *repression* of the masturbation complex.

If, in the course of advancing psychosexual development, pathological masturbation is subjected to a normal, automatically carried

[2] See Minutes 109, this volume.

through repression (sexual repression), this process, because of the abnormality of the masturbation, does not move forward smoothly but by way of a violent struggle. As the first psychological manifestations of this struggle there appear sexual guilt feelings, so well known to us in cases of masturbation (the belief that others are taking note of the masturbation, etc.). If this defensive struggle constantly increases in intensity, it finally results in the *conscious rejection* of masturbation (as unhealthy, degrading, etc.). This conscious rejection, which we might express in the formula, "You must not masturbate," proves too weak to counteract the inclination, and is therefore repressed into the unconscious. The place of the prohibition formula is then taken in consciousness by a disavowal of the fact, by the perpetual concealment of the truth—namely, that the person still continues to masturbate.

The unconscious compulsion to lie (to conceal the truth) thus comes about as a reaction to the fact of masturbation—which, even though it has become unbearable, the person in question is too weak to overcome. This is conjoined with a displacement from the sexual to another realm—a process that comes close to being a spreading out of veils [*verhüllende Erweiterung*].

The compulsion to lie is a reaction formation in so far as the individual has to establish, so to say, again and again, "It is not true (that I masturbate)," because he is not at all sure of his victory over the drive. Thus, in these people, the constant disavowal of the fact of their masturbation has become fixated as its characterological replacement; the mechanism of this process is similar to that shown by Freud for the anal character.

The sublimation in the mendacious character consists of the fact that the compulsion to lie is turned into its opposite; this results in a conspicuous love of truth, an inclination to frankness ("honest Joe"). The kind of character that will develop depends on the way in which masturbation was practiced, how it was concealed, and especially how it is broken off. Just as the compulsion to lie becomes fixated as a replacement in consciousness, only after the defense against the masturbation complex has become unconscious, the truth-loving character is probably determined by the *holding in consciousness of defensive thoughts* and by the conscious suppression of masturbation (one positive and three negative observations support this [formulation]). The prohibition formula "You must not masturbate" operates consciously, but it has a counterpart, so to speak, in the unconscious "You must not lie," that is, the compulsion to tell the truth.

During the course of the examination of his topic, the speaker has strayed from his theme and come closer to a *psychology of the masturbator*. The character of the masturbator, whose most prominent traits will be enumerated below, has much in common with the anal character, not only in regard to its mechanism but also in regard to its content:

1. *Cleanliness* that can be of anal origin just as well as it is of masturbatory origin, whenever it takes the form of a washing compulsion (in men it is perhaps more likely to be of anal origin, in women of genital origin).

2. The tenacious holding on to a lie, and stubbornly persevering in it, calls for a great amount of defiance.

3. In *avarice*, we find a curious analogue to the character of the masturbator—specifically in frugality, which includes the passion to collect. Indeed, the link with money is by no means characteristic of the anal zone alone; the speaker once made the attempt to arrive at a psychology of prostitution on the basis of a link between money and the genital zone.

This parallelism between anal and masturbatory character does not come as a great surprise to us. In both cases, we are dealing with the repression of a piece of infantile erotism, in two erotogenic zones that initially had equal value. Yet it is not impossible that these conformities flow from a more general autoerotic character.

Accordingly, independent masturbatory characteristics would be:

4. The *punctuality* so frequently encountered in neurotics. (This may very likely still be part of the anal character's passion for order, closely connected with the compulsive deadlines onanists set themselves, which seem to be some kind of overcompensation: *from now on*, to miss no more deadlines.)

5. *The tendency to making a business of keeping things secret*, which leads to concealing everything in the most ridiculous manner, to doing everything alone and without witnesses (artists who can work

only when alone; Irma, in Binswanger's analysis, who can eat only when she is alone) [see below].[3]

6. *Shyness* and its opposite, which correspond [respectively] to lying and the fanaticism for the truth.

7. A special trait: almost all *suicide attempts* in the puberty period are connected with the inability to overcome masturbation, to put an end to it by setting a fixed date. Perhaps it is the repression of this compulsive idea of a fixed date that produces the unconscious compulsion to set a last and indeed, an effective deadline.

8. *The urge to steal or to appropriate things.* To pathological lying, in all its characteristics, corresponds kleptomania (no external reason; the act is committed out of an unconquerable desire; frequently it is energetically denied, confessed with shame, etc.).

Stekel, following Otto Gross, has already indicated the "sexual root of kleptomania." Gross' formula was: secretly doing something forbidden; Stekel added: this forbidden thing is unfaithfulness, adultery, the temptation to which is fought by women who are not satisfied in their married life; and in the course of this struggle, they appropriate penis symbols. This is certainly correct, but it is only superficial. This temptation to commit adultery, strong as it may be, can never produce a pathological compulsion symptom, such as kleptomania; only an infantile sexual affect is capable of rendering the whole reaction pathological, and this affect is given in masturbation and its repression. "To do the forbidden thing in secret" always referred, at first, to masturbation. The struggle against the temptation to be unfaithful is nothing but the struggle against the temptation of the forbidden (masturbation), a struggle now continued in the realm of heterosexuality. And, indeed, it is the women who masturbated excessively in their youth who cannot be satisfied in marital life. Moreover, the search for the penis fits better into the picture of defense against masturbation than into that of adultery. The fact that most of these kleptomaniac women are at the same time pathological liars does not surprise us. We welcome this confirmation of our viewpoint. Just as the pathological lie serves to conceal masturbation (defense), so, on the other hand, the symptomatic act of kleptomania betrays the fact that the person is still masturbating—that is, that she is "doing the forbidden thing in se-

[3] Ludwig Binswanger: *Versuch einer Hysterieanalyse. Jb.*, 1:174-356, 1909.

cret." Thus the pathological lie and the pathological urge to steal are the unconscious manifestations of the drive and the defense against it: the repressed defense manifests itself in lying, the repressed drive in the urge to steal.

In Grillparzer's case, for instance, the simultaneous occurrence of pathological lying and the urge to steal (see his diaries) becomes comprehensible in terms of his masturbatory character; it is perhaps no accident that the poet who fought masturbation with the greatest effort and the least success, Kleist, gave us, in the tale of "Michael Kohlhaas," the tragedy of the excessively honest man who is afflicted with a painful sense of righteousness almost bordering on the pathological. This, however, leads us too far afield.

The purpose of this paper was merely to draw attention to the connection of the mendacious character to infantile masturbation and the form of its repression; even if the proof of this was not successful in all points, yet the fact was forced upon us through the observation of several individuals.

Binswanger's analysis helps greatly to confirm the conception set forward here with regard to this process: masturbation plays a much more important role in it than comes through in the case history. The patient has displaced the entire masturbation complex to the oral zone. She sets herself fixed dates for fasting as a penitence for her *lies* [just as the masturbator sets himself deadlines for breaking off the habit] (pp. 188 and 315).[4] "Lie" here stands for masturbation; this confirms the unconscious connection. Binswanger correctly interprets her hunger as sexual hunger; her fasting is, then, sexual abstinence—that is, a defensive struggle against masturbation (especially p. 185). The patient's washing compulsion is itself evidence of her excessive masturbation (p. 253). The patient offers the information that she has never had anything to do with masturbation; apart from being [a manifestation of] resistance to treatment—and throwing new light [on the nature of her resistance]—this assertion is to be explained in terms of her mendacious character. The fact that the patient gave this information without affect (a fact that Binswanger stresses, and which probably misled him into stopping where he did), also points

[4] These and the following page references refer to Binswanger's paper (see footnote 3 above).

to the fact that her assertion has its source in her mendacious character; indeed, the lies are presented as the truth, and therefore must not betray themselves through affects.

The tale of "Our Lady's Child" (Grimm #3) offers a second confirmation: the stubborn perseverance in the lie, linked with the transgression of the sexual injunction (the symbolism of the forbidden door = masturbation; compare also [Grimm's tale] #9b) is a brilliant representation of the etiological conjunction.

DISCUSSION

STEKEL is not yet in a position to pass judgment on what we have heard; in any case, we cannot flatly reject it without having tested its correctness.

It is his impression that the speaker enormously overrates masturbation. From two cases Stekel learned that for the child, when he lies, it is only a question of doing something forbidden, something that his parents have indicated it is impermissible to do. That is how the concept of lying becomes conjoined with that of sin.

Stuttering, Stekel says, is merely a specific form of lying. In addition, the child is led to lie by his desire [to find out] whether or not his parents guess what he knows; it is a question here of testing the adults (Hans). This may refer in many cases to masturbation. One of his cases subsequently indulged in intensive masturbation.

For the time being, Stekel would not accept what Rank said about conscious repudiation.

All poets were great liars; perhaps they also all masturbated? Lying is the first stirring of creative power.

The fairy tale, until now unknown to him, is interesting, inasmuch as it shows how the first contact with the problem of sex releases anxiety.

PROF. FREUD does not wish the paper to be submitted for publication, because it involves an unwarranted sort of scientific work and, in addition to [making] various minor mistakes [also makes] some gross methodological ones.

This difficult topic can be dealt with only by way of analysis, and its problems can be resolved only on the basis of careful and painstaking observations. Although it seems quite probable that these things are true, it would be methodologically altogether incorrect to communicate them to others.

Speculations such as those presented today are for us without value. Our concern is with far-reaching certainties, and these can be attained only through analytic work. There is no merit in having bright ideas; those are easy to come by. As far as possibilities are concerned, Freud can offer some others, which would shift the problem.

The paper was far too long, and the speaker did not succeed in making the state of affairs clear to us. That children's lies are simply conjoined with masturbation was pure supposition; of a demonstration of this, we heard nothing. As far as children's lies are concerned, it is by no means a matter of course for the child to lie; it is a matter of course to tell the truth.

The specific difference between normal and pathological masturbation is not evident. The effects on the character [discussed by Rank] must arise from masturbation in the first years of life.

In lying, the child imitates the adults, who conceal the sexual facts from him, and who lie by giving him false information about these facts; it is from this that the child assumes his right to lie. Of course, this is connected with sexuality, but there is no direct connection with masturbation. Lying must of course be strictly distinguished from fantasy activity.

The comparison with the anal character suffers from a particular defect. If one speaks of the masturbatory character, it remains doubtful—in contrast to the anal character—whether this term refers to the character of the person who masturbates or to the character changes that result from the overcoming of masturbation.

Gross' and Stekel's papers on kleptomania do not claim to be definitive statements.

The washing compulsion, according to analytic investigations, appears first as a compulsion to wash the genitals. It occurs in persons (mostly women) who became sexually excited when their genitals were washed in infancy. Thus it is only indirectly connected with masturbation.

In spite of all these objections, it cannot be denied that the speaker touched very intelligently upon a series of the most interesting problems—e.g., that infantile masturbation and the feelings of guilt present a great problem, and what the sources are of the terrible importance that neurotics attach to masturbation. Rank was right in touching upon these questions: what are the consequences of infantile masturbation, and why does it stir up such a great feeling of guilt? There is no doubt that something results from the overcoming of infantile masturbation, that a character change does take place. But one must also show what happened to the masturbation.

The speaker stressed the strong point in the subject: namely, that it is a necessary condition that masturbation be successfully concealed; then there develop truth fanatics of the sort of Zola; this, Freud can confirm. However, he does not know what complications now become possible. Nor are the preconditions so simple: the castration complex betrays to us that masturbation may be just as frequently detected as not. An analysis always goes far enough for us to determine whether masturbation was or was not detected. In the history of the latter case, there is always a great "secret"—and that secret is masturbation.

ADLER too stresses the importance of the problem. By way of reminiscence, he mentions that, as one of the lecturers in the "Society," he spoke about the psychology of lying: at that time he was interested in pinning down the relationship between lying and truth. He also argued that lying is necessary for the preservation of a certain psychic equilibrium; he still maintains that opinion today.

Adler would question some of the fundamentals of Rank's paper—for instance, his statements about the significance of organic repression in masturbation, his taking leave of the instinctual life—a practice that, according to experience, one has no right to engage in. On the contrary, with regard to lying it can clearly be demonstrated that its starting point is connected with the scoptophilic instinct, which seeks a psychic overcompensation, when it is not gratified in its passivity.[5] The further course of development is characterized by a certain cowardliness, to which Adler referred in his discourse on the instinct of aggression. In general, the problem of lying cannot be resolved without a consideration of the instinct of aggression. Furthermore, there is a connection between lying and sensitivity. It does not matter that, as a result of sensitivity, one can just as well lie as tell the truth. It is

[5] Adler seems to refer to exhibitionism. This passage of the record is again very difficult to understand.

always the constellation at the given moment that is decisive. Theoretical considerations lead to the conclusion that both elements are always present: that is, in all cases of exaggerated love for the truth one finds at the same time the habit of lying, and the other way around.

When Rank attempted to shake the specificity of the anal character, a good deal [of the problem] was seen correctly. Adler likewise sees the analogy, only from a different standpoint. There exists no neurotic in whom one could not discover the anal character. Freud was wrong in narrowing it down to one definite type; it also appears in mixed forms. The reason is to be found in the fact that there take place transferences from the anal to the sexual sphere and vice versa. Therefore Adler could approve of this assertion of Rank, although with some modifications.

FEDERN thinks that the speaker has discussed "normal" and not "pathological" lying. Rank's "pathological liars" are not at all frequent. The fact that neurotics are generally no more given to lying than other people, while masturbation plays an incomparably greater role in their lives, seems to speak against a connection with masturbation. People lie most when they have a secret to conceal. This certainly happens frequently with onanists.

The washing compulsion of one of his patients, an excessive onanist and an anal character par excellence, proved to be of anal origin.

Federn believes that those who are burdened by a secret develop an urge to tell the truth.

SADGER first of all would like to defend the speaker against the totally unjustified attacks [upon him]. What Rank lacks is a gift for popular presentation. As far as the content is concerned, he has made very valuable suggestions.

It is true that Rank said little that was new about the pathology of lying, but he broached another topic: namely, which psychological traits are characteristic of the masturbator? Sadger was struck by this topic while he was making a study of Kleist, that typical onanist. In the literature he found nothing about this topic; Rank said some pertinent things about it. On the basis of his own experience, Sadger would like to add that the so-called *Flegeljahre* ["the raw, unpolished years," a German term for the period of later adolescence] are also pertinent here. Those who are in the midst of pubertal development will abuse someone to his face, protesting that they are merely telling the truth. It seems that, with the reappearance of masturbation, an exquisite urge for the truth sets in, evidently as a reaction to the secret [that is being] concealed from everybody. Sadger himself [at that period] had really taken advantage of the words "true" and "genuine," and he had found the same thing in Kleist. However, it does not seem to him, as it does to Rank, that the passion for truth appears only with the suppression of masturbation. Rank correctly set forth quite a number of other symptoms of masturbation.

Rank's formula for the origin of pathological lying would have been correct, if he had not limited it to masturbation; in all probability the pathological lie is connected with the concealment of a sexual complex, but this does not always have to be masturbation. Besides, it may well be that those persons who, in childhood, had a rich fantasy life, are the ones who are inclined toward pathological lying; perhaps they have forgotten how to distinguish their fantasies from reality. Rank correctly recognized the fantasy-and-wish-fulfillment character of lying. The urge to steal ultimately goes back to being in love with one's parents.

HITSCHMANN has the impression that one really cannot approach these problems without having examined patients. The theory that lying is connected with repression seems plausible enough to him.

Pseudologia phantastica should not have been neglected.

Hitschmann recently saw a case that fits into this area and nicely agrees with much that Rank touched on.

RANK concludes that, actually, his ideas have not undergone any direct or factual refutation; rather, his belief in the validity of his findings and assumptions has been confirmed by the fact that some of the gentlemen (Stekel, Sadger, Hitschmann) agreed with his views, their concurrence being in part quite open and in part concealed by misunderstandings. He was particularly gratified by Professor Freud's affirmation of his main point—the fanaticism for truth.

Now that some misunderstandings have been cleared up and several controversial points set right, Rank expresses his appreciation for the active interest in his paper and in the discussion.

76

SCIENTIFIC MEETING *on April 21, 1909*

Present: Prof. Freud, Adler, Bass, Federn, Heller, Hitschmann, Hollerung, Rank, Sadger, Steiner, Stekel, Dr. Karpas.

A GENERAL PRESENTATION OF FREUD'S THEORIES

[*Propaganda among Physicians*]

SPEAKER: DR. HITSCHMANN

The speaker takes as his point of departure the fact that the Freudian School can rightfully be reproached for not having done enough toward [producing] a brief compilation of Freud's theories. The need for such a compilation is brought home if one considers the opinions common among most of our colleagues: they believe that with the reading of the *Studies* [*on Hysteria*] they have exhausted all there is to know; they think that [the insights] do not hold for all cases; moreover, they consider them to be nothing new; they reproach Freud's pupils with being fanatics; etc., etc. To be sure, such a survey should steer clear of trying to persuade the great masses of the general public, especially in view of the fact that there exists a group of people who really cannot muster any interest in sexual matters (in contrast to a second group who react continually and strongly to the sexual complexes). This propaganda writing should, therefore, be directed mainly to the body of physicians. They certainly give us ample reason for doing so by their bringing forward over and over again such objections without understanding as: nothing in Freud's theories can be proved empirically, or (as an objection against analysis): how could a woman possibly disclose her most intimate feelings to the physician? and so forth. Such propaganda should also serve the function of bringing Freud's points of view to the attention of specialists, who are so often confronted with neuroses. On the other hand, only the main body of practitioners can begin work on the preventive measures that are so desirable.

All these and many other closely related considerations challenge us to write an integrated compilation of Freud's ideas, somewhat schematized and nonhistorical in character, similar to Ferenczi's paper,[1] parts of which could be taken over unchanged; it should be written in popular form, in which there are, at every important point, illustrations of a schematic character, and it should be somewhat more detailed at those points where the usual trite objections are ordinarily raised.

Such a compilation (which the speaker has sketched out) should begin with a brief description of the present status of research in neurosis (such as the speaker gave in his paper on "Neurosis and Toxicosis"[2]), which culminates in the statement that nothing remains but the sexual neuroses (and the accident neuroses). Next there should be a report on Freud's wholly new explanation of the actual neuroses (an understanding of the anxiety neurosis is immensely significant for the practitioner); it is a matter of making offprints of the article in question. From the anxiety neurosis a transition could be found via anxiety hysteria to what is called psychogenic, a point that is not yet completely clarified.

[1] S. Ferenczi: "Actual- and Psycho-Neuroses in the Light of Freud's Investigations and Psycho-Analysis" (1908). *Further Contributions to the Theory and Technique of Psycho-Analysis.* London: Hogarth Press, 1950. Abraham said of this paper in the *Jahrbuch*: "A detailed report into which the author has inserted some of his own experiences."

[2] Cf. Minutes 65, this Volume.

The difficulties in understanding the psychoneuroses are rooted in the concept of the unconscious and in infantile sexuality, which must be substantiated in terms of a purely empirical science. One would have to range quite far in enlarging upon the [concept of the] unconscious, and go into some detail about its virulent [illness-provoking] role. At the same time one could bring forward some things that [it is] necessary [to know] about dreams, jokes, and everyday life.

Finally, one should touch on analysis briefly, as the only method by which one can learn something about the unconscious. About this (the unconscious), one would then have to make the following statements: first of all, the extent to which it contains repressed material (Bleuler: "Unbewusstes und Assoziation" ["Unconscious and Association"][3]); secondly, that we cannot understand the unconscious without [a knowledge of] the phenomena of hypnotism, suggestion, and double consciousness. One could describe the origin of hysteria and obsessional neurosis in the same way as Ferenczi did in his paper. Finally, one must touch on the connection with the psychoses, and, in conclusion, say a few words about the methodology of analysis.

The speaker believes that the publication of such a pamphlet would be very successful in winning over interested people. His few remarks were intended merely to lead to a discussion and to get the gentlemen to indicate their attitude toward this question.

DISCUSSION

FEDERN thinks that this is a truly necessary and worthwhile undertaking against the needless attacks by those who do not know [anything about analysis]. The size [of such a pamphlet], he thinks, should be about the same as that of an issue of the *Wiener* or *Berliner* [*medizinische*] *Klinik.*

Sexual impotence (total impotence, or anaesthesia) should be mentioned as a counterpart to the partial repression that occurs in all cases of neurosis.

This compilation should deal only with matters of which we have

[3] Hitschmann is probably referring to Bleuler's contribution to Jung's *Assoziationsstudien* (1906), the correct title of which is "Bewusstsein und Assoziation" ["Consciousness and Association"].

sure knowledge; in this way it would also be of historical significance, in so far as it would show where Freud's theory of neuroses stands at the present time.

Of course, such a pamphlet will influence only healthy clear-sighted people, not those whose entire lives are based on sexual repression.[4]

PROF. FREUD says that he can put several things at Hitschmann's disposal if he wants to carry through this undertaking. First of all, the assurance that years ago the demand for such a compilation had already been voiced (Bleuler); furthermore, Freud can supply a publisher, for Deuticke has repeatedly approached him with such a request. The task itself not only can be carried out, but would be of great value. However, it would have to be undertaken by a *single* person; Freud himself is not only ready to assist that person with his experiences and counseling, he would also give such a work his authorization. But certain conditions would have to be observed. For instance, one would have to turn aside from the temptation to offer a closed system, to admit frankly, for example, that the position of hypochondria is still suspended in darkness. Also, one would have to draw explicit attention to the limits of our knowledge (repression too still lies partly in darkness). Furthermore, this work would require that the writer refrain from expressing any of his own ideas.

A short chapter should deal with the differences between our views and the ones now commonly held. And one should not fail to make a few comments on the mistakes and the misunderstandings and [to include] refutations of the most usual objections. Prof. Freud thinks that Hitschmann, since he had the idea, would be best qualified for this undertaking.

SADGER too thinks that this is an excellent idea, but has his doubts about the possibilities of a popularization. He tried to give a brief excerpt of Freud's theories in the *Zeitschrift für Psychiatrie und Neu-*

[4] It took fifteen years before Federn, together with Heinrich Meng and a host of collaborators, published a popular presentation of psychoanalysis on the basis of the views expressed here. The work appeared as *Psychoanalytisches Volksbuch* [*The Layman's Book of Psychoanalysis*], with a Foreword by Prof. Freud, in 1926. In 1956, a fifth edition was published. Innumerable popular presentations of psychoanalysis have been published since, each of which poses anew the problems discussed here. It is to Hitschmann's credit that he raised the question of a popular presentation of the body of psychoanalysis, and that he attempted it shortly thereafter (see fn. 8).

rologie[5] but did not meet with any particular approval. The greatest interest was engendered by his examples, and he cannot stress too emphatically the persuasive value of illustrations by contrast with theoretical arguments. He considers it indispensable to supplement this propagandistic pamphlet by a short, stenographically recorded analysis in order to demonstrate how the patient himself arrives at his ideas.

Sadger is convinced that the revolution in this field must come from the large body of practitioners.

DR. KARPAS (New York) alleges that in the U.S. Freud's teachings are little known and for the most part only from superficial reports. Such a publication would therefore be highly desirable there.

STEINER would agree with Sadger with regard to both the need for propaganda and his skepticism about its success. Whoever is interested in these things is going to read the standard works; some matters just cannot be made easy for people. What one says briefly, one may thereby say falsely.

BASS remarks that the speaker has expressed a wish fulfillment for him. He does not share the opinion of the previous speakers who hold that the subject would suffer from brevity—which should serve to whet the appetite even more. Moreover, one should have regard for the fact that laymen seem to be more interested in Freud's teachings than the professionals. Certainly, illustrations should not be missing. The whole project should be begun at once.

ADLER considers the question already settled, since there is someone who is willing to do the work and since the others, Prof. Freud in particular, have given their consent. He personally considers it desirable that it be Hitschmann who presents it to the public.

HELLER too is of the opinion that there is a need for such a pamphlet (in the sense of: "How do I tell it to my family physician?"); at the same time he believes that the beneficial effects that are looked for may fail to materialize. First of all, the majority of physicians are

[5] Reference is made here to the paper "Die Bedeutung der psychoanalytischen Methode nach Freud" ["The Significance of the Freudian Psychoanalytic Method"], *Zentralblatt für Nervenheilkunde und Psychiatrie*, 41, 1907.

people who have built their entire lives on a considerable amount of sexual repression. It is not likely that the pamphlet would contribute more to getting rid of prejudice or facilitating understanding than the works that came before it. As to the value of illustrations, especially in reference to Freud's teachings, Heller's experiences were the opposite of Sadger's. An illustration is convincing only to the extent that a person really feels inwardly compelled to open himself up to such teachings.

STEKEL too is skeptical with regard to success. He recalls that he was the first to undertake propaganda on a grand scale; he encountered very great understanding and did not find the subject itself so difficult [to handle]. His writings recruited many adherents to our cause among physicians as well as among lay people. But propaganda can be carried out only if it succeeds in making an artistic presentation of the materials. That is why he must maintain a veto against shorthand protocols. It was impossible for him to read Sadger's analysis of a homosexual in Hirschfeld's *Jahrbuch*[6]—an impossibility that many others [also discovered]; whereas the history of Dora,[7] artistically worked up, makes a deep impression.

It is doubtful, he thinks, whether the book will be useful; to be that it would have to be a great work. But for that it would have to be written out of a wealth of experience.

SADGER defines more accurately his proposal (to give an analytic case illustration): of course, he had in mind the kind of case in which, during the first few weeks, the patient himself, almost without resistance, develops everything. Such cases are far from being uninteresting.

FEDERN states that the question of publishing case histories should be strictly separated from Hitschmann's proposal. In that, it is a question of a brief *clinical* presentation of these kinds of diseases, as he (Hitschmann) at present understands them.

STEKEL announces his intention of writing a kind of popular dream interpretation.

[6] "Fragment der Psychoanalyse eines Homosexuellen" ["Fragment of the Psychoanalysis of a Homosexual"]. *Jahrbuch für sexuelle Zwischenstufen*, 9, 1908.

[7] S. Freud: "Fragment of an Analysis of a Case of Hysteria" (1905). *S.E.*, 7:7-122.

PROF. FREUD thinks that one should not underestimate the objections of Steiner and Sadger. There is no very easy way, no *via regia,* into this new and very difficult field. However, such a pamphlet would not have to be convincing; conviction comes only with one's own experiences. The purpose of this pamphlet would be above all to prevent people from talking about something they really know nothing about.

Case histories could never serve—as Sadger thinks—as *introductions.* Furthermore, he fully agrees with Stekel that case histories that are not worked over are completely indigestible. A scrupulous but "artistic" presentation, such as that of Dora's history, is the only acceptable possibility. In any event, the use of illustrations in this work should be sparing.

Freud himself made the attempt to approach the writing of a compendium of such topics as the hysterical attack and the hysterical symptom.

HITSCHMANN remarks that in this book he would never pretend to offer his own ideas; actually he would have to do nothing but copy. The purpose of the pamphlet would be to induce physicians to concern themselves with the etiology and pathogenesis of these illnesses.

The understanding of the significance of these problems would thereby gain enormously in the whole circle of medicine. The significance of neurosis in life, in the family, and in medicine cannot be rated highly enough.

He hopes to succeed in writing the pamphlet during the summer.[8]

[8] Hitschmann's book, then entitled *Freuds Neurosenlehre: Nach ihrem gegenwärtigen Stande zusammenfassend dargestellt,* was published by Deuticke in 1911, and in English as *Freud's Theories of Neurosis* by Nervous and Mental Disease Publishing Co., in 1913.

77

SCIENTIFIC MEETING *on April 28, 1909*

Present: Prof. Freud, Heller, Hitschmann, Joachim, Rank, Rie, Sadger, Steiner, Karpas as guest.

Reviews and Clinical Communications by All Members Present

HELLER reports on the recently published collection of entries in the prize-competition of the *Dürerbund* for the best solution of the problem of the sexual enlightenment of children.[1] The outcome of that event has surpassed our worst fears. The only point of interest for us is what Bahr[2] considered to be interesting in every such questionnaire. "We do not learn anything about the subject in question, but quite a bit about the persons who reply." And in this sense the answers provide a quite interesting image of what today's spokesmen in this field understand to be sexual enlightenment.

[1] "Betrachtungen, Ratschläge und Beispiele als Ergebnisse des Dürerbund-Preisausschreibens" ["Reflections, Suggestions and Examples in Response to the Dürerbund-prize Contest"]. *Am Lebensquell: ein Hausbuch zur geschlechtlichen Erziehung* [*At the Source of Life: a Manual on Sex Education for Use in the Home*]. Dresden, 1909.

[2] Hermann Bahr, Austrian writer of the first two decades of this century.

Not a single one of the contributors attempted to consider the problem from an objective, natural-scientific point of view. On the contrary, it would seem as if the contributors had set themselves the task of even further obscuring the whole [question of] sexuality. Thus the book can make no contribution other than to help smooth the path for neuroses. For those with this viewpoint, the book merely proves that the task of imparting purely objective sexual enlightenment to a child cannot be fulfilled.

SADGER gives a brief report on [Karl] Birnbaum's *Psychopathische Persönlichkeiten*[3] (review in *Wiener klinische Rundschau* [23, 1909]).

Sadger then reports about a curious complication in transference: the case of a hysterical patient, now in treatment with him, who—long before the treatment began—had been secretly in love with him and had made him the object of her fantasies.

PROF. FREUD, in this connection, calls attention to a problem which, in some cases of hysteria (like this one), causes one for a moment to become confused about our theoretical presuppositions: one asks oneself: where is the sexual repression in this case? By way of more precise inquiry, one finds the answer. This is how it goes: one may have a number of sexual impulses that manifest themselves not in conscious actions but in symptoms, without a sexual repression being present at that moment, for this repression has taken place earlier. The present impulse may be a *derivative* of the unconscious. Such cases therefore demonstrate the peculiar power of the infantile.

RANK mentions a passage from Bleuler's latest essay ("Sexual Abnormalities in Children" [*Jahrbuch der Schweizer Gesellschaft für Schulgesundheitspflege*]) which confirms Rank's own view regarding the connection between masturbation and the trait of lying (p. 630).[4]

Rank further reports on an imbecile boy who had a phenomenal memory for dates (Meeting of the *Verein für Psychiatrie und Neurologie* in Vienna). As Bleuler and Jung indicated in another context

[3] Correct title: "*Über psychopathische Persönlichkeiten: Eine psychopathologische Studie* ["On Psychopathic Personalities: A Study in Psychopathology"]. *Grenzfragen des Nerven- und Seelenlebens.* Wiesbaden: Bergmann, 1909.

[4] See Minutes 75, this volume.

(Bleuler: *Bewusstsein und Assoziation*[5]), these feats of memory can be understood only as achievement of the unconscious. The enormous affects that produce such an interest probably arise from the sexual sphere, and the special interest in the calendar, days, dates, etc., is connected with masturbation and the breaking off of this habit (fixed dates and deadlines [for breaking off]; comp. "Psychology of Lying").

PROF. FREUD thinks that the distinction between conscious and unconscious cannot be applied to memory. Remembering something has nothing to do with consciousness.[6]

RIE comments that this fact need not be an achievement of memory; it could be one of intelligence; he knows a cretin who is a chess champion.

HITSCHMANN replies that, by questioning the patient, it was established that this boy's achievements were solely the work of memory.

PROF. FREUD can well imagine that the boy acquired his proficiency by constant preoccupation with calendar calculations. In general, he would like to caution against being so categorical in assuming sexuality to be the mainspring. His contribution to the question will be limited to a case in which memory and interest were not quite as extraordinarily concentrated [in one area], yet the case still presented some similarities to the above-mentioned one. The case is that of a young homosexual who in his childhood was dominated by strong heterosexual complexes. He had both a predilection for the calendar and a memory for it. In this particular case, of course, Rank's supposition could well be to the point. The young man had marked the red-letter days and had a quite special interest in them as well as in everything connected with them. The periodic return of the red [letters][7] had captured his attention, and it was not difficult to guess what this had originally referred to.

[5] E. Bleuler: "*Bewusstsein und Assoziation*" ["Consciousness and Association"]. In: *Diagnostische Assoziationsstudien*, ed. C. G. Jung. Leipzig: Barth, 1906.

[6] Consciousness has no memory; the preconscious has a memory. See Freud: *The Interpretation of Dreams* (1900). *S.E.*, 4 & 5.

[7] The original protocol has "*Die periodische Wiederkehr des Rotwerdens, . . .*" lit.: "of becoming red."

STEINER had always had the idea that there is a relationship between sexuality, memory, and mathematics. It is striking that all children have a good memory; it is equally striking that women with a pronounced sexuality do not understand mathematics. It is well known that memory grows weaker in puberty. Obsessional ideas in people are also often connected with numbers.

The calendar performance mentioned here is, after all, not an extraordinary feat, but within the reach of anyone [who uses] a formula that can easily be retained by a good memory. (To this argument, many [discussants] object that it has been established as a fact that the boy did not make use of any such formula.)

PROF. FREUD suggests that our normal forgetting may be the scene of lively activity for our ungratified repressions; therefore the boy with few repressions had a good memory at his disposal. Remembering is no puzzle; it is forgetting that is the problem; a feeble-minded individual can accomplish prodigious feats in this respect [remembering].

RIE remarks that this is perhaps the key to the amazing memory of hysterics for foreign languages. For the time being, repression in them was very likely occupied in other ways.

PROF. FREUD comments further that we are quite justified [in saying] that sexuality and mathematics are opposites, but this remains wholly unexplained.

JOACHIM reports about his own phenomenal memory in childhood.

SADGER remarks that this [such a memory] is probably characteristic of those who do not masturbate. (FREUD: in the latency period.)

STEINER reports two minor observations from his practice.

The inability to work on the part of one of his patients was disclosed to be a kind of "delayed obedience" to his father's oft-repeated statement: "You will never amount to anything."

Another patient experienced pain in his left knee when he was sexually excited and during urination. The equation of urination and the sexual act goes back to his childhood. As far as the pain in the knee is concerned, all that could be found out was that the patient at the age of eight chased his younger sister with the intention of lifting her skirts, and in this pursuit hurt his knee.

HITSCHMANN states that a pain in the knee during sexual excitement occurs in people who have varicose veins.

He tells about a very successful application of the association experiment to criminal psychology (reported in *Monatsschrift für kriminelle Psychologie und Strafrechtsreform*, edited by Aschaffenburg); it was carried out according to a method described by Bezzola[8] in the *Revue de Psychiatrie*: he has the subjects go on associating until a kind of hypnoid state sets in. In such a state, the murderer involved in the experiment made an indirect confession. The similarity between this hypnoid state and the dream is very interesting.

In Ziehen's *Monatsschrift* there is an essay by Dr. Risch, "Über die Verkennung psychogener Symptomenkomplexe der frischen Haft und ihre Verwechslung mit Katatonie" ["On Misunderstanding the Psychogenic Syndromes of Persons Recently Imprisoned and Confusing Them with Catatonia"].

Hitschmann then briefly reviews a book by [Georges L.] Dreyfus, *Über nervöse Dyspepsie* [*On Nervous Dyspepsia*], 1908, which deals with this problem without any reference to sexuality or to the work done by Freud and his associates, though we find repeated intimations of the fact that the author knew something about our doings.

PROF. FREUD comments: whoever accepts out of our findings the concept of psychogenesis, but without admitting [the role of] sexuality, will certainly get nowhere.

RIE suggests that the dyspepsia of bride and groom is probably the result of a crude chemical process related to frustrated excitement.

HITSCHMANN calls attention to the connection between anxiety and vomiting in children. (FREUD: Vomiting is a form of anxiety.)

PROF. FREUD finally discusses a few *dream problems*. Proud as he was not to have found much to add when the second edition of *The Interpretation of Dreams* was being prepared, the book is nevertheless incomplete in one definite respect: the role of sexuality deserves to be enlarged in the statement of the dream problem. The better one under-

[8] Swiss neurologist.

stands dreams, the more one is forced to assign to the sexual material a decisive role.

The formulation should be extended to the effect that the dream represents the fulfillment of disguised *sexual* wishes.

A second extension is necessary because of the fact that far too little importance has been ascribed to the fixed symbolism of dreams: indeed we are approaching the time when a book of dream symbols will become possible. Freud has already begun to collect material for such a book and to search out the meaning of the recurrent elements, with the presupposition that, when nothing else can be uncovered, we have to assume [the presence of] something sexual.

After these preliminary remarks, Prof. Freud puts the following question (tied in with a communication from Jung) to the group: What does a *flight of stairs* mean in a dream? (A man dreams that he walks up a flight of stairs, at the end of which there is an abyss.)

SADGER, in the light of his experience with a patient, interprets it as climbing up on the mother and falling into her vagina.

STEINER mentions the recently discussed climbing dream of the short man who was married to a tall wife.

HITSCHMANN imagines that a displacement from below upward might be involved.

PROF. FREUD remarks that the dreamer, whose family life is well known to Jung, would certainly have been greatly embarrassed if after communicating the dream, he had been asked whether it was not true that his wife had refused to have intercourse with him for quite some time. The stair dream is really a coitus dream, the stairs being intercourse cut into stone (the jerky mounting of the stairs represents the rhythm of intercourse; in both cases, one winds up being short of breath, etc.). The abyss at the top represents a transformation into anxiety of the feeling that "above" there will be bliss. Verifications of this typical interpretation of the stair dream would be most welcome.

Other typical symbols: geographical dreams represent, with incredible regularity, genital landscapes.

78

SCIENTIFIC MEETING *on May 5, 1909*

Present: Prof. Freud, Bach, Federn, Hitschmann, Reitler, Sadger, Steiner, Stekel, Wittels.

PRESENTATION

Heinrich von Kleist

SPEAKER: DR. SADGER

The paper will be published this summer in Löwenfeld's *Grenzfragen des Nerven- und Seelenlebens.*[1]

DISCUSSION

WITTELS points out that the speaker uncovered a series of connections which are, at first sight, clear.

However, it might be more important to make certain general points of view in regard to pathographies the subject for discussion. If

[1] For this reason Rank did not record the paper. See *Heinrich von Kleist: eine pathographisch-psychologische Studie.* Wiesbaden: Bergmann, 1909.

nowadays analysts write pathographies, they should do so from a scientific standpoint. Above all, one should, by way of induction, establish certain general principles of pathography. One should compile [a list of] those things that are found to be common to all poets, in order to save oneself the trouble of continually repeating long recognized facts (e.g., feminine habitus; or certain perversions, such as homosexuality, which—in view of Freud's findings—we are not surprised to find in poets). One might even say that a perversion that is not practiced by the poet must find expression in his works. In contrast to Sadger, one would also have to consider, of course, those works that would permit us to draw conclusions with regard to these suppressed perversions. However, since a poet's work cannot be subjected to a regular analysis, one would have to limit oneself to interpreting only that which has already been firmly established by analysis.[2] We would by all means wish poets themselves to give analytic interpretations of their works, because in that way we might hope to obtain helpful explanations.

With regard to specific factors, Wittels remarks that the speaker, while offering penetrating interpretations, disregarded the milieu and its influence. It cannot surprise us, for instance, that Kleist, a citizen of the Prussian Reich, puts such special stress on virtue; and this need not be, as Sadger believes, a reaction to his infantile vice (masturbation). Patriotism in the midst of the German Reich seems also to be a matter of course. One should be very circumspect in dealing with the psychology of masturbation, because masturbation is very often an expression of the sexual drive.

STEKEL comments that the *manner* in which Sadger treats the topic makes these things rather unattractive for the general public. As far as the content is concerned, Sadger's views are certainly justified, though some exaggerations have crept in. Stekel subscribes word for word to the general standpoint expounded by Wittels; only a short time ago Stekel again stated publicly that every poet is a neurotic (Stekel: "Dichtung und Neurose" in Löwenfeld's *Grenzfragen*, No. 65).[3]

[2] It is not quite clear to what "firmly established" refers. Symbols? Family relationships?

[3] See Minutes 64, this volume.

FEDERN first of all wishes to draw attention to the contrast between what Kleist has told us about himself and Sadger rationalized or, rather, rendered commonplace for us.

No doubt there were strong neurotic components in Kleist's makeup. But neurosis is always an impediment to the artist, and it was a terrific creative gift that enabled the poet to produce his works, not his neurosis.

Federn thinks that Wittels is wrong in his conception that we find all kinds of perversions in every poet, and just as wrong in what he said about giving vent to these perversions. A person can practice a perversion and still remain ungratified.

The connection between homosexuality and being in love with one's mother exists only in Sadger's head.[4] Even though there might be some truth in this, it is still not always the sole and ultimately decisive factor. Nor will it do to trace things back to masturbation in this way. This man simply lived to a quite incredible extent in his fantasies; but this is absolutely not true for persons who are given to excessive masturbation. On the contrary, fantasy is frequently the substitute for physical masturbation. Nor is this connected with feelings of guilt; indeed, in his work Kleist is not particularly "in search of guilt," not a moralist. We find suppressed sadism breaking through in his works, and there is also evidence of disturbed family relationships, but not a trace of masturbation. Thus all of Sadger's particular assertions remain unproven; nevertheless, everything that he has affirmed (homosexuality, masturbation, mother complex) must be taken into consideration.

HITSCHMANN characterizes the discussion as a toil of Sisyphus, for it will have no results. The manuscript will still go to press unchanged. There is no reason for an analysis of Kleist, particularly since so little is known about the poet's first twenty years (and especially nothing about his mother and her relationship to him). But if, in addition, the investigation is conducted—as it is here—without any reference to his works, then nothing at all will happen. In these circumstances it would be more advisable to make a patho-

[4] Later on, Sadger was proven to be completely right.

graphic study of a writer such as Gogol[5] whose sexual pathology (onanist) is notorious. In the psychology of the onanist we do not find the self-reproaches, the hypochondriacal notions, the evidence of somatic symptoms—all of which are connected with it.[6]

Hitschmann expected Sadger to put emphasis on Kleist's love for his sister, which probably played the greatest role.

The whole paper left a very unsatisfactory impression.

REITLER would like to come out in favor of the paper. Kleist is not at all unsuitable for such a study; one can draw upon his works [to show] that he was a severe neurotic. The only question is whether his biography provides us with sufficient material for an analysis. If we keep in mind that the neurotic has remained arrested at the level of infantile sexuality, we may assume that the love for the mother plays a principal part. On the other hand, Sadger did not give sufficient evidence to prove this was the case with Kleist. In other respects, however, Sadger did a commendable job, even though it would be desirable for some details to be changed (especially before publication).

Rank repeatedly referred to the relation between the artist, the neurotic, the criminal and the pervert. Kleist has all these psychic peculiarities. In *Käthchen von Heilbronn* and in *Prinz von Homburg* he portrayed—infelicitously to be sure—hysterical absences. Both homosexuality and sadism are too apparent to require discussion. There are paranoid traits in *Die Familie Schroffenstein;* this drama is indeed considered to be the tragedy of suspicion. The poet also reveals paranoid and criminal tendencies in "Michael Kohlhaas."

RANK remarks that he has a personal aversion to pathographies and therefore cannot go into details today. In general he shares the viewpoint defined by Wittels, a viewpoint which he tried to realize in the following way: using a typical motif (the incest motif), he demonstrated that all significant poets have certain complexes in common and that these should be established by comprehensive studies of that

[5] Nikolai V. Gogol (1809-1852), Russian novelist and dramatist.

[6] Rank has again apparently abbreviated too much. Obviously, the sentence should read "In Kleist's psychology, which Sadger presented as that of an onanist, we do not find the self-reproaches . . . which characterize a masturbator."

sort (Rank accomplished this in regard to the homosexual complex). It goes without saying that such investigations must draw on the poet's works. Otherwise an inquiry such as that presented today has little value, because the person studied could just as well have been a statesman. If one approaches topics of that kind analytically, one has to introduce a different way of looking at things, "from within" (Jung), as it were; the traditional form of pathography is not capable of taking hold of contents that have been worked through analytically.

PROF. FREUD says that, from his standpoint, he can only repeat what was expressed in the discussion.

Why is it that, even though Sadger makes assertions that must be accepted as correct, his communications feel strange to us, sometimes even offensive? That is the enigma that Freud would like to try solving. The first reason lies in the fact that in such a psychological analysis of a creative writer one does not find any point of contact with our image of the man's personality, and that is why the analysis seems strange. One simply cannot do justice to a personality if one stresses only its abnormal sexual components and does not make an effort to establish their close ties with the individual's other psychic forces. In that case, as has been said here, one might just as well have written a pathography not of a creative writer, but of anyone else you could think of, someone unknown to us who—by the way!—left a number of works of creative writing.

Details: Sadger begins with the statement: "homosexuality and masturbation played an important role in our poet's life"; it would be desirable for the juxtaposition of these two factors [to be set forward] more precisely. Homosexuality is a component of sexuality—actually it is not quite that, but merely the existence of a special aim; masturbation is a manifestation of the sexual instinct.

Sadger must also be reproached for having a special predilection for the brutal. However, our task is not arbitrarily to speak new truths, but rather to show in what way they can be arrived at. A certain degree of tolerance must go hand in hand with a deeper understanding, especially of unconscious phenomena, if life is to remain at all bearable. Sadger apparently has not acquired this tolerance, or at least he is not capable of expressing it. And this lack of tolerance, which manifests itself in a moralistic pathos, is the second repellent aspect of his paper.

Quite apart from these general weaknesses, this work seems to be wholly unreliable. Factual material is totally lacking, and with it the evidence for a number of things. All we can see is that Kleist, one of the most creative poets in our literature, was at certain periods of his life an awkward boy; aside from that, we were shown which sexual aberrations he had.

But even the specific explanations are a complete failure: for instance, the fantasy of becoming a peasant (interpreted as the desire to flee from the father into solitude along with the mother); the fantasy of dying together with a beloved person, etc. Sadger's attempts at analyzing Kleist's works are also very weak; Reitler's few remarks contained, substantially, a great deal more than the entire elaboration. The general public is right in rejecting this type of analysis—and this refers in part also to Stekel (*A Dream Is Life*).[7] In such elementary analyses all finer distinctions of structure manage to get completely lost, and so does the understanding of the poet.[8] One just cannot ignore the value of the object employed in such research. For a mere demonstration that every human being typically has these basic emotions, our poets are too good.

Some technical errors crept in—e.g., in regard to the masturbation complex. Masturbation is nothing but a very many-sided activity. Moreover, in these creative individuals the character of the masturbator does not become fully formed. Nevertheless, with regard to some derivations, Sadger was very successful (e.g., the pedagogical inclination traced back to the teacher, the search for true friendship, etc.); but alongside this, we find so much banality that one can only regret the effort spent.

STEKEL emphasizes that the idea of "dying together," which also appears in neuroses, was an especially interesting topic in tonight's presentation. Here death has a symbolic meaning: it symbolizes the actual enjoyment of love and life. Just a short time ago, Freud inti-

[7] See Minutes 54B, this volume.

[8] This sentence was probably not accurately recorded. Freud must have said "In such elementary analyses all finer distinctions of structure must get completely lost and *therefore* also the understanding of the poet."

mated that suicide is, for some persons, the last act of love. In one analysis, a patient meant "the act of love" when he spoke of "dying." (PROF. FREUD: "to die together" means: for once he would like to have intercourse.)

SADGER justifies his paper by stating that its purpose is not to furnish contributions to the psychology of a poet's creativity, but to write the natural history of the *dégénéré supérieur*. In this endeavor analysis is used for the purpose of differential diagnosis—that is to say, by way of analysis to separate out what has its source in sexual activity. Nor has it been in the least Sadger's intention to interpret the poet's works; rather pathographies serve to bring the poet closer to us as a human being. The two aspects that Freud stressed as seeming strange are due mainly to the fact that a number of things intended for the broad public were omitted from today's communication, because Sadger was concerned only with bringing out the essential core of his conception. On the basis of his analyses, he tried to find possibilities for the explanation of various points: he willingly admits that there turned out to be quite a few weaknesses, because the most essential material about the poet's childhood and family is missing. As to the discussion, he must regretfully state that actually he did not learn anything essentially new.

Finally, the speaker tries to disprove specific attacks. For instance, in view of Brokes'[9] fragment of a letter, the probability of Kleist's masturbation cannot be excluded (Kohlhaas, by the way, also goes back to Brokes), etc.[10]

The speaker did not intend to contribute anything to the psychology of the poet, nor would he have the courage to say anything about this work of the future. He merely presented a number of problems in the poet's life and tried to find their solutions; the attempt to make any improvements on this was missing from the discussion.

[9] Ludwig von Brokes, a close friend of Kleist.

[10] It was not Brokes but Ernst von Pfuel who called Kleist's attention to the Michael Kohlhaas theme.

79

SCIENTIFIC MEETING *on May 12, 1909*

Present: Prof. Freud, Bass, Federn, Graf, Heller, Hitschmann, Joachim, Karpas, Rank, Rie, Sadger, Steiner, Stekel.

DISCUSSION

Sexual Enlightenment

HELLER: From the *Lebensquell* (Collection of Answers in the Prize Contest for the Best Solution to the Problem of Children's Enlightenment)[1] he presents various sorts of enlightenment grouped according to general points of view.

Then he reads aloud cases that rest on actual events, and could therefore serve as a foundation for the discussion.

RIE briefly reviews Bleuler's essay "Sexual Abnormalities in Children." Actually, Bleuler only gives the reasons for the necessity of enlightenment and says little about its quality. The best information about the pamphlet's content is conveyed by the eight introductory theses by Bleuler, which the speaker reads [to the group].

[1] See Minutes 77, this volume.

Rie does not discuss the objections [that could be raised] against Bleuler's moral-philosophical conception. He is particularly struck by the fact that, as thesis #1 shows, Bleuler's mind is closed to [the idea of] autoerotism. As to the masturbation of the later period—for the avoidance of which he considers enlightenment to be necessary—Bleuler is inclined to attribute to the psychological many elements that can be explained somatically. Furthermore, according to Bleuler, only children with a morbid disposition turn to masturbation; it is the opposite that is more likely the rule.

As far as the reviewer's personal view is concerned, he is opposed to enlightenment at school; in Rie's opinion, however, the other way of enlightenment is no longer to be discussed, for this would have to be dealt with from case to case.

STEINER stresses the fact that, despite the new reports on this already discussed subject, no new points of view have been arrived at; this shows how difficult it is to come close to the problem. To be sure, we are entitled to be amused by attempts at a "botanical" solution (*Lebensquell*); but, at least as far as Steiner himself is concerned, we are at a loss when it comes to showing how to do better.

The greatest damage must be ascribed to the stork; to drag him into the matter was not only altogether superfluous, it was also disastrous.

For [the task of] enlightenment, only parents should be considered, and their chief task consists in avoiding unnecessary lies. If children really have to be enlightened, this should not happen in a forced manner, but always in a way that is suitable to the child's ability to grasp things. When we see how defective are the ideas that many adults have about coitus, even after sexual intercourse, one will certainly despair of giving the child a correct knowledge of this process in a way that will not do any harm.

PROF. FREUD turning first to Bleuler's essay, points out that a misunderstanding with regard to anal erotism has crept into it; the character traits Bleuler mentioned appear only *after the victory* over anal erotism, as a substitute for it. Hence, among persons in whom the original *Anlage* is still left, there would be a striking lack of these traits (in contrast to Bleuler's examples). On the question of masturbation, Bleuler says many interesting things. Personally, Freud is more and more inclined toward the view that it is not masturbation that—as the patients assert—is the source of all these neurotic sufferings; the essential factor is what lies behind masturbation—namely, the primitive masturbation-fantasies. For these are not suppressed along with the suppression of physical masturbation; with the accumulation of libido their effects are all the stronger. Neurotics are persons who in fantasy have not arrived at a detachment from their first objects; and it is from this *content of the primitive fantasies* that all these feelings of repression follow. For persons who can detach these fantasies from father, mother, etc., masturbation has no psychological consequences. They also make an early transition to real objects. Thus the harmfulness of masturbation goes back to the incompatibility of the first object choice. If Bleuler believes that childhood masturbation (4-5 years) can be overlooked, he is mistaken. In normal children, to be sure, it soon disappears. On the other hand, Freud considers the statement to be altogether correct that certain individuals have a repugnance toward the masturbation they have practiced until then; suddenly, and independently of external influences, it becomes impossible for them to masturbate. This moment marks the turning point in their development. Shortly thereafter, hysteria usually sets in. To find out what makes it impossible [for them to masturbate], one has to enter more deeply into the matter. It is probably a faint recognition of the *social* significance of love relationships and of the responsibilities that result from them. Thus the impossibility [of masturbation] seems to be connected with a step forward on the way to the finding of an object.[2]

With regard to enlightenment, one must agree fully with Steiner. In their "botanical" explanations, people do nothing but repeat the process of finding words for sexual matters (semen, fertilization, etc.). In the case of [Little] Hans,[3] too, enlightenment was not carried

[2] I would like to call special attention to this contribution to the discussion. It contains, in a nutshell, the whole problem of masturbation.

[3] Freud: "Analysis of a phobia in a five-year-old-boy" (1909). *S.E.*, 10:3-149.

through to the final riddle; at times, one can very well be content with an incomplete explanation. How enlightenment about intercourse should be given is a problem that Freud would like to leave open for discussion.

On this occasion one should also say a word in *favor* of [enlightenment at] school. The practical reason for doing so lies in the fact that most parents are in general not equipped to be educators. Another reason is that children do not at all want to obtain enlightenment from their fathers. To orient the child in life is among the responsibilities proper to the school, and sexual problems are an important part of this orientation. Naturally, enlightenment should not be, like a shower, suddenly poured over a child; but sexuality should, from the beginning, be recognized and treated as a significant area, along with so many others, of human and animal actions and experiences. The model, ment that is tied in with a child's questions. We simply do not under-that man too is a mammal, the child will be able to draw the correct conclusions by himself.

From analyses we can learn quite a bit about the kind of enlightenment that is tied in with a child's questions. We simply do not understand children, and only since [Little] Hans do we know what a child thinks. The child has two incorrect notions about the origin of children: (1) that children are born because the parents ate a certain dish; this is an infantile sexual theory, of which the forbidden fruit of the Bible—which must not be eaten—is clearly an echo; (2) the sadistic conception of sexual intercourse (fighting, assaulting, overpowering). The child who asks a question wants first of all to know whether his idea is correct. Consequently, the enlightenment of these very young children need not explain something of the complicated mechanism of biological processes, etc.; that is not at all what the children want to know; enlightenment may content itself with contradicting these infantile theories. Children do not ask questions out of a need for causality but for the gratification of certain interests. Enlightenment should above all make it clear to them that this is a matter of acts of tenderness, that [in the process] their parents love each other very much; then the children will not make any demand at all for specific details of enlightenment. As to the process of coition the older children should find out about it in school, in their science lessons.

HITSCHMANN believes that this topic needs to be viewed from several additional angles, inasmuch as it should include the prevention of nervous diseases. It would also be worthwhile to discuss the question of by what means, enlightenment included, nervous illnesses could be prevented; especially what, in view of the most recent experiences with Little Hans, should be done about it in education. Perhaps some things might be done in character education: the child should have less [occasion for] secrecy and, as a result, a sense of confidence instead [in the adults]; also, one should accustom him at an early age to bring to bear upon feelings of pleasure a sense of renunciation; this would later make it easier for him to give up masturbation. That enlightenment at school is quite feasible is shown by the fact that even now it takes place at school—to be sure, by way of schoolmates. Furthermore, the enlightenment of only one generation would suffice. The ideal of sexual education would actually be to induce late awakening of sexual need.[4]

Solving the ultimate riddles by referring to mammals may also have certain disadvantages—as, for instance, the image of coition from behind, etc.

BASS starts with his own experiences: his little boy talks about these things only with his mother. The child knows that one need not be married to have a baby, yet he thinks that all that is necessary is for a woman to have looked a man in the eye. One cannot start early enough on the instruction of children, and since most parents are not qualified to do this, it should be carried through at school. Of course, this presupposes a special training of the instructors. Enlightenment may also be of great importance toward helping to detach children's affects from their parents. With regard to the technique of enlightenment, one cannot establish any rule: the enlightener must be fully equal to the situation. Enlightenment could be most appropriately carried through within the context of instruction in biology.

[4] If this could really be achieved, it would be of enormous value in our society.

STEKEL hesitates to express his heretical opinions. It is a mistake to believe that the child asks his mother for enlightenment; he is testing his mother with his questions. The fact is that children do not want to be enlightened by adults: enlightenment by adults is a trauma for the child; it is just as impossible at school as it is at home. The best enlightenment is actually by way of a trauma; Stekel knows of cases in which a trauma prevented a neurosis. Enlightenment is most suitably taken care of by [other] children. The problem is: how do we protect the child from incestuous thoughts, which are the most fundamental cause of all neuroses? If we knew [the answer to this question], we could perhaps render a service to mankind.

With regard to Freud's view about masturbation being given up out of a social instinct, Stekel has to remain skeptical. We have no justification for assuming such an instinct in children.

REITLER refers to Bleuler's assertion that only children with morbid dispositions, abnormal children, start to masturbate before puberty; in a certain narrower sense, this is quite correct. Before puberty, a child normally "masturbates" at various erotogenic zones (the zones of later perversion); this masturbation has no pathognomonic significance. A child's premature genital masturbation, on the other hand, must be regarded as a perversion, which permits us to infer an abnormal sexual constitution (Freud's conception of the genesis of homosexuality). We are interested in sexual enlightenment only as [a means of] preventing the development of neurosis; this, however, would require a transformation of our educational methods; children should be brought up in such a way that they would not be in need of enlightenment. For this, school comes, of course, too late. As far as early instruction and frankness at home are concerned, the case of [Little] Hans offers us a very good opportunity to observe whether and to what extent education toward a harmless conception of sexual enlightenment helped him. Undeniably, mistakes were made in his education, and these were indeed responsible for his neurosis. The discovery and the cultivation of the feeling of shame are in contradiction to the harmless conception of sexuality to which the child was accustomed at home. And thus the neurosis begins as a result of his inability to suppress [the desire for] exhibition; the resolution of the phobia then took place by way of civilization—that is, by way of its acceptance: the boy no longer exhibited in the open but on the toilet.

KARPAS reports that recently Stanley Hall,[5] in a lecture at the Association of Teachers, said that it was their duty to bring these matters before the children in the course of teaching them biology. However, in America these efforts come face to face with an enormous repressive complex.

RANK would like in a modest way to call attention to the fact that a premature and comprehensive enlightenment of children may eventually prove to be harmful to them, with regard to their intellectual capacities in later life (sexual curiosity = thirst for knowledge, zeal for learning; brooding about sexual problems—philosopher; sexual curiosity—plastic artist, etc., etc.).

Referring to Steiner's question, Rank then points out the mythological origin of the stork fable (stork = swan = bringer of souls, and bird of death = bringer of children. The soul as a bird, etc.).

BRECHER [as a guest] emphasizes the difficulty of contributing anything new to a subject as complex as this after so thoroughgoing a discussion; he can only indicate his attitude toward the arguments presented. He is in favor of enlightenment, in spite of Stekel's objections and Rank's doubts; it has not been proven that enlightenment does away with the energy that, in a sublimated form, asserts itself as thirst for knowledge. But even if that were so, the ensuing damage would be of less consequence than that which would be brought about by the omission of enlightenment. Enlightenment would, of course, have to take place at school in courses in the natural sciences. One should first go into an explanation of the processes at birth; later one could also take up coition and attempt a synthesis. An over-all scheme cannot be established, in view of the constitutional differences [among children]; this may also account for the fact that some children do not want to be enlightened by their parents, whereas others call upon them directly for it.

With regard to masturbation, Brecher would point to the signifi-

[5] G. Stanley Hall, founder of experimental psychology in America, and the president of Clark University, Worcester, Mass., who invited Freud to give a series of public lectures at that university.

cance of its somatic aspects; he has the impression that a continuous discharge of the products of inner secretion is taking place, which surely influences the psychic processes, and vice versa.

SADGER too first reports some observations made on children. The question of why some children ask questions and others do not, could probably be connected with their being in love homosexually or heterosexually. A boy who regards his father as a rival will not ask him for sexual enlightenment; he will ask his mother, if he is in love with her; but he does not know why he is asking. Matters are probably more complicated than we now suspect them to be.

It is doubtful, he thinks, that teachers are the suitable persons [for the sexual enlightenment of children].

The giving up of masturbation seems to be connected with the child's becoming conscious of his being in love with his mother (or homosexually).

FEDERN: In the enquiry conducted by the *Lebensquell*, he misses any data about the success of enlightenment.

As to the "normality" of infantile masturbation, he would speak against both points made by Reitler: later masturbation at other zones is merely a substitute for genital masturbation. The differences between the "masturbation" of the normal child and the autoerotic activity of the child who is predisposed to neurotic illness seems to be that the normal child obtains from the discharge normal pleasure but not sexual lust, as the future neurotic does; for the latter, the interweaving of discharge with sexual sensations is characteristic. As far as the development of neuroses is concerned, one can surely undertake successful preventive measures.

GRAF comments, in connection with Reitler's remarks about the case of [Little] Hans, that it is a progressive process of curiosity in the boy. Referring to Freud's remarks that [Hans's] enlightenment was not carried through without anything being left over, Graf says that the boy should have been told the last fact too, with a certain degree of clarity. The child now feels that several pieces are missing and asks his father more and more for explanations of natural events. In the course of time this will accumulate and demand an answer. In matters of sexuality, he has detached himself from his parents.

The value of plants for enlightenment should be by no means underestimated; the processes of plant life offer the most suitable natural examples [*Naturexperimente*] of the procreative processes. The school could collaborate very effectively in [the task of] enlightenment by way of its natural history classes, the goal of which need not be full knowledge, and yet they should take that as their direction. However, long before [they enter] school (during the first three years), children must be brought up in the right way—which means that they do not feel awkward about asking questions.

Hans' illness developed, in Graf's opinion, on the basis of his strong sexual predisposition (*Anlage*), which awoke a premature need for love; this in turn became too strongly linked with his parents.

PROF. FREUD also thinks that Reitler did not do justice to the conditions in Hans' home; not *that* many mistakes were made, and those that did occur did not have *that* much to do with the neurosis. The boy should only have been refused permission to accompany his mother to the toilet. For the rest, neurosis is essentially a matter of constitution. If, like Hans, one brings along with one a strong disposition to sexuality, then either a very early development takes place or else the basis for a conflict is established and then the fate of mankind is repeated in the individual. Mankind must go through neurosis and then arrive at a tolerable position;[6] the same thing holds true for the child with a strong sexual need. In view of the therapeutic means at our disposal, we may in this sense change our attitude toward the neuroses; the conviction that neuroses are unavoidable will also influence our opinion about the possibilities of prophylaxis.

In the expectation that the story of Little Hans will be subject to all sorts of attacks, Jung is preparing, for the second half of the *Jahrbuch,* the analysis of his eldest daughter's phobia, which took a very similar course; in this case, the parents do not have the slightest imprudence to reproach themselves for. This little girl, too, produced a characteristic phobia after the birth of a brother. She attributed her inability to leave the house to the fear of an earthquake, which was at that time justified by the Messina catastrophe. One sees here of what

[6] Rank so abbreviated Freud's words here that it is difficult to understand what he meant.

secondary significance is the specific content. She, too, fell ill from aggressive impulses against the mother; because the illness resulted from aggression, in both cases the neurosis consisted of prevention of movement. The explanation that a child grows in the mother's womb put an end to the phobia within three days.

Finally, Prof. Freud adds the most important argument in favor of sexual enlightenment at school, an argument which, he says, should have been included in the paper on "Civilized Sexual Morality."[7] The main damage done by neglecting [to enlighten] children lies in the fact that, for the rest of the child's life, sexuality is afflicted with the character of the forbidden; this can be countered only if children obtain enlightenment at the hands of a person of authority. This character of the forbidden later on plays an important role in married life; for these persons can find sexual enjoyment only in what is forbidden; they are disappointed in married life and are therefore "anaesthetic." This stigma, above all, should be removed from sexuality.

[7] "Civilized Sexual Morality and Modern Nervous Illness." *S.E.* (1908), 177-204.

80

SCIENTIFIC MEETING *on May 19, 1909*

Present: Prof. Freud, Adler, Federn, Graf, Häutler, Hitschmann, Hollerung, Joachim, Rank, Reitler, Sadger, Steiner, Stekel.

PRESENTATION

On a Specific Type of Male Object-Choice[1]

SPEAKER: PROF. FREUD

PROF. FREUD begins with something that he has had frequent opportunity to observe during the past two years: namely that male patients have repeatedly shown certain peculiarities in what he has termed "prerequisites for love." By this is meant the fact that, for every person, there are certain prerequisites, usually unknown to him [or her], whose fulfillment is the precondition to falling in love. To one

[1] This appeared under the title "Über einen besonderen Typus der Objektwahl beim Manne," as the first of Freud's "Contributions to the Psychology of Love (*Jahrbuch* II, 1910). The paper recorded here was laid out on a much broader basis and contains ideas that were not included in the published version. (Strachey translated the title as "A special type of choice of object made by men.")

girl, for instance, the prerequisite for love was for someone to prefer her to her sister; and when a young man, on comparing their photographs by chance, did just that, she fell in love with him immediately. Another case of a more deep-going prerequisite for love was recently related by Paul Lindau in a feuilleton in the *Neue Freie Presse:* a man, writing to his friend, tells him the story of his love affair, which he himself finds completely puzzling. The man, who, since his mother's death, had led an altogether solitary life, one day became engaged to a young girl, who was loveable in every respect. Accompanying her is a plain-looking girl, a close relative of hers, to whom he does not pay the slightest attention. One day, the young man rescues this [other] girl from the sea and when she, almost benumbed, is restored to life, he falls in love with her and [ultimately] marries her. To the psychoanalyst, there is nothing at all to question about this affair; for this man, the prerequisite for love is a [dead] body that one can love; in the man's introductory remarks, there is already an intimation that this refers to the dead mother. The subject of prerequisites for love is quite interesting; yet it is not a central part of today's discussion, to which the speaker now turns.

There are some men with the following noteworthy prerequisites for love, which can be grouped schematically under four headings:

1. It must be the wife of another man. Thus these men are much more likely to fall in love with married women than with unmarried girls, and with the latter only when they are just about to belong to another man.

2. The second point concerns the way in which the men behave toward these love objects. Their behavior is quite contradictory: they cling to these women with great fidelity, and have difficulty in freeing themselves from them. On the other hand, however, they show an inclination to form a series [of such attachments], which is, of course, in contradiction to the idea of fidelity. This contradiction is resolved by the fact that these objects replace one another perfectly, that they are, in fact, identical.

3. The third point is the most striking of all: the woman has to be sexually notorious; she must have a bad reputation. From this prerequisite one can draw the conclusion that these men can be fully in love only when they can be jealous. Here we find a certain organic

connection among the different prerequisites: on the one hand jealousy is connected with point 1, on the other hand, with sexual suspiciousness.

4. The fourth point sounds like a secondary consequence of point 3, but it is really not: it is the need to wish to rescue this person. This fourth point, too, is quite well combined with the previous ones, and there is secondary, artfully construed connection among them. If the woman is sexually disreputable, she is in danger of falling—this is, from another direction, his justification for holding fast to her.

The speaker now proceeds to survey these four prerequisites together. This type [of object choice] cannot be represented as a crystal, which always appears in perfect formation; the various facets are sometimes more, and sometimes less clearly defined. The last point is also interesting from a literary point of view; it may well be that it is related to the characteristic attempt to save the prostitute, which is so often found [in literature].

Besides, these persons can neither be called healthy, nor are they neurotics; in this respect, at least, the cases Freud observed were not neurotic; in other respects they were, in that, among other things, they also showed these peculiarities in their love life. As for the explanation of this coincidence of peculiarities, at first it is disappointing, for it contains something long known to us. But it may be just this circumstance that is our stimulus to dig more deeply into this problem. These are persons whose libido was fixated onto the mother. From this we assume that with all men object-choice starts with the mother, and that in the case of neurotics it is, for a particularly long time, fixated upon her. Thus, for the specific understanding of the case at hand, one must observe the following: it is a matter here of a person whose libido was, for a long time and intensively, fixated upon the mother, but did detach itself from her and become transferred to other persons. Alongside the persons described above one must, without further ado, distinguish two other types:

1. Those whose libido has remained fixed to the mother even up to the present and who have not at all detached it from her. These are neurotics who have no object-choice at all.

2. Those who are neurotics too, but whose libido did not remain fixed to the mother for a particularly extended period; they detached

their libido from her in due time and chose other objects; but as the result of other influences, they became neurotic later on and their libido consequently reverted to the mother.

In the case under discussion, however, in which the libido did become detached from the mother and transferred to other persons, the prerequisite for the object—that it be like the mother—is tightly clung to.

The speaker now proceeds to a detailed explanation of the four prerequisites already referred to.

The first point is to be explained, by itself, as the case of the mother; this prerequisite—the taking away of the wife of another man—could perhaps become easily intertwined with a man's sadistic tendency, without the fulfillment of this prerequisite coming to be regarded as a sadistic triumph.

About the second prerequisite, there is not much more to be said. Great fidelity corresponds to the great significance of the mother, the attachment to her, etc. In these individuals, one can pretty regularly trace the marriage fantasy. They do not, to be sure, marry easily; yet, whenever they fall in love, the fantasy of marrying the woman is always there, even though, as a rule, it is a question of people they cannot marry. Dreams and fantasies of these people tell of the "secret league" of their boyhood years, which ultimately always has the meaning of marriage.

In this point we can already observe the formation of series, the transition to those persons who can detach themselves easily and can bring into being a long series. The point of departure for one type of person is the mother from whom he cannot detach himself; the other type searches constantly for the irreplaceable one—which also leads to series formation.

3. This is the most interesting and the most puzzling point. What seems strange at first is the [apparent] contrast between this prerequisite and the image of the mother. And yet it is precisely this prerequisite that is modeled upon the mother. Here we can demonstrate the transition to a common [pattern of] behavior. One can often observe that young folks make sexual evaluations along two different lines: on the

one hand they feel great respect toward women, and even adoration for them; occasionally they also fall in love, but pretty nonsensually.[2] They have separated psychic and sensual love from each other; in their upbringing the purely sensual was presented to them as forbidden and contemptible. If their sensuality becomes strong enough, it breaks through "on the side," as it were: they have sexual intercourse only with those who are held in contempt. Developed to the extreme, this type of person arrives at a state of psychic impotence; this is always the sign of a respect that renders the person incapable of relating crude sensuality to the beloved woman.[3] This is the case in general. Now, if the sexual need is very intense and this condition has persisted for a long time, some kind of compromise is established. The woman of dubious reputation provides this possible compromise, which permits a reunification of [the tendencies that produced] the original schism in his love life. It is along these lines that we can explain the raising of disrepute [as a prerequisite]. Analyses have taught us that there are times in puberty when boys will imagine their mothers in all sorts of relationships and even impute to them love affairs. This prerequisite for love, then, mirrors their early fantasies. Just as the sadistic component takes part in the creation of the first prerequisite, so the masochistic component takes part in the creation of this one. These women of ill repute, of course, very easily provide the motivation for jealousy, and the desire to suffer from this jealousy is a singularly masochistic trait. Thus an individual's other character traits also benefit from the formation of these prerequisites for love.

4. This is the most interesting trait—rescue. It is only a rationalization if one tries to derive this prerequisite solely from the interest that many people have in the improvement of those who are not sexually irreproachable. On closer observation, it turns out that it [the need to rescue somebody] is a completely independent trait, which has become linked with ill repute. It would be worthwhile to make a little study sometime, titled: "Motives of rescue and redemption in fantasy

[2] The "on the other hand"—the purely sensual evaluation of a sex object—is missing in the protocol.

[3] Freud described this type in *On the universal tendency to debasement in the sphere of love* (1912). *(Contributions to the psychology of love II) S.E.*, 11.

and neurosis." The deliverer motive goes back to the struggle against masturbation and signifies the yearning for the woman who will put an end to masturbation. If the deliverer in this fantasy bears maternal traits, there are good reasons for it. Among neurotics, we frequently find the fantasy that the mother should give herself up to her son so that he will be able to free himself of masturbation. In the story of Rousseau's youth, this is quite explicitly stated as a fact in his relationship to Mrs. Warrens. The individual deliverer (*not* the world-saviour, the deliverer of mankind) who appears also in Wagner's "Flying Dutchman" and elsewhere in literature, can be regularly traced back to the mother, [who comes] in the wish-fantasy to liberate [the son] from masturbation. But the motif of rescue has another source. In *The Myth of the Birth of the Hero,* the motif has been fully elucidated, in connection with its counterpart. To cast out a body (which regularly means birth) and to rescue—these belong at their roots together. Hence the complex of rescue has something to do with giving birth. The rescue is the thanksgiving, the equivalent of being born; it is the [fulfillment of the] obligation toward the parents, for the gift of birth, and in a very simple way: the rescue is offered in return for being brought into the world. This motif underwent various [forms of] development: with regard to the father, it took on a different meaning from the one it took on in regard to the mother. In relation to the father, it is the fantasy of rescuing the father (emperor or king). In analyses, one sees how the old fantasy became interwoven with a new motif. This fantasy comes into consciousness during a period of rebellion against the father, when one finds it irksome to have to be thankful to him for one's life. Thus, in regard to the father, the motif acquires a hostile connotation, whereas in regard to the mother it has a connotation of tenderness. This fantasy of rescuing a woman from water is especially frequent in dreams; in terms of the analysis of the symbolism of water, it means: to make a child with mother, in return for the gift of one's own birth to give her a child. It is especially interesting in this context to consider those dreams in which plunging into the water, etc., consistently means birth. The dreams of rescue are, in most instances, dreams of inhibition; they are easily understood if one considers the interpretation (to get the mother with child). In a dream reported by Pfister (*Evangelische Freiheit*),[4] we find an interesting variation of such a dream, which is evidence for the correctness of the interpretation. The woman who, in that dream, jumps into the water rescues herself; the interpretation reveals that the woman symbolizes the Madonna: she, of course, needs no one to "save" *her.* At this point, we should take note of the interesting fact that the motif of the drowned body [lit., "water corpse"] (Lindau's story) also belongs in this context and consistently refers to the mother. The bloated drowned body is used as a symbol for the pregnant mother, and it is understandable that the life-giving mother is thrown together with the corpse. In many cases, it is the mother's death that allows this complex to come into the foreground. Finally, it is worth mentioning that in most novels rescue plays a role as a prerequisite for love; it is constantly used by poets.

DISCUSSION

STEKEL first fulfills the task of thanking the speaker for the wealth of stimulation.

The topic has always occupied Stekel's mind, the more so because it is striking that the physician upon whom transference is always established in treatment seems to fulfill the prerequisites for loving in *all* patients. This contradiction however, is resolved when one probes more deeply into the subjects; these people do not love the individual

[4] "Ein Fall von Psychoanalytischer Seelsorge und Seelenheilung" ("A Case of Psychoanalytic Pastoral Care and Psychotherapy") in *Evangelische Freiheit, Monatsschift für die kirchliche Praxis in der gegenwärtigen Kultur* (1909). (*Evangelical Freedom,* A Monthly Magazine for Clerical Practice in Present Day Civilization, 1909.) Pfister himself gives a summary of this article in *Jahrbuch* II.

"The book describes the cure of a youth of nineteen-and-a-half, who for almost four years had been suffering from the obsessional idea that he would have to die in an insane asylum, after leading a useless, morally despicable life. During the previous year, his impulses to commit suicide had turned into decision. A plethora of hypochondriacal brooding regularly brought on headaches. This case belonged in the parson's domain because the youth, who had been brought up in the spirit of free Protestantism, felt powerfully drawn toward Catholicism in spite of the strenuous objections of his own reason, and practised a veritable cult of the Madonna. This abnormal situation was rooted in domestic conditions and scenes which brought about an inner detachment from father and mother. To cite only the most important among numerous conditions, the obsessional fears about his own future issued from his father's threats. In the Madonna and in the venerable figure of a bishop, the patient found substitutes for mother and father. The cure was effected in the course of a few conferences and has lasted up to the present. (June)"

as such, but only in the costume in which they clothe him. This, then, should be added to the Professor's presentation—that, when these prerequisites are not offered by reality, the person produces them in fantasy. Herein also lies the source of the delusion of jealousy, which is needed by the persons involved. Stekel himself is acquainted with several such cases; he relates some instances that fully substantiate the presentation.

It is striking what trifling matters play a decisive role in the choice of a love object (as, for instance, a slight echo of the vowel-system in a sister's name, etc.). Names especially have a definite ability to evoke illusions and to provide disguises; perhaps women's predilection for fancy-dress parties can be explained in this way. It is a well-known fact that men readily fall in love with certain costumes that evoke echoes of childhood memories (e.g., the Gipsy woman, etc.). We need only point in passing to the great ability of girls for slipping into various psychic costumes.

As to his own prerequisites for love, Stekel has not been able to arrive at any conclusion. The prerequisites probably move toward two extremes: they either coincide with the infantile ideal of love, or they are its direct opposite. This may perhaps explain why Jewish men are so ready to marry Christian girls (as the antithesis to their mother).

As for the prostitute, it is true that a number of neurotics are potent only with such a woman; but even then, they do not often succeed with the same woman. As soon as the relationship threatens to become a stable one, marriage fantasies enter the scene.

The neurotic fantasy of turning the mother into a prostitute not only eliminates the rivalry with the father, but also increases the chances of her being attainable. The mother's influence in the early childhood of every human being is so strong that, in this regard, a sexual trauma at the hands of a strange person must be considered a great blessing, since the child is thereby detached from the family.

The feeling of respect is surely a most significant root of impotence. From his own experience, Stekel can confirm the meaning of the redeemer motif. Heretofore Stekel has not known that rescuing means a child. An incident in Wagner's Clinic[5] bears out the symbolism of

[5] The psychiatric clinic of the University of Vienna, under the direction of Wagner-Jauregg.

water; a psychotic patient refused to take a bath, saying, "I do not want to lose my innocence."[6]

Pfister's dream could also have a masturbatory meaning.

STEINER thinks it is evident that the prerequisites for love go back to earliest childhood; since at that time the parental complex is predominant, one can only go through the same train of thought one has already gone through before.

Steiner points to the child's notion that father and mother were related to each other even before marriage, from time immemorial—a mechanism that might continue to be a determining factor in later life. It would seem, in general, that in childhood many things are closer to consciousness, which later on become unconscious.[7]

The fact that, in the love lives of most people, a person who is unattainable and belongs to someone else plays a large role, is a phenomenon which, psychologically, may not need any closer argumentation. Always, and in all areas, one loves that which one can least [easily] have. The resistance of parents plays an important role, too, as an incitement to getting married; psychologically, this may go back to the parents, especially to the mother.

FEDERN stresses that one cannot comment critically on Freud's comprehensive investigations.

He can present a contrast to the type discussed, in his own person. His mother played no role whatsoever in his life; her place was taken by his grandmother. In contradiction to Stekel['s presentation], Federn must stress that it is just as great a lack when the relationship to one's mother is so utterly disturbed. While Federn never had water-rescue fantasies or dreams, he did have a great number of other rescue fantasies. His own prerequisite for loving was that the woman had to be totally unattached. Nor did he ever have the wish to elevate a woman or to save her; he had rather the need to be elevated by the woman—which may perhaps go back to the masturbation struggle.

[6] Stekel may have misunderstood this patient. Schizophrenics often express their thoughts by saying the opposite of what they mean. To take a bath has also, among other meanings, the meaning of being cleansed, having one's innocence restored. If this patient says "I do not want to take a bath because I do not want to lose my innocence," the words, most probably, mean "I *do* want to lose my innocence."

[7] Rather, one would now say that it is almost impossible to make a clear distinction between preconscious and unconscious in early childhood.

In the prerequisite of shifting, even with regard to the prostitute, Stekel definitely went too far. In such cases, we may have to deal with persons with perverse fantasies, which were repressed with great effort; it is because of these perversions that the man cannot look at the prostitute again.

SADGER comments that one cannot grasp at once the full meaning of today's paper and immediately express an opinion about it. One is taken by surprise by the new and interesting things one has heard today. He would like to add only a few remarks.

While he was listening to the four prerequisites for love, a drama, "Unattainable," by Wilbrandt,[8] came to mind. It deals with the first point. There is a bit of homosexuality in it, too—which does seem to have been alien to the poet, in terms of his own experience.

On the basis of his [professional] experiences, Sadger can confirm the existence of fantasies about the mother as a prostitute, and the desire to be saved by her from masturbation. The problem of the love-relationship to the dead mother found new clarification today. Kleist too, for instance, is constantly in search of the grave; his mother died when he was ten years old, and it is conceivable that his wish goes back to this experience, to the fact that he could not free himself of the memory of his dead mother.

ADLER stresses, to begin with, the significance of today's paper. Prerequisites for love should be discussed in detail, even though not all of them may be equally important—such as, for instance, that the girl must be older or taller or smaller, etc. Some persons find their prerequisites for love in the contrast to their own physique. Of greater importance is the prerequisite about which we have heard today; we cannot be satisfied only to establish this concept, but will also have to lay stress on the psychic phenomenon to which this prerequisite for love owes its significance. And this is all the more advisable, since one can find the same phenomenon over again in most other prerequisites brought forward today.

With regard to that type, which unquestionably exists, Adler would like to be permitted to make a small limitation [of concept]: if one considers this more precisely, it seems that similar prerequisites are

[8] Adolf von Wilbrandt, 1837-1911, Austrian poet.

to be found in every neurotic. This does not come as a surprise to us, since all these prerequisites have their source in the relationship to the mother. Duration, intensity and reaction may well determine the final result which, in the mature individual, looks so significantly different; these differences threaten to disappear, however, when we agree upon the mechanism. One can also find situations that are the reverse: for instance, a predilection for prostitutes, which later on can turn into its opposite. It often happens that individuals make the "rescue" attempt once and thereafter it disappears. It would seem that, for the most part, all cases exhibit these points, not always with the same degree of precision, but still by unmistakable clues. In neurotics, one of the most common prerequisites for love is the woman who brings the neurotic love.

Adler's analyses of impotence demonstrate to him the opposite of what Freud described. The patients most often fail because of the absence [on the part of the women] of any coming forward to meet them, and their missing fire with the prostitute is always the condition for a disturbing moment. The desire for another man's wife is very frequent. It follows from this that these people manifest such aggression, not only with regard to their love lives, but that, in the rest of their lives, they are [people of] forward, aggressive dispositions.

In describing this type, Freud showed us only the archetype; the dynamic element begins to enter into it when we approach the train of thought that, in other cases too, [enables us to see what] is playing the most prominent role: [the fact that] the state of *sensitivity* in all these people, which here manifests itself only in this particular form, is invariably a return to the earliest condition under which their sensitivity was stimulated (usually by the inaccessibility of the boy's mother, who does not turn her tenderness entirely toward him). It is this sensitivity that first makes it clear to us how the prototype of the relationship to the mother begins to have its dynamic effects. Adler knows of the case of a woman who begins to love her hitherto unloved husband as soon as he falls in love with another woman—which, moreover, is a common thing. She was certainly ready to leave him, but she cannot tolerate his leaving her. In general, one gets the impression that what is called love is something very rare, and that sensitivity plays in it an almost more important role than the normal sex instinct.

Fidelity and attachment might be traced back to the urge inherent in these characters to fulfill to a certain extent their sense of purity, and even this trait must be based on sensitivity. In order to maintain an equilibrium in the psyche, certain reactions are appropriate—one of which is the consciousness of one's own fidelity.[9]

It is all the more difficult to hold on to this mechanism of sensitivity where it is a question of ill repute. Stekel is quite right in maintaining that fantasy always plays tricks on these individuals; we can only add that the neurotic's enormously increased watchfulness will always find details that are adequate [to arouse] jealousy. As to the ill repute of the woman, Adler can cite experiences from his analyses that elucidate the significance of the patients' sensitivity for this point too. This is a question of persons who have doubts about their own value. They are oppressed by the consciousness of the fact that the woman stands on a higher level than them; in the [effort to] degrade her, they proceed, step by step. They do not come at once, in their search for a substitute, upon prostitution.

This last point, while it strengthens Freud's view more than any other, at the same time fits Adler's own view. The fantasy of the wish to rescue could certainly stem from the prototype too, but again only by way of the inclination of these people toward doing something significant, a wish that has its origins in their increased sensitivity.

Towards an insight into the complexity of all these relationships, Adler considers the evidence of the sensitivity of all these persons to be quite justified and, in his opinion, of the greatest importance.

STEKEL remarks that in his book *Poetry and Neurosis* he had the word "sensitivity" (to neurosis) in mind when he suggested the term "Disturbance of Affectivity." To this ADLER replies that his own paper in which he set forth the significance of sensitivity for the neurosis was presented half a year ago in the Society for Psychology, and that, moreover, the term "Affectivity" stems from Bleuler.

PROF. FREUD, in his remarks closing today's discussion (which will be continued at the first opportunity), appends a biological aspect, which belongs to the incest fantasies: namely, that in these fantasies

[9] This whole paragraph is only vaguely intelligible. We cannot determine whether this is due to Rank's confused recording or Adler's own confusion in thought.

the old family inbreeding lives on; at one time, it was certainly real, and therefore it is an archaic trait in neurotics.

Prof. Freud welcomes as amplifications the various sorts of reactions [of the discussants] to the prerequisites of this type, suggesting even its negative formation, which his paper did not go into. Stekel made a valuable contribution in pointing out that the prerequisites are supplemented in fantasy. Freud based his description of the type on the normal individual who, at least in this respect, is not a neurotic.[10] Stekel's supplement holds true for the neurotic. And the fact that transference (the fulfillment of the prerequisite for love) takes place regularly in treatment, is due precisely to the fact that one is dealing with such neurotics.

Adler now brings to our attention something quite worthy of note, which does not come to light in our presentations. We always follow up the sexual drives and their effect on the psyche; a complete description requires the relationship of the ego-instinct, and Adler demonstrates this part [of the picture] of behavior. This is the censorship that the ego exercises over the actual sexual situation; it is the real cause of repression. In only one point, Freud cannot agree with Adler: Adler's view that the dynamic element is regularly furnished by the ego-instinct; this assumption seems not only arbitrary, but also to involve a grave underestimation of sexuality, which can just as well cathect certain forms with its energy, as is true of our case here. So long as it is a question, for example, of sadism, we cannot determine whether we are dealing with a part of the ego instinct or with a component of the sexual instinct.[11] Where, however, it is a question of masochism, there the purely sexual aspect is rather evident.

[10] This statement seems strange. Neurosis, according to Freud, is based on a libidinal disturbance. How, then, can a neurotic be "normal" in respect to love relationships? It is probably that Freud's statement was in some way garbled in being recorded.

[11] In this deliberation Freud cannot yet decide whether sadism—that is to say, destruction—can be placed as an independent instinct, side by side with the sexual instinct. This he later did in *Beyond the Pleasure Principle*.

81

SCIENTIFIC MEETING *on May 26, 1909*

Present: Prof. Freud, Adler, Federn, Graf, Heller, Hitschmann, Joachim, Rank, Reitler, Sadger, Stekel.

CONTINUATION OF LAST MEETING'S DISCUSSION

On a Specific Type of Male Object-Choice

HITSCHMANN happily hails the fact that at last a way out has been found—and the evidence for it—from the continual reference to being in love with mother. Now one can say in what way [someone is] in love, for how long, when, whether pathologically or normally, etc.

The statements themselves one can, of course, only appreciate. Had someone else described this type, one would have put forward some objections with a little more self-confidence—for instance, that the four characteristics are in part correlates of one another. If a man can love only women who are not free (1.) it is understandable that he would sooner stick to women of bad reputation; then again the wish to rescue is easily comprehensible. Yet, if he arrives at a series-formation, this is generally due in part to the way [of life] of these unrespectable women, and in part to the mode [of existence] of the bachelor. And if one considers how frequently promises of marriage and such are made, one should say that the marriage fantasy too may not be so markedly characteristic of the type. But Hitschmann withholds all these objections, being convinced that the structure is much too close-knit for such commonplace objections to have any significance.

As to Lindau's story, which Hitschmann already knew, he suspected that the love for the girl companion was awakened when the man saw her in the nude; on the other hand, through the frequent predilection of men for servant girls in subordinate positions. Hitschmann has no explanation for the fact that it is precisely the sight of the dead mother, whom the man had certainly loved earlier, that becomes a precondition for loving. By the way, this type reminds him of Molière's "Misanthrope."

REITLER begins by saying a few words about the discussion, the level of which stands in an inverse relation to that of the lecture. This, however, is not meant as a reproach, since objections cannot be brought forward, but only confirmations. As to supplementations [to Freud's exposition], only Stekel and Adler have up to now brought them forward. Stekel touched upon the supplement of the neurotic's fantasies, and it would be interesting to inquire into the reasons why neurotics deviate from the ideal type. If we were able to fathom [the nature of this] differentiating among the prerequisites for loving, we would also come very close to the reason for neuroses. Adler's contribution was only partially correct, and is therefore incorrect. At present he seems preoccupied with new terminologies, which basically say nothing new; for, what he calls "sensitivity," we have called "egocentricity" or the "attitude" of the neurotic.

Reitler has strong resistances to the subject itself, for he is himself such a type [as has been discussed], although with some variations:

1. He got married, and he now recognizes that the motif of rescue, in a social respect, was the determining factor.

2. The prerequisite of disrepute is displaced here, in that his wife was an illegitimate child.

HELLER also has nothing to say in criticism, but he does have a contribution to offer, on the basis of self-knowledge. It is not quite clear to him whether the type was described as being very widespread, that is, as normal or not normal. For some of the traits of the type are present in his own psychic life, too, but only if their distinguishing characteristics are taken in a broader sense.

Point 4, rescue, is distinctly characteristic of him—not, however, in reference to sexual disrepute, but as rescue from real or imagined misery. Just as distinctly characteristic is the symptom of series-formation, along with fidelity to one person. Freud's explanation that in such a series-formation the objects replace one another did not offer much clarity to him, because in his case the objects are quite differentiated, and it is just this that is the motive for the formation of a series. One point was not mentioned at all, [although] it too plays a great role: that the object lost value in proportion as the possibility of possessing it drew closer.

JOACHIM: The expositions about the prerequisites for loving might at first glance appear to be self-evident. On closer examination, however, one sees that something new was presented. These are not prerequisites in the ordinary sense, such as lie within the individual, but rather such as lie outside, so to speak. Thus someone may, for instance, fall in love either with a person whom he already knows or with one whom he does not yet know at all, if [the fact] that she fulfills one of his conditions for loving is brought to his attention. This may perhaps explain why some love-affairs seem so absurd to someone who considers them: he takes into consideration only the persons, and obviously pays no attention to these prerequisites. Afterwards, of course, people often notice such a love reflex and try to find reasons for it ("love at first sight"). People in love are not philosophers, as many have assumed; and the essence and root of love do not consist in penetrating into the essence of the person beloved.

It may perhaps bespeak a certain superficiality on the part of persons in love that they are moved to love by things that are not essential —that, for instance, identity of names is often enough to awaken love. This is, of course, not to be understood as meaning that one can fall in love if only a single prerequisite is fulfilled, while one has, in other respects, a complete aversion [toward that same person]. But where the relationship is otherwise congenial, such a [single] prerequisite can settle the matter. To illustrate this point, Joachim tells the story of a colleague who fell in love three times with so-called "Sisters" (nurses). Upon being asked whether this might not be a matter of love for his [own] sister, he answers that he and his sisters are enemies! His last love, also a nurse, was called Nelly; a guess that one of his sisters might have had this name was not confirmed, either. But now he had a dream in which he called the "nursing sister" Helly. This, however, is his youngest sister's pet name and the English version of the name Helene. A frequent prerequisite is someone's becoming convinced that another person is in love with him. Perhaps this, too, goes back to the maternal root, for the mother indeed offers her love to the child.

A frequent motif in legends and myths is the awakening of the hero's love at the instant a maiden offers him a drink. Related to this may be the medieval love potion, in which secretions of the female body were mixed. It is not inconceivable that this prerequisite for loving goes back to drinking at the maternal bosom—[that is, drinking] a secretion of the female body.

It was pointed out that, for someone who is in love, the beloved object loses its attractiveness as it becomes attainable. As the antithesis to this, one must remember that the person in love very often tries, in his fantasy, to elevate his object to ever higher levels, in the end so high that he alienates it altogether from himself. Thus Goethe, in a sonnet celebrates his beloved, first as his daughter, then as his sister, as his beloved and finally as his princess—which probably also goes back to maternal etiology: the princess is probably his mother.

GRAF can confirm the fact that in many cases falling in love is occasioned by a name or by something that is connected with it by association.

RANK, from his study of the psychology of poets during his investigations into the "Incest-motif in Poetry and Saga" can furnish a dazzling and in all respects pertinent confirmation of the actual existence and the frequency of this type—even if in its development in fantasy.

Type 1. Don Carlos, for whom it is a question of love for the wife of another man—in this case, of the father. On that pattern, an enormous number of dramas have been fashioned; indeed in all of dramatic literature the taking away of a woman is always involved, and it is this that, as a rule, results in the conflict.

Type 2 is not so clear-cut, but can also be demonstrated in going more deeply [into it].

Type 3 is a quite frequent, almost regularly recurring motif in the form of a division: the completely chaste [on the one side] and [on the other] the object of ill repute and lesser worth (the motif, generally known in literature, of the hero who stands between two women: Carlos between Elisabeth and Eboli, Hamlet between Ophelia and Gertrude, Emilia Galotti and Orsina [Lessing's tragedy *Emilia Galotti*], Louise Miller and Lady Milford [Schiller's *Kabale und Liebe*], etc. etc.).

Type 4 is also frequent, as Stekel, for instance, demonstrated in *Traum ein Leben*. In *Kabale und Liebe* (Act II, Scene 6), one finds a form of the rescue-motif that completely confirms Freud's view.

A typical motivation for the mother-rescue in almost all poets is the conviction of the loving son that his mother is unhappy in her marriage to the aging father and must therefore be rescued from this marriage.

As this survey has already shown, this mother etiology can be demonstrated in all great poets—at its finest, perhaps, in Schiller, in whose own love life and poetic work the incest complex found its most perfect expression; Rank proves this by several examples, and it will soon be seen in the work already mentioned [1912].

Just as one type of love life can be derived from the behavior toward the mother, so several types of social behavior can be derived from the behavior toward the father (cf. myth, anarchism).

Finally Rank touches upon a case which shows how, within the framework of this type, [we may find] variations that go as far as a reversal into the opposite. It is Don Juan, who has been already frequently mentioned: he demands in all respects the exact opposite of these prerequisites for loving; nevertheless, the complete turnabout that these now demonstrate proves that they too surely go back to the mother. This is probably connected with the fact that in him the original aggressive component of love life has gained in strength, whereas in others—especially neurotics—it is repressed and thus produces the rejection of sexuality. This causes these persons to flee from the elevated, chaste object, either to persons who offer them their love (prostitutes) or into fantasy (poets).

ADLER: In examining Rank's expositions in conjunction with Professor Freud's, one may be allowed to point out once again that more or less distinct traces of these relationships can be found in everyone. We are not therefore surprised to discover them in poets, too. That is why Adler would like to plead in favor of not creating a strictly defined type on the basis of these prerequisites, but rather of setting wide limits. He wants to add several prerequisites, even though they can be inferred from the material. For instance, representatives of this type show very pronounced sexual envy, which in fact coincides with several of the points mentioned (for instance, 1). A character trait that is rather more difficult to understand—it represents a variation—is the turnover into misogyny. We find traces of this in every person who persists in the rejection of sexuality. The relationship to the mother needs only to become subjected to a reaction from which it emerges in the form of the rejection of women and the result will be misogyny—which may even go so far that the person concerned wants to exclude women from every profession. An examination of political attitudes in general that started from this point would be most interesting. Particularly with regard to the antifeminist movement, we might be able to throw some light by starting from this standpoint; and from this we could move further to the homosexual tendencies of these persons. In such cases, the detachment from the mother in the reaction could be accomplished by way of a person who, in our civilization, is always available—such a person as a tutor (Adler was able to follow through on a case of this kind), a friend, the father, etc.

Finally Adler wants to point to the female counterpart of this type, a counterpart which, in consequence of the so distinctively female culture, may not correspond [to the male] in every aspect but is striking in several—particularly in regard to the demands involved in the prerequisites for loving. To illustrate this, Adler now enlarges on his report about the woman patient, mentioned in the first part of the discussion, for whom it was a prerequisite for loving that the man receive a proposal from another, in this case from a married woman.

STEKEL mentions that he recently discovered the rescue fantasy in a boy he is treating. Also, he came across a poem by Theodor Koerner, which has to do with the rescue of a woman and with a wedding fantasy.

FEDERN tells about a young man's prerequisite for loving which has to do with his father; the young man's wife has eyes that closely resemble his father's.

PROF. FREUD confines himself to adding a few remarks without going into everything that has been brought forward. First he would like to define more exactly the position of his paper within the system. It is a matter here of taking hold of something striking within an area that has not yet been investigated by analysis. Freud encountered this type several times, but he does not consider it to be a very frequent phenomenon and would by no means call it normal.

From the modifications and additions that have been made [in the discussion] it can be seen that what he offered is in no way something complete, but has stirred up, as it were, a great number of related ideas; it was meant to provide a stimulus for going beyond the already somewhat dreary formula of the mother, and for not losing sight of the abundance of psychic happenings, which yield the most diverse results. Soon the main interest will turn from the fact itself to the modifications and the processes that lead to them. There is no doubt that here neurotic and normal happenings touch each other closely and that from here worthwhile insight might be gained into the most diversified processes.

Only a few remarks: Hitschmann set forth the seeming interrelationship of these points. These are the well-known rationalizations that can be compared with the seeming connections in dreams, but in no way exclude the unconscious motivation. The problem of why it is precisely the corpse-prerequisite that is attached to the object in Lindau's story is explained in this way: that this is a prerequisite for loving that first appeared only later; as long as his mother was alive, the man did not need any prerequisite for loving at all.

In general, it should be added that, for the numerous variations, that point of view must be set forth that will be generally decisive for a more refined investigation. It is indeed the vicissitudes of the libido that are involved, and among the vicissitudes the libido's localization will be particularly stressed. This could perhaps be grouped according to the following polar viewpoint:

whether in fantasy or in reality,
whether in consciousness or in the unconscious.

In the development of the different forms, the determining factors are duration and intensity.

Dr. Reitler is to be thanked for the frankness of his communications and we must remember our self-evident obligation of discretion.

Heller related an interesting modification, which is to be evaluated as a contribution similar to that of Stekel—that is to say, with regard to the localization of the libido. The series-formation belongs to the modifications of the type, and not to its characteristics.

Finally, a few words about the other topics, which were touched on only incidentally—for instance, the prerequisites for loving. Knowledge of these is of great significance for [an understanding of] the state of being in love and permits us [to form] a judgment about [the kind of] falling in love [it takes] to conclude in marriage. The prerequisites for loving prove to us that falling in love consists in the fact that an old ideal, which dates from infancy, is realized in another person (Joachim), and that it thus makes sense to say that "marriages are made in heaven."

The significance of names can be borne out in [a study of] cultural history. Among orthodox Jews, there exists the curious prohibition against the son's choosing a girl who has the same name as his mother. The lawgiver obviously knew that the mother stands as the model behind the object-choice. In [the work of] poets, too, we find the prerequisites for loving being taken into consideration in an artful way; for instance, in Shakespeare's *Midsummer Night's Dream,* juice dropped on a person's eyes has the effect of making him fall in love with the first woman he sees upon awakening: the first woman one sees is actually the mother. The same motif, but with a tragic outcome, appears in the Jephtha saga, where the first woman must be sacrificed. This entire complex explains the case of Linda Murri, too, in which the brother becomes a murderer because he wants to "save" his sister.

In some cases Freud came to know of the transition to homosexuality in a different way. A young boy, who, until well in pre-puberty, had been strongly attached to his mother and had no friends, suddenly felt hatred and jealousy toward other boys, because the beloved mother once praised another boy in his presence. In puberty the mother is repressed into the unconscious, which is accomplished by means of identification with her: from then on he too likes boys.[1] If, in a concluding process in consciousness, one part is repressed into the unconscious, then a change also takes place in the other, the [still] conscious part; thus, at one and the same time, he represses his jealousy of the boys and transforms it into love. Another case showed the same characteristic; nevertheless this is not to deny the possibility of a process such as [the one] described in Adler's case.

Finally, in order to exhort caution [in dealing with] these delicate psychological matters, Prof. Freud reports an example from his personal experience that illustrates the role a name can actually play in such a choice of a love object; but often this occurs in a much more subtle way [than has been yet discussed], by association of content (the preference for the name Eve is replaced by attention shown through the gift of an apple).

[1] This is the first indication of the development of a type of homosexuality which was elaborated on later by Sadger.

82

SCIENTIFIC MEETING *on June 2, 1909*

Present: Prof. Freud, Adler, Federn, Hitschmann, Joachim, Rank, Reitler, Steiner, Stekel, Karpas (New York).

On June 16, 1909, a social gathering took place on the *Konstantinhügel* [Hill of Constantine].

PRESENTATION

The Oneness of the Neuroses

SPEAKER: DR. ADLER

In his introductory remarks, the speaker stresses the difficulty of speaking about this subject as early as now; on the other hand, he expresses the hope that through this paper and the discussion of these lines of thought (which are still very much in need of forbearance), we may be able to make a small step forward in the understanding and therapy of neuroses. Then he turns to the subject itself.

It is with old and long since established facts that we must begin—facts that clearly [demand to be recognized] as one of the bases of neurosis, and must be taken into consideration in any summary view of neuroses. Adler is referring to what he has put together under the concept of *organ inferiority*. He has already explained all this, time and again; he would like now to add only that this concept would seem also to furnish the basis for an understanding of instinctual life, inasmuch as instinct, too—as Adler recently explained in a lecture—can be understood only in terms of a theory of evolution. Tied in with organ inferiority is the peculiarity of a more powerful instinct, and a later [than usual] fitting into the norm—from which there follow alterations that consistently come into conflict with the demands of civilization. These peculiarities are reflected in psychic life, with the result that we encounter inhibitions of development in the psyche, too, but also more significant achievements that rise above the average. Thus the following proposition has some justification: greater achievements of an organic and psychic nature take place on the basis of this organ inferiority, as long as it forces no more than the proper compensation and additional growth. Or perhaps one could better express it, from the point of view of practice, by saying that, under favorable circumstances, certain defects in a child create a disposition toward greater performance.

There is a second point—and it too is only a recapitulation of previously discussed relationships—which assumes importance in instinctual life insofar as here, too, the psychic inhibitions of development become manifest. It is to be looked for in the sphere of what the speaker has put together under the name of *aggressive drive*. The scope of this concept is known, too; and for the purposes of today's discussion Adler wants only to mention briefly that what is involved here is an achievement of civilization that was necessary for the development of mankind, inasmuch as the capacity to think ahead and to feel ahead could come about only by way of this detour over inhibited aggression. This inhibition in turn has its origin in a fearing ahead, such as we find, once again, as a rule in neuroses. The difficulty in fitting together all the neuroses into this sphere lies in the fact that their forms of expression are so varied that in many cases one finds only traces of one form (e.g., anxiety), while in other cases one finds such clear features that everything else disappears. But it will always be possible to trace the diverse forms back to the instinct of aggression. Thus here too we find once more the existence of a common etiology and therefore we may venture, from this angle too, to undertake to bring together all neuroses.

A third factor that Adler found prominent in all the neuroses that he could subject to analysis is *oversensitivity*—one of the most conspicuous characteristics of all neurotics. In textbooks it is mentioned cursorily. The analysis of this trait seems to be by no means the simplest thing to accomplish. Adler has already explained that what is involved is a surprising [ability to] utilize to the fullest the zone of sensitivity. The patient is sensitive in areas of his psyche that, in the case of a halfway normal person would not enter his thoughts, [as areas] in which sensitivity plays a role. The connection with the instinct of aggression is rather evident here; other connections are not so easy to recognize. The origin of this sensitivity lies in the transformations of the instinct of aggression. Knowledge of this contributes greatly, to begin with, to an understanding of the patient's personality and character; in the second place, it is indispensable to the analysis of individual attacks, which we are able to understand only if we know in which area of his psyche the patient is sensitive. The ascertaining of this area not only [indicates] the path for the analysis but also [provides] a certain unburdening for the patient. His confidence in the physician becomes enormous as soon as the patient feels that his sensitivity is understood and allowances are made for it. By the same token, most patients who break off treatment do so out of a wounded sensitivity.

Adler now turns to a consideration of the beginnings of instinctual life and of the character that has developed therefrom. This is a point which, at the moment, it is difficult for him to discuss. This is a question of the section that Freud has comprised under the term *anal character*. Adler has already mentioned several times that, as a rule, he finds the anal character in his analyses, though not always with such sharp features as Freud has presented it to us, and perhaps with some additional traits; yet it certainly appears in connection with the points previously mentioned: organ inferiority, aggressive instinct and extraordinarily intensified sensitivity. The latter in particular is so intimately linked with the anal character that it cannot possibly be severed from it; indeed, some of the anal character traits enumerated by Freud have their basis in this sensitivity—for example, stubborn defiance.

Avarice, too, Adler was repeatedly able to trace back to sensitivity. On the other hand, this sensitivity is strengthened by the causes for the development of an anal character. Ultimately, sensitivity goes back to a fear of soiling, which in the earliest childhood years surely represents a phenomenon of civilization, and goes directly back to the anal character. The latter develops regularly as a component of the human character; from this point of view, too, we cannot therefore be surprised to discover it in all neurotics. At this point, Adler cannot go into more detail, but [he asserts] that that which we see as fear of soiling and, in a figurative sense, is fear of degradation, offence, wounding, loss of cultural level—this stems from a reaction to the anal character and generally turns into sensitivity.

The same [sort of] expansion should be permitted with regard to the other point on which Freud spoke recently—i.e., the connection of neuroses with the *relationship to the parents* (to father or mother). This relationship, too, is not absent from any case; if it is not so pronounced in all cases, it can still always be found in hints.

In the normal individual, too, but especially in the neurotic—and here would be the moment to put together the five points into one—under the pressure of these various impulses, there will arise inner conflicts which the psyche will attempt to balance out in one way or another.

Now the next task—and this is the most difficult part—would be to develop once again from these bases the common characteristics of the neuroses. The second, even more difficult, question that emerges is this: what now happens to the concept of the *choice of neurosis?* Since all this really belongs to the program of the future, for the present we can only make a modest contribution [to the subject]. The material shows that the confluence and collision of instincts is of the greatest importance [in the choice of a neurosis]. The fact that organ inferiority plays its part here too can be seen consistently from the analysis of certain functional symptoms. These encounters, and the conflict of instincts that are especially pronounced, yet not free for cultural utilization, as well as the degree to which aggression is restricted—these certainly play their part in the choice of a form of neurosis; but it cannot possibly be that this is all, or we would have to suppose that even a small difference in the strength of an instinct suffices. The most important factor in the choice of neurosis, however, is definitely the stage of the child's development at which this clash occurs—the clash among separate instincts [or of these] with civilization, with the external world—briefly, at what point the inner conflicts make themselves heard. The speaker almost doubts that he can demonstrate in abstract form what this is all about; he will therefore discuss the circumstances [to be found] in an example.

This is the case of a woman patient who, as a child, showed distinct signs of an inferiority of the eyes which is also found in [other members of] her family. A precocious childhood, sexual impulses and seduction—and especially the fact that the patient's ambition had already in early childhood assumed tremendous proportions. This girl then goes further. Led by love for her father, she develops a fantasy in which he is the greatest man in the world. She then shows an overflowing overestimation of her father, of which she has not been able to rid herself to this day. This often causes her, in her sexual relationships, to seek as a prerequisite that the man be very prominent, but this connection is not accessible to her consciousness. During the course of her analysis, it becomes clear that the patient has been unhappy in her married life because her husband did not fulfill the prerequisite of being the most outstanding man of all. Adler has quoted this small fragment only in order to demonstrate at what stage of the development of instinctual life the inhibition of aggression exercises its effect. It is evident that in the case of this patient the inhibition of aggression lies in her relationship to her father; there remains in her fantasy, as a very important element, this residue: that it is the most outstanding man that she must choose. The fact that sensitivity is directly connected with this, especially in all transferred sexual relations, is easy to see. We must assume that the inhibition of aggression (i.e., the formation of the fantasy and its repression) occurs at the time when the child becomes conscious of various relationships to the father; out of this is developed the prerequisite that the beloved man must have an affair, must be a scoundrel, etc. etc.—even if these conditions existed originally only in the child's fantasy (the product of her distrust, etc.).

Even though no choice of neurosis can be demonstrated in this case, nevertheless variations in symptom formation can be observed. The questions here are: at what stage of development this inner conflict comes to light in the child, at what point in his psychological development repression takes place, and what intellectual level the child has then reached. These conditions Adler deliberately expressed, he says, in such a vague form; now he would like to mention only one determining factor: namely, the fact that what is involved is a number of psychic performances by the child, which have to do with: (1) his ability to react to the outside world, that is, the effectiveness and developmental strength of his instinct of aggression; and (2) the strength of his capacity to react to himself—that is to say, how far he is in a position to overcome unpleasant trains of thought, to repress them or to transform them into their opposites.

While preserving the principle of the oneness of neuroses, one may say that the choice of neurosis is quite generally conditioned by these factors: when and in what state the sounds of his inner conflicts reach the individual, i.e., in what state he encounters the inhibition of aggression—or in more generally understandable terms, in what mental condition the repression of fantasies takes place. In this process, as has already been stressed, the strength of the reaction toward external as well as internal experience plays a principal role. From this, one point becomes evident, a point which should be given some weight: a neurosis must be traced back to the time before the repression occurred, something that Freud did regularly, and which is confirmed when one considers the anal character. The latter concerns the stage of development at which, as mentioned before, the fateful event occurs. Thus it is clear that it is in fact a question of an innate instinct, and that organ inferiority is in the background; organ inferiority cannot, to be sure, decide the choice of neurosis, it cannot by itself lead to a neurosis; but consideration of it is indispensable to an understanding of the choice of neurosis and of the symptomatology of the neurosis that occurs later.

The speaker then offers a further example that has to do with the choice of neurosis, in order to demonstrate the total picture by way of an individual case. This case shows the characteristics of the relationship to the mother very closely, and in all respects. The patient, an extremely ambitious child, later underwent an intensification of these prerequisites. He wants not only to be in his father's place but—out of his pre-neurotic ambition—he is striving [ultimately] to surpass his father. Thoughts about his father's death and the inheritance that would then fall to him play a large role. But his father enjoys rather good health; and as the neurosis sets in, the patient develops a buying compulsion—that is, a striking compulsion neurosis. This can be traced back to the fact that the patient, in order to drown out his fantasies and to avoid the psychic pain caused by his oversensitivity, moves himself into the time when he will already be heir to his father; he thus brings the situation much more sharply into focus: he is in possession of the fortune, he can do whatever he likes, and if he is in any way hurt in his sensitivity he tries to soothe his feelings by making large purchases, which go far beyond his means. Here we find the conditions of vanity, of ambition and of over-sensitivity to pain connected with the reaction to the self. This patient acquires his obsessional neurosis on the basis of the same experiences that in another case lead to hysteria (hysteria with states of depression) and not to obsessional neurosis; otherwise, that case shows the same elements except for ambition, and certainly a lesser degree of sensitivity to pain.

From this vantage point, it will be possible later to clarify our view. The patient in the second case, for instance, tries to achieve control over his fantasies not so much by means of actions based on the aggressive instinct as by forgetting, by amnesia; this is a difference that certainly goes back to the first years of life.

The speaker closes by pointing out that he has kept his word in so far as he was able to offer an outline, the chief purpose of which was to show that even today we are in a position to draw from our analyses a justified conclusion as to how one has to envisage the choice of neurosis, and that in fact the preconditions exist for putting all neuroses together under one uniform viewpoint.

DISCUSSION

PROF. FREUD sees little to find fault with, in the details of Adler's unusually lucid and consistent train of thought, but he must confess that in general, he has a different standpoint. It is interesting to compare these standpoints with each other and thus to throw light on the problems from various sides.[1]

Taking into account Adler's request for an attitude of forbearance toward his ideas, which are not yet fully ready for decision, Freud asks for an analogous attitude toward his criticisms.

The most general objection is that Adler, almost as if by design, has eliminated the sexual factor, which cannot be omitted when one considers the oneness of the neuroses. Adler is essentially occupied with the psychology of consciousness and with that portion of psychology that he (Freud) has neglected; one might call it the psychology of the ego instincts. The whole of psychotherapy is ranged on the side of the other, the erotic instincts, so as to render an individual capable of the other interests. The etiology of neuroses is on the whole sexual. As a complement to it, writing about the ego instincts and their behavior with regard to the sexual instincts that are to be warded off, is a matter of extraordinary importance; it is [in fact] indispensable. But one must oppose the view that the description of this part of psychology represents the characterization of the neuroses; it is the characterization of the ego.

Organ-inferiority and Freud's personal view about it have already been discussed repeatedly. (Point 1.)

As to the instinct of aggression, Freud objected to the view that hypostatizes the instinctual character of all instincts as a particular instinct, and then allots to all other instincts only formal content. (Point 2.)

As for his position on Adler's third point, oversensitivity, it is that this is a specific character trait not of the neurotic individual but of certain ego instincts in the individual. In the oversensitivity of an individual one can see only motivations for repression. It denotes to us the loci of repression, behind which the pathologic complexes are hidden. As such, it provides a welcome completion [of the picture]. In general, the third point cannot be regarded as a characteristic of neuroses, [although] perhaps it may be regarded as a characteristic of the neurotic. Sensitivity could be compared in a way to a libido of the ego instincts.

[1] See: *On the History of the Psycho-Analytic Movement* (1914), *S.E.* 14.

With reference to the universality of the anal character and of the relationship to the parents (points 4 and 5), Freud is in full agreement with Adler's opinion. These then are not characteristics of neuroses but of all human beings. By the way, it surprised Freud to find that even Adler confused anal erotism with anal character. Freud himself wanted only to show that certain character traits have this erotic origin; but this has nothing to do with the neuroses. The universality of the relationship to one's parents belongs just as little to neurosis, but rather to the general prerequisites for civilization. The last two points are, therefore, especially unsuited for establishing a oneness of the neuroses.

With reference to the problem of the choice of neurosis, Freud must grant that in Adler he has found several of his [Freud's] own conclusions. Adler sees as the prerequisites [for the choice of neurosis]: (1) organ inferiority; (2) the confluence of instincts and (3) the stage of psychic development at which the conflict befalls the child. Freud would like to express his opinion about these points in the following way: his own attempts to explain the choice of neurosis have failed until now; an enormous number of factors have to be taken into consideration. Organ inferiority is thought to be decisive in the choice of a symptom, that is in the localization. The choice of neurosis, however, is totally independent of somatic compliance. Freud does not think it improbable that confluence of instincts plays a role in it. The stage of development has found in his own reflection a somewhat different role, in which the time of life is the determining element. Generally, however, the time of life corresponds to different stages of development, and it is not the absolute number [of years] but the stage of development that has been reached in it that is the essential factor. It seems that hysteria is connected with the earliest [stages], obsessional neurosis with the ongoing [stages], and paranoia with the last stages. The time at which the conflict arises coincides with the outbreak of illness; it is not, however, the time at which the choice of neurosis takes place.

The choice of neurosis depends, however, on other elements, and the determining factor is not among the three named. Freud himself has abandoned the idea of the time of life; what caused him to do so was the way in which the neuroses develop out of one another, and give way to one another. What happens most frequently is that, in analyzing an obsessional neurosis, one encounters certain forms of hysteria in the individual concerned; this would also tally with the earlier acquisition of hysteria. But what is one to do with cases in which, for instance, a girl of sixteen or seventeen begins with an obsessional neurosis and then half a year later develops a hysteria? What [is one to do] with those cases, so frequent and on which so little research has been done, in which for a rather long time the illness is regarded as a hysteria and gradually a dementia comes to light? Or with persons who, having had a hysteria for years, suddenly change to a paranoia? These are conditions that cannot possibly be explained in terms of those three points. Freud has the impression that Adler's abstractions have little life [in them], and that his attempt to solve this problem did not succeed.

The most interesting fact, however, is that the oneness of the neuroses does not now need to be searched for, because it has existed for a very long time. Freud himself conceives of the neuroses as substitutive formations for the repressed libido[2] and explains their differences in terms of the different mechanisms of the repression and of the return of the repressed. The disposition for the choice [of a specific form] of neurosis lies, according to his view, in the vicissitudes of the libido, some of which we have met with, and which seem to take their course through various inhibitions of development. Here again the element of time makes itself felt, so to speak. The most generally accepted pathological point of view is [to equate] inhibition of development with disposition, and regression with the mechanism of falling ill; that which gives it its impetus, however, is the libido and its vicissitudes.

ADLER first turns back the reproach of having eliminated the sexual factor, by pointing out that he did not talk today about etiology and thought he could forgo stressing the importance of sexuality. Moreover, this gap too seems to have been closed by the fifth point. In reference to hypersensitivity, he is planning a major work that may clear up this point. It is by no means a question here of the ego-instincts forming a barrier against the sexual instincts, but of a permanent state of mind [*Stimmungslage*] which immediately intervenes with all

[2] The original has: "*Verdrängung der Libido*" = "repression of libido," which does not make sense.

means at the organism's disposal, as soon as a more sensitive spot is touched; it is evident that this means more for the understanding of neuroses [than the ego instinct]. He cannot enter into a critique of instinctual life; it is, however, easy to show that an instinct does not have a formal character at all but can be understood only from its developmental history. Adler does not believe that he has committed an error with regard to the anal character; he is glad to see that Freud also views the anal character as universal.

Points 4 and 5 should be considered together insofar as, under certain conditions, they lead to an inner conflict; this conflict should rather be designated as primary conflict, for it was not the conflict that precipitates the outbreak of illness, that he had had in mind.

As to the choice of neurosis, there is a certain difference between saying that time determines it, and that the stage of development does. If Freud emphasizes that the rise of neuroses depends on the development of the libido and its disturbances, this question is justified: what are the causes of these developmental disturbances? Adler recalls a case from which it is evident that this developmental disturbance does not necessarily have to be congenital, and yet also stems from that constitution. One need not by any means have recourse to the innateness of a libido. The determining factor for the formation of neuroses, as well as for the choice of neurosis, is this primary conflict, in which the contradictions come to light. It follows from Adler's view that the oneness of neuroses goes more deeply than the etiology of the individual neuroses, which hitherto have received a separate examination. The principle of oneness must disregard the choice of neurosis; that is a matter of differentiating, which grows out of the psychic constitution, so that actually it does not make any fundamental difference whether an individual becomes a neurasthenic, a hysteric or a paranoiac. In regard to the turning of one neurosis into the other, one must state, from the viewpoint of the significance of the developmental stage, that there can exist a stage at which it may happen, as the result of an inner contradiction, that a mixture of all neuroses can appear.

FEDERN: Just as Goethe set himself the task of showing what kind of human being Hamlet was before he had the terrible experience with his father, so Adler has asked himself what kind of person the neurotic is before he experiences the primary conflict, before he succumbs to the formation of the neurosis. One could start from the other side, and investigate how it is with neurotics who have been cured, and thus find out whether they show specifically constitutional differences. Adler looks for these constitutional differences in a localized hypersensitivity of the ego instinct. The oversensitivity would then have to continue to exist even after the cure. Adler considers the man who is already a neurotic when he comes to see him, and it is evident that he [the neurotic] must always show the various symptoms of local hypersensitivity. The latter is already implied in the unpleasure-toned feelings of neurotics.

Sensitivity as intensified reaction to a minor stimulus is already familiar to us. The question is whether this hypersensitivity is due to the fact that certain instincts of the neurotics are displaced or repressed, or whether there is a constitutional element. Often one encounters among normal persons an unheard-of hypersensitivity, and yet they remain normal because they are not disturbed by abnormal part-instincts. Thus [the theory of] "sensitivity" cannot be upheld (except insofar as it is a consequence of repression); it is too general a concept for often even the intensity of feeling implies hypersensitivity. As to whether it is by elements of time or of developmental history that the choice of neurosis is determined, Federn believes that this "primary conflict" can arise at any time, whenever one of the part-instincts becomes unbearable.

STEKEL, having heard Adler's discourse only in part, cannot go into it, and would therefore like to present his own standpoint on the question of the choice of neurosis and of the oneness of the neuroses. Sometimes he thinks that there is only one neurosis, which comes into being through repression, and that what we characterize as different types of neurosis are only different forms, which we have fashioned ourselves. There is something unfathomed out of which the various pictures crystallize. He believes only in a repression-neurosis, which we call hysteria; and it is this that—according to the constitution, as Adler has pointed out—can express itself [in different ways].

In regard to compulsion neurosis, Stekel recently made a discovery: the genesis of doubting goes back to the fact that in childhood these persons and their love were placed between two persons (for instance, mother and governess, father and tutor, etc.).

To Stekel, what is characteristic in the formation of neuroses is only one factor, which Adler has emphasized and which Freud also stresses: neurosis does not owe its origin to a sexual trauma, nor to early sexual experiences, but to the relationship of early sexuality to the parents, to whether it was more strongly or more weakly fixated on them. The simplest formula would then be: the causes of neurosis lies in the relationship of infantile sexuality to the parents' sexuality.[3] In this sense, he is a supporter of the theory Adler presented; he, too, believes in the oneness of the neuroses. Neurosis is a disturbance of affectivity which results from the fact that the child, at any early age, had to repress its true affects toward its parents, from which has come disorder in its emotional life. The concept of hypersensitivity does not express this with precision. The neurotic reacts abnormally for this reason—because with minor stimuli one can arrive at a complex that is marked by strong affects.

HITSCHMANN is inclined to characterize Adler's standpoint as being fruitful in its opposition. He has the feeling that for Adler those questions emerge again and again that one easily finds to be banal. Everyone is agreed that these sexual causes always have to meet with a certain character in order to become pathogenic. It is therefore quite justified to attempt to inquire into what sort of character is necessary for the formation of neuroses. Hitschmann always had the idea that it is the way in which the individual reacts to sexual inquiries and what he makes of them that permit a certain neurosis to form. And in this one cannot deny the significance of a kind of innate character, or inherited characteristics. What Freud has always called "psychosexual constitution" is one note, it goes without saying, in all our discussions. The attempt to see whether there is something homogeneous behind it is certainly justified.

Hitschmann does not have enough experience to offer a definitive judgment about what has been presented. In general, he feels rather unsatisfied. In particular, hypersensitivity is found in perverts to the

[3] This formulation does not jibe with what was said before. Stekel may have intended to say "to the parents as sex objects."

same degree; so too with psychopaths, who have glided past a neurosis. If the main characteristic of neurosis lies in repression, one must construe an instinct of repression, which does not exist in others [non-neurotics]. Does this instinct perhaps come close to "sensitivity" or does it perhaps even correspond to it?

REITLER comments that just as, by postulating the instinct of aggression, Adler takes from the sexual instinct the element of drive, so he endeavors to strip the instinct of self-preservation of its driving force by detaching from it hypersensitivity as a *movens*. This is connected with a misunderstanding that developed in relation to the concept of part instincts. It appeared as if these part instincts could lead a separate existence—the sort of impression that could have been avoided if one had used a different nomenclature (such as "instinct segments"). In this way it became possible to strip the entire sexual instinct of its instinctual character—which, of course, is nonsense.

Anal character and relationship to parents is common to all men and not only to neurotics.

As far as the choice of neurosis is concerned, organ inferiority is decisive for the symptom formation and perhaps also for the attack; the same holds true of the confluence of instincts (which, by the way, should rather be called instinct fusion). There is no evidence to confirm the assertion that the stage of development is the determining factor.

With regard to the oneness of the neuroses, Reitler has long had his own ideas. Hitherto we have sharply distinguished the neuroses from one another; now we shall have to study developmental history. Reitler is convinced that the neuroses known to us develop one out of the other, that they are developmental stages of a series. The primary stage is the anxiety neurosis, in Freud's sense; the second stage is the psychic superstructure over the anxiety neurosis, the anxiety hysteria. The third stage, the obsessional neurosis, is nothing other than an anxiety hysteria in which we find a number of reactions (protective measures, penitences, etc.) to the suppressed, anxiety-generating ideas. Obsessional neurosis is thus to be regarded merely as a more fully developed anxiety hysteria. Conversion hysteria must be viewed as parallel to the obsessional neurosis: obsessional protective measures in conversion hysteria are identical with the obsessive deeds of neurotics. The confirmation of this view can be seen in the fact that behind every compulsion neurosis can be found an anxiety hysteria, and that the resolution of a compulsion neurosis always takes its course over an anxiety hysteria. The going over from one neurosis into another is not a "sudden shift," but is to be interpreted as a developmental process.

ADLER has only thanks for the attention and thinks that he has been relieved of the obligation to go into most [of the points raised]. There is only one point that he would like to mention. Hitschmann thinks that hypersensitivity is found in others, too. This argument can easily be refuted, for there is no pervert who does not show neurotic symptoms. The same holds true for psychopaths in general. Thus Adler holds fast to his theory of hypersensitivity, to a very great extent.

PROF. FREUD makes in closing a few comments that were stimulated by the discussion.

The oneness of neuroses has meaning only if one also has regard for the diversity of neuroses: and this rests on the diversity of the conditions under which repression takes place. The forms are not, as Stekel thinks, unessential and conventional. Differences in therapy, in judging the neurotic in actual life, and perhaps also in prophylaxis, correspond to the differences in the mechanisms of repression.

In response to Stekel's remarks about doubting and the "incestuous thoughts" of every neurotic, Freud would like to say the following: The explanation of doubting in terms of an accidental impetus in an important period of life, is, as he can assert on the basis of well analyzed cases, too shallow. As far as the parent complex is concerned, one must, despite all due recognition of Stekel's "scent" [for the unconscious], raise an objection. The oneness of the neuroses surely has accidental reasons, too insofar as much of their uniformity arises out of similar origins. The complex that forms the core of neuroses contains the incest-fantasy, but a few other things as well; what is unsatisfactory in Stekel's explanation is the fact that it is merely a wall behind which further vistas open up. It is possible to analyze it further; the customary explanations remain quite a bit behind the essential complex.

To say that the oneness of the neuroses lies in their etiology is not sufficient either, because this coincides with the etiology of our psychic development in other respects. The question of why one becomes ill has evaporated during the course of our analytic efforts[4]; once and for all, such a single cause does not exist, there is no such general etiology. Whether or not an individual falls ill is determined solely by quantitative relationships.[5]

[4] Freud's remark that the question concerning the etiology of the neuroses has "evaporated" in the course of the discussion is somewhat puzzling. The problem of the choice of neurosis, i.e., of the specificity of a neurosis, has not been fully mastered to this day, whereas Freud himself has given us some understanding of the etiology of the neuroses. He has often stated—he does subsequently in this very discussion—that the question of the etiology of neuroses is a question of quantities. This means that an excessive amount of instinct frequently cannot be mastered even by a normal ego, and thus becomes a cause for neurosis; however, an overly weak ego is just as incapable of mastering a normal quantity of instinct energy and can thus lead just as well to the development of a neurosis.

Several years later Freud found the law of the etiological complemental series: constitution and external influence (trauma) complement each other. The stronger the constitution, the more powerful the trauma must be to bring about a neurotic disturbance; the weaker the constitution, the less the traumatic energy that is sufficient to bring about this result.

All of this leads to the conclusion that there is not a single etiology of the neuroses but several etiologies, a conclusion that Freud expressed in this discussion, just as he did on many other occasions. The multiplicity of etiologies may perhaps also explain the specificity of the choice of a neurosis.

[5] In this meeting the latent discords with Adler become manifest for the first time. Freud acknowledges what should be recognized and criticizes what goes counter to his own conception. But he is always fair. How generously Freud acknowledges the part taken by the ego in the formation of neurosis, as is stressed by Adler! But, he says, Adlerian ego psychology is not a psychology of the unconscious; it is a psychology of consciousness.

83

SCIENTIFIC MEETING *on October 12, 1909*

EIGHTH YEAR OF THE SOCIETY 1909/1910

Roll of current members (October 1909): 23

Prof. Dr. Sigmund Freud
Dr. Alfred Adler
Dr. D. J. Bach
Dr. Alfred Bass
[crossed out in the original]
Dr. Guido Brecher
Dr. Paul Federn
Dr. Alexander Ferenczi
Dr. Max Graf
Dr. Hugo Heller
Dr. Eduard Hitschmann
Dr. Edwin Hollerung
Dr. Albert Joachim
Dr. Otto Rank
Dr. Rudolf Reitler
Dr. Oskar Rie
Dr. Maxim Steiner
Dr. Isidor Sadger
Dr. Hugo Schwerdtner
[crossed out]
Dr. Wilhelm Stekel
Dr. Rudolf Urbantschitsch
Dr. Fritz Wittels

Dr. Josef K. Friedjung
Dr. Carl Furtmüller
Dr. Victor Tausk
Dr. David Ernst Oppenheim
Dr. Ludwig Jekels
Dr. Margarete Hilferding
Dr. Stefan Maday
Dr. Baron Franz v. Hye
Dr. Richard Nepallek

Tuesday, October 12, 1909: This year's first meeting was held for the purpose of welcoming members and took place at the Hotel Residenz.

Present: Prof. Freud, Adler, Bach, A. Deutsch, Federn, Graf, Heller, Hitschmann, Hollerung, Rank, Reitler, Rie, Sadger, Schwerdtner, Steiner, Stekel, Urbantschitsch, Wittels.

Guests: Dr. Eitingon, Imperial Councillor Freud, Phillip Frey, Dr. Friedjung, Dr. Furtmüller, Dr. Kahane, Dr. Nepallek, Dr. Rosenberg, Dr. Tausk.

Unable to attend: Bass, Ferenczi, Häutler, Joachim, Prof. Königsberg, Meisl.

SCIENTIFIC MEETING *on October 20, 1909*

Present: Freud, Adler, Bass, Federn, Hitschmann, Hollerung, Rank, Reitler, Steiner, Sadger, Stekel, Wittels.

Guests: Dr. Eitingon, Dr. Tausk.

Proposed for membership: Dr. Friedjung, Dr. Furtmüller.

PRESENTATION

Experience and Emotional Experience

["Erfahren und Erleben"] [1]

[*Encountering experience and living through an experience with awareness and affective response*] [2]

SPEAKER: OBERSTABSARZT DR. E. HOLLERUNG

DISCUSSION

FEDERN emphasizes that the main reason why he could not go into all the details is that, in the first place, as the speaker himself has

[1] The English expression for the German *Erfahren*, as well as for *Erleben*, is "to experience." *Erfahren*, as used in this paper, means to *encounter an external experience;* it does not imply the subject's emotional involvement and participation. *Erleben* means to *live through an experience* with full emotional participation and awareness. Except in those passages where we have used a still fuller characterization of these concepts, we have translated *Erfahren* as "meeting with a practical experience" and *Erleben* as "living through a personal experience."

[2] No protocol has been preserved of this paper by Hollerung, just as none exists of his paper on Semon's *Mneme* (Vol. I, Min. 6). Hollerung presented the same paper

pointed out, some of his theses are arbitrary assumptions. To Federn the essential thing seems to be that the speaker very correctly has made a distinction between *Erfahren* and *Erleben* ["meeting with a practical experience" and "living through an experience with emotional involvement"]. This distinction could be of great value in regard to the formation of neuroses. Several symptoms of neuroses seem to be characterized by the fact that the neurotic is capable of both meeting experiences and going through them in the same situation in which, for the normal individual, either one or the other is no longer possible, or else has not yet become so.[3]

One part of the disposition to neurosis may be seen in the fact that these persons, as the result of their precocious development of drive and instinct, live through emotionally, at an earlier period, what others can merely meet with as an external experience; and only later do these others become capable of living through them emotionally. Psychoanesthesia could be explained in terms of the individuals merely *having* [meeting with] experiences, instead of living through them. The neurotic, on the other hand, has inner experiences without preceding external ones; we can define analysis, also, in the following terms: by way of providing external experience, at a later point, we attempt to blunt the effect of these inner (earlier) experiences.

STEKEL states that he went through an emotional experience today without having met with an external experience. His negative attitude toward these organic things has rendered him incapable of apperception. Nevertheless Stekel joins the last speaker in expressing his thanks [for the presentation].

WITTELS comments that he too was able to follow these in part abstract and psychophysical trains of thought only partially, since this direction is very foreign to him. Moreover, one would have to reflect

---

two days later, on October 22, 1909, to the Society for Psychology [*Gesellschaft für Psychologie*] in Vienna. It was published in 1910 by Leuschner & Lubensky in Graz. It is noteworthy that none of Hollerung's works—he published at least one other article, "The Application of the Principle of Causality in the Medical Sciences," in the *Wiener Medizinische Wochenschrift*, 1906—has ever been mentioned in any psychoanalytic bibliography.

[3] Actually, it is the opposite that would be true.

longer about these things in order to be able to express an opinion about them.

ADLER has the impression that the speaker has prepared a great surprise for us. To be sure, Adler considers the statements, in their present form, to be pure fantasy; but this does have perspective, and for this reason it would be very much to be desired that the work be forthcoming soon *in extenso*. He would like to single out one thought that he had himself been at the point of expressing: that the brain, the central nervous system, have become subject, with regard to their accomplishments, to a certain overestimation; and that we would do well to recall their development, which shows that the cerebrum is essentially not very different from the sense organs.[4] Perhaps here too we are dealing with an organ that acts merely as a registrant and not autonomously.[5]

There are a good many perspectives; but we want to refer to only two specifically: (1) that, especially in our investigations of neuroses, we are steering more and more toward the idea that we are dealing with chemistry, a point to which Freud has also made reference. The second perspective has to do with the problem of heredity (the sexual cells too are continually touched on). In numerous works of the last decade (Pavlov too will be mentioned), it is shown how intimately chemistry is connected with psychic life; similar inquiries into the changed chemistry of the blood and the sexual cells are unknown to him, and for that reason he regards today's paper as a valuable contribution.

DR. TAUSK (as guest), in contrast to Adler who regards the physiological problem as the main point of today's paper, would like to make the problem of knowledge the focus. If one speaks of a chem-

[4] The German text runs as follows: ". . . die das Grosshirn nicht weit von den Sinnesorganen stellt . . ."; this, literally translated, is: ". . . which places the cerebrum not far from the sense organs. . . ."

[5] Adler, when he says that the brain is essentially not very different from a sense organ, seems to have in some way absorbed a view held by Freud, but to have missed the point of it. In *The Interpretation of Dreams* Freud already says that the conscious is the organ of perception; and later he developed the idea that the sense organs (eyes, ears, etc.) are protrusions, as it were, of the cortex, which have their psychological representation in the Ego and Superego. See Freud's metapsychological works, as well as *Beyond the Pleasure Principle* (*S.E.* 18), *The Ego and the Id* (*S.E.* 19), and *A Note Upon the Mystic Writing Pad* (*S.E.* 19).

istry [of the body], one can understand this only as an analogy: namely, that the psychic processes unfold in accordance with those universal laws that hold in general for the mechanical processes. What has not been spoken of is quality; how does this chemistry function so that the *quality* comes into being? This is the whole question of the theory of knowledge.

(Adler would like to set matters straight, because it is here a question of the fact that the impressions from the external world must first pass through the blood in order to appear as sensation.)

REITLER thinks that the paper on the whole left a strange impression because it has the significance of a preliminary communication; for that reason, it is to be desired that it be submitted *in extenso*.

At the moment, Reitler would like to single out only a few details. It is striking that the reporter spoke against the belief that animals have an ego-consciousness. It was not made clear how the speaker differentiates between feeling and sensation. There is no doubt that the chemistry of the blood influences the brain (as evidenced by states of intoxication, anaesthesia, etc.); however, Reitler would doubt that that necessitates [the assumption of] a secretion [*Absonderung*][6] from the brain. Finally, one must energetically reject the dictum that [the concept of an] unconscious psychic material appears to be like the concept of wooden iron.

HITSCHMANN feels the need to say a few kind words about the paper, which obviously required much effort. He would like, however, to put forward his hesitations about the presentation of psychic processes by means of charts; the incommensurability of the psychic processes prohibits these presentations. He cannot help having the impression that this paper represents a combination of the psychological society at the University (of which Surgeon Major-General Hollerung is a member) and our association. Hence the strong aversion to the unconscious psychic. The views that Adler raised about chemistry and heredity do not seem to offer anything new. From the paper as a whole, Hitschmann was not able to learn anything.

[6] Without detailed knowledge of the paper, Reitler's remark simply cannot be understood. The original has: dass das eine Absonderung vom Gehirn notwendig mache, möchte er bezweifeln = lit. he would doubt that this necessitates a "secretion" of (or a "separation" from) the brain.

DR. EITINGON (from Zürich, as a guest) is quite willing to concede that [new] perspectives have been opened up; these refer, however, to areas that are not ours. It is no accident that there is no room for the unconscious; since the ontological has been touched upon, he would like to allude to the methodological. Again and again attempts are made to sanction the whole [psychoanalytic] movement by trying to demonstrate its physiological probability. Thereby, however, our problems lose their precise character, and something indistinct is the result. All of Adler's hints were correct, it is true, but they lead into other spheres. The question about the methodology of psychoanalysis is the only one that is still to be posed and answered. Does an analyst have to believe in psycho-physical parallelism? I think that he has no need to; he should not and he does not have to. Pluralism is best here: everyone sees how to carry on his work so that, in his own field, he can arrive at good problems and satisfactory solutions. Hypotheses of that sort [should be applied] where they find use in being fruitful, and not where they eliminate precisely what is essential. That was a methodological blunder on the part of the speaker.

PROF. FREUD [feels that he] has good reasons for maintaining a modest position. Above all, because it is a question of a theme and an elaboration that he is not equal to. He does not venture to combine biological and psychological thinking. In this sense, he would like to express his appreciation and admiration for the fact that the speaker found the energy to begin working on problems that may be on the agenda a century after us.[7]

Prof. Freud was astonished to find an Aristotelian argument in the Surgeon-General's speech: the brain cannot mediate any sensation because it itself has none. One must not forget that to the Greeks the proposition itself had logical value.

Semon's suggestions, from which the speaker took off, seem to be greatly overrated.[8]

We must point to one gap in the train of thought, which [when it is bridged] may bring the brain back into esteem. It is true that a feeling

[7] In this remark Freud apparently anticipates his later utterance that a time may come when the psychoanalyst will ask the chemist to give him the specific drug for the corresponding psychological situation.

[8] Cf. Minutes 6, in Volume I.

originates inside the body; but does that mean that something originates there that is perceived elsewhere as a feeling, or does it mean that it itself is perceived where it originates? In the first case, we have a break in the continuity of psychic processes. A feeling must be perceived by the brain. What we call a feeling must somehow reach the brain, otherwise it cannot have any effect on other performances.

The remark that [the concept of] the unconscious psychic seems to be contrary to sense comes down to a dispute over words, which is of no scientific interest.

Surgeon Major-General Hollerung remarks, in closing, that he believes that he was misunderstood in his reference to the Unconscious. He himself adheres to the standpoint of agnostic monism. He is an opponent of dualism, on which present-day psychology relies. One cannot speak of psychology as a science; it is not feasible to ignore the objective, the somatic factor. That which we call psychic is only a small part of the expression of the organic system.[9] It is precisely repression that can be best elucidated from this side. Hollerung is convinced that what we call unconscious processes are material changes.

He is aware of the fact that his expositions are hypothetical, but hypotheses are unavoidable. His attempt is exculpable in that it aims at comprehending the psychic from one unified standpoint.

[9] Freud formulated this problem with especial precision later in his "An Outline of Psychoanalysis" (1938), *S.E.* 23.

84

SCIENTIFIC MEETING *on October 27, 1909*

Present: Prof. Freud, Adler, Federn, Heller, Hitschmann, Joachim, Rank, Reitler, Rie, Sadger, Steiner, Stekel, Wittels.

Dr. Tausk proposed as a member.[1]

Dr. Friedjung and Furtmüller become members.

PRESENTATION

Analysis of a Hysterical State of Confusion[2]

SPEAKER: DR. WITTELS

DISCUSSION

REITLER: Thanks to the distinguished analysis of this brilliant case and especially to its synthesis, he finds it so clear that there is no criticism left for the discussion.

[1] Dr. Tausk became one of the most gifted of psychoanalysts. He had first been a judge in Croatia, and then a stage director in Germany; finally, he studied medicine, and became a psychoanalyst. He was able to study medicine only because several members of the Society provided him with the necessary means.

[2] The record of the paper itself has not been preserved. As Wittels' concluding remark will show, copies of the manuscript had been distributed among the members of the audience.

HITSCHMANN must also grant that the analysis was carried out with ingenuity, but thinks that the patient was sicker after the treatment than he was before it. Whether he is now cured and to what extent we have not been informed, any more than how matters now stand with regard to his psychic impotence. The question must also be opened up of whether the patient did not needlessly complicate the treatment by his intensive reading of Freud's works. Here and there among the otherwise ingenious solutions, there seem to appear some arbitrary interpretations. All in all, it would have been interesting to learn to what extent "expected ideas" of the patient's were presented and how far he came by himself. One has the impression that it would have been possible to cure the patient in a shorter way.

FEDERN is not in a position to react immediately to this overwhelming declaration. He does not find the interpretations arbitrary in any respect but altogether consonant with the unconscious material. He has the impression that this is one of the most severe hysterias, and the patient certainly could not have been cured in a different way or in less time. Cases of this kind occur in persons who grew up under such favorable external circumstances [as described by Wittels] and whose later neuroses have their root cause in earliest childhood, in precocious sexual feelings [which appear at a time] when consciousness is not yet capable of working up the [concomitant] experiences and fantasies. The patient is one of those persons who, at an early age, have already repressed their entire sexuality. Such patients produce almost no associations at all, and for this reason it was necessary here too to interpret the dreams in part quite arbitrarily in order to bring at least some material into the patient's consciousness. The anxiety must be the reaction to libido that cannot be utilized in any way. By way of this anxiety affect, sexuality has an effect once again upon the total consciousness.

Behind each confusion there seems to be a strong defensive reaction that is, a sudden "impossible-to-endure-any-longer" attitude toward reality.

The patient's becoming engaged at the beginning of his treatment certainly rendered it more difficult.

SADGER thinks that, as agreeably as the speaker's broad vision may strike us, nevertheless his method has many disadvantages; the greatest one is the fact that he does not let the patient find everything himself. Thus [the explanation] of the two psychotic attacks seems to show gaps, although the basic features on the whole were correctly developed. Several of the solutions, attractive as they are at first glance (for instance, interpreting symbolically the feeling of being cold), seem a little strained. Lastly, Sadger would like to point to two minor items: (1) The patient supposedly at first hated the physician and became fond of him only later. The reverse may have been true, as evidenced by his compliance after the first session (he immediately followed the advice to become engaged). (2) It was undeniably a technical blunder not to interpret the complex of anti-Semitism on the spot. Such a postponement does not help at all; one makes the work harder for oneself and increases the resistance. On the whole, the physician used too much ingenuity.

STEINER had, as a listener, a feeling of the greatest satisfaction with a splendid paper. As a physician, however, he cannot speak lightly of a cure. (But this is not to the point here.) It is not the physician, as was said, but rather the patient who should have had less ingenuity; such patients are better able to cure ten other patients than themselves. Patients of this kind suffer from too much intelligence [*Intelligenzkranke*].

In order the better to see through many symptoms of neurosis, one can, in dealing with man, make use of an expedient, i.e., to transfer [in one's mind] the symptoms from man to woman. This then could be a case in which one would wish the man were a woman; then the whole intellectual superstructure would fall away.

PROF. FREUD would like first to divulge the previous history of today's paper. Wittels made his further concern with this case, as well as with analysis in general, dependent upon his being accepted [as a member]. Since Wittels provoked a judgment, Prof. Freud is glad to be able to say that anyone who can see through and present such a case in such a way has the right to expect to become a master of analysis. And one can only wish that he may continue to interest himself in this subject.[3]

The difficulties in the case lie in the fact that: (1) the patient is a very intelligent man, and (2) one could no longer tell him very much that was new to him because, unfortunately, he had brought theoretical knowledge along with him. This latter fact eliminates the reproach that the physician gave him too much information. The analysis is being carried through with first-rate technique and the various objections come to nought. In [the treatment of] this patient, one has to deal with peculiar kinds of resistance, to whose analysis no clue had ever been given; and it is amazing that a beginner could find these ways by himself.

It would be best to distinguish three modes of development in [the treatment of] cases:

1. Difficulties emerge at the beginning; later the treatment progresses smoothly.

2. In the beginning the treatment goes splendidly; the difficulties come later.

3. The typical case—the difficulties appear in the middle [of the treatment].

The first is characteristic of the severe but instructive cases; the second, the insoluble cases; the third, the typical ones.[4]

Some cases show the so-called "negative reaction"—i.e., each solution brings with it a [temporary] worsening of the illness. In the case presented, there is indifference:[5] for a long time the patient brings no material at all; then he brings up things intellectually, but without affect; at the end come the great outbursts of affect. These "supplementations" of affect are already well known. This case also shows distinctly in what way religious instruction acts upon the lives of

[3] Freud was very fond of Wittels, and had a weakness for him. When, in the year 1929, the question came up of whether Wittels should be reinstated as a member of the Vienna Society—some members refused to accept him—Freud came to his defense, closing his recommendation with the remark, "The man has ideas."

[4] These are important technical hints; they should be observed conscientiously. Freud often stressed that one cannot determine at the beginning of a treatment whether a case is severe or light.

[5] What Freud obviously must have said is that in this case the initial resistance manifests itself in indifference.

Catholic children. How many a germ of psychosis enters the child's brain along this path! The Christ-fantasy that is clearly present in this case also goes back to that. It is this that gives the attack its character as ecstasy. As far as the psychotic attacks themselves are concerned, they are necessary reactions to the [therapeutic] intervention, reactions that are not as such provoked, and which involve no danger at all for the patient.[6]

This patient is a man who has sexualized thinking itself. The emphasis has shifted from the content of thinking to the act of thinking itself; it is for this reason that he is so pleased with being in analysis. The large number of dreams in a single night (7-8) corresponds to just so many sexual acts. The misuse of terminology implies a spoofing of the physician. All in all, this is a child who wants to do better than his father.

The general therapy of cases that offer such difficulties is as follows: one cannot do anything but use as much patience [as is needed] until the transference has taken shape as a force; with persons on whom fate never inflicted particular pain, one has to make use of special means: one must try to play fate in their lives. Assured of the powerful transference, one must suddenly threaten them with the withdrawal of love, as a result of which the outbursts of affect begin.[7] An intervention of this sort took place when the treatment was interrupted by a vacation. The psychotic attacks were brilliantly interpreted. Many a philosophical thesis by someone who is seriously considered to be a man of science is likewise nothing other than a veiled sexual fantasy—which is the case with this patient.

In general, neuroses are much more centered [around one point] than we thought. In this case too it is the typical problem, the same story as has been disclosed in Oedipus and in little Hans. In this case

6 "Psychotic" symptoms suddenly appear here and there during treatment, but in most cases have no broader significance. They are a kind of temporary symptom, inherent in the treatment.

7 Intervention of this type today would be termed "active analysis." Of course, one must know exactly what one is doing and just what one wishes to accomplish; Freud always stressed this. We find in the remark a first indication of the technique which led to setting a date for the termination of analysis. Much later Freud elaborated this idea in the paper, "Lines of Advance in Psychotherapy," 1918, *S.E.* 17, and referred to the above as an example of active analysis.

we are confronted with a very far removed distortion of this core complex of infancy.

But what makes this case particularly difficult and is, moreover, not typical, is the fact that in the transference the patient has the physician change sex: the physician first represents to him the father, but then the mother and the betrothed. With regard to this point, the speaker might accept a supplement to his interpretation. This is something unusual, not in the nature of transference. It could be the reflection of a certain part of the childhood theories, the part that constitutes the core complex. The child's theories of birth are, as is well known, varied. If he has seen how his mother brings a child into the world, the role of the child-bearing woman is established. There then remain two wishes to the child: (1) to get the mother with child (2) to obtain one himself from his father. With this the role of the physician as father has been established.

If, however, a patient has not seen his mother giving birth, he is very unsure in regard to the question of who gives birth; he may then develop the further theory: (3) to desire to obtain a child from his mother. It is only in this case, however, that a patient is in a position to have his physician play the bisexual role. Such special circumstances seem to be needed, in order for the patient to expect that change of sex on the part of his physician.[8]

As against the preliminary publication of the analysis, as desirable as it may seem in other respects, Prof. Freud would like to set forth considerations of a pedagogical character. Once the case is completed, publication should follow.[9]

STEKEL, must admit that, "unenvious as always," he envies the speaker this analysis. In the face of this brilliant achievement, a lack of understanding such as has been shown in certain objections is truly incomprehensible. To go into details is impossible; only some minor items are to be singled out. It seems to be detrimental to the analysis to call in Prof. Freud as a consultant. No higher authority should stand above the attending physician.

[8] The role of bisexuality in transference is most instructively presented here. See Nunberg: *Curiosity.*

[9] It was not possible to establish whether Wittels ever published this case.

The great number of dreams produced is merely a form of resistance (PROF. FREUD: not many, but long dreams): the patient wishes that this conversation with the clever man of whom he has become fond could last as long as possible.

Behind the father and mother are hidden other matters. The incest conflict is merely the frame into which everything else is inserted. With the detection of this frame nothing has yet been accomplished. Wall- or door-meaning of the resistance must be translated as man (wall) or woman (door).[10] For the father's death the patient substitutes "wedding." In Schubart's dreambook it was already noted that a corpse may signify a wedding.

In the course of his most recent analyses, Stekel came to realize the great significance of religion for the development of neurosis. There are two kinds of persons who cannot fall ill with a neurosis: the absolutely devout and the typically amoral. Skeptics most often fall prey to neurosis. In most people piety is not based on logic, but is an affect.

Finally, he would like to make a plea for the publication of this paper.

ADLER can be brief, all the more so since part of what he would have to say will soon appear in a paper. He could go along with Freud's remark that the difficulty in this case lies in the patient's enormous drive for knowledge. Such cases are not hard to handle: this one was well grasped and will no doubt proceed well. One of the principal points of resistance is the fact that the patients really want to know everything better themselves; one must energetically call their attention to this. This urge to know stems from the childhood constellation; it is the primary cause leading to the confusion of which the patient is still capable even now. In his childhood he must have been governed by a most highly confused state, which must have led him as well to the birth fantasies.

Most likely the patient must have had the impression that Wittels, too, is in some sense castrated (circumcised); thus his representation as a woman (in the transference) signifies also a degradation. *Traces* [of these ideas] can be found in all patients.

[10] This passage is unclear.

One has the impression that even today the patient is always under a compulsion to masturbate, and it is not impossible that it was an attempt to masturbate that introduced this state of confusion. In his confusion the patient plays the role of a child, at one level deeper than in the neurosis. At the same time, however, he demonstrates that the main point has not been understood. The patient shows his physician again and again: you do not understand, there is something more involved here. He insists on exploring the proximate cause of his confusion.

In his attacks of chills and vomiting, he seems to be imitating his mother, who probably suffered from such symptoms at the time of her menstruation. That view is also supported by the monthly occurrence of these attacks.

WITTELS, in his concluding words expresses his gratitude for the numerous suggestions.

The dream that the patient had after reading his analysis contains appreciations as well as criticism, both of which Wittels has experienced here today.

(PROF. FREUD: The dream means "He (the patient) could do that better").

85

SCIENTIFIC MEETING *on November 3, 1909*

Present: Prof. Freud, Adler, Federn, Friedjung, Furtmüller, Hitschmann, Rank, Reitler, Sadger, Steiner, Stekel.

Eitingon and Jekels as guests.

Dr. Tausk becomes a member.

Dr. Bass resigns.

PRESENTATION

A Case of Multiform Perversion, Part I

SPEAKER: DR. SADGER

This is the very complicated case of a thirty-two-year-old Swedish baron (an archaeologist) who, coming from a quite degenerate family, suffered even as a youth from epileptic seizures. For the past two years he has been living with a former prostitute, in an alliance so intimate that it lacks only a church ceremony to make it a marriage. A few weeks ago he fell in love with an insignificant young man, a waiter, and wanted to travel with him to Ostend. The family physician who sent him to Vienna to be cured of this peculiar attraction, stresses in his covering letter mainly the factor of degeneration and epilepsy, and gives less weight to the homosexuality. In the psychoanalysis, which was carried through for five months, it was revealed that it is not the severe hereditary taint, but the *vita sexualis*, that stands in the foreground. During the course of treatment, his epileptic attacks were fully interpreted and cured[1] but it became evident that, in addition to homosexuality, a number of other sexual aberrations dominated the clinical picture—for instance, some forms of autoerotism, onanism, narcissism, a sort of autocoitus, extensive anal erotism, exhibitionism, voyeuristic tendencies, an infatuation for statues, sadomasochistic desires, etc.

The speaker now presents a brief biographical sketch of the patient, and then immediately proceeds to discuss the phenomenon that stands in the foreground, the

Homosexuality. Concerning his infatuation with the waiter, the patient declares that he desired only to be near him and to have light bodily contact; this in itself was sexual pleasure for him. "For, with me, sensations are aroused mainly by way of the eyes." Later he admits that one of his chief pleasures consists of reaching for his partner's testicles. He loves two kinds of men: (1) Youths of 17 or 18, with vivacious eyes and a feminine type of deportment. However, they must not be homosexual, because, he says, everything that is contrary to nature is repugnant to him. (2) He is somewhat less but still attracted by men of twenty-five to thirty years, of a sexually powerful nature, but only by those who have a drive toward the female sex, a trait that he [claims to] recognize in their expression. While he has feelings of love for the first type, he does not feel attracted toward the second, but is merely strongly interested in him. The patients adds to the first type some supplementary features, which bring it rather close to the second type. The two have in common youthfulness and the quality of their eyes. Upon encountering young men of either type he always asks himself: what shape does his sexual problem take? He would like, he says, in this way to learn how he himself should go about it. Later, a third type emerges, the man of science.

It became evident that the patient had fallen in love homosexually with quite a number of persons before the waiter; above all with his

[1] Probably it was not genuine epilepsy.

father and with the latter's brother, an archaeologist. According to his account, he did not become aware of his homosexuality until, at 18, he had a love-affair with a seventeen-year-old friend of the first type, a cadet. In all his homosexual love-affairs, the main role is played by his looking at and admiring the man, i.e., by the feeling of love aroused through the eyes; further, a desire to lie naked beside the love-object (as was the case with the cadet), a repulsion toward sexual intercourse and, finally, the passive trait of letting himself be loved and fondled. In relation to the waiter, crude sexual fantasies also came to light, which left him no peace.

Often and gladly he loves and works *en trois,* in "a triple alliance" as he calls it; he also loves the number three generally, in parties, etc. With his present wife, too, he feels at ease only when a third, his wife's lover of the moment, is present. He thinks that his former living together with his two sisters is the basis for this. In actuality, it stems from his wish to be third in the alliance with his mother.

The *family* of the patient. He intensely loved his uncle, the archaeologist, who had great influence on him and also determined his choice of a profession; this attraction was manifest when he was 15 or 16 years old. At that time, the uncle behaved like a mother toward the boy; he was also an influence in the development of his inclinations toward exhibitionism.

His *father* is said to have suffered from melancholic depressions and from absences, with which a fall from a horse was thought to have had some connection. Later the patient hysterically imitated these attacks, as well as his father's poor eyesight and hearing. At first, he admired his father. Later on, he compared him with others and began to criticize him. Political differences (a visit at court was involved, in which the son did not want to participate) led to their estrangement; from then on, he visited his father only twice a yaer. His last and most serious conflict with his father was brought about by his illegitimate relationship with the prostitute. The causes lie deeper, of course, and go back to the mother.

The *mother* plays, in the life of this patient—as with every homosexual—the decisive role. She is pictured as being proud of her noble birth, bigoted, and of little intelligence. From the beginning, the patient had been her favorite child. When he was about 15 or 16 years old, an estrangement developed between him and his mother because the patient no longer felt that he was "understood" by her. Subsequently he began to hate her, allegedly because she had raised her children the wrong way; however, behind this assertion one must look for the reproach that she brought him up badly as far as sexuality is concerned. The patient also describes her as being stingy in a mean sort of way and unbearably crotchety in matters of orderliness, in all of which we can find indications of the mother's anal erotism. In addition to these chief symptoms of anal erotism, she displayed some less known ones: she had no confidence in others; no one was capable of doing things nearly enough to suit her. She is constantly afraid of getting cancer of the intestines, from which her mother died; she suffers from constipation and frequently gave enemas to herself as well as to her children. When he was 13 or 14 years old, the patient became sickly and weak, and the family physician conjectured that the patient was indulging in masturbation, which he steadfastly denied when confronted by his mother. He was hurt by his mother's imputation (actually, he had unconscious masturbatory feelings); when, at 15 or 16, he consciously began to masturbate and his mother spied on him in whatever he did, that was when, it seems, his hatred for her set in.

The *sisters:* The older sister, who later became a nurse, exercised less influence on the patient's life than the younger one, who also showed a number of pathological traits. She suffered from severe spells of loss of consciousness and, during the course of the last two years she has allegedly been going blind as a result of nervousness. As a child, she was exhibitionistic for a long time. When he was four, the patient saw her female genitals for the first time while she was urinating. This younger sister's character, too, is decidedly anal: she sits on the toilet for unusually long periods, frequently uses an enema and early in life already showed a strong stubborn character. Of stinginess, she allegedly has none at all. Instead, she shows another symptom: she has the theory of the chaste man. When the patient was about twenty-four or twenty-five years old, he had undisguised incestuous wishes in regard to his sister. He thought he would do her a great service by having intercourse with her, because otherwise she would lose her bloom as an old spinster. He gave her veiled hints, but she rejected them because he was not chaste enough for her, having sullied himself in intercourse with prostitutes. At the age of ten, this sister already hated her mother, whereas she was extraordinarily attached to her father.

As in all cases of homosexuality, so the members of this patient's family, too, show indications of this disposition. The patient himself is a man with pronounced childlike traits. The father is decidedly masculine, but in earlier times liked to embroider. The archaeologist uncle is enthusiastic about household matters and kept house for the grandfather like a woman. He behaved like a mother toward the children (especially toward the patient), not only figuratively speaking (he washed them, combed their hair, etc.). Moreover, various other relatives show homosexual characteristics.

Heterosexuality. By no means was the female sexual object alien to the patient. We already know about his intercourse with the prostitute; we are aware of his love for his mother and his incestuous thoughts with regard to his sister. Thus the patient can only be characterized as bisexual, with a predominantly homosexual instinctual orientation. Of deeply incisive importance for his life was the nursemaid. She came to the patient's home when he was 3 years old and stayed there until he was 17; she had more to do with his upbringing than did his mother. One of his earliest memories at the age of 3 is that he embraced her tightly with arms and legs; in doing so, he had a feeling of tension in the small of his back. From his seventh or eighth year comes a recollection of the fact that while washing him she took his penis in her hand; [he recalls that] he became angry and forbade her to do that. She had healthy coloring and large blue eyes, both of which turn up again in his first male type.

His drive toward the other sex, which appeared very early, was quite clear. He loved a type of woman who was sixteen to eighteen years old, such as seemed to him to be embodied in a second cousin. Even earlier, around 5 to 7 years of age, he loved two girls. But his love-affairs were always platonic; the eye played the leading role—for the patient it was, to use Freud's expression, an erotogenic zone. Later there were a number of girls whom he loved, of the same type. One of these girls had a fiancé, a medical student, with whom the patient also fell in love; now, in addition to being this girl's husband, he is the patient's physician.

The speaker now turns to the most interesting and most important chapter: *the relationship to prostitutes.* The patient states that he suffered from severe depressions and that, during such periods, without any sexual longings, he would go to see a prostitute, merely in order to sleep alongside her. He liked always to visit the same girl. Up to his twenty-fifth year he masturbated regularly. Thereafter he visited prostitutes always in the company of friends, which may go back to his father. His desire, initially, was only to sleep beside the prostitute, to be able to pour out his heart to her and to be introduced into the mysteries of love by her. At the age of thirty, he at last succeeded in performing intercourse, with his fourth prostitute (before that he was always afraid of ridicule)—which changed his entire being. This fourth prostitute, a pretty young girl, pleased him so much that he lifted her up, carried her into bed, and immediately had intercourse with her. Once, at 18, as a way of showing his strength, he had lifted his mother, and also his sister, high up in the air. When he did the same thing with the prostitute, he was able to have intercourse with her because there was a link from her to the mother. A pulmonary disease made it necessary for him to go away for some time; when he returned, the prostitute was no longer there and all his searching for her was fruitless. In this period there emerge incestuous thoughts toward his sister; these disappear only when he finds a new, his fifth, prostitute—whom, at the beginning [of his treatment], he had claimed to have been his first. She was rather old, and intercourse with her was successful only because the patient played a passive role in it.

His *wife* he liked very much from the first time he saw her; her kind nature, her strong sense of justice and her tasteful manner of dressing made an agreeable impression upon him. Later, their relationship almost broke up because he had intercourse with one of her colleagues. He does not want to have his wife alone, but only together with a third person, a friend.

With this the speaker closes today's account of the case. There are two points that he would like to throw open to discussion: (1) the relationship of [hereditary] taint to sexuality; (2) a few new ideas on the subject of anal erotism.

Ad 1. The inclination to depressions mentioned before (attacks of melancholia for periods of one to one and a half months) and the lack of moderation in his emotional life (fits of anger) are typical symptoms of hereditary taint. Only through sexual factors, however, is it fully unfolded. The patient usually has intercourse with his wife every fourth day; if it happens that he does not have intercourse for six days, he immediately becomes depressed. The depressions, by the way, also appear for homosexual reasons. In his depressed states, he would be calmed by a visit to prostitutes, even if he merely talked and had no intercourse—which points back to the mother. Likewise, it is to his mother that his frequent belief seems to go back that a woman did not want to have intercourse, although he had no [objective] reasons for thinking so.

The interrelationship between a hereditary taint and the sexual factors that favor it and set it in motion is very important; however, an exposition of this relationship does not yet exist in terms of a large body of material. All these depressions are produced no less by psychosexual factors than by factors of the anatomy of the brain.

Ad 2. The three characteristics of anal erotic individuals that Freud has stressed seem mainly to be derived from men. The speaker would like to add some experiences concerning women. In women, meticulous cleanliness and neatness seem to be more pronounced than the other characteristics which, in several cases, are altogether missing. Corresponding to the woman's activity, anal symbolism seems to have its specific forms of expression. For instance, to many women cleaning is an end in itself and has a pleasurable tone. Frequently such women keep their children for a long time from gaining anal independence: they persist in setting them on the pot and accompanying them to the bathroom.

A girl with sublimated anal erotism shows (just as the patient's sister does) the fantasy of the man who must enter married life chaste.

Another characteristic often found in anal erotics is the thought: nobody else can do it as well as I myself (i.e., can evacuate his bowels as well = do as I can). Again, there are others who postpone everything until the last minute. Finally, the habit of sitting on the toilet for a long time, engaging at the same time in reading.

DISCUSSION

STEINER remarks that one cannot debate vis-à-vis facts. As far as the two points are concerned, the speaker went to the trouble of discovering America all over again. The relationship between disposition and sexual elements has not become clear to Steiner; besides, he could not see anything new in it. As far as the anal erotism of housewives is concerned, Freud, in the Dora-analysis, has described it[2] as "the housewife neurosis" (Federn interrupts: but not on an anal basis). Moreover, the speaker has neglected to differentiate between anal character and anal erotism.

FURTMÜLLER would like to have an explanation of one of the few cases of anal character in the circle of his acquaintances, a case that does not seem to fit the description. The case is of a colleague who suffers from attacks of complete loss of consciousness and who shows all the traits of an anal character. He also presents indications, however, of recent anal erotism. It would seem therefore that symptoms of repression can exist side by side with remnants of the actual preoccupation with the anus (erotism).

FEDERN stresses the likeable impression that the patient creates. The speaker's techniques of presentation is an unusual one; it may very well be correct, yet we are accustomed to listening to a historical presentation. A technique such as the speaker's may evoke the impression that connections have been arbitrarily established.

To interpret the younger sister's gardening as symbolic sexual activity is a crude way of expression. In every calling one can find sexual aims being substituted for. In Federn's opinion, it is incorrect to relate housecleaning to the anal sphere. One must caution against imprudently characterizing certain symptoms as anal erotic. The same thing might happen as happened with our initial overvaluation of sexual traumata, whose effects later were forced to be [recognized in our theory as] more limited. Some of the relationships assumed by Sadger do, by the way, appear to be rather plausible.

The lifting up of the prostitute Federn would this time like to inter-

[2] This must be an omission in the record. It should be: "excessive tidiness."

pret in a non-Freudian way, as a simple expression of sheer pleasure in the girl.

With regard to the question of [hereditary] taint, Federn can offer a nice example of three brothers who had different reactions to the sexual harmfulness of coitus interruptus—which establishes the likelihood of Sadger's assertion that anxiety neurosis appears more easily in persons with a [hereditary] taint. It may be that a predisposition of the heart is involved here. Otherwise, anxiety neurosis has little connection with what we call degeneration. One can hardly raise any objection to [the assumption of] a relationship between hereditary taint and sexuality. In four cases of serious climacteric depressions, Federn has observed that, in individuals with a hereditary disposition, excessively protracted harmfulness (for instance, masturbation continued for a long period) can lead to melancholia.

RANK can confirm by the example of a fully developed anal character the view that the habit of putting off everything to the last minute is one of the features of an anal character.

HITSCHMANN finds in what was imparted today only the conscious anamnesis of the patient. What is pathological is rather the degree of his inclinations [than the inclinations themselves]. Homosexuality fits in very well with the interest in ancient art (Winckelmann), and the study of historical costumes may perhaps also play a role here. The theoretical objections (like those of Federn) seemed often to have really little foundation. This case again shows how little is proven if one demonstrates: the man loved his mother. Here too the degree is always the decisive factor. "He loved his father homosexually" is a pleonasm: how else was he to love him? The desire of a married couple for a third person is very frequent, and has the most diversified reasons (especially, the wife's anaesthesia).

In depressions a lack of sexual gratification may also play an important role—particularly in connection with masturbation.

Tracing the idea of the "chaste man," as well as excessive tidiness in housekeeping, back to anal erotism does not seem plausible. The washing compulsion, however, does seem to have a connection with masturbation.

The question is what the disposition to actual neurosis consists of:

masturbation may play an important role just as the vasomotor does in anxiety neurosis (Curschmann).[3] The examination of the patient's sex organs by the attending analyst Hitschmann considers to be absolutely necessary and it is a sign of prejudice if Sadger failed to do this. Clues might well be found that could be taken into consideration as indicative of an inferiority of the sex organs in neuroses (especially in homosexuals).

JEKELS believes this evening's most important topic to be the one touched upon by Steiner—namely, maintaining the lines of demarcation between anal erotism and anal character. Jekels would be grateful for a clarification with regard to this problem.

In [the discussion of] the relationship between [hereditary] taint and anxiety neurosis after *coitus interruptus*, one circumstance was overlooked, which Freud long ago emphasized: anxiety neurosis in men appears only when they feel concern for the women's gratification.

FRIEDJUNG would like to raise the question of whether it is necessary to make such a sharp distinction between anal character and anal erotism. Is it not possible that in *one* and the same individual, indications of sublimated anal erotism and, on the other hand, residues of primary anal erotism could be found side by side? Or that perhaps, even later, anal erotic phenomena make their reappearance via sublimation—for instance in a physician who becomes a proctologist?

REITLER thinks that Federn went altogether too far in his criticism and that Hitschmann was right in accepting the determinations of certain factors (gardening, lifting).

The interpretation of housecleaning as an anal characteristic may perhaps be correct in this case; but one must not generalize it, for in other cases this characteristic may also be traceable to masturbation. It would be understandable, as well, as a component of the household neurosis that originates in lack of sexual gratification.

The confusion between anal character and anal erotism in this circle is grievous. Friedjung's assumption that mixed forms also occur is absolutely correct.

[3] Hans Curschmann: "Vasomotorische und trophische Erkrankungen des Nervensystems" ("Vasomotor and trophic illnesses of the nervous system") in *Lehrbuch der Nervenkrankheiten*, Berlin 1909, Springer.

Anticipating the analysis, Reitler would like to ask whether rescue fantasies did not also play an important role in this patient. If so, Freud's description of the type (of maternal etiology) would be fully corroborated.

PROF. FREUD has no objections to make to Sadger's statements. The analysis is carried out with thoroughness and promises to yield interesting results.

As a result of the incompleteness of today's report, a good many objections, which rest on insufficient information and misunderstanding, fall away. Reitler has given an indication of the direction in which the rather simple solution of this case should be looked for.

What Sadger calls a taint [*Belastung*] we call hereditary [*Heredität*]. During the course of the psychoanalytic investigation, one part of the significance of what has been experienced has reverted to the constitution which, however, can be further distilled from the vague concept of hereditary to sexual constitution. It is, indeed, in the reduction of sexual disturbances to experiences and to the sexual constitution that we have found our real sphere of activity. With this, however, the importance of the non-sexual constitution is not denied.[4] These two are quite compatible with each other, and there is no need to replace one with the other. Concerning the relationship between [hereditary] taint and sexuality, it is necessary for there to be adequate and precise evidence of what the unmistakable signs are and how all this is interrelated—from what one is able to recognize these non-sexual factors in neurosis. Heller has made a highly promising beginning. On one point, Sadger can be shown to have contradicted himself: in contrast to his present assertion that such a taint is extraordinarily conducive to the formation of an actual neurosis, he has come to think only recently that those with a severe hereditary taint do not acquire an actual neurosis (Lenau),[5] because the hereditary taint kills it.

As far as anal erotism is concerned, Sadger's statements were faulty; otherwise, they were not so much new as they were estimable and detailed. He is to be reproached for having neglected to make distinc-

[4] Freud obviously implies here that the sexual constitution must meet up with the non-sexual (the ego constitution) for the disposition to neurosis to develop.

[5] See: *Aus dem Liebesleben Nikolaus Lenau's* ("From Nikolaus Lenau's lovelife"). (Cf. Vol. I, Min. 8.)

tions. It is a question of the destiny of this universally maintained anal erotism. The character developed from it in the publication is the type in its most extreme form. The fact that this transformation can occur partially and can be incomplete was stressed by Furtmüller. The case of the patient's mother is of this sort; here one finds a well-utilized anal erotism. In the care of infants, this initially actual, later sublimated, anal erotism is again directly utilized. This above all is the formula for maternal bliss: the possibility of reverting without reproach to the repressed infantile [drives]. We see here too how, in this process, the character of the mother changes, how the hitherto firmly established character formation, [when it falls] under the influence of the newly erupting eroticism, regresses a bit.

The interesting problem of why it is that in some persons this character-triad [orderliness, stubbornness, stinginess] does not completely develop, could be pursued and answered in the spirit of certain Adlerian considerations. In women, pedantry and the passion for tidiness are frequent, but not stubbornness and stinginess. Stubbornness probably does not develop when a confluence of instincts is not present, and this, as a rule, is what is missing in women. The sadistic component, powerfully suppressed in the normal woman, probably works against the formation of obstinacy. The remoteness from any concern with money on the part of a woman of good family will most likely be responsible for the fact that money does not take on any great meaning for her. One does not come to dealing with such questions if one does not sharply differentiate between character and erotism. But this sharp conceptual separation has nothing whatever to do with their co-existence.[6]

Physical examination is certainly most desirable but unfeasible in analysis; it must be done by another physician.

Regarding masturbation, one must never forget, as Hitschmann did today and Sadger recently, that it is only the carrying out of an action and not an instinct; it cannot therefore be referred to as an etiology. It is not the fact of being accustomed to masturbation that makes it so difficult to overcome, but rather that of being accustomed to particular objects, particular fantasies, whose contents cannot be replaced

[6] Freud was *always* intent on separating the instinctual drives from character, i.e., from the ego-drives.

by real love-affairs. Masturbation is not an instinct, it is merely a matter of the activity of the individual concerned, an activity that is to his advantage; the one who only fantasises is farther removed from normality than the onanist. The reference to the vasomotors (Hitschmann) is due to a confusion of physiological mechanisms with psychological etiology.

The interpretation of housecleaning was too determinate a statement; one has to prove in every individual case that this activity is anal. Nor does it always correspond to sexual repression (Reitler). The reaction to contamination through a sexual act (masturbation) expresses itself on the subject's own body; if the reaction refers to objects of the external world, it may perhaps be of anal origin.

86

SCIENTIFIC MEETING *on November 10, 1909*

Present: Prof. Freud, Adler, Federn, Hitschmann, Friedjung, Furtmüller, Rank, Reitler, Sadger, Tausk.
Eitingon, Jekels as guests.

PRESENTATION

A Case of Multiform Perversion (Part 2)

SPEAKER: DR. SADGER

The speaker begins with the remark that, because of the large scope of this complicated case, whatever does not strictly pertain to the topic must be omitted; for instance, the patient's pseudoepilepsy, the analysis of which proceeds along the same lines as that of the first case (already published),[1] and yields the same results; further, his intolerance to alcohol, which has its homosexual as well as heterosexual roots, etc.

The speaker now moves on to a discussion of the influences of the

[1] "Fragment der Psychoanalyse eines Homosexuellen" ("Fragment of the Psychoanalysis of a homosexual"), *Jb. f. Sexuelle Zwischenstufen*, 1908.

patient's upbringing. As a child, the patient had no companions; his first playmate, when he was 10 years old, was a cousin, with whom, however, he was not bound by any genuine ties of comradeship. He always felt a need for older boys, for "protectors" as he called them. His later search for comradeship is undoubtedly a reaction to his former lack of it. Frequently one finds that people who later become homosexuals have spent their entire youth almost exclusively under female guidance.

Up to his fifteenth year, no one had talked to the patient about sexual matters; between the ages of 15 and 17, he received his first sexual enlightenment from schoolmates; this information was supplemented when he was in the army. Even at the age of 16, he still slept and bathed together with his sisters. Up to his seventh year, he also looked on frequently when his father was bathing. His mother's behavior in his presence was just as uninhibited; in the presence of the 12- and 14-year-old boy she would sit on the chamberpot to urinate. This sitting down on the pot the patient later imitated in his hysterical attack. It was from his mother's behavior that the patient's previously mentioned scoptophilia got its satisfaction. As one symptom of anal character, which is found in the patient's mother, Sadger refers to the habit elderly women have of lifting their skirts extremely high in order to keep out of "mud." During the treatment, the patient recalls his mother's sitting on the chamber pot in terms of her lifting high her nightgown.

Homosexual impulses in earliest childhood:

The patient had a special liking for cylindrical objects. He would embrace the stove passionately; he loved his mother's tailor's dummy dearly, and embraced it, too. (Somnambulists often embrace a stove and climb up on it). It has already been pointed out that he saw his father's genitals in the bath. The forbidden curiosity about them expressed itself in a symptom: *disuria psychica.* When he urinated simultaneously with his father, he would compare the genitals and, in so doing, forget to urinate himself. This seems to be a typical root of *disuria psychica.*

It is significant that the patient's interest is in testicles, which attracted him more than the penis. He wants to grab hold of the waiter's testicles from behind and below. Probably that was the way his nursemaid and even earlier his mother had taken hold of him, although he does not distinctly remember that. Thus, as a homosexual, he identifies with his mother as a woman who wants to bring her lover gratification.[2] This interest in testicles, by the way, also has a homosexual root. When he saw his father bathing, he had the wish to cut off the latter's testicles (an obvious castration wish, which goes back to the mother). Besides, he had read that onanists have weak testicles. The contraction of a man's testicles when he touches them is proof to him that the man has some feeling for him. He himself is calmed by [the act of] touching. He had wished that his own testicles would not hang down as they did and tried in various ways to keep them from doing so.

This interest [in the testicles] could conceal itself very well [behind anything else]. The scruff of the neck, for instance, reminds him of testicles (which are openly exposed); so do powerful shoulder muscles. Even as a child he was very much interested in the Zulus: he was particularly fascinated by their powerful muscles, the loin-cloth, and the clean-shaven head, which also attracted his especial interest when he saw clowns and Pierrots in the circus. This interest in the testicles is also the basis of his liking for statues, which is determined by his fully developed scoptophilic instinct and his interest in the genitals.

Linked with his scoptophilia is its counterpart, exhibitionism, which became apparent in his fourth to fifth year. He made himself a loin-cloth and, naked, practiced muscle exercises. At 15, he began to sketch himself in the nude, if possible with an erect penis. Drawing to him was a means of idealizing himself. In recent years he used to be totally undressed during the summer when at home. To wash his hands, he would undress completely in front of his comrades. Then he would engage in a sort of sexual gymnastics, in which he was also totally naked.

The patient had a whole series of the most horrible sadistic and masochistic fantasies which, for the most part, were directed toward his parents.

Next to the scoptophilic instinct, *anal erotism* was most pronounced

[2] This observation is an important contribution to the etiology of homosexuality. The idea seems, however, to stem from Freud. Cf. Sadger's earlier papers: "On the aetiology of homosexuality," *Medizinische Klinik*, 1909; "Is homosexuality curable?" *Ztschr. für Sexualwissenschaft*, 1908; and "Fragment of the psychoanalysis of a homosexual," *Jb. f. sexuelle Zwischenstufen*, 1908.

in the patient. As a child he went through a prolonged enteritis, which, according to Czerny,[3] (*The Physician as Paedagog*) frequently lays the groundwork for subsequent depressions. The patient also suffered from fecal incontinence. He had a *prolapsus recti* and constantly played around in the anus with his finger. At 15, he read about pederasty. In "practicing pederasty" (finger in anus), he felt a sensual pleasure and had erections; later he combined masturbation and "pederasty." Even at present, he still has feelings of pleasure while moving his bowels. He is in the habit of regurgitating the dishes he likes best; this goes back to the childhood experience of having swallowed a worm. It seems to be a disguised form of coprophagy. In contrast to the idiosyncrasies of other children, he used to prefer those dishes that are like feces in appearance.

Some general remarks:

1. Above all, the lack of *sexual enlightenment* is of greatest import for the development of neuroses and perversions. Anaesthesia in a girl can frequently be attributed to the fact that the most innocuous sexual matters are not permitted to be discussed in her family; the same result follows when masturbation in young girls is handled with excessive severity. In boys, such conditions form a basis for psychic impotence.

2. *Homosexuality*, as a rule, appears most forcefully in puberty, at the earliest in the tenth or eleventh year. For it to occur there must take place a significant event, one that is capable of taking the mother out of the picture. For this there can be many reasons: in Kleist's case, it was the mother's death; in another case, a disfiguring illness; in a third a financial catastrophe, which caused a [temporary] withdrawal of maternal love. In the case at hand, it is the mother's unsuitable behavior with regard to masturbation.

The fact of being brought up for a long time in female company, as well as of having no childhood companions—all this, as has been said before, plays an important role.

To whom the individuals concerned turn after the elimination of the mother, also depends greatly on external circumstances. As a rule, they turn to a somewhat older comrade, someone through whom they

[3] Adalbert Czerny, 1863-1941, well known pediatrician, author of *Der Arzt als Erzieher des Kindes*, 1908 ["The Physician as the Child's Educator"].

can be enlightened and introduced into the mysteries of sexuality; or else they turn to a somewhat younger boy, whom they themselves can enlighten and toward whom they can play the part of the mother. It is rarely that they turn to the father or to another older man.

A large role is played by autoerotism in the form of narcissism. In the types of people that the person loves one can recognize, in addition to the characteristics of the individuals who are loved homosexually or heterosexually, traits also of the person himself. Another of Sadger's patients still loves the type that evolved in him at the time when he came to do without the love for his mother. At the bottom of this kind of narcissism, there seems to be a flight from the mother who is no longer [toward him] to the mother who once admired and loved him. Together with the repression of the love for the mother, most individuals also repress the love for the entire female sex. Freud has called attention to a case in which the man's turning away from the mother and his inclination toward boys go back to jealousy of a boy whom his mother had praised.[4] This situation has been found to be true in several other cases.

3. Obviously, the case of the patient under discussion reminds one of the type of maternal object choice described by Freud, although not all the requirements agree here exactly. The wish to rescue, which, according to Freud, means [the wish] to make a child, appears in the patient in a repressed form. He constantly broods over the problem of whether he, as a degenerate, has the right to get his wife with child; as a precaution, he uses a condom. Furthermore, he has no thought of marriage. In other aspects, too, this case is more complicated than the "type," by the presence of homosexuality, scoptophilia, exhibitionism and anal erotism.

The patient reproached the mother for—and later was always resentful of—the fact that she never talked to him about sexual matters, any more than his father did. [In his analysis] it turns out that he had the idea that his father should have enlightened him about masturbation in his struggle against it (when he was 19), and should have taken him to girls. Because his mother earlier had neglected to give him enlightenment, he now turns to the father (the man), where

[4] Cf. fn.1, Minutes 81.

it is easier for him; in the army, he is brought to prostitutes by his comrades. He turns to the prostitute because it is her task to introduce him into "lovelife"; this is, as he himself clearly says, her real function. His mother on the other hand, had implanted in his mind the view that intercourse with a woman is something sinful.

As to direct thoughts of coition with his mother, the patient cannot recall having had any. After his treatment was completed, he wrote that he had caught himself daydreaming about this. The eyes of his sister, about whom he had incestuous thoughts, played a part in the type [of men he loved].

The patient has little resistance; it becomes stronger only in connection with one point, and that is anti-Semitism.

The speaker is well aware of not having given all the explanations; homosexuality in particular still remains unexplained. Nevertheless, he believes that he has offered one or another new idea; particularly with regard to the fancy for statues, he has to some extent solved the question, and perhaps has also contributed a few new points toward [an understanding of] the genesis of homosexuality.

DISCUSSION

ADLER stresses that the things that have been brought forward come to light in almost every analysis (aside from the symptoms). One should, therefore, actually have pursued the path farther back. For this reason it also seems that many of the explanations of the symptoms are derived from much too late an age (from the 15th or 16th year). If one goes back deeper into childhood, one is much more likely to arrive at a synthesizing summation of the various symptoms (behind which there almost always lies the same thing). On the basis of the experiences up to now, one could approach such a case with a dictionary, as it were; and the speaker seems to have made more than ample use of that expedient. This has also had the effect of making the synthesis more difficult, for in this way one gets only up to that point that was to be anticipated. For instance, that kind of approach can be used successfully in most cases of anal character. However, it is not only the effects produced by the anal zone that take part [in the formation of anal character], and in some cases one even has to posit their presence, for while the anal character is there, yet one cannot infer the eroticism from the analysis. It may be that there are relationships and excitations experienced by the child that can form an anal character, yet have their origin in entirely different situations—and not always in organic situations alone. In general, it is a feeling of inferiority that dominates the child; and this feeling is still so strong in the actual neurosis that it can explain why the neurosis lasts so long. The feeling of inferiority is very marked in this patient.

The interrelationship between inferiority and hereditary taint has been so frequently examined—and Adler himself has made some contributions to this—that one can regard these questions as having much more of a basis. It cannot be enough to attempt to maneuver from the standpoint of hereditary taint over to the psychic sphere; one must also demonstrate how the two are connected. Organic insufficiencies cause this feeling of inferiority in a child; he therefore approaches the sexual problem with greater tension than do other children. Today one can already express as a conviction the idea that only those who are organically inferior, those who have a hereditary disposition of a certain category, are capable of developing a neurosis.

In today's paper, the most important topic appears to be homosexuality. To find a preliminary solution to this problem, one must go further back in time than to the period when the boy renounces [his attachment to] his mother. This event, as a rule, does not have that effect, or at least it does not necessarily have it. We cannot explain why the boy simultaneously represses women in general. Homosexuality probably comes about only if the child's sexual enlightenment is so deficient at the time when his sexual impulses are awakened, that he cannot distinguish between father and mother in regard to sex. Interest in the male member (as a consequence of insufficiency), along with deficient enlightenment, seems to be the prerequisite for later homosexuality. Since the child is totally ignorant, a fixation onto the father takes place at this time. That in addition to this fixation there can also occur a fixation onto the mother must be assumed for all cases. In the patient presented here, this uncertainty is most prominent (Exclamations expressing objections.).

EITINGON follows with the remark that he too cannot find uncertainty here [in this paper]. The patient's homosexuality has become generally dubious to him. Behind everything there is the lack of satisfaction with the patient's own genitals. The narcissism in this case, too, is merely a construction and does not seem at all to be an autoerotic sex activity.

FRIEDJUNG would like only to make some brief remarks. As to the relationship put forward by von Czerny, between early enteritis and the development of character, he has not been able to find any confirmation of it, at least not in that manner. Anal prolapse does not seem to be a purely organic and accidental illness; on the contrary, according to his experience, it is probably conditioned by anal erotic motives and has a considerable amount of active help on the part of the child as its presupposition.

Friedjung himself had previously ascribed too little importance to sexual enlightenment as a means of preventing neurosis.

Adler's remarks about the origin of homosexuality seems to be of basic importance. Freud too has already called attention to it; the case of the girl who regards the "blood mixture" during menstruation as sexual intercourse and in this belief risks a homosexual attack is a telling example.

FEDERN first emphasizes the thoroughness of Sadger's work as well as the wealth and value of the material. In regard to some details, however, Federn must contradict him. The interpretation of the skirt-lifting seems arbitrary to him, and it would have been much more plausible to trace that back to the extremely clear exhibitionism. On the whole, the mother's anal erotism should not have been treated at all in this analysis. Federn does not contest the methodology, as he was accused of doing, but its misapplication. Insufficient enlightenment can, of course, be only *one* of the preconditions of impotence. Besides, as Freud once indicated, only those persons remain completely unenlightened in whom the development of the sexual drive is not altogether in order.

In regard to the two cardinal points, detachment from the mother and choice of an object, Federn must contradict Sadger. It does not become evident in this case that the detachment from the mother carried such weight; there are signs of homosexuality much earlier than that. Of greater importance is the early interest in the father's testicles. Men are often very sensitive in the region of the perineum; if this is true of the patient, then there was a strong stimulus for his interest in the male genitalia. The defense against incest cannot be the cause of homosexuality in a man in whom the incest-wish has remained current. Nor does the lack of comradeship in the patient's childhood fit in. The lack of sexual enlightenment, on the other hand, is a most essential factor; but it is only a supportive factor and not a specific one. In contrast to Eitingon, Federn thinks that the narcissism has to be recognized as autoerotism. And one must also agree that intensive autoerotism must lead to homosexuality.

Federn too cannot find the patient corresponding to the mother-type (Freud).

PROF. FREUD cannot see, with regard to its technical aspect, any particular achievement in this analysis. The complexity of the case is nothing extraordinary; indeed we have only uncovered the regular constitution of all men. The speaker did not succeed in mastering the material and in arriving at a synthesis of the case.

The assertion that growing up among women does not lead a man to an intensive love for woman but frequently to homosexuality is correct. The effect on a woman of such a childhood [growing up among women] is often that she remains [thereafter] with a woman.

The interpretation of the oven as a female body, which was challenged by Federn, is completely correct; there is confirmation of it in mythology. To the men of antiquity, the oven was a female genitalium; this becomes fully intelligible only if one knows that a flame was a phallus to them. One comprehends why the vestal virgins were not permitted to marry: they were already married—to the flame-phallus. Also, a punishment for adulteresses was a burning chip forced between the thighs into their genitals. Dream symbols that did not find a similar corroboration in myth, fairy-tale, popular custom, etc., would have to be [regarded as] questionable.

It is distressing that an education as liberal as that enjoyed by the patient, had no better results. This is explained, however, by way of the insight that, as the outcome of this education, the man did not become a neurotic, but simply a pervert. In this context, one looks in vain for indications as to why and in what way he fell into a neurosis in certain respects.

A primitive interest in the testicles to the exclusion of the penis is nevertheless possible. But what appears to us superficially is this: the interest in the testicles is displaced from the mammae. The interest in arches seems also to be such a displacement from the woman onto the man.

The notion that the [process of becoming a] homosexual coincides with the repression of the mother is absolutely correct; it occurs by means of identifying with the mother. The boy rids himself of his mother by way of identification, which here coincides with repression.[5] The ultimate causes of homosexuality are not made accessible to us by way of analysis, because it cannot solve for us the problem of whether the sexual impulse turns in a positive or a negative direction. To determine at what point what circumstances a person turns toward a certain object comes to be a work of speculation. The participation of organic disposition will play a decisive role.

The man [presented here] is of the type in which protracted sexual development is particularly evident, as well as an infantility that is long held to.

Sadger's comment with regard to narcissism seems new and valuable. This is not an isolated phenomenon but a necessary developmental stage in the transition from autoerotism to object love. Being enamoured of oneself (of one's own genitals) is an indispensable stage of development.[6] From there one passes over to similar objects. In general, man has two primary sexual objects, and his future existence depends on which of these objects he remains fixated on. These two sexual objects are for every man the woman (the mother, nurse, etc.) and his own person; and it follows from this that [the question] is to become free from both and not to linger on too long with either. Usually, one's own person is replaced by the father—who, however, soon moves into a hostile position. It is at this point that homosexual-

[5] This is one type of homosexual. Subsequently, Freud described another type in "Certain neurotic mechanisms in jealousy, paranoia and homosexuality" (1922) *S.E.* 18.

[6] See Freud's later essay "On Narcissism: an Introduction" (1914), *S.E.* 14.

ity branches off. Man does not set himself free of himself so soon, as this case very beautifully demonstrates.[7]

REITLER thinks that the speaker has left out the most important factor—that is, the neurotic symptoms. All we have heard is the anamnesis of an invert and pervert, and there is not much of an analysis present.

One would have to say: detachment from the mother failed [to take place].

Uncertainty with regard to sexual theory plays an important part, but in this case, it is not pertinent.

A striking characteristic of homosexuals is the development of a remarkable stubbornness: if they don't get everything, they renounce everything. Perhaps this too goes back to the fixation onto the mother: since he could not get her, he renounced everything. Reitler is acquainted with a patient who initially showed narcissism, and later homosexuality.

Reitler was glad to see Freud clearing away the expectation that analysis can explain homosexuality.

Observing and practicing the injunction against masturbation is not to be held responsible for women's anaesthesia; we know, on the contrary, that intensive masturbation often results in anaesthesia toward normal intercourse.

TAUSK found that, in young people who masturbate and have fantasies of intercourse accompanied by emissions, traveling by carriage or railway often takes over the role of coition; in their dreams, they try to avoid stepping into a carriage in order to avoid emission.

In reference to homosexuality, Tausk tells about a five-year-old boy who attempted intercourse with a little girl, believing that she had a penis. Only in puberty did he become enlightened about this.

In therapy there is something that seems to play a role, which Tausk would like to call secondary culture: it may perhaps not always be advantageous to go back to the primary recollections (father and

[7] These remarks show how early the concept of narcissism was recognized, as well as the significance of object choice in regard to future health or illness. This choice can lead to two end results: heterosexual love (in pathological cases hysteria, phobia, etc.), or narcissistic love, which can take the shape of homosexuality or paranoia.

mother, etc.) if one can help the patient by releasing the affects of the secondary culture.

HITSCHMANN thinks that, if the patient could stay only for five months, one should perhaps have gone about the treatment differently. One does not know whether this was a therapy or an exploration, during the course of which someone happened to get better. More likely, it was the former. The improvement is obviously due to the fact that the patient found deliverance from the labyrinth of sexuality, by being able to speak freely of it.

Several details were no doubt of value; nevertheless, one must caution against too hasty generalization.

Interest in the circus is an exquisitely sadistic trait.

As an internist, Hitschmann would also caution against so readily ascribing every [instance of] clinical constipation to anal erotism.

The patient is a polymorphously perverse hypersexual, who cannot be characterized as an invert. That he wanted to take the waiter along with him is only [an expression of] a moral weakness.

That the enlightening mother is always the model for homosexual friendships seems unlikely; such friendships would rather seem to replace the enlightening father.

The motive, "I want to be normal," certainly plays a part: hence the longing for enlightenment.

In reference to anal erotism one should, perhaps, also adduce the negative characters.[8]

[8] It is not clear what Hitschmann means by "negative character." Probably he is referring to negativistic character traits, such as stubbornness, spitefulness, etc.

87

SCIENTIFIC MEETING *on November 17, 1909*

Present: Prof. Freud, Adler, Federn, Friedjung, Furtmüller, Heller, Hitschmann, Rank, Reitler, Steiner, Stekel, Wittels.
Dr. Jekels, Dr. Deczi (Budapest) as guests.

PRESENTATION

What Can Pediatrics Expect from Psychoanalytic Research?

SPEAKER: DR. FRIEDJUNG

The speaker begins by mentioning a paper of his from 1908,[1] in which, in spite of his familiarity with the Breuer-Freud *Studies,* he made no use of them, because he did not know how to.

Besides, the outpatient clinic of a hospital, on which he had to rely at that time [for observations], gives a distorted picture; one first begins to learn something about children only when one sees them in their own milieu, at home. A further difficulty is that in most instances

[1] The reference probably is to "Die sexuelle Aufklärung des Kindes" ["The Sexual Enlightenment of the Child"], which was published in 1909 in Vienna, but may have been presented as a lecture at an earlier date.

one obtains the anamnesis from someone else [than the patient himself]; as a rule, it is presented in a very subjective manner (by parents) and is full of gaps.

Only by observations made on the child in his milieu does one realize how great an influence his surroundings exercise. For instance, one can see how someone's announcement that the child is going to resist ("he will not let you take his temperature") "justifies" his resistance, and how, as soon as the "suggesting" parents have left the room, a complete change takes place. In such instances, it is not infrequent that, to inquiries as to whether the child sleeps poorly, whether he suffers from enuresis, anorexia, fear of strangers, thunderstorms, dark rooms, one receives an affirmative answer.

From the "naughty" behavior of children to pathological psychogenic symptom formation, there is an infinite number of transitions.

The speaker now cursorily discusses some of these clinical pictures. The monosymptomatic character of infantile neuroses is, in his experience, only apparent. In any case, through the solidity of the one symptom, they show a great multiplicity [of symptoms].

In the foreground we find:

I. Phenomena in the *digestive organs,* which, having been particularly stressfully taxed, are readily inclined to illnesses. Besides, both ends of the alimentary tract are significant erotogenic zones.

1. *Anorexia,* which already appears in infancy, may be organically determined and is frequently encountered in older children. It is likely that hysterical and melancholic anorexias in adults have their prototype in this anorexia of infants. Fear of poison plays a role in them.
2. Habitual *vomiting,* which is carried over from early infancy into later childhood years. Such children start any and every illness with vomiting. Pathological, habitual vomiting in children who have just become of school age is of particular interest; it often appears in the first grade as an epidemic.
3. *Constipation* and its counterpart—i.e., frequent, yet normal, moving of the bowels—which is evidently meant to obtain greater pleasure-gain. In some cases the psychogenic cause of constipation can be demonstrated without difficulty.

4. *Prolapsus,* which in many cases must be assumed to have a psychogenic origin. Generally, this symptom seems to be distinguished by over-determination. Perhaps in older girls, it conceals a fantasy of parturition; in children who are little loved or believe themselves to be so, a passionate longing to be cared for may perhaps play a role.

5. *Attacks of pain.* Frequently, [symptoms of] an *ulcus rotundus ventriculi* are imitated; in most instances, what is involved is identification with a female relative who has been suffering from this illness. No organic bases can be found for attacks of pain located in the abdomen, and then can easily be modified by therapy.

II. *Respiratory Organs.*

1. *Choking* [*Verkeuchen*], which appears to be psychically determined.

2. *Asthmatic bronchitis:* it is not inconceivable that this, too, is psychogenic in character.

3. *Pertussis,* which, in neurotic children invariably accompanies bronchitis; in most instances, it is feigned or aggravated.

4. Other phenomena of the respiratory organs, merely suggested: hiccups, belching, spasms of screaming.

5. *Speech defects*

a) total mutism; very frequent, open to suggestion, readily accessible to influence.

b) aphasia, the same as in adult hysterics.

c) stuttering, which appears suddenly in one who hitherto spoke fluently, mostly in the only or youngest child; upon being taken out of their milieu, they often speak quite well and fluently.

III. *Urinary Organs.*

1. *Enuresis nocturna,* in spite of Fuchs,[2] cannot be excluded from this group; case of a girl in whom enuresis was a substitution for emission.

2. *Pollakisuria,* not infrequent in children between one and a half and three years.

[2] We have been unable to establish a reference for this.

IV. *Spasms.*

1. *Grimacing.*
2. *Squinting.*
3. *Stereotypes;* a somewhat theatrical form of masturbation.
4. *Spasms of the diaphragm* (Case of a girl).
5. *Grand attacks.*

V. *Paralyses,* which in children show peculiarities.

1. *Astasia-Abasia,* very frequent and easily cured.
2. Following diphtheria.
3. Following an injury.

VI. *Psychic Alterations.*

1. Poor sleep, in children who have been taken into their parents' bed, or carried around for a while.
2. Excessive apprehensiveness, which is very transparent; and there is no need to say anything more about it.
3. *Pavor nocturnus,* about which nothing conclusive can yet be said.
4. States of anxiety and phobias, with which the speaker has had some experience. States of anxiety following poliomyelitis.

The method of research is difficult and will certainly have to be different from the psychoanalytic method. Above all it is necessary to collect, with the greatest thoroughness possible, objective observations instead of subjective statements; and then *per analogiam* to draw conclusions from our knowledge of adult states about these conditions which, after all, are characterized by a relative simplicity.

These clinical pictures are of great importance in that they can be put to good use in pedagogy and prophylaxis. Once pediatricians, paedagogues and nurses are familiar with these conditions, the number of adult neurotics will be considerably diminished.

Therapy has not so far been neglected. In many cases, it is sufficient simply to change the milieu or the influence exercised by those around the child, in order to effect the disappearance of symptoms. However, it is possible that by these means nothing is cured other than the symptoms, which later can appear once again. At first one sees a satisfactory therapeutic result, since at this early age conflicts are seldom severe. Where that is the case, however, this therapy fails. Moreover, the child's ability to sublimate plays an important role in the cure; he must be able to succeed, in a changed environment, in sublimating his pathological inhibitions.

The field of research here is enormously big, and one man's working capacity is not sufficient to accomplish even a part of the task.

DISCUSSION

HITSCHMANN stresses that in the method of the paper one could recognize the authentic practitioner. A different way of considering problems might perhaps have led to broader points of view. Pediatrics, insofar as it deals with the psychology of the child, can settle greater questions. When one thinks how naively the child used to be looked at, in times past, and how, by way of our investigations, people have been brought round to the feeling that the child is heavy with destiny! Surely, in addition to sexuality, other factors will be found that have a share in the child's character formation and in his development.

It will have to be established which of these phenomena and symptoms are ubiquitous, which pathological, and what is indicated by the degrees [of intensity] of the individual symptom. Concerning the feasibility of analysis of the child, there is a passage in Freud's earlier writings in which it is declared to be impossible, or rather that a method has yet to be found for it.

A few supplementary observations should be made; for instance, that children may also vomit because of fear, that prolonged lingering on the toilet is a very frequent occurrence. Is there not also something of the nervous behind the pseudo-croup? The neurotic factor in pertussis can be only a relative one. What the speaker said about prolapsus does not seem very probable to Hitschmann. Most interesting are the hysterical children who, in a certain sense, seem to contradict the theory, since their hysterical symptoms are formed without reminiscences.

REITLER has the impression that psychoanalytic research may expect a great deal from Friedjung. He would like to see as the main task the ascertaining of the neurotic states of infants. The basic question of whether there exists an infantile hysteria he would be inclined to answer in the affirmative; he has at his disposal several cases of this kind, which are explainable, of course, only by having recourse to heredity. The psychogenic element must lie in the preceding generation. Among the forms of illness that must be referred to a sexual basis we must also count migraine; we interpret it as [a result of] autointoxication through one of the secretions of the sex glands. Reitler himself has suffered from severe migraines throughout his life, and had, it seems, suffered from them even as an infant.

A second important point would be an investigation into when erections first occur, whether in such children they appear particularly early (observed in an infant of five weeks), and when they re-occur after infancy (at four to five years).

A detail out of a case history to corroborate the assertion that enuresis is a substitution for emission: a patient intensely fixated on his mother goes to her grave after her death in order to shoot himself there. However, he gives up his intention and leaving the cemetery, enters a men's room; while urinating, he has the hallucination that this is happening on the mother's grave. In this way he performs sexual intercourse with her in an infantile manner.

Children's injuries, in most cases are likely to have to do with falling, which to them is equivalent to the Fall of Man [*Sündenfall*].

HELLER can confirm some of what has been said from the observation of his own children; for instance, vomiting in school—which never occurred when they were still staying at home. The digestive symptoms were also strongly in evidence: the "long-sitter" mentioned by Hitschmann is Heller's boy. In his third or fourth year he developed in addition to vomiting, a compulsion to bite (directed against his brother), which disappeared again after some time. He also has a noteworthy aversion to kissing and being kissed.

ADLER remarks that a debt of gratitude is due the speaker for the material presented, even though he has not in all instances given sufficient explanations. It will not do to take many symptoms as substitutes for coition or acts of emission. To be sure, something analogous is involved, but what is missing is the proof that one is dealing with a substitution. It is equally unsatisfactory to assume that many of the symptoms are released by a single affect (anxiety), because other affects rank just as high (rage, anger). In regard to some of the symptoms, one has no choice but to accept the explanation he [Adler] has given: an original, congenital inferiority, which is especially prominent in symptoms of the first childhood years. About 90-95 percent of all children show signs of stuttering in their second or third years; it is therefore just not enough to declare this to be a manifestation of a neurosis. Organic anomalies of the speech organs are to be found side by side with stuttering. This connection becomes even more important if one takes heredity into consideration; Adler has seen cases similar to Reitler's. Perhaps it turns out that such a primary development [organ inferiority] of the child returns in the neurosis with a totally different meaning, of course, with other determinants and in a neurotic sense.

The same may be true of enuresis, and many other childhood defects, of which vomiting deserves special emphasis. In infants, however, it cannot be considered a neurotic symptom. It seems that primary inferiorities of the alimentary tract are involved, which later, as the result of certain conditions, become capable of entering the neurosis and playing their part in it. One must take notice of this difference in the evaluation of such a symptom, because otherwise it becomes enormously difficult to differentiate between childhood defects and neurotic symptoms.

Children sleep poorly because they have fantasies in connection with events of the day, fantasies that soon lead to certain questions: for instance, in a boy they led to the question of what would become of him after his death, a question that concealed the problem of where he had come from. For the first time the child is caught up with the problem of the origin of human beings. But because this formulation of the question is based on the boy's ignorance, one cannot say that the question is a neurotic symptom; in the adult, it is utilized only in its reappearance as a neurotic symptom.

PROF. FREUD: The question as to what psychoanalysis expects from the pediatrician can, in general, be answered to the effect that it expects from him its confirmation and its verification. All the things that we assert go back to childhood, but were not, of course, discovered in the child—these are matters that will be beyond doubt only when the pediatrician confirms them.[3]

Among the special questions there are some that should be stressed, to which continued observation could easily supply the answer. These are questions of basic significance: (1) Above all, does such a development as we postulate, toward later normalcy and civilization, actually take place? The pediatrician has to observe to what extent the so-called later perversions appear in childhood, when they disappear and what may by chance take their place. (2) Is the part played by heredity over- or underestimated nowadays; how much [of what is called heredity] is actually pseudo-heredity, i.e., results from parental influence during the first years of life? (3) What is the relationship of congenital inferiorities to later developmental disturbances and functional defects? This is a relationship which, in a child, it will be easy to ascertain. The transition from functional deviations to a later neurosis must be determined precisely. For the pediatrician it is comparatively easy, because of the ease with which he can survey the child's milieu, to give us definite answers to these questions, and we will have to guide ourselves thereafter by them.

We anticipate that it may turn out by chance that adult neuroses have their prototype in child life (concerning which Adler was right in pointing out some dubious interpretations on the part of the speaker); we would then see in the developmental disturbances of children the germ of later neuroses. This is evident, for instance, in obsessional neurotics. At the age of 6 to 8 this neurosis is almost monosymptomatically focused on one point, and is already fully developed. It is a question whether everybody has not shown a kind of elementary neurosis in childhood; whether the relationship is not a much more intimate one than we envisage—i.e., that not only the elements but even the patterns stem from childhood; whether the later neurosis is not merely an enlargement of something like a neurosis into a characteristic creation of later or middle childhood.[4] Then we would have a

[3] Direct observation of "Little Hans" brought the first striking confirmation of Freud's assumptions.

[4] The ideas tentatively expressed by Freud here were later (in the *Introductory Lectures, S.E.* 15), formulated positively in the assertion that every adult neurosis is preceded by a childhood neurosis.

clear understanding of the origin of the neuroses and, between the core complex and the later adult neurosis, we would have to insert the elementary neurosis as an intermediate stage. The pediatrician is in a position to make the distinction definite between the psychologically conditioned strata of neurosis and a core that falls into the earliest years of life; he can further determine, with regard to this core, what [aspects] should be shifted over to development and what should be ascribed to heredity. Perhaps it will appear that behind all psychologically conditioned phenomena there lies something else.

The objection that infantile hysteria does not seem to admit of reminiscences has been raised also by Jung. Two instances of neglect occurred here: (1) In an infantile hysteria that appears in the sixth to eighth year, the prehistory must be in no way underestimated, since the decisive impressions are received in the second to fourth years of life. As far as these reminiscences are concerned, the fact that only a short period has elapsed is counterbalanced by the magnitude of the changes that occur within this short time. (2) We assume that there is no repression that does not have an organic core; this organic repression consists of the substitution of unpleasurable sensations for pleasurable ones. Probably man's detachment from the soil is one of the basic conditions for [the formation of] a neurosis; the olfactory sense is prone, as a consequence of this detachment, toward repression, since it has become useless. The repression of coprophilic tendencies begins in the same way: the bigger the child gets to be, the further it rises away from the ground. In this organic repression psychic factors as yet play no role; it is the repression of pleasurable sensations [and their transformation] into unpleasurable ones that we characterize as a portion of civilization. This repression can also make possible a hysteria in an infant, indeed even in an animal. Where the limits are to be drawn here, only observation can say. The entire theory of the neuroses is incomplete as long as no light has been shed on the organic core of repression.[5]

In reference to anxiety, one must keep in mind that the child first feels anxiety as a consequence of the act of birth. It is noteworthy also that every affect initially presents itself as an hysteric attack. The affect

[5] As far as I know, up to the present time no one has taken up this point as a subject of research.

is but the reminiscence of an experience;[6] the pediatrician must, therefore, give us information also about the origin of affects. Most children have one trauma from which point on they behave like hysterics; this trauma is: being weaned from the mother's breast; it is a trauma of psychological significance in relation to the pleasure taken in nourishment. From here repression begins—which, as we see, may be based on an unpleasant reminiscence (as is also true of psychic impotence). These individuals, for instance, have an aversion from then on to milk.

The pediatrician would also do well to include in the clinical picture certain circumstances of the child's life: whether he is the first or last child, what happened just before he fell ill (birth, death, etc.); in short, the entire family status. In this way it will turn out which part of the psychic phenomena is to be attributed to the organic illnesses described. Our task is not to take the place of organic pathology, but to trace the psychic contribution everywhere.

Finding a technique for this study of children is not as hopeless a task as it may seem. One will avail oneself of the help of a skillful nurse (in especially favorable circumstances, of the mother herself), who must observe the child continuously and report everything that seems to be of importance; thus, as in the case of deranged persons, this would be indirect observation.[7]

For some time to come child research will have to let itself be guided by the experiences gained in the treatment of adults. This, however, is not the ideal set of circumstances.

The therapy of a child's nervous states will always have [to contend with] one great difficulty: the parents' neuroses, which will form a wall in front of the child's neurosis.[8]

[6] As we can see from these remarks, Freud had already at that time traced anxiety back to birth: he saw in the affect at birth the prototype of later anxiety. This view was subsequently distorted and misused by Rank. For the history of the evolution of Freud's theory of anxiety, see Editor's Introduction to *Inhibitions, Symptoms and Anxiety, S.E.* 20.

[7] Freud offers here a suggestion for child analysis that was later taken up and worked out by his daughter Anna. At the same time Freud seems to suggest a method for the treatment of psychotics which may not differ essentially from the treatment of children.

[8] Anna Freud has conducted a research project aimed at finding out in what way a child's neurosis is dependent upon the parents'—especially the mother's—neuroses. According to my own experience, in some cases of infantile neurosis the mother's analysis renders an analysis of the child superfluous. See also: Nunberg, "A Dream

WITTELS has the impression that Friedjung is the right man—even in a field that allows fantasy so much latitude—for holding on to the natural scientist's instinct for acute observation. This advantage is counterbalanced by the disadvantage that Friedjung has given far too little consideration to general points of view; for instance, the question of what pedagogues can learn from the results hitherto arrived at by psychoanalysis. Concerning this question, Wittels has repeatedly defined his own stand: one ought not educate children, because one cannot educate them. One should not concern oneself with children at all.

In addition to the consequence of weaning stressed by Freud, Wittels would like to point to its "ethical" consequence: the fact that the individual is forced into a pervasive pessimism; that this trauma places the kernel in the child's heart of an especially deep indignation, which can manifest itself later in the adult's spiritual life as a certain "primary indignation" (as of a satirist, who must become indignant every day about something different, etc.). Therefore, a very slow and cautious weaning seems to be indicated, perhaps even none at all.

Today one cannot psychoanalyze a child; later on, one may perhaps succeed in treating neurosis in its incipient stages in the child.

FURTMÜLLER, being a layman in medical matters, would like to confine himself to the field of education. Wittels' principle that one ought not to educate is valid only insofar as Wittels really means by "education" *bad* education. What educators should expect from Freud's point of view as a whole is [to obtain] clues for a *sensible* education, such as foresees the conflicts in store for the child and builds against them in due time. The systematic warding off of certain noxae can also be called education. Therefore the most important goal, that which is nearest at hand, must be the education of parents and other persons who take care of children; from this would, of course, result an influence upon the child.

DECZI would like to comment only on a few minor questions. Czerny does not believe that pertussis is an infectious disease. (HITSCHMANN: It has been so proven by experiments on animals.)

---

of a Six-Year-Old Girl," (1926) *Practice and Theory of Psychoanalysis.* New York: International Universities Press, 1948.

Deczi has seen erections in a child of six or seven months. In reference to the repression of certain areas of sensation (such as the nose), a remark of the animal psychologist Zell should be kept in mind, to the effect that there are eye animals (man, ape) and nose animals.[9]

Observation of the child outside his usual milieu should supplement his being observed at home.

In reference to the question of how long a child can be called a "suckling," Bunge's observation should be mentioned; he establishes a connection between the capability of nursing and a certain excess of iron in the liver.[10]

STEKEL cannot imagine what Freud means by organic repression; as far as he is concerned, there is only a psychic repression into the organic. Weaning may perhaps be a trauma. An aversion toward milk, however, is not, according to Stekel's clinical experiences, to be brought into connection with weaning. The aversion is usually felt toward the skin on the [boiled] milk; it seems to stem from the fact that children have drunk the "milk in the skin" (from the mother's breasts); when this becomes unpleasurable, they stop drinking milk.

All children who suddenly stop eating have been doing their parents a favor by eating, and they take revenge upon them by stopping. To observe children's fantasies is one of the most important tasks of the pediatrician.

Stekel will admit that children do vomit when they begin to go to school. They are afraid of getting to school late, gulp down their breakfast and then vomit. This anxiety must be characterized as anticipatory anxiety. In such states, nausea or emissions appear; both these processes are thus unmasked as sexual ones. For these children are anticipating something else entirely than what new and special experiences they are going to have at school. These are children who at night have been observing and anticipating with tension what father was

[9] Theodor Zell (1862-1924) discusses the difference between the visual and the olfactory type of animal in his book *Ist das Tier vernünftig? Neue Einblicke in die Tierseele.* [*Is an Animal a Rational Being? New Insights into the Animal Mind*] Stuttgart, 1910.

[10] Gustav Bunge, physiologist (1844-1920), "Die zunehmende Unfähigkeit der Frauen, ihre Kinder zu stillen; die Ursachen dieser Unfähigkeit; die 'Mittel zur Verhütung' "; ein Vortrag, München 1900; neue vermehrte Auflage, 1908. ("The Increasing Inability of Women to Nurse their Children; the Causes of this Inability the Means of Prevention"); a lecture, Munich 1900; new, expanded edition, 1908.

going to do with mother. To this is added the father's replacement by the teacher.

Children's attacks of pain in the digestive tract are frequently [an expression of] birth fantasies (pseudo-appendicitis).

JEKELS thinks that it may be useless to try to remove, with the help of sublimation, constitutional symptoms of infantile neuroses; rather, here too analysis will be in place. Just as little is there to be accomplished by changing the milieu. As to Wittels' opinion about the complete hopelessness of education he too shares it. The education of parents and teachers may perhaps have the result that freer human beings will be brought up, because many will realize that one must not brutalize children the way one now does, in order to make them as submissive as possible to their environment.

FRIEDJUNG: On the question of infant hysteria, about which he remains skeptical, a large amount of material first has to be collected.

What Friedjung said about stutterers has been misunderstood: he had in mind only those children who had already spoken well.

It is surely no accident that some children acquire the habit of vomiting; no doubt there is an organic, and perhaps even an inherited, basis for this symptom. Friedjung does not want to go into the question of education today.

The boundary between infancy and later childhood seems to be determined by the teeth; by the fact [of having teeth] the child is directed toward a different [type of] nourishment. Weaning has the effect, in most cases, of a trauma—even if it is carried out gradually; sudden weaning may perhaps be less harmful.

88

SCIENTIFIC MEETING *on November 24, 1909*

Present: Prof. Freud, Adler, Federn, Friedjung, Furtmüller, Graf, Hitschmann, Jekels, Joachim, Rank, Reitler, Sadger, Steiner, Stekel, Tausk, Wittels.

PRESENTATION

Theory of Knowledge and Psychoanalysis

SPEAKER: DR. TAUSK

The speaker begins by giving a brief overview of the history of the theory of knowledge and the problems it has set for itself. First of all, one must keep two subjects separate: the function of perception and the function of the instincts (affects, etc.). The subject of the theory of knowledge is the investigation of the functional. The series of philosophers of the theory of knowledge who have occupied themselves with [the problem of] perceiving in a narrower sense begins with *Aristotle,* and then proceeds via *Spinoza* to *Hume,* with whom the *theory of knowledge* actually begins. After him comes his successor, Kant, who taught us how to perceive the function of perception itself.

Aristotle starts off with the question: what is the content of the

Form? What is the relationship of content to form? These are questions that nowadays seem to us inadequate, because we have learned that form is content. Aristotle discovered the laws of rational functioning and put them down in his [works on] logic. But his immediate successor, Plato [sic], was no longer a logician. He wanted, even then, to find room for the affects, an endeavor that later on was repeated again and again (Scholastics-Spinoza; Kant-Schopenhauer), and which appears understandable to us if we bear in mind that what is always involved is to obtain from the theoretical insights that had been gained what is best and most agreeable for mankind and for oneself. The real difference between these two kinds of thinking becomes immediately apparent in Aristotle and Plato. The latter thought that the laws of logic must have validity for all that happens in the universe; since the harmony of logical thinking does not come forward on our earth, there must be a region [lit., a possibility] somewhere else where all things are in harmony. That world exists in the world of the Ideas, and our world is but a reflection of this harmonious world. Thus this euphoric way of thinking misled Plato into postulating the existence of a world of Ideas. He did not take into consideration the great difference between the function of perception and Being.

From there the path leads to the founders of religion, to the dogmatists, who said: "Man *shall* be such and such"; this "shall" is a feeling with which we are going to become acquainted later in the form of anxiety. In order to establish the "shall," they have, quite naïvely, referred to a Supreme Being.

While Plato, in the sense indicated, continued [sic] Aristotle's teachings (as Schopenhauer later continued Kant's), Spinoza's ideas are fundamentally in contrast to those of the scholastics. Spinoza did the same thing that Plato did, but in a different way; his pantheism is only a formula; to him the vessel in which all the laws act in harmony is God. The outcome of his entire deliberations is the equalization of logic and ethics—which in Weininger's work returns in the same way.[1]

After Spinoza, there is, up to Hume, no longer any talk of investigating perception and the affects. The theosophists and mystics are of no interest here; they want to prove that what the Church Fathers said is

[1] Otto Weininger (1880-1903), author of *Geschlecht und Charakter* [*Sex and Character*].

logical. Only with Hume do we find once again an important problem of the theory of knowledge: the function of causality is to be psychologically explained. The question is: how do we know that everything happens that way? That one thing necessarily follows from the other? As to his answer, Hume is only in part correct. He stated: it is from the fact that one thing follows from the other in so many cases, that we come to know the law of succession. To him, then, it is purely a matter of experience. He could not give any other answer at that time, because he did not yet have a psychology of perceiving; it was Kant who first furnished that. Kant posed the problem: what am I in relation to these things that appear here? Are they dependent on me or not? Are the contents perceived inherent in the things, and what are the ultimate conditions under which we perceive? Kant answers: the relations of things (time, space, causality, quality, quantity, etc.) exist only in our mind, by which it is that we determine the things and their relationship to us. We function in such a way that things appear to us in such a way; that is how we function *a priori*. This was the first psychology of a theory of knowledge. Subsequently, Kant elaborated this theory into a fine systematic structure, and he thus diluted it and adulterated it. Later we learned from Freud, as shall be shown, also about the priority of becoming subjected to affects.

Schopenhauer again erected an ethical structure on top of someone else's logical edifice. He applied the Kantian logical categories to the affect-function, and very beautifully and almost without contradiction carried out a sharp division between the theory of knowledge and the affect-function right through to the end. Eventually, he put them together so that they were in harmony with each other. Since it was necessary for him to leave off [following] his own will (instinctual drive), he wanted to utilize Kant's findings first of all in the service of his own euphoria. And thus he, exactly as Spinoza had, came to a denial of affect. We are meant to be nothing but logic; we are prevented from this, however, by our will. Therefore we are not to have a will, but only to perceive. This is the division between "the world as will and idea." Not until Weininger is an attempt again made to turn the logical experience into an ethical one.

The error of all these thinkers lies in the material of the topic itself: logic has a content that is clearly harmonious. These harmonies of thought cannot be applied to imperfect organisms, which must indeed come into conflict with everything in order to be able to exist.

The entire development, in terms of historical facts, as well as of the outlook of the individual person, should be considered in a way that enables us to rediscover in it and to apply to it the psychological laws established by Freud—at least, to begin with, the principal laws: those of repression and of anxiety, which appears as a necessary ingredient of adaptation. Repression furnishes the *material* which is the sublimated symbolical content in all these theories. The motive force, however, is anxiety.

The speaker then proceeds to talk about consciousness and its functions; further, about optimism and pessimism, and also about the concept of metapsychology, created by Freud.

The subjects of the theory of knowledge are consciousness and instinctual life. Consciousness has the function of recognizing the unconscious;[2] it is an organ for making available unconscious experiences.

Consciousness develops by way of the differentiation of feelings, a differentiation that is conditioned by the difficulties presented by the milieu. Consciousness originates therefore as a means of the struggle for existence and bestows upon an individual superiority over those who aim only at the instinctive satisfaction of their needs. The question of the relationship between consciousness and the unconscious first found an answer through the disturbance of the function, which gave the impetus to an investigation of the law of functioning. The disturbed function is one that is grasped on its way to adaptation.

From here the path leads to the theory of the transcendental unity of the ego—a theory that culminates in an explanation of the conscious and the unconscious.

It is characteristic of consciousness that it admits only those elements that are supposed to contribute to the individual's well-being. The character [of an individual] is determined by how much of the unconscious is made conscious and how much of this is consciously utilized in the struggle for existence.

[2] This definition should not be confused with Freud's conception of consciousness. According to him, consciousness is an organ for the perception of external events as well as of inner processes, e.g., preconscious or unconscious ideas, feelings, sensations, emotions, etc.

The functional elements of consciousness are: pure reason as the cognitive factor, and practical reason as the organizing factor.

Freud has shown the adaptation of affects to be an *a priori* function. The regulation of affects occurs *a priori* only by way of the possibilities disclosed by Freud. The transformation succeeds in maintaining the individual's well-being in his mileu. The most perfect adaptation is that which we find in the genius, in that he himself creates his own milieu.

Pessimism has no other meaning than that the content of life is the possibility of adaptation. Philosophy and every science stem from the suffering of life.

Concerning the origin of consciousness, as a question [to be answered in terms] of milieu, it can be said that the weakest (of a certain quality) will be the first to create this consciousness for themselves. Civilization is a civilization of the weak. The energy for the generation of consciousness is furnished by the sexual instinct. Similarly, when this instinct is turned away from [the goal of] sexual well-being, it creates social well-being. And this is not a sublimation but a substitute formation, a means for obtaining sexual pleasure anew.

To this then is added anxiety: the individual is frightened by his ego, because he stands in fear of losing it. This is fear of death—a fear that one has only when one thinks that one is not going to be able to satisfy fully one's capacity for [sexual] pleasure.

Finally the speaker remarks that he is aware of the incompleteness of his exposition; but he believes, nevertheless, that he has shown here and there how he has applied the Freudian laws to that way of thinking.

(The concept "metapsychology" is not formed correctly; the term should be "transcendental psychology," in that it is a psychology that discloses unconditional functions.[3])

DISCUSSION

FRIEDJUNG hopes that the speaker, who himself thinks that much has been left unsaid, may perhaps have the chance to supplement this

[3] The reader who is not well versed in philosophy may well find it difficult to understand this paper. Besides, Rank seems to have rendered the lecture too cursorily, which may have contributed to the obvious gaps.

Faithful to our principle, we have here, too, avoided expressing our views even when we have felt that the speaker in some respects deviated from Freud's theories.

on other occasions. This is particularly true of the role played by anxiety and repression in these philosophers' theories of life. Also, the speaker touched briefly on the nature and source of pessimism, without discussing its correlate, optimism. On the other hand, Friedjung would like to raise an objection to the statement that civilization is invariably an accomplishment of the weak. On the contrary, actual civilization is always a civilization of the strong. Further, Friedjung found any detailed and direct reference missing to the deepened insights into the problem of free will, such as we have gained, thanks to Freud. It is only now that it seems self-evident to us that the will is not free, in that we have come to know its source.

ADLER stresses that, in this vast area, it is worthy of thanks if someone even so much as broaches an individual problem. In view of the huge [scope of the] material, it was to be foreseen that the speaker would be able to touch upon the problems only sketchily, without achieving their solution. Therefore it is embarrassing to go into certain matters of detail. One might perhaps have sought out a broader goal than the speaker has done. Adler himself, in the first year of these meetings,[4] attempted to consider the philosophical systems from the point of view of our approaches. In [the case of] some philosophers, it can be clearly shown with what problem they have been wrestling. Again and again these turn out to be the same problems that occupy us theoretically as well as practically. The problems of causality call to mind the attempts, which develop early in the life of the individual man, to establish and perceive a causal relationship—attempts which, according to Freud, go back to the child's reflections on his origin, to his desire to fathom the sexual relationship and their consequences.[5] What we perceive as a philosophical problem is therefore actually nothing more than the substitution, the sublimation and the psychic superstructure of perceived deficiencies and inferiorities.

On other systems there is impressed, in addition to this penetration of the world in a causal respect, a special standpoint from which various things can be brought into question. Hegel, who enabled the idea of evolution to make a breakthrough in philosophy, places in the foreground [of his philosophy] his conception of dialectics, i.e., the trans-

[4] Records of these meetings do not exist.

[5] Freud: *Three Essays, Leonardo da Vinci.* Nunberg: *Curiosity.*

formation of one thing into its opposite, of the thesis into the antithesis —matters that occupy us continuously. From this we must conclude that in the life of this philosopher, the problem of his personal dialectics played an uncommonly large role, to the point where it became to him the most important problem in all of development.

As far as Schopenhauer is concerned, Adler tried as early as six years ago to explain that the origin of his pessimistic conception of the world lay in his relationship to his mother, toward whom he developed a harsh opposition at an early time (probably in the process of repressing a longing for her). We see a direct continuation of this in his attitude toward the world.

The speaker may perhaps have raised too high our expectations with reference to anxiety and its significance for philosophy. It does in fact play an enormous role; but the transformations and metamorphoses of the problem of anxiety in the human mind are frequently so far removed from any relation to anxiety that one can hardly be aware of the connection offhand. The fact that ethical principles and religious laws spring from the same source has already been stressed. Adler himself has traced these laws back to an affective state [*Affektlage*]; thus not much can be expected from studying them, since they develop under compulsion.

In reference to the pessimistic outlook, too, one can go a step further than the speaker. Analysis invariably discloses that the pessimistic outlook emerges under the pressure of the struggle for existence, but presents only one form of this struggle: it is the reaction of an individual who, under [the burden of] guilt feelings, cannot develop to the level of activity (aggression)—an individual who has remained arrested in his development at a point at which punishment or calamity has become an expectation. Pessimism cannot be considered apart from its opposite, optimism. The individual arrives at optimism when he succeeds in achieving mastery over this fear of punishment, this sense of guilt. The distinction lies in the orientation of aggression, which finds expression in both these outlooks—as a result of which, however, both will lose their place in our consciousness.

HITSCHMANN would like to refer to the few words that were spoken at the meeting welcoming the membership, on which occasion much that pertains to the topic was already touched upon. It is highly questionable whether ideas such as these, so long as they are not clarified, have anything to offer. If one attempts to relate [the concept of] repression to the [physical] law of the attraction and repulsion of matter, it will not have any meaning since this concept is indeed formed by "leaning upon" such ideas.

PROF. FREUD would like in the first place to correct a historical error. Plato is not a successor of Aristotle; he was the older man, and a student of Socrates.

When the problem of form was discussed, Freud recalled a definition that is not generally applicable but for certain (especially artistic) conditions is appropriate: form is the precipitate of an older content. A content has, as a rule, its history; the earlier stages of the present content have left behind their form.

As far as the paper as such is concerned, Freud can indicate his position only generally. Personally, he has particular difficulty grasping such abstract ideas as were presented in the lecture, ideas that should have been presented in a much more elementary manner. It would be interesting to find out whether a philosophic study [of a question] would yield more than a mere translation into a language difficult to understand, or whether one could perhaps expect a further simplification and the achievement of clear results. Various accidentally impeding circumstances (illness, etc.) have made it impossible for the speaker to satisfy this curiosity; moreover, the task is such that it could not have been accomplished in the limited time. The philosophic mastery of our experiences is actually going to yield new results; whether the time is yet ripe for it, Freud cannot judge. The speaker, however, seems to be the right man for that undertaking. It would be desirable if, despite today's misfire, Tausk would make it his task from time to time to present to us single parts of this broad constellation, in a clear, detailed, and elementary fashion.

GRAF would not like to suppress a wish whose fulfilling he wants to suggest to the speaker. The most difficult intellectual problems, if they are well thought out, can be presented in a language that comes a bit closer to common usage. It is asking too much [to expect a reader] to learn one single individual's language as well. Schopenhauer and

Nietzsche have shown that one can in fact deal with the most difficult problems in an aesthetic way.

From the paper, the course of the speaker's development can easily be recognized. He is at this point still in process of fermentation, in which he wants to link his grasp of the theory of knowledge to the teachings of Freud. It seems, however, that there is still too great a distance between them. Some time in the future one will perhaps work from Freud toward philosophy. On the whole, Graf has the same respect for this discourse as he has for any honest and completely devoted piece of work.

FEDERN believes that the weariness of the speaker when he was proceeding from Kant to Freud, and declared that he could not go on, was more deeply determined. Tausk established copious links, but as to the synthesis that he had in mind, he did not succeed in achieving that. In view, however, of the enormous [amount of] material and the difficulty of the problems, one cannot reproach him for this. The most important task is to show first what are the unconscious motives that enter into [the thinking of] individual philosophers, and secondly to what extent the philosophies, measured against our criteria, stand up.

With some individual points, Federn concurs in part, and in part disagrees. The assertion that consciousness is a creation of the weak is in accord with Adler's ideas, but it is contradictory to our feelings. One should rather say that it comes into being when, during the course of the struggle with the external world, a weakness appears. But it is only the strong ones among human beings who live under the same circumstances, that will cultivate consciousness.

REITLER, expressing his fullest appreciation, waives his turn to speak.

FURTMÜLLER stresses the point that in the foreground of the problem is [the question of] how far repression, anxiety and, in general, the motives that analysis has recognized to be operative, play a role in the [development of] philosophical systems. It should, furthermore, be disregarded that this problem has nothing whatever to do with philosophy in general, and in particular with the history of philosophy. We must, after all, distinguish between the psychological conditions requisite for an achievement and its logical value. The philosopher does not have to be content with the fact that we analyze him psychologically; on the contrary, he does demand to be shown whether or not he has committed a logical error. In mixing these two viewpoints, the speaker has to a great extent wronged the philosophers. His entire interpretation of the philosophy of Plato does not sufficiently take into account the scope of its importance. We must not view Plato's conclusions as only a play of his affects. A similar attitude in reference to Kant is just as inadmissible.

It is not so certain that our present insights into the theory of knowledge will necessarily, as the result of psychoanalytic research, be forced to change in the near future. Philosophy and the theory of knowledge have only to acknowledge these facts; and even the refusal of official psychology to recognize the Unconscious is not a basic obstacle to that, for it is purely a question of the interpretation of concepts.[6] It seems self-evident that the wealth of psychological understanding [gained by psychoanalysis] will in its turn have effects on philosophy; but there is nothing in the present state of affairs that could compel us to seek an immediate change.

Prof. Freud finally proposes to the speaker that in his next paper he make use of the material saved for his concluding remarks.

[6] The German original has: . . . *denn das ist rein nur eine Frage der begrifflichen Besinnung.*

89

SCIENTIFIC MEETING *on December 1, 1909*

Present: Prof. Freud, Adler, Federn, Friedjung, Furtmüller, Graf, Heller, Hitschmann, Rank, Reitler, Sadger, Steiner, Stekel, Tausk, Wittels.

Dr. Jekels and Stein from Budapest as guests.

PRESENTATION

A Fantasy of Leonardo da Vinci[1]

SPEAKER: PROF. FREUD

The speaker's attention was drawn by chance to the possibility of Leonardo's becoming an object for psychoanalytic investigation; and to be sure, there are quite definite singularities in Leonardo's character, which justify this psychoanalytic importunity.

Leonardo was born in 1452 and died in 1519 in his sixty-seventh year. He is esteemed as one of the greatest artists and was so esteemed by his contemporaries. Yet, side by side with this, from the start of his

[1] Cf. Freud's essay: "Leonardo Da Vinci and a Memory of His Childhood," published in 1910. *S.E.* 11.

career, a certain strangeness of his personality counted against him; they could not quite understand him and he was considered to be an eccentric, as much for his own nature as for the nature of his occupation. He was at the same time a great investigator, and was more interested in natural science than in his art. For instance, fifty years before Copernicus he had written down [in his notebooks what were to be] the latter's discoveries; he made the best anatomical charts, was the first to calculate according to geological periods, etc.

There are two principal character traits that provide the occasion for psychoanalytic concern with Leonardo: the first is that he never finished anything, a trait that recalls the neurotic; the second is the lack of regard with which he treated his creations: he had no interest in them and did not concern himself with what became of them. As a consequence, most of them have been ruined or are close to it.

We shall, of course, first inquire into the man's sexual life in order, on that basis, to understand the peculiarities of his character. About it, not much is now known; still, there is enough to propel us on to a certain path [of inquiry]. It is certain that no woman ever played a role in his life, and therefore homosexuals claim him for themselves. In fact, as a youth he is said to have been charged with homosexual intercourse. But on the basis of all we know about him, it seems out of the question that he should have been active in sexual matters.

Probably, he is to be regarded as an inhibited homosexual, or one who is homosexual in thought only. He did select young and handsome pupils, but there is nothing at all to signify that he had any direct sexual relations with them. On the whole, he seems to have been a man who was completely lacking in activity, the aggressive instinct, and who had attained a very high degree of mastery over his affects. He shows an extraordinary sexual repression, of which one sentence in his notebooks offers particular confirmation: "The act of procreation and its organs are marked by such malformations that, were it not for the beauty of the rest of the body, the human race would have long since died out."

Leonardo did not eat meat.

One of his favorite occupations was to buy up birds and then let them fly free. His chief hobby was the desire to fly, and even in his old age he still hoped to be able to solve the problem [of flying].

For us it is obvious that these character traits are connected with his *sexuality;* we expect to find in Leonardo's sexual development the single solution for the four enigmas of his life: (1) that he was such a great investigator; (2) that he did not persevere in any one thing, but left most of his works unfinished; (3) that he dealt with his works so badly; and (4) that his peculiar kind of inactive sexuality prevailed throughout his life.

We shall not err further in presuming that we can, on the basis of his *childhood,* explain how it came about that a character with precisely these peculiarities took shape. But where are we to get the material? It seems as if we have to be satisfied with saying: the inactivity that he shows in relation to art is connected with his sexual inactivity. However, this inhibition of energy was not general but a limited thing, for he was, indeed, also an investigator.

About his childhood, as we stated before, little is known. He came from a family of philistines; for four generations, his forefathers had been notaries, who had never particularly distinguished themselves. His father sired him, while still a young man of twenty-three, with a peasant girl named Caterina: Leonardo was an illegitimate child. In the year of Leonardo's birth, his father married a woman of high rank. The next thing we know about Leonardo is that at five years of age he was living in his father's house in Florence. Since the marriage remained childless, it seems plausible that the father, with his wife's consent, took his illegitimate child into his house. The father married four times in all (by his third and fourth wife he had altogether ten children) and died at eighty some odd years.

In his treatise about the flight of birds, a scientific essay, Leonardo suddenly becomes fanciful and says: "It seems that I have always been destined to occupy myself with the flight of birds. In my earliest recollection of childhood, it seems to me as though a vulture had flown down to me, opened my mouth with his tail, and several times beaten it to and fro between my lips."

This cannot, of course, be a childhood memory, but a fantasy about his childhood. If we apply our psychoanalytic skill here, we must declare this to be a homosexual fantasy, the meaning of which could perhaps be: to take the penis ("tail"; in Italian, it means precisely that) into the mouth and to suck on it.

We know that dreams of flying originally have invariably the meaning: I can mate [like a bird], I am a bird, I am sexually mature. There is something of that kind here too.

Now, there is another strange path that leads a little step further into the story. In hieroglyphic writing, the vulture[2] stands for something quite definite—i.e., the mother—and indeed the pronunciation of that character is "mut." If we attempt to insert this into the fantasy, then it would mean that his mother bent over him, put her penis into his mouth and there moved it to and fro several times.

We know that in girls the fantasy of sucking a penis goes back to suckling at the mother's breast. We could, then, imagine that a homosexual reworking of this sucking at the mother's breast may by chance lead to something like the fantasy that we find in Leonardo. We would therefore say that at the bottom of this there is the recollection of an extremely intense [pleasure enjoyed in] drinking at the mother's breast (the intensity being indicated by the tail's briskly moving to and fro), and that this recollection has been reworked in a homosexual sense. We can also take into consideration something else: the Egyptians had a deity that was called Mut and was represented as having a vulture's head. Now, there is no other Egyptian deity that has been so frequently represented as an androgyne (that is, with a penis). Thus the primitive idea of the child, which ascribes a penis to the mother (infantile sexual theory), has also remained alive in folk experience.

This makes it easier to understand how this mother-fantasy was reworked in a homosexual sense. This first lost penis of the mother plays a large role; and foot-fetishism, which we have been able to trace back to the suppression of certain coprophilic drives, must also have some connection with a search for and a happy recovery of this lost penis of the mother.[3]

Thus we are inclined to suppose that, in Leonardo's case, an enor-

[2] After Freud's publication of *Leonardo Da Vinci and a Memory of his Childhood* in 1910, the criticism was voiced that in his notes Leonardo used an Italian word that does not mean "vulture" but "keith," and that therefore Freud's interpretation of Leonardo's fantasy was absurd. Aside from the fact that a "keith," like a vulture, is a bird, an answer to this criticism, especially as put forward by Meyer Schapiro, can be found in Dr. K. R. Eissler's book *Leonardo Da Vinci* (New York: International Universities Press, 1961).

[3] In foot- or shoe-fetishism the son in a way also endows the mother with his own penis; he projects onto the object what he himself possesses.

mous mother fixation took place at an early age; that (as Sadger has shown in reference to homosexuals) he adored his mother and in repression of this love became a homosexual. The memory of both attitudes would be retained in this fantasy.

Now however the objection presents itself that hieroglyphs could not have been known to Leonardo because they were deciphered only in the twenties of the last century. Yet it can be proven that Leonardo was acquainted with the vulture as a symbol of motherliness, through his reading of Greek authors, who were thoroughly steeped in Egyptian culture. One of these Greek authors even indicates the basis for this symbolism: the ancients thought that there were only females among vultures, and that their impregnation was the consequence of the fact that they opened their vagina during flight and let themselves be impregnated by the wind. This fable was popularized by the Church Fathers, who wanted by way of it to confirm the possibility of immaculate conception. We may, then, imagine that one day Leonardo read this story of the vultures and then the following fantasy struck him: was not my mother also such a vulture, just such a poor bird without a male? We recognize that his illegitimacy was not without influence on this fantasy, which represents a recollection of his having been without a father during his childhood.

A child's growing up solely among persons of one sex is, as we now know, one of the strongest contributing causes of homosexuality; there was thus ample reason for this fantasy to be recast homosexually. We are then entitled to imagine that this fixation onto the mother did take place in Leonardo, and that he, awakened [sexually] at an early age by the tenderness of his deserted mother, had a brief but very intensive love-affair with her. We venture further to supplement what is traditionally told about him, to the effect that he may have spent his first four to five years with his mother, and may have been taken into his father's house only after the latter's marriage had proven definitely to be barren. The years from two to four, however, are the decisive ones; it is during this period that children produce their theories. The first and most important circumstance for Leonardo to ponder was why he had no father, as other children did. From this constellation stems his urge to investigate and to ponder; with his innate and enormous ability he had in earliest childhood translated his libido into the drive to investigate, and so it remained. With this, the greatest part of his sexual activity was exhausted for all time to come.

This first exploration by a child must, of course, fail because of his lack of sufficient cognitive capacity. The failure to complete this first exploration leaves behind a paralyzing effect on his whole life. The fact that Leonardo could never finish his later works is the stigma of infantilism, and renders it probable to us that his investigations actually go back to these matters, to his first fixation onto the mother.

These character traits of the necessity to investigate and the inability to complete can be further demonstrated in other traces of his life and work. It fits in amazingly with his sexual life. The development of certain cases of homosexuality shows, during the first period [of life], an intense fixation onto the mother; then its repression comes about, and with that the great transformation sets in. Homosexuals are separable into two groups, depending on which of the primitive sexual objects they choose; these two primary objects are the woman (mother, etc.), and the subject himself. Those of one group search throughout their lives for the woman with the penis, whom of course they can find in the male; in the others, such as Leonardo, the course is the following: simultaneously with the repression, an identification takes place: they themselves become feminine, become like the mother. That is their way of ridding themselves of the mother; then they search for themselves, love their own childhood ego. This is the root of the *love of young boys* of the genuine homosexuals. Leonardo, too, according to the reports of his biographers, behaves like a mother to his pupils: he teaches, advises, clothes them. He selected them, as his scanty successes show, not according to their talent but according to his own personal liking.

Leonardo kept a diary, which we may view as a neurotic trait. In the pages that have been preserved, he addresses himself, strangely enough, always by the intimate form of "You." This is obviously a substitute for an intercourse he had once had. The precursor and model of every diary seems to be the child's evening confession; in both cases one does not tell the real truth. This intimate "you" of the diary is to be equated with the aural hallucinations of the neurotic. The internal voices that tell them something are meant to be a substitute for the persons they miss: they are father and mother once again (sometimes also teachers). Conscience clothes itself in a figure. The "demon" of Socrates, too, is probably nothing else. In paranoia, these parental voices are replaced by those of colleagues, "the others." All voices use the intimate "you" (as in hysterics). In paranoia, they use the third person: they are the envious siblings, the prototypes of the subsequent persecutors.

In the second volume of his trilogy, *Antichrist,* of which Leonardo is the subject, Merezhkovski, carried away by his fantasy, sought to guess more about Leonardo's childhood and the rest of his psychic history than had been reported. What he says coincides very closely with our investigations. He has the little six-to-eight-year-old Leonardo often escape at night from the estate of the Vincis to his mother's hut nearby, slip into bed beside her, nestle against her and tell her everything he did during the day. That, of course, cannot be taken as proof, yet it throws an interesting light upon the interpretation of the fact that later he kept a diary.

In this diary, we meet a man who has completely mastered his normal affects. He has none where we have them; to him, everything is an object of investigation. The downfall of his greatest benefactor he records with meager words; similarly, the account of his father's death is recorded as an arid entry, which refers to the hour of the death only twice. In such trifles these covered-over affects betray themselves. Among these notes we find here and there, in a very detailed and petty fashion, records of insignificant matters. For instance, the expenses for the burial of Caterina (his mother), among which, in a most ridiculous fashion, he notes down the smallest items. Apparently this is the way in which he expresses the fact that he has been affected. Another account refers to a coat which he had had made for one of his pupils. A further reckoning is a list of things stolen from him by another of the boys. It is characteristic that these pedantic accounts appear to refer only to two types of persons—namely, his love objects. With such a displacement onto the smallest things, he cannot help giving expression in his diary to his suppressed affects.

In addition to these hints of the [role played by the] relationship to his mother in his sexual life, there are also certain clues in the painter's works, and the record of these could have the effect of making the so far actually unproductive work, for the first time, valuable. The greatest impression that one receives from his paintings is the famous Leonardo smile, so clearly evident in the *Mona Lisa,* the *Saint Anne,* the *Bacchus* (probably his last work), the *Leda* and many others. The *Mona Lisa* is a portrait on which he worked for four years. It is hardly likely that he himself added that feature to her countenance; one might therefore imagine that this woman had left a deep impression on him, and that, since that time, he had retained her smile, as it were.

This smile is most strikingly and most beautifully shown in the face of St. Anne, yet that composition had been created many years before the Mona Lisa. Therefore, Leonardo can have had only inner reasons for his predilection for this smile. Vasari reports that, among the youth's earliest works, there were busts of women who were smiling in this same way. This smile, it is to be assumed, stems from some person [who was part of] his childhood.

The painting of St. Anne with two others offers a curious composition, such as does not exist again in the Renaissance. The Blessed Virgin sits as a mother in the child's position on the lap of St. Anne, and bends down to the small Christ child. Both women have this strange smile, but St. Anne's is the more beautiful. It has generally been noted that Leonardo has canceled out the natural age difference between the two women. We recognize in this picture something from his life story. There are two mothers present, one of them somewhat farther away and the other an older woman. If the smile was the mother's, then it must be possible to explain this composition with reference to it. This picture is a condensation of two features that are true only for Leonardo: he really had two mothers, one of whom stood between the other mother and the child. But the second chapter in the history of his childhood is also contained in the picture: in his father's house in fact, he found, in addition to the second mother, also a grandmother, and both women are said to have been very kind to him. This grandmother he now portrayed, not as an older woman but as a second, more distant mother.

This smile has always been regarded as most mysterious (in the *Mona Lisa,* it has an odd effect): it is the blissful smile of the vulture as it bends over the child. The fact is that it contains a secret, a secret that is clearly revealed in the Bacchus, who is androgynous. This smile represents the bliss of mother love as being simultaneously the supreme sensual gratification. This blissful-sensual smile represents the achievement of union with the mother: it is the child's triumph in possessing his mother; it is the artistic representation of this triumph.

There still remains the problem of why he dealt so badly with his works. Here we come upon the third characteristic of his sexual life, the vestige of masculinity that had been left to him. In searching for his mother's smile, he feels himself to be, in a certain sense, masculine. He is able to express the residue of his masculinity in a process of identification with the father. There is no doubt that this identification did exist. He always played the great gentleman, or tried to play this role even when he lacked the means to do so. This served to compensate for his illegitimate birth. But it is also meant to [serve as a way to] surpass the father, to outdo him, to show him how one really acts the great gentleman. However, in this too, fate persecutes him: in his eyes, the father committed a grave misdeed, for which Leonardo never forgave him: the father created a child and then did not trouble himself about it; Leonardo does exactly the same thing with the works he has created. In this respect—to his own and the world's disadvantage—he is successful in really copying his father, and with his behavior he renews the reproach against the father again and again.

The same man who created these objects of incomparable beauty also had an indomitable desire to collect caricatures and objects of ugliness. Possibly, the hatred [he felt] toward his natural mother's husband, his step-father—whom we may picture as an old and ugly peasant—may be behind all this.

DISCUSSION

FRIEDJUNG is embarrassed to enter into a discussion of this captivating paper. One thought has been newly evoked by it. One can well imagine that this exploratory activity [on the part] of the child, which can gradually expand into the adult's investigative work, could be tied down by an education based on enlightenment and thus run aground.

JEKELS should like only to ask whether the binding of affects could be traced back to infantile sexuality. (PROF. FREUD: to the enormous process of sublimation.)

GRAF has the feeling that this frittering away of artistic potency is not in keeping with a creation of the quality of *The Last Supper*. There is apparently a kinship with Michelangelo, who likewise left so much unfinished, although for different reasons. The characteristics of painters, the typical situations they depict, always have a connection with their preferred sexual objects.

Today's paper is so conclusive and so well thought out that one could hardly raise any pertinent objection. Graf would only offer an opinion in opposition to the underestimation of Raphael. It is difficult to get close to these harmonious geniuses; yet the same elements are found in them as in problematical natures, and perhaps even something more; perhaps they are after all, a higher type.

(PROF. FREUD concedes that, of Leonardo's creations, the "Last Supper" gives least evidence of these characteristics; nevertheless, it has remained unfinished and, as a result of Leonardo's carelessness while working on it, is now in a state of decay.)

HITSCHMANN, too, thinks that a critical discussion is out of the question. The whole paper makes a very great and very beautiful impression. As to minor doubts, one is all the more inclined to suppress them, in so far as, side by side with the things that have been assumed here, there stand experiences gained from patients, which take a parallel course. In regard to the diary, it is easy to understand that one cannot give expression to truly deep emotions.

HELLER would like only to join the others in an expression of gratitude. As far as the neglect of works is concerned, perhaps in addition to the unquestionably correct and wonderful interpretation derived from the individual case, a [certain] role is played also by the general underestimation of the completed work that we find so frequently in important artists.

(PROF. FREUD thinks that this might possibly be a component of the father-relationship in general.)

STEINER stresses that Freud has succeeded [in presenting] consistent circumstantial evidence, and it would be difficult to say anything against it. Just a few minor remarks: the wind represents to all peoples something expressly masculine. In the fertilization of plants it plays, in fact, an important role. In those pedantic calculations there is also concealed a reproach—that, with regard to the person [in question] (usually one who has died), one has done too little. A child does not consider his mother to be old—he knows nothing of age—nor does the mother grow older in the child's eyes. In reference to the artist's antipathy toward his work, Steiner can confirm what Heller has said: The relationship of the artist to his work is not that of mother and child; rather, for the artist, the act of creation is really a sexual act.

REITLER quotes a passage that shows Leonardo's conscious attitude to the vulture and is such as to present the direct opposite of maternal tenderness and concern, and thereby the aspect of repression (the vulture [is the] personification of envy; he leaves his own young without food). An impulse to conceal [*verhüllen*] also expresses itself in his childish puzzles.

Leonardo plays the mother's role vis-à-vis the boys and is betrayed (robbed) by them as his mother was by his father.

(PROF. FREUD now adds an important point: Leonardo's investigative activity has been determined by his relationship to his parents. He is ahead of his time, above all by way of his sexual repression, which is otherwise unknown to the Renaissance. On the other hand, he is also one of the freest persons who has ever existed. But this absence of prejudice too is determined by his relationship to his parents: all along he endeavors to free himself from old age [i.e., father] and to return to Mother [!] Nature—principles that he repeatedly advocated in public.)

STEKEL, too, can make only a few minor remarks in reference to the presentation. It is amazing how the deciphering of a few hieroglyphs has had the effect of bringing us much closer to an understanding of the artist. Stekel can, on the basis of an observation, confirm the idea that the foot is the mother's lost penis. A man has the fantasy of walking along the *Ringstrasse* barefooted, and with an enormous big toe. In Leonardo, too, it is striking that he places the big toe so far apart; he does the same thing to individual fingers (as in the *Bacchus*, and many other works).

The subject of how growing up in an environment [that includes persons] of only one sex encourages [the development] of homosexuality deserves a thorough discussion, as does the subject of the stepmother.

The non-completion of things could, in addition to its infantile root, also contain a hint of psychic impotence.

In *Leda and the Swan* the fantasy appears; the swan brings his beak close to Leda's lips. The mouth as an erotogenic zone plays here, as [it does] also in the blissful smile, an enormous role.

Antipathy toward what one has created is by no means typical; there are also contrary traditions. (Fräulein v. Scuderi.)[4]

RANK also can only add his own thanks for today's presentation. In reference to Friedjung's ideas concerning enlightenment, albeit admitting their justification, one must consider whether, for mankind as a whole, it would not be more advantageous above all for there to be fewer neurotics, even though perhaps at the cost of preventing [the development of] geniuses, and instead to have an average type of greater merit. It appears that the normal process of development has been going in that direction, so that it would be merely accelerated by purposeful efforts at enlightenment.

ADLER would like to select a few points and attempt to shift them to the field of the neuroses. We would, for instance, characterize Leonardo's neglect of his works as "slovenliness," a trait that we find very frequently in neurotics, although in most cases together with its opposite, a marked exactness, which is expressed in Leonardo's fussiness over minor details. Pedantry, however, does not play the only role and, as Steiner does, one will have to assume also [the existence of] a feeling of guilt. In regard to the inability of artists to complete their works, a quite frequent phenomenon, it is evident that they are not pleased with their work, that they can never do things to their own satisfaction. From this it is not far to the great oversensitivity that is, indeed, also very significant in neurosis. This oversensitivity goes back to the very earliest years.

From the fantasy with the vulture one might infer that the manner in which hunger is gratified also plays a great role in Leonardo's life (he being a vegetarian).

[4] E. T. A. Hoffmann: *Das Fräulein v. Scuderi.*

As to the foot-fetishism, it must be emphasized that some cases could be traced back to the fact that these persons as children sucked their big toe; all these foot fetishists were also thumb-suckers. In a man such an emphasis on the mouth necessarily leads to a feminine point of view; from this there would seem to be a much simpler and more correct approach to homosexuality.

The problem raised by Friedjung plays an important role in education. One should not disregard [the fact] that enlightenment should not be started before it is necessary; one should wait until the displacement of sexual curiosity onto the urge for knowledge has taken place, and offer enlightenment only when one notes that the child has psychological difficulties. Premature enlightenment, prior to the displacement, can hardly be carried through without causing harm. Proof of this is the children of the lowest classes, for whom enlightenment takes place by way of the child's involvement in all marital processes.

TAUSK has received the impression that the paper is a great critique of art as well a great psychoanalysis.

There is a passage in his diary where Leonardo directly speaks of his great love for his mother.

A characteristic but vulgar analogy to the impregnation by the wind is the saying the Croatians have for an illegitimate child: "he has farted a child into her."

There is an interesting difference between Italians and South Slavs,[5] in regard to the sexual and the excremental: the Croatians curse only in sexual terms (fornicate, etc.); so do the Italians. The South Slavs, on the other hand, curse only in excremental terms. Nor do they have an expression that means both tail and penis (FRIEDJUNG: this is the case in Czech.).

As far as enlightenment is concerned, one can observe that children, even if they have been sexually enlightened, are nevertheless intensely interested in other matters and go beyond enlightenment.

Tausk himself used to keep a diary, in which he addressed himself in the third person (by the initial of his given name). This goes back to the fact that as a child he was always eager to listen in when his

[5] Before the first World War, the designation "Yugoslavs" was not yet in use. One distinguished "Serbs," Dalmatians, etc.

parents, who often quarreled on his account, came to terms again; they talked about him, of course, in the third person.

STEIN merely expresses his thanks for the wealth of suggestions and for having been invited into this circle.

He should like simply to pose the question, whether not finishing one's works is to be interpreted as a symbol of sexual inactivity.

SADGER expresses his admiration for the achievement of having clarified so much about a man of whom so little is known. The smile invariably signifies, as Sadger knows from a patient, secret erotism. Laying the main stress on trifles in order to conceal affects seems to belong to the psychology of the dandy.

FURTMÜLLER would like to mention two things. If one derives man's drive to investigate from the child's urge to know, one must not overlook the second logical possibility that both can be effects of a common cause.

The poet's relationship to the work he has created should not be considered to be in all instances the same. The poetic faculty can be used by an individual for the solution of entirely different psychic problems. There is a difference between the artist who wants to rid himself of a problem by means of his work and the one who wants to create for himself an ideal that he cannot find in real life. And that determines the relationship to the finished work (Pygmalion).

FEDERN had earlier had the impression that Leonardo was a restless, fantastic human being, not without cruelty (FREUD: these are misunderstood traits).

His leaving his works of art unfinished could be explained rationally in terms of his special interest in the problem of flight, for which he cared more than for anything else.

Another possible motivation of his incapacity to finish lies deeper. The bisexual *Anlage* of the genius has often been emphasized: that the great artist must be not only father (masculine, the begetter of ideas) but also the mother who carries to its completion what she has received and brings it into the world. Thus in order to create to the point of completion [*ausschaffen*] a certain amount of female sexuality must be artistically sublimated. Leonardo did not succeed in this sublimating of the qualities of the mother, which were left in the realm of sexuality, and it was for this reason that the male element could beget in him more than the female component was able to deliver.

PROF. FREUD in conclusion expresses his thanks for the attention and active participation and is only sorry that the discussion has not placed more material at his disposal.[6]

[6] It is striking that in spite of the fact that Freud had delivered his paper on obsessional neurosis shortly before this meeting, neither he himself nor any of the discussants called attention to Leonardo's obviously compulsive character traits.

90

SCIENTIFIC MEETING *on December 15, 1909*

Present: Prof. Freud, Adler, Federn, Friedjung, Furtmüller, Hitschmann, Rank, Sadger, Stekel, Tausk.

Dr. Karpinska[1] and Dr. Jekels as guests.

PRESENTATION

Education or Fatalism?

SPEAKER: DR. FURTMÜLLER

STEKEL: At the beginning of the session Stekel presents a case of traumatic neurosis, adding the remark that, as a result of the trauma (a fall from a rather low height), an old neurosis, which lay ready in the patient, reached [the point of] outbreak. With the establishment of this fact, the link from our hysteria to the traumatic neurosis seems to have been discovered.

PROF. FREUD comments that one is not entitled, from this case, to draw any conclusions about genuine traumatic neurosis, insofar as the patient let himself fall; that was a hysteria.

[1] Dr. Karpinska (Ph.D.) of Warsaw was a psychologist.

FURTMÜLLER would like only to offer some problems for discussion and to ask for hints on how to continue his work in this direction. Because of his limited acquaintance [with psychoanalysis], he begs to be excused if his paper should contain several things that have long since become common knowledge among us, and others that are far removed from our field.

The speaker takes as his point of departure the strong resistance that Freud's statements on the child's inner life have encountered, a resistance which, in view of their surprising character, they were bound to encounter. First of all, the instinctive empathy with which we project the psychic processes evoked in us by an object into that object, has given us a distorted picture of the child. This at first purely conceptual difficulty is at once intensified by virtue of our processes of will. The paradise of childhood—like that of mankind—is nothing but a retrogressive wish-fulfillment. Parental egotism and parental presumptuousness stand in the way of the recognition of the child's impulses of rebellion and rivalry. The ultimately effective force by which insight into the most decisive factor—i.e., the sexual life of the child—is blacked out, is the fact that the relations of the parents to the children also have a sexual coloration. In taking no note of children's sexuality, parents avoid, for understandable reasons, making any judgment on this psychic condition of their own.

Having thus seen that theoretical understanding is blocked off by elements of the processes of will [*Willensleben*], we may surmise that the same harmful influences will also make themselves felt in the practice of education. The long-standing criticism of the prevailing educational system has, by way of Freud's inquiries, gained in inner cohesiveness and depth. The whole danger inherent in this educational method, however, became clear to us only after we learned that, between rebellion and submission, there exists still a third way: neurosis. It is this insight, above all, that forces us into a profound skepticism regarding problems of education. And since we lack the theoretical knowledge necessary for setting a lofty and positively attainable educational goal, it really seems that everything forces us into a deep-going rejection of education.

The speaker then attempts to demonstrate that this standpoint is untenable in practice, and that there are ways of modifying the educational method employed till now, so that its harmful effects can be in some measure avoided. If one understands education as the "conscious and intentional influencing of the development of an individual," one passes up, to begin with, the use of force. The goals of education can be placed into three separate groups: it is a question either of the present welfare of the child, or of the interests of those around him, or of the future welfare of the individual. The first point is, in principle, altogether beyond discussion. The criticism made of educators, that they want to make things too easy for themselves, seems, in two respects, to be unwarranted. First, harm is done, as a rule, if parents make life very uncomfortable for themselves and for their children. On the other hand, having consideration for the adults is something that is absolutely justified and necessary. By far the most important and most difficult problems are those of the third educational goal: concern for the future. We know that, within a few years, the child has to cover a [process of] development for which mankind as a whole has needed millennia; that between the natural instincts of the individual and the demands of civilization stretches a chasm that has to be bridged by the child's entirely psychic work. In the evoking of these processes, the imitative instinct plays an important role—but only if it obtains a definite direction; and this again presupposes that the child has been brought face to face with value judgments. If, for this transmission of value judgments, the mere fact of living in a social community proves to be no longer so effective as it used to be, the totally changed conditions of our economic life are to be blamed. In earlier times a child lived within society; at present it lives outside of and alongside it. Therefore, just as an intellectual preparation for living in society has become necessary by way of instruction, so too has a general psychological preparation by way of education. Herewith the new path for education seems in principle to have been set forth. It must replace natural growing into society by artificial preparation for society. Education will best succeed in this endeavor by placing the child in circumstances in which society in its general conditions is reflected in a simplified form.

Nowadays, it seems that the highest principle is obedience—that is, subordination to the individual will of the educator; consequently, the whole educative process is resolved into a chain of particular acts of obedience and resistance. In contrast to this, continuity, uniformity and imperceptibility ought to be the chief characteristics of the previously noted process of accustoming [the child] to social living. Education will have to renounce, from the start, the use of brutal means of coercion, since it has recognized their dangers. That does not mean, of course, that one must come to a halt before the child's every resistance; to do so would, indeed, be poor preparation for social life, which is so rich in restrictions. All it means is that one must limit direct coercion to a minimum and give preference to indirect coercion, which makes the winning of pleasure dependent on submitting. In respect to this, Adler has offered remarkable suggestions as to how the child's need for affection can be turned to pedagogical advantage.[2]

From this standpoint, the formation of the milieu becomes particularly important. The dangers of too much or too little tenderness are indeed sufficiently well known, and so is the [importance of the] relationship between the parents themselves as well as the relationship between them and the child. With the formation of the milieu, however, we come up against a limit on the entire work of education, for the milieu is dependent on influences of so many kinds that it will hardly be possible for us to set forth an ideal milieu. Above all, parents will have to carry out some educative work on themselves.

Finally, the speaker takes up sexual education in more detail. For this we lack, above all, a fuller knowledge of the dynamic processes of psychic life. And probably this most personal part of human life will draw back from the educator's intervention. Nevertheless, when an abnormal development of the sexual instinct becomes apparent, one must not give up, without further ado, attempting an intervention; especially where the processes of repression are involved, one will obtain good results by placing psychic aids at the child's disposal.

As to the question of sexual enlightenment, the speaker shares Adler's view that one should not acquaint a child with such matters before the child really feels a serious need for them. Adler's argument, however, does not seem to the speaker to constitute a proof—namely, that one must wait for the displacement onto other spheres of the sexual drive to know, so as not to endanger the child's intellectual

[2] A. Adler: "Das Zärtlichkeitsbedürfnis des Kindes." ["The Child's Need for Tenderness"] 1908 *Monatshefte für Pädagogik.*

development. Considered historically, the drive to ask questions appears so early in the human being that its derivation from the sexual drive cannot have taken place.[3]

If this is true, the drive to ask questions belongs to the inborn psychic faculties of man and, at the first suitable occasion—which comes mostly from the sexual sphere—will undergo development. Nor can one see why the sexual drive to know should be inhibited by sexual enlightenment, which indeed never can go so far as to open up for the child full insight into all relationships. He will always still find problems enough, especially since there are, indeed, a number of insoluble problems and these are the ones with which the child is preponderantly concerned. For the time being, we must disregard the question of whether these continual reliefs and assistances that are afforded the child in this way might not hold back in some cases the development of exceptional initiative. In this sphere, the point is to do what is most beneficial for the average. The genius will still encounter the "less favorable" conditions that he seems to need for his formation and development.

DISCUSSION

TAUSK wants to take issue with the remark that Freud has offered merely interrelations and deepenings of things about which there have long been surmises. He has instead pointed out real motivations and sources, which have up to the present not been dealt with. The problem of repression, the problem of anxiety: each of these is in itself a problem of education as such; the task of the ideal educator would be to follow through and observe these processes. That we become inhibited by our knowledge is surely correct, as far as practice is concerned; but this is only because we do not know how to listen, for the child invariably gives the answers.

Society [in the eyes of] the child is nothing more than a given fact. The child should become familiar as soon as possible with the relationship between right and duty; he should find his place [in society] and develop all his reactions. Tausk cannot accept the principle of continuity and habit.

[3] See Nunberg: *Curiosity*. New York: International Universities Press, 1961.

One should protect the child from the feeling of guilt by warning him that certain things could become harmful to him.

The basically philosophic question has also been raised, of whether the drive to ask questions is not an independent instinct. In connection with this, there is no need to suppose a disguising of sexuality; the urge to ask questions appears secondarily as a component of the sexual instinct itself, of the search for an object. It is certain that enlightenment does not cause any inhibition of the child's emotional life.[4]

PROF. FREUD emphasizes that he has always, as far as possible, avoided drawing conclusions—least of all, issuing prescriptions—for education on the basis of our findings. Therefore, he cannot take issue with the legitimacy of the problem and would be glad to receive for the *Sammlung* an essay that would reflect the impressions of a pedagogue gained from his encounter with psychoanalysis.

In today's paper one can, to begin with, observe a psychoanalytic façade, behind which there are very liberal and promising views about education. Two sorts of things could be expected from its publication: first of all, on the basis of the psychoanalytic standpoint, to define anew and to regroup the tasks of education. Then our present knowledge will surely be able to exert an influence on some particular problems of education. The task [of education] itself could be divided into three strata, the educator's attention being distributed among three different epochs of the child's life. In the first epoch, the psychoanalytic results could be utilized for the support of the organically determined and hereditarily fixated repressions occurring at that time; that is to say, a forcible support for these processes in the form of the breaking of habits, suppression of sexual libido, etc. In the second stage of education, when the child can already talk and feels himself to be an individual, it would be a matter of guiding the processes of repression. In this, Adler's proposal will hold up—to educate the child by means of love, to wrest from him, in return for love, a part of his temperament. This principle might perhaps come to naught, but only if the child perceives that, no matter what happens, he is still loved. In the third phase, the development of social feelings and obligations, education would have the task of preparing and supporting the necessary

[4] See Nunberg: *Curiosity.*

detachment from the parents. The last two phases can be compared with similar stages in our treatment, in which too it is a matter first of supporting all impulses toward a powerful transference, and later of the difficult task of dissolving this transference, of making the patient once again independent.

With regard to the lack of concern and the absence of ceremony on the part of some parents, who allow the child to take part in everything, "since he does not understand anything anyway," one must not forget the fact of deferred recall and understanding. About things that the child may perhaps not understand today, some years hence the understanding may suddenly turn up.

The goal of education can be described, from the point of view of psychoanalysis, as the overcoming of forepleasure. By referring to a great ultimate pleasure, one has to induce the child to renounce the momentary forepleasure. This promised ultimate pleasure then moves out ever more widely until it is dissolved into the well-being of humanity.[5]

The imitative instinct in the presentation appeared somewhat strange to us because its relationship to the motives disclosed by analysis was not touched upon. The imitative instinct is nothing but an expression of the intensive infantile desire to be "big."

How enormous a role is played by education is evidenced by the phenomenon, so frequent in neurosis, of deferred obedience. The repressing force, which makes its appearance as self-punishment, often disguises itself as deferred obedience: he [the patient] now carries out what he was earlier threatened with.

The illness is often only the echoing voice of parents and educators (in another sense, of course, it is also always a fulfillment of the bad instincts). Thus everything that, in education, seems to have no consequences, may nevertheless become very significant if the individual becomes neurotic.

In the matter of sexual education and enlightenment, Freud does not share Wittels' negativistic views. But what one is to do, and how [to do it]—that is a very delicate business. In general, it is better to delay making direct proposals until we know more about the child.

[5] See Freud: *Unlust, Lust, und Realitätsprinzip.*

ADLER thinks that it is not easy to speak in a general way of recommendations for education, since everyone presumes to be capable of solving all [such] problems. This is surely connected with a peculiarity of the human psyche—the phenomenon of contradictory currents of thought, in line with which one and the same person, in [dealing with] the same matter, can at different times come to different conclusions. Moreover, Adler can confirm, on the basis of experience, that people who have arrived at identical theoretical solutions, nevertheless in their practice proceed differently; and one can observe how at times one's own temperament plays a trick on oneself. The educator also must reckon with such difficulties, and a solution will easily be found if one takes the educator's individuality into account.

It does not seem superfluous to direct attention to how necessary it is to win the child's trust and how difficult it often is to succeed [in doing so]. Above all, one must endeavor to bring children with strong instinctual predispositions to the point where they learn to endure restrictions. Perhaps the solution of this task lies only in the continuity of education. It does not seem to be a disadvantage for the child to perceive that, no matter what happens, he is loved; often, what matters to him is the measure of love at the moment. One might even lay down the demand that the child must always have this consciousness, as well as the other—that one is always telling him the truth. Misunderstandings, especially those brought on by the language to which a child is often exposed, can have consequences that, in analysis, frequently become recognizable to us through symbolism.

As far as the instinct to ask questions is concerned, to a certain degree Adler accepts what has been said. The question-instinct, when it already makes its appearance before "sexuality," seems to be connected with scoptophilia. Nevertheless, an intensive interest must go along with it, for the instinct of questioning to become connected with the principle of causality and to remain with it forever; and that is acquaintance with the sexual problem.[6]

RANK believes that, for the time being, it will be fully sufficient, and will produce plenty of good results, if the findings of psychoanalysis are applied to education in a negative sense—i.e., if one endeavors

[6] It is very difficult to understand the meaning of this sentence as it stands.

to protect children from all the hurts that up until now have been considered to be not harmful or unavoidable. Meanwhile the findings and the time needed for the [establishment of the] needed reforms will be gained. For that negative intervention, however, an "education" and theoretical enlightenment of the adult generation is necessary; but one must not fail, during the course of this process, to impress upon the adults that the lessons that have had to be forcibly crammed into them because of their deep-rooted prejudices, are not to be passed on to their children in the same rough-cast fashion.

FEDERN makes the point that our judgment in questions of education must necessarily be distorted by the fact that we are dealing with sick people. We do not, at present, know how to answer a great many questions of detail, and can only suppose that education under normal circumstances will be satisfied with being exclusively sexual education. The question is: How do I protect the child who is not yet integrated from his own instincts, especially from the part-instincts? It is certain that sexual enlightenment must at all times, in response to a direct question, offer a frank answer. There is no sense in making the exploration of sexuality such a difficult problem for the child. The difficulty is only that the normal circumstances that we took, a while back, as a basis are very rare. The basis for a neurosis lies in two conditions: (1) in something which one could call "nest-filth" and (2) in the possibility that the parents are abnormal in two respects: (a) either they have sublimated abnormally or (b) they have individual perversions, which they have been unable to master. Among the latter it is mainly sadism and anal erotism that come into consideration. Such parents cannot bring up their children.

SADGER would like, to begin with, to defend the much attacked Wittels. Sadger, too, is of the opinion that it would be better for children if less educating were done. The best education is, in general, to leave children to themselves and to take the lead [by setting them] a good example. Those who are best in this are the born pedagogues, who act instinctively; those who set about their work consciously and theoretically, usually have badly brought-up children.

Freud has taught us to obviate certain dangers of sexual life, and this factor should be accorded increased attention. However, it is very difficult to combat, for instance, a masturbatory activity that rests on an organic basis and has become a habit. Excessive masturbation, by the way, almost invariably has an obsessive neurotic character. With regard to sexual enlightenment, most parents are in the habit of side-stepping it; the fear of a child becoming prematurely aware of the sexual problem is slight. The urge to know does not first have to do with the question: where do children come from?; it is the appearance of the genitals of the other sex (of the parents) that first excites the child's curiosity.

HITSCHMANN: Much as Furtmüller's consideration of Wittels' remarks is to be welcomed, because it has led to today's paper, Hitschmann would still like to prevail upon the reporter not to attach so much significance to such aphoristic statements.

To refrain from educating remains an utopian idea, which is simply not practicable. Example and imitation do exist; there is a question of a drive to educate in the adult and a contrasting drive in the child.

To begin with, of course, the educators have to be educated, and that shifts the entire problem back by one generation. This task requires persons with healthy instincts and great knowledge. It is not only the child who is to be sexually enlightened, but sexual knowledge must later still be diffused. Prevention is the main point in education as well as in enlightenment. It would also be interesting to find out how cases of immorality develop. One could be made skeptical about education by the fact that two individuals raised in the same way often have entirely different fortunes, as well as by the fact that pedagogues of a theoretical bent usually have very badly brought-up children. Förster[7] has also advocated the utilization of infantile desires for education (e.g., the desire to grow up, etc.).

Worthy of imitation is also the American educational principle of bringing children up to their social obligations by having them form a society themselves.

Another problem is what to do if a child shows too little or too much ambition.

Excessive masturbation can best be combatted by the turning of

[7] Friedrich Wilhelm Förster, 1869-?, German psychologist and educator.

intensive love (on the part of the mother, for instance) toward the child.

FRIEDJUNG would not like to regard tonight's topic as a theoretical question. The pediatrician's activity can hardly be separated from that of the educator any longer. One does not get very far with theorizing [alone]; one must make up one's mind what one wants to achieve by education. It is obvious that this activity must nowadays be individualized. Love is, no doubt, the most important vehicle of sexual education. It is not a question of whether or not a child should be enlightened; one simply has to choose who is to do it: father, teacher, physician, or the servant girl and the child's schoolmates. The imitative instinct cannot be regarded simply as an imitation of the grown-ups; children sometimes imitate the younger ones in order to be able to enjoy the same benefits they do.

STEKEL thinks that matters are not so simple as all that. When children ask questions, they already know a great deal; above all, they have a definite motive for their questions: they want to see the genitals. Sexual enlightenment at the hands of adults is a severe trauma; the best enlightenment is still the one that has been customary until now: by domestic servants and playmates. The most important means for making children healthy are an education that makes them independent and deliverance from the feeling of guilt. This consciousness of guilt appears in two forms: religious and ethical. It is the religious feeling that plays an especially important role. The obsessional neurotic's superstition, for instance, is a consequence of the fact that he is really a believer. The ethical consciousness of guilt arises in those instances where the child grows up in the warm hothouse atmosphere of the parental home, surrounded by the love that Adler has cited as ideal. The children are then unable to turn away from the parents. The servants, however, manage that. The main point is that the children in their sexuality do not remain fixated onto the parents. Thus education by love can become severely damaging.

From rebellion and obedience, the two reactions of a child toward his parents, stem all the great social movements in our world.

The "turning off" of masturbation is a difficult matter. In severe cases, one will not accomplish much with coercive measures. The only possibility lies in occupying the child with things that interest him and that compel him to transfer part of his energy into other fields.

FURTMÜLLER first expresses his thanks for such a rich fulfillment of his expectations of a rounding-off [of what he had done] and stimulation [to go further]; today, however, he cannot go further into the essence, but must be satisfied with the discussion of some details. In education by love, it is the educator's skill that will be of paramount importance. To show a child that one does not love him is dangerous. Just as little can one approve education by pleasure-premium (particularly in the form of money: STEKEL); it would probably damage the development of character.

91

SCIENTIFIC MEETING *on December 22, 1909*

Present: Prof. Freud, Federn, Friedjung, Furtmüller, Hitschmann, Joachim, Rank, Sadger, Stekel, Tausk.

Dr. Jekels and Dr. Karpinska as guests.

REVIEWS AND CASE REPORTS BY ALL PRESENT

TAUSK would like to return to the definition recently advanced by Professor Freud, of form as the precipitate of a content that preceded it [in time], and comment that this cannot apply to the so-called pure forms; the pure forms are the forms of our functioning. One should have to succeed in tracing back the affective movements as well to such pure experiences. These pure forms cannot be a precipitate of previous experiences; instead, they are generally the precondition for an achievement of this sort coming about.

PROF. FREUD observes that what the philosophers have in mind is not what he had in mind—i.e., artistic form; if one were to include space and time, etc.—that is, the pure forms—it would mean bursting the limits of [*sprengen*] the concept of form.

DR. KARPINSKA remarks that Kant's hypothesis belongs to the theory of knowledge and it is impermissible to apply it to affectivity.

HITSCHMANN emphasizes that all these subjects of functioning and pure thinking are nothing but words, to which, upon agreement, a certain meaning is attached. No one has yet proven that pure thinking exists; after all, affects and will always do play a part in it.

Hitschmann would refer Tausk to Mauthner's[1] works about language, in which is presented this misuse of words, behind which are sometimes concealed very valuable thoughts (Mauthner: *Spinoza*).

FURTMÜLLER cannot share the opinion of Hitschmann, who underrates the work of philosophers. Certainly these words can be misused. But science is aware that, in the concept of "pure thinking," it is using merely an abstraction. It is precisely for this reason that Furtmüller considers it somewhat dangerous to mix psychology and philosophy, for their justification consists only in the fact that they contemplate the same things from different points of view. If we declare form to be a precipitate of a content that existed before it, the problem, as a result of this understanding, is merely moved back one step; we must, after all, reach a point where the form took shape.

FEDERN maintains that Prof. Freud referred only to the form of presentation and not to the forms of thought. But these forms of thought as well once had to be acquired. Kant thought them to be *a priori* forms, because he did not know anything of the great line of heredity in the human race. Weininger displays the influence of Kant's teachings on psychology in a pathological form; and yet, there is something correct there.

TAUSK once more stresses his opinion that these things can really be brought together.

PROF. FREUD lastly insists that these things cannot be disposed of so casually. We need not see a disadvantage in shifting the problem back (Furtmüller); we are accustomed to designate something of this kind as progress; for in our explanations we generally do nothing other than trace problems back.

Prof. Freud gives two examples of the elucidation of obsessional

[1] Fritz Mauthner (1849-1923), *Beiträge zu einer Kritik der Sprache* [*Contributions to a Critique of Language*]. Vol. I, *Zur Sprache und zur Psychologie* [*On Language and on Psychology*]. Vol. II. *Zur Sprachwissenschaft* [*On Philology*], Vol. III. *Zur Grammatik und Logik* [*On Grammar and Logic*].

ideas in order to call attention to the singularly disguised ways in which infantile sexual impulses can be encountered. Both examples are derived from a patient who suffers from a severe obsessional neurosis.

1. She is constantly afraid of running over a child.
2. She is afraid of splinters (of glass splinters).

These two seemingly so different ideas, both of which severely restrict the [movements of the] patient, admit of the same solution.

She is a woman who has no children and it was because of her disappointment in this hope that she fell ill. She has (1) a phobia; like every phobia, it corresponds to a wish—in this case, a wish of a sadistic nature. How does she come by the desire to run over children? Being childless herself, she is envious of all others who have children. This strange wish, born of envy, has come down to us in the story of Solomon's judgment, in which it is used for identifying the real mother. Aside from its roots in vengeance, phobia (1) has still another meaning. "Running over" is, as we know from dreams, a very frequent symbol of coition (taken from the movement). In this translation, the phobia would mean: the wish to have sexual intercourse with a child (to use it sexually). This makes sense when a simple substitution is made. In her fantasies, the patient is both man and woman. The desire for vengeance is the feminine wish, the other the masculine wish. She wishes that some man would abuse some child sexually: that man is her father, and this intentionally vaguely defined child is herself. The regret over not having been [sexually] used by her father is the content of her neurosis. She is the eldest of five sisters, and, her attention having been directed at an early age toward the processes of birth, she wanted a child by her father. This, in conjunction with a clear jealousy of her mother, led to a slight obsessional neurosis which, during her puberty, concluded in great piety. When she learned that she could not have a child, her desire turned back to her infantile libido. Her phobia does not contain an actual fear, but she has an undefined sense of having run over a child. The phobias of obsessional neurotics never contain an anxiety about something [that may happen]. What is always involved is an anxiety that is attached to the sense that it *has* happened: it is a *delayed* anxiety.

(2) Motivation is purely infantile—that is to say, other motivations

are commonplace. The patient spontaneously recalls that as a child she had been told that the stork brings babies through the window. It so happened that actually, on the occasion of a birth, she did see a smashed window. The phobia thus conceals the wish to see splinters—in which would be proof that there is a child. This she now ardently wishes for, whereas at that time, in childhood, she was vexed when a new little sister arrived.

STEKEL also found, in suicidal attempts to be run over (and in fantasies of that kind) the symbolizing of a sexual act. This fantasy invariably indicates *intercourse* in the form of *rape*—which can absolve the individual involved of any feeling of guilt. During the course of the analysis, an additional determination of the splinter-anxiety may come to light—namely, the wish that a child might die because of a splinter. The most valuable contribution is the remark about the anxiety of obsessional neurotics. Stekel has repeatedly found that their anxiety consists in this—that they project some past experience into the future.

JOACHIM, in connection with anxiety about a past experience, recalls the "Rider on Lake Constance."[2]

HITSCHMANN sees a contradiction in the fact that the patient still believes in the stork, and yet wants a child by her father.

FEDERN, in order to characterize this neurotic anxiety, draws upon the term "qualms of conscience" [as used] in our language, and points to the fact that the fear of being run over is typical of and normal for children.

PROF. FREUD can only confirm the occurrence of the rape-fantasy (Stekel) but notes that, in view of children's sadistic conception [of intercourse], this assumption is, even without that, self-evident. The contradiction pointed to by Hitschmann is explained by the fact that the fantasies appeared at different times.

[2] Reference is made here to a poem "Der Reiter und der Bodensee," by Gustav Schwab, which tells of a man who rides for hours over a snow-covered plain until he finally comes upon a house. When he learns that, unknowingly, he has ridden across the frozen Lake Constance, he dies of shock. "To feel like the rider on Lake Constance" has become a standard expression in German.

FURTMÜLLER believes that, from his work on Pascal and especially on Pascal's posthumous notes, which were meant as preparatory work toward an apologia of Christianity, he could conclude that Pascal would be an extraordinarily profitable object for consideration from the psychoanalytic point of view. His very change to the religious is noteworthy. In the short biography by his sister, there is recounted a youthful experience that is interesting enough: for several days Pascal was bewitched by an old woman. Furthermore, we are struck by a certain restlessness, which throws him into diverse fields of activity; in each of these he produces more than ordinary achievements, and then he goes in search of a new field. At first, he devoted himself to mathematics and physics ("free fall"); then for several years he plunged into social life; then he became religious and finally a mystic-humble Christian, who foreswore all things intellectual.

Furtmüller would like to solicit some hints as to a deeper penetration of the subject, and first of all to ask whether it is in general promising, indeed possible, since there exists such very scanty biographical material.

STEKEL considers the undertaking to be poor in its prospects. Before his utter piety, Pascal had a period of temptation, of doubt.

PROF. FREUD remarks that the question could be answered sooner, if it were posed more precisely. Charcot mentions a phobia from which Pascal suffered: he frequently had the sensation of walking along the edge of a deep abyss.

STEKEL relates minor items. The frequent symbolism of railway stations in dreams has, in addition to the meaning of coition, which is common to all rides, another meaning. The arrival and departure of trains symbolizes birth- and death-fantasies (the wish that someone should depart = die). (To run over someone else with a car frequently means to outlive that person; to pass someone is to outstrip him, etc.)

Card dreams are also very frequent. They signify, to begin with, play; like all play in a dream (playing the piano or violin, etc.), they mean sexual play. To this is added the secret symbolism of card-playing that is familiar even to conscious thinking (the king trumps the queen, the little one; the "pagat," the knave, etc. It is especially the ace of spades that plays an important role). Even more frequent are maps that correspond to the maplike designs on underwear, which betray masturbation.

In regard to foot-fetishism, it could perhaps also be considered that, through contact with the sex organs, the foot can become an erotogenic zone; in several cases it could be established that such contact had taken place. Often the desire refers to the foot of a gunner [*Kanonier*] (FEDERN also knows such cases), the interpretation of which is simple enough. In these cases the struggle against foot-fetishism coincided with the struggle against masturbation; "Kanonier" means "ka onanie" [Viennese dialect for "no masturbation"] (in one case this association was overdetermined by an uncle who was a "canon").

A violinist who suffers from a neurosis often comes to a halt when playing A-major runs. Among his recollections there is a joke which he heard on some occasion: between two feet has she't.[3] He is also afraid that, because his hands perspire so much, the strings might tear. This refers to escapades:[4] he believes that he owes his life to an escapade on his mother's part. Among musicians, by the way, conscious sexual symbolism also plays an important role.

In reference to Pascal's abyss: every patient who is afraid of going out into the street suffers from fear of an abyss—which is connected with the Fall of Man. Schrau[5] of Munich found that all neurotics suffer from strabismus when they are at a height; this was able to be corrected by the use of prismatic spectacles, with the result that the neuroses improved. In one of his own cases, it turned out that the patient had played frequently with prisms during his childhood, and when he looked through them, he had an abyss before his eyes.

FEDERN doubts that with every fear of space is linked the fear of an abyss.

[3] The joke can be fully understood only in German: *zwischen zwei Füss* (*fis*—f double sharp) *hat sie's* (*cis, gis*—c sharp).

[4] Again, the association is based on a play upon words. The German word for string (on a musical instrument) is "Saite," for escapade it is "Seitensprung," of which the first syllable is obviously consonant with the word for string.

[5] No reference could be found.

PROF. FREUD first of all would like to caution against these wonderful therapeutic successes. It is important, in considering all determining factors, to distinguish the accidental from the basic. Freud, too, would deny that, in agoraphobia, the abyss plays an essential role. In agoraphobia a widely ramified complex is translated into spatial concepts; the most diverse trains of thought are represented spatially, especially ambitious ones. And thereby one first observes how many faded spatial expressions are part of our speech (to get ahead, to make one's way in life, etc.).

The foot that is sought for and adored by the fetishist is a woman's penis (in Freud's sex theories).

TAUSK points out that maps also have to do with the place of birth, and quotes as pertinent to this a dirty joke.

In reference to running over: a carriage very often symbolizes the female genitals (FREUD: as chest; see "Little Hans").

Tausk has seen a case of fear of locale in which the space to which the fear referred was a prison.

SADGER cautions against the one-sided interpretation of map-symbolism; in one dream maps signified buttocks.

JOACHIM asks for practical suggestions in reference to one of his cases. It concerns states of anxiety in a woman who was married at seventeen, had a child in the first year of married life and since then has practiced coitus interruptus. Her husband gives her sexual satisfaction by masturbating her; during intercourse, she is anaesthetic. She levels reproaches at herself, which go back to infantile reproaches for masturbation. She is apprehensive that, as a consequence of this abnormal form of gratification, she has fallen ill. Masturbation one must forbid, of course, in order to permit normal intercourse. How is one to act in this situation?

STEKEL would only liberate the patient from the fear that masturbation is harmful to her.

FREUD does not consider that to be sufficient, since masturbation is actually harmful to her. If, upon the elimination of the sexual harmfulness, her condition does not improve, an analysis must be performed; for people recall little and act out most.

JOACHIM adds that the patient is a woman of thirty-nine who has a kind of paranoia; she hears voices and it is interesting how her self-reproaches (because of masturbation) are materialized in them (for instance, she hears [someone saying] "slut!").

FEDERN tells of a case in which the main symptom was psychic impotence (1), but in which the patient suffered besides from compulsive laughing (2) and sweating hands (3).

Ad 1. The patient had intensive sexual experiences during the first years of life. Later he occupied himself a great deal with his sister, had incestuous fantasies that referred to her; at the age of twelve and a half he had completely repressed his sexuality; analysis succeeded in resolving his psychic impotence.

Ad 2. This refers almost exclusively to absurdities connected with the intestinal tract; defiance against the scatologic father, at whom he always had to laugh.

Ad 3. has nothing to do directly with sexuality nor with anality, but is connected with enuresis. The patient had been a severe enuretic. The perspiring hands merely expressed embarrassment; it would be saying the obvious thing, if one were to explain this in terms of commonplace reasons—that he became embarrassed precisely because of his perspiring hands. However, his embarrassment is disclosed as being the primary factor. The main root of his embarrassment is the enuresis for which as a child he had often been laughed at, so that every morning, when he woke up, he found himself painfully embarrassed, and for his own comfort he imagined he had merely been sweating "down below." This sweating he has displaced from below onto his hands; it was a comfort to him: "I have merely perspired, not urinated." At the same time it was a substitutive formation for enuresis as well as a symptom of embarrassment.

STEKEL mentions a violinist whose hands redden. The symbolism of dry and wet plays an important role in perspiring. Stekel does not doubt that it can be influenced by psychological means.

RANK quotes a passage out of Schopenhauer's *World as Will and Idea* (Vol. 2, Chapter 32 on insanity), as a precursor of the Breuer-Freud theory (*Studies on Hysteria*); in it Schopenhauer establishes a connection between the origin of will and the forcible "knocking something out of one's head."[6]

A poetic, very subtly motivated slip of the tongue from the *Merchant of Venice* (III/2) is Portia's first words: "One half of me is yours, the other half yours; mine own, I would say." Profound psychologist that he was, Shakespeare has Portia make this slip precisely when she wants to conceal from her beloved that her whole being belongs to him, and it is this that the slip of the tongue betrays.

One of Rank's own experiences from the psychopathology of everyday life: An acquaintance by the name of Gold, on coming toward him is unconsciously noticed, and worked up into a fantasy of gold; it is when Rank looks at him that the man is consciously recognized.

From the autobiography of the English novelist Anthony Trollope (Vol. I, p. 56), a passage in which he describes his erotic-ambitious childhood fantasies and makes them responsible for his having turned poet; this description tallies beautifully with Freud's essay on the poet and fantasying.[7] There is an essential difference between the fantasy of the dramatist and that of the novelist—a difference that probably goes back to a fundamental difference in autoerotic sexual activity. The daydreams of healthy individuals and those of neurotics seem to bear resemblance mainly to the fantasies of novelists, to whom Freud also refers in his essay; the dramatist has other fantasies.

PROF. FREUD has referred to the middling novelists, because the point in this essay was to bring to light not the artistic problem but the psychological core. Toward the direct communication of daydreams we would feel only indifference; that limitation it is for the artist to overcome. Real art begins with the veiling of the unconscious. The "inartistic" poets are the ones who display most clearly the things for which we are looking. The third problem has not yet been broached at all. The complications resulting from the sexual constitution are the means that the poet makes use of for artistic presentation. In any case,

[6] "Schopenhauer über den Wahnsinn" ["Schopenhauer on Insanity"] related by Otto Rank, *Zentralblatt I*. The passage mentioned here is: ". . . As a consequence of the statements made previously, one can understand the origin of insanity as being a forcible 'knocking something out of one's head,' which however is made fully possible only by 'setting up something else in one's head.' "

[7] "Creative Writers and Day-Dreaming" (1908). *S.E.* 9.

this much can be said about the dramatist: he is a sadist.[8] The pleasure derived from drama rests essentially on sadistic effects.

JOACHIM thinks that the dramatist shows the change over from autoerotism to object love.

PROF. FREUD: Drama clearly shows how the multiplication of the actor in Greek tragedy developed: these are split-offs from the same person. Jung has called attention to a paranoid novel: *Imago* by Spitteler.[9]

RANK: One's own person as a love object is almost typical for painters, as is proven by the fact that a great many—in fact, almost all—artists paint self-portraits.

PROF. FREUD confirms this, and adds that young artists lend their own features to the figures of others that they portray.

RANK mentions finally that the Oedipus story contains, in addition to the incest complex, its counterpart as well, homosexuality; and the Sphinx with a female upper part of the body, the hindquarters those of a male animal, presents the "woman with a penis," that infantile sex theory that here clearly refers to the mother. It fits in quite well that the foot plays such an important role [in this story].[10]

HITSCHMANN reports the titles of several new papers: Meyer: "On somatic manifestations of dementia praecox"; in the latest issue of Brodmann's Journal, "On Hysterical Twilight States."[11] From the *Archiv für Rassen und Gesellschaftsbiologie:* "On the origin of homosexuality as seen from the basis of the theory of heredity."

In reference to the significance of the foot, a case of a mother who uses her child to keep her feet warm.

The envy of the childless: a lady without children who is head of a

[8] This statement is important for an understanding of the form of artistic presentation. It seems to be true that dramatic representation is used by the writer for overcoming his sadism. The working of sadism is quite clear in tragedy; in some types of comedy it is disguised, in others very obvious.

[9] Karl Spitteler, 1845-1924, Swiss poet.

[10] Oedipus = swollen foot.

[11] Bernard Schwarzwald: "Beitrag zur Psychopathologie der hysterischen Dämmerzustände und Automatismen" ["Contribution to the Psychopathology of Hysterical Twilight States and Automatisms"]. *Journal für Psychologie und Neurologie,* 1909.

boarding school frequently dreams that the children entrusted to her come down in a crash with the elevator.

An anesthetic woman who has dreams of being raped.

At present Hitschmann is treating an agoraphobic young man who shows peculiar traits; one sees that agoraphobia is, after all, not so closely connected with the eyes.

92

SCIENTIFIC MEETING *on January 5, 1910*

Present: Prof. Freud, Federn, Hitschmann, Rank, Reitler, Sadger, Stekel, Tausk, Wittels.
Dr. Jekels as guest.

PRESENTATION

A Case of Multiform Perversion III

SPEAKER: DR. SADGER

SADGER presents a supplement to his case of multiform perversion [Minutes 85-86] and discusses the neurological aspect: intolerance to alcohol and [hysterical] absences. The entire analysis will be published in the next issue of the *Jahrbuch*.[1]

DISCUSSION

HITSCHMANN thinks that the interesting expositions surely provide a new proof of the value of taking stenographic notes during an

[1] "Ein Fall von multipler Perversion mit hysterischen Absenzen" ["A Case ot Multiple Perversion with Hysterical Absences"]. *Jahrbuch II*, 1910.

analysis. He has long-standing resistances against brain anatomy and the attraction of a brain phantom has been often enough rejected here. The conception of absences as equivalent to maximal feelings of lust is not new; Freud long ago showed that to be so. The patient's posture during his absences is reminiscent of certain forms of childhood masturbation (between the thighs). Case of a female patient who, in a similar position, had a discharge. Undoubtedly, there are attacks that seem like epileptic attacks and yet are neurotic ones. For the practicing physician, this direction [of inquiry] is very important.

The conscious *a posteriori* interpretation on the patient's part does not actually mean much. It is questionable whether these things are to be taken as real. The patient had indeed no desire of any sort to yield up anything unconscious. Patients say a great deal, in the state of "extended" consciousness,[2] which indeed is not actually unconscious. How far the patient is influenced in this by his physician does not stand out clearly.

TAUSK believes that this patient is duping the physician in that it is not until the interpretation that he develops certain fantasies—for example, coprophilia; he thereby withholds from the physician his actual experience. This secondary phenomenon should be, first off, the object of interpretation.

JEKELS thinks that one cannot form any opinion so long as Sadger does not bring out the analytical details.

STEKEL does not take up the theoretical appendix; he is not conversant with brain anatomy. As far as the analysis is concerned, Stekel must comment as follows: if it is always emphasized that an attack is a sexual equivalent, then this is not what is to be demonstrated; this we have already learned through Freud. The ultimate content of the absences in this case has not been analyzed. There must be some particular motive that compels the patient, who is already consciously such a swine, to flee with his fantasies into the unconscious, into the attack. About these presumably horrible fantasies, which occur during these absences, we have heard nothing.

[2] In those years, even Freud spoke about the consciousness becoming "extended" as a result of analysis. Hitschmann probably has in mind the fact that preconscious and not directly unconscious material enters into consciousness.

Tausk's remark is to some extent justified; it seems that the patients serve to Sadger the things that he asks for.

The stenographic detail smothers what is most important. The material is certainly highly interesting and has, to be sure, its own great value. But it would have been more important to show why the patient needs to fall into his absences and what goes on in them.

FEDERN would like to come to the speaker's defense. Sadger has disclosed a great deal of the content and relationships of the absences. In order to interpret an attack, with all its complications, in the way that Freud has indicated, one would have to have seen these absences; to interpret them merely on the basis of the patient's accounts will not be possible with any ease.

As to the theoretical part, one has the impression that some individuals are intolerant toward sexual excitations. Sadger's theory characterized degeneration as an illness in the sphere of body sensations. These cases draw one's attention to the fact that what is involved here is a falling ill of the higher sphere, which is not in any position to master the overwhelming instinctual life. In this one cannot but see a certain inconsistency in Sadger's theory.

It does not always have to be the desire to linger with sexual fantasies that is the motive for the flight into absences; it could be also a flight away from [the pursuit of] sexuality (from memories of impotence, homosexual inclination, etc.). In regard to this perverse individual, it would be likely that he flees into sexuality, not away from it (PROF. FREUD: The two are the same).

WITTELS would like to take issue with several things brought forward in the discussion. What was said by the patient was not brought forth quickly and effortlessly, as it would seem from the paper. Moreover, one must credit an experienced analyst with the ability to know when a patient is trying to make sport of him and when he is really offering explanations. Further, one has to agree unconditionally with Federn's view that one must have seen the attack in order to be able to interpret it fully.

REITLER also believes that past absences are difficult to interpret. But this patient also had such attacks during his treatment, and they should have been examined. There is no doubt that it is not a conscious sexual excitement that can lead to absences, but only an unconscious one.

TAUSK, referring to Wittels' remarks, asserts that he did not mean to say that the patient is making fun of the physician. But the patient succeeds in doing something in his analysis which he should not succeed in doing, if he is to be cured, and through it he evades the affect.

PROF. FREUD confesses that the first presentations of Sadger's papers always leave him with a poorer impression than when they come out in print. The reasons for this antagonism lie for the most part in the subjects that Sadger usually has. This patient is an absolute swine, a case of infantile and homologously inflated sexuality; we have so many repressions within ourselves that, when faced with that, we feel aversion.

Other motives for antagonism lie in the speaker himself, above all on account of the overwhelming mass of details that he presents, when he should be presenting only the results. Furthermore, all these things are still matters for debate; if one now makes a detailed application of these still unsettled foundations, that is something that we have no need of today. Sadger overrates the power of proof inherent in these things. *We* certainly recognize that all we have heard today is possible. For instance, it is certain that the attacks of suddenly arising (in addition to the organic factor, which is unquestionably involved) represent the fantasy of erection; during these attacks the patients perspire, blush—in short, behave as if they were a penis. This, however, is only one of the many conditions that produce the state. The isolating of these purely fantastic and sexual moments is apt to call forth resistance. It would be necessary to direct toward our own selves the admonition that, simply because these things have an offensive effect, we are not thereby to regard them as untrue. Artists indeed do the same things as neurotics or other individuals do in their fantasy (compare the pictures of living penises, etc.).

In his remark about absences, Stekel seems to have hit on something deeper and more correct. The fantasies that bring them on spring from an act of perseveration; the absence represents a dwelling upon and elaboration of a preceding fantasy (stimulated immediately before), not the transition to a new one.

It is a technical fault in Sadger's presentation that he recounts matters so smoothly that the impression must be created that the patient had brought them forth equally smoothly (Wittels). Thus one has in fact the impression that Tausk put into words.

The explanation of absences has, in fact, long since been given and can already be found in the paper on the anxiety neurosis[3] (1896).

It is striking how frequently certain attacks and neurotic states occur after meals. In spite of everything, however, the decisive factor does seem to be organic conditions, which are, of course, symbolically disguised. One must refer to the fact that many persons, after a meal, feel a need for sexual activity (a case in Stekel's book about anxiety states.[4]).

The first part of the theoretical presentations summarizes what Sadger has read in the pertinent publications (anxiety neurosis, hysterical attack). As to the leap into brain anatomy, Freud would like to dissuade against it on grounds of principle.

RANK reports a young girl's dream, which consists of two separate portions; the second portion, as the result of its frankness as an emission-dream, takes some details of the first portion and, without any information on the part of the dreamer or any efforts on the part of the observer, interprets them as being infantile-sexual.

STEKEL has the impression, despite the confused form [of presentation], that the most important points have been unobjectionably interpreted. If one is thoroughly familiar with symbolism, one can already recognize, after the first sentence, where the dream will wind up. The beginning is the most important part of a dream and often betrays its entire program. The "Chinese dress" is—like everything "Chinese" in a dream—a symbol of bisexuality (because of the braid worn by men). Here it is the vacillating between father and mother, man and woman.

All the persons who appear in the dream are again and again reducible to the dreamer.

[3] Freud: "On the Grounds for Detaching a Particular Syndrome from Neurasthenia Under the Description 'Anxiety Neurosis'" (1894). *S.E.* 3.

[4] *Nervöse Angstzustände und ihre Behandlung.*

JANUARY 5, 1910

PROF. FREUD remarks that the bisexual character of the dream is very clearly an element of wishing. The dream says: If I were a boy! It has a certain theoretical significance, but has not been sufficiently interpreted; if its interpretation were more complete, one could publish it for the sake of that self-interpretation.

93

SCIENTIFIC MEETING *on January 12, 1910*[1]

Present: Prof. Freud, Adler, Friedjung, Furtmüller, Graf, Heller, Hitschmann, Joachim, Rank, Reitler, Sadger, Steiner, Stekel, Tausk, Wittels.

Dr. Jekels, A. Deutsch, Dr. Karpinska as guests.

PRESENTATION

The "Fackel"-Neurosis

SPEAKER: DR. WITTELS

The speaker takes off from the question of the purpose with which we undertake pathographies of artists; he sees as the reason for our doing so the fact that we wish to find out how art and neurosis are related, and how the one passes over into the other. In this sense Wittels wants today, in an incomplete way, by means of a case that is well known to all of us, to attempt to show how extraordinary talents are produced; how through neurotic countercurrents, they are inhibited,

[1] Entry in the attendance book: Prof. Freud proposes Dr. Oppenheim for membership. This year's congress will take place on March 30th and 31st in Nuremberg.

or under certain conditions promoted; and how at one time these talents come through with art and at another time remain neurosis. The case referred to is that of the Viennese writer Karl Kraus, and his periodical *Die Fackel* [*The Torch*], which may be regarded as a diary of its editor.[2]

Kraus is the youngest of several children in the family of a Jewish merchant. He was always a superior student, and as a young man had already thrown himself into a journalistic career and got as far along in this field as the *Neue Freie Presse.* Then suddenly he threw himself into reverse, and for years railed against journalists and carried on a bitter fight against journalism, directed especially at that paper to which he had originally wanted to become a contributor.[3]

The *first problem,* then, is that a man who seemed to have become a journalist of his own inclination—and for whom all paths to that goal had been smoothed out—suddenly shifted gears, because of some personal motive, to become an "anticorruptionist."

The *second problem* is that later he changes again: journalists interest him no longer; he throws himself into the problem of sexuality and, in so doing, comes very close to the problems we deal with.

The *third problem* is that he again changes and—during what is, for the time being, the most recent and still continuing period—becomes a writer of aphorisms; he is content with a form of expression that is the most unimpassioned [of all] and is not suitable to permit so volcanic and high-spirited a writer to give full vent to his feelings.

Preoccupied with [finding the] ways of solving these problems, the speaker [Wittels] one day had a vision in which he saw his own father reading the *Neue Freie Presse.* This newspaper is an immense power in Austria, especially in the Jewish community; it belongs, so to speak, among the household effects of the bourgeois family; it is, as it were, "the father's paper." A friend who was told about this

[2] See Minutes 24 (Vol. I), fn. 3, pp. 195-196.

[3] Politically Kraus was an Independent, closer to the Socialists than to the parties of the middle class. In what were the sharpest satires of his time, he lashed out against conditions during World War I. (*The Last Days of Mankind* appeared in 1919.) It was typical of Kraus that, under the impact of the Nazi terror in Germany, he went over to the side of the Austrian clerical-authoritarian regime (Dollfuss-Stahremberg), which stood for everything that Kraus in his earlier years had bitterly fought against. In *The Third Walpurgisnight,* the sequel to *The Last Days of Mankind,* Kraus foresaw in a visionary way the horrors of World War II.

vision remarked that the *Presse* is the father's organ, which corrupts the whole world; the *Fackel*, on the other hand, is but a small organ, which is, however, capable of destroying the big organ. The speaker would rather not enlarge upon these symbolic hints, because there is no chance that they will meet with the slightest degree of understanding outside this circle. It would be such a nice demonstration, if the publication of this magazine turned out to be the reaction to the father's death. Now this is not so, for the *Fackel* had begun to appear a year earlier; nevertheless, in the child's unconscious, the death-wish could have gained, in anticipation, sufficient intensity.

Several other points corroborate this interpretation. The publishers of the *Presse* were named Moritz Benedikt and Bacher. Kraus attacked the former almost exclusively, although the latter exercised just as great an influence on the makeup of the paper. Kraus' father's name was Jacob: the "blessed one" of the Bible; in the Vulgate, "Benedictus." Added to this is the fact that for a long time Kraus had been treated in Benedikt's house like one of their own children. Next to Benedikt, it was mainly Hermann Bahr, the fatherly friend of young talents—who had befriended Kraus, too—whom the *Fackel* persecuted for years with the greatest vehemence. Bahr's supporter, Bucovic (see the trial[4]) also had to suffer these attacks. Further objects of Kraus' rage to persecute were Julius Bader, who at that time was looked upon as the foremost satirist in Vienna, and the operetta librettist, Bernhard Buchbinder. It is striking that all these names begin with "B," a fact that the speaker cannot explain, since he is too little acquainted with the family relationships and does not even know the mother's name. One can, on the basis of analogous facts in the life of neurotics, surmise that this conspicuous feature must have a reason. To one patient, for instance, A and 1 symbolize the male genital organ, B the female organ.

The *Presse* is the father's organ, which the little one does not have; the father is superior to the son, inasmuch as he can read; the little one is just learning to read, and still mistakes one letter for another. We may assume that the child was already making puns at an early age; a pun is made by changing one letter, with the result that sense

[4] We do not know what this refers to.

is turned into nonsense and what is serious becomes a joke. In this may be seen one root of Kraus' later playing upon words. For years he wrote a regular column dedicated to "nailing" the misprints, errors and mistakes in the *Neue Freie Presse* ("Pithy Items from the *Neue Freie Presse*"); and for a long time it was the greatest fun to him to smuggle into the columns of the *Neue Freie Presse* some nonsense that was at first taken literally.

From all of this, it is evident that it was a *neurotic* attitude toward one particular newspaper that was the starting point of his hatred for journalists. He has been pretending to be fighting against the evils of the newspaper, but he has not done so in those areas in which the influence of the *Presse* actually could be harmful, i.e., the fields of politics, political economy and art. In order to understand this neurotic hatred of his, one need only to remember that the origin and starting point of every neurosis is the Oedipus motif. That it had its effect in this case too has already been suggested. One of Kraus' compulsions was to insult the busts of his parents. His relationships with his parents, as well as with all his siblings, are filled with enmity. He hates them, a circumstance that may perhaps explain a motif that was always recurring, throughout his life: he attaches himself to someone in passionate friendship, which later turns into the bitterest enmity. This is a generalized repetition of the first problem; it has happened seven or eight times in his life. He himself evaluated it in the following words: "I am really the only man in Austria and all [others] are dashed to pieces against me." This can be interpreted only as being the language of the unconscious; as such it is easily understood. All those whom he fights in this fashion Kraus calls "merchants" [*Commis*],[5] although this designation seems out of place when it is applied to a man of letters, even if he is not altogether first-rate. The use of the term becomes understandable, however, when one knows that his brothers are all merchants, and that he is the only man of letters among them. Thus the interpretation forces itself upon us that the continual repetition of this game [friendship-enmity] in Kraus' life is the representation of the relationship of his brothers and himself to their father. His brothers—that is to say, his best friends—become his

[5] In Viennese usage, *Commis* has a disparaging connotation.

enemies because they do not agree with him. The capstone to this chain of evidence is the fact that the senior Kraus was a manufacturer and produced pulp for newspapers.

The speaker then passes over to the second period which, in contrast to the first, rather prudish phase of the *Fackel*, openly reveals acquaintanceship with sexuality. For this second period, an external cause was decisive. Kraus had made the acquaintance of love; he had fallen in love with an *artiste*, who had since died; her "unfaithfulness" had hurt him. The death of this actress can be connected directly with the change in the *Fackel*'s direction. Altenberg,[6] who was Kraus' most faithful friend, showed him how he could overcome his pain and, in fact, expressed it in a memorial address to this actress in the *Fackel*. He set the intellectual genius of man in contrast with the aesthetic (sexual) genius of woman. At that time, the appearance of the magazine was interrupted for the summer, and it has remained so ever since. One would be tempted to look for the explanation of this unusual state of affairs in the fact that the father does not spend the summer with his family in Ischl, but out of business considerations remains in Vienna.

In this second period of the *Fackel*, it is Kraus the artist who is speaking; his private neurosis has become linked with the general neurosis of the time. In this phase Kraus has, in some respects, himself lived through much of what Freud has found out by way of scientific work, and has presented it in an artistic form. The pathography ought not speak about this phase of the *Fackel*, for it is art, and of Kraus' neurosis almost nothing is left, although in a few instances the fundamental neurotic scheme betrays itself. The farther Kraus progressed in his understanding, the more evident became an involution back into neurosis. Finally, he asserted that, except for the woman who gives herself to everyone, all women are hysterical. Freud has shown that such views of life represent the reversal of a previous overvaluing of the mother and being disappointed in that love. In later years, Kraus had in fact such a wretched attitude toward his mother that his brothers were able to put the blame on him for her death.

Kraus' association with Wittels falls toward the end of this second

[6] See Volume I, Minutes 24, fn. 3 (p. 196).

period. Kraus was lacking in the scientific foundations to be able to evolve a theory out of his views, and he took pains to trumpet forth this deficiency as his greatest strength. Later, when he had broken off with Wittels, Kraus didn't want to have anything to do any longer with the whole business of sexuality. He adopted the point of view that there are no opinions but only form. With this, the third period sets in, the period of artistic sterility, which leads to neurosis and is associated with an impoverishment of thoughts and temperament. If one assumes that the artist—like anyone who does anything with passion—sexualizes his activity and thereby brings forward that passion, then Kraus first sexualized the newspaper, and then fled into the general neurosis; now it is *form* that he sexualizes: the only thing that matters to him is *that* he writes and *how* he does it, not *what* he writes. But whoever sexualizes form must come at once to aphorisms. Kraus defends this form as artistic, by contrast with journalistic. He takes the idea of the journalist in a broad sense; one could perhaps define the man he has in mind as one who at an early age became linked with the general neurosis, so that he stands amidst his contemporaries on one foot, as it were. Thus the neurotic and the journalist stand at the two ends of art.

Finally, the speaker touches upon several general points that may perhaps lead beyond the problem of this single individual. Above all, the problem of the satirist: Kraus is a misshapen man, as was Voltaire, and as court jesters are described as having been. Mockery seems to be linked with physical deformity, and in that way to be suitable as a special domain of the Jews, in accordance with a remark Freud made in the analysis of the phobia of a five-year-old boy.[7] (Castration complex—circumcision). Kraus differs from Voltaire in the inconsequentiality of his accomplishments, which has as its basis the imperfections of his education. Similarly, Harden[8] actually fights without any real effect against the king, whose power he extraordinarily overrates.

Another art that merits unraveling from this point of view is acting. Initially, it was confined to the representation of the royal family; in its roots, it seems to touch the satirist's talent. German dramatic art, after all, did have its beginning in the figure of "*Hanswurst*" (the

[7] Freud, "Analysis of a Phobia in a Five-Year-Old Boy" (1909). *S.E.* 10.
[8] Maximilian Harden, 1861-1927, German journalist.

jester). In its first form, it enables a young man to play the father (the king) vis-à-vis his mother. Kraus' great dramatic-parodistic talent is well known, indeed.[9]

The speaker remarks in conclusion that he is quite conscious of the incompleteness of his exposition, but that he wanted only to demonstrate by means of one specific example how, out of neurosis art emerges and out of art once again neurosis.

DISCUSSION

TAUSK thinks that, for the final synthetic section [of Wittels' paper], the problem of the revolutionary, who is an organ for the sensing [*Fühlung*] of decay, would be very important. The real harmfulness of the *Presse*, its vulgarization of thinking and feeling, Kraus rightly does battle against—and this is his greatest merit. Tausk himself does not have a real feeling for seeing in the relationship to the *Presse* a mirror-image of the father neurosis. Perhaps at the bottom of this there is the fear of that which has been printed, formed, completed—which one cannot get at. It is a significant fact that Kraus began as an actor. Because of his physical appearance he was rejected, and from this too stems one part of his rebellion. Dramatic art is actually the journalistic one among the arts, because it achieves its effects by means of all kinds of expedients in the crassest way.

We have learned from Freud that overcoming the father is in keeping with the character of the great man, and we should not reproach Kraus in any way for having made the attempt. Kraus' neurosis is that he measures everything against his ideal. On the other hand, this is also the way to greatness. Kraus is quite far from being an aesthete; in complete contrast to one, he is emotionally involved in everything he experiences.

On the whole, Wittels has not given enough points from which one can draw conclusions [*Angriffspunkte*]. The scientific method is not always the best for illuminating a personality; art is often better suited for that purpose. Only the last part of the exposition was really fruitful.

ADLER is not in a position to go into the topic itself. He has all along had [no more than] an infinitesimal interest in the *Fackel*. From

[9] Kraus' dramatic recitals, in which he took all the parts, were famous.

the start Adler had the impression that this man is a philistine run wild, for whom the path to adequate self-indulgence became cut off. The question of his talent and of his capabilities is not under discussion. We are interested only in [finding out] where the compulsion and the urge to attack have come from. Adler has quite often found this type among his neurotic patients. These are the people who feel themselves to be the unique ones. The characteristic trait of this type has already been mentioned today—[they are] the type of people characterized by Freud as wanting to surpass their father. At bottom, they are actually feminine persons. They arrive at that out of an inner feeling of weakness, which clearly betrays the stamp of hypersensitivity. It seems to be the type so frequently encountered in neurosis; one could denote it as a compulsion to [produce] a hypertrophically masculine fantasy.

JOACHIM would rather consider Kraus from the psychiatric point of view. The limitless overrating of his own ego; his mania for making puns (often based on purely associative sounds), as well as his abnormal irritability—these things justify so doing. One gets the impression then that this is a question of a maniac.

Wittels' explanations, interesting and ingenious as they were on particular questions, overshot the mark; this was especially so in relation to the *Presse*. What has been said about the connection of pugnacity and the passion for satirizing to infantile father-hatred, one can employ as a general principle. Especially in maniacs is this trait of understanding everything better, of knowing and doing everything better than anyone else, an expression of that infantile endeavor to surpass one's father.

HELLER regrets that Wittels did not enlarge further upon the transference from the father onto the *Presse* (which he reads). In that way, some knowledge could perhaps have been gained about the relationship of the new generation to the old one in general, as well as in this individual case. One character trait has not been sufficiently stressed: in all of Kraus' carryings-on, there is a markedly sadistic trait, which also explains the lasting relationship with Altenberg, who allows himself to be mistreated and enslaved by Kraus. To try to explain Kraus objectively, as Tausk did, just cannot be done by us, for Kraus is a definitely pathological character.

GRAF expresses his gratitude to Wittels for having taken a distinguished journalist as a way of unfolding the entire problem of the satirist. Graf himself has been acquainted with Kraus since high school [*Gymnasium*], and he has the impression, personally, of a certain morbidity in Kraus that seems to indicate an actual mental disturbance. Wittels was fully justified in explaining the problem of the satirist in terms of the father-problem and in seeing, in the most important life relationships, reproductions of the relationships to father and mother. As a youth, Kraus once played the part of Franz Moor,[10] and the choice of this role already points in itself to that complex. The talent for imitation and parody is as a rule first tried out on the teacher, wherein the transference from the father is obvious. Kraus' hatred in the first period of the *Fackel* is directed against the entire world of his father: this is District I. One brother is a robust, actively sexual person, and in Kraus' hatred for him sexual envy most likely plays an important part.

His relationship toward women is interesting. The relationship with the actress Kalmar has already been mentioned. But even as a high school student he had fallen in love with a then popular actress, who resembled Kalmar. What captivated him in Kalmar was the fact that, for all her talents toward becoming a great tragic actress, she was used as a luxury [*Luxusdame*] by the Viennese smart set. That is how the fantasies about his mother attach themselves to her; he might also have believed that his mother was abused by his father. The same is true of the first actress, who played a role [for Kraus] similar to that played by Kalmar. The first period, then, is characterized by the relationship to the father; the second, by the relationship to the mother; and the third by decadence, a shrinking of his talent, and a delusion of grandeur, in which the infantile wish fulfillment can be only too clearly perceived.

STEKEL finds that by and large the speaker has succeeded well in his demonstration. There is no doubt that in so doing he has abreacted

[10] One of the two protagonists (the villain) in Schiller's drama *Die Räuber* [*The Robbers*], a play of fraternal jealousies and rebellion against the father.

some of his own emotions. Kraus gives the impression, initially, of being an enormously envious person and, in fact, it was out of envy that he dropped Wittels, too. From a psychiatric standpoint, he impresses one rather as a paranoiac with a marked megalomania. His last aphorisms evoke the impression that the writer has succeeded in presenting something nonsensical in such a way that one might suspect that there was sense in it.

The attitude of a man toward his newspaper is in itself an interesting topic. It won't do to pass judgment on newspapers and journalists in as simple a fashion as Tausk did.

PROF. FREUD can only agree with several of the views expressed till now. We have reason to be grateful to Wittels for making so many sacrifices in disregarding quite a few circumstances—above all, that it is a man who is still living that is involved. Analysis is, indeed, supposed to make one tolerant, and such a vivisection could justly be reproached as being inhumane. Wittels' second sacrifice is that he had to overcome so much of his own personal feeling, and he will surely guard against making his affects accessible to a wider circle, who would not have scientific esteem for them. In the third place, it is praiseworthy that Wittels carried out this self-control with so much discretion. And yet he did not fully win out over the painful [aspects] of the affair.

It is one of the customary illusions that the actor must identify with his role. In those roles with which he identifies too well, he fails. In a certain sense, he must remain above his role, and it would be worthwhile to ascertain the limits of this process of identification.

Some of the points Wittels adduced are undoubtedly correct: the father complex, the character of the milieu, Jewishness, the return of enmities as neurotic character, etc. But we forget too easily that we have no right to place neurosis in the foreground, wherever a great accomplishment is involved.

Freud's personal relation to Kraus was such that, even before Wittels became one of our collaborators, he had had the idea that the cause [of psychoanalysis] could obtain an effective helper in Kraus. Later on, Freud had recognized this to be an error in judgment. Kraus has an extraordinary talent, together with a character that has not attained great heights of development. He lacks any trace of self-mastery, and seems to be altogether unrestrictedly at the mercy of his instincts. Freud can evaluate him only in a phenomenological, and not a moral, sense. He cannot find, by the way, that Kraus' accomplishments in this most recent period have declined so greatly.

The most important thing is the clue that by nature he is an actor. Freud personally finds distasteful Kraus' intellectual dependence on Peter Altenberg, who represents the aestheticism of the impotent.

The "B's" are interesting. Such cases are, in fact, frequent in neurosis. For example, a patient whose friends' names had to begin with an H, and for whom more than ten instances fulfilling this condition could be shown to have occurred. The explanation was that the person who was the archetype of these friendships had a name with this initial, a fact that the patient himself arrived at. In order to find an explanation in Kraus' case, one would have to be familiar with the family history. It is probable that these manifold enmities go back to his brothers and in particular to one of them.

As far as the play upon the words, Jacob-Benedictus, is concerned, in such matters a certain degree of caution is in order. We like to draw conclusions on the basis of such indications, which are usually treated with disdain; the bridge is there, it is true, but it does not always hold up. In [dealing with] neurosis, we are more certain about such matters. There we make use of the bridge only if an intimate relationship, justified by its content, exists in the unconscious. If such a serious connection is uncovered, then one may show in addition that in the neurosis it is reflected in this word bridge.

HITSCHMANN refers to the fact that the envy [characteristic] of the youngest brother certainly plays an important part in Kraus. He thinks that the topic of the person who pokes fun at everything and of the satirist has really gone by the board. A person is witty when he is also otherwise aggressive. In addition, however, anal erotism undoubtedly plays an important role. An aphorism is, as it were, a refined joke.

FRIEDJUNG, too, is of the opinion that Kraus suffered predominantly from the brother complex. His pedantic sense of form is perhaps to be derived from the fact that, in his parental home, German was not always spoken correctly and purely.

FURTMÜLLER should like to put forward a general comment. He cannot help seeing a danger in Wittels' paper. The question is whether analysis is to be considered a structure of dogmas or a method of working. In today's paper it was rather the first conception that held sway; the result, therefore, is not very convincing and a good deal was neglected; all of which has actually led us in a certain sense to a misunderstanding of this man. A man like Kraus cannot find a place on the *Presse*, even without a neurosis.

94

SCIENTIFIC MEETING *on January 19, 1910*

Present: Prof. Freud, Adler, Federn, Friedjung, Furtmüller, Hitschmann, Rank, Reitler, Sadger, Steiner, Stekel, Wittels, Tausk.
Dr. L. Binswanger,[1] Dr. Jekels, Dr. Karpinska as guests.

PRESENTATION

A Contribution to the Psychology of Doubt[2]

SPEAKER: DR. STEKEL

The speaker refers to Freud's latest publication about obsessional neurosis[3] and hopes to be able to contribute to those fundamental expositions, which are so rich in content, some modest supplementations, as well as a few new things.

Before going into his actual topic, Stekel reports briefly on two

[1] Dr. Ludwig Binswanger was the owner of a sanitarium in Kreuzlingen on the Bodensee.

[2] Appeared as "Der Zweifel" ["Doubt"], *Zeitschrift für Psychotherapie und med. Psychologie,* 1912.

[3] The reference doubtless is to the "Ratman": "Notes Upon a Case of Obsessional Neurosis" (1909), *S.E.* 10.

cases that he has seen recently. The first case has to do with a patient who, having made some purchases (furs), spent a whole night without sleep, not knowing where he would get the money to pay for the merchandise. It turned out that his doubt had nothing to do with the merchandise, etc., but with a girl whom the man (he was married) desired. The doubt, as well as the sleeplessness, then, cannot be accounted for by actual circumstances but were evoked by a hidden affect. Thus we see here the regression from acting to thinking (Freud), and learn that doubt is an affect; while this is not something new, for many it is still strange.

The second example, a case of a young obsessional neurotic, shows that the affect of doubt arose out of insincerity. This is what distinguishes the doubt that we can throw some light on today from that which is usually called doubt but should rather be known as skepticism. This latter is the state in which one succeeds in mastering one's doubt and in contemplating matters without affect. Connected with this is the fact that the doubter is not actually an agnostic; as long as he is doubting, he is battling against a positive belief.

Anyone who has much to do with anxiety states will note that in almost no case is doubt absent; perhaps it is simply a question of one and the same psychic phenomenon. Anxiety is, according to the speaker's definition, the reaction to the advance of the death instinct, caused by a suppression of the sex instinct. Now, there is no anxiety that would not be tied in with questions containing doubt. It is chiefly in three forms that these questions appear: shall I? can I? may I? The answer to these questions is given to us by phobia, which replies to the questions with an energetic no. To overcome anxiety, a strong imperative is needed—an imperative that also overcomes the fear of death. Similarly, the neurotic's doubting ends in an imperative, which in most cases also contains the death clause (Cf. Freud's analysis) [see Footnote 3]. This death clause already comprises the problem of anxiety *in nuce*. Thus, as Freud has demonstrated in the analysis of little Hans, phobia too is an imperative that puts an end to a tormenting condition. Phobia is thus an anxiety hysteria, in which the component of doubt has been replaced by a negative imperative. Doubt no longer exists; if it sets in again during the course of treatment, this is to be considered a sign of improvement. The only task then remaining is, by the dissolution of doubt, to bring about belief. For, every doubt is doubt about oneself; the same thing holds true for belief. Doubt and belief are the same affect; doubt is a negative belief. In a person who is suffering from anxiety hysteria, it is belief in himself that has been shaken. Hatred, anxiety, doubt—all these are transformations of the libido. In anxiety, it is a matter of a somatic symptom; in doubt, of an intellectual symptom.

More important is the question: how does doubt arise—i.e., when does anxiety develop, and when doubt? The speaker now attempts to investigate this connection with the help of practical examples. Doubt develops, first of all, from a confusion between seeming and being, between symbol and reality; of this, doubt is the balance.[4] But doubt is also a battle of the intellect against the affects and instincts (regression from acting to thinking). The obsessional neurotic mentioned above vacillates, in his identification, between father and mother—which is typical. A projection of one's own inner uncertainty onto other persons is also characteristic of every doubt (jealousy); it leaves all others in the position of doubting and standing between two objects. That is the root of jealousy. In this vacillation in love, the vacillation between man and woman—exaggerated by Adler[5] (*Jahrbuch I*)—also plays a role. Doubt is of a rather complex nature, indeed. It shows a vacillation between symbolism and reality, between man and woman (father and mother), between two women or men (the homosexual component), and besides, a doubting of each of these beloved (hated) persons.

Yet, one can arrive at a simple formula: in anxiety neurosis, it is anxiety that is the strongest force, replacing doubt by a negative imperative (phobia). In obsessional neurosis, doubt is the stronger element, and anxiety is replaced by an imperative that we call the compulsive act. This becomes evident also in the fact that it is in connection with the failure to carry out the obsessional command that anxiety makes it appearance (Freud).

The next most important factor is the wavering between two love

[4] This is a literal translation of a rather obscure sentence.

[5] "Über neurotische Disposition, zugleich ein Beitrag zur Frage der Neurosenwahl" ["On the Neurotic Disposition; a Contribution to (the Etiology and) the Problem of the choice of Neurosis"]. *Jahrbuch I*, 1909.

objects (Freud), which is, however, only one of the forms of doubt and does not by any means exhaust [its modes of expression]. Every doubter shows a tendency toward bipolarity of symptoms, an oscillating between sadism and masochism, cruelty and compassion, man and woman, right and left, etc. This bipolarity can be proven [to exist] in the compulsive acts, most clearly in religious doubt, in which atheistic or blasphemous periods alternate with great piousness and faith. All neurotics are believers. The affect of faith is firmly anchored, in that it is fused with the parental complex (God = father). One of the roots of doubt is the wavering between belief and unbelief, between intellect and affect, between conscious and unconscious (for example, the case of a patient who, at the age of 8, already felt doubts about whether in case of danger—robbers, etc.—he should first save himself or his father). Also frequent are those forms in which the doubt appears to be repressed, and never becomes manifest. For instance, in the case of the person who drinks urine, this passion is a compulsion and the doubt about whether to do it or to leave it undone never enters the patient's consciousness. This compulsive impulse is an imperative carried forward from childhood, a delayed obedience, in this case referring to the fact that his mother had forced him to eat, even against his will and under conditions of nausea. It is a kind of defiant obedience to the mother's insistence that he overcome his nausea. The anxiety is displaced therefrom onto normal intercourse.

There is also a close relationship between doubt and cheating: every doubter is actually a cheater. In doubt, the repressed criminal instincts come forward, and it is no accident that obsessional neurotics are for the most part lawyers and judges or philosophers. They are occupied with the question: what is the right thing? the right way? The lawyer wants to become a defender of his own criminal ego, the philosopher seeks to find, by way of cogitation, the path to what is right.

Freud has assumed that, in the preconscious of the obsessional neurotic, there are two complexes that fight for dominance; this can explain the bipolarity.

The speaker closes with a case that demonstrates the neurotic's consciousness of guilt and then summarizes his expositions in the following theses: doubt is—as Freud has shown—doubt of love. An obsessional neurosis comes into existence if the "parents' imperative" is disobeyed at too early a period, when a child vacillates in his love between his parents and a stranger. As soon as the question begins to be asked whom he loves more, the foundations of a neurosis are laid. The first doubt is a substitute for the missing libido—just as the first anxiety is. From this first love there emanate anxiety and doubt as consequences of the first "sin." The commanding voice of the parents is replaced by doubt. In almost every case of obsessional neurosis, the aftereffect of the "imperatives" of the first authorities (father and mother) can be shown to be operative, making themselves felt as delayed obedience or else as defiance. Obsessional neurosis is the imperative of the parents; doubt is the question directed to the parents: may I? can I? should I?

DISCUSSION

FURTMÜLLER is not altogether clear at this point about the distinction between the doubt of which the speaker wants to speak, and philosophic doubt (skepticism). One difference is immediately evident: neurotic doubt is a practical matter, whereas skeptical doubt is theoretical. It is true, to be sure, that neurotics too are prone to theoretical doubt (Stekel's cases); on the other hand, we must assume that philosophic doubt (of the reality of the world) has an unconscious and not a logical root. Perhaps one should pursue both phenomena together and try to fathom why at one time theoretical doubt, and at another time practical doubt, succeeds in expressing itself.

Bipolarity must be mentioned as an inherent quality of our entire psychic complex, even in the normal person.

FRIEDJUNG doesn't have much to say, but rather more to ask. He would like to limit himself to Stekel's emphasis on the fact that all these phenomena have their roots in childhood, and to comment that, in the face of these phenomena, he is at a loss, in two respects: first, one cannot elicit anything from children; and secondly, one cannot take any preventive measures. Friedjung would be very grateful for suggestions in this respect.

To TAUSK, doubt appears, on the whole, to be nothing but the expression of the function of anxiety, as it presents itself, in terms of the intellect, toward the outside world. If we approach this as a problem of cultural history, it is correct to go back in general to the first possibilities of doubt. We shall ask which of two basic instincts would be capable of making a living creature uncertain in his selection of the means of gratification. Obviously, the sexual instinct (for the instinct to eat is, to begin with, satisfied by the parents). The child is prevented from choosing; one kind of libido must be repressed. It is this that yields anxiety[6] and it is this that makes the selection a matter for doubt. The primary stage of doubt, then, would be anxiety. Doubt always presupposes an unconscious knowledge of what would be best suited to the gratification of the instinct. It is only later that the achievement of censorship is to create a symbol.

In reference to philosophic doubt, Tausk would side with Furtmüller against Stekel. In philosophic doubt, he sees nothing but a carrying forward of that primitive doubt: philosophic doubt is determined in its choice of themes by sexual doubt.

The remark—correct as far as philosophy is concerned—that the doubter is a cheater, would be even more to the point if it were reversed: a cheater is a doubter. Lastly, the statement that doubt is an affect should be rectified: doubt is not an affect; at most, it is a clash of affects.

SADGER has several objections to Stekel's statements, which are frequently only a juggling with words. Above all, as has just been mentioned, doubt is not an affect, but behind it lie affects. Doubt has to do with love (cf. Lenau), and not with oneself. Vacillating between beloved persons is characteristic of every neurotic, not only of obsessional neurotics. According to Sadger's experience, doubt represents not the question directed to parents (can I, etc.), but: does the beloved person love me or not?

Finally, Sadger mentions briefly the case of a two-year-old girl, which shows that children who have such early symptoms are open to explanation of them.

HITSCHMANN finds Stekel's formulations somewhat too difficult, and in many instances merely a paraphrasing of what Freud has of-

[6] At that time psychoanalysis still tried to understand anxiety in terms of libido, as Freud then did.

fered. Regarding a connection (?)[7] between anxiety and doubt, it is questionable whether it can always be found. Many of Stekel's interpretations lose their power of proof by virtue of the fact that this primitive doubt can be displaced onto any conceivable objects, with the result that the later objects are not equivalent [to the primary objects]. Nor is the primitive doubt, as Sadger sees it, doubt about whether one is loved but rather, according to Freud, doubt of one's own love.

It seems, too, that there is a relationship between doubt and the rejection of sexuality. The question is whether one can always find actual complexes (as Stekel does), or whether these things are not older and do not have to be pursued back to their first appearance.

L. BINSWANGER comments that he was particularly interested in and stimulated by the case reports, and also that he could fully follow and understand the interpretations. In the theoretical section, Binswanger found too strong a tendency toward generalization, and nothing new in relation to Freud's statements. Moreover, several things were presented too quickly and unclearly.

For instance, doubt was declared to be the opposition between conscious and unconscious, between intellect and affect; and these sets of opposites were placed alongside each other, as though they were synonymous. There is, no question, however, that there are unconscious processes of the intellect and "conscious" affects. In general, in Binswanger's opinion, there is not so sharp a division between intellect and affect, on the whole. The problem in each case is what is prevalent, and Binswanger shares Bleuler's view that in neuroses the affective factor predominates. Hence to him the problem of whether doubt is an affect or not does not seem of basic importance. These matters are in general rather shadowy, and perhaps unfathomable.

PROF. FREUD first remarks that it was the purpose of his most recent publication (on obsessional neurosis) to stimulate others to collaborate, and in this sense he is glad that the stimulus was successful. In general, he shares the impression that was voiced by some of those who spoke before him. Stekel's expositions are, as always, strong and interesting, as far as case reports are concerned; but in the theo-

[7] We do not know why Rank inserted a question mark at this point in the minutes.

retical section, they are weak and blurred. This is doubly blameworthy in this area, where the sharpest possible definition of wavering concepts is a basic requirement. In obsessional neurosis we are dealing with a particularly uncertain object. The most striking thing about it is the compulsion. Yet Loewenfeld could assert that compulsion is inherent in every neurotic symptom; indeed, that the obsessional character is linked in general with everything psychic. With this, we completely lose sight of what is typical of obsessional neurosis. Now, the same thing holds true of doubt; doubt, too, belongs to all neuroses, just as it does to normal thinking. We do not wish to know what doubt is in and of itself, but what is this specific doubt in that neurosis. And it is specifically the main characteristic of this [kind of] doubt that Stekel has overlooked. It is not the customary doubt but a *doubt of reality,* and refers to something that has been consummated, that has happened. The doubt seen in Stekel's first case (the one about furs) is, therefore, not an obsessional neurotic doubt but an anxiety delirium, the content of which is determined by what is standing behind it. In this instance, it appears that Stekel mixed up cases of anxiety hysteria and obsessional neurosis. One misses an explicit reference to the relationship between anxiety and doubt. The conscious theoretical evaluation of things is not so easy for Stekel as is the tracking down of unconscious symbols, in which one's own unconscious serves as divining-rod.

"Every fear is fear of death"—an aperçu without content. The same thing applies to the sentence: "Every doubt [is] a doubt of oneself." We ought never to neglect the fact that every effect has a number of causes. On the other hand, we have not yet learned to comprise in a single act of thought the processes of the ego and the unconscious. Stekel's definition of doubt belongs to the psychology of the ego, which we have had to neglect up to the present, because we have been describing solely the processes of repression and of the repressed.[8]

[8] In this passage Freud clearly expresses the fact that he is *not yet* ready to deal with the psychology of the ego, that he wants first to understand fully the mechanics of repression. However, it proved to be not really feasible to postpone concern with the ego. Freud's metapsychological papers (*The Ego and the Id* and others) give evidence of the fact that he was aware of that fact; but, as was mentioned in the Introduction (in Volume I of these Minutes), he did not wish to be disturbed in his program.

Freud did not wish to close before citing some points as representing a convincing and legitimate continuation [of our trains of thought]. In that regard, "bipolarity" of symptoms [does not] any longer describe something new, and is not a happy choice. The remark that each individual compulsive action has an infantile prototype is valuable, although it is doubtful whether this can be generally demonstrated. There appears to be a tendency in the patient to trace back each compulsive act to such an infantile prototype, and in some cases this is accomplished. Equally valuable is the statement that the compulsion starts with the parents.

DR. KARPINSKA would like also to take issue with the statement that doubt is an affect. Philosophical skepticism to her too seems to spring from sources similar to those of neurotic doubt; it is sublimated, and thus does not encroach on practical fields.

FEDERN is not clear about the relationship between anxiety and doubt. It is difficult to discuss Stekel's views because he does not use words in their precise meaning. In general he did not present, outside of a few details, anything new. If Stekel, with his great experience, makes assertions, one may assume, to be sure, that they have passed through the unconscious and therefore must have a certain degree of correctness. Yet this [Stekel's] explanation of doubt is not the only one.

It is interesting how neurotics connect compulsion with doubt. The compulsion is not always the answer to (the settling of) doubt. These individuals have detached their libido from the object to such an extent that it is concentrated on the process of thinking; they have to repeat over and over again in a conscious way what others unconsciously decide.

RANK would join with the discussants in regard to the closer relationship between neurotic and philosophic doubt. In certain developmental periods of philosophic thought, one sees how a doubter (a skeptic) is succeeded by an "obsessional" system, which puts an end to the doubt by means of a categorical: "This is how it is!" After this there usually follows the antagonist, who claims: Only the opposite of that can be true; and then comes all over again a new doubter of all these postulates.

ADLER as the last speaker would like to go into mainly what no one but Stekel has touched upon. Adler is referring to his own derivation of doubt, which is that it stems from a child's position between his parents and his confusion regarding the difference of the sexes. The proofs of this assertion he must reserve for a special presentation. He is familiar with all the relationships that Stekel mentioned; they are superficial and traceable to the one primary doubt. In one of the cases quoted by Stekel, the patient's doubt apparently has to do with whether he should behave as a man or as a woman. We can trace back the whole business of doubt, wherever we find it, to this single basis; this is true of even its normal manifestations, which we are accustomed to handle otherwise. We know, indeed, that every neurosis, not only obsessional neurosis, can be reduced to the infant's situation.

Just as the path from doubt to compulsion can be pursued, so can that from doubt to anxiety. In compulsion, the male character appears; in anxiety, the female. Vacillation between two love objects has homosexual significance; it is the vacillation between man and woman, wherein either one of the two has to be regarded in the Freudian sense as a reenforced contrast.

STEKEL remarks that he is already accustomed to the fact that everything new that he offers encounters great resistance at first, only to be accepted in many instances after publication—above all by Professor Freud. Stekel believes therefore that, despite all opposition, something of what he has said will be lasting. The new viewpoint is that, in anxiety hysteria, doubt has been replaced by a negative imperative, whereas in obsessional neurosis it is anxiety that has been exorcised by the imperative. These are not fantasies but follow from the material (cf. the anxiety of failing to perform an obsessional command). A further new viewpoint is that the imperative for every compulsive action stems from childhood, from the father.

His opposition to Freud rests on the fact that Stekel endeavors to wipe out the transitions between the neuroses, as well as the differences between them; in actuality, he recognizes only a single neurosis.

95

SCIENTIFIC MEETING *on January 26, 1910*

Present: Prof. Freud, Adler, Federn, Friedjung, Hitschmann, Oppenheim, Rank, Reitler, Sadger, Steiner, Stekel, Tausk, Wittels.

PRESENTATION

Clinical Reports Bearing on Obsessional Neurosis

SPEAKER: DR. HITSCHMANN

The speaker reports on several cases of obsessional neurosis examined recently which showed marked analogies to the case published by Freud, even though they also revealed differences in details.

I. A young man in his twenties, who has some feminine somatic characteristics, complains that in his work, as well as everywhere else, he is disturbed all day long by the fear that his father might die, or that something was happening to him at the moment. This fear set in, he says, in his thirteenth year. At nineteen, he created for himself a short and fervent prayer as a protective measure against this obsessional fear. The correspondences with Freud's case become clearly evident if one surveys the patient's developmental data in historical order.

In his third and fourth years, the patient suffered from *pavor nocturnus;* he had a recurrent dream in which an old woman with a shawl pursued him across the Aspernbridge.[1] His greatgrandmother played a role in this.

Up to his twelfth year, the patient often got into his father's bed; never his mother's. Altogether he was far more affectionate toward his father; and when there was talk of divorce (at a time when he was six), he decided without hesitation in favor of his father. He also remembers two isolated incidents of being chastised: once, in his sixth year, for unseemly laughter, which he defiantly continued; and then, later on, a slap in the face. At that time, he said to himself: if only I could die, so that my father would feel the pain!

As a small child, and later on as a boy, the patient was very religious; this was intensified at the time of his confirmation (at thirteen).

He was a *voyeur* to an extreme degree, with a very strongly marked urge to know, as well as scoptophilia, and with an "abundant and effective sexual life." He carried on various [sexual games] with his sisters, eavesdropped upon his mother and upon both parents together, watched his grandmother while she undressed, etc.

He was enlightened about the act of birth when he was six and a half years old, on the occasion of a cow's calving. However his enlightenment, especially in reference to procreation, must have been incomplete, for he retained the idea that egg yolk comes from the female genital and egg-white from the male, and that both flow together into a "small box."

At 7, he fell in love with a little girl.

At 12, he had a striking oedipal dream in which he masturbated in his mother's genitalia with his finger, whereupon the egg yolk flowed out. Emission; severe reproaches.

At 15, the desire appeared to be a hermaphrodite. An uncle had told him that, in his thirteenth year, every individual changes his sex.

It is typical that in this story almost no mention is made of the mother; as in Freud's case, the patient's relations with his mother are quite cool.

[1] A bridge over the Danube in Vienna.

The actual traumatic occasion is described by the patient as follows. Led on by another boy, he had begun to masturbate. The first attempt at mutual masturbation failed: he got no erection. It was at that time that the first doubts about his sexual power set in; they have remained with him to this day. Soon he began to feel pain in his left knee and testicles and confessed to the father about his masturbation. His father said, in a severe tone: "I forgive you, but swear to me upon my life that you will never do it again." Under the great impact of this scene, the patient took the oath. He was brought by his father to a physician, and examined for a hernia (the physician had him cough); from then on the patient had a hysterical cough. He then fought energetically against the desire to masturbate, but after three months he was no longer able to resist: he masturbated. Then, in a condition of enormous excitement, he went through an abnormal state for two days, during which he prayed continuously that the consequence (in accordance with his breaking of the oath) should not appear. (The reproach, translated from the wording of the oath, runs as follows: "if I masturbate, my father must die"; and this corresponds completely to the fear in Freud's case). Since then he has had the obsessional fear.

The speaker did not have an opportunity to make penetrating inquiries of the patient about feelings of hatred toward his father. Nevertheless, several details could be easily ascertained. For instance, at about his twelfth year, he put on theatrical shows with playmates; he was the one who obtained the plays. In one of them, he took the part of an orphan who mourns his father's death; in another, a youth who killed his father with a flute. After the incident of the injunction [against masturbation], he was no longer able to perform in these plays. Not infrequently, he also has anxiety dreams that have to do with his father's death.

Six years ago he became engaged, out of fear of the dangers of sexuality. Several attempts at intercourse failed. Up to half a year ago he masturbated. His particular precondition for loving is a woman who gives all of herself. His relationship to his fiancée is full of resistances and doubts of his own love. His excessive love for his father prevents him from fully and unreservedly loving his fiancée. Some homosexual traits of the patient are also connected with the grotesque form of love for the father. Toward his sisters, he showed sadistic impulses.

In describing his obsessional fear more exactly, the patient mentions that his prayer appears in the most varied situations, often in a most troublesome way. Generalization also appears in it, inasmuch as the prayer to God to keep his father alive also extends to mother and siblings. When the patient feels better, his fear grows stronger (Polycrates-idea).[2] In this sense, it is a pleasure to him to be ill or in danger. In the evening, when the desire to masturbate is most intensive, he prays several times. Around that time he is tormented by death-wishes; he has the fantasy that he is dying after a fight. In this sense, he uses as an excuse for masturbation the intention to harm himself. His prayer is sometimes so trying that he must make motions that are reminiscent of the child's form of masturbation.

He shows still other, minor traits that reveal his compulsion. He reads obituary notices very precisely, in relation to his father's age. Strikingly often he dreams the examination-dream, which would fit in with his psychic impotence. He is a very beautiful example of the splitting of a personality.

In the course of a psychoanalytic treatment of only short duration, the patient was completely freed of his compulsion and anxiety. He still needed treatment for his psychic impotence; yet he kept away from it, nevertheless.

Finally, the speaker reports upon the patient's very typical dreams, among which a singular form of the oedipal dream is quite striking.

II. The second case has to do with the brief observation of a ten-year-old girl, who likewise suffers from an obsessional neurosis. This child, too, shows the splitting of personality: in her normal state she is gay, carefree and childlike; she is sad, ill-humored and brooding in the neurosis. Her mother is an elderly woman with a second husband by whom she has had three daughters; her other children are by her first husband. The father is cold and unfriendly, as the mother was in the previous case. The child is considerably fonder of the mother.

[2] The reference is to Schiller's poem, "The Ring of Polycrates," whose motif is the idea that the Gods will punish the mortal who is too fortunate and that therefore sacrifice must be made to placate them. This is a theme of Greek literature and the Greek view of life. The story of Polycrates, tyrant of Samos, was first told by Herodotus (III, Chap. 39-44).

In historical sequence, the consequences are as follows:

In her fifth year, she was beaten as punishment for stubbornness; at about the same time, she slept with her mother in the parents' bed.

In February of last year, for the first time, her parents went out by themselves. The child paced back and forth uneasily in her room, looked under all the beds, and then sat down on the chamber pot; all the while, she was breathing audibly and weeping softly. Then she went to bed. As a reason [for her behavior], she mentions that she was sad because of the mother's absence.

In March she suffered from shortness of breath. At about the same time she had a dream—apparently of masturbatory content—that recurs as a daytime hallucination.

In July the obsessional neurosis broke out. She began to drag her foot when she went over a threshold, and started [to display] compulsive repetitive acts when she was climbing stairs. At that time, she spoke of death a great deal.

At the end of the year, her present illness broke out. During her evening prayer, which in its content closely resembles the compulsive prayer of the previous case, she was suddenly overcome by anxiety, began to scream, continually repeated the prayer for hours on end and could be calmed down only with difficulty. She states the following: when I am praying and thinking of Father, then something like a black veil comes [over me], and I am afraid that I must die. Then at another time she does not believe that she has to die. She never repeats her prayer without thinking of her father. She must repeat it "because she has done it once"—this is her answer to all [questions about her] repetitive actions. She must count up to a certain number, because otherwise something could happen. What could happen? Her mother or her sister could be run over. She also displays a peculiar repetitive urination, accompanied by a certain shivering that is reminiscent of infantile masturbation. Several dreams reveal hostile wishes against the mother.

General comments:

Hermaphroditism really seems to play a rather considerable role, constitutionally as well as clinically. Whether it is related to the illness or to the formation of the doubt cannot be decided on the basis of this single case. The splitting of personality is evident in every case. The first, the ethical-religious personality, must stem from the period of "primary defense," in order to have somehow remained preserved. It may perhaps have developed in the struggle against incestuous desires. The problem of death plays an important role in every case. It is clear that in both these cases the death wishes directed toward other persons (Oedipus-complex) were—as is often true—turned back upon the subject himself. This may perhaps be one of the methods of repression.

If one approaches the problem of compulsion altogether naïvely, one gets the impression that compulsion is nothing but sexual compulsion. Moreover, Freud's proposition that the obsessional wish later becomes the obsessional idea is proven to be true. (Prof. Freud, referring to the first case: the wish that the father should die, so that I can masturbate without interference.)

The inability to make a decision is in fact based on this struggle between love and hatred (at first *vis-à-vis* the father). A secondary source of doubt is the vacillation between sexual desire and rejection of sexuality.

In conclusion, the speaker refers to a case [of obsessional neurosis] that has developed from hypochondriacal anxiety; that is, the content of the secondary defense becomes the illness.

DISCUSSION

FEDERN does not have much to say; these are cases like those that are already familiar to us, and they do not have anything essentially new to offer. The first case of psychic impotence shows that the inhibition (properly speaking) has remained limited to sexuality, and that therefore no complex psychic superstructure has been erected. This has its reason in the fact that the sexual conflict appeared at a time at which the boy's psyche already had matured enough so that he understood his sexuality ([was able to] master it). The death wish directed against one's own person is the most beautiful example of what one can call *defense.*

What has been said about the frigidity of one parent is important. The proportion of homo- and heterosexual inclination in a human being, apart from his own constitution, certainly also depends on who among the persons around him evoked [in him] a higher degree of sensuality.

Where does the element of compulsion come from? The abnormal [aspect of it] is that, in spite of the indubitable facts of experience, the patient does not arrive at the realization that what he dreads never materializes. One actually has the impression that the compulsion derives its force from sexual compulsion.

FURTMÜLLER finds it difficult to make any comment when purely clinical matters are presented. It did strike him as strange, however, that in the history of the ten-year-old girl, the older sister and the patient's relationship to her were not discussed at all, even though this sister probably played an important role as a rival-substitute for the mother (she sleeps in the same room as her father).

REITLER considers the first case to have been superficially analyzed. In similar cases, he found the father's dying to be a symbolization of the detumescence of the penis (possibly fear of impotence). One of Reitler's homosexual patients wanted to be an hermaphrodite. During intercourse, he imagined that the penis belonged to the girl (castration-fantasy).

OPPENHEIM can confirm Reitler's statement that a cursing of the penis (death-wish) is not alien to the folk spirit. The sexual interpretation of forest and meadow in dreams has its analogy in Greek mythology, where the birth-goddess Artemis was worshipped on meadows. The second utilization of [the symbol of] the key that opens closed doors is familiar from the Bible. The South Slav symbolization of the penis as a bald head may belong in [the same category as] dreams of decapitation.

ADLER lays stress on the diligent and honest work of the speaker, who by way of his cases has confirmed what has been well known as the result of previous expositions. The shortcomings of his analyses must be in reality be stressed for all analyses: i.e., that one has not succeeded in showing what is compelling in neurosis.[3]

Today, Adler is interested in taking up two points, the detailed discussion of which however is reserved for a special paper: namely, that indications of hermaphroditism are to be found in every neurosis, but that they cannot represent the compelling element either, unless per-

[3] See Minutes 94, this volume.

haps, out of the entire structure of this psychic hermaphroditism, there might result a compulsion. The same thing holds true for the splitting of the personality.

If one relates dreams of beheading to the penis and to castration, the question arises of why it is there that the castration complex has had an effect, and what explains its importance in these instances. The fear of castration is not sufficient motivation. Nor is the discovery of psychic impotence sufficient, as far as the examination-dreams are concerned; here too psychic hermaphroditism is at work.

TAUSK has the feeling that everything Hitschmann presented is already known and solved. He is surprised that all of this has been brought forward as a new problem. Adler has spoken on the oneness of neuroses, and there is really no need to separate off a single symptom of illness by itself; one complex passes into another. What is compelling in a neurosis, has to one day be given artistic form and experienced as Nietzsche perhaps might have done. Finally, Tausk gives a report on the obsessional ideas he himself has met.

RANK calls attention to the dreams in which the head (face) is veiled; unveiled, these are seen to be incest dreams. This veiling of the head is a pre-stage of beheading; certainly the castration complex is operative in it, as has already been suggested by the connection [of these dreams] with the Oedipus complex. The sexual symbolism in Greek culture of meadow, field, and garden, etc. is well known; these expressions were used facetiously to denote the female genitalia (according to Winckelmann's *Antiquity*[4]).

STEINER would reproach the speaker on technical grounds, for having mixed the historical and the analytical detail with one another, so that they have become indistinguishable. The fact that compulsion is of sexual origin is in this circle no longer a matter for discussion. The form of compulsion that is determined by the sexual form may perhaps be a question.

There is no doubt that in every woman the desire to be a man plays a role. Hence it is understandable that to some men, too, a similar wish for a change of sex is natural. From this point of view, castration

[4] Johann Joachim Winckelmann: *Geschichte der Kunst des Altertums* [*History of Art in Antiquity*], 1764.

dreams gain in significance. In the second case, the dreams afford beautiful verification of the Theory of Sexuality.

FRIEDJUNG comments only on the second case, which is closer to him. The separation of the historical from the analytical is not altogether possible. Hitschmann's report offered almost nothing analytical; in view of the difficulty in coming close to the child, this is understandable. Hitschmann did all he could while tapping all the various possibilities with the child. The actual analysis should, however, start at the point at which Hitschmann stopped. Compulsive smiling is encountered frequently, and its etiology would be worth knowing.

STEKEL stresses that all these cases demonstrate the importance of the religious factor for the exploration of neuroses and, secondly, that all obsessional fears are linked with the "death clause." Thirdly, it is worth stressing that every obsessional idea is a parental command. Hitschmann did not draw everything out of his cases; it all depends upon the way one looks at one's material.

PROF. FREUD emphasizes that not only the honesty but also the correctness of the observations must be praised. The reproach that Hitschmann did not penetrate into the deepest layers is taken care of by the fact that he himself is fully aware of this, and that he had no intention whatsoever to extract more than the analogies with the other cases investigated. These analogies are, in fact, sufficient for several points to be established beyond any doubt. Above all, it must be stressed that in both cases the hostile impulses come to the fore. The first case in particular calls for such a supplementary assumption of an early hostility toward the father. It is true, to be sure, that the oath has to be regarded as purely incidental, this oath that from the beginning sets up a relationship that others must struggle hard to produce by themselves.

Details: We have not got very far as yet in the art of interpreting dreams without the dreamer's associations, and it is indeed to be doubted whether we shall ever succeed in doing so. As for an interpretation of the head-dreams, what is lacking till now is material.

The involution of the death-wish [onto the subject] is the general mechanism of these fears.

Federn's remark about the influence of the more affectionate (or, in some cases, cooler) parent is important; the significance, in relation to the sexual development of the child, of the extreme situation of lack of one of the parents has already been appreciated (Theory of Sexuality). In this sense one could speak directly of the significance of the father for the prevention of homosexuality. In relation to the obsessional character of the neuroses, Federn labors under a misapprehension, which he shares with Löwenfeld and Adler. That is to say, all neurotic phenomena have this compulsive character. This is connected with the fact that all of them are of sexual origin, and indeed sexuality is a compulsion. The compulsive character of obsessional neurosis is something specific, something totally different, and it requires a specific explanation.

The search for the compelling motive of neuroses (Adler) we take to be settled—in the sense that there is no compelling motive, since all motives have only a relative etiological significance. Whether or not a neurosis develops from these etiological factors depends on purely quantitative relations, which we cannot estimate. The oneness of neuroses is not a new discovery either, but rather the presupposition of our entire work: all neuroses have similar mechanisms; it is only the outcomes that are different. But the oneness of the neuroses in no way diminishes the value of distinctions, and we should not on that account neglect the differences [among them].

Nor does the emphasis on the religious factor (Stekel) enrich us with any new insight; we already know that religion is the universal obsessional neurosis,[5] but as to the nature of this neurosis, it will not bring us any enlightenment.

The fact that the death clause is universal is fairly certain, and is the best proof for our conception of the obsessional neurosis.

One would like to place a question mark after the "parents' imperative." It makes sense, in any case, only as far as *obsessive acts* are concerned.

Freud can contribute some corroboration to the sexual-symbolic interpretation of the Chinese (Stekel); it shows that a pigtail is in fact a sex-symbol. A woman's pigtail is the missing penis and those who

[5] See Freud: *Obsessive Acts and Religious Practices.* (1907) *S.E.* 9.

lop off the plait of hair actually create women (cf. the monkey's curling tail in "Little Hans").

The disbelief concerning Stekel's interpretation of the gasometer (as vagina) has been reinforced in consequence of a recently completed analysis of an obsessional idea of the same kind (doubt whether the gasometer had been turned off), in which, however, no role was played by a woman. The fear of not having turned off the gascock is equivalent to the fear of causing a fire at night, a fear that unquestionably goes back to enuresis. In similar circumstances, others may have the examination dream.

SADGER regrets the fact that, as last speaker, he has to tell the truth candidly to the reporter: that his work was no analysis but merely an ordinary anamnesis, which included matters of sexuality in its inquiry. As to throwing any light on the symptoms and the finer psychological relationships, that he has left completely undone.

Hermaphroditism is found, as a rule, in every hysteria—all of which are bisexual in nature.

HITSCHMANN at first replies to these remarks by saying that only some kind of envy can make someone emphasize the shortcomings of his (Hitschmann's) work in that tone and that manner, shortcomings that he himself had acknowledged. The first case, on account of compelling circumstances, was in treatment only a short time; the second has not been under treatment except for a few weeks. Moreover, the speaker did not present a great deal that he considered to be self-evident. All he wanted was to emphasize the analogies to Freud's case; he never asserted that he had offered anything new.

The historical [mode of] presentation was chosen only as a short-cut, and as a better overview for purposes of comparison.

The connection between compulsion and sexuality he had meant differently: the action that lies behind the neurotic's dream thought is sexual action. (PROF. FREUD: But that does not explain the obsessive character.)

96

SCIENTIFIC MEETING *on February 8, 1910*[1]

Present: Prof. Freud, Federn, Friedjung, Furtmüller, Heller, Hitschmann, Rank, Sadger, Stekel, Tausk, Wittels.

REVIEWS AND CLINICAL COMMUNICATIONS BY ALL PRESENT

STEKEL reports briefly on an analysis by Maeder that has had fine results (*Gauppsches Zentralblatt*).[2]

Several minor items from clinical experience: If a patient comes with the complaint: I cannot (. . . do this or that, etc.), this always refers to sexual incapability.

Toward the interpretation of dreams: Various vehicles, as is well known, always have sexual significance ("sleigh" is a female); but "railroad" proves in some cases to have still other determinations. For

1 In the attendance book there is the following entry: Congress invitations. Mrs. Oppenheim (Dr.) invited.

2 Alphonse Maeder: "Psychoanalyse bei einer melancholischen Depression" ("Psychoanalysis in a Case of Melancholic Depression"). *Zentralblatt für Nervenheilkunde und Psychiatrie*, 1910. An abstract of this work by the author himself appeared in 1911 in the third volume of the *Jahrbuch*.

one patient the most important thing was the "pull," the pulling.[3] To another patient, the locomotive had a bisexual meaning (a machine-beast, which satisfies itself); this indeed does play a role in the masturbatory fantasies of neurotics, who frequently gratify themselves as man and woman at once.

WITTELS can relate a similar interpretation by one of his patients, to whom the railroad train signified the masturbatory complex. The question is whether one is entitled to generalize this. Closely related to this interpretation is the tunnel. Further, the desire of every boy to become a conductor perhaps corresponds to the entire autoerotic complex of the child.

To another patient school had an anal meaning, by way of the verbal bridge, "school-stool" [*Schulzwang-Stuhlzwang*].

FEDERN, referring to the interpretation of the train engine, comments that every neurotic has hermaphroditic dreams; but they refer to the sexual aim and not to masturbation.

HITSCHMANN reviews an interesting report of a dream (*Frankfurter Zeitung* of 30/1/1910) by Buchner.

Then he raises the question of whether, in every actual-neurosis—and this is the most recent claim (especially on Stekel's part)—a psychic conflict must also be operative. In many cases, it seems to be missing and even where it is found, one must not forget that often, through treatment of the actual noxiousness, the entire neurosis disappears.

STEKEL adheres to his view that in all actual-neuroses a psychic conflict has a role. The doctor's way of proceeding in such cases is worth discussing. One ought not, as some doctors think one should, advise the unsatisfied woman to take a potent lover. We have no right to intervene in this way in a marriage.

TAUSK would, in relation to this, proceed radically.

FEDERN comments that one frequently encounters actual-neuroses without psychic conflict; and where a psychic conflict is present, the neurosis was already present before that.

[3] The German for a railway train is "*Eisenbahnzug.*" *Zug* means "train" as well as "pull."

WITTELS advises in such a case of an unsatisfied woman to wait, cautiously, until the patient herself has discovered the cause of her suffering; then one can help her very much by making clear all the factors that are involved.

FRIEDJUNG thinks that one cannot lay down general rules for dealing with such a situation. The way in which one proceeds is determined by each individual case.

PROF. FREUD would have spoken against Stekel if Friedjung and Wittels had not done so first. It is inconsistent to say, "I must not impart this or that." This simply cannot be said in such a general way. It is evident that the technique can be practiced with understanding and tact, or otherwise [but in that case without success].

The problem of the conflict in actual-neurosis is well worth a thorough examination.[4] Prof. Freud himself has not subjected to strict examination a sufficient number of cases during the past fifteen years.

If one wants to find out whether some conflict belongs among the actual-neuroses, it is best to turn to men, in whom the finest actual-neuroses, without any conflict, can be observed. In women, of course, the conflict readily supervenes. All cases will have been accounted for if one says that in the actual-neurosis a psychic conflict can be present, as well as absent. But there is no evidence at hand that it is always present.

The definition of the actual-neurosis refers to its symptoms, which are not determined by that same psychic disturbance by which they are determined in psychoneurosis. The deviation can have a psychic, as well as a purely technical, somatic cause; anxiety, therefore, occasionally also arises without sexual etiology. In this, one must distinguish between sexual etiology and sexual mechanism. What is disturbed and produces the symptoms is the sexual mechanism.

STEKEL has seen, among his numerous cases, no pure actual-neurosis. Men, too, struggle with the temptation (conflict) to take the

[4] Freud dealt with "actual-neuroses" first in "On the Grounds for Detaching a Particular Syndrome from Neurasthenia under the Description 'Anxiety Neurosis'" (1895) in *Neurologisches Zentralblatt.* Only in a later work, "Sexuality" in the *Aetiology of the Neuroses* (1898) did he introduce the term "actual-neuroses." Freud asserted that the actual-neurosis is of somatic origin; Stekel, that it is of psychological origin.

liberty of normal coitus and, as soon as this is made possible (for instance, because the wife is already pregnant), the temptation (the conflict) vanishes. According to Stekel's experience, even with a commonplace etiology (exhaustion, etc.), the psychic conflict always supervenes. It is difficult to decide which comes first.

HITSCHMANN, finally, speaks about a young man, nineteen years old, who is in treatment because of a troublesome ring fetishism. In addition he has, in relation to his father's death, a compulsive command and suffers from compulsive urinating. According to the insight gained up to now, the fetish first involved a lorgnon (two rings), and seems to go back to the infantile conception of the woman (mother) with a penis. The ring together with the finger has a similar meaning. The patient also is somewhat homosexual (transference dream!).

TAUSK reports the analytic solution of a doubly determined eating conflict in a young man who suffers from a curious feeling of fullness in the mouth. This could be traced back to the following: he—who considered his penis too small to fill a vagina—thought that during fellatio the woman would at least have her mouth full. The patient's feeling of a full mouth subsequently—when it had become almost impossible for him to eat—could also be related to anal erotism. The patient had, indeed, as a boy of seven to eight years eaten a lot, filled his mouth in order to increase the pleasure during evacuation.

On the symbolism of riding in a vehicle: a Bosnian saying—"Watch out, little one; the carriage is coming." (Symbolism: shaft = penis; the two wheels = testicles).

On bisexual masturbation: a young man, while masturbating, spreads his legs apart, and thinks of himself as having intercourse both as a man and as a woman.

Lastly Tausk refers to Fliess' book *On Life and on Death*,[5] which offers wide perspectives if the author's thoughts are extended from the organic sphere into the psychic (limitation of the psychic energy given an individual).

STEKEL finds the anal solution too far-fetched, and is of the opinion that Tausk, by too quickly communicating the interpretation in

[5] Wilhelm Fliess: *Vom Leben und vom Tode, Biologische Vorträge*, Jena, 1909 [*On Life and on Death, Biological Lectures*].

terms of fellatio, has aroused the patient's disgust with that activity.

PROF. FREUD counters that displacements of that sort—from below upwards (anus-mouth)—can be confirmed without difficulty.

FRIEDJUNG calls attention to the fact that to children the connection between a large food intake and large evacuation becomes clear at a much later period.

RANK reports on an otherwise normal girl who apparently has visual and auditory hallucinations, that have to do with her beauty and with flatteries that some gentlemen whisper to her or express by their glances. This is a degree of vanity that already has a paranoid character. This feminine vanity is, so to speak, what might be called a still normal degree of paranoia (Prof. Freud's example of the little girl who, on wearing her new dress for the first time, believes that all eyes are turned on it). Or rather, in paranoia, this vanity has taken a pathological turn. The contents of the hallucinations tally with this: the girl hears words of flattery concerning her beauty and virtue; the paranoid (for instance, Freud's published case) hears words of invective.

The same girl shows an acutely marked anal character, in which the component of stubbornness is in fact, as Freud thought, supported only by the sadism that has remained unrepressed (Adler's confluence of instincts).

This girl also clearly confirms the theoretical expositions that appeared in *The Artist*,[6] according to which, as a result of the withdrawing of libidinal energies in puberty, there develops out of sadism (the active instincts) the contrasting instinctual series (compassion, etc.).

Finally, Rank suggests that *being surprised in a dream* ("I was surprised that . . ."), in addition to the specific meaning for the dream, seems always to have a typical, universal meaning.

FRIEDJUNG tells about his four-year-old boy, who recently very manifestly fell in love with the nursemaid, a situation which is still increasing in intensity.

SADGER reviews two books which he accepted for this purpose: Bumke: *On Somatic Phenomena Accompanying Psychic Processes*

[6] Otto Rank: *Der Künstler. Ansätze zu einer Sexualpsychologie*. 1907.

(Wiesbaden, 1909), and Lange on the same topic.[7] The latter of these, though not mentioned in the former, is the more important, by far; yet both books show that in psychology one does not get far with exactitude.

From case reports Sadger selects two, which show that unusually early (up to the second year) and extraordinary expressions of erotism can be observed in children. One can see in such cases also how certain psychotic states are directly prepared in the child.

HITSCHMANN remarks that erections in a child's first year, even in the first half-year, are not rare.

FURTMÜLLER considers it dangerous to influence small children by means of energetic coercive measures. Perhaps more damage is done by such strong measures of repression than if one permits childhood defects to become balanced out slowly and fade away.

TAUSK mentions that enuresis plays an important role taken in conjunction with sexuality.

HITSCHMANN refers to the significance of the neck of the bladder as an erotogenic zone.

HELLER would like to return to a passage in Bumke's book in which it is stated that it is possible, from the unconscious (involuntary) movements of the lips during the process of thinking, to read off the contents of the thought; this casts some light on certain types of fortune-telling and miraculous training ("clever Hans").[8]

Heller further calls attention to an interesting novel by Frederik van Eden:[9] *The Blessings of Storms* (Original: *From the Cool Waters of*

[7] Carl George Lange (1834-1900): *Die Gemütsbewegungen, ihr Wesen und ihr Einfluss auf körperliche, besonders auf krankhafte Lebenserscheinungen; eine medizinisch-psychologische Studie* [*Emotions, Their Nature and Influence upon Physical, Especially Pathological Phenomena; a Medico-Psychological Study*]. 2nd ed., Würzburg, 1910. The first edition appeared in Leipzig in 1887, the Danish original in 1885.

[8] Clever Hans was a miracle horse, which could seemingly think and do sums. Oskar Pfund: *The Horse of Mr. von Osten* ["Clever Hans"]; *A Contribution to Experimental Animal and Human Psychology.* New York, 1911. [*Das Pferd des Herrn von Osten; ein Beitrag zur experimentellen Tier- und Menschenpsychologie.* Leipzig, 1907.]

[9] Wilhelm Frederik van Eden, 1860-1932, famous Dutch author. In its English translation the novel referred to is entitled *The Days of Deliverance.* The Dutch original was published in 1900, the English translation in 1902, the German version in 1907.

Death). The author, a neurologist by profession, shows a curious course of development. After a fine first book, *Little Johannes* (1887), a period of withdrawal from life set in; then he became the founder of a religion; promoter of a sect; socialistic communist; finally, he wound up as a sort of follower of Tolstoy. The book under discussion falls into the time of his mania for founding a religion, and rather accurately depicts, with embellishments of realistic detail, the case history of a hysteric. Van Eden is familiar with Freud's works, which he rejects; yet, contrary to his will and his conscious awareness, he corroborates them in his novel.

FEDERN tells of an exception to the interpretation of the dream within a dream; in this particular case, the dream within the dream merely shows the resistance, in treatment, against the therapy.

On Ferenczi's *Introjection:*[10] Susceptibility to hypnosis may also depend upon whether, as a child, the individual was easily lulled to sleep by a beloved person.

FURTMÜLLER reviews a pamphlet in Loewenfeld's Collection, "Kant and Swedenborg,"[11] referring to Kant's *Dreams of a Seer.* An attempt is made in this brochure to prove that Kant's valuation of Swedenborg was unjust. The brochure itself is unscientific; everything that has been reported the author simply takes to be really so. Hoffman has become convinced that Swedenborg possessed telepathic faculties. Of interest is the reference to the man, his life and his diary, in which Swedenborg is said to have entered all of his (for the most part, sexual) dreams.

HITSCHMANN would like to point out that psychoanalysis really seems to be suited in part to elucidate occult phenomena. In regard to

[10] S. Ferenczi: *Introjection und Übertragung* [*Introjection and Transference*]. *Jahrbuch I.*

[11] Richard Adolf Hoffman: *Kant und Swedenborg*, Wiesbaden, 1909, p. 24: ". . . a diary which Swedenborg wrote on a trip via Holland to England in 1734-1744, thus as a man in his middle fifties. These intimate notes were published in Stockholm as late as 1859 under the title 'Swedenborg's Drömar' in the original Swedish version." An English version of the "Drömar" was published by R. L. Tafel: "Documents Concerning the Life and Character of Swedenborg," collected, translated and annotated, 1875-77.

See also: C. G. Jung, *Zur Psychologie und Pathologie sogenannter okkulter Phänomene.* Leipzig, 1902.

graphology, too, analysis is suited to show how much and what [aspect] of its claim may be justified.

PROF. FREUD has still seen only incorrect graphological judgments. However, some miming is doubtless involved.

STEKEL calls attention to his repeated assertion that some sexual symbolism appears, rather undisguised, in every handwriting.

A long informal discussion then ensues about the phenomena of spiritism, occultism and clairvoyance, during the course of which Stekel proposes to present a woman patient who is favorably disposed as a medium.

PROF. FREUD agrees to this proposal, remarking that, if such things exist at all, they are physiological and not psychological. Besides, it seems that, *subjectively*, the impulse to cheat must always be present.

98

SCIENTIFIC MEETING *on February 23, 1910*[1]

Present: Prof. Freud, Adler, Federn, Friedjung, Furtmüller, Hitschmann, Oppenheim, Rank, Reitler, Sadger, Steiner, Stekel, Tausk, Wittels.

Dr. Jekels as guest.

PRESENTATION

Psychic Hermaphroditism[2]

SPEAKER: DR. ADLER

The speaker is well aware of the fact that, in the topic announced, he is touching upon the most delicate point in the area of psychoanalytic investigation. He reserves a presentation of his work *in ex-*

[1] The 97th protocol has not been preserved. Those present at that session were: Freud, Adler, Federn, Friedjung, Furtmüller, Heller, Hitschmann, Oppenheim, Rank, Reitler, Sadger, Steiner, Stekel, Tausk. Mrs. Oppenheim and Dr. Jekels were guests. Dr. Oppenheim presented a paper on "Fire as a Sex Symbol."

[2] This paper was published under the title "Der psychische Hermaphroditismus im Leben und in der Neurose" ["Psychic Hermaphroditism in Life and in Neurosis"] in *Fortschritte der Medizin,* 1910. An English translation has appeared in *The Individual Psychology of Alfred Adler* by H. and R. Ansbacher (Basic Books, 1956).

tenso for the Congress at Nuremberg, and would like in this circle to define only briefly the view [presently] taken of this old problem, as well as to discuss some individual questions.

The term psychic hermaphroditism and its essence have a rather considerable past. In addition to Freud's *Three Essays,*[3] which deal thoroughly with this question, we must refer to Halban's[4] view that every human being is hermaphroditic, a trait that expresses itself either directly in the genitalia, or in the secondary sex characteristics, or in psychic life. This view is, in a certain sense, in accord with Krafft-Ebing's[5] view (masculine and feminine brain center). Fliess'[6] conception is in essence also the same, although Fliess called attention to the peculiarities of the hermaphrodite, mentioning especially that he is more readily susceptible to neurosis. Fliess believed that the man falls ill because of his feminine tendencies, the woman because of her masculine tendencies. The bridges from the view to those of Weininger and Swoboda[7] are certainly known, and familiarity with Freud's conception is also taken for granted; from the latter we want to single out in particular only the statement that every neurotic shows homosexual traits. Attention should also be called to one of Sadger's remarks—that every hysteric displays masculine and feminine fantasies—an assertion that was somewhat narrowed down by Freud. The

[3] *Three Essays on the Theory of Sexuality* (1905), *S.E.* 7.

[4] Josef Halban, prominent Viennese gynecologist: "Schwangerschaftsreaktionen der foetalen Organe und ihre puerperale Involution" ["Reactions in Pregnancy of the Foetal Organs and Their Puerperal Involutions"], *Ztschrft. für Geburtsheilkunde und Gynaekologie,* 1909.

[5] See Minutes 10 (Volume I), fn. 10. Freiherr v. Krafft-Ebing: *Psychopathia sexualis, mit besonderer Berücksichtigung der konträren Sexualempfindungen* [*Psychopathia Sexualis with Particular Reference to the Antipathetic Sexual Feelings*]. 1st ed. in 1886, 37th ed. in 1907.

[6] See Volume I, Minutes 21, fn. 1. Wilhelm Fliess: *Der Ablauf des Lebens. Grundlegung zur exacten Biologie.* [*Course of Life. Basic Principles for an Exact Biology*], Leipzig, Vienna, 1906.

[7] For Hermann Swoboda, see Minutes 21 (Volume I), fn. 4. His work: "Die Perioden des menschlichen Organismus in ihrer psychologischen und biologischen Bedeutung" ["The Periods of the Human Organism and Their Psychological and Biologic Significance"]. Otto Weininger (1880-1903), philosopher, became famous with his book *Geschlecht und Charakter: eine prinzipielle Untersuchung* [*Sex and Character*]. One of his tenets was the psychological and ethical inferiority of women. He, too, plays a role in the Fliess-Freud controversy. See "Origins of Psychoanalysis," *Imago,* London 1950. Concerning the problem of bisexuality, compare the section "Masculine, Feminine," in Nunberg, "Problems of Bisexuality as Reflected in Circumcision," *Imago,* London 1949.

speaker himself has proven, on the basis of dreams, that homosexuality is present in prostitutes.[8]

The speaker now advances the following hypothesis: that the disposition that belongs to the opposite sex seems to present itself as a component of the sexual instinct and is more or less doomed to being either atrophied or sublimated. In order to explain this proposition, Adler refers to his work on the aggressive drive and its transformations, which play the most important role in neurosis. This conception suffered from the defect of being a biological one and not suitable to a complete understanding of neurotic phenomena. To this end, one must consider a conception of the neurotic that is most highly personal and judges phenomena in a way that does not admit of definition in biological terms, but only in psychological terms, or in terms of cultural psychology.

In viewing neurotic phenomena from these standpoints, which is in essence the current standard procedure, it is a question of what the neurotic understands by "masculine" and "feminine." It turns out that by "feminine" he understands almost anything that is bad, certainly anything inferior, and that in this way he attempts to avert what is pathological.

The speaker refers to his latest work in which he has been able to show that the "disposition to neurosis" lies in the feeling of inferiority, the fear of being slighted, which stems from the earliest times in which a child encounters the problem of sexuality; this is a feeling that is later formulated as: "I am not fully a man." In this matter of the fixating of the feeling of inferiority through the sex problem we are dealing with infantile and not at all with biological values. In that valuation, it seems that everything that is active is regarded as being masculine, everything passive as feminine.

It is Adler's proposition, then—consonant with that of Freud—that in every neurotic (in every human being) we find masculine as well as feminine traits, whether it be in a mixed (compromise) formation, or one alongside the other. The sublimated form of this conception is the problem of freedom or the determination of the will. Despite our inner conviction that the will is determined, we behave as if it were

8 "Zwei Träume einer Prostituierten" ["Two Dreams of a Prostitute"], *Ztschrft f. Sexualwissenschaft*, 1908.

free; the fault lies in the posing of the problem. In a similar way, these two distinct conceptions are felt by the neurotic, and all character traits can be traced back to that fact.

From here the speaker throws a bridge to the view that he set down in his study on organ inferiority. According to his conception, as he developed it there, achievements that are recognized as being inferior are felt to be unmanly, thus feminine. The effort to get rid of these "feminine" traits is experienced as "masculine." The female child, too, sees her ideal in the man, albeit with the limitation that she has to become a man by feminine means. In stressing that it is the task of analysis to bring to light the woman within the neurotic man and to show that all his pathological traits are suffused with these female tendencies, one is probably saying nothing new.

We are acquainted with phenomena, that occur during the development of the child, which are in a position to support these trains of thought in the child—above all, for instance, his lack of understanding of the sex problem (see false sex theories, Freud). In addition, there are the instances of tickling and feelings of pleasure in certain parts of the body (particularly mouth and anus), which increase a child's uncertainty in regard to his sexual role. (This is the reason why young men, right up to the time of puberty, often prove to be uninformed about their sexual role.) If one turns back to the parents, one finds—especially in neurotic families—the character of bisexuality to be very pronounced; but aside from this inherited tendency, the milieu of the child's rearing undoubtedly also plays a role. Further support of this uncertainty is to be seen in every seduction to perversion.

What has been said also applied to female neurotics, in whom one can invariably show the presence of the wish to be a man and who for the most part had already in childhood betrayed masculine traits.

A further point is the question of homosexuality. Analyses of overt homosexuals and of neurotics disclose that the male homosexual always has the feeling of being a woman. The question of how it is then that there are active homosexuals can be answered if one considers this to be a secondary stage—the masculine protest, as it were, of these inverts. But in neurotics too, this protest of masculinity can always be shown to be present (for example, in reference to the character trait of sensitivity). A neurosis is established only after this masculine protest has failed. And it is bound to fail in the neurotic for the following reasons:

1. because his feminine characteristics invariably become dominant (masochism, anxiety, irresolution, doubting, pessimism, feeling of guilt);

2. because the demands that he makes in order to feel himself a man are hypertrophic: he must overcompensate for his feeling of inferiority because otherwise he feels unsatisfied; on the other hand, by this overcompensation he is prevented from finding satisfaction;

3. because our society is not adapted to fulfilling demands that invariably go too far and that is the point at which the neurosis becomes manifest.

Under particularly favorable circumstances, these hypertrophic demands achieve success, and then performances of genius may ensue, whose close connection with the neuroses is indeed well known to us.

Those phenomena of neuroses that we call compromise-formations in the true sense of the word—such as doubt, sadomasochistic traits, all forms of the inhibited or perverted aggressive instinct, the phenomena of compulsion and anxiety—these are derived and obtain their power from the battle between the feminine foundation and the masculine protest. A further form of this battle is stubbornness. The stubborn adherence to childhood defects that are felt to be unmanly also represents a compromise-formation between a trait that is felt to be "feminine" and the attempt at a masculine protest. All manifestations of inferiority in this way experience a secondary realization. In many cases, compulsion should be understood in these terms; this applies, for instance, to continuing enuresis, masturbation, to frequent emissions, etc. The same explanation holds true for the compulsive habit some boys have of holding on to their penis while falling sleep—a symptomatic action by way of which they demonstrate doubt in their masculinity. In general, it seems as if this doubt would play a frequent role in symptomatic acts. In neurosis, it is the tendency to develop away from the feminine to the masculine. The fact that in dreams all these phenomena of the feminine, as well as the tendency to move toward the masculine, play a role—this is, in terms of Freud's work, self-evident. In this sense every dream provides the occasion for understanding the tendency to develop from woman into man. The dream also indicates the point at which the pathogenic situation expressed itself, at which the child fixated his sexual role and at the same time mobilized all of his masculine tendencies in order to "become somebody" in the world. The same is true of fantasies, although it seems that there are also purely female fantasies. Individual phenomena of sleep and dream also have their place here (for instance, not being able to go away from one spot). That doubting in dreams is traceable back to this chief doubt, between masculine and feminine, can be demonstrated by dreams.

This conception seems suited also to throw some light on certain forms of fetishism (on garment fetishism in particular, both male and female garments).

The theory of periodicity is secondarily included in [the discussion of] the problem of hermaphroditism, because woman has a [menstrual] period and is tied to it.

Lastly, the speaker briefly recapitulates once again the essentials of his discourse: the child's infantile comprehension compels him to look upon everything inferior as unmanly and to conceive of it as feminine. This infantile identifying of inferiority with femininity develops as a result of incorrect sex theories, and of the sensations in mouth and anus that induce the child to perform intercourse-like manipulations. Although we follow Halban to a very great extent in assuming that hermaphroditism is congenital, we are nevertheless compelled to take cognizance of the impression that is evoked by the phenomena of infantile neurosis and to make use of psychological elements for the elucidation of the problem of neurosis.

DISCUSSION

TAUSK would raise only one cardinal question: where does the criterion of "masculine" and "feminine" start from in neurosis? All of this is only a matter of repression and refers simply to sexual activity.

FURTMÜLLER: The same question came to his mind. It seems important also to ask what part of this hermaphroditism is a constitutional phenomenon and what part is historical. In the conception of the feminine as inferior, there is certainly also much that is merely historical. One cannot see why the duality of our attitude to the problem of freedom of will should also hold for the situation in which we vacillate between man and woman. The illusion of freedom of will is like the illusion by which the moon seems to be moving when clouds are passing in front of it.

HITSCHMANN was not quite able to follow the lecture because of an indisposition.

FEDERN thinks one could actually agree to every sentence and yet put a question mark after it. Adler endeavored to further develop the theory of inferiority in its application to the development of neuroses. In so doing, however, he failed to distinguish organ inferiority significantly from (1) abnormalities of sexual development, and (2) the feeling of inferiority.

The observation that hermaphroditism appears with greater regularity in neurotics is nothing new and can hardly be contradicted. Certainly, the feeling of inferiority can become, subjectively, a cause for repression—just as, on the other hand, because of the intensified impulses that are appropriate to the opposite sex, more desires must remain unfulfilled. Now Adler asserts that neurotics suffer subjectively from their hermaphroditism; he thinks that they feel the rest of their deficiencies as also belonging to the opposite sex—an attitude that makes their position even more difficult. If this is correct, then it seems to make for a new conception of the neuroses. Federn himself has not yet observed that patients regard as "feminine" everything that they feel to be deficient; it is a question whether Adler does not exaggerate when he places the factor of bisexuality at the midpoint. There are hysterics who become so without any feeling of inferiority. Bisexuality, like so many other conditions, can be a promoting factor; but it does not belong at the center of a theory of neuroses.

Holding on to his penis is simply a boy's masturbatory way of putting himself to sleep.

OPPENHEIM wants to content himself with referring back to Tausk's question of what, in a psychological sense, is masculine and what is feminine. One can conceive of the masculine and the feminine only in an anatomical sense; their transposition into the psychological world is difficult. Oppenheim would doubt that it is a scientific concept rather than a historical one, based on value judgments.

FRIEDJUNG would also like to return to the question of how much of this is to be ascribed to constitution and how much to upbringing. According to his experience, the latter is of great influence. It would be interesting, in relation to that question, to study those neurotics who were raised by one parent only, and were thus completely withdrawn from the influence of the other sex.

The explanation for the retention of childhood defects is the pleasure gain that it provides.

SADGER appreciates Adler's honestly thought out work and his inclination to rise above the subject matter, but regrets that notwithstanding these merits of the paper, Adler's inclination toward theorizing came so much to the fore. The infantile conception that what is inferior is feminine, which Adler has stressed, Sadger has not yet found in his analysis. A child, in his rivalry with the father, always indeed feels inferior. Moreover, it is a question whether the child invariably finds the woman to be the inactive partner. In the analyses of homosexuals, almost regularly the patient turns out to be the child of an "active" woman and a weak, reserved man. The invert's feeling of being a woman goes back to his identifying with his mother. It is a striking fact that in the child and among old people homosexuality often becomes prominent.

Adler's dream criterion cannot be confirmed by Sadger.

REITLER does not consider everything that was presented to be correct; what was correct is already contained in Freud's works—for example, the indication that every human being has, before puberty, a homosexual period. If everyone is supposed to see his ideal in the masculine, then one must decide to whom this ideal is meant to refer: to the subject's own person or to that of the love-object. It does happen, after all, that a man retains the desire to be a girl, that he does not want at all to be masculine and yet sees his ideal in man. One must also deny that all girls, especially at a later period, see their ideal in the masculine. Just as little could one find confirmation of the assertion that dreams and fantasies invariably reveal this tendency toward man. In childhood, bisexuality always plays a role; the determining factor in regard to neurosis is the development after puberty.

JEKELS has too little experience of his own to be able to appreciate Adler's views, which are derived from numerous analyses; all he can say is that the paper appealed to him very much, even though the uncertainty about the valuation of masculine and feminine (Tausk) was striking. The paper is a logically incontestable and consistent continuation of Adler's views about the significance of the aggressive instinct and of the theory of organ inferiority.

STEINER remarks, about the question of the criterion between masculine and feminine: these are not contradictory but complementary concepts. The opposite of masculine is infantile.

As far as the paper itself is concerned, one must distinguish between matters of dogma and hypotheses; Adler has failed to prove the latter. Under present-day conditions, it is not incorrect to present as dogma the inferiority of what is feminine. Besides, there are innumerable times when one can hear women express the wish: "If only I had been born a man!" Whether it is true that the neurotic always has the feeling of being a woman must still be verified; nevertheless, it seems to be confirmed that in the neurotic this bisexuality, a trace of which is present in every human being, goes somewhat to the extreme.

RANK is not in a position today to take up the paper critically in its entirety; he only mentions, with reference to the analysis of a dream, that each situation could be interpreted as being bisexual (masculine as well as feminine). To extend this, as Adler thinks, to all dreams is perhaps risky, since there are undoubtedly dreams—as Freud has shown with regard to symptoms that in general are also bisexual—that have a monosexual basis and can be so interpreted. Yet, one has the impression that many dreams, especially those of neurotics, are to be interpreted bisexually.

As far as the development of homosexuality is concerned, it proves to be ever more probable that, under usual conditions, the first love in both sexes is for the mother; whether this inclination is maintained, or in what way and how intensively it is repressed, is decisive with regard to either homosexuality or heterosexuality.

PROF. FREUD always finds in Adler's papers a sum total of sagacious remarks, which are conceptually well separated [from one another], and above all throw a sharp light on the facts. On the other hand, Adler has been denied the gift of facilitating for others the sympathetic understanding of his thoughts. Besides, one faces his expositions with a certain feeling of alienation, because Adler subjects the psychological material too soon to biological points of view, thus arriving at conclusions that are not yet warranted by the psychological material.

It is noteworthy that three speakers who were actually not psychoanalytically oriented—Tausk, Oppenheim, and Furtmüller—placed their emphasis on what is decisive: that in the area of psychology we do not know what we should call masculine and what feminine. The example of Fliess, who offers a biological characterization, has misled many. Fliess saw in the unconscious the elements of the opposite sex. This is wrong. It is true that in the woman one does find in neurosis repressed masculinity, but in the man one finds only the repression of "masculine" impulses and not of "feminine" ones. Neurosis always has a "feminine" character. But the concepts of "masculine" and "feminine" are of no use in psychology and we do better, in view of the findings of the psychology of the neuroses, to employ the concepts of libido and repression. Whatever is of the libido has a masculine character, and whatever is repression is of a feminine character. Psychologically, we can present only the character of activity and passivity.

Important as hermaphroditism is to the conception of the neuroses, nevertheless we must not forget that, first of all, all kinds of psychic hermaphroditism can exist without neuroses. Also, it is in contradiction to some impressions to shift the core of the problems of neuroses into this mixed formation; however, a full development of the "mixed formation" is undoubtedly a supporting force, as are so many other factors. In early childhood, which is indeed the time when the foundation for a neurosis is laid, the difference of sex plays a very minimal role. These are later conscious processes, projected back into childhood. In addition, one must keep in mind that libido develops in several thrusts (Rank: *Artist*). First of all, as a purely active impulse, which subsequently changes into a passive one; with the following thrust, not only the active paths but also those that have become passive are cathected with masculine libido (make a virtue of necessity). If one substitutes here the concepts "masculine" and "feminine," then the result is what Adler has described. It is a change of nomenclature through which we lose clarity. The same thing holds true for interpreting the dream as representing a striving away from woman toward man: the dream has no more than the striving to fulfill a wish, and this striving is a matter of libido, is active.

On other points, we can only agree with Adler; for instance, in reference to the compromise-character of the object of homosexuals. There are, by the way, more ways than one that lead to homosexuality. One of them has become known to us through Sadger's and his own (Freud's) investigations: i.e., that the boy attaches himself first to the woman, then identifies with her (thereby repressing the love for woman) and, by way of "narcissism," self-love, seeks himself in the male objects. The conception of paranoia, it seems, is also determined by this suppressed object-component (the homosexual one). One can say that sublimating becomes sexual once again and asserts itself by way of the paranoia.

Being raised by only one parent (Friedjung) frequently leads to homosexuality in both sexes.

STEKEL believes that psychic and physical hermaphroditism are the most significant factors toward an understanding of neuroses. In this basic sense, Adler said nothing new, but he did add significant details. The identification of "inferior" with "feminine" must be verified. Stekel can, on the other hand, confirm the bisexual character of dreams, without which in actuality no dream can be understood (PROF. FREUD offers, by way of objection, children's dreams!). The riddle of reversal in dreams means: the dream is to be read as it is and also the other way round. Indeed, it must be possible to read every dream "as it stands written"; it must already, even without interpretation, have a meaning.

The most important insight gained from [the examination of] the problem of psychic hermaphroditism has to do with masturbation. Homosexual fantasies play the main role, if an individual is not capable of abandoning masturbation (SADGER: And other perverse fantasies, too.).

Not everything that is underrated is characterized by us as feminine. There are neurotics who overrate woman (lyricists, etc.). Adler's presentation suffers in general from its one-sided, male point of view; the same would have to be applicable, vice versa, to the woman. Nor should one forget the bipolarity of symptoms, which show that neurotics do not feel only masculine. On the whole, a neurotic has a larger range of action than a normal individual.

ADLER refers to his Nuremberg paper for more explanatory and more relevant statements. He stresses that several discussants made the mistake of wanting to pin him down to the biological point of view. He believes that he was less biological than [he would have been] if he had pursued the vicissitudes of the libido and of the innate sexual constitution. Besides, the conception of the libido as being masculine has itself fallen prey to the valuation discussed before; he, after all, did not create it; it simply exists and the objection raised against it, that it is a historical valuation, is of no importance. Moreover, Adler has sufficiently emphasized that this valuation is the infantile one; actually, however, it is quite general.

In regard to the problem of will, Adler meant that its being "tied down" is perceived as feminine; freedom, the possibility of making decisions, as masculine. In general, the valuation is subject to fluctuations; as for us, however, the valuation by the neurotic is all that interests us.

The most important problem passed over in the paper, cannot be gone into now either; but Adler stresses his firm impression that the incest problem is but a secondary phenomenon and is based on these fundamentals. This will also make understandable the fact that the homosexual *a priori* identifies with his mother.

In regard to some points, Adler can gratefully welcome Prof. Freud's remarks as well as Stekel's agreement with his conception of homosexuality.

99

SCIENTIFIC MEETING *on March 2, 1910*

Present: Prof. Freud, Federn, Friedjung, Furtmüller, Heller, Hitschmann, Joachim, Rank, Reitler, Sadger, Steiner, Stekel, Tausk, Wittels.

PRESENTATION

Developmental History of the Neurosis

SPEAKER: DR. REITLER

For a long time the speaker has occupied himself with the question of whether a patient can really fall ill primarily as a result of either an obsessional neurosis or a conversion hysteria, or whether all the forms that are known to us do not rather represent stages in the development of psychogenic neuroses. The mixed forms, which are so frequent, seem to speak for this [latter] view. The speaker in no way underestimates the theoretical and prognostic value of differentiating sharply among the individual forms of neurosis—although, from the purely therapeutic point of view, we could dispense with this, since our method of treatment is the same for each of the different variants of neurosis. The prognostic value of a differential diagnosis would even be enhanced, if the speaker's idea that one form of neurosis develops from another according to laws, should prove to be correct. The neurosis that is further along in the developmental series would, at the same time, also represent the more severe form of illness.

The speaker then stresses that he has come to his conclusions not by way of the psychoanalytical approach, but by way of speculative construction; however, the building blocks of his edifices were taken throughout from the results of the investigations by Freud—who, although he did not express precisely the idea of the evolution of neuroses, nevertheless suggested it in several passages. The speaker now turns to the representation of the "family tree" of the neuroses. The fundamental condition for the development of a neurosis is formed by the "abnormal psychosexual constitution" (Freud), whose most essential symptom is sexual precocity. The latter in turn manifests itself in the child's genital masturbation, long before the onset of puberty. The speaker believes that, on the basis of Freud's theory of sexuality, he must ascribe to this premature masturbation special significance for the development of a later neurosis, in the sense that, according to Freud, the sexuality of children is in contrast to that of adults. Because the child, before puberty, is normally polymorph-perverse (autoerotic), he has at his disposal, for the gratification of his autoerotic libido, all erotogenic zones, with the exception of the genital zone. In accordance with the child's immature stage of development, the genital zone should normally be still absolutely inactive. If, then, a child masturbates quite exclusively at the genitalium, there is present in such a case a sexual precocity that is an expression of an abnormal psychosexual constitution; with this is provided the fundamental condition for—even the eminent danger of—the formation of a neurosis. Whether a neurosis in fact develops depends, according to Freud, "on a quantitative factor"—i.e., on the total stress the nervous system must sustain in proportion to its power of resistance. Now, if the nervous system of the child who masturbates prematurely is overburdened, obviously there will appear primarily the form of neurosis that we should expect in the adult too, as a consequence of abnormal masturbation: i.e., *neurasthenia* (cf. the "family tree"). However, that is not the end of the matter; very soon a struggle sets in against masturbation, in the course of which the child can avail himself of only two possible solutions (both of which are equally disastrous): either *abstinence* (which in most cases is probably only partial), or *continuation of masturbation.* If the child succeeds at least partially in the struggle against his desire to masturbate, the consequence will be an anxiety neurosis, according to Freud: "Those who have become neurasthenics as a consequence of masturbation, as soon as they desist from their [habitual] type of sexual gratification, fall into an anxiety neurosis. These persons have rendered themselves particularly incapable of tolerating abstinence" (Cf. "Analysis of the Phobia of a Five-year-old Boy.").

If the child retains the original neurasthenia as a result of continuing masturbation, the further course is, in both cases, nevertheless the same. For now the *psychological* factor comes in, and with it the great leap is made from the two primary neuroses to the psychogenic neuroses. To this leap [the situation] must come sooner or later, since in every human being there is enough psychic material for the development of complexes that are hostile to consciousness, but whose repression must fail, simply because the sustaining power of the nervous system has been substantially reduced by the already existing actual-neurosis. And therefore, as the result of the approach of psychic determinants, a neurasthenia—that is to say, an anxiety neurosis—must turn into an *anxiety hysteria.* This course of development is not only theoretically a logical result; it is in many cases also demonstrable in practice. Pure forms of the actual-neuroses are extremely rare, indeed; almost always, in analysis, a superstructure of anxiety hysteria can be demonstrated. The anxiety that is, at first, "objectless" changes, relatively quickly, into the "fear of something definite." It becomes *phobia.* This transformation is set in motion by an individual's understandable striving to ease his situation. Phobia, however, already includes the earliest beginnings of *compulsion,* and in fact the evolution of the psychogenic neuroses takes its course from anxiety hysteria via phobia to *obsessional neurosis.* Proof: if an obsessional neurotic is prevented from carrying out his "ceremonial," an attack of anxiety is brought on. The anxiety is released that the patient successfully endeavored to exorcise by his ceremonial. In the treatment of the total neurosis, however, one can make similar observations.

In addition to obsessional neurosis, a parallel offshoot, conversion hysteria, branches off from anxiety hysteria and phobia. In it, too, the patient's tendency is unmistakably to create for himself a better psychic situation. With regard to the choice of somatic discharge, the speaker expresses the conjecture that it very likely depends on the degree of intelligence whether an obsessional neurosis comes about, with its highly complicated psychic performance, or a conversion hysteria, with its relatively minimal psychic display, for which only a certain compliance of the organ systems involved is required.

In support of the contention that conversion-hysteria, just like obsessional neurosis, is derived from phobia and anxiety hysteria, and that both represent, to a certain extent, parallel phenomena in psychic and organic areas, the speaker refers to the fact that the somatic symptoms of hysteria have an obsession-like character. And at the time when a conversion hysteric is being brought toward recovery, finally there appears, in place of the physical symptoms, the anxiety that had been previously converted. The obsessional neurotic, just like the conversion hysteric, goes back in his cure over the same path along which, during the course of development of his neurosis, he had made his way forward. Both first become phobics, anxiety hysterics; only thereafter do they get well again. These stages of retrogression, which by the way may last only a very short time, are demonstrable in every case in which the psychoanalysis has been completed.

In conclusion, the speaker refers to the most severe of all forms of neurosis—genuine hypochondria—which, as the final member in the developmental series, arises by way of the confluence of obsessional neurosis and conversion hysteria. Less significant forms of hypochondria appear, by the way, in all gradations of shading during all the stages in the development of neuroses; but they lack throughout the [element of] compulsion, whereas that is exactly what is typical of *hypochondria vera* (cf. Stekel). In this there is involved a conversion hysteria, the somatic symptoms of which, as a result of the confluent obsessional neurosis, meet with a compulsively stressed consideration.

DISCUSSION

STEINER begins by stressing how clear and lucid the presentation has been, and also that the foundation of the edifice is in principle incontestable. It is very doubtful whether the neurosis in every case covers all these stages. And also one could not then understand why certain people even at a very late age stay at [the stage of] neurasthenia. Furthermore, there is often no lack of intelligence, and yet no obsessional neurosis develops; on the other hand, conversion hysteria does not occur only in people of limited intelligence. Another weak point is thus to be found in the schematization of the whole work.

FURTMÜLLER, as a layman, finds it quite fascinating to see all these phenomena linked together, by way of their development, into one dramatic sequence. He can only express the hope that the expositions will find confirmation. It seems questionable to him that, merely because a child occupies himself with his sex organ, he is to be stigmatized as being abnormal.

SADGER would like to limit himself to a bare reproduction of the impression made upon him by this new and engagingly presented train of thought. In general, masturbation is not especially prominent in the precocious child; the pleasure gained from urinary and fecal functions plays a greater role. One must, furthermore, not forget that masturbation can be interrupted and taken up again several times before puberty without leaving behind particular damage. Indeed, in most instances masturbation passes without leaving any trace. What matters is how often an individual masturbates. The speaker endeavored—just as Stekel did—to blot out the boundary line between anxiety neurosis and anxiety hysteria. However, the existence of pure cases of anxiety neurosis can be deduced from the fact that numerous cases are, for all practical purposes, cured.

There are, to be sure, no unintelligent obsessional neurotics, but patients endowed with intelligence can also come to conversion hysterias.

On the whole, one has the feeling that the whole thing might be, after all, only a theoretical construct; the most hazardous connecting link seems to be phobia.

JEKELS comments that Furtmüller anticipated the most striking point when he raised his objection against the valuation of childhood masturbation. One really cannot understand why the growing pleasure the child gains from genital masturbation should be so decisive, as against all other autoerotic activities. The speaker obviously hit upon this schematized conception because he had once again taken up the earliest works of Freud, which assert the existence of a sharp separation between the somatic and the psychic. Freud himself has lately been allowing room for the supposition that the influence of psychic factors in these somatic neuroses should not be altogether ruled out.

STEKEL thinks that at first glance there is something novel and attractive in the argument as such, but in practice it proves to be incorrect. In some cases it may correspond to the facts, but there is no doubt that one can see an obsessional neurosis coming into existence spontaneously. That there are very intimate and regular connections between anxiety hysteria and obsessional neurosis, Stekel has explained in his paper on doubt. One must take a stand against Reitler's model because he has constructed it in such a way that every neurosis begins with neurasthenia. Stekel himself has never seen this neurasthenia. As far as hypochondria is concerned, he has seen one case in which there were neither obsessional-neurotic ideas nor anxiety hysteria. A number of psychic symptoms contribute to the fixation of attention on physical phenomena.

There is something attractive about the idea that a conversion hysteria reveals itself in people of low intelligence, but one also finds exceptions to this.

Moreover, the harmfulness of children's masturbation is by no means agreed upon yet; only the way in which individuals react to the traumata is decisive for the neurosis. This decision is probably made as early as the first year of life.

FRIEDJUNG doesn't have much to say that has not already been said, but he would like to stress some things from his own experience. The unqualified assertion that genital masturbation in the period of childhood is what is decisive for a neurosis does not appear to be right.

Nor can the speaker's further expositions be brought into harmony *a priori* with actual conditions. [For if they could], then all of mankind [would have to be] neurasthenic or tormented by anxiety. Very seldom is neurasthenia seen in children; in most cases neurotic phenomena in children are combined with anxiety.

WITTELS: It is precisely the attractive character of the paper that arouses his mistrust.

With regard to masturbation, we ought not to be at all surprised if the genital zone is involved at an early age. It is a question whether one should go so far as to deny the erotogenicity of a child's genital zone. The criterion of intelligence is incorrect. One could rather say that obsessional neurotics are for the most part intelligent people, and that conversion hysterics are both intelligent and unintelligent. In general one must say that this direction for speculative endeavors, just like the other direction, which involves going back to the organic causes, brings more harm than gain to our system.

PROF. FREUD agrees in principle that one occasionally speculates and goes beyond observation—provided one is conscious of it. Freud has personally never made an effort to construct a complete system; he has instead focused on the gaps—for example, those that exist in our understanding of the actual-neurosis, which still lags behind our present knowledge. Today's paper can be regarded as only a "fantasy of the future," insofar as our present knowledge is still too full of gaps to entitle us to a decisive opinion on these questions. With this a serious valuation of this interesting schema would actually be disposed of, were it not for the fact that it provides the occasion to tie together a number of doubts and suggestions.

Above all, as has already been stressed in the discussion, the foundations for the whole argument are unstable. In the theory of sexuality [Freud's], a viewpoint contrary to Reitler's position is represented—namely, that masturbation at certain periods of childhood is requisite for later normality, and that definite forms of neurosis are traceable to other quite definite erotogenic activities. Stekel underestimates the harm done by masturbation and by sexual activity in general, although abstinence undoubtedly has a more harmful effect than gratification. One must take note of the fact that neurasthenia invariably proves to be a consequence of excessive masturbation, a statement that cannot be reversed. The problem of masturbation as such is a highly complicated one and has many obscure elements in it; it is the outlet for children's sexual activities, and in each case one must first find out what lies behind it.

The family tree seems oversimplified. It is a question whether only one tree-trunk grows out of abnormal psychosexual conditions. Obsessional neurosis seems to have an autochthonous origin; the intermediate position of phobia is very artificial. Yet there is a path that leads behind this schema; it suffers from the fact that it is purely phenomenological, and does nothing but bring the forms of illness into relationship with each other. It would be conceivable for the psychological forebears of all these forms to have had such relationships. What is wrong in the views about the forms of illness might perhaps be correct, if one put in what we already sense about the separate pieces. One would have to take into consideration the predisposition to neuroses, an hypertrophy of an instinct, the age at which the fixation occurs, the stage of development at which the child finds himself, and finally the mechanisms of repression, by which the individual neuroses differ essentially from one another. If one could get at what lies behind the factors that create the disposition for a neurosis, as well as behind the repression, one would perhaps come upon relationships similar to those that Reitler has brought forward.[1] Besides, there is something correct that is to be sought out behind Reitler's personal conviction. The basic idea of his theory is quite meritorious, even though it has no practical significance. The basic idea is: everything that we call psychoneurosis must go back to an infantile actual-neurosis; we must add: whether or not it now becomes manifest.

As far as the value and meaning of a separation of the individual forms of neurosis is concerned, this separation is not only a theoretical necessity, but also pragmatically meaningful. The technique of psychoanalysis is not the same for every form of neurosis and a few suggestions in this respect can already be given: for instance, one will have to treat a phobia differently from a conversion hysteria, in which the simple introduction of therapy is sufficient. For the phobic patient has not only the symptoms, but also a psychic protective structure; as long as he has it, he does not yield the material out of which this protective structure is made. One must therefore develop in him the

[1] See discussion about the choice of neurosis, Minutes 82, this volume.

courage to learn gradually to renounce this forestructure: he must expose himself to the anxiety the avoidance of which had been the [purpose of] producing the phobia. Thereby, he will gain the material that is needed for the resolution of his anxiety. In obsessional neurosis, other changes of technique will have to be undertaken.[2]

HITSCHMANN is of the opinion that the speaker took the easy way out in explaining the choice of neurosis, nor did he always use genuine Freudian building blocks for his structure. The speaker overlooked the fact that children's masturbation may indeed automatically cease to exist; that it normally disappears of itself organically; and that this latency period, just like the period of masturbation itself, is a normal stage and can spread out to various zones. Hitschmann can say nothing about the organic neuroses in children, but it seems likely that the want of any sexual discharge in children ought to make these organic neuroses not correspond fully, after all, to the actual-neuroses of adults. One cannot see why anxiety hysteria in children should always be assumed to have a masturbatory prestage.

One could as well say that obsessional neurotics are intelligent because they have an obsessional neurosis.

FEDERN believes that the relationship between intelligence and obsessional neurosis is correct; but there are also intelligent conversion hysterics.

Reitler's formula would be more correct if it were expressed in the following way: every child who reacts to infantile masturbation with neurasthenia is predisposed to neurosis. Neurasthenia in children is very familiar to us. Federn considers it to be a correct observation that, in fact, with every solution of a conversion hysteria, anxiety is released. (PROF. FREUD: The development of anxiety is to a great extent absorbed by way of the mechanism of the treatment [transference], so that the largest part of the anxiety has to be overcome in the form of resistance to the transference; the treatment compels the patient to take a different way back in the solution of the neurosis.)[3]

[2] In these remarks we see the first indication of the "active" technique. We can also gather what Freud means by this technique.

[3] Again a technical hint. It is to be recommended that one read Freud's remarks in this discussion very carefully, because they are, on the one hand, difficult to understand, and, on the other hand, very important.

MINUTES 99

REITLER feels that he can be brief in his concluding remark. All he wanted to do was to suggest, as an idea, that the neuroses could after all be explained in terms of developmental history. He would consider of the greatest importance, just as Freud did, the observation that the psychogenic neuroses of adults go back to infantile actual-neuroses.[4]

[4] Later, Freud does not talk any longer of actual-neurosis in childhood, but of the infantile psychoneurosis.

100

SCIENTIFIC MEETING *on March 9, 1910*

Present: Prof. Freud, Adler, Federn, Friedjung, Furtmüller, Hitschmann, Oppenheim, Rank, Reitler, Sadger, Steiner, Stekel, Tausk.

PRESENTATION

The Infantile Preconditions of Masochism[1]

SPEAKER: DR. FEDERN

DISCUSSION

TAUSK, who is not well-informed in the area of masochism as a psychic phenomenon, finds two new and noteworthy ideas in the paper. (1) Masochism is the condition, prepared in infancy, that expresses itself as a perception of an inner tension that has no possibility—whether in thought or in reality—of attaching itself to an object. From these ideas, the [clinical] pictures of masochism can easily be derived. (2) The image of carrying and being carried is an expression of psychic masochism that can be traced in the history of culture,

[1] There is no record of this paper, nor has it been published. The ideas in it were worked up into Federn's "Contributions to the Analysis of Sadism and Masochism: "I. The Source of Male Sadism" (*Internationale Zeitschrift für Psychoanalyse*, 1913) and "II. The Libidinous Sources of Masochism" (1914).

philosophy and religion (where it also appears in its active form). We need only call to mind that Christianity has made a postulate of carrying (the cross, suffering, original sin). It is probable that the feelings of guilt that are supposed to express themselves in carrying provide a considerable contribution to masochism.

The separation of the concepts of masochism and algolagnia also seems important to Tausk. He finds the term "pleasure-toned misery" most appropriate for characterizing what he must now imagine masochism to be.

OPPENHEIM would like to follow the suggestions given by the preceding speaker only in those areas that are more familiar to himself. It would be worth examining whether such features of Christianity can really be brought into relation with the manifestations of masochism. The striving for debasement seems also to have found expression in the Christian choice of names in those times.

FURTMÜLLER, in connection with these remarks, would only like to mention tentatively a few phenomena from literature. Until now, he had thought that masochism and algolagnia [sensual pleasure in pain] were very closely related. (Holofernes in Hebbel's *Judith;* some of the characteristics of Goethe and of the *"Stürmer und Dränger,"*[2] for whom not only joy in pain, but also joy in every other emotion, played an important role.)

PROF. FREUD begins by commenting that, in the second edition of the *Theory of Sexuality,* he has, indeed, treated the problem of sadism and masochism very warily. The literature contains such a muddle of, to be sure, estimable points of view, but no indication of the end from which one should unroll the problem.

As a result of the technique of today's presentation (reading to the audience), it was hardly possible to follow everything; and Prof. Freud can therefore go into only individual points. In general, he thought that the speaker added to the difficulties of the subject and contributed nothing toward order in this field. One point deserves special em-

[2] *"Sturm und Drang"* is the name given to the period in German literature that was characterized by the greatest emphasis on feelings and emotions, and the enjoyment of all facets of life with all one's senses, as opposed to the immediately preceding period of enlightenment. The young Goethe, the young Schiller, and Herder were among the representatives of that movement.

phasis: the significance of the point of view that, the more intensively an individual is enamored, the more generally dependent upon the sex object he becomes. For a significant rule for analysis can be developed from this: while the patient attaches himself to the physician, the physician is subject to a similar process, that of "countertransference." This countertransference must be completely overcome by the analyst; only this will make him the master of the psychoanalytic situation; it makes him the perfectly cool object whom the other person must lovingly woo.[3]

ADLER: From the mass of material offered, the impression forces itself upon us that a path was taken here that is familiar to us. The elements that the speaker tried to show as being contained within the masochistic complex are in fact present there, but their reduction has not been altogether successful. However, this chapter is so difficult that a great deal of work will still be required to achieve that goal.

With the basic conception that derives masochism from undischarged tensions, one must take issue. After all, no child is successful in getting rid of these tensions. Equally unsound is the assumption that the masochist did not masturbate [in his childhood]. Federn let himself be blinded here by the greater sensitivity of the genitals, but that is not the root [of masochism]. Masochism is rather to be traced back to the child's dependence, which is felt to be feminine. In his paper on psychic hermaphroditism,[4] Adler has shown in what way this feeling is intensified: by sensitivity of the anus and the mouth, by fantasies about these, by confusion about sexual life, by a lower degree of activity and the inhibition of activity, because of a feeling of guilt, that appears at an early age. (Tausk)

The overvaluation of an object, to which masochism is attributed, does not itself appear to be elementary; it is encountered also later as a tendentious attitude, which makes the goal appear to be difficult to attain, so that the subject feels wholly a man when he reaches it.

In the principle of bearing and enduring suffering, the masculine protest also seems to come to light. The entire neurosis, with all its

[3] Again an important technical hint! The concept of countertransference is subsequently developed further. Freud is said to have discovered countertransference during his treatment of a phobic patient.

[4] See Minutes 98, this volume.

disagreeable sensations, exhibits that trait of proving to oneself and to the environment how much one is capable of enduring. Here, too, it becomes evident that the masochistic complex is intermingled with sadistic traits, which direct themselves against the subject's own person.

HITSCHMANN has little experience in this field. In any event, one always sees masochism and sadism appearing together; it is difficult to separate them. The classic case of Rousseau really fits in with what has been said about the genitals and inferiority. One must probably distinguish between those who satisfy themselves only masochistically and those who can also have intercourse. It would have to be shown, too, what this renouncing of the act comes from, whether it is really a weakness of the genital apparatus that is involved here.

STEINER would have liked the presentation to be more lucid and to have been organized more in accordance with a systematized outline: (1) masochism as perversion; (2) as fantasy; (3) as sublimation. (*Ad* 1) Masochistic activity occurs in such a way that the opposite sex is always involved, never the subject's own. (Objections). (*Ad* 2) In masochism as fantasy, it seems to be that the man sees himself as a woman; the woman, in turn, as a man. (*Ad* 3) To this belongs everything that means enduring, suffering, pain; this cannot be organized into a system.

SADGER wants to defend Federn, who was the first to apply psychoanalytic points of view to *psychopathia sexualis.* Sadger himself has had only one case in which masochism, side by side with inversion, was in the foreground. Federn has discovered some noteworthy things, even though he seems to have erred in some details. The idea that masochistic children do not masturbate is just not so.

Some points to which Federn did not call attention: what is called patting, something between striking and fondling, and from which children derive great pleasure, plays an important role in the genesis of masochism. The same applies to alcoholism in parents, who often beat their children without measure and then usually treat them twice as affectionately. This establishes an early and organic connection [between being beaten and love]. Sadger could not find that an inferiority of the genital apparatus, in Adler's sense, is involved in it.

REITLER finds [Federn's] work valuable and probing, even though, in certain passages, it does lack clarity. Federn did not give sufficient consideration to sadism, which one cannot imagine separated from masochism. In every case both tendencies are found, and not in temporal succession, but for the most part united in a single act.

Krafft-Ebing seems to be right, as opposed to Federn, in thinking that "algolagnia" must be [considered] linked up with psychic masochism. The enduring of pain can at the same time be a psychic humiliation. And this may well go back to patting (Sadger). The idea that masochists are not autoerotic genitally can hardly be maintained. It seems very plausible, on the other hand, that in all of these cases overvaluation of the object is involved and object-love is pronounced. The "bearing of a cross," too, in this sense is not purely masochistic, for the suffering is to be endured out of love for the godhead, etc.

PROF. FREUD makes the supplementary remarks, that one source of our deficient explanation of the derivation of sadism and masochism lies in our lack of knowledge concerning the nature of pain in general, with its half-psychic and half-physiological determining conditions. This enigmatic character [of pain] is very clear in children, who often seem not altogether to know whether they should regard something as painful, and in whom, on the other hand, one can, to one's own surprise, eliminate organically warranted pains by suggestion.

It should be emphasized that masochism in our civilized society is increasing extraordinarily. If one is interested in the infantile impressions that are at the root [of this phenomenon], one discovers that it occurs for the most part, in children who have not been beaten[5] enough or not at all.

[5] This is a foreshadowing of the later theory that, where real gratification fails, gratification is created in fantasy.

The work with children undertaken by Anna Freud has revealed that children who have been brought up in "complete freedom" produce more feelings of guilt than those who were brought up with more or less stringent restrictions, and are thus better prepared for adaptation to reality. Children themselves desire guidance.

In "Instincts and their Vicissitudes" (1915), *S.E.* 14, Freud regarded masochism as sadism turned inward (thus, reversed sadism).

In "A Child Is Being Beaten" (1919), *S.E.* 17, he continued along the same lines and, in addition, found masochism to be reinforced by femininity.

In *Beyond the Pleasure Principle* (1920), *S.E.* 18, he saw the possibility of the existence of a primary, independent masochism.

In "The Economic Problem of Masochism" (1924), *S.E.* 19, he expressed the con-

STEKEL feels disappointed in the paper, which did not even approximately touch upon the topic, as he had conceived it. If we ask ourselves why it is that pain is valued as pleasure, we must take into consideration the fact that there are people who value every pleasurable sensation as pain. The problem has a simple solution: it is a question of stimuli, and the threshold for stimuli is different in each person. True, the problem is complicated by the fact that there is, in addition, a psychic superstructure. The increase in masochism has its explanation in man's increasingly deep sense of guilt. It is a punishment that people inflict upon themselves. This also explains why those who were not beaten in childhood are rather prone to masochism: they catch up with the punishment that their parents did not visit upon them. The circuitous route is explained in the following way: everything that is supposed to be punishment becomes erotic, and if it is erotic then it is pleasure. In this sense neurosis as a whole is nothing but an expression of masochism: the patient punishes himself for his guilt through the neurosis, and it is no wonder therefore that he clings to the illness. Nor should one forget in these considerations the bipolarity of symptoms: the fluctuating between the delusion of grandeur and that of insignificance.

Of great importance is Freud's remark about the countertransference; Stekel can fully confirm its existence.

FRIEDJUNG has little to say and would like only to remark that Federn gave much too little attention to the influence of upbringing upon sadism and masochism. It appears as if the only child is more inclined toward sadism. The concept of countertransference can be extended to medical practice in general, and it may perhaps explain the successes of "brutal" physicians.

FEDERN finds missing in the critique sufficient clarity to demonstrate to him what objective mistakes he made and what had not been understood [by the audience]. As to Freud's reproach that Federn had allowed his topic to become disorganized, he would reject it. As against

---

viction that there is a primary masochism. Now he discerns three kinds of masochism: (1) primary or erotogenic; (2) feminine; (3) moral.

The problem of masochism occupied Freud's mind almost to the end of his life.

(See also Introductory Remarks by J. Strachey to "The Economic Problem of Masochism," *S.E.* 19.)

it, he refers once more to the homogeneous fundamental idea of his exposition—that the child's immature psyche reacts to these tensions with fantasies of this kind and that under this main viewpoint all manifestations of masochism—from the normal component to the most abstruse excrescences—can be subsumed. This irrational masochism Federn has described in detail, and it is only of this that he has asserted that at its roots lie strong tensions minus sexual activity (masturbation). Federn has mentioned in addition that masturbation can supervene, and that in rational masochism sexual tension is also necessary, but that various external impressions may participate therein as determining factors. He has also stressed that only in irrational masochism can one explain the autochthonous genesis in terms of the relationship of the primary psyche to sexuality. It was Federn's intention only to give a psychoanalytic explanation of the most sharply marked masochism.

The idea that the sense of guilt should be among the causes of masochism seems plausible; yet there are cases in which it is absent.

Federn is hopeful that this conception, when tested on larger material, will prove to be correct.

101

SCIENTIFIC MEETING *on March 16, 1910*

Present: Prof. Freud, Adler, Federn, Friedjung, Furtmüller, Graf, Heller, Hitschmann, Joachim, Oppenheim, Rank, Reitler, Sadger, Steiner, Stekel, Tausk, Wittels.

REVIEWS AND CLINICAL COMMUNICATIONS BY ALL PRESENT

JOACHIM gives an example that shows that patients' contradictions often signify unconscious assent. A woman who disavows any hatred for her husband immediately thereafter relates a dream that fully confirms that hatred.

He goes on to tell of a nice example of symbolism in a psychosis. The patient has a very strong, square-built husband, and quite a number of her symbols refer to this shape of his: she wants to eat only out of a broad, square cup; wants to wear square-checked material; thinks that her husband forces her to squeeze her square-built foot into a tight shoe (sexual symbol), etc. It is interesting that the patient herself characterizes this thinking as symbolic.

FRIEDJUNG reports on a paper on "Association Experiments with Children," presented by Goett in October of last year at the *Münchner*

Gesellschaft für Kinderheilkunde [publ. in *Zeitschrift für Kinderheilkunde* I, 1910]. Further, he relates details of hysterical states in a six-and-a-half-year old boy who, after a dream, began to utter grumbling sounds at brief intervals. In his dream, a big black man had thrust a pole into the boy's chest. He sleeps with his father and says that the latter always clasps him tightly. It would seem that on that occasion the boy had felt his father's erect penis, and that the dream has this very meaning. Nor would it be out of the question that the boy had overheard a coition, during which his mother uttered a sound similar to the one which the boy has since been producing. Identification with the mother occurs, in fact, in sleeping with the father as well as in the dream. One could not elicit more from the boy without asking suggestive questions.

PROF. FREUD comments that in such a case, if one wants to come up with anything, one cannot avoid asking some leading questions. Besides, the patient can be influenced only in a direction that suggests itself to him. One has to take the risk of being at first misled by the patient. For in neurosis, the reality is that of thought, and not that of the external world. One can never see to what extent the symptom is externally conditioned; it is true, to be sure, that the symptom must always have a certain external point on which to lean. A clue for further probing into this case could have been found in the boy's seemingly harmless remark that the father had made a gift of this or that to him; with this remark the child seems to imply: in return for my allowing him to hug me, he gives me that.

ADLER, too, considers such a procedure as Freud suggests here to be important; one could, however, go even further, perhaps, and continue to deal with associations of the gifts. Among these the mouth-organ is outstanding, because the child's symptom also has to do with the mouth. The mouth-organ is a sound-producing instrument, and it is probable that in this child it is a question of specific anal sensitivity. The goal of the child's neurosis is to get away from the father and come to the mother; and one wonders whether the reported significant improvement cannot be traced to the fact that Friedjung had ordered separating the child from the father. The dynamics of the case have to be imagined along the following lines: the boy plays a dual role;

he would like to behave toward the father in a feminine manner, but has the feeling that he must not or should not do so, and accordingly turns to the masculine role (toward the mother).

FREUD, who acknowledges these suggestions to be very fruitful (relative to the connection with the anal zone), raises the question of whether Adler believes that this child would not have become neurotic if he had slept with the mother; there is no doubt that he would have, of course, since we know enough cases of that sort. The introduction of these biological viewpoints into the process of comprehending psychological processes seems premature; such consideration of his sexual role has no significance at all for the child himself, so that a child's becoming neurotic cannot be traced back to that sort of change in his sexual role.[1] In boys it seems rather plausible, because in them repression coincides with femininity; but for the woman and her neurosis, this is certainly not true at all.

STEKEL calls to mind that, with such children, his technique of having the patient say words has proved very effective.[2]

SADGER is of the opinion that, as far as practice is concerned, the association experiment does not lead to any shortening [of the treatment] nor does it make it any easier. (FREUD confirms that this is also his point of view, but says that nevertheless the employment of this method should not be rejected out of hand.)

REITLER relates the case history of a patient who demonstrates *ab ovo* the developmental history of the neuroses as set forth in his last paper. It is a question of a severe obsessional neurotic; from his fourth or fifth year on, the patient practiced genital masturbation; he fixated his libido at a very early age onto the mother, in whose bed he slept, and from his sixth or seventh year he masturbated with fantasies about the mother. In his eleventh year, he was seduced by a homosexual and misused for mutual masturbation. However, he succeeded in getting out of this distressing affair, stopped masturbating, and after a quarter of a year fell ill with an abstinence anxiety neurosis. This was soon intensified psychically (becoming an anxiety hysteria with *pavor noc-*

[1] Freud repeatedly cautions against confusing psychology and biology; this was his paramount objection to Adler.

[2] This is a reference to the association experiment.

turnus and terrifying dreams). At first, he was afraid of his seducer, whom he imagined he encountered everywhere; then he cut down the extent of his anxiety and became afraid of those streets that led to the seducer's apartment. After that, the phobia became generalized and he could no longer leave his house at all. From this situation there developed a transition to obsessional neurosis.

His ritual now consisted of his having to walk exactly the same routes coming as going (in the street as well as in his own room); indeed, it went even so far that soon he had to put on and take off all his clothes, and generally had to do everything forward and backward. With this he signified on the one hand that he was a masturbator (back and forth—signifying masturbation); on the other hand, it implied the wish to cancel out everything. As the result of external obstacles, the treatment had to be abandoned without having been successful.

PROF. FREUD is at present treating a woman patient whose illness has taken a similar course. Through a trauma in her married life, she acquired an anxiety neurosis. Soon there were added phobias from an anxiety hysteria. Subsequently, a new occasion evoked the appearance of obsessional neurotic symptoms. This is a development which—in addition to the autochthonous cases—not infrequently leads to the outbreak of an obsessional neurosis. It does give the impression of a development, but there is another conception that is also possible.

It seems clear that this patient's obsessional neurosis provides expression for the same thing as do her anxiety symptoms. It also seems, however, that other new motives were awakened in her, which favored the transformation of the one neurosis into the other. In the anxiety hysteria, she had essentially fought temptations. Then a motive of vindictiveness, which stemmed from her childhood, supervened (her sexual life had begun very early, with sadistic manifestations). This would then not be a spontaneous change from one form into another, but a transformation by way of a change in the psychic beginning.

HITSCHMANN reminds us of his case of a ten-year-old girl who gave transitory evidence of anxiety at one time, before her compulsion appeared. On the other hand, he now has in treatment an obsessional neurotic, whose obsession appeared spontaneously when he was five years old.

OPPENHEIM, referring to the new topical problem of students' suicides, discusses an article by Swoboda in the latest issue [Vol. XXII, 1910] of *Österreichische Rundschau*. Its point of departure—quite in harmony with the reporter's own ideas—is a defense of the school. Swoboda distinguishes between "motive for" (conscious reason) and "cause of" the suicide (what is actually operative in the psyche). The cause of suicide, according to Swoboda, always lies in sexual life, whether it be in hyper- or hypo-gratification (abstinence). He does not furnish a more detailed explanation of why this should be so, and one must definitely speak out against this exaggeration of what is certainly a correct viewpoint. There are cases, no doubt (the historical ones of Cato, Saul, etc., etc.) in which the (conscious) motives must also be considered as causes. Oppenheim himself can suspect the existence of a connection with sexual life, in a case in which there is involved an external concurrence of a failure ("slump") in school and suicide; and this is probably true of all student suicides. Besides, the factor of suggestion very likely plays an important role in them.

STEKEL proposes, in view of the great importance of the problem, to arrange a particular evening for the discussion of suicide, especially of young persons.[3]

FEDERN reports on a paper by Jones concerning the explanation for nightmares (nightmare-apparitions),[4] which can be shown to be anxiety dreams. Jones emphasizes that these phenomena show a characteristic triad: (1) anxiety like death, contained in the dreams; (2) difficulty in breathing, combined with the sensation of something sitting on one's chest; (3) total paralysis. Previous explanations have been satisfied to lay their emphasis on organic phenomena (somatic stimuli). As Jones sees it, the reasons for the so far deficient explanations lie in the fact that the authors who dealt with these phenomena

[3] See Minutes 104, 105, in this volume.

[4] Ernest Jones: "On Nightmares," 1910, *American Journal of Insanity*. This essay is the first chapter of Jones' book, *Der Alptraum in seiner Beziehung zu gewissen Formen des mittelalterlichen Aberglaubens* (*Schriften zur angewandten Seelenkunde*, 1912); it was first published in German, and then much later, in 1931, in English, under the title *On the Nightmare* (Psychoanalytic Library) in England, in America under the title *Nightmare, Witches and Devils*. Federn's review of the book appeared in *Intern. Zeitschrift für Psychoanalyse*, 1913.

had suffered from such dreams themselves and had not recognized the anxiety neurosis at their root. Jones believes the dreams to be attacks of anxiety during sleep, coming on more easily in these circumstances because conscious inhibitions are absent, that is to say, less strong.

In explaining the dream images, Jones alleges that pressure on the chest always corresponds to the notion of coition (any physical stimulus may, of course, take part as an occasional cause herein). It is for the most part the feminine (masochistic) component that, through its repression, produces these dreams; that is the reason why they occur so much more frequently in men. It is interesting that the significance of abstinence in relation to the emergence of such nightmares is mentioned, albeit not with full clarity, in early case histories (e.g., in Paracelsus).

OPPENHEIM mentions that, in the identification of anxiety dreams with nightmares, the sexual element is already expressed. For according to modern as well as ancient interpretation, these are the kinds of erotic powers that seek to take possession of the human being sexually in his sleep (cf. Roscher: *Ephialtes*).[5] Mythologists are merely not aware of the psychological connections and the erotic elements. A certain connection with the sadistic component must also be surmised (vampire). An ancient picture shows the typical representation of such a nightmare: a nude woman riding on the chest of a sleeping man.

FEDERN remarks that the sexual is not so obvious in all cases, but Jones also derives the thoroughly distorted dreams from the same feeling of pleasure (*Lust*).

PROF. FREUD comments that the vampire-saga has not yet found any explanation.

FEDERN mentions Hock's monograph on this topic.[6]

ADLER in his research on psychological hermaphroditism came across nightmares too, which are found, by the way, equally often in

[5] Wilhelm Heinrich Roscher, 1845-1923, *Ephialtes, eine pathologisch-mythologische Abhandlung über die Alpträume und Alpdämonen des klassischen Altertums* [*Ephialtes, A Pathologic-Mythological Treatise on Nightmares and Demons of Classical Antiquity*], Leipzig, 1900.

[6] Stefan Hock, 1877-1947, *Die Vampyrsage und ihre Verwertung in der deutschen Literatur*, Berlin 1900 [*The Vampire-saga and its Utilization in German Literature.*]

both sexes and even in entirely healthy people. One can, however, understand the phenomenon only after one has become convinced that the nightmare is not an isolated phenomenon but has neurotic ramifications. Jones seems indeed to have anticipated the understanding of them. It has become evident from the witch trials that these matters were always looked upon as intermingled with sexuality (Incubus). The opposite, the succubus, is what Adler has called the masculine protest. It is found in women who have intercourse only in a reverse position. A similar interpretation holds for not being able, in a dream, to go forward. This is closely related to the paralysis that is tied in with nightmares: it is a symptom that seems to represent a transition into the feminine, a loss of activity.

There are many patients who cry out in their sleep; this is either the starting point of the nightmare or a residue of it. It seems that this crying out always reflects the female situation. A woman patient [with this symptom] had already felt herself to be a man in her childhood.

HITSCHMANN says that if one dream can be designated as typical of anxiety neurosis, it is the dream about animals and burglars.

STEKEL comments that this is not the only form of such dreams, and that dreams of being run over, birth dreams, etc., also belong in this group.

HITSCHMANN: In connection with the relationship between disturbances of motility and muscular pleasure in motility (*Theory of Sex*), Hitschmann reports the case of a girl who often wants to run at night; one has the impression that this represents something of a sexual nature. He also relates the case of a young man with a poor physical constitution, who suffers from agoraphobia; his father and brother also suffered from it, a homogenous inheritance, as can be observed frequently in obsessional neurosis. The patient can go out only if accompanied by his mother (or possibly by his aunt), who must also wait outside during the treatment. Masturbation is absolutely denied.

Whereas the patient previously suffered from emissions (in dreams), this has no longer been the case since the outbreak of agoraphobia. His dreams almost invariably have the same content: the room is changed (he is lying in a strange room); then he screams for his mother and awakens. It is easy to perceive that he had sexual wish-dreams concerning women (perhaps his mother). Upon medical advice, the patient had intercourse; he was accompanied by a friend, and the experience left no particular impression on him; yet his condition improved significantly. Ambition-fantasies could not be detected in him.

PROF. FREUD remarks that the case is easy to understand. The father's death is the fundamental precondition of the whole thing. As the result of it, the way to the mother is unobstructed; the patient wants to come to her but is greatly afraid of this. He now wants to turn to other women, yet he cannot do so because he does not wish to become unfaithful to his mother. That is the conflict: he screams at night and wants to go to her. Social ambition really seems to be lacking in this case, even though erotic ambition is not altogether missing. Agoraphobia sometimes has the sole purpose of preventing the patient from going to prostitutes.

FURTMÜLLER would like to refer to a recent remark with something he picked up from reading. The remark was that phrases that seem to have arisen out of an individual's momentary whim turn out to be from an old fund of myth and vocabulary. It also becomes evident that turns of expression that seem to be but a passing trope can often have deeper significance. Since in our circle the attempt has already been made to derive the entire development of the investigatory drive from the sexual instinct of asking questions, the idea comes to one's mind that to many scientists the metaphor of *nuda veritas* often really does have the meaning of a woman; that the sexual revealing that he would like to carry out in relation to the woman, the scientist performs on a scientific object. A passage in a letter by Multatuli[7] very beautifully confirms this connection, in regard to one of the most abstract sciences, mathematics.

OPPENHEIM thinks that the sexual origin of the investigatory drive is expressed in the story of paradise (even linguistically: to know = to copulate). The biblical saga of paradise simply depicts how coition started (apple, tree, snake, etc.). The punishment, too, is a talion. In

[7] Pen-name of G. D. Dekker, 1820-1887, Dutch author.

retribution for having tilled the woman's field, Adam must work the real soil; and woman, in retribution (for coition), must bear children.

SADGER reviews Ostwald's book on *Great Men.* A distinction is made between two types, the romantic and the classicist, a division that corresponds in actuality to the four temperaments. One of the distinguishing marks of the later great man is mental precocity.

PROF. FREUD offers an example of an unusual symbolism. A patient who, in an institution, is working the soil gets an attack of anxiety at the moment when the sun shines on him. The patient explains this by saying that he had been working around in "Mother Earth," and it was quite natural for him to become anxious when Father (the sun) was looking on.[8] The same patient also suffers from agoraphobia; he always has the feeling that the ground is uneven, etc. This also goes back to the symbolism of "mother Earth" and to the time when as a child he would climb all over the "uneven" mother. This curious symbolism of the sun is corroborated by the following, which was reported by the patient: While he was still well, in answer to the question where his father was planning to go for the summer, he would quote from *Faust* (Prologue in Heaven): "And the course prescribed to him he will complete with thunderous pace." Here he did in fact compare his father with the sun.

As a result of the experience gained in this case, it was possible to detect the same symbolism in another case. That was the case of an asexual man with latent homosexual feelings. All along he had as his ideal to sit inside of four walls in conversation with a dear friend. He has an older brother whom he first loved homosexually. He loves him too much to rob him of his birthright (in fantasy) and has therefore made him merely his twin brother. The fantasy related above means, then, to sit together with this brother, as his twin, in the mother's womb. Of late this patient has been coming with a complaint: that he has a room with a southern exposure, into which the sun shines, and this he cannot stand; moreover, it is impossible for him to manipulate the venetian blinds. Here again there appears the same sun-symbolism: he is in the mother's womb and the father intrudes (venetian blind

[8] See Freud: "Psychoanalytic Notes on an Autobiographical Account of a Case of Paranoia (*Dementia Paranoides*)" (1911), *S.E.* 12.

[German phrase: *Jalousie*] = symbol of jealousy). Some of the patient's dreams clearly show him as an onlooker at parental intercourse, while he is in the mother's womb.

In this sun-symbolism is comprised the whole conception of mythology, which sees the sun as the progenitor and the earth as the impregnated partner.

TAUSK demonstrates by an example that those who write their signature with a special flourish are inferior or, one might better say, dependent individuals. A young man uses in his signature characters from the signatures of the three persons whom he most detests (his father and two teachers).

Pfister is perhaps committing a mistake in his "therapy," as far as the ultimate intentions of psychoanalysis are concerned. He carries out the so-called "relief from guilt" in such a way as to take everything away from these people, but to burden them in increased measure with a feeling of responsibility toward God, parents, etc.

GRAF speaks of a fine poetic figure in D'Annunzio's novel *Lust* [*The Child of Pleasure*]: at a crucial point, and in a characteristic context, while talking with the person whom she had loved in her youth, the heroine plays with her wedding ring and absentmindedly pulls it off her finger.

In an earlier paper on *The Flying Dutchman*, Graf tried in vain to find an elucidation of the motif that plays such a crucial role in Wagner's poetic work and in his life: intruding into a marriage and snatching the woman away toward himself. Graf is now in a position to offer an explanation for this. It was repeatedly rumored that Geyer, who married Wagner's mother when the child was six months old, was Richard's father. Wagner himself spread these rumors abroad, and one gets the impression that a fantasy of Wagner's is involved in this. If this is true, then that Wagnerian main motif is to be traced back to an identification with Geyer (throughout his life Wagner wore the painter's garb that was characteristic of Geyer)—whom he assumed to have committed adultery with his mother.

PROF. FREUD remarks, in reference to the passage from D'Annunzio, that, in the second edition of the *Psychopathology of Everyday Life*, he (Freud) quoted the same symptomatic action as an accomplishment of Duse's, and that therefore one of them must have taken it from the other (GRAF: *Lust* was written before D'Annunzio got to know Duse). The Wagner-motif goes back to the "maternal aetiology": (1) the wife of another man; (2) ill-repute = fantasy of adultery.

102

SCIENTIFIC MEETING *on April 6, 1910*

Present: Prof. Freud, Adler, Federn, Friedjung, Furtmüller, Graf, Heller, Hitschmann, Oppenheim, Rank, Reitler, Sadger, Steiner, Stekel, Tausk, Wittels, Jekels.

Federn proposes Dr. Margarete Hilferding, and Stekel Dr. Frischauf for acceptance as members.

An Epilogue to the Congress

PROF. FREUD opens the session with a brief review of the Nuremberg Congress and the resolutions on organization passed there; the implementing of these resolutions will signify a new period for the activities of our society. The requirement that we fall into line with the general association as a whole, as well as into competition with other local groups, changes some of our previous arrangements. The members of the society have been up to now Freud's guests; now this is no longer feasible. The society must constitute itself and elect a president; at the same time this offers the opportunity to undertake some other changes. Freud would rather not be president of this new society, because the society would in some respects thereby be hampered. He deems Adler to be the personality suited to take over the leadership and therefore proposes his election.[1] There are two wishes that Freud would like to impart to the new society: (1) that personal relationships be better cultivated; up to the present this has not happened in the way that would be desirable. The second wish would be that an opposition not be created between Vienna and the other centers, but that the Vienna group remain on good personal terms with them. He will be glad to cooperate as a member of the new society.

ADLER, in order to dispel certain misunderstandings, gives an account of the happenings at the Nuremberg Congress and of the ensuing conduct of the Vienna School; it was forced into a position of opposition by a clumsy memorandum against which one had to defend the Vienna school, and its younger members in particular, and to protect them. Adler now criticizes the reasons for this entire action, which originated with Freud, and comes to the conclusion that some of these reasons were undoubtedly exaggerated; in this overestimation of perils, there lies a sort of self-underestimation. On the basis of all these deliberations, the Vienna school tried at the Congress to eliminate the harshness of this "Memorandum," and for the most part was successful.

We can therefore say today that from now on we belong to an association that chooses its president in a free election by members with equal rights, like every other association. The intentions of the memorandum were bound to force us to take a definite stand, and with this the demands of which Freud has spoken are already fulfilled. At the Congress, the feeling was unanimous that we must band together; this is the first step forward that will bring us closer to the others and will surely make itself felt to a still higher degree in our further works. If we wish to progress further in our intentions, we must take measures some of which are, to be sure, "music of the future" [*Zukunftsmusik*], but others can and should be discussed even at this time.

1. We must give up our seclusion and seek to bring suitable persons to our meetings and to let them take part in our work. With the increase in our numbers, and the strengthening of our productive capacity, our influence among the body of physicians and in society will grow. The realizing of this perspective is likely to come into collision

[1] The fact that Freud proposed to make Adler president of the Society, despite considerable differences in their outlook, is one more proof of Freud's great tolerance.

with some of our cherished customs. Above all, we have to concern ourselves with an appropriate meeting place.

2. As far as the scientific work itself is concerned, our pleasure in working [together] will unquestionably increase, as soon as we feel we can have confidence in one another. And this will enable us to enjoy in the future too the so far unchallenged reputation of the Vienna school as the leading scientific force. No one among us has any plans for a direction that is hostile toward that of any other group; on the contrary, we shall gladly learn from them, as well as give them support as far as we can and as they wish. Above all, we must strive to further precisely our scientific training and to lay main stress on it, for nothing will protect us as effectively from unjustified attacks. To make more concrete proposals at this time would not yet be in place.

Our group is planning to publish a monthly journal on psychotherapy and analysis. The journal will, of course, be open to everyone, but the Viennese first of all must be asked to collaborate. Finally it will become necessary for suitable individuals occasionally to offer courses on psychoanalysis and its application.

Thus there are opening up rather large perspectives, about which everybody present is asked for his advice.

Finally, regarding Freud's proposal to elect him (Adler) as the leader, in his opinion this would be a superfluous act. Freud ought to retain the leadership, but should be relieved by a committee from the oppressive troubles of administrative duties.

PROF. FREUD wishes to add only a few words, mostly by way of concurring. Above all, he is pleased to hear that we legitimize both steps now that they have been taken, and it gives him particular satisfaction that we are forming a personal union. He wants to disclose now that he would never have handed over the leadership to Zürich, had it come to that point two years earlier.[2]

[2] Freud's decision to hand over to Jung the leadership of the psychoanalytic movement seems in the first place to have been a consequence of his disappointment in the Viennese body of physicians, who treated him so badly, and also probably a consequence of some disappointment in the Viennese members of the society, who did not completely fulfill his hopes and expectations and often quarreled among themselves. On the other hand, Jung was a representative of academic psychiatry and of a respected University clinic. These circumstances led Freud to hope for a better reception of psychoanalysis in legitimate university circles.

It was not the fear of danger that prompted him to this resolve, but one personal and several objective motives. First of all, he feels the need of putting himself in the background. Then, he does not consider Vienna to be a fit soil for something [like this] to thrive in. It was Ferenczi, under Freud's own influence, who drew up the memorandum that was so unfavorably criticized; censorship was not present in these proposals, nor was it intended. In one respect, certainly, the statement was positive: it concedes to the president the right of representation on the outside, and the right to exercise an influence upon controversy.

Prof. Freud suggests the election of a three- to four-member committee, that would engage in the working out of detailed proposals.

STEKEL cannot imagine how we would exist [as a society] without Freud—who seems to harbor deep hatred toward Vienna. Stekel is the last who would not gladly accept Adler [as leader of the group], but do we really have to give up Freud? Perhaps a compromise could be created to the effect that Freud retains the leadership, as he has up to now, and that Adler function as vice-president. Circumstances demand reorganization; there exists the will to work together and intensively. In establishing our central organ, we have no intention of opposing Zürich; but we do want to make use of our experiences, in which we are ahead of them, and to show that Vienna is the soil in which analysis first flourished. Stekel's proposal is the following: that Freud retain the intellectual leadership, and that Adler join as vice-president, to function [also] as organizer and business manager. The only form through which to make possible continued work is, to be sure, the election of a committee.

FEDERN, too, stresses the absence of any hostile intentions toward Zürich and justifies the conduct of the Viennese at the Congress by referring to some offensive stipulations contained in the Memorandum. If one can speak of a discord between Vienna and Zürich, the reasons lie in the aloof behavior of the members from Zürich.

Even though it is difficult to imagine the old patriarchal relationship ceasing to exist, surely Freud has good reasons for his decision, and to fight against them will, he supposes, be in vain.

Federn's *proposal* aims at the following: if Adler is made chairman (and Federn would propose this title), Freud should be elected honorary president, which offers the opportunity for him to preside in our circle as before.

TAUSK expresses his feeling that something very saddening is taking place. He cannot make any positive statements because he did not take part in the Congress, and therefore would like only to express his view with regard to some of what he heard here today. No soil is so well suited as that of Vienna for the dissemination of Freud's teachings, and that is, probably, precisely because it is a sick soil. It won't do to consider psychoanalysis merely from the medical standpoint; this does not offer a true picture of what our conception of psychoanalysis should be. Tausk then makes a comparison with Darwinism, which was a scientific religion just as psychoanalysis is; no society for the dissemination of Darwinism was founded, and yet today it is part of the consciousness of every civilized man. It is out of these considerations that the speaker expresses his opinion against the formation of an association. At best he would evaluate the founding of a society as an expedient for maintaining the decorum of individual members. In any event, no one, under any circumstances, wants to give up Freud's participation. If the organizational direction is to fall to somebody else, then as far as Tausk is concerned, too, Adler is the only one to be considered.

SADGER thinks that he has observed that Freud has been fed up with the Viennese for the last two years now. However, the fact is that we need him. If we are ahead of the Zürich group, that fact must be attributed to Freud's steady leadership, instruction and advice. Stekel would therefore like to second Federn's proposal to make Freud honorary president.

HITSCHMANN gives his impression of the Congress, which is that the Zürichers, as a breed, are totally different people from us in Vienna. But for all of that we do not underestimate our inner qualities.

As far as the reconstitution [of the Society] is concerned, we have nothing against that form so long as, with this change, we do not have to do without Freud's personal influence. The rest is after all purely a matter of form, since the society will not act against Freud's wishes in whatever may be involved.

From all that has happened we can learn the lesson that we must take our cause more seriously, must impose upon ourselves somewhat more self-discipline in regard to our scientific work, and must not permit ourselves any blemish.

FREUD, in order to dispel some misunderstandings, once more gives the reasons why he regards Vienna as an unsuitable soil; he explains for how many compelling reasons Zürich seems to be disposed in advance to be the location of the center.

He explicitly stresses that it is a mistake to think that he is considering withdrawing from working together and from personal relationships; all of that is to remain completely [as it has been]. The proposal to make him honorary president cannot be carried out, simply because the society makes no provision for such a position. We are concerned here with organization, and it would be useful if a younger worker were to step to the head. Adler would be in many respects unhampered with regard to the others. This freedom is our compensation for the transfer of the center to Zürich.

STEINER calls attention to the fact that the discussion has not taken us any further than we were before, the more so since it has already been established that Freud does not in the least wish to retire.

However, even for purely external reasons it is altogethr unthinkable to number Freud simply as one member among others. One must therefore establish from the start that Freud is honorary president.

WITTELS makes a comparison between the Zürichers and the Viennese, a comparison in which he goes into the different conditions under which psychoanalysis is taught here and there. The Zürichers are trained clinically to become Freudians; they would probably champion any other doctrine with the same righteousness and the same tearful tone. The Vienna society, on the other hand, has grown historically; each one of us has a neurosis, which is necessary for entry into Freud's teachings; whether the Swiss have, is questionable.

Wittels shares Tausk's impression (his own characterization) of something terribly sad taking place. Up to the present we were pretty much the opposite of a society, and what is sad is simply that we should now become a society.

The speaker then raises the question of how we could test people, in order to make it impossible for such people as the Swiss, who belong [among us] in only a superficial sense, to gain admission.

Whether or not we found a society is of secondary significance. The favorable aspect is that we are stimulated to do scientific work.

FURTMÜLLER, too, is in favor of the honorary presidency for Freud, whom one could not very well carry along as a simple member. The present speaker does not see any danger arising from the fact that the common people might get into the society as the consequence of its broadening out, and that they would then spread the doctrine in a distorted form. This has happened to all great ideas; it was the only way in which they could succeed at all. One could, first, separate the narrower circle of workers from the larger circle of those members who are merely studying and "listening in."

FRIEDJUNG, as one of the youngest members, finds the melancholy mood all the more understandable, but thinks that it ought not to influence our further decisions. Whether the foundation of a society is the right thing, the future will have to show. We cannot ensure Freud's leadership by making him our honorary president, but rather by making him want to continue to be our leader. It does not matter in what form this occurs. It is a spur for us to work more intensively and more critically than up to now, so that we can stand up in front of Freud and the general public.

REITLER also had an impression of sadness at the beginning of the discussion, but during the course of the evening the mood has become brighter. The foundation of the society is to be welcomed as opportune. But to plan mass enrollment of members would be decidedly detrimental.

Finally, he suggests that we first found our society and then nominate Freud as honorary president of the entire association.

STEINER agrees fully with the previous speaker's opinion about mass enrollment, which he too considers to be very harmful. The conditions for admission should remain as strict as they have been up to now.

FREUD refers to the fact that his resignation is not only a nominal one. In order to shift away from one aspect of the discussion, he declares his readiness to take part in the society's work in the following form: we forgo any title-giving and accept him as "*scientific chairman*," whose function would be, of course, strictly distinguished from that of the president.

Freud is elected scientific chairman by acclamation.

FREUD now makes the following proposals:

1. election of a committee
2. election of a president

Ad 1. following Freud's suggestion, Adler is elected president of the local Vienna group by acclamation.

Ad 2. Adler, as president, moves a resolution concerning the committee, which should consist of the following gentlemen: Messrs. Federn, Hitschmann, Rank, Steiner, and Stekel.

ADLER asks all the other gentlemen to forward wishes and suggestions in writing to the committee—that is to say, to the secretary.

FREUD moves that the discussion be continued next Wednesday, and for the time being places at the society's disposal the meeting place used up to now. Scientific work has to rest, of course, until the formal matters are disposed of.

STEKEL then unfolds the plan, which had already been suggested in Nuremberg, for the foundation of a journal of psychotherapy and analysis. This journal is intended to be a supplement of the *Jahrbuch* and, in addition to original scientific papers, is to contain brief communications, the reports of our meetings, and full-length reviews. Adler and Stekel should sign as the editors, and on the title page the names of Freud, Jung and others will be listed as permanent collaborators.

SADGER proposes to elect an editorial committee.

FREUD would like to offer a few suggestions concerning this plan. Above all, one ought not turn this journal into an "opposition" to Zürich but let it stand open to everybody to join in its work.

Deuticke is willing to extend the scope of the *Jahrbuch* to a journal that will appear bimonthly. This would make it possible to place without any difficulty those papers of which Stekel spoke and to take on editorial functions. Should this proposal seem unacceptable, a second would be to publish this monthly as a supplement to the original

Jahrbuch, and it would not be a hopeless undertaking to try to win over Deuticke to this proposal, too.

Freud suggests the title *Zentralblatt für Psychoanalyse.*

FEDERN repeats Sadger's proposal to appoint an editorial committee that should be as many-sided as possible, and suggests as its members Messr. Oppenheim, Furtmüller, Sadger, and Reitler.

FREUD remarks that next time, as in all business meetings, Adler will chair the meeting. The speaker further reminds the members that reconstituting the society should not cause any shifts in our secretary's position, and that he should be considered for the secretaryship of the *Zentralblatt.*

ADLER, in reference to the suggestion of an editorial committee, remarks that he is reserving the right, in case of need, to appeal to the gentlemen also in this matter and to appoint them to the editorial committee as advisers.

STEKEL, finally, moves that Sadger be nominated to the working committee that was elected provisionally. No objection is raised to the proposal.[3]

[3] Much of what was, one might say prophetically predicted in this discussion—by Tausk and Wittels—subsequently proved to be true: especially the fact that the so-called "Swiss"—Jung and his circle—despite all their positive beginnings, did not distinguish themselves in psychoanalysis.

103

SCIENTIFIC MEETING *on April 14, 1910*

Present: Adler, Federn, Prof. Freud, Friedjung, Furtmüller, Hitschmann, Joachim, Oppenheim, Rank, Reitler, Sadger, Steiner, Tausk, Wittels.

Reorganization of the Society

AGENDA

1. Presentation of and deliberations on the draft of the bylaws
2. Election of the executive committee:
   a) vice deputy-chairman
   b) treasurer
   c) librarian
   d) secretary
3. Election of the budget officer
4. Report on a meeting-place
   a) Charite (Hitschmann)
   b) Cafe Pucher, Cafe Siller (Adler)
   c) Premises of the *Gesellschaft für Kinderheilkunde* [Association for Pediatrics]
   d) Cafe Arkaden (Rank)
5. Report on the planned Monthly Journal (Adler and Stekel)

6. Proposal for a medical meeting (Adler)
7. Motion concerning the urn (Federn)
8. Suggestions for publicity (Jekels); in writing
9. Discussion of the Kraus affair (Adler)
10. Various proposals and questions (Rank):
    a) Housing of the library
    b) Establishing a library committee
    c) Proposal concerning the acquisition of a typewriter
    d) Membership list
    e) Agenda
11. Motions and interpellations[1]

ADLER introduces the draft of the bylaws with the admonition to be as brief as possible in its discussion, since the matters involved are in large part purely formal and will have no further influence on the course of our work. Nevertheless, there are a few points on which opinions may differ.

The paragraphs of the proposed bylaws will be put to individual vote, after possible discussion and proposals for changes.

Paragraph four gives rise to an extensive discussion in reference to the question of the admittance of new people into membership.

SADGER makes a motion and gives his reasons for retaining the present system of admission, and not accepting the three-quarter majority rule suggested.

STEINER is of the same opinion.

PROF. FREUD considers acceptance of the three-quarter majority rule to be more to the point under the new conditions, but proposes that three-quarters of the members of the society be required to declare themselves positively in favor of an applicant for admission [in order for him to be admitted].

FRIEDJUNG proposes a three-quarter majority of the votes cast.

STEINER proposes an amendment that provides that first the executive committee in their small circle shall decide about each applicant;

[1] In the original transcript, the eleventh point was at first: *On the Sense of Authority* (Adler). This, however, was crossed out and replaced by the eleventh point in our text.

then, if they consider the applicant acceptable, they are to place his name before the plenary session.

TAUSK makes the following suggestion: each candidate for membership is to be registered with the executive committee, who will then invite all members to make known any objections to the applicant that are factual and can be substantiated.

ADLER requests that this suggestion be noted in the next Agenda. In the balloting on this point, the following motions are carried: three-quarter majority of the votes cast, with the Steiner-Tausk amendment.

Adler proposes the following explicit supplement to paragraph 9: any undertakings on the part of individual members that take place in the name of the society, must have the approval of the executive committee.

FRIEDJUNG is opposed to this explicit guardianship; the matter is understood, in any case, by itself.

HITSCHMANN agrees that this wording would raise difficulties.

ADLER withdraws his resolution.

FRIEDJUNG moves that [a motion for] the dissolution of the society be added to those exceptional resolutions that can be passed without absolute majority, as set forth in paragraph 10.

FURTMÜLLER, in reference to paragraph 12, draws attention to the fact that, under the conditions [as indicated], the court of arbitration would be a game of chance, since the president would be elected by lot.

TAUSK concurs.

RANK proposes that, in order to prevent such a situation from happening, two arbiters be chosen by each disputant.

FEDERN proposes that the resolution on having one arbiter for each disputant be left as it is, but that an election of the president by lot be ruled out.

Federn's proposal passed.

Item II of the agenda: provisional selection of an executive committee.

Chairman: Adler
Deputy-chairman: Stekel
Treasurer: Steiner
Librarian: Hitschmann
Secretary: Rank

Item III: Selection of auditor: Federn

Item IV: Meeting-place

Resolution: To leave the final decision to a committee composed of Messrs. Adler, Friedjung, Hitschmann, and Steiner, the general membership having decided in principle in favor of a place that could be rented from some other scientific society (not a restaurant or a cafe).

Item V: For the present, Adler cannot yet report anything definite about the planned journal, since Jung's reply to the announcement of our plan as well as to Deuticke's proposal to have the *Jahrbuch* appear monthly, has not yet been received.

SADGER emphasizes that the prospects of success for the journal are so good that we are not dependent on Deuticke.

Item VI: ADLER stresses the need for a medical meeting in order to establish fundamental rules.

On item VII, FEDERN moves that the compulsory discussion, the order of which was set by lot, be abolished and that a free discussion be allowed, in which the speaker is at liberty to reply immediately, and counter-reply and rejoinder are also permitted.

PROF. FREUD no longer has any objection to doing away with the urn.

He moves to leave the details and the whole form of discussion to the chairman.

Furthermore, he proposes the nomination of several—possibly three—chairmen, who would alternate regularly, and suggests for this position the president, his deputy and the scientific chairman. Besides, the president should be at liberty to let any member of the society chair certain scientific meetings.

Freud's motion carried after a lengthy debate.

Item VIII: Jekels proposes, in writing, the motion to consider intensive publicity; as appropriate measures, he suggests:

1. Courses for physicians, pedagogues, etc.
2. Touring lectures in various Austrian cities
3. Lectures, especially in young people's academic associations

ADLER is of the opinion that these very noteworthy proposals cannot be taken up in today's discussion; debating and implementing them must be kept for a more propitious time.

Item IX: Regarding the attack that was made in the last issue of the *Fackel,* Adler comments that no reaction whatsoever should be forthcoming out of this circle.

FREUD adds the further admonition to avoid in private conversation, too, making any remarks about this matter. For the Vienna Psychoanalytic Society, "The Kraus Affair" does not exist.[2]

In large part, there is no discussion on point X:

a) The library will be housed in the new place.

b) The library committee has been replaced by a librarian.

c) A revision of the membership list will take place on the occasion of the collection of the annual dues for the *Internationale Psychoanalytische Vereinigung* [International Psycho-Analytic Association].

d) Points on the agenda are to be discussed as the need arises, and the specific resolutions are then to be gathered together.

Item XI: STEINER proposes establishing an account for the Society at the *Postsparkasse* [Savings Bank] in order to simplify [finances] and to make the financial management less expensive.

JOACHIM proposes Dr. Weiss, director of the Institution in Rekawinkel, as a member.

[2] From then on, Kraus remained maliciously antagonistic toward psychoanalysis.

FEDERN proposes Dr. Hilferding, and suggests an amendment to the effect that all candidates for membership may attend the meetings as guests before their definitive acceptance.

ADLER considers this suggestion important and entirely worthy of approval. He proposes to reserve two evenings for meetings with guests.

STEINER is opposed.

PROF. FREUD indicates the possible disadvantages of such meetings with guests:

1. In the first place, they will occur too frequently.
2. We may not be sufficiently careful in the registration of guests.

Another possibility would be to give applicants for membership an opportunity to present a "trial lecture," so that one could become informed about their scientific capabilities.

In the balloting, the following motion is carried: applicants for membership may attend the meetings only after their acceptance. In appropriate cases, the president may request a trial paper.

During the debate about the nomination of Dr. Hilferding and Dr. Weiss, SADGER declares himself to be opposed in principle to the admission of women.

ADLER would be in favor of admitting female physicians, as well as women who are seriously interested in the subject and want to collaborate with us.

PROF. FREUD would take it as gross inconsistency, were we to exclude women on principle.

In the test balloting conducted after Freud's remark, it turns out that three out of eleven votes are opposed on principle to the admission of women; this will oblige the president to proceed with extreme caution on this point.

PROF. FREUD could only lend his support to the candidacy of Dr. Weiss—from the standpoint of science. However, with regard to his personal character, Freud does not consider him to be trustworthy. Moreover, his appearing on the membership list may not be a matter of indifference to Dr. Weiss.

JOACHIM describes Weiss' character as altogether trustworthy, but will ask him again whether, in view of the prospective publication of his name, he wants to maintain his candidacy.

ADLER calls attention to a resolution passed a few days ago in Hamburg by the neurologists of Germany, to boycott those sanitaria in which Freud's method of treatment is employed.

Dr. Hilferding's candidacy is referred to the executive committee.[3]

[3] We append the first two paragraphs of the statutes which became effective on October 21, 1910:

"Paragraph 1. Name and seat of the Society.

"The society is called *Wiener Psychoanalytische Vereinigung* [Vienna Psychoanalytic Society], and has its seat in Vienna.

"This society presents itself as an independent society affiliated with the scientific association: *Internationale Psychoanalytische Vereinigung.*

"Paragraph 2. Purpose of the Society.

"The society aims to cultivate and further the psychoanalytic science founded in Vienna by Prof. Dr. Sigmund Freud, to take in the area of pure psychology as well as the application of psychoanalysis in medicine and the arts. The society is a scientific one and has the further purpose of supporting among its members all endeavors that are directed toward the acquisition and spreading of psychoanalytic knowledge. The society has the additional task of maintaining intellectual contact and the interchange of scientific ideas with the International Psycho-Analytic Association and with the other affiliated societies."

Paragraph 4 of the first section is as follows:

"Members of the Society

"The society is composed of actual and honorary members. Everyone can become an actual member, who upon the proposal of an actual member or an honorary member and after prior deliberation of the executive committee, has been accepted by the plenary assembly by a three-quarter majority of secret ballots, and has been declared admitted by the executive committee. The names of candidates are to be made known to all members of the society at least a fortnight before the election is to take place; votes may also be cast in writing. A candidate will be notified of rejection without being given the reason for it."

104

SCIENTIFIC MEETING *on April 20, 1910*

Present: Adler, Federn, Freud, Friedjung, Furtmüller, Heller, Hitschmann, Oppenheim, Rank, Reitler, Sadger, Steiner, Stekel, Tausk, Wittels.

Philipp Frey as a guest.

PRESENTATION

A Report on Dr. Baer's Publication Suicide in Childhood *(Leipzig 1901) Followed by a Discussion of Suicide in General*

SPEAKER: PROF. OPPENHEIM

AGENDA

I. Report on a meeting-place; resolution.
II. Resolution concerning the library.
III. Registration of new applicants for admission:
   1. First lieutenant Dr. Stefan Maday (Adler).
   2. Dr. Ludwig Jekels, Bistrai (Rank).
   3. Dr. Hilferding (Federn).

IV. Communications by the president.
V. Proposal to announce the lectures in medical journals (Stekel).
VI. Report of the secretary.
VII. Motions and Interpellations.
VIII. Prof. Oppenheim: Report on von Baer, *Suicide in Childhood*, followed by a discussion about the topic of suicide in general.

Point I.

ADLER reports that 12 Kronen per evening will have to be paid for the rental of the premises.

STEKEL expresses misgivings about this new financial burden.

STEINER finds the premises as well as the rent quite acceptable and moves: (1) to institute a subscription; (2) to raise the membership dues—that is to say, to create two categories of members. For those who are practicing psychoanalysts, the total yearly contribution (including dues to the International, as well as library and other expenses) will amount to K 60; for laymen, K 30.

The treasurer announces that an anonymous gift of K 200 has been received to start the subscription.

ADLER puts to a vote Steiner's proposals, which are in accord with everybody's thinking; both motions are passed.

FEDERN stresses that the division into two classes of membership cannot, of course, be strictly enforced, and that the executive committee can certainly decide about possible further reductions.

Ad II. The librarian is authorized to purchase a bookcase and to have the library shipped.

Ad III. Adler moves to vote on Drs. Hilferding and Jekels next time. Votes will then be cast anonymously; those members who are absent, all of whom will have been notified, may vote in writing.

First-lieutenant Dr. Stefan Maday is nominated for admission; available information about him is to be directed to the executive committee.

Ad V., Stekel's proposal, SADGER believes that this will cause difficulties.

FURTMÜLLER thinks that it might entail the registration of a number of guests, whose introduction it would still be preferable to leave to personal recommendation.

ADLER proposes to remove this point from the agenda temporarily, and to postpone it for discussion at another time.

PRESENTATION

Suicide in Childhood

(on the basis of Dr. A. Baer: *Der Selbstmord im kindlichen Lebensalter*[1])

SPEAKER: OPPENHEIM

The problem of suicide among children is only a part of the great general problem of suicide in general; but it is in part a problem of a certain [degree of] independence, and thus also capable of being dealt with separately.

If every act of suicide, insofar as it negates the strongest human instinct—that of self-preservation—is felt to be something counter to the norm, this [latter] feeling is infinitely stronger where the suicide of children is concerned. And this emotional judgment is fully sustained by the findings of statistical studies of suicide, which show that the overwhelming majority of suicides occur at past fifteen years of age. Thus, among the abnormal contemners of life, the young represent an abnormality carried to the second power. It follows from this that an explanation that is sufficient for adult suicide does not thereby include a solution to the riddle of suicide in children. If we consider in addition that the [present] increase in the frequency of suicide among children is not parallel to an increasing frequency of adult suicides, we become convinced that a particular sort of causation is responsible for the suicide of a child. These specific causes, however, ought to be investigated individually.

Baer believes that he can narrow down the problem even further.

[1] Dr. A. Baer: *Suicide in Childhood*. The manuscript of Oppenheim's review is enclosed in the Minutes of this meeting. The translation was made from this manuscript.

Among the suicides under fifteen years of age, those under ten are, again, a vanishing minority. Therefore, they cannot be the subject of an investigation that aims at establishing laws; such an investigation must concentrate on the most frequent cases—those that belong to the age group between ten and fifteen years.

This being the age at which school is the center of a child's life, one can be, from the standpoint of whether the school exercises any influence on the suicide of schoolchildren, actually quite satisfied with this limitation.

But whether it is justified in the face of the insight gained by Prof. Freud—the insight into the surpassing significance of the first years of life for all later development, particularly all development that is contrary to the norm—whether it is not precisely the rare cases of suicide in tenderest childhood that are the most informative ones, that question I can only raise. Its solution I must leave to those who are better qualified than I.

In any case, however, fundamental to a solution of the problem is what forms a major part of Baer's investigation—i.e., ascertaining the distribution in place and time of the phenomenon that is to be explained.

As far as regional distribution is concerned, the suicide of children is a frequent phenomenon, not only here but also in Germany, Switzerland, Italy, France, and England; it is therefore a subject for statistical observation.

Accordingly, one can judge our Viennese journalists who, on the occasion of the most recent suicides of schoolchildren, acted quite as though causing them were exclusively the national privilege of Austrian high-school [*Gymnasium*] Professors.[2]

The important question of whether child suicide occurs more often in certain countries than in others, Baer has no answer to. On the other hand, he does discuss the distribution between city and country and, on the basis of the Prussian statistics, comes to the conclusion that the oft-repeated assertion that suicide is more frequent among children of industrial districts and larger cities has not been corroborated by statistics.

[2] In Austria, a [*Gymnasium*] high-school teacher is called Professor.

If the geographical survey of suicide among children leaves open quite a few questions, the organization of facts from the chronological viewpoint appears all the more telling.

It cannot be asserted that the suicide of children has become prominent only recently. Even the philosopher Montaigne, in the sixteenth century, mentions it as a sad sign of the times. In Prussia, statistics about child suicides can be traced back to 1780. But it is only in the nineteenth century that the cases have become frequent; an increase from year to year is clearly apparent. In Prussia, for instance, from 1869 to 1898, the annual average increased from 38 to 65. If one computes how many out of 100,000 children under 15 years of age perish in one year by suicide, the result is, for 1871, a figure of 1.2; for 1898, it is already 2. There is, therefore, an increase in the frequency of suicide among children as well as among adults; as has been mentioned before, however, no analogy is demonstrable.

A correspondence between the two stages of life does become evident, however, with regard to the proportion of the sexes.

Among adults, 80.05% of the suicides are men, 19.95% women. Among the youthful suicides, there are 78.91% boys and 21.09% girls.

A shift in this proportion, which is controlling for all stages of life, occurs only in the period from 15 to 20 years of age. In that period, the proportion of girl suicides goes up to 32%. That this is due to the more rapid pubertal development of girls did not escape even Baer's attention, although he is otherwise rather blind to the significance of the sexual factor.

With this we have already come upon the core problem: the question of the motive for child-suicide.

On this point too, the official statistics, based on the official inquiries that are made into every suicide, offer continuous records.

From these Baer first takes the fact that, in the kingdom of Prussia, of 979 suicides under fifteen years of age during the period from 1884 to 1898, 79 (8.07%) were mentally ill. But this proportion undergoes a considerable rise if the number of suicides as a result of indefinite causes is deducted. That number is 351—that is, 36% of all cases. Of the remaining 628 cases with known causes, 79 are mentally ill—that is, 12.57%. Actually, however, the number of mentally ill persons among youthful suicides is still greater, since it is precisely among those whose motives remain unknown, that there may be concealed many with psychic defects that are difficult to recognize.

Baer specifies criteria according to which, he believes, one can recognize, from the circumstances of the deed itself, mental illness as its motive. Employment of unusual and cruel means of commiting suicide—such as burning oneself to death in an oven or by means of gasoline; repeated suicide attempts; obvious, long-lasting vagrancy—place on a suicide the stamp of the pathological.

Another and larger number of youthful suicides, after a more thorough examination of their total behavior, must be assigned to the category of the psychically inferior or the degenerates. This, to be sure, seems to be a rather motley crew. For, in Baer's own words, one must think of, as included in it, "all shadings of innate and acquired weaknesses" of the nervous system, the various degrees of congenital psychopathic disposition that Koch[3] brings together into the concept of "psychopathic inferiorities," and Magnan, Möbius, Strümpell[4] and others into the concept of congenital degeneration. I, with my layman's understanding, cannot help being astonished that acquired nervous debility is placed without ado on the same footing with congenital debility, or is even represented as disappearing altogether behind the latter. For Baer lays all his stress on the inferiority that is due to descent from inferior parents, especially alcoholics. But what to the speaker seems to be the essential point is that an inferiority is present at all. For whether it be acquired or congenital, it will have the effect that any discord, any minor vicissitude in a child's life is not met by an equivalent power of resistance; becoming "sick of life" is the

[3] J. L. A. Koch (Cannstadt): *Die psychopathischen Minderwertigkeiten*, 3 vol., Ravensburg, 1890-1893 [*Psychopathic Inferiorities*].

[4] Valentin Magnan (1835-1916), French psychiatrist. *Psychiatric Lectures* (translated by Möbius), Leipzig, 1891-1894. The speaker refers to the second and third issue: *Über die Geistesstörungen der Entarteten* ["On the Mental Disturbances of Degenerates"], 1892.

Paul Julius Möbius (1835-1907) *Über Entartung* [*On Degeneration*] Wiesbaden 1900. (cf. Vol. I, Minutes 14.)

Ludwig Strümpell (1812-1899) German psychiatrist: *Die paedagogische Pathologie, oder die Lehre von den Fehlern der Kinder. Versuch einer Grundlegung für gebildete Eltern, Studierende der Paedagogik, Lehre, sowie für Schulbehörden und Kinderärzte.* [*Pedagogic Pathology, or the Theory of Children's Defects. An Attempt to Present Fundamentals for Educated Parents, Students of Pedagogy, Teachers, School Authorities and Pediatricians*] Leipzig 1st ed. 1890, 4th ed. 1910.

immediate result. Without knowing, however, Baer himself considerably limits, in my opinion, the significance of inferiority when he admits that, even in normal children, a quite trivial motive, such as fear of punishment, may lead to suicide—because the child's thinking, weak as it is in its ability to differentiate, and because of the sparseness of its associations, easily overestimates the importance and the range of phenomena.

But suicide does not always occur on a given occasion, with explosive suddenness; often it also appears as the result of chronic melancholic depression, during the course of which suicidal ideas force themselves again and again upon the person's mind. Such depressions may have a thoroughly pathological character. Baer reports, for instance, about a fourteen-yaer-old girl, a shoemaker's daughter, who, affected by a disposition that was given to excesses, fell prey to continuing anxiety, and, as a result of this anxiety, felt constant impulses to commit suicide. Now she wanted to throw herself from a high place, now to thrust a knife into her heart, now to jump into the water. After fighting against these ideas for four weeks, the child recovered—that is, for the time being. In her later life, the impulse to destroy herself returned and gradually passed over into insanity. But if melancholia is rooted in grief, privations, continuous maltreatment, then it is actually the appropriate reaction to the circumstances of life; suicide that issues from that emotional state would seem to be a heroic cure rather than a manifestation of illness.

So too, in regard to the suicide who is given to melancholic reflections, I find missing in Baer's work the distinction between a manifestation of a pathological state of mind and what can be understood in terms of a normal psyche.

If, then, Baer in the statistical material differentiates those cases in which the deed was preceded by a depression of long standing from cases in which an acute affect was the cause, then he is seizing upon an entirely external criterion and not the psychical characteristic of suicides.

However, I believe that I must go even further and declare that, from statistical data, no information whatsoever can be obtained about the motives for suicide. I can save myself the trouble of offering detailed criticism if I let the matter speak for itself—i.e., if I read to you the in part meaningless, in part ambiguous, in part synonymous headings; in the Prussian statistics for the years 1884-1894, the following are ticked off:

repentance, shame and remorse, anger and strife, mental illness, passion, weariness with living, physical suffering, grief, vice, unknown causes.

More valuable than a thousand cases pigeonholed under such schematic headings would be a real understanding of just a few. Dr. Baer sensed that too, and he therefore followed the data of official statistics with a compilation of his own of twenty-five cases, the more intimate circumstances of which he tells in detail.

But if he reports, in a journalistic vein: "Because of fear of punishment, the ten-year-old girl R. jumped out of the kitchen window of her parents' apartment on the fouth floor. The child suffered multiple serious injuries," that is not a real contribution, but merely a paraphrasing of the statistical data.

And the point at which Dr. Baer stops is indeed the point at which the problem of the psychologist only begins.

Why was the child so excessively afraid of punishment—which, to be sure, belongs among the normal unpleasantnesses of child-life—that she fled from it into death?

On the basis of subsequent statements about the influence of the family on youthful suicide we could, of course, think that ill-treatment that the girl had suffered from her parents on previous occasions had intensified her anxiety to such a degree that she resolved to destroy herself. Surely, however, we may also consider the possibility of psychic inferiority. However, we cannot come to a decision [about this] because, for us to be able to do so, the author would indeed have had to provide us with more material.

With what lack of understanding the author passes by the real problems is especially clearly shown in the section mentioned previously, in which the influence of the family on child suicide is discussed. He says there that the death of a beloved member of the family can bring a child to the sudden resolve to depart from life. As evidence thereof he tells of a fifteen-year-old boy who after his mother's death, sank into melancholia and was subject to compelling ideas of suicide; further, of a thirteen-year-old girl who threw herself into the Seine because, without her father, who had disappeared a year earlier, she did not want to live any longer.

Whoever stands on the ground of Freudian psychology will suspect the existence of an erotic conflict in this suicidal love of the girl for her father and of the boy for his mother, and will then be able to understand how the life instinct is overpowered by the biologically equivalent sex instinct.

Baer believes, by contrast, that the increase in children's suicides must be tied in with the growing precocity of our over-sophisticated youth, who have become blasé, as a consequence of their enjoyment of all kinds of pleasure.

I find these considerations not very convincing. If there are really no children any longer, but only younger or older adults, then "child suicide," as a particular phenomenon alongside that of the suicide of adults, does not exist either. And yet, the statistics of suicide, as Baer himself has shown, does give evidence of the independent existence of this group [of suicides].

Our author, by the way, is not prevented by his strongly moral and religious principles from acknowledging that it is precisely religious promises of a blissful life after death, as urgently preached by sentimental mothers and nurses, that are quite capable, under certain circumstances, of furthering the flight from life on earth.

In this context, the author expresses another important set of ideas whose significance Prof. Freud has shown for other problems of child psychology. For Baer asserts, with reference to other researchers, that youthful suicides do not feel a disproportion between the triviality of their motives and the gravity of their decision, because they imagine death quite differently from the way in which we adults do. Yet it does not seem to me to be beyond doubt that this conception of the harmlessness of death, which attracts children to death wishes against relatives, also has the power to achieve a victory over the instinct of self-preservation, which is altogether without reflex.[5]

However, unreserved agreement is due to Baer's exposition of the roles played by imitation and suggestion in the causation of child suicide. Since the child's spiritual life is lacking in independence, any

[5] It is not clear what is meant here by an instinct without reflex.

more powerful impression that reaches him from the outside will have a compelling effect. Thus the report of an acquaintance's suicide or that of a relative or of someone the same age can imbue a child with a longing to imitate the deed. Indeed, even among adults, as has been observed in the case of prisons, suicide occurs epidemically. The same thing happens much more frequently among children. Our experience is not lacking in cases of the strongest power of proof. A fourteen-year-old boy, according to Voisin's[6] story, hanged himself after painting three crosses on the opposite wall and putting a jar of holy water at his feet. His uncle, who had often been drunk, had hanged himself in exactly the same manner after breakfast four weeks earlier. At the funeral of a boy who had hanged himself for unknown reasons, one of the choirboys who followed the casket said to his companions that he, too, was going to kill himself by hanging, and four days later carried out his threat (Durand-Fardel).[7]

One of the most powerful media of suggestion produced by the development of human civilization is the modern press. Only the Catholic Church, in its best days, had a similar power of suggestion at its disposal, and only it was hated with the same ardor, by atheists who strive after independence. *Ecrasez l'infâme,* Voltaire's fearfully blasphemous words, could exercise retributive justice if today they were aimed at the new despot in the realm of the spirit, the press.

Gentlemen, you will be amazed at this sudden outburst of deep rancor; but you will immediately recognize how well founded it is precisely at this point.

The press, which reports with lamentations each new schoolchild suicide, which with cries of rage searches for the "murderers" of the child and invariably finds them among the teachers—this press itself sees to it by means of this noisy clamor that new victims are always succumbing, and for them the material for new lamentations and new accusations keeps on growing.

Thus, I have arrived at the problem that to me represents the core of the entire question of suicide, because it concerns my own life so

[6] Either Felix Voisin (1794-1872) or Auguste-Felix Voisin (1829-1898) is referred to here. Baer does not indicate his source.

[7] Maximilian Durand-Fardel (1815-1899), "Etude sur le suicide chez les enfants," *Annales médico-psychologiques,* 1855.

painfully closely. I refer to the problem of the suicides of schoolchildren.

Is it the school, with its disciplinary system and its disciplinary measures, the subjects and the methods of its teaching, its examinations and certificates, that drives so many schoolchildren into suicide?

The evil magic of words, which not only in fairy tales and in the dark practices of superstition, but also in broad daylight, in everyday life, exercises its gigantic powers—this ancient sorcerer with whom old Socrates already struggled—if valiantly, still not always successfully—in his dialectics, wants to force a "yes" upon our tongue. School? That is, after all, many pupils. And if schoolchildren kill themselves, who should be responsible but the school?

For the man who lives from one day to the next and thinks and writes in terms of the present moment, the question is very likely settled by this magic incantation. Dr. Baer, fortunately, does not belong in that category; he has examined the problem seriously and thoroughly. And of his findings, the very first is especially valuable to me: denouncing the upper school for the suicides of schoolchildren neither dates from the present nor is it "an Austrian specialty"; all the more so, in that it was practiced in the far more disciplined Prussia, and in the last century, at the beginning of the eighties. In order to determine the justice of these accusations, the then Prussian Minister of Education, von Gossler, had a survey prepared in 1883: no less a man than Virchow[8] was among its authors. On the basis of the statistics for the years 1869-1881, the experts declared that they could not discover the slightest indication of the widely assumed increase in the number of suicides among students at institutions of higher learning.

It is much to be regretted that Baer did not give more particulars of this specific statistical survey, and did not supplement it by new material.

The path by which to reach an incontestable result is indeed clear enough. Alongside all the suicides who went to a secondary school, one has to place all other suicides of the same age-group, who attended

[8] Rudolf Virchow, the famous pathologist, (1821-1902) and Carl Westphal, psychiatrist: *Gutachten der königlich wissenschaftlichen Deputation für das Medizinalwesen, betreffend die Überbürdung der Schüler in den höheren Lehranstalten* [*Expert Opinion of the Royal Scientific Commission for Medical Matters, Concerning the Overburdening of Pupils in the Institutions of Higher Learning*] *Vierteljahrsschrift für gerichtliche Medizin und öffentliches Spitalwesen*, 1884.

other schools or were already engaged in a practical occupation.[9] One determines the proportion of the secondary-school students who have committed suicide to the total number of their colleagues, and in the same way the proportion within the other categories of youthful suicides. If the result is that proportionately no more suicides are committed among secondary-school children than among differently occupied children of the same age, then it is fully proven that the secondary school does not provide its pupils with any special motive for suicide.

Baer has unfortunately failed to conduct his investigation along these lines; for this reason the absolution with which he frees the secondary school of the responsibility for suicides is not very persuasive. What was done, however, is that our Ministry of Education, motivated by the latest suicides of schoolchildren, made an official statement to the effect that the percentage of suicides among secondary-school pupils is no greater than it is among pupils of other schools or among apprentices. Regrettably, a short declaration that is not even official appears in the newspaper; in it, only results are presented, and these not in figures. This is not equivalent to an investigation by the Central Bureau of Statistics. May we not have to wait too long for such a complete explanation! For the time being I believe that, as the result of Baer's statements and of the corresponding declaration of the Ministry, I have enough evidence to be justified in denying an even relative preponderance of secondary-school pupils among youthful suicides.

Secondary school is, then, no "specific" for suicide; it does not drive [a student] from life. But it would fail in its supreme goal—that of preparing children for life—if it did not itself include a part of this life, of this hard life, with its constant struggles, its severe defeats and its hard-won victories. Whoever sees school in this light—and one ought not scold him for being a word juggler, if he describes his conception as "alive"—may demand that no more responsibility be ascribed to the microcosm of school for youthful suicides than is ascribed to the macrocosm of society for that of adults.

How great this guilt, then, is evaluated as being is determined solely by the judge's *Weltanschauung*. The followers of the compassionate Schopenhauer will surely judge it to be infinite.

[9] School attendance was compulsory only up to the age of fourteen.

Is school then—and the life that was snuffed out—to find solace in the strong-spirited teachings of the superman Nietzsche? I do not know; my only advice is that school await the time when the world-reformers bring it, too, to absolute perfection.

DISCUSSION

The Chairman (Adler) points out that the speaker, by emphasizing the important points, has opened up the path to a discussion in which the personal experiences of each man with regard to this interesting topic will surely be dealt with.

In summarizing, Adler would like to mention the following points as being particularly important:

1. One must talk about "disposition";
2. The psychology of the suicide will have to be elucidated;
3. The question of motives is of great importance;
4. The problem of the influence of suggestion (press, school, etc.).

HITSCHMANN mentions as an especially gross contrast to our way of thinking the recently published work of a pathological anatomist,[10] who established certain anatomical conditions in suicides; Hitschmann would like to show that, even in such a paradoxical manner, relationships can be established between congenital characteristics and the fact of suicide.

In addition to the individual motivation, heredity unquestionably plays an important role in suicide; it is well known that, in some families, suicide is hereditary. Hitschmann reports a particularly gross case of this kind.

The theme of death and sexuality, and their close interrelationship, was often touched upon. It must also be mentioned that a compulsion can in fact lead to suicide. Attention should also be called to states of depression, about which even the family often knows nothing. Being slighted (stepchildren) will surely frequently contribute to the decision to commit suicide.

The psychology of the problem [of suicide] could also be more

[10] The anatomist referred to is probably Julius Bartell and his work: "Zur pathologischen Anatomie des Selbstmordes" (*Wiener Klinische Wochenschrift*) 1910 ["On the Pathological Anatomy of Suicide"].

closely approached by taking as a starting-point certain dreams that often represent a slump, a fall, a suicide.

In children's suicide, vindictiveness against the parents is often a factor. Some hurt is to come to them through it.

It is probably in a small number of cases that a motive of long standing is involved; in most instances, suicide is an impulsive decision, which—if that were possible—would gladly be reversed.

Hitschmann reports in closing, on the suicide of a woman teacher, an "old spinster." He was able to gain partial insight into her motives; here, too, it turned out that complex reasons were the determining factor. For fifteen years, she had entertained a platonic relationship with another teacher, who then became engaged; shortly afterwards, she committed suicide by hanging herself. Not long before, her mother had died, and she was to have taken over the management of the household, for which she had no inclination. Aside from all this, motives relevant to vanity and to health played a part.

SADGER distinguishes two sections in the paper: one of a general, and one of a more personal character.

As far as the former is concerned, the speaker recognized very well that Baer's expositions are quite superficial and presented in too general terms.

The most important cause (of suicide), in children as well as in adults, is sexuality. No one gives up his life who has not abandoned the hope for love. The factor of heredity certainly cannot be denied, yet the precipitating factor in every case is lack of love.

The suicide psychosis *kat' exochen* is melancholia; but that is an illness predominantly of older people who, on the one hand, take note of a decrease in their natural capacity to love, and on the other hand can look forward to little love from others (Hitschmann's case). With regard to suicide mania, which occurs in some families, it may be that heredity has a part in it; but the essential factor is the identification with other family members.

As far as the suicides of schoolchildren in particular are concerned, to begin with they occur most frequently at puberty, which is marked by an enormous accretion of the need for love. It is precisely in this phase, however, that the estrangement from the parents also usually occurs. There is invariably a period in which the child opens his heart to his parents, even if he does not do so in a direct manner. Most parents, however, do not understand this behavior of their child: disappointed, the child turns away and looks for understanding and love elsewhere. His good fortune if he finds them!

In puberty, the need for homosexual love (for the father) also increases; as is well known, this is transferred from the father onto the teacher. If the boy, disappointed at all turns in his hope for love, cannot gain the love of his professor either, this often provides the final impetus to a complete despair of any prospects of love, and therewith to suicide.

In summary, Sadger states: even though the accusation leveled by the press against the professors—that they are directly guilty of their pupils' suicides—is not justified, there is still a small grain of truth in it. The school ought to have more consideration for the fact that children are in a period of a great need for love, and that a certain friendly kindness, if only of an external character, should be shown them. By these means, many a schoolchild's suicide could be prevented. It would be unjust to ascribe to the professors any maliciousness in this respect; they neglect this friendly kindness out of ignorance; enlightenment of both parents and professors would be the best prophylaxis against schoolchildren's suicides.

PROF. FREUD expresses his appreciation of the paper and can only agree with the critique that the speaker exercised in regard to Baer's book. Freud is particularly in agreement with the opinion that, from the customary statistics, no judgment can be made about the matter, and that a careful examination of individual cases will contribute more toward an understanding of this difficult problem. It is, of course, above all the *attempts* at suicide that must furnish the material suitable for such an investigation, even though some of these attempts were from the beginning not intended to be effective.

It is hard to tell what share the school has in the attempted suicides of schoolchildren; we do not have enough investigations at our disposal to form such an opinion.

Only some separate comments can be made on this question.

First of all, some less frequent cases of attempted suicide: among these, the psychologically most significant one is the case, already mentioned by Sadger, of the identification with beloved persons (imitation on the basis of the same etiological demand).

Two other, rarer, conditions are the following:

1) One gets the impression that in many cases it is the fear of incest itself that drives [children] into suicide. This was true in one case in which the child put up a terrible battle against being punished at home. The boy was a masochist, to whom being punished was a full equivalent of sexual union. The idea of being spanked by his mother had the same effect as if she had held out to him the prospect of seduction.

2) Another case showed how difficult the examination of the etiology of such cases can be. This involved a young secondary-school student, who attempted suicide with a gun and severely wounded himself. This mentally normal and highly intelligent boy could not answer the question of why he had done it: he did not know, he said. When he told his family history, some time later, it turned out that his sister, having married and become pregnant, had come to visit her parents' home and that it was immediately after her departure that he had tried to shoot himself. He had, then, attempted suicide because he had not been able to bear the sight of his pregnant sister, but he had not the faintest notion of his motive for this. Subsequently, there appeared a strange corroboration of the correctness of this resolution. The young student, who had begun to be interested in psychoanalysis, discovered in the most unlikely passages of poetical works fantasies about the womb; he had a special talent for spying them out.

With regard to the psychological formulation of the preconditions for suicide, we stand only at the beginning. For the moment we can accept without hesitation the speaker's proposition that in suicide the life instinct[11] is overwhelmed by the libido. That this is no empty phrase follows from our most general psychological definition of neurosis, which we regard as a conflict between the ego instinct and the sexual instincts. The problem is, under what conditions is this over-

[11] "Life instinct" must be an error in recording. Obviously the phrase should be "ego instinct." Subsequently, Freud changed his view about the dynamic processes involved in suicide. In later works, particularly in *Mourning and Melancholia*, he reformulated his conception to the effect that the libido or life instinct is overwhelmed by the destruction or death instinct.

whelming possible, and when does it result in suicide, instead of a neurosis? According to this conception, suicide would not be so much a result of, as a substitution for a psychosis, although the two forms can, of course, combine with each other in any proportion.

These definitions, of neurosis as well as of suicide, take the duality of the human psyche more into consideration than is the case if sexuality by itself is taken as a basis, and the assertion is made that one is its masculine, the other its feminine aspect.

As far as the second point is concerned—the suicides of school children—Sadger has already said much that is pertinent. It would be interesting to ascertain whether, in point of fact, despair about the prospects of being loved is in every case the precondition of suicide; there is something alluring about that formula.

The speaker has come to the defense of the school with the idea that it should be a likeness of life, with its harshness and its struggles. To this, one must reply that school should *not* be that; it ought not forget that it does not have before it mature individuals; school must represent only the *transition* from the parental home to life. The teachers, however, take matters with bitter seriousness, whereas they would do better always to maintain toward their pupils a certain benevolent superiority.

One can fully approve of what Sadger mentioned, and perhaps add some thoughts. Teachers concern themselves too little with the question of the child's sexuality. Their duty must not be considered to have been fulfilled if they merely do not drive the child to suicide; there is more to be done than that; they must also exercise a life-maintaining influence. [The function of] school is to give the child, in this stage of his detachment from his parents, a new footing within a larger relationship. The reason why so few teachers nowadays are adequate to this task, why they slip into the mistakes just condemned (i.e., taking things tragically and ignoring the sexual factor), is connected with the growing proscription of homosexuality in our time. In suppressing the practice of homosexuality, one has simply also suppressed the homosexual direction of human feelings that is so necessary for our society. The best teachers are the real homosexuals, who actually have that attitude of benevolent superiority toward their pupils. If, however, a teacher with suppressed homosexuality comes face to face with this demand, he becomes sadistic toward the boys; these teachers hate and persecute the children because they make those "sexual demands," thereby irritating the teachers' sexuality. Just as the homosexuals are the best teachers, so the repressed homosexuals are the worst, and the strictest.

Teachers, however, have an even more difficult task. Analysis teaches us that transference is by no means unequivocal but shows, side by side with tender emotions, hostile ones, too. The teacher also has to know and to understand that; he must accomplish the intricate task of not losing his authority, even when he knows that he is the object of his pupils' mockery and scorn. This task will best be mastered by one who is also equal to the first pedagogical demand.

FRIEDJUNG likewise emphasizes the fact that statistics and case material for this subject are insufficient in all directions. Things are never as simple as they might seem to be, on the basis of such reports. In support of this view, he relates the case of a young woman who did indeed come from a family with a severe hereditary taint, but for whom the preconditions mentioned by Freud and Sadger were also true. The absence of any prospects for love are demonstrated with special clarity in this case.

Similar preconditions may perhaps be traceable for the suicides of melancholics.

From his own high-school student days, Friedjung recalls a perfect example of the homosexual professor, under whom all students studied well and with pleasure.

FURTMÜLLER thinks that, in considering the problem of suicides, the question must first be raised of whether one would not have to exclude from among the cases of suicide a large portion in which one could not speak of such an overwhelming of the life instinct; for the unsuccessful *attempt* at suicide is not rare, either.

With regard to the psychology of suicide, it must be kept in mind that man's psychological condition is such that he is unable to imagine the opposite of life.

Pupils' suicides can no longer be treated from a purely psychological viewpoint, but must be considered also from social points of view. The school is not so much guilty because of its individual teachers, as it is as a whole institution.

As against the comparison of the school with life and the challenge to this idea by Prof. Freud, the speaker would speak with more sharpness: school is not only like life; it is harsher. Not one of us could endure with equanimity the fact that, every half-year, judgment was to be passed on his activity and his general achievement.

The main point therefore remains: to remodel the institution of the school as a whole. But that is what one is not willing to do, because one lays the greatest stress on the privileges acquired by way of school. As long as that is the case, there will be little accomplished in the psychological training of teachers. In addition, one must take into consideration the fact that every modern school is a mass institution and ought not to count upon born pedagogues.

ADLER proposes, in view of the late hour, to adjourn the discussion to the next time and for the remainder of the evening to leave the floor to the speaker. Adler would also like to raise the question of whether the valuable suggestions and conclusions of this discussion should not, under the direction of a committee, be published as a pamphlet.

STEKEL expresses his willingness to present an accompanying report.

Adler's moves are carried.

PROF. OPPENHEIM, having clarified a few misunderstandings, would like to exercise an influence upon the continuation of the discussion, insofar as he would, falling back to a previous remark, set up two categories of suicides: those in whom the obvious motive appears to be fully sufficient (heroic suicides, of which history and fiction is full), and those in whom this is not the case, and for whom a deeper psychological investigation would therefore have to be instituted. Can two categories be distinguished in this way?

105

SCIENTIFIC MEETING *on April 27, 1910*

AGENDA

I. Voting on Dr. Hilferding and Dr. Jekels.
II. New Applications:
  1. Dr. Stefan Maday; voting at the next meeting.
  2. Dr. Baron Franz von Hye (Proposed by Stekel).
III. Discussion about the publication of a pamphlet on suicide.
IV. Report of the Librarian.
V. Report of the Secretary.
VI. Proposals and Interpellations.
VII. Continuation of the discussion on suicide.

Present: Freud, Adler, Federn, Friedjung, Furtmüller, Hitschmann, Oppenheim, Rank, Reitler, Rie, Sadger, Steiner, Stekel, Tausk.

Dr. Frischauf as guest.

Ad point I. SADGER moves that a letter from Wittels be read aloud, in which he expresses his opinion with regard to the first point on the agenda.

ADLER is opposed, giving as his reason that a vote that is not secret is contrary to the by-laws. After a rather long debate, he proposes to have the letter read in unofficial session.

The result of the balloting is: of fifteen valid ballots (including Wittels' letter), for Jekels thirteen yea, for Dr. Hilferding twelve yea, two nays (Ballot counters: Furtmüller, Hitschmann). Both candidates are elected.

Ad II. ADLER proposes that the voting on Maday take place next time. Furthermore, he announces the candidacy of Dr. Richard Nepallek, and STEKEL that of Dr. Baron Franz von Hye.

PROF. FREUD recommends Nepallek in every respect.

IV. Upon Adler's suggestion, a committee is appointed, composed of Messrs. Adler, Furtmüller, Hitschmann, Sadger and Stekel.

V. Books received.

VI. RANK raises the question of how distribution of the minutes should be carried out; as a result of the increasing number of out-of-town members, it has become increasingly difficult.

HITSCHMANN moves that a typewriter be bought; the motion is seconded by most, and carried. Steiner, Stekel and Rank are entrusted with the purchase.

CONTINUATION OF THE DISCUSSION

FEDERN stresses that one rarely finds a neurotic who has not at times suffered from ideas of suicide, and every psychoanalyst knows that, with regard to neurotics the danger lies in suicide. To the question of why neurotics, nevertheless, so seldom commit suicide, Federn would answer: because they are not sufficiently normal.

In Federn's opinion, suicide is a *normal* reaction to negative experiences in life.[1] This idea is consonant with what Prof. Oppenheim stressed in his conclusion, when he spoke of the two categories of suicides.

Neurotics certainly think of suicide often, but, in the way of their actually doing it, stands: (1) the instinct of self-preservation, and (2) fear (of the deed). One might think that the two are the same, and that the fear is nothing but a manifestation of the instinct of self-preservation; but we also know that neurotic anxiety originates in

[1] This was an opinion shared by many psychiatrists of that era.

repressed sexuality and that, therefore, it is more likely that the neurotic, once cured, may kill himself.

If the formula has been advanced that suicide is an overcoming of the instinct of self-preservation by the libido, it must be added that libido is also to be found on the side of the life instinct; the more there is of free libido, the more the joy in living. An individual whose libido has been disappointed will without much difficulty find a substitutive sublimation.

At this point, the suicides of schoolchildren come into question. Parents and teachers are hostile to libido and make transference difficult; hence, at least a part of the basic reason for suicide in schoolchildren lies in the teachers. To be sure, this is not the entire cause; that is a general antipathy to life. This has to do with those cases in whom suicide is not a neurotic symptomatic act, but in whom the joy of living can no longer, as a totality, endure life's torments; an insignificant incident of everyday life (school) provides the final push.

Side by side with sublimated homosexuality, the sadism of teachers plays the main role.

Finally Federn mentions a compilation of statistics by Masaryk, according to which [the frequency of] suicide is related to the decline in religiosity, and calls attention to the fact that, at the congress, Freud asserted the same thing about neurosis.[2]

STEKEL cannot corroborate Federn's experiences, according to which suicide is the reaction of a normal individual. Nor is the danger of suicide to be feared in treatment; as long as the patient has any hope for recovery he may, it is true, toy with (the idea of) suicide, or even threaten it, but he will not carry it through. On the basis of his material, Stekel can confirm Freud's statement that suicide is one of the terminal forms of neurosis.

One circumstance has not been taken into consideration up to now, although it plays an important role: the principle of talion. The suicide is tormented by a deep sense of guilt; no one kills himself who has not wanted to kill someone else. All the rest is only a precipitating factor.

Statistics show that fewer suicides are recorded in very religious countries.

[2] See: *The Future Prospects of Psycho-analytic Therapy* (1910) *S.E.* 11.

The limitation on the number of children also provides the occasion for suicide by way of increased affection.

Sadger was right in saying that hopelessness in love drives one to suicide; but he did not thereby fully exhaust the sexual aspect of the problem. There are many who commit suicide because they cannot muster the courage for sexual activity. That is the first point. The second is the one stressed by Freud—i.e., that the problem of incest is in the foreground. A third factor becomes evident in the fact that, with all suicides, suicidal ideas and attempts occur because masturbation has been given up. Suicide is nothing but the final masturbatory act ("To lay one's hand upon oneself"). Freud has called attention to the fact that masturbation acquires its significance only through fantasy. These fantasies are, in most instances, however, repressed incest fantasies.

All these factors that have been mentioned were, in cases analyzed by him [Stekel], causes for attempts at suicide. He gives a brief survey of these four cases and concludes with the case of a student whom he analyzed only today and who reveals these preconditions with particular clarity.

Thus one cannot simply say that school and the teachers are to blame. It is true, however, that school could prevent suicides if, like psychotherapy, it could bring about a transference.

TAUSK distinguishes between two different questions within the problem:

1. the question of the meaning of suicide;
2. the question of the psychic mechanism of suicide.

The two questions, however, may merely represent two different ways of viewing the problem.

Ad 1. Tausk refers to Schopenhauer's exposition on suicide, in which the philosopher says that "life is a stance." In that case suicide is an individual's illogical action *kat' exochen.* The discussant now tries to express the logical meaning of this attitude in biological terms, through which it also gains meaning for psychological consideration.

Tausk then discusses thoroughly the concept of the sense of guilt, and with this sets forth, separately, the psychological foundations for any further conflict that must lead to suicide. The sense of guilt reduces itself to the demand of civilization, which obliges us to achieve either sublimation or the repression of instinct. The father appears as the agent who expresses this demand, which on the whole he imposes the more harshly, the more guilty he has been [of failing] to fulfill it. The child soon finds this out and unconsciously criticizes the father; that is how this basic conflict comes about.

What elements in the psychic mechanism lead to the transformation of this negation into a positive factor, is not for us here to examine more clearly. That they are sexual elements is certain.

Tausk speaks, in conclusion, about several suicides by professors that occurred while he himself was at school. In many instances, teachers do become the precipitating motives for a suicide, because they are not permitted to see that the children are "loaded" with sexuality.

It is noteworthy that the Turks do not have suicide at all, because they believe in a real future in the beyond.

REITLER distinguishes three categories of suicides:

1. those in which it is a question merely of suicidal impulses;
2. those in which attempted suicides and playing with suicide are involved;
3. those that are the really serious suicides.

To us only the first category is of specific interest. Federn was right in stressing that most neurotics are tormented by suicidal impulses, which have a definitely obsessional character.

Reitler attempts to explain, along the lines of his presentation of the developmental history of the neuroses, the origin and derivation of the fear of examinations: out of the anxiety without object of the actual-neurosis (abstention from masturbation), this fear constitutes itself as a phobia, by way of anxiety hysteria; for this, there is indeed sufficient material on hand (incestuous masturbatory fantasies; father-teacher; sexual meaning of examination, according to Stekel). There is only one way out of the phobia left to the child, i.e., avoiding the examination, either by playing truant or by simulating illness; or else the obsessional impulse turns into suicide: the student must kill himself in order to escape the examination.

ADLER stresses that the problem is so complicated that all relationships of human life, as well as all psychological phenomena, come up for discussion. Some among them are so important that almost everyone has touched upon them and he too must refer to them again.

Statistics, although they certainly have their shortcomings, should not be underestimated. As for the pathological findings (Bartel),[3] it seems that in fact each and every form of organ inferiority appears in suicides (including inferiority of the sex organ). In the prehistory of suicides, one encounters exactly the same psychic causes as one does in neurotics, and therefore we must not be surprised that in analyses we so often come across the intent to commit suicide and the effort to do so. The psychic feeling of inferiority that arises out of organ inferiority is particularly prominent in childhood, and is subsequently answered by an overcompensation, in which a striving after special distinction is often manifested, a striving that leads these individuals to become excessively dependent upon the external world. Other relationships are also found besides these. Thus one could not say: persons who are so constituted must come to commit suicide.

One motif brought out in the discussion has a certain compelling quality: these are usually people in whose childhood there was already apparent the effort to punish the parents by means of illness, etc.

It would be interesting in cases of [unsuccessful] attempts at suicide to ferret out why the individual did not carry it off. In one case, the patient said that he had had no example to follow. But the fact was that he was much too feminine to kill himself. Here we come upon an important point in the psychopathology of suicide: suicide is the last attempt to perform a masculine deed. The suicide shows a strongly marked homosexuality, which is also true of the neurotic. In male suicides, one regularly encounters rebellion against the father (which again is connected with [school] examinations, inasmuch as persons are often forced [by the parent] to enter a specific field of study).

The reporter finally turns to the presentation of some of the attempted suicides that he was able to analyze.

In one girl, attempts to commit suicide were directly connected with

[3] Cf. Minutes 104, fn. 9.

masturbation, of which she was unable to rid herself. It could be demonstrated that suicidal attempts regularly followed an onanistic act. Thus there is involved a struggle against masturbation, by which she feels disgraced (feeling of degradation, of inferiority). Basically, every suicide has its source in this feeling, if one scrutinizes the material equipped with "neurotic equations" (Stekel). At the root of many female suicides, committed at the time of the menstrual period (or in Spring, or on Sundays and holidays, when the number rises considerably), there also is this feeling of degradation; in the case of the woman, it lies in the fact of being a woman.

The question of what school and teachers have to do with the suicides of schoolchildren is to be answered to the effect that, in these cases, the suicide takes from the school material what he would otherwise have found elsewhere. Nor does the suicide kill himself because of an unpleasant professor; the situation is far more complicated, almost the other way round, as was revealed in the last student suicide that Adler had the opportunity to investigate. The boy killed himself because he believed his capabilities to be unequal to the demands [placed on them]. In some of these suicides, what is involved is actually the reproduction of the relationship to the father, not in such a way that these children could refer to actual experiences of neglect, but that, out of the neurotic situation, they wanted actually to punish their teacher.

Adler then talks about three suicidal attempts that he was able to analyze and, in summarizing them, he makes the following points: suicide is the attempt at a masculine protest, of course in persons whose femininity is beyond question. These are persons who bring with them from their childhood a deep-seated feeling of inferiority and, arising out of it, unlimited ambition, of which they themselves are often completely unaware; in analysis, however, they learn to understand it very well.

PROF. FREUD is far from expressing a final opinion; yet he cannot conceal his impression that, in spite of the merit of what has been said and the sum total of suggestions given, an actual solution of the problem, in our sense, does not seem to have been found. It must not be forgotten that suicide is nothing else than a [sort of] exit, an action, an end to psychic conflicts, and that our job is to explain the character of the deed and the overcoming of the resistance [against the act of suicide].

Among the gaps one must be singled out that seems to be unavoidable. Prof. Oppenheim has set us a problem for solution; is suicide in *every case* to be interpreted as a reaction of the ego to the overwhelming power of the libido, or should one assume that there is, in addition, a suicide that results *purely* from the ego? We did well to give no answer to this question; for these matters have not become accessible to research. The approach to the complex of suicide from a study of the ill lies in *melancholia,* and at the moment nothing is known about its nature; its mechanism, especially, has not yet been studied at all.[4]

FEDERN comments that the normal individual reacts to a failure of the libido with ill-humor. The highest degree of ill-humor is melancholia. In two cases of melancholia, an excessive masturbation was demonstrable, continued into married life and to very old age. It would not seem impossible that people who react to masturbation with ill-humor become melancholics at the climacteric.

STEKEL mentions two analyses of melancholics that show the sense of guilt to be substantiated.

PROF. FREUD: The sense of guilt is encountered also in other neuroses, in all cases; the question is the specific mechanism of melancholia.

PROF. OPPENHEIM cannot consider it to be his task really to bring to a conclusion such a rich discussion, to combine all the varied suggestions under unifying points of view and to state the positive results. He can only go into entirely separate points.

First it must be established that the basic question has been left unresolved—whether the suicide is to be classed with the neurotics. In Federn's argumentation, there is a certain contradiction. Besides, the assertion that sadists tend toward [entry into] the teaching profession is indeed difficult to substantiate.

[4] It is interesting to note how cautious Freud is, even though he seems to have an idea of the solution. Indeed, guided by the key of melancholia, he later solved this problem, at least in part.

There is some interest in Stekel's thought about the talion, which finds cultural-historical corroboration in forced suicides (Orient, Athens, period of the Roman emperors). An essay, *A History of Suicide in Antiquity*[5] discusses in detail the fact that this form of killing is based on the talion principle: the punishment is supposed to cover the crime, and thereby to undo it, as it were.

Concerning the question of the relationship between suicide and religion, history gives us many explanations. The different religions oppose suicide with severe injunctions. Lichtenberg[6] remarks that suicide is more frequent in Protestant than in Catholic countries, and relates that fact to confession.

Suicide is perhaps not a problem that can be solved through consideration of the single individual; it is a mass phenomenon, and in the endeavor to understand it, one must also (as work by Hirzel[7] shows) take into consideration the conditions of place and time ("Werther fever,"[8] suggestion). The effectiveness of suggestion was, by the way, well known in antiquity (Portia imitated her father Cato when she committed suicide, and there are many other instances). Antiquity makes a curious distinction between suicide and self-immolation (self-immolation stands, indeed, at the center of Christianity). Thus here, too, new component problems arise, which may yet promise to lead to the core of the problem.

The CHAIRMAN (Stekel) thanks the speaker of the evening and all other speakers in the discussion and requests that what has been said be put together in a pamphlet.[9]

[5] K. A. Geiger: "Der Selbstmord im klassischen Altertum. Historisch-kritische Abhandlung" ["Suicide in Classical Antiquity. A Historical-critical Essay"], Augsburg, 1888.

[6] Georg Christoph Lichtenberg (1741-1799), German physicist, essayist, and aphorist.

[7] Rudolf Hirzel (1846-1917), classical philologist. The reference is to his "Der Selbstmord" ["Suicide"], *Archiv für Religionswissenschaft*, 1908.

[8] The publication of Goethe's *Die Leiden des jungen Werther* [*The Sorrows of Young Werther*] was followed by a wave of suicides, for which the novel was thought to be responsible.

[9] The pamphlet was published under the title *Über den Selbstmord, insbesondere den Schülerselbstmord* (*Diskussion der Wiener Psychoanalytischen Vereinigung*) 1910 [*On Suicide, with Special Reference to Suicides of School Children*]. See Freud's contribution, *S.E.* 11.

106

SCIENTIFIC MEETING *on May 4, 1910*

Present: Adler, Federn, Freud, Friedjung, Furtmüller, Heller, Hilferding, Hitschmann, Oppenheim, Rank, Reitler, Sadger, Steiner, Stekel, Tausk, Wittels.

Guests: Dr. Frischauf, Mr. Friedmann.

AGENDA

I. Voting on the admission of First Lieutenant Dr. Stefan Maday.
II. Announcement of the voting to be scheduled for the next meeting, concerning Messrs. Dr. Richard Nepallek and Baron Dr. Franz von Hye.
III. Report of the Secretary.
IV. Report of the Pamphlet Committee.
V. Proposals and Interpellations.
VI. Dr. Joseph K. Friedjung: Review of the book by Strohmayer: *On the Psychopathology of Childhood.*[1]

[1] Friedjung's review of the book (its original title is *Vorlesungen über die Psychopathologie des Kindesalters für Mediziner und Pädagogen*) was published in the first issue of the *Zentralblatt für Psychoanalyse*, 1911. Strohmayer was a member of the German Psychoanalytic Society for a short time. (Cf. Jones, Vol. II.)

After welcoming Dr. Hilferding, the Chairman proceeds to the agenda.

Item I. Maday elected, with thirteen votes out of the fifteen (two unmarked).

Item IV. The special committee has resolved to suggest to Prof. Freud that he write an introduction [to the discussion on the suicide of schoolchildren], and is hopeful that he will also give permission to publish his contribution in the pamphlet. The other discussions will then follow, perhaps under the title "Psychic Disposition and Motives for Suicide." It has been proposed that Oppenheim write an introductory chapter about the suicide of students. As the concluding chapter, a discussion by Furtmüller about the connection between pedagogy and suicide is planned.

OPPENHEIM expresses formal as well as objective doubts, but finally declares his willingness, with the proviso that he might possibly write under a *nom de plume*.

STEKEL and ADLER suggest that he present the topic, so to speak, without any reference to the book.

ADLER proposes that the end of May be set as the deadline for the manuscripts of the individual contributions.

STEKEL announces that Bergmann in Wiesbaden has agreed to be the publisher of the collection; he will pay 60 Marks per sheet.

Stekel further suggests that the size of the editorial committee be reduced, and once and for all the title, as well as the editorship, of these discussions be established.

ADLER nominates Sadger, Stekel, Hitschmann and himself as the members of the committee (motion carried), and moves to postpone the question of the title.

V. STEINER reports on the gratifying progress of the subscription, which was considerably augmented by a contribution from Urbantschitsch (K 200).

Further, he moves to settle the secretary's salary beginning with next year, and to establish the sum of K 800 per year for this.

STEKEL reports on the Monthly Journal, the publication of which —thanks to Freud's intervention—seems to be as good as assured.

Bergmann in Wiesbaden has practically accepted; the first issue is to appear in October. By then, three issues will have been prepared for publication. The Monthly Journal is to include: (1) brief original papers; (2) brief communications stemming from practice; passages from literary works, etc.; (3) reviews. All members of the society are, of course, invited to collaborate diligently. Prof. Freud will sign as editor; he will share the responsibility with the two co-editors, and will also exercise a corresponding influence upon the paper. A paper by Freud on the prospects of psychoanalysis will open the first issue.[2]

PRESENTATION

A Review of the Book: Lectures on the Psychotherapy of Childhood *by Strohmayer*

SPEAKER: DR. FRIEDJUNG

FRIEDJUNG first gives a general survey of the contents of the book, and an evaluation of the work as a whole: by and large it is to be welcomed with great joy, because the author moves entirely along the lines of the new research; yet, on the other hand, the book gives rise to a feeling of regret, for Strohmayer does not consistently think the problems through to the end, and, especially in his final judgment, rather holds back. If one compares this to the works published heretofore, the fact that Strohmayer has read Freud's work without prejudice and has made use of it (there is a nice example of this on page 86) is to be praised as a step forward. But the inconsistency already mentioned is particularly noticeable in the sections on acute mental illnesses and on therapy. More carefully thought out are chapters on prophylaxis and psychopathic constitution, which the reviewer discusses in more detail. In these sections, Strohmayer proves himself to be a good psychologist, who has read Freud to advantage.

With regard to the problem of *heredity*, Strohmayer essentially holds

[2] "The Future Chances of Psychoanalytic Therapy" (1910), *S.E.* 11. (Freud read this paper at the Congress in Nuremberg, 1910.)

Adler's views, without quoting him, however; the author also approaches the question of overwork.

Then he discusses extensively the effects of the *milieu,* and how childhood defects in the presence of unfavorable influences can grow into psychopathic symptoms. As to the origin of these childhood defects, some of which already have a pathological meaning of their own, Strohmayer is not always clear.

Then the author passes on to the influence of *education;* he attaches importance to the disciplining of emotional life. Not only conscious impressions, but also those that have become subconscious, exercise an influence on the psychopathic constitution.

Strohmayer then proceeds to the discussion of *sexual life.* On the interpretation of sucking as a manifestation of sexuality, he expresses himself with great reserve. On masturbation he says much that is reasonable: masturbation is not the cause of nervous disorders; it is coordinated [with them]. What is involved here is sexual precocity: the genital zone is readily stimulated, a characteristic trait of many hereditarily nervous children. He speaks, further, about the attitude of children who masturbate at an early age (shy, bashful, conscience-ridden, brooding), an attitude that results from the exhausting effort of repression directed against the erotic images. If the repression fails, the result will be elements of hysteria and of compulsion, such as are so often encountered in children; the affect of disgust is displaced upon food or materials (a case, Furtmüller's, of a boy who displayed an idiosyncrasy against touching certain materials; this idiosyncrasy was based on an unsuccessful repression of masturbation).

Strohmayer considers it very important that sexuality not be stimulated in psychopathic children. He refers to Stekel's work on anxiety neurosis (nuptial bed, *pavor nocturnus,* governess). Then he calls attention to the fact that perverse *Anlagen* frequently reach far back into childhood.

He cautions, in general, against corporal punishment of children whose emotional reactions are pathologically heightened. Overwork, too, leads to disturbances of emotional reaction and of the moral qualities, and, not infrequently, to suicide.

In discussing the *psychopathic constitution,* Strohmayer limits himself, to a great extent, to description; nevertheless, he adds a few interesting hints about its pathogenesis. He points to the disharmonies of feelings and affective life in such children (rage, fear, egotism, hypersensitivity to pain, hypochondria).

Then he depicts the intellectual behavior of psychopathic children with their onesided, yet often also universal talents. Frequently, one can also observe a periodicity in intellectual achievements. Such children are particularly imaginative; they tend to lie, but also to produce genuine delusions.

The author refers to the frequency of obsessional ideas in psychopathic children, yet does not consider sufficiently the more recent of Freud's findings (an example of compulsive doubting; compulsive fear of getting verdigris in his mouth; obsessional idea of having to stab his mother).

There follow superficial discussions about bashfulness and modesty as precursors of neuroses; Strohmayer makes an untenable distinction between the individual of an especially frigid nature, on the one hand, and the person with an abnormally strong sexuality on the other, without grasping the actual identity of these two types.

The author further points to the urge to collect, which has to do with the strongest and most worthless objects, and can often develop into kleptomania. He also mentions the frequent sleep disturbances in psychopathic children (Stekel), disturbances that sometimes have a connection with sexual excitation (lulling to sleep by means of masturbation).

Then he speaks about tics of all kinds (nail chewing, plucking of the skin and hair-pulling), and expresses in full his opinions about bedwetting, which are in harmony with Freud's. Yet he does accept the vague assumption of a weakness of the bladder, which is seldom likely to be the cause; in most cases, bedwetting is of psychogenic origin. The same is true of spontaneous voiding of the bladder when a strong affect is present (laughing, etc.)—at which time certain inhibitions also seem to disappear.

In connection with this topic, the author discusses other pathogenic phenomena, which can simulate anatomical illnesses (vomiting, diarrhea, idiosyncrasies).

The section on acute psychoses is especially weak, because it is predominantly descriptive; in the hands of the psychoanalyst, the cases mentioned would have yielded a rich crop. In particular, Strohmayer neglected to call attention here to the sexual relationships. It is striking how often he uses the word "meaningless" in this section. Freud has called attention to the fact that these phenomena are meaningful; we simply do not yet understand their meaning.

DISCUSSION

SADGER cannot share the speaker's favorable judgment. The much-praised "thoroughness" moves along well-travelled roads. Analytic technique seems to be foreign to Strohmayer; he brings up sexual matters only because it has now become the fashion, and only insofar as they are obvious. The deeper relationships he did not uncover. And, indeed, there is nothing more sexual than a normal child. Sadger himself has collected a number of observations of children, which show how early and with what enormous force sexuality appears in the child. The most valuable information about children is given by people who have themselves gone through psychoanalytic treatment. Sadger relates briefly a number of such observations, which shed light upon the anal erotism and scoptophilia of some children. In addition, one could observe something for which he would propose the term urinary erotism, a topic about which he has already announced a full-length paper for the end of May.

It is not infrequent that children practice the retention of urine with obvious feelings of pleasure; even erections appear on these occasions. Children who show urinary erotism often urinate excessively and, by comparison with other children, have intensified feelings of pleasure.[3] They have periods during which they wet themselves and cannot be trained. These are periods of enhanced libido. Later, this same phenomenon is called enuresis. The most reasonable things seem to be those that Strohmayer said about masturbation, although he left out the extremely important fantasies. Other important relationships, such as those between tics and sexuality, he has completely overlooked.

It is to be wished that Strohmayer would make himself more familiar with analytic technique and use it more courageously; for it is out

[3] The same applies to incontinence in laughing, coughing, etc. (This is a footnote in the original.)

of the analysis of the child's first impulses that there will come the most significant contributions.

ADLER, in contrast to the preceding speaker, thinks that in spite of all it is gratifying that a beginner ventures with a certain degree of courage into this field. Strohmayer's book is composed with a tolerable [degree of] knowledge of the subject, even though it remains superficial.

One of the most striking case histories in the book is the one of the boy who has the obsessional idea that he must die, in conjunction with a notion that verdigris gets into his mouth. This phobia is very widespread. According to Adler's experiences, which coincide with a hint of Freud's, involved in ideas of poisoning are fantasies about pregnancy. Strohmayer's case is one of a boy who has a feminine phobia. The idea that one must die is a phobia that many girls connect with pregnancy. (There are similar notions, according to which sexual activity is likely to be followed by tuberculosis.)

In reference to enuresis, everything the authors say about organic inferiorities is correct. Gaining pleasure from urination and defecation seems to be a rather fleeting thing. One does not find a patient who would have clung to this pleasure-gain for a long time; the anomalies, however, he has clung to. These find their explanation only when they are viewed as expressions of stubbornness; it is on this that the strongest stress falls. The case of a patient who had enuresis as a child is mentioned: during her treatment, she produced an enormous enuresis, which proved to be borrowed from her brother, whom she had believed to be her mother's lover. The enuresis, then, was the equivalent of her love for her mother and at the same time of her defiance. This interrelationship is most clearly expressed in those dreams of enuretics in which girls dream that they are urinating like boys, and boys like men.

STEKEL would like to support Adler's critique, and to caution generally against condemning a book on the basis of a review.

He, too, can confirm the connection, detected by Freud, between ideas of being poisoned and ideas of pregnancy. In a case of obsessional neurosis, the phobia of poisoning had to do, in addition, with a fear of infection of a sexual nature. Green, as the color of hope, is particularly suitable for expressing this relationship.

Strohmayer does not, it is true, present deeply penetrating analyses; yet one must give him credit for having referred at all to these matters. The future of psychoanalysis lies in what we learn from [the study of] children.

TAUSK thinks that the verdigris-fear comes from the very widespread habit children have, of putting pennies into their mouths. He was particularly interested in a thought that he had on the basis of a general reflection about analyses of children. It would be a task for analysts to agree upon a *Weltanschauung*. For where is it to lead, if one tells children things, in analysis, that contradict the present outlook of civilization? To heal neurotics means, indeed, to give them a basis that will enable them to establish a link with society. The child must be given a *Weltanschauung;* and the question is, how does this *Weltanschauung* look, that is based on Freud's teachings, when it is expressed in a general formula?

HILFERDING calls attention to the real basis of verdigris-fear, for tin-plated copper implements were formerly used almost exclusively in the household.

SADGER explicitly emphasizes the fact that his sharp criticism—which he maintains—is meant only for this intimate circle. It is self-evident that, vis-à-vis the public, one is not going to step forth against anyone who shows a willingness to concern himself with sexuality.

PROF. FREUD characterizes Strohmayer as an independent mind, who at an early age already made remarkable discoveries (he guessed correctly the derivation of obsessional impulses from repressed sadistic impulses[4]). On the other hand, however, he is a man who cultivates the wrong kind of independence; he is afraid of losing his independence if he concedes too much. Moreover, he is prevented by personal complexes from getting any further with analysis for the time being, just as everyone in general gets only as far as his personal complexes will permit.[5]

4 Strohmayer: "Zur Charakteristik der Zwangsvorstellungen als 'Abwehrneurose'," *Zentralblatt f. N. u. P.*, 1903 ["On the Character of Obsessional Ideas as 'Defence Neurosis'"] and "Über die sachlichen Beziehungen der Sexualität zu Angst- und Zwangszuständen" ["On the Factual Relations of Sexuality to States of Anxiety and Compulsion"] *J. f. P. u. N.*, 1908.

5 This is an early indication of the necessity for the psychoanalyst himself to be analyzed.

In his new publication, "On the Analysis and Prognosis of Psychoneurotic Symptoms,"[6] Strohmayer proves to be deficient in two points: (1) in regard to the estimation of the value of dream-interpretation, to which he prefers the association-experiment; (2) he believes the essence of psychoanalysis to consist in giving the patient conscious knowledge; he has never succeeded in evoking affects.

As far as the facts are concerned, his opinion about this book will turn out to be not much different from Sadger's, who declared his opinion with the relentlessness that is characteristic of him.

Some minor remarks: in the case of the boy with the verdigris-fear and the obsessional idea of stabbing his mother, the difference between the sexual-biological view that Adler has expressed and the purely psychoanalytic view can be very nicely demonstrated. The boy's symptoms are nothing but the complete expression of the Oedipus complex, in the language of the obsessional. To stab one's mother means (in the sadistic conception) to have sexual intercourse with her; in this, the boy identifies with his father. The fear of having to die arises, in the same way, from this identification with the father, for whom he had wished death. Every neurosis in boyhood years begins with the death-wish against the father. Longing and fear of pregnancy are intermingled in the fear of verdigris. The boy wishes to beget a child with his mother, and at the same time, in his identification with her, there is the fear of getting a child himself. It is thus an Oedipus complex that is still rooted in infantile sex theories. At the bottom of the fear of poisoning there is, of course, the infantile sex theory of conception taking place by way of eating.

Putting pennies into the mouth is connected with the idea that money must be that particularly valuable something that one must put into one's mouth in order to get a child.

As far as the idiosyncrasies are concerned, their entire mechanism and significance can be elucidated with the help of an example. This example has to do with the younger healthy brother of a patient, who can relate only one nervous symptom out of that brother's childhood: he was unable to eat red-currant croissants. The patient gives the following explanation for his healthy brother's idiosyncrasy: when the

[6] "Zur Analyse und Prognose psychoneurotischer Symptom," *Zeitschrift für Psychopathologie und Psychologie*, 1910.

brother was between twelve and thirteen years old, he was caught by his mother in a situation in which he held a red-currant croissant in one hand while reaching under the housemaid's skirts with his other hand. From then on, he could no longer eat red-currant croissants; the other business he did not give up, as a neurotic would have done. The idiosyncrasy is therefore an act of repression, shifted to the individual's advantage—i.e., displaced from the important to the unimportant; as the result of it, the individual keeps his sexuality free.

There are other idiosyncrasies, against certain foods that remind one of feces, in children who have not completely overcome their coprophilic impulses. These, too, are displaced repressions.

If, in the interest of prophylaxis, the rule is given: one must not stimulate sexuality too much, the better aid to an effective prophylaxis lies in not exerting too much pressure on such children [of the sort that will lead] to repression. The best thing is, of course, to do both.

Lastly, the present speaker would like to offer a suggestion that is remotely connected with the topic. He is referring to the communication of an idea about the emergence of "moral insanity"; with this communication, he renounces his claim to priority regarding that idea. Undoubtedly, here as everywhere, a specific organic basis exists. Our next task, however, would be to establish the share of accident and biography [in that development]. On the basis of certain intimations, the following possibilities can be assumed to be present. The individuals involved are often very intelligent persons, in whom moral inhibitions, such as are usually developed in the latency period, do not come about. Genetically, the process would be as follows: the development of these barriers is interrupted early, as the result of an experience of the child's: e.g., a breakdown of parental authority in the sexual respect because of the child's having witnessed actual sexual misbehavior, especially on the part of the mother. It would not be impossible that the child, [in response] to this example by his parents, were to say to himself: if they do not need it, I do not need it, either; thereupon, the development of these moral constructions ceased to take place. Another detail observed in our practice supports this view: the lying of children who in general do not lie and are by nature truth-loving. They tell lies from the moment when they see their parents lie.

HITSCHMANN reminds us of the fragment that he presented some time ago of the analysis of an obsessional-neurotic child, in whom the fear of dying was also connected with the Oedipus complex (mother).

At the present time, Hitschmann has in treatment a fifteen-year-old girl who shows striking moral weakness. It turns out that the mother had an affair of many years' duration, and that the daughter is correct in considering herself an illegitimate child. She suffers from a compulsion to ask questions, especially in relation to the mother (her mother must repeat the answer a certain number of times); behind this compulsion, there is probably concealed the urge to put an end to all doubt about that subject.

STEKEL on the basis of his own experience can confirm Freud's assumption by an interesting case (the mother has an affair; the boy, moral insanity). It should be mentioned that some individuals also react in the opposite way, i.e., with a great supermorality.

FEDERN has also seen several cases of moral insanity that developed under the same circumstances. In contrast to this is the case of a young man who, from his earliest childhood, suffered from an extraordinary shamelessness, and committed suicide at seventeen; he came from an extremely philistine family, where nothing [nothing of that kind] could have taken place. He was excessively attached to his mother.

It must be stressed that Sadger's material about children stems from patients, and that it therefore concerns pathological children. It may easily lead one to assume a hypersexuality [in general], which does not correspond to the facts.

ADLER comments that Freud's valuable suggestion must be pursued further. It is doubtful whether Freud's understanding of the lie can be fully maintained. Not only the example of parents but that of the entire environment plays a role in it. There is no child who would not, at least for a short time, lie.

Lastly, Adler cannot concede that his conception of the obsessional case as a sexual-biological one should be contrasted with the psychological view. The Oedipus complex cannot explain the case completely. There remain two possibilities, either the one developed by Freud—that sexual aggression against the mother becomes so strong that the child is driven to repression and tries to satisfy his love through the father (homosexuality); or Adler's opinion, that the child develops two aspects: (1) he turns his sexuality toward the father and behaves like a girl, or (2) he turns toward the mother, which occurs, however, only after he has begun to defend himself against his sexual role in relation to the father.

PROF. FREUD believes nevertheless that it is the amorality of a child's *first* sex-objects that induces him to lie. Strangers probably do not play such a role in the first years of [the child's] life. Freud, on the basis of his own experience, could by no means assert that all children tell lies.

107

SCIENTIFIC MEETING *on May 11, 1910*

Present: Brecher, Federn, Freud, Friedjung, Furtmüller, Hilferding, Hitschmann, Joachim, Oppenheim, Rank, Sadger, Steiner, Stekel, Tausk, Wittels.

Guests: Dr. Frischauf; Mr. Friedmann.

I. Dr. Richard Nepallek and Baron Franz von Hye are elected unanimously. The latter will not become officially a member until the fall.

II. Stekel, who is chairing the meeting in Adler's place, announces, in reference to the *Zentralblatt für Psychoanalyse,* that the contract with Bergmann has already been signed. The first issue is to appear in the middle of September or at the beginning of October. The distribution of material to be reviewed will be made in the near future. The editor's office, for the time being, will be in his apartment; many contributions are expected from all members.

III. Librarian Dr. Hitschmann reports the [titles of] books that have arrived, and urgently requests the return of all borrowed books, journals and Minutes, since it is planned to catalogue the library.

MINUTES 107

Since Dr. Sadger's paper is scheduled for publication in the *Zentralblatt* this fall, only its most essential points are reported here.

PRESENTATION

Is Bronchial Asthma a Sexual Neurosis?[1]

SPEAKER: DR. SADGER

The speaker first discusses the two prevailing theories of bronchial asthma, and the common causes provoking the malady, some of which seem quite understandable (climatic factors), whereas others defy understanding (attacks on certain days, etc.) and indicate psychic connections. Other circumstances also testify to the existence of psychic connections (therapeutic effectiveness of hypnosis, inducement of an attack through its mental image, etc.). Strümpell[2] recently called attention to the fact that the development of asthma is not infrequently traceable back to early childhood, and that persons with this affliction, according to Czerny's experience, often have exsudative diathesis.

In the view of the precipitating conditions mentioned above, the sexual factor is consistently neglected.

The speaker has not found the harmful sexual factor missing, in one single case of asthma among the many that he has observed in his practice, ever since Freud taught us to take note of the asthmatic symptoms among the symptoms of an anxiety neurosis. (The speaker cites three typical cases.)

Just as many cases of a seemingly typical anxiety neurosis have turned out under closer scrutiny to be an anxiety hysteria, so, it appears, a large number of cases of asthma also admit of a similar diagnosis. In the case of a twenty-three-year-old youth with homosexual tendencies, who showed a wealth of hysterical symptoms, in addition to his inclination toward inversion, exact psychoanalytic evidence could be given of the fact that his attacks of asthma, which reach back

[1] "Ist das Asthma bronchiale eine Sexualneurose?," *Zentralblatt für Psychoanalyse* I. Vol, 1911.

[2] Adolf von Strümpell (1853-1925): "Über das Asthma bronchiale und seine Beziehungen zur sogenannten exsudativen Diathese" ["On *Asthma Bronchiale* and its Relations to the So-called Exsudative Diathesis"], *Medizinische Klinik*, 1910.

into his earliest childhood (the first attack occurred when he was about five years old)—attacks for which he holds the customary causes responsible—were, without exception, called forth by sexual factors. And these factors pertained not merely to the present, but—in keeping with the character of a hysterical symptom—they were also infantile experiences of a sexual sort. He had an extremely affectionate father, whose erotic (homosexual) caresses gave him utmost pleasure, which has since been repressed into the unconscious, but still lives on as an undying desire; it is materialized in occasional asthmatic attacks, whenever the patient is again incited in a similar manner by a sex object of his own gender. A second (heterosexual) infantile root has to do with the habit of the patient's mother (and also his grandmother) of hugging him with excessive ardor in moments of tenderness.

Just as the patient's suffering was induced by sexual desire, so, on the other hand, it could be removed, either momentarily or for some time, by sexual satisfaction, or by a corresponding equivalent. By contrast, however, his analysis also revealed that, despite its unpleasant symptoms, attacks of asthma can be prolonged out of conscious or unconscious motives of love, a connection of which the patient seems to have been in part aware.

Finally the speaker discusses the relation of bronchial asthma to the nose and to exsudative diathesis. He calls to mind the interrelations between sex organs, sexual activity and the nose. These interrelations, according to his experiences, appear to exist even more extensively than Fliess[3] showed us, years ago. The connection exists also in the patient [under discussion], whose attacks of asthma usually terminate with a great deal of secretion and expectoration and who, in any case, was not unfamiliar with exsudative diathesis. This connection, however, is sustained in addition by psychosexual roots. The patient himself, even as a child and entirely spontaneously, equated the nose with the member, and in analysis equated rubbing his nose with masturbation, and sneezing with ejaculation.

By way of summarizing, the speaker finally brings out the conclu-

[3] Wilhelm Fliess: *Die Beziehungen zwischen Nase und weiblichem Geschlechtsorgan, in ihrer biologischen Bedeutung dargestellt.* [*The Relationships between the Nose and the Female Genital Organ, Presented with Regard to their Biological Significance*], Leipzig and Vienna, 1897.

sions of his exposition: in asthma there is always present an inborn, although up to that point only hypothetical, disposition. In addition to that, a condition of exsudative diathesis is certainly present (nose, bronchia, etc.). As far as acquired factors are concerned, afflictions of the upper respiratory tract create a disposition to asthma (nose-sexuality). It is to be stressed as something new that the asthmatic condition was called forth only by circumstances of a purely sexual nature. These were at first topical in nature, but by analysis they could be reduced to infantile sexual experiences, which had provoked a physiological shortness of breath. The bronchial asthma, then, would be a monosymptomatic hysteria reaching back into childhood; a hysteria, however, that differs from any other with regard to its specific somatic conditions and in terms of the particular infantile sexual elements mentioned above, which produced a genuine shortness of breath.

DISCUSSION

FRIEDJUNG finds the expositions, particularly insofar as they concern the specific case, very interesting; he himself has leaned toward such a view of asthma for a rather long time. Nevertheless, he wants to express certain doubts, the more so since it is a question of conclusions that are drawn from the findings in one single case, and refer to an illness whose picture is still far from being fixed. Friedjung can confirm that asthma in children sometimes goes back to a very early age (two years), and that these children belong among those who have exsudative diathesis (Czerny). Bronchial asthma is seen more frequently in the children of the well-to-do and for the most part in the only, or especially pampered, child.

It is precisely in whooping-cough that the influence of nervous conditions—in contrast with Sadger's example—should not be underrated; the disease takes its mildest course when the child is removed from his milieu.

HITSCHMANN mentions that, in singling out asthma from the rest of the illnesses, the general difference between nervous and non-nervous diseases should have been stressed as being already historical. Since Freud's findings, we no longer doubt that asthma belongs in the category of the anxiety-neuroses; but it will not do to overlook its chronic effects, and to neglect those states of illness that are similar. Nor is one justified *a priori* in asserting that, since asthma in certain cases goes back to sexual causes, this is true of all cases. The symptoms of anxiety neurosis can develop from organic causes, too. And there is no basis for rejecting the vagus theory. The same thing applies to the rejection of hay-asthma. Furthermore, there is missing, of course, any negative proof in regard to details—i.e., whether all these sexual harmfulnesses were not effective at times when the patient had no asthma.

What is so restrictive about asthma, by comparison with a nervous symptom, is its characteristic profile, from which there is no transition to the healthy state, as is true of nervous symptoms. The discussant refers to his paper on "Neurosis and Toxicosis,"[4] in which he emphasized that the actual-neurotic element is pushed into the background as they have been.

Concerning the remarks about the nose, the discussant believes that he has observed repeatedly that it does, in the manner described, have a connection with the sexual organs.

BRECHER can report on a case of bronchial asthma, however, without being able to give any information about the psychogenesis of the attacks. All that came to light was that the severe attacks appeared as equivalents of other hysterical states.

The discussant also has the impression that bronchial asthma and psychoneuroses have something to do with each other, in some way; but one must be very cautious about estimating their mutual relationship. One could very well imagine that asthma is present for some reason or other, and that hysteria then finds available a mechanism that it uses for the representation of various fantasies. This neurosis, into which hysteria is, so to speak, converted, is no psychoneurosis but an actual-neurosis (sexual neurosis).

The fact that the vagus is stimulated at the same time would not be in contradiction to the psychogenic theory; for this is but a path of discharge for the psychic excitation.

STEKEL gratefully welcomes the impetus that the speaker has given to the discussion of this important topic by way of such a very instructive example. Since Stekel wrote his book about conditions of nervous

[4] See Minutes 65, this volume.

anxiety, the literature about this topic has grown immensely. His conviction about the psychogenic nature of asthma has already been generally accepted, and the last great book by Sänger[5] derives asthma directly from a trauma in childhood.

It seemed strange that Hitschmann should oppose the rejection of *vagus* neurosis; the *vagus* is, indeed, only the executive organ. It is to Sadger's credit that he called attention to the psychogenic factor (after the book on conditions of nervous anxiety).

By contrast with Hitschmann's assertion, there are gradations from the simplest to the most severe cases, as the discussant can confirm from his own material.

One patient produced the asthma artificially; it gave him intense feelings of pleasure and sometimes terminated in emission. In another case, the asthma proved to be a reproduction of the pleasure he had felt when his wet-nurse pressed him to her body.

Contrary to Brecher's supposition, asthma occurs far more frequently in men, even though it is actually a "female" disease. In a number of analyses, asthma was revealed to be an imitation of the breathing disturbance that occurs during intercourse, especially in the partner who lies underneath—that is, the woman (mother). Nightmares, and the like, too, are identifications with the person who lies underneath, as in men of a homosexual nature. That mucous secretion takes place then can be explained by the fact that, for the neurotic, the neurotic equation: mucus = sperm = milk, etc., is valid.

Various bad habits would deserve a separate discussion: rubbing one's nose, nose-picking.

FEDERN objects to representing Sadger's conception as meritorious. The psychogenic conception and treatment of asthma was first made public (after Stekel's book) by Stegmann.[6] What Sadger presented today was a relationship of sexual activity and abstinence accompanying the appearance and disappearance of an anxiety neurosis. It is a matter of a patient in whom an anxiety neurosis is com-

[5] Moritz Sänger: *Über Asthma und seine Behandlung* [*On Asthma and its Treatment*], Berlin 1910.

[6] "Zur Aetiologie des Asthmas bei Kindern" ["On the Etiology of Asthma in Children"], *Med. Klinik*, 1908.

bined with bronchial asthma; this case cannot prove to us that bronchial asthma is sexually and psychogenically determined. We know, certainly, that all somatic states of excitation can be provoked by sexual excitement. If Sadger wanted to demonstrate that in asthma hysterical conversion is also involved, one would have to raise the objection that the patient was indeed not a hysteric at all, but a pervert.

The connection between the swelling of the nose and sexual tension Federn had found in many cases. In order for asthma to supervene, much more would probably need to be present.

Bronchial asthma must be seen in connection with anxiety neurosis, but it has nothing to do with hysteria; in any event, Sadger's case does not show any evidence whatever in that direction.

JOACHIM has frequently encountered in psychotics the substitution of the nose for the genitalium; a case in point: stereotyped nose-rubbing, which could be reduced to a symbolic substitutive act of masturbation.

RANK can confirm this relationship by way of the symbolism in fairy tales.

PROF. FREUD stresses the difficulty of the topic, which necessitates the exercise of restraint. He declares Sadger's observation to be quite significant, since it provides proof of the infantile roots. Regarding the conception of the case itself, Freud would differ from the speaker in several essential points. Especially disturbing is the leap that invariably occurs with Sadger, from the thorough observation of detail to the abrupt pasting on of the theory, like a façade.

In dealing with nervous asthma, it seems obvious to take a look at similar conditions; there is, first, migraine; then, certain forms of neuropathic edema, and certain forms of stuttering. Most conspicuous is the similarity to the edemas that neurotics often get under circumstances in which others do not. There can be no doubt about the psychic factor in these attacks, just as there can be none in the case of migraine, in which the characteristic also occurs of being displaceable and psychically induceable. Migraine is not a hysterical symptom, but, so to speak, an organic suffering; normally, it follows its own periods of recurrence, but it can be shifted to specific times by the individual.[7] All of these are syndromes in which, alongside the organic conditions, the psychic element also takes a major part; the question is how these two factors share in the causation, a question that must be handled with a great deal of caution.

Sadger's communication shows its incompleteness in two points. The first one Stekel has correctly singled out. If the patient chooses as his love objects boys between eleven and twelve years of age—that is, himself at that age—analysis must show us why it is that he chooses himself at precisely that age, what happened to him at that time and which satisfactions fall into that age-span.

Secondly, the question arises whether this patient, too, became homosexual by the mechanism described by Sadger (early attachment to the woman, soon thereafter repression of this inclination, finally identification with the woman and object-choice on the basis of narcissism) and what role the father's caresses played in that development. In this case the assumption seems more likely that these caresses of the father made him homosexual. This gap in the analysis justifies the question of whether we are confronted here with a new type of homosexuality.

The aforementioned leap consists in the fact that the speaker, having in the first instance traced the intimate psychogenic roots and shown that each time there was a sexual cause, in a single leap goes over into the organic; and, in postulating as a precondition for bronchial asthma the exsudative diathesis and a bronchial affliction, without further ado joins in with what those physicians say, for whom sexuality does not exist. Exsudative diathesis is nothing new; it is identical with what was previously called lymphatic diathesis, and there is no reason, on its account, to give up our fundamental concepts.

The assumption of the necessity of a bronchial affliction for the development of asthma is likewise a sudden turnabout. According to the theory initiated by Freud and continued by Adler, in these phenomena are involved organs that inherently have a specific disposition, the nature of which could be imagined as follows. They are organs

[7] On the basis of my own clinical experience, I can add that, in anticipation of specific events, some epileptics are able to delay their attacks. For instance, it quite often happens that patients in institutions postpone their attacks until after the Christmas festivities are completed.

that greatly exaggerate their erotogenic function, alongside of their other biological functions. One must assume that all organs originally carry with them such erotogenic capabilities, in addition to their physiological ones. During the course of life, however, they are more and more forced to restrict their erotogenic function, and that can cause a great many disturbances, if it does not proceed smoothly. Adler's extensions [of Freud's theory] have brought to it a certain degree of penetrating illumination. These organs, for which Adler uses the very unfortunate term "inferior," would be completely sufficient for the disposition. For instance, in the case of stuttering, this is quite plausible, as is shown by the case of a stammering patient whose son at ten years of age suffers from bronchial asthma.

We employ the word "psychogenic" in an incorrect sense. Only that can be called "psychogenic" which is based on impulses that have become unconscious. But what we have found to be pathogenic in neurosis is always a sexual process that has two aspects: it has psychic effects (psychogenic); but it also has somatic effects and for these we have no term. One could call them "sexual-neurotic." Migraine, edema, bronchial asthma would be sexual-neurotic symptoms of that sort—that is, such as to presuppose a strong organ disposition, a high erotogenicity, but on the other hand to be capable of combination with various psychogenic disorders.

Sadger's case permits an even deeper insight, although one is not going to draw general conclusions from it at once. Owing to the predominance in certain families of such syndromes (for instance, in the region of the throat), one becomes inclined to suspect that they are of a constitutional and hereditary nature. However, one has experiences that indicate that it may be simply childhood *rearing* that has succeeded in turning these zones into erotogenic ones. If one goes farther, however, the matter once more becomes doubtful. The caresses of children by adults (in Sadger's example, the father's) very likely depend on the erotogenic zones of the adults (the father kisses the boy on the neck, because it is one of his own erotogenic zones), so that probably both influences, the constitutional and the accidental, here too have a combined effect.

The markedly erotogenic character of the nose, particularly during development, is incontestable. There are nose-swellings that are equivalent to erection and with sexual excitement do not appear but disappear.

The most doubtful aspect of the speaker's exposition seems to be the fact that his presentation arouses one's suspicion that he overrates the significance of sexual fantasies in sexual-neurotic symptom complexes. It appears as if Sadger thought that the patient forms the symbolic idea that his nose is a penis, and that this equalizing then calls forth the symptoms on the nose. But the true state of affairs is altogether different. The biological and sexual-neurotic connection lies at the root of the symptoms, no matter whether the patient does or does not form the symbolic idea. It is the perception of the biologic material that causes the patient to form the idea, which is nothing but the reaction to the unquestionable biological fact. Therefore one must not shift the causation of the symptoms onto the fantasy; this is the case in hysteria, although there, too, somatic compliance plays an important role.[8]

SADGER, in his concluding words, expresses his thanks for the numerous suggestions, especially those of Prof. Freud. He admits that the organic preconditions are the weak point in his work. In that regard, Prof. Freud said totally new things, which completely explain somatic compliance and must now be digested.

The misunderstanding with regard to the fantasies is due to the abridged presentation; the speaker regarded the view stressed by Freud as self-evident.

As far as homosexuality is concerned, the speaker asserted a long time ago that the mechanism that he could demonstrate is found in every case. It is true that lately he has had the experience [of seeing] the father play an important role. Frequently, the father is the more loving parent (he behaves like a mother), whereas the mother is cooler. With this is connected the fact that all homosexuals have, in addition to the ego-type, a father-type, which, however, is often, as a result of the rivalry for the mother, later repressed.

Friedjung's remarks were interesting.

Hitschmann's and Federn's objections can be easily refuted.

[8] In these statements, Freud lays the foundations for the so called "psycho-somatic" pathology, a conception of certain illnesses that was later on to be gravely misunderstood and misused.

PROF. FREUD lastly makes two remarks about homosexuality, which have to do with the paper. One should have distinguished between two types: (1) those who take themselves as the love object, and (2) those who choose the father. It is probable that the genesis will not be the same in every case.[9]

Between the extremes of the father as the more loving parent, and the mother as the more loving parent, lies a contradiction; the relationship must be clarified; they cannot simply stand in a complementary relationship to each other. From individual cases one can see that, for homosexuality to appear, the father does not have to be present in person. There are those who grow up without a father and yet become homosexual. In any event, the problem of the causation of homosexuality in childhood is extremely complicated.

STEKEL sees as the essential factor in its causation the flight from the mother to the man.

HITSCHMANN on this occasion emphasizes how difficult it is to gauge the degree of parental affection. In any case, it is a grave contradiction that he has found both etiological factors in one and the same case. It would not seem impossible that in those cases in which a father is missing, the fantasy created by longing for him plays an important role.

[9] See Nunberg: *Homosexuality, Magic and Aggression* (1936).

108

SCIENTIFIC MEETING *on May 18, 1910*

Present: Adler, Brecher, Freud, Friedjung, Furtmüller, Heller, Hitschmann, Nepallek, Oppenheim, Rank, Reitler, Sadger, Steiner, Stekel, Tausk.

Dr. Frischauf, Mr. Friedmann, as guests.

ADLER requests that the gentlemen who took part in the discussion on suicide deliver their contributions, since the deadline for publication is approaching.

Then he moves to conclude the activity for this semester in the middle of June. (Motion carried.)

It has been proposed that the next meeting's discussion be on the harmfulness of masturbation.

STEKEL reports that he is going to carry out psychoanalytic treatments in Dr. Samueli's sanitarium in the Hinterbrühl[1] this summer, on a trial basis. He invites all his colleagues to make use of this opportunity.

[1] Hinterbrühl is a small township near Vienna.

PRESENTATION

On the Feeling of Strangeness in Dream and in Life

SPEAKER: DR. STEKEL

As his starting point the speaker takes a work by Löwenfeld, which appeared several months ago in *Gauppsches Zentralblatt* (Volume 32, No. 15, 1909) and treats of "Dreamlike and Related Conditions." The topic under discussion is the feeling that some patients complain of, that things are strange and dreamlike; this is a feeling that—by contrast with the frequently treated problem of *déjà vu*—is only occasionally mentioned and still awaits psychological clarification.

The speaker reviews Löwenfeld's work in detail[2] and emphasizes that two states are intermingled in it: one group of patients complains that everything appears to be strange and changed, whereas to another group everything seems like a dream.

The speaker further discusses Löwenfeld's attempt, carried out with expert knowledge, to provide a survey of the hitherto published literature on this topic, which has been treated by Janet, Pick, Strohmayer, and Jung. *Janet*[3] lays the blame for the loss of the sense of reality on a lowering of psychic tension. *Pick*[4] similarly thinks that the impression of something being strange has its origin in the fact that the patient has lost the feeling of familiarity. *Strohmayer*[5] goes a bit deeper when he traces the phenomenon to a deficiency in ego-feeling and especially emphasizes the connection with states of anxiety. However, this does not yet represent a psychological explanation. *Jung* (in his work on dementia praecox[6]) singled out one of the most important

[2] A review by Stekel of Löwenfeld's work appeared in *Zentralblatt*, Vol. I.

[3] Pierre Janet, 1859-1947, French psychiatrist, an opponent of Freud.

[4] Arnold Pick (1861-1924, professor of psychiatry in Prague): "Zur Pathologie des Ich-Bewusstseins. Studie aus der allgemeinen Psychopathologie." [On the Pathology of Ego-Consciousness. A Study in the Field of General Psychopathology"].

[5] Wilhelm Strohmayer, Professor in Jena.

[6] C. G. Jung: *Über die Psychologie der Dementia praecox.* Halle: Marhold 1907 [*The Psychology of Dementia Praecox, 1909*].

elements when he stressed that only those ideas that form a complex[7] have attracted full attention. Finally, Löwenfeld first attempts to give a physiological explanation of the problem on the basis of the assumption that the cerebral performances are reduced; then he looks for psychological support of this view and, like Strohmayer, finds it in a dormant condition of the ego-feeling.

We would be inclined to assume that what is involved is a strong affect, which brings about a narrowing of consciousness and makes it blind to the diverse impressions of the external world. Löwenfeld, however, leaves this line [of thought] and is of the opinion that the feeling of unfamiliarity can be broken down into categories: in one of these, the feeling rests on the indistinctness of perception, and in another it has to do with the reproduction of previous events. It follows from this that there are two [different] kinds of disturbances: in the first instance, the object appears strange; in the second, it appears merely new, rather than changed.

All in all, Löwenfeld's conception is a hodge-podge of what earlier writers have said. He introduces one single new point of view, by his allotting to states of anxiety an essential role in evoking those feelings, but he himself concedes that the puzzle is not solved by this assumption.

One day, after Stekel had read this work, a patient who had been in psychoanalytic treatment for six months came in with the complaint that suddenly everything seemed strange and changed to her. It was possible in this case to resolve the feeling of strangeness completely by psychoanalysis. Before starting to present this case, the speaker again emphasizes that one must distinguish sharply between the feeling of strangeness and the feeling that things are dreamlike. The latter feeling is also evoked in normal persons by particularly strong affects, which are either joyous or painful; this feeling has been celebrated again and again in the work of poets (Grillparzer, Calderon). Neurotics find themselves having this feeling of the dreamlike under quite

[7] In his association experiments, Jung noted disturbances in the course of associations—for instance, extended reaction times. Pursuing these disturbances to their source, he found that at their root are trains of thought that are held together by an affect; Jung named these formations "affectively toned complexes" or briefly "complexes." The discussant is obviously referring to the complex in Jung's sense.

specific conditions. If the unconscious breaks through forcefully, they will often have the feeling that the secondary ego (the unconscious) has taken over control for a while; each breakthrough of this kind generates the feeling of the dreamlike. It should not surprise us that these states are connected with anxiety, for we know that forbidden wishes are active in the unconscious. The feeling of the dreamlike is therefore to be explained as a breakthrough of the unconscious.

Something altogether different, however, is the actual loss of the feeling of reality, of which the speaker cites some examples. For instance, a patient, upon going out, often has the feeling: this is not a street. What is involved here, without question, is the confusion of symbol with reality. For this agoraphobic patient, the street is really not a street, but a vagina; this also explains his particular fear of particularly narrow streets, or of alleys that taper off at the end, etc. It is noteworthy that he was seized by this feeling in the *Heinrichsgasse* (his name is Heinrich; *gasse* = road). Homosexual feelings also play a role in that instance. In a second case, the confusion of street and its symbolic meaning is also involved.

More interesting is the next case: a man who states that for some time everything has been appearing strange and different to him. He lives in strife with his relatives: it is on his mind day and night. These conditions have existed since his marriage, which was supposedly for love. Soon after the wedding, he reproached his wife with not being a virgin, and he now distresses her relatives constantly with demands for money. He had his first attack on a street in Rotterdam; it turns out that this is connected with his passion for *rote Damen* ["red ladies"]. He had loved such a lady before his marriage in Brussels; and this lady (Christine), whom he prefers to his wife, has now become a stranger to him.

Two jokes that come to his mind support these associations.

When he comes home, he says, everything appears strange to him—except his wife and his child. Here it must be remarked that all these symptoms appear either openly or in masked form. In this instance, analysis revealed that the feeling of strangeness referred precisely to his wife and children, from whom he would like to become estranged, whom he would like to forget. But his sister too has become estranged from him, by his marriage; and even more, his mother, to whom he is deeply attached. Above all, however, he has become a stranger to himself, and he displaces this feeling of his own recollection[8] onto his environment, onto the external world.

Stekel then discusses the dream of a patient who also complained about the feeling of strangeness. In the dream, what becomes evident is her desire to become estranged from her parents and also from her fiancé, to forget those persons whom she once loved very much, not to know them any more. In reality, she is incapable of detaching herself from those persons and of achieving psychic independence. The feeling of strangeness corresponds in this case to a powerful wish.

Finally, the speaker takes up the case of a patient who was mentioned at the beginning of this paper, to whom suddenly—right after a dream—everything seemed strange. A note from her prehistory should be referred to here: the patient, whose husband has been showing the first signs of general paresis, was completely cured of her agoraphobia by psychoanalysis. Stekel had promised to visit this patient at her summer residence, but did not keep this promise. On the evening preceding the dream, the woman sat at a table; in front of her was the picture of the physician (Stekel), as well as the picture of her father, who was also named Wilhelm and was a physician. She was annoyed at the physician's lack of interest and said: "My father would not have done anything like that." During the night she had a dream, the content of which was the dissolution of the identification of the physician with her father, and the former's identification with the unloved husband. The feeling of strangeness in this patient is, then, induced by a breakthrough of the fervent desire to forget someone whom she loves and to become estranged from him. If *déjà vu* is based on an identification of symbol and reality, the feeling of strangeness is occasioned by a *differentiation* between them. Whenever one love dies and another is about to develop, or if even merely the desire for a new love exists (or some other affect), than this feeling of strangeness appears. A decrease of ego-feeling certainly plays a part in it, for the feeling of self-esteem is quite badly hurt in these persons.

[8] It would seem that what Stekel wants to say is "the patient's feeling toward the recollection of his former self. . . ."

DISCUSSION

ADLER stresses the fact that, from Stekel's discourse, we have come to know a great number of relationships, which were in part familiar, in part less so. The feeling of strangeness is found in almost every case of neurosis. But every normal individual, too, will have had this feeling occasionally upon awakening from sleep and finding himself unable to orient himself in his room. In a poem by Chamisso,[9] this feeling is described [as taking place] at the death of a cherished person. The speaker reports some cases from his experience that are not covered by Stekel's formula (loss of love). In the first case, that of an ambitious lieutenant, the feeling of strangeness made itself known in the form of obsessional ideas—such as whether an acquaintance of his was not merely an idea of his. This doubt of the reality of objects and men is connected with a celebrated doubt that plays an important role in philosophy (especially in Schopenhauer's). At that time, the patient had to withdraw from a marriage because he had acquired syphilis, and he believed that it must without fail be followed by paralysis. When he was informed about his error, his condition improved spontaneously.

A number of childhood defects were involved [in the patient's fear of paralysis], including the feeling of physical inferiority in relation to his brothers, a feeling out of which a dialectical development took place, of increased ambition and self-esteem. If this is what Strohmayer had in mind with his "reduction of ego-feeling," then Adler must agree with him.

A second case shows another aspect of the problem. This is the case of a neurotic who since childhood had displayed mild disorders. When he entered school, it took him a long while before he could comprehend the real meaning of school; he thought that the whole thing represented a comedy staged by his parents. If one investigates further, with reference to the patient's feeling of strangeness, one learns that when he was a child, being afflicted with a congenital heart condition, he had been extremely spoiled and had tyrannized over his entire environment. This, of course, was no longer possible at school. If one

[9] Adelbert von Chamisso, 1781-1838, poet.

compares this finding with the first case, one sees that the intensive wish that everything should not be real arises solely from the feeling of vanity on the part of the ambitious person, who does not want to be exposed to hurt of any sort.

Another problem is also of special interest; concerning it, however, Adler has little experience: the sensation, for instance, that, a patient's arm was lost; she was searching for it when she awoke at night.

Now, it would suit us very well if we could clear up the feeling of strangeness, as we have many other symptoms, if we could show with what childhood condition this feeling is connected. The analysis of several cases of this type reveals the same basis: fear of degradation and the individual's painful feeling that he will not be able to fulfill his ambitious desires. In order to evade failure, these persons place, between themselves and failure, anxiety. This anxiety is, then, a protection; it is the advantage that the patients gain from their illness. The source of these phenomena is the fear, on the part of certain children, of anything strange and new: these are children who have a feeling of inferiority, children who with every new event fear scorn, punishment, slight, etc.

Most important—this is also what Stekel most emphatically stresses—is the meaning of this symptom and the nature of its dynamics. From Stekel's cases, too many different possibilities seem to follow. If the patient's surroundings seem strange to him, surely, as Stekel put it, a wish lies at the basis of this feeling; but one must investigate what advantage the patient gains thereby.

Finally, the discussant would like to call attention to a case in which the mechanism seems to be clear: plagiarism in which something that the plagiarizer knew seems foreign to him. The mechanism of plagiarism, which Adler once set forth in great detail, surely leads back to the same root: to unsatisfied ambition, to the feeling of inferiority, and a feeling that can be verbalized in the following way: I cannot bear not to have been the first to say a certain thing.

REITLER makes the point that an investigation on the roots of the feeling of strangeness must not start with the individual objects that appear strange; the essential factor is the [general] reaction of the patient to the external world. That feeling comes under discussion during the course of every psychoanalytic treatment; it arises also, during the treatment, in the transference onto the physician. In transference, childhood wishes have become effective, in a form that is not compatible with adult life. It is to this conflict that the discussant would trace the feeling of strangeness.

In a patient, who resembled the "Rotterdam" case, quarrels about an inheritance proved to be a displacement from sexual to social life: the patient had already accepted the sexual bequest of another, when he married a woman with an illegitimate child.

PROF. FREUD first emphasizes that this topic is a good example of the inadequacy of the questions that are posed by those to whom our psychological points of view are alien. They single out something as a symptom (inhibitions, impulses); since they are ignorant, however, of its place in the totality of psychic life, they set about investigating it in the most awkward fashion. Stekel's not very extensive attempt to explain this phenomenon along psychoanalytic lines, already shows how much more fruitful is such a way of considering the question.

Adler's wish to hear the dynamics of this phenomenon explicitly stated is not hard to fulfill. In any event, what is involved is an endopsychic perception: consciousness here gets to know something of those processes that are otherwise concealed from it (unconscious). This endopsychic perception can correspond to various processes.

Jung sees the character of dementia praecox in this feeling of strangeness which, as Stekel has remarked, must be sharply distinguished from the feeling of the dreamlike. Jung came to that erroneous view, because in these cases [of dementia praecox] essentially what is (endopsychically) perceived is that for which Stekel has suggested the (quite superfluously new) term 'differentiation"—namely, a *detachment of affect*—which means that, from an object to which it had been attached, the libido is shifted to some other point.

Stekel should have summarized a little the points of view and the findings; the present speaker will try to do that for him now.

In the feeling of strangeness there is involved, then, the *endopsychic perception of a detachment of affect* that, in cases of hysteria, is either attempted or desired or temporarily successful, and can shift onto indifferent objects (for instance, from the person to the inanimate environment, etc.). This is a process in which superficial associations play their part as well as symbolism and wish-fulfillment, as is the case with all other symptom-formations for which it is essentially the path of associations that paves the way.

In hysteria, detachments of affect occur without any further ado; furthermore, they occur in the unconscious, just as among normal people they occur in consciousness. The most difficult detachment of affects forms the content of mourning, from which, too, the way leads to an understanding of melancholia.[10] Dementia praecox corresponds to successful withdrawal of the libido from its objects.

One comes upon a further problem if one turns one's attention to the mutual position of the two basic instincts with regard to this phenomenon. The libido withdrawn from the object can be consciously held in readiness, in the same way as it can be held in the unconscious. In any case it can remain at the disposal of the sex instinct, as in hysteria. It is characteristic of dementia praecox that the libido returns to the ego. The demented person has no feeling of inferiority; he develops megalomania, in which he enlarges his ego by means of the libido that he has withdrawn from objects.[11] Adler can never do justice to the psychoanalytic facts, because his interest is focused on the ego and the conscious processes; psychoanalysis, however, takes hold of matters on the basis of the unconscious and the libido, which are, indeed, what produce a neurosis.

Reitler called attention to the fact that what is involved is the relationship between the ego and the external world; we could say: the relationship between the conscious ego and the condition of the libido in the unconscious; thus we arrive at a new contradiction. *This* feeling of strangeness is as a rule traceable to a change in the ego. A number of disagreeable experiences have appeared unreal to such individuals, and have therefore made no impression upon them. In these cases, the basis was not a weakness of the ego, but an insolence of the ego: it feels so strong that it dares to reject the external world. These circumstances result in a second type of feeling of strangeness; what the two

[10] It is amazing how early Freud recognized the relationship between mourning and melancholia. His work on this topic did not appear until as late as 1917. ("Mourning and Melancholia," *S.E.* 14).

[11] See Freud: "On Narcissism: An Introduction" (1914), *S.E.* 14.

categories have in common, however, is obvious. Vicissitudes of the libido are always involved, whether they be cathexes that the individual does not want to set in motion or cathexes that he withdraws.

One of the most striking examples of this feeling [of strangeness] is that words that one has been for decades in the habit of using suddenly appear completely strange.[12]

The feeling of becoming alive, which Löwenfeld quoted in this context, does not belong here; it derives unquestionably from the complex of erection.

Janet's *sentiment de la réalité*—behind which something of importance is concealed, although in a different sense from the one Janet had in mind—belongs to the realm of the psychology of the ego, to which Adler refers again and again. This is a field hitherto rather neglected by psychoanalysis. In that *sentiment de la réalité*, it is a question of the conflict between fantasy and reality that permeates our whole psychic life, a question of the two principles that guide the working of our psychic apparatus. Initially, that apparatus works according to the pleasure principle, and only when we are forced by bitter experience do we develop our intellectual capacities—our thinking apparatus—and work in accordance with the reality principle. The psychological role of this principle becomes known to us only [when we examine] the obsessional neurosis. The neurotic withdraws from life insofar as he works on the basis of the obsolete currency of pleasure and neglects reality testing.

TAUSK comments that Freud's example of a familiar word that has suddenly lost its meaning, can be explained in terms of divesting this word of the affect that it possesses within the sentence—that is, in the complex.

On the basis of his own experience, Tausk suspects that the sense

[12] Cf. Nunberg: "States of Depersonalization in the light of the Libido Theory." In this article, which was written without knowledge of the existence and contents of this protocol, I expressed similar ideas: I traced the feelings of depersonalization and strangeness to a loss of libido that is, of course, accompanied by a change in the ego. On the basis of this fact, I drew the conclusion that, for a *normal* perception of the external world, as well as of the internal world, a libidinal cathexis of the ego is necessary.

A patient whom I treated long after the publication of "States of Depersonalization" described those states as a "cellophane bag feeling"; this seems to me a very apt characterization.

of estrangement is combined with a feeling of guilt. Perhaps the feeling of strangeness means nothing but this: if I recognize myself, then I must kill myself. Adler's schoolboy belongs to this category. As a counterpart, the discussant quotes the saying, often quoted, that the whole of society is nothing but a comedy. Here, too, a deep feeling of guilt lies at the base.

In the psychology of this matter [feeling of strangeness], one must distinguish whether the objects that appear strange are generally unrecognizable, or whether something specific has happened to them (whether something particular has been added or subtracted, etc.); each of these alternatives will, again, have its specific meaning.

As a supplement to the topic of the feeling of unreality, Prof. Freud mentions the story of Tartarin de Tarascon[13] who, while traveling through Switzerland, refuses to believe that the Alps are dangerous. Philistine that he is, he cannot become accustomed to anything else but his Tarascon, and therefore refuses to bring to bear, on the new that he meets, the affect cathexis; in that moment it becomes "unreal" for him.

ADLER quotes, as a further example from literature, Don Quixote and his confusion of the real external world [with his fantasy]. What is operative here is a compulsion of the individual to raise his self-esteem by transforming the external world; Tartarin achieves the overvaluation of his own person by playing down the external world.

Referring to Freud's statements with regard to Adler's view, Adler thinks that one cannot stop short with Freud's formula of the endopsychic perception of the detachment of an affect, but must ask why the detachment takes place. Adler tried to find an answer to this question: the detachment takes place so that the patient can protect himself against a degradation. This, however, is not drawn from the psychology of consciousness. The feeling of inferiority is not conscious to the neurotic to the degree that it is effective—that is, in its dialectical consequence as megalomania. Nor is it conscious to the patient to the same degree that it exists. There are even cases in which the patient is directly aware of almost nothing at all about it. It is also with regard to the insolence of the ego that the patient protects himself

[13] Alphonse Daudet, 1840-1897, *Aventures prodigieuses de Tartarin de Tarascon.*

from degradation by means of the mechanism of estrangement. The way in which the feeling of inferiority penetrates into the feeling of strangeness can be seen in micropsia.

STEKEL declares that this time he cannot fully go along with Adler's views; and in particular Stekel cannot grasp how Adler could find himself in such full disagreement with Stekel's view of his cases, since no analyses at all were involved in Adler's. Stekel does not believe that in all cases the feeling of strangeness is a protection of the ego.

Freud's comprehensive formulation, on the other hand, met with Stekel's full agreement, and he can accept it fully. He believes that, with it, the problem has been solved for us.

PROF. FREUD, in order to support his proposition, would like in conclusion to present the continuity of one of those cases concerning which he had said that the feeling of unreality has been caused by the refusal to transfer affects onto the outside world. This young man was convinced of his great charm (of which he had been persuaded in his childhood), and now he thought that nothing could happen to him —just as before—that everyone would do everything to please him, etc. That is a frequent placement of the libido (narcissism). There was no trace of a feeling of inferiority. Prof. Freud must concur with Adler in the view that the feeling of strangeness must have a tendency. But the economic gain does not shed light on the nature of the phenomenon itself. Freud would speak against the assertion that what is involved therein is a megalomania, which is compensating for a feeling of inferiority.

Lastly, a correction should be made: the example of Don Quixote, quoted by Adler, is a case of the opposite [character]. He [the Don] does not deny cathexis to the outside world but rather overcathects it; he is an illusionist.

109

SCIENTIFIC MEETING *on May 25, 1910*

Present: Adler, Federn, Freud, Friedjung, Furtmüller, Graf, Heller, Hilferding, Hitschmann, Joachim, Nepallek, Oppenheim, Rank, Reitler, Sadger, Stekel, Tausk, Wittels.

Frischauf as guest.

DISCUSSION ON THE HARMFULNESS OF MASTURBATION

PROF. FREUD, in his capacity as scientific chairman, points out that the editors of the *Zentralblatt* intend to publish the discussions on the harmfulness of masturbation as one issue of the *Wiener Diskussion.* He then proceeds, in one sentence, to call attention to the manifest aspect of the problem. This is the contrast between the extraordinary harmfulness of masturbation, as assumed and energetically defended by the patients, and the fact that the majority of physicians consider it to be, in all probability, harmless. Why it is that, in some cases, masturbation seems to be so injurious, whereas, in other cases, it doesn't do any harm at all; and whether it is masturbation as such that matters or what matters is what is at the bottom of it—these are the questions that should be answered.

HITSCHMANN takes as his point of departure the idea that doubt about the harmfulness of masturbation is in part a [form of] resistance to Freud's teachings, insofar as the objection is frequently raised against the sexual etiology of neuroses that so many people have not been harmed by masturbation. In fact, there are a number of people who are not harmed even by masturbation that is practiced daily, as the speaker was able to observe recently in the case of a young colleague. And there are numerous other individuals who have remained well, up to the time when they stopped masturbating.

Hitschmann would classify the consequences of masturbation as (1) psychic changes, and (2) the organic changes that follow in its wake.

Ad 1. To these people the sexual has become something wrong—a secret—and sexuality has become blemished forever. Furthermore, we should mention those disturbances that can be gathered together under the term of "psychosexual parallelism"; individuals [so affected] lack self-confidence, they do not have the necessary social aggression at their disposal, etc. In extreme cases, neurotic symptoms emanate directly from masturbation; a special role is played in this by the notion that one can read masturbation on a person's face, a notion that should perhaps be taken in consideration when we deal with psychogenic disturbances of the eyes. In general, certain peculiarities—such as certain ways of looking in the mirror (Ibsen carried a mirror inside his hat)—are rather suspicious.

Indirect psychic harms inflicted by masturbation are due to the fantasies that accompany masturbation and determine the direction of sexual life. Severe psychic changes are based on the fact that the individuals involved become sufferers from nocturnal emissions. The question arises as to what connection emission has with neurosis, and why it is that there are so-called excessive masturbators who don't have an emission of that sort in their whole life, yet there are so many others who, while practicing masturbation to a comparatively moderate degree, suffer from frequent emission. One would be inclined to believe that the latter have an erotogenic zone at that place;[1] frequently, they are people who suffered from enuresis in childhood (dreams). Sub-

[1] This sentence is not clear; the penis as such is an erotogenic zone, anyway.

sequently, they become very much afraid of emissions and arrive at the idea of "saving their sap" (*masturbatio et coitus interruptus*).

The psychic change at the time of more frequent emissions is to a neurotic hypochondria.

Among the organic changes that are brought about by increased masturbation, there belongs above all the actual-neurosis of neurasthenia; here again one must point to the question, as yet unsolved, of whether these patients may have some organic defect in the *urethra posterior*.

In dealing with the problem of masturbation, one must above all distinguish among different ages. On the question of whether autoerotism should be prevented altogether, [or] whether it is only the excessive masturbation of a child that should be fought against, there is much to be said. As to the fact that excessive masturbation in puberty should be brought to a halt, there cannot be any doubt. It is true, however, that one must consider how difficult it is for parents to discover the presence of masturbation, especially in earlier childhood, when masturbation is practiced on other erotogenic zones. Except for excessive cases, one will aim at halting masturbation by loving and calm treatment. Once masturbation has been given up, pollakiuria not infrequently sets in.

Finally, the consequences of *not* masturbating must be mentioned: according to a statement made by Freud, more than half of those people who are psychically impotent had not masturbated, and this would signify that far more of those individuals who have not masturbated fall ill.

PROF. FREUD would like to suggest for this topic a mixed type of discussion: a brief interchange should be permitted after each main speaker, in which directly critical objections, questions for clarification, contradictions, etc., could be voiced.

Accordingly, he would like to ask Hitschmann how the young colleague who masturbated daily fared in married life; until one knows this, one cannot say anything about the case. (The young man is still unmarried.)

FEDERN, in contrast to Hitschmann, has seen only one single case in which masturbation did no harm: a man of forty-two, who from seventeen to thirty-four masturbated regularly. At that time, he began to suffer from the involuntary discharge of semen during defecation—a condition that was treated without success—but otherwise he showed no psychic injury whatsoever, and in a later affair proved to be completely potent.

OPPENHEIM has the impression that Hitschmann considers the physical harmfulness of masturbation as having been established, and he would like to raise the question of the relationship of this assumption to the way in which Prof. Freud posed the problem.

HITSCHMANN replies that perhaps an abuse of a gland may be involved, or an increased metabolism. Some patients undoubtedly overrate the effects of masturbation, which can sometimes remain harmless, even if it is practiced frequently. In other cases, the result will be neurasthenia with a psychic superstructure; at times, organic damages to the *urethra posterior* will ensue too.

ADLER would like to stress, in regard to these delicate points, that both extremes are found among masturbators, as well as among those who suffer from nocturnal emissions: great sensitivity, but total insensitivity as well. Curing by probing is a complicated process; it must by no means be regarded as primary.

For purposes of evaluating the harmfulness of masturbation, REITLER would like to divide the topic according to certain principles. One should take into account: (1) whether it is a normal or neurotic individual that is involved; (2) at what period masturbation occurs; and (3) whether it is practiced upon the genitalium or upon another erotogenic zone.

Masturbation is the result of an autoerotic sexual stimulus, and one will first have to find out when and how sexual excitations come about during the various stages of human development. Through analysis we are well informed about these questions, as far as neurotics are concerned, but we are still very much in the dark with reference to normal sexuality.

It is established that there are sucklings who even then have erections (secretion of milk, "witches' milk" [*Hexenmilch*], also occurs). The speaker is inclined to ascribe the infant's sexual excitement, which lasts only briefly, to certain chemical products that he has brought along from his mother's body. Once these are used up, the period of (apparent) latency sets in (Freud); this lasts until puberty, when the individual is capable of producing these chemical substances himself.

The speaker now comes to his view, expressed several times previously, that *genital* masturbation before puberty does not represent something normal, but is rather a symptom of a neurotic disposition. Gaining pleasure from other erotogenic zones before puberty, on the other hand, is normal, because it is merely a forepleasure-premium for other functions. This would make no sense as far as genital masturbation is concerned, nor has any observer yet seen this type of mastubation before puberty under normal conditions.

Example of a boy five years and nine months old, who had a distinctly anal character, which had developed from intensive repression of anal erotism (he was trained too well by his mother). As the consequence of this renunciation of "perverse" pleasure, the boy came to genital masturbation all too soon.

After puberty, on the contrary, masturbation must be regarded as the normal biological sexual function, in the normal as well as in the neurotic person. The normal child may under certain conditions react to it with an anxiety neurosis, and the hereditarily encumbered child with a psychogenic neurosis. At this time, the [male] masturbator should be taken to a woman as soon as possible; as far as girls are concerned, there is nothing else to do but let them masturbate; only, they must tolerate it well. The speaker would go so far as to regard this as the criterion for recovery from neurosis: whether or not masturbation is tolerated.

PROF. FREUD objects that the distinction in principle between normal and neurotic individuals now appears to be something that is in principle debatable; that distinction, however, lies beyond the problems occupying us at present. Nor does he believe that the latency period begins as early as the first weeks of infancy. Between the third and the fifth year, there occurs a pronounced increase of sexual activity, with erections and masturbation, even in the wholly normal child.[2]

[2] This discussion took place before the stages of development of libido organization had been recognized by Freud.

STEKEL remarks that one cannot accept as evidence the fact that no observer has reported on genital masturbation in children; this may be because it is self-evident.

FURTMÜLLER sees a misuse of teleology (because genital masturbation suits no purpose, it does not exist). Genital masturbation is probably just as well known as is thumbsucking, but it is just as little understood as being of a sexual nature.

FRIEDJUNG would take issue with the view that children display a particularly lively sexuality [shortly] after birth.

TAUSK mentions a recently published book on the life of the South Sea islanders, in which there is talk of the normal masturbation of small children.

SADGER has been collecting, for some time, observations in this sphere, which, despite various works specifically devoted to it (Rohleder,[3] etc.) is still rather unclear in regard to its symptomatology, as well as to the question of its usefulness or harmfulness. The speaker would like to confine himself to discussing this latter point, about which there are, according to Freud's observation, two opposing views.

The physicians' opinion about the relative harmlessness [of masturbation] is based on the familiar physiological considerations of the minimal loss of protein; moreover, most of the doctors recall their own masturbation, which did them little harm indeed. Finally, they consider the fact that it is, in general, such a widespread habit that, if it were harmful, everybody would have had to become ill. Neurotics, on the other hand, overrate the pathogenic effect of masturbation and —this is especially characteristic—are ashamed of it. Besides, they are afraid that their masturbation can be detected [from their appearance].

In the analyses of neurotics, one proceeds every time from the consciously remembered masturbation of puberty, or sometimes even childhood, to the unavoidable masturbation of early infancy, which was effected by the nursing person (in most instances, the mother). This masturbation is of great significance; it is at the bottom of the tenaciousness of later masturbation. In all instances, it is nothing but

[3] Dr. Hermann Oskar Rohleder (1866- ?): *Die Masturbation. Eine Monographie für Ärzte und Pädagogen*. Berlin, 1899. A ninth edition of this book appeared in 1921.

a return to the beloved mother, and everything else is merely a substitute for it. If a man gets rid of masturbation, that is because he has succeeded in finding in another woman a full substitute for the mother; if he does not succeed (i.e., if masochistic, fetishistic and other fantasies are also involved), one finds that such a person, even when married, must masturbate after intercourse.

This meaning of masturbation can best be studied in homosexuals: the homosexual plays the role of the mother, who masturbates the other person; in mutual masturbation, the homosexual (simultaneously) plays the child and has the other (partner) masturbate him.

If masturbation appears with increased intensity in persons who have a severe hereditary taint, then it is a form of obsessional neurosis; this may be its only symptom, just as psychic impotence may be the only symptom of a hysteria.

For the boy in puberty, masturbation is the only way out; whoever does not masturbate during the course of puberty is neurotic. The only patients who have demonstrably not masturbated during puberty are severe obsessional neurotics.

The speaker verifies his statements by two cases in which he succeeded, by elucidating some of the sexual fantasies, in eliminating part of the harmfulness of masturbation.

The connection with emissions already mentioned by Hitschmann, as well as erections at an early age, had to do with urinary erotism, which corresponds to anal erotism, and, like it, is based on reinforcements of certain constitutional factors. Such psychopathic children have erections when urine is retained. Urinary erotics are almost invariably intensive and persistent masturbators.

HITSCHMANN finds that some of the statements that have been made are not yet fully proven, nor does he regard them as convincing—especially the assertions concerning mothers and homosexuals. It should be mentioned that there also exists a masturbation without fantasies, something that affords a purely localized pleasure.

The most significant consequence of masturbation, as far as married life is concerned, is the fact that intercourse is very quickly over; masturbation thereby indirectly becomes the cause of neurotic marriages and, with it, also of nervous children. Similarly, the inability to tolerate *coitus interruptus,* abstinence and unsatisfied excitation, is a result of masturbation, which must therefore be considered to be, as it were, the cause also of anxiety neurosis.

What Adler found by dealing with the ego instincts should be added as a supplement to the psychic consequences: that stubbornness, lack of self-confidence, and some other character traits are also connected with masturbation.

TAUSK remarks that up to now we have heard nothing about the physical harm done by masturbation, and he himself cannot make any statement about that. About the psychic aspect, however, he has learned some things that he believes he should formulate.

He relates the case of a hypochondriacal young man who pictured intercourse as the overcoming of a strong resistance and who, having practiced a peculiar type of masturbation (he thrust his penis through a sheet of newspaper), became a pursuer of virgins; thus he did not relate to the woman herself, but only to the hymen. Another man, with homosexual tendencies, had intercourse without any thought of the genitalium. His homosexual disposition seems to have been fixated by masturbation. The most significant harm done by masturbation is the fact that the masturbator loses connection with the world in general, because he cannot find any connection with women. As a result, the ego becomes impoverished; this is equivalent to the loss of a zest for living, to hypochondria.

In one case Tausk did suspect masturbation to be a substitute for the mother.

FEDERN refers to Wittels' description of the psychic consequence of masturbation:[4] it impedes the sublimation of autoerotism.

STEKEL mentions that the newspaper plays an important role in symbolism (especially in the symbolism of masturbators). It is, as Wittels showed, a substitute for the father, and like time[5] in general, has some relation to the mother; the saying that "everything is in it" also plays a part.

FURTMÜLLER comments that even those who do not want to admit the harmfulness of masturbation nevertheless talk about the

[4] Fritz Wittels: *Die sexuelle Not,* Vienna and Leipzig, 1909.
[5] The German term for newspaper is *Zeitung; Zeit* = time.

masturbator's feeling of guilt. It seems, however, that this feeling of guilt comes about only when certain states of depression in childhood have become anchored [in the child's mind] in masturbation.

The Catholic Church's purely intellectual view that masturbation is reprehensible because it represents a squandering of the semen destined for propagation, seems, according to some stories that are told in the *Anthropophyteia*,[6] to be traceable to an inner experience during the act of masturbation.

We must not ask: does masturbation lead to a neurosis? Neurosis is, indeed, nothing but the manifestation of defense against excessive demands by civilization. Even if someone has not become neurotic as a result of masturbation, he still will display an inhibition of aggression that is culturally not helpful. Masturbation will be harmful whenever it remains a permanent state, and is not chosen merely as a temporary expedient.

TAUSK believes that the person who overcomes masturbation may also become a cynic.

OPPENHEIM mentions that the Cynics[7] actually had a higher opinion of masturbation than of normal intercourse.

ADLER, in reference to the question raised by Furtmüller, reads excerpts from letters written by two girls who are suffering from the consequences of masturbation. However, in view of the fact that cases of this kind are so frequent, one must be cautious in speaking of the consequences of masturbation. The ideas of these patients cannot be regarded as the results of masturbation. Masturbation does not become something independent later on, either in neurosis or in the psychology of the normal individual; it is merely utilized. We must separate what we call harmful consequences from this utilization.

FRIEDJUNG, in a brief description of a young man, adds to the evidence of the harmful influence of masturbation on the development of character.

6 See Minutes 46, Volume I.

7 Oppenheim refers to the Greek philosophic school of the Cynics, founded by Antisthenes.

RANK would like to caution emphatically against overrating accidental influence (for example, the "enlightening" book). These are merely means and subterfuges that are used by psychic development.

HITSCHMANN mentions female anesthesia as a consequence of masturbation, and cites Bruckner's[8] masturbation in old age.

GRAF also speaks about Bruckner's masturbation, which he continued until the end of his life, and about some of his obsessional symptoms.

RANK recalls his attempt to derive the pathologically mendacious character type from a very definite form of repression of masturbation; its successful repression, on the other hand, brings about the opposite and socially highly esteemed character of the truth fanatic. In view of these two contrasting consequences of masturbation, one will have to state, in reference to today's problem, that the usefulness or harmfulness of masturbation, as well as the degree [of either] will depend on whether masturbation is suppressed, at what period this happens, and above all in what way the repression succeeds or fails. That again will depend upon all the other conditions of repression.[9]

STEKEL would merely like to let a man who is absent speak today, and to read those passages that refer to masturbation from the book by the Russian physician, Dr. Gutzeit,[10] who is, in a certain sense, a precursor of Freud.

Stekel finally stresses that the topic was not dealt with altogether along the lines of the problem as posed by Freud. The question that induced Freud to raise the problem, has to do with a reexamination of the nature of neurasthenia: the question is whether masturbation is

[8] Anton Bruckner, 1824-1896, Austrian composer and organist.

[9] See Minutes 75, this volume.

[10] H. L. von Gutzeit: *Dreissig Jahre Praxis* [*Thirty Years of Practice*], Vienna 1873. Stekel reports briefly on this book in the *Zentralblatt für Psychoanalyse* I. Dr. Gutzeit regarded masturbation as a natural and healthful means of sexual gratification for girls and women who cannot have normal intercourse or who do not want it. He believed that vivacious girls, who often begin to menstruate as early as twelve years of age, show menstrual abnormalities at about eighteen or nineteen years, if they neither have sexual intercourse nor masturbate. Gutzeit declared himself to be strongly opposed to any medical or moral advice or measure that was aimed at preventing masturbation.

harmful, whether it produces neurasthenia. This is the point that should be given chief attention next time.

PROF. FREUD admonishes the members not to neglect, in their discussion, the usefulness of masturbation, in addition to considering its harmfulness. He remarks, further, that for [a better understanding of] some very uncertain points about male masturbation, it would be quite in order to turn to female masturbation, which represents, indeed, a certain simplification.

The Chairman closes the meeting by putting his impressions into words: judicious, varied and rich in content as the individual expositions have been, they still do not warrant publication in a special brochure. The discussion should strive for a higher level and for greater depth.

110

SCIENTIFIC MEETING *on June 1, 1910*

Present: Adler, Federn, Freud, Friedjung, Furtmüller, Hilferding, Hitschmann, Nepallek, Oppenheim, Rank, Reitler, Sadger, Steiner, Stekel, Wittels.

Dr. Frischauf and A. Deutsch as guests.

COMMUNICATIONS

The CHAIRMAN urges the discussants to speed up their working out the discussions on suicide.

Since no communication about the "International Association" has been received up to now, the decision has been made to inquire in Zürich whether the date of the founding of this Association can be made public. Should Zürich's intention be to delay the announcement for some time, the Vienna group would constitute itself as an independent society for the time being, and join the "International Psycho-Analytic Association" as a local branch later.[1]

The LIBRARIAN lists the books received.

STEKEL reads several replies to the invitation for collaboration and asks for contributions to the Journal [*Zentralblatt*].

[1] The delay in officially founding the Association seems already at that time to have been due to Jung's hesitation.

CONTINUATION OF THE DISCUSSION ON THE HARMFULNESS OF MASTURBATION

The scientific Chairman (SADGER) emphasizes that the discussions have gone along rather sleepily up to now and points out that Freud himself is partly responsible for this, in that he has anticipated much of the topic in previous discussions[2] and, moreover, has this time circumscribed the topic too narrowly. It is true that he has mitigated this defect by his invitation to discuss the usefulness of masturbation, as well as masturbation by women. The speaker himself would like to add the request not to go too far afield in the discussion.

STEKEL takes an actual experience as his point of departure. He saw two brothers recently. The one who looked fresh and vigorous turned out to be a masturbator, whereas the other one, who looked pale and sickly, timid and embarrassed, did not masturbate but has intercourse regularly.

Under the term "masturbation," we gather together a number of processes, which we have no right to regard as identical, either psychically or organically. Among the autoerotic processes, there are those that are harmful and those that are not. To begin with, we can distinguish two main groups of masturbators:

1) those who practice masturbation without friction, merely by acts of fantasy (beautiful speeches, reading, or certain affects), so-called "mental masturbation"; and

2) those who practice masturbation with friction; the latter is performed in several ways:

- a) by purely mechanical stimulation, without fantasy;
- b) first by fantasy, which is then followed by friction;
- c) in the particularly harmful forms of *masturbatio prolongata*, and
- d) *masturbatio interrupta.*

All these forms are analogous to corresponding forms of emissions.

There are, furthermore, a number of autoerotic processes that emanate from erotogenic zones; these we must characterize as masturbation.

[2] See Index, Vol. IV (Index to the Minutes).

The question of what forms are harmful must be answered as follows: those forms are harmful in which fantasy is employed frequently and emission is delayed (type: anxiety neurosis), in which fore-pleasure is extended and end-pleasure postponed.

Pure friction without accompanying fantasy is absolutely harmless, if it is not practiced excessively; it helps people considerably in getting through a period of abstinence.

In regard to neurasthenia—which, according to Freud, is caused by excessive masturbation—Stekel must continue to advocate the view he stressed earlier—i.e., that we find no neurasthenia at all, but only anxiety neuroses. Nor is neurasthenia—that is to say, anxiety neurosis—directly connected with masturbation. The speaker attempts to demonstrate by means of two cases that what is involved is solely a psychic conflict, which implies a deeply repressed sexual desire.

Ejaculatio praecox has various causes. It occurs in persons with strong affects, in those who cannot tolerate prolonged tension, and free themselves from it by premature emissions. It also occurs in people who have an especially small amount of libido; for instance, a man may have a premature emission during intercourse with his wife, yet be completely potent with a mistress.

The harmfulness of masturbation has to do with a totally different area: it lies in the severe psychic battle that masturbators must carry on, once they have been informed about the damage wrought by masturbation and its objectionable nature. Their self-reproaches do not refer to the act [of masturbation] itself, but to the fantasies that were originally connected with it. Of these fantasies, the following play a special role: (1) the homosexual ones (simultaneously playing man and woman; symbolism of the hand), (2) incest-fantasies, and (3) perverse fantasies. Originally, these fantasies are present in full clarity; later, however, they change to such an extent that they are no longer rcognizable, even to the autoerotic himself. A particular symbolism is designed to disguise these fantasies. Yet it is possible to diagnose them from the point in time (the precipitating cause), at which masturbation was started. Whether masturbation is given up easily, with difficulty or not at all, is connected with the fantasies that have become linked with the act.

The speaker now relates several (six) cases that provide information about the usefulness and harmfulness of masturbation; they demonstrate that even masturbation that is continued for many years—indeed, excessively practiced—is [sometimes] tolerated without particular detriment to potency and the sexual sphere.

It should be mentioned that there are individuals who exhibit the opposite of a sense of guilt, who associate with masturbation the idea of a religious act—i.e., of something especially holy.

A neurotic who has never masturbated is a very severe case; he has such powerful inhibitions that the prognosis is bad, as well, for his being cured.

If Freud believes masturbation to be injurious because of the psychic short-circuit that it establishes, one must object that this conclusion of his represents a reversal of the actual fact. Masturbators have a strong instinct and weak inhibitions, and they show a corresponding type of behavior in relation to women, too. Proof that these conditions are a consequence of masturbation is still missing.

Masturbation is the return to man's first attainment of pleasure; it is an infantile process. It is directed toward the mother, or to another person who has since then been repressed, and is now retained in the masturbatory fantasy. Whether masturbation will be given up depends on one's success in moving the patient away from his first pleasure-gain and making him move forward.

A prophylaxis for masturbation is unnecessary. It is the task of upbringing to spare the child all the traumata that will subsequently repeat themselves in the fantasies that accompany the act.

HITSCHMANN would like to bridge the contradiction between his and Stekel's expositions. If Stekel denies the existence of neurasthenia, he overlooks the fact that, in the case of the two brothers, for instance, the patient fell ill with a hysteria in the form of a neurasthenia, a phenomenon that Freud has already mentioned. It is nothing new, either, that even a person who masturbates excessively may remain healthy; this is no evidence at all against the finding that frequent emissions are a cause of neurasthenia. Nor is it a new discovery that a continuation of a moderately practiced masturbation is often better than its sudden complete abandonment. People who cannot fall asleep without masturbating and who [still] have this impulse are simply old masturbators; this phenomenon is a symptom of their previous habit.

Ejaculatio praecox cannot be explained in terms of a single factor, but probably has psychic causes as well; it is most frequently provoked by so-called "mental" masturbation.

STEINER does not find Stekel's exposition satisfactory: what was good was not new, and what was new was not good.

FEDERN would like to establish that, in his view and despite Stekel, neurasthenia continues to exist. *Ejaculatio praecox* cannot represent a self-help of nature because, when patients are cured of it, they are able to endure the tension very well. In reference to the "short circuit," the opposite of Stekel's argument is true: masturbators have strong inhibitions and little instinct. . . . If masturbation is a return to man's first pleasure-gain, then this is true of each and every [later] pleasure.

REITLER believes that Stekel was on the right track but, in discussing the forms of masturbation, he stayed too much on the surface. It does not matter whether masturbation is practiced with or without friction; in the main, one must adhere to the view that it is not the act that is the determining factor, but the fantasy. Masturbation with friction and without fantasy does not correspond to the normal type but is a narcissistic [variety]. It is interesting that, for the hysteric, giving up masturbation entails severe harm; this is so because he has not yet learned to control his part instincts, and his troubles increase as soon as he cannot give expression to them in masturbation.

ADLER finds that some statements have crept into Stekel's discourse that cannot be sustained. For instance, spermatorrhea cannot be considered to be analogous to masturbation, although it is true that genuine spermatorrhea is a form of emission. As far as the non-existence of neurasthenia is concerned, Adler must agree with Stekel's views.

PROF. FREUD agrees with Stekel's statements, as far as some details are concerned; with regard to other points, Freud is inclined to continue advocating opposing views.

Masturbation purely by friction is in all likelihood practiced only in childhood; later it is probably always accompanied by a fantasy, even though it may be an unconscious one.

Concerning neurasthenia, it must be conceded that this point needs most careful verification. Hitschmann has already clarified the misunderstanding about the etiological role of masturbation. Tracing back masturbation to the battle of weaning does not help us to understand why the struggle is so hard for the masturbator, and what produces his feeling of horror when he succumbs in that struggle.

STEKEL would like to clear up a number of misunderstandings. The struggle is so hard for masturbators because of the terrifying threats and the self-reproaches that they heap upon themselves as a consequence of their fantasies. It is a battle for their independence in erotic life.

We know very little about the influence of masturbation on dream life; we know hardly anything about the symbols of masturbation.

The harmfulness of masturbation does not lie in the act itself, but rather in the ethical, religious and esthetic inhibitions [that surround it].

It will no longer be possible to maintain the concept of neurasthenia; Freud does not see any [neurasthenia] because there is no longer any to see.

STEINER thinks that, in studying masturbation, one should proceed from the natural conditions; one should also examine its physical aspect. Stekel has made a start; it is certain that not all forms are harmful; the more closely masturbation resembles coition, the less harmful will it be. If it is practiced for a long time, however, this form of masturbation too will produce an overexcitation of the *pars urethra posterior*.

In many instances, nocturnal emissions and masturbation are, in fact, to be considered equivalent. The patient generally falls asleep with a fantasy, and then it takes only a small stimulus to bring about an emission.

The existence of neurasthenia cannot be denied; the speaker daily sees a number of cases of pure actual-neurosis. Just as little can there be any doubt of the physiological bases of *ejaculatio praecox*.

One does too much honor to masturbation, if one makes the masturbator a special type. Masturbation is no illness; it is not even a symptom. The harm is not inflicted by masturbation but by neurasthenia.

ADLER sees in Steiner's argumentation a contradiction, inasmuch as Steiner first stressed the relationship between masturbation and neurasthenia, and then later did not want masturbation viewed from the standpoint of usefulness and harmfulness, but only as a symptom; this latter is Adler's point of view, too.

STEKEL commits himself to analyzing any neurasthenic and uncovering the repression at the bottom of the neurasthenia. There are also nocturnal emissions that take place without any sexual excitation having occurred during the previous evening.

HITSCHMANN considers it self-evident that, in the analysis even of an actual-neurotic, one will also find various complexes and conflicts, which are indeed [to be found] everywhere.

REITLER objects, offering the opinion that masturbation that resembled coition as closely as possible could also be harmful, just as there are also harmful coitions. What always matters are the fantasies and the instincts that lie at their root.

FRIEDJUNG would like to confine himself to the [problem of] masturbation in small children, a subject that he knows from his particular [medical] experience. He has frequently observed masturbation in small children only five to six months or a year old. It is true, however, that in these instances there are involved masturbatory acts in the broadest sense, and it is questionable whether one can put such acts on an equal footing with the masturbation of sexually mature individuals. For infantile masturbatory acts generally occur without erection or orgasm. With regard to the question of harmfulness, the speaker has not yet encountered a case of masturbation during earliest infancy, in which harmfulness would have been unquestionable. Nor did he see, among the older children of five to ten years, any case in which masturbation was the immediate cause, for instance, of looking bad, and in which recovery was brought about therefore when the masturbation stopped.

Friedjung, too, can confirm that a nocturnal emission was not caused in every instance by sexual excitation before falling asleep. There are emissions that do not come about in such an innocent manner, without physical assistance on the part of the dreamer. In cases such as these, the dreamer performs motions of coition in his sleep.

ADLER wants to emphasize that this phenomenon is found in neurotics; one of his patients very appropriately termed it "masturbatory dream motion."

He further wants to stress that he was the first to assert the psychogenic unity of all neuroses (including the actual-neuroses).

PROF. FREUD calls attention to the fact that the establishment of the existence of masturbation is not always an easy thing to do, and that, in this respect, he himself does not believe any patient before he has had him in treatment for three to six weeks. The number of people who continue to masturbate in their sleep is much greater than one thinks, so that many individuals who know nothing of masturbation nevertheless have actually masturbated. Prof. Freud can see no advantage in postulating the oneness of the neuroses, since the libido, which is at the basis of all neuroses, itself establishes their oneness.

ADLER recapitulates his assertion to the effect that no psychic difference can be shown to exist between the character of an actual-neurotic and that of a psychoneurotic.

STEKEL refers to the fact that he was the first to claim that neurasthenia does not exist and that in anxiety neurosis there are psychic conflicts.

ADLER objects to this, in that in his book Stekel does make a distinction between anxiety neurosis and anxiety hysteria.

PROF. FREUD does not have anything final to say in regard to this question [of masturbation], nor does he wish to offer a decisive answer to the various problems; he wants only to present a number of formulations in order to bring forward his own point of view. In so doing, he will restrict himself to the consideration of genital masturbation and the essential question about its damaging effect.

It must be said, to begin with, that masturbation is mistakenly regarded as a clinical syndrome, and that the essential thing is the fantasies.

The question of whether masturbation is a symptom, a state of illness, or the cause of illnesses, proceeds from an unintelligent presupposition—as though excessive masturbation could come into being by accident, and did not itself have deeper causes.

Early masturbation is a sign of great sexual need; whether it does harm or is tolerated depends on the relationship of the sexual instincts to the ego. The question about the harmful effects of masturbation makes sense only if one compares masturbation with other forms of sexual activity. Otherwise the question of the harm that is inflicted by masturbation is equivalent to one about the harm that is inherent in sexuality in general, sexuality being one of the most dangerous activities of the human being.[3] And so, then, the subject of the possible harmfulness of masturbation crumbles away; what remains is only the consideration of the harmful effect of masturbation as a particular kind of sexual activity. Cases in which masturbation is not injurious cannot of course, as negative cases, decide the question of the harmfulness of masturbation.

If, then, masturbation is harmful (the preconditions for this lie outside our topic) it does harm in the following ways:

I. somatically
II. psychically

Ad I. There are simple points of view:

Masturbation does harm (1) in that it offers an opportunity for excessive sexual activity;

(2) in that it represents an inadequate form of sexual activity (Steiner), which employs only a few types of stimuli, and is thus not without effect upon the composition of secretion;

(3) in that it gives rise to an impairment of normal potency. That many masturbators have retained their potency does not prove anything against that statement. A certain amount of usefulness is attached to masturbation; of this we will speak later.

Ad II. The injuries are more extensive and transparent; they come about:

(1) through the setting of a pattern in which the individual becomes accustomed to reach the satisfaction of his needs, not by means of great efforts but by means of a "short-circuit";

(2) through loosening the individual's interconnections with his

[3] In his later writings, Freud again and again stressed the dangers of sexuality, to which the ego reacts by repression.

fellow men; masturbatory gratification is an antisocial act; it brings the individual concerned into opposition to society.

(3) through the preponderance of fantasy life over reality, a situation that forms a pattern for a number of other functions.

(4) through the excessive demands that the individual concerned, as the result of being spoiled by his fantasy, makes upon reality, which can never satisfy him.

(5) through the individual's inability to tolerate sexual restrictions, which life—especially married life—makes unavoidable.

(6) as a result of the fact that masturbatory activity is to be regarded as identical with the preservation of the infantile condition in every respect. Therein lies the main psychic harmfulness of masturbation, because with it there has been created the basis for a psychoneurosis, which sets in when conflict and rejection are added.

(7) through the general debasement of sexual life, which results from the cheapness and easy availability of the sexual act and the social disdain attached to it. Masturbators of this type are thereafter unable to have intercourse with persons whom they love and esteem, but only with those whom they disdain.[4]

An additional factor appears in women, in whom a sexual conflict arises in connection with the practice of masturbation. Whereas man's resistance is mainly of a social nature, in the woman it is a straight sexual conflict. Woman's masturbation, while being an infantile activity, has in addition a masculine character.[5]

Summarizing all points of view under the heading of two chief categories, one can say: excessive masturbatory activity brings disturbances in an individual's social behavior, and in his attitude toward reality, over which the reality of thought (fantasy life) predominates.

One must not imagine that, with the removal of masturbation, its harmful effect is also removed. Masturbation is merely the phenomenon behind which other forces are concealed.

In addition to the harmful effects of masturbation, its advantages must not be neglected. They consist in the fact that:

[4] See Freud's essay: "On the Universal Tendency to Debasement in the Sphere of Love" (1912) *S.E.* 11.

[5] Freud obviously refers to clitoris-masturbation. (Clitoris = penis.)

1) masturbation counteracts abstinence and, after all, does represent a sexual gratification that discharges the sexual tension that otherwise would often have a pathogenic effect;

2) it brings about a reduction of potency, such as is necessary in our civilization if the conditions of married life, etc. that have been set up by society, are to be met;[6]

3) it makes it possible for a young man during the second (cultural[7]) period of latency [after puberty] to devote himself to other tasks.

It should also be mentioned that sexual freedom and the independence from parents that it implies are indispensable preconditions.

As a last point [in favor of masturbation], the avoidance of infection must be cited.

STEINER adds to the enumeration of the advantages of masturbation a better formation of fantasy life (artistic production).

STEKEL is pleased that some of the thoughts that he expressed were contained in Freud's statements. There is, however, still another way of looking at the problem. For coition, to certain individuals, is an inadequate form of gratification.

Because of the sense of guilt, masturbation is not always the easiest and cheapest way of gratification, either.

Concerning female masturbation, it is to be noted that there are cases in which masturbation is started directly at the *introitus vaginae* [entrance into the vagina] (and not at the clitoris).

FEDERN asks Prof. Freud to set forth his viewpoint in regard to neurasthenia.

FURTMÜLLER, in view of Stekel's assertions, would like to raise the question as to why it is precisely masturbation that is so terrifying —why, for instance, the much more concrete dangers of illegitimate sexual intercourse do not deter people, whereas a mere description of the far more remote dangers of masturbation make such a deep impres-

[6] Cf. Freud's essay on "'Civilized' Sexual Ethics and Modern Nervous Sickness" (1908) *S.E.* 9.

[7] "Cultural" in this context obviously means "required by our cultural conditions."

sion. Evidently, there must be something inherent in masturbation that makes the individuals concerned so sensitive to that fear.

PROF. FREUD first speaks against some of Stekel's objections and emphasizes that, in discussing the harmfulness of masturbation, one can, of course, consider only the positive cases and not those in which masturbation did no harm.

If Stekel believes that the entire harmfulness of masturbation stems from the notion of the individual involved that he has done harm to himself by masturbating, this is a derivation of deep-rooted psychic effects from the conscious psychic surface. The person involved must first have accepted the terror [attaching to masturbation] for deeper reasons (Furtmüller).

Concerning Stekel's contention that potency is unharmed, it must be stressed that even the individual who is cured [of his masturbatory habit] is considerably less potent, in comparison with other men.

It is most unlikely that women start to masturbate directly at the vaginal opening; childhood masturbation was probably overlooked when that assertion was made.

One must fully agree with the statement that a goodly portion of the "psychic harmfulness of masturbation" (formation of conflicts) stems from the opposition of parents and teachers in childhood (castration complex); this coincides, however, with the parents' general attitude toward sexuality.

Regarding Freud's view about neurasthenia, it has changed much less than is generally believed, and he still adheres to the essentials of his former standpoint. By contrast with Adler and Stekel, he is firmly convinced of the difference between actual- and psychoneuroses (Steiner). Freud is quite prepared to assume that psychic processes are added on to purely physiological ones. On the other hand, it must be denied that the symptoms of neurasthenia are hysteric; they are symptoms of a purely toxic nature, and their possible symbolic meaning (*Stekel:* pressure in the head—birth fantasy) is a psychic superstructure. Similarly, the differentiation between anxiety neurosis and hysteria must also be maintained. The complications have already been indicated in Freud's first paper on the anxiety neurosis: the anxiety neurosis supplies the material upon which a hysteria can then develop.

Besides, the theory of the neuroses never was a purely psychological one, for sexuality is, indeed, also an organic factor.

THE CHAIRMAN: Since there are still several members who have asked for the floor, the chairman proposes to continue this discussion next Wednesday.

111

SCIENTIFIC MEETING *on June 8, 1910*

Present: Adler, Federn, Freud, Friedjung, Furtmüller, Heller, Hilferding, Hitschmann, Nepallek, Oppenheim, Rank, Reitler, Sadger, Steiner, Stekel, Tausk.

Dr. Fr. S. Krauss [Editor of *Anthropophyteia*], Dr. Brauchbar, Dr. Frischauf as guests.

The chairman informs the group of a suggestion he has received. Since it is not likely that the hope for joint publication of the discussions on masturbation will materialize this season, individuals who want to publish their contributions separately should do so along the lines they have expressed. There are others who also intend to publish independent papers [on this topic].

STEKEL raises the question of what should be done with the additional honorarium of K 100, which Bergmann is paying for the editing of the *Discussion*.

ADLER would like to leave the decision on that matter to the editorial committee, but would propose that the *Discussion* appear as "edited by the Vienna Psychoanalytic Society."

STEKEL proposes to donate the honorarium to the Society.

CONCLUSION OF THE DISCUSSION ON THE HARMFULNESS OF MASTURBATION

ADLER does not intend to present a full-length treatment of this topic from his point of view; he has spoken about this problem several times before, most recently in his paper on psychic hermaphroditism,[1] in which masturbation appears as one of the forms of the masculine protest. This becomes evident even at the starting-point of masturbation, in the mechanism of sexual excitation: through the stimulation of an erection and through the emission.

The speaker then proceeds to examine how this point of view tallies with the harmful effects of which we have heard. There is no point in asking what harm masturbation entails, because (1) in each case, masturbation encounters a different disposition, and (2) one always has to take into consideration a large number of countervailing conditions.

Everything the neurotic expresses by means of masturbation, he expresses also in other ways. And all the harm that appears in masturbation, and that could be traced back to it, can just as well be traced back to earlier conditions.

The speaker now tries to demonstrate this latter point in particular, by way of several cases in which other colleagues saw harm coming from masturbation. This is also true, for instance, of neurasthenia, the preconditions for which exist before masturbation is begun. Concerning the fear (conscience) that is supposed to make the masturbator sick, it can be shown in every one of these cases that the sort of persons involved are terrified in the same way by other things, too, both before and after [the onset of] masturbation. A similar point of view holds true when it is asserted that masturbation makes an individual incapable of tolerating [sexual] abstinence; such individuals have long before shown themselves to be incapable of tolerating abstinence of any other kind, either. This incapacity is traceable to organic inferiorities that are connected with instinctual life. In respect to antisocial attitudes, one must employ the same argument—i.e., that persons of this type are noticeably timid and retiring, even at an early age. Such indi-

[1] See Minutes 98, this volume.

viduals, when they meet with deceptions, etc., leave the straight path of aggression and surround their fantasy with safeguards (masturbation).

This secondary function might be regarded as being beneficial for the neurotic; however, it is also harmful. On the one hand, masturbation restores to the neurotic his equilibrium; on the other hand, it is easily available. But neither the harm nor the benefit is to be taken seriously, because they can come about just as well by other means.

DR. KRAUSS would like to ask how the speaker would classify those individuals who masturbate not out of nervous weakness but, for instance, for magical purposes.

ADLER thinks that these people want to impress themselves with their masculinity.

KRAUSS comments that if masturbation were actually as harmful as it is claimed to be, all of mankind would necessarily have become neurotic long ago.

PROF. FREUD wishes that, when Adler examines the problem, he would also take into consideration the neurosis of women.

Freud thinks that the engaging in masturbation (in Krauss' sense) does not go back to an overestimation of the sexual act, but to a specific archaic evaluation of symbols, phrases, fantasy-formations. To these persons, the word is magic, a fact that is probably the basis of all art. Masturbation is surely nothing but the image of coition in fantasy. To the primitive man, the symbolic action is the guarantee of the real one.

STEKEL finds that Adler falls into the error of applying his (certainly significant) principle to everything. Masturbation, to Adler, is for both sexes masculine protest; but Stekel knows cases for which this is certainly not true, cases in which masturbation is practiced while being accompanied by the most definitely feminine fantasies.

REITLER, in opposition to Stekel, is inclined to agree with Adler that the harm done is frequently traceable to earlier conditions, in the same sense as the neurotic symptom rests on previous experience. It is true, however, that neurasthenia cannot exist prior to masturbation.

Reitler cannot accept masculine protest as being the *movens* ["motive force"] of the entire problem.

TAUSK would like to reply to Stekel's objection with the comment that the reproach to Adler remains unjustified, so long as it has not been proven that man-woman is not the central problem of neurosis. It is true that the matter cannot be clarified in terms of biology. The sphere of influence of the female is as strictly circumscribed in nature as is that of the male, so that there is no need for a masculine protest.

When Tausk spoke of antisocial attitudes, it was in the sense that the woman carries on a competitive battle for sperm; we are completely heterosexual in our orientation, and the withdrawal of that tribute is regarded as a disgrace.

KRAUSS, in connection with Tausk's remarks, mentions masturbation as a children's game in Bosnia.

ADLER believes that he recognizes a masculine protest in these games, too, since they are about who is finished more quickly and has developed great strength in ejecting the sperm. Similarly with urinary games. These points of view can be utilized just as easily with women, but are more difficult to explain in their case. The biological basis is not to be taken into consideration; the infantile (neurotic) valuation is alone what counts. Besides, the biological foundation can be seen in the theory of inferiority.

As far as concerns those people who, while masturbating, feel themselves to be like a woman, it is precisely this that is a clear manifestation of the psychic harm [inflicted by masturbation]. Regarding the question of compulsive masturbation, Adler with Sadger (and against Stekel) acknowledges that there is such a type.

FEDERN brings to the forefront the question of whether neurasthenia is caused by the masturbation [itself], or whether (as Adler and Stekel believe) it originates in the cultural valuation on the part of the outside world, i.e., in the conflict engendered by it. Federn shares Freud's opinion, even though certain observations would seem to speak against it.

One must point to the fact that we have to regard masturbation as an unsatisfactory terminus to a frustrated excitation; we must continuously examine what persons are subject to more or less frustrated excitations, and whether or not these persons are capable of reaching the stage of masturbation. In the first case, [masturbatory] activity is not going to be harmful, because it represents a gratification. This is a direct indication of when one can permit masturbation and when one cannot.

The feeling of guilt is not dependent exclusively on the cultural valuation; it is a manifestation of the ill-humor that proceeds from the unsatisfying masturbation, in which the instinct of aggression is, indeed, curtailed.

HITSCHMANN mentions the case of a woman who masturbates excessively and cannot find full satisfaction in intercourse; she shows symptoms of an anxiety-(cardiac)-neurosis but none of the typical symptoms of an actual neurasthenia.

ADLER emphasizes that the feeling of guilt exists long before masturbation and merely acquires new content [with it].

TAUSK: In accordance with previous expositions, Tausk would like to see the [concept of] "guilt feeling" reduced to the actual meaning of the words; it is not to be thought of without [the presence of] a demand. The masturbator violates the demands of our heterosexual culture.

FRIEDJUNG calls attention to the dilatations of the heart that occur in puberty, which are considered to be a consequence of masturbation (between the ages of twelve and seventeen).

PROF. FREUD can only confirm Adler's opinion that the feeling of guilt subsequently fuses with masturbation. In the feeling of guilt, the anxiety is psychically bound (in the same way as in a phobia); this is the anxiety that arises as a consequence of the development of moral inhibitions. The feeling of guilt, then, is to be derived from an unsuccessful, quantitatively too strong suppression of instincts; no masturbation need have preceded it.

FURTMÜLLER is of the opinion that Tausk, in interpreting the unconscious intellectually, is pursuing a path that leads in a direction opposite to that of psychoanalysis.

Furtmüller would like to ask Adler why he believes masturbation so well suited to become the symbol of all these harms.

ADLER had only wanted to state the fact that masturbation is so suited.

HITSCHMANN, too, mentions the well known "masturbator's heart," and the stomachaches that masturbators have, which cease immediately as soon as masturbation is stopped; these pains can also be successfully treated by way of the nasal conchae.

HILFERDING can relate only some scattered experiences, particularly in regard to masturbation in females. She has frequently noted a complex of symptoms in girls shortly before the appearance of menstruation: (1) increased urge to urinate; (2) slight discharge. In such cases, vulvitis has also been seen. Upon inquiry, it has invariably turned out that some kind of masturbation has been practiced. In other cases, masturbation resulted from sliding to and fro on the seat when the bladder is too full (at school), or from stimulation by garments that fit too tightly. In these cases, there is no feeling of guilt, either.

The speaker then passes on to the cases in which masturbation is practiced for strictly sexual reasons; this she saw only in the period following menstruation. And in these cases, too, the speaker could not find any feeling of guilt; it is true, however, that she was not able to penetrate deeply enough. In other cases, there was a feeling of guilt—after the reading of books [that are apt to arouse sexual excitation]. Whether the masturbation that is practiced for the purpose of resolving sexual tension is in fact primary, or whether perhaps it goes back to infantile masturbation, the speaker could not learn until now; further, she doubts whether information will be obtainable, because of the amnesia.

The speaker reports on the masturbation of two sisters, one of whom was [physically] well developed and yet displayed timidity, a feeling of inferiority and a sense of guilt; the other girl was rather frail, and did not display any of the other traits, either. The question then arises as to whether the symptoms are really to be traced to masturbation, or whether they originate in a neurotic disposition.

Another ill-effect of masturbation is frigidity in women; in this instance, too, one should investigate to what extent it is either a primary disposition or related to early masturbation.

In the case of women, it does not happen that they find in it a kind of sexual release. Nocturnal emissions in women cannot be considered to be exactly analogous to emission in men.

PROF. FREUD, in conclusion, would like to state his impression in words, without offering a final opinion. He would advise against publishing anything for the present on the problem of masturbation; instead, one should begin anew to collect observations. In this, it will be necessary first of all to make a study of masturbation in women, which offers far more favorable conditions. Thereafter, one will have to separate the different forms according to their different clinical conditions and psychic consequences.

There are two kinds of masturbation in women. One is analogous to the masturbation of men, practiced with the hand. The other is practiced by means of pressure of the thighs; this has no doubt developed unintentionally. Holding back of the urine in particular provides the occasion for it (Hilferding).

As far as the man is concerned, one should separate the cases of pure masturbation from those who suffer essentially from nocturnal emissions. As far as the causation of neurasthenia is concerned, the conditions are the same in women as in men.

STEKEL closes the discussion with the comment that, even though it did not come up to our expectations, nevertheless the discussion did establish that a unified opinion on this subject is not [yet] prevalent. By and large, however, the majority of speakers have supported the view that masturbation is harmless.

112

SCIENTIFIC MEETING *on June 15, 1910*

Present: Adler, Federn, Freud, Friedjung, Furtmüller, Heller, Hilferding, Hitschmann, Joachim, Nepallek, Oppenheim, Rank, Reitler, Sadger, Steiner, Stekel, Tausk.

Krauss as guest.

COMMUNICATIONS

THE CHAIRMAN reports that no notice concerning the foundation of the International Association has been received up to the present, and therefore proposes to carry through the independent foundation of the [Vienna] Society.[1] 1. The Association intended to publish a pamphlet. 2. It is so easy to found a society that one cannot understand the long delay. Perhaps by our act of independence we can finally effect the founding of the International Association.

PROF. FREUD is of the opinion that nothing will be lost if we wait through the summer; Jung has a number of personal difficulties.

FEDERN refers to the validity of the Nuremberg resolutions and agrees with Freud.[2]

[1] See Minutes 110, this volume.
[2] See Minutes 102, this volume.

STEKEL fully agrees with Adler.

FURTMÜLLER suggests a compromise; one should wait a little while longer, but in any event the founding of the Association should be accomplished before October.

STEINER concurs, and adds the suggestion that the Chairman be entrusted with this matter.

FREUD accedes to the modified Furtmüller-Steiner proposition, with the amendment that the Chairman of the International should be notified.

ADLER brings the Freud-Furtmüller-Steiner proposal to a vote; it is carried, 11 to 1.

If the Society is going to send a third letter to Jung, the secretary should be delegated to do this.

The work on the materials of the discussion on suicide has been completed; it will be sent to Bergmann tomorrow.

THE LIBRARIAN requests the return of all borrowed material.

THE TREASURER then asks for the transfer of the Mk. 100 of additional honorarium.

THE CHAIRMAN announces that this is the final meeting [of the year] and requests that all communications concerning the Society be directed to him; the date of the next session will be announced by mail.

PRESENTATION

On Urethral Erotism[3]

SPEAKER: DR. J. SADGER

Taking as his starting point the anal erotism brought to light by Freud, the speaker focuses attention on the equally significant erotism that has to do with the urethral apparatus and its products. This latter erotism must be understood in a broad sense, just as anal erotism is by no means limited to the anus.

The concept of "urinary erotism" takes in the erotogenicity of the entire peripheral urethral apparatus, from the bladder to the *orificium*

[3] Sadger's paper was published under the title "Über Urethralerotik" 1910 in *Jahrbuch II.*

externum urethrae, as well as the erotogenic relationships that appear later on, and that stem from the actual genital organs and their physiological products. These latter relationships should be classed with urethral erotism, because it happens frequently that erotogenic relations radiate directly from the urinary organs onto the sex organs, and also because the products of the two organs have been shown, by psychoanalysis, to be taken to be identical. That the peripheral urinary apparatus is predestined to become a pleasure-zone can be explained, as far as the masculine sex goes, by the existence of the *corpora cavernosa urethrae* (thus, typical organs for lust), and—in both sexes—by the fact that urine washes over the peripheral genitals.

If one does not succeed in completing a child's toilet training before the end of his first year, or at the latest during the course of the second year, that is proof of a strong urethral erotism. Such children are already subject to pollakiuria during the first weeks of life; later, they show symptoms that betray that micturation in and of itself is pleasure-toned. Just as pleasurable to the child is the washing of his body with urine (skin erotogenic); subsequently, these children may bestow [this pleasure] on other beloved persons, urinating upon them as a proof of their love. For children of this type, urinating as such is pleasurable—which also explains any enuresis that lasts beyond the physiological[ly normal] time. For the same reason, some children yield their excrements only in *dosi refracta;* one patient stated that during childhood he liked to interrupt his micturating repeatedly, for the purpose of obtaining pleasure thereby. Such children take along into their later years the impulse to interrupt emission (*in coitu et masturbatione*).

Another symptom of urethral erotism is an abnormally early excitability of the *corpora cavernosa urethrae* by the retention of urine; in infants, this not infrequently leads to the opposite of micturation, i.e., to retention. Just as in the adult the necessity of urine retention causes a certain amount of sexual excitation (erections in the morning), so the child gets an obvious stiffening of the penis when urine is retained—which, in turn, impedes micturation and makes help by the mother imperative (a new source of pleasure). In these children, there frequently develops a regular negativism, which seems to set the pattern for the corresponding behavior in *dementia praecox.*

Since, as has already been mentioned, children of this type micturate upon persons they love—and the same thing holds true for feces—it is only natural for them to interpret their parents' intercourse as consisting of the father micturating upon the mother. If, subsequently, the wish-fantasy to have a child by the beloved person is added, then drinking her urine is the appropriate means. It follows that, for the child, urine is a sexual product.

The seemingly contradictory statements of authors who write about the erotogenicity of the peripheral urethral apparatus are striking; one author always finds hyperaesthesia in his cases, whereas another author as a rule finds anesthesia. This becomes clear when one keeps in mind that the two phenomena are two sides of the same coin—urethral erotism. The erotism of the peripheral urinary apparatus also betrays itself, apart from the rather ready excitability of the already mentioned *corpora cavernosa urethrae*, in quite frequent tickling sensations in the urethra; further, in acute urethral pains, which appear without any anatomically observable reasons; finally, in emission-like sensations with or, at first, without discharge.

Then there are a number of symptoms that seem to refer exclusively to the genital sphere, yet nevertheless actually represent a *continuation of urinary erotism into puberty.*

Viewed from this standpoint, phenomena that are still puzzling in many instances, of premature as well as of delayed emission, of an increasing number of emissions and *spermatorrhoea*, of *congressus interruptus* for the purpose of prolonging pleasure, of psychic impotence (model: *retentio urinae;* injunction against urinating on the mother), of nervous urethral disorders, of neuralgias of the peripheral genitals in adults—all these phenomena acquire a new meaning. Habitually practiced urine retention is also a pre-stage of later masturbation.

These transformations *can* take place but do not by any means have to; infantile urethral erotism can remain isolated, causing no difficulty. But what then becomes of infantile urethral erotism? In one aspect, it remains fairly unchanged (urinary games of boys); in another, it receives a sexual-symbolic covering (theory of coition; *potatores*, drinking of urine). Urethral erotism is then further modified along the lines, indicated in speech, of making urine equal to water (water games, etc.). Sublimation should also be mentioned; not infrequently, it determines the choice of games, sports and professions (swimming, sailing, becoming a sailor or a dike construction engineer).

A disposition toward urethral erotism is determined by heredity and upbringing. On the paternal side, as well as on the maternal side, there frequently appear urethral disorders. Diverse influences during a child's upbringing—especially if there is playing with the child's genitals on the part of an adult, or if the mother (by reason of her own anal erotism) continues to set the child on the pot long past the proper age—will reenforce the hereditary disposition.

A prophylaxis would have to start with treatment of the parents and attempt to mitigate these harmful influences of upbringing. The therapy [to be applied] is the psychoanalytic one, during the course of which the entire psychic covering is undone.

Lastly, the speaker cites several cases—one of a homosexual, another of an obsessional neurotic with two small children—that illustrate what has been said.

DISCUSSION

FRIEDJUNG would like on behalf of the children to move up the age for toilet training to a later point; very few children are really trained before the end of their first year.

He would not at all regard a child's urinating upon another person as being always a proof of love. Lastly, Friedjung refers to the popular notion that children urinate when they are frightened.

DR. KRAUSS mentions that, as has been shown, there was, among the ancient Greeks, no difference in the value assigned to anal erotism and to heterosexuality; this is in harmony with the view of all Oriental peoples, as well as of some Slavic peoples. Urinating upon another person also often has the meaning of derision.

He then refers to the widespread custom of urine-drinking (peoples of the Negro race; Eskimos; Japanese mussel soup).

FEDERN suggests to the speaker that he refer to the essential works of Freud and Adler that preceded him. The latter did call attention to the significance of pharyngeal reflexes, the relationships of hyper- and hyposensitivity, and, in particular, heredity and the psychic superstructure (water sports, etc.).

On the whole, the paper was quite valuable and instructive. Drinking of urine returns, in the infantile sex theories, as an infantile conception of the sexual act; it also casts some light on the masochistic practice of allowing urine to be passed into one's mouth.

One must keep in mind that not everything that takes place around the genital organ is urinary erotism. We must distinguish the following: (1) that along with premature sexual excitation of the urinary tract, there occurs at the same time an excitation of the sexual sphere; (2) that the feelings of lust are not located in the urethra, but in the as yet undeveloped sex organs; (3) that there are rare cases in which urinating in and of itself engenders lustful excitement; these are persons who feel sexual pleasure, however, even with a limp penis.

The speaker then briefly mentions several cases that demonstrate that scoptophilia also benefits from urinary erotism. Urinating together [with another person] is one of the earliest sexual excitements to involve an object. Anxiety does not precipitate the urge to urinate. All kinds of excitement release libido (anxiety) in the child, and that libido then increases the urge.

NEPALLEK comments that the urinary apparatus often remains an erotogenic zone later on as well, especially in women; cases are known in which masturbation into the bladder has occurred. The expression "pumping ship" [*schiffen* = urinate] also belongs under the heading of "sublimation of urethral erotism" (navigation, etc.).

The only thing TAUSK learned from the paper was that the genital apparatus is involved in micturation.

HITSCHMANN feels that the paper is quintessential Sadger. This time he has functioned as a methodical thinker and has really cleared up much in this field. It is true, to be sure, that every one among us would have interpreted the subject in the same way, but it is important, too, for others to see [these ideas] brought together in this form. That Sadger's patients are invariably such swine is probably due to the fact that, under a close going-over, every neurotic simply looks like that.

Hitschmann then refers to a connection with the *urina spastica* of hysteria.

FURTMÜLLER calls attention to the fact that a popular superstition attributes healing power to urine. There is a classical example of the infantile conception of the sexual act as urinating upon or into the sexual partner in Grimmelshausen's *Simplicissimus*.[4] The explanation given of the predilection for water sports will probably arouse opposition among the uninitiated, an opposition that could be mitigated. That predilection may be something that, under certain conditions, can become anchored in urinary erotism.

HELLER makes reference to the curious ritual, connected with urinating, that one can often observe in children.

A tickling stimulus may perhaps be connected with the onomatopoetic way of inducing children to urinate.

OPPENHEIM would like to bring into the discussion two facts from antiquity. The relationship between urine and procreation is expressed even in language; this double meaning is utilized in the saga of the procreation of Orion.[5]

ADLER would not like to take the paper as a point of departure for theoretical deliberations that are far removed from those of the speaker. What Sadger offered does not show sufficient acuity and does not bring to light the connections. The analogy between urination and the act of procreation is not necessarily much more than an analogy.

Adler thanks Federn for having referred to his [Adler's] paper,[6] in which the relationships with heredity, and furthermore with water and fire sports, exhibitionism, homosexuality, are already set forth; there are differences, to be sure, so that Adler would exempt Sadger from the obligation of citing him.

Adler would like, further, to dispute the assertion that homosexuality invariably stems from the love for the mother; he would say that this love—in the case discussed today, too—is the masculine protest. In the urinary activity, the feminine aspect becomes manifest.

The fear of being taken by surprise cannot be identified offhand with

[4] Hans Jakob Christoffel von Grimmelshausen (1625-1676), German writer: *Der abenteuerliche Simplicissimus.*

[5] Orion's father, Hyrieus, who had become impotent, prayed to the gods for a son. They ordered him to sacrifice a steer, urinate upon its skin and then bury it in his wife's grave. Nine months later, Orion was born from the earth. [According to Robert Graves: *Greek Myths.*]

[6] The reference is probably to Adler's *Der psychische Hermaphroditismus im Leben und in der Neurose* (1910) [*Psychic Hermaphroditism in Life and in Neurosis*]. See Minutes 98, this volume.

a corresponding wish. Precisely the opposite is the case; these are people who, all along and in every respect, like to hide themselves.

STEINER expresses unreserved appreciation for the paper, the value of which is not diminished by the fact that its main points have been stated previously by Freud. On the basis of his observations, Steiner can fully confirm the paper's contents; the interrelationship between urethral erotism and sexuality one sees again and again. Frequently a patient will speak only about his disturbed urinary function, instead of about the sexual function. Man's behavior at the time when his sexual function comes to an end is also typical. Those who suffer from prostate trouble repeat almost the same things that we have observed in infants. Students' urinary habits and the piggishness they indulge in at their beer-drinking bouts unmistakably betray their origin. Various compulsive acts, too, can be readily interpreted in this way (opening water-taps).

To wind up, the significance of urethral erotism for the joke should be mentioned; it proves that these complexes are deeply rooted in our unconscious. The only fault one can find [with this paper] is the complete neglect of the organic.

HILFERDING believes that pollakuria is not infrequently provoked by upbringing. Where coquettish little girls are concerned, the question does arise of whether an organic ailment was not present after all. Cases of small children (2-3 years old) who are subject to frequent changes of environment and fail in their bodily functions cannot be interpreted as cases of urethral erotism; the truth is rather that, as a result of these changes, the artificially established control of the instincts breaks down.

In relation to the analytical therapy of pollakiuria, Hilferding reports on the case of a child who often had to "leave the room" at school: after receiving a physician's note of permission to do so, he no longer feels an unusually great urge to urinate. This child, then, was merely afraid that he would have to urinate, and it was this fear that had provoked the increased urge. Children often urinate on total strangers; in such cases, it could not be a token of love.

A ritual in connection with micturation can also be the result of upbringing and external circumstances.

STEKEL can go into only a few details. The paper offered a great many sound observations, but also quite a number of exaggerations and incorrect statements. Stekel knows examples of cases in which water games have nothing whatsoever to do with urinary erotism. He would not introduce the term urethral erotism. What was described in this paper is what Adler has already described as the character of the enuretic; all the rest takes place in the genitals. Urolagnia does not become clear if it is explained in terms of urinary erotism.

The precondition for loving that consists in the fact that the penis must be touched presents a complex problem; it goes back to infantile stimulations (Hans). Stekel would not be inclined to see a relationship between anxiety and urethral erotism. It is incorrect, too, to trace emissions and coitus interruptus back to such manipulations with urine. Typical of the enuretic ritual are fantasies of the mother's womb and ideas about swimming in the amniotic fluid.

FREUD has been deterred from working on the problem of urethral erotism by the fact that, in both sexes, the anatomical apparatus is mixed up with the sexual organs, so that it is difficult to deal separately with the specific characteristics of urethral erotism. Sadger was too biased in doing so. The clitoris, for instance, cannot be regarded as a part of the urethral apparatus.

Federn has voiced the chief objection to the paper, which was rich in content and [in many instances] quite correct; a distinction should have been made between the erotic feelings that refer to the organ and those that refer to the function. In Sadger's paper, the organ came off badly. Moreover, he ignored one of the basic problems: how far general organ pleasure can be identified with sexual pleasure. The observation that provides the strongest evidence for the existence of an independent urethral erotism is that of urinating upon another person as a proof of love. The objections raised against that are surely justified; nevertheless the fact is not to be denied (case of a ten-year-old boy who urinates on his nurse). It is true that often this micturation also has the negative character of the component of love (stubbornness, hatred, scorn).

Urination [of the baby into the woman] is not a primary sexual theory of children; it may perhaps come about early in urethral erotics (frequently in girls). Urethral erotism is significant in regard to pathology, because it gives rise to a social phobia: girls [so affected] cannot endure staying in closed rooms, because a sexual excitation once caused them to feel the urge to urinate. Dysuria is a good example with which to illustrate the statement that the erotic function of an organ is apt to disturb its social function.

Steiner's suggestion is valuable, that one can see a portion of erotism reflected in jokes.